D0984358

One Thousand Thoughts

FOR

Funeral Occasions

Introduction by

RUSSELL H. CONWELL, D. D.

HARPER & BROTHERS PUBLISHERS

NEW YORK AND LONDON

Republished by Omnigraphics • Penobscot Building • Detroit • 1999

Library of Congress Cataloging-in-Publication Data

One thousand thoughts for funeral occasions / introduction by Russell
H. Conwell.
   p. cm.
   ISBN 0-7808-0303-5 (lib. bdg : alk. paper)
   1. Funeral sermons. 2. Sermons, American. 3. Homiletical
illustrations.
BV4275.05   1999
252'.1—dc21   99-28070
                                         CIP

Printed in the United States of America

INTRODUCTION

BY RUSSELL H. CONWELL.

The seeds of the forest seem wasted when the land is already overgrown. But the waste appears trivial compared with the loss of good thoughts and comforting messages which have been beautifully and thoughtfully expressed by the wise and good and which no kind friend of man has preserved.

In this volume some of the most helpful ideas have been saved from oblivion and some of the best messages preserved for further use. Men are what they think: and he who furnishes mankind with inspiring thoughts is their noblest benefactor. This book is a good deed. This collection of thoughts and sermons will help those who do the work of ministering angels, to do more of that work and do it better. We cannot do less than to express our gratitude to the compiler and the publisher. The seeds of blessing contained in this book have been transferred from the shade and rocks to the barren fields and planted where they are needed, and where they will find favorable environment to develop into the largest fruitage.

What a sermon this volume is, as a whole, when we appreciate the exhortation it suggests to save and promulgate Christian ideas. How few are the manuscripts, books, inscriptions recovered from the libraries and tombs of Babylon, Egypt and Greece! Oh, if we had the literary treasures of all the ages intact! What an array of good deeds could have been shown today, if many had done what so few tried to do, and had preserved all the best compositions of all the great and good.

We cannot hope to be original and creative in all directions, and the busy heart-loaded pastor has but little time to dig the ore for his plow or sword. David in distress needed Goliath's sword already forged and polished. He who preserved the sword and gave it to David seems entitled to love and honor with him who wielded it in defense of his country. Let us not give way to pride and say foolish things because they are our own. But it is wisest and most devotional to think of the mourner and the hopeless, and give to them the best things no matter who may seem to have uttered them first. One cannot avoid the thought that the authors of these sermons and addresses will be glad even to know that the servants of Christ are using effectively still the messages they supposed would die with their delivery. They may feel grateful to those who renew the life and beauty of these children of their hearts.

Of all the multiplied forms and places in which Christ appears this volume shows him most emphatically as the Comforter. This phase of his divine character can be most effectively shown to the weeping, and can be studied and copied with the sincerest devotion. May these messages be "links in the chain which binds Earth to Heaven."

Russell H. Conwell

CONTENTS

SECTION I

ILLUSTRATIONS, POETIC SELECTIONS, OUTLINES.

SECTION II

FUNERAL SERMONS AND ADDRESSES.

SECTION II.

FUNERAL SERMONS AND ADDRESSES

PUBLISHER'S FOREWORD

The Funeral Service is the most trying duty of the pastor. To the sorrowing friends there is no loss so great as their loss. If the pastor's address does not appreciate this, and if he does not pour oil into the wounds, he has failed them at the most critical time.

With from ten to twenty or thirty funerals each year, he needs to watch against treating them as something common. He therefore needs all the help and suggestions that he finds in preparing his regular sermons.

The choice thoughts and especially the Poetical Quotations will be treasured in the hearts of the bereaved for years. There will be requests for the pastor to write out copies of them.

He will be repaid for his efforts of preparation in this ministry of comfort, by remarks like these:

"I will always remember Rev. ————. His remarks at John's funeral were so beautiful." "It seemed as if I could not live through my loss, but the poem quoted by our pastor gave me a new hope."

That this volume will meet all the needs and requirements of these trying services is the expectation of the publisher. For the co-operation of leading pastors in furnishing copies of addresses the publisher is thankful, and the readers will appreciate the service.

F. M. Barton

SECTION ONE.

I. DEATH—GENERAL.

REFLECTIONS AND ILLUSTRATIONS.

Life, Death, and Love (1).

A woman lay with closed eyes and quiet breath waiting to welcome an angel whose presence seemed to overshadow the white-curtained room. A man knelt beside the bed, the woman's hand pressed close against his cheek, while his lips moved as if in prayer.

In the room were Life, Death, and Love.

"What have you given her?" questioned Death of Life.

"I brought her my best gifts," answered Life; "youth, health, beauty, joy—and love."

"Has Love brought her good gifts?" again asked Death.

Said Love with wistful eyes: "I brought her brave, bright hours, sunshine and laughter, happiness and glory in living and then a heavy cross. The sunshine she shed about her, even with the fading of Life's glory; the cross hidden deep in her soul cast out self and made a new radiance and beauty there."

"Let her come to me," said Death. "Life had much to give, but peace and rest are not for Life to bestow. Love would give all, but must reckon with the human heart. I will crown and glorify and bless her."

Life fled from the quiet room with a sigh and one whispered, tender word; but Love lingered, brave even in the full presence of Death.

"What of him?" said Love, pointing to the kneeling figure.

"He made the cross?" Death asked.

"Yes," said Love weeping.

"We must teach him," said Death, "what he could not learn from Life."—The Outlook.

Intertwined Lives (2).

Man builds his life into the tools, the arts, the achievements of his city, until our earth becomes very dear. When that Grecian traveler landed on the Enchanted Islands and pulled the bough from the myrtle tree he heard a cry of pain and saw a branch exuding blood; and so closely is man's heart entangled in friendships and homes and industries that when Death lifts a violent hand the soul cries out and the heart bleeds through mutilation.

Death Touches Only the Body (3).

In proportion as the body falls into ruin, the spirit is disengaged; like a pure and brilliant flame, which ascends and shines forth with additional splendor in proportion as it disengages itself from the remains of matter which held it down, and as the substance to which it was attached is consumed and dissipated.—Massillon,

Death Not Frightful (4).

It is a great thing to leave this world, and yet I cannot think it a specially frightful thing. True, we make a plunge into the unknown, which is so far appalling, and yet even that is somewhat of a fiction. We do know a great deal about the matter after all. We know Christ, which is to know pretty much everything; we know what He is and can be to us, so that if we knew all about the city and the river and all the paradisiac figures it would not add much to our knowledge. It comes indeed to this, that our plunge into the unknown is plunging into a sea of knowledge—the same we have been sailing in before, only in a coasting way. May God be with you and help you to be lifting your sail gladly.—Horace Bushnell.

Dismantled (5).

An old business block is being taken down, just across the street from where we sit. It was built many years ago. It has been the home and headquarters for many a flourishing business. It has had a long and varied career. Now it is in ruins. Some one might croak out a complaint that buildings might as well not be put up, if they are to come to such an end as this. He might ask the use in erecting a block if it is to be turned over to a wrecking company to be destroyed. But there is much use in it. That building has sheltered many shiploads of merchandise. The proprietors have sustained their families for half a century from the profits of the business carried on here, and thousands of families have found here what they needed in their homes. There has been a great deal of reason why the old building should exist. A better building is to rise. It will be twice as high as the old one, much more attractive and convenient and sturdy. It will shelter a larger business than the old one ever did. It will occupy the ground to much better advantage. It will be better adapted to the needs of modern life and business, and will correspond with its present surroundings much better than the shabby building did in the old age.

So it is to be with the children of God. We are to lay aside the flesh and bones of this earthly body, but we are to have a better, more excel lent, more appropriate and better conditioned body in days to come. We are not to be wrecked and ruined by death. We are not to be stripped and left homeless and unsheltered. We are not to be unclothed, but we are to have new and better clothing. We are not to be homeless, but are to have a better and nobler mansion in which to live. We are not to be turned out into the void and dreary space, without a habitation, but are to rejoice in the cheer and comfort of the new home, into which our souls will be tenanted as they leave this.—Selected.

The Fear of Death (6).

The fear of death, which has been so enormously exploited in dramatic literature, sacred and otherwise, is said to be almost without existence in sickness. Most patients have lost it completely by the time they become seriously ill.

Death and sleep are both painless, according to Dr. Woods Hutchinson, and cause neither fear nor anxiety by their approach. It is one of the most merciful things in nature that the overwhelming majority of the poisons which destroy life, whether they are those of infectious diseases or those which are elaborated from the body's own waste products, act as narcotics and abolish consciousness long before the end.

Familiarity With Death (7).

Familiarity with death is apt to alter one's conceptions of it. Two ideas are very generally accepted which experience shows to be false. One is that the dying usually fear death, and the other, that the act of dying is accompanied by pain. It is well known to all physicians that when death is near its terrors do not seem to be felt by the patient. Unless the imagination is stimulated by the frightful portrayal of the supposed "pangs of death," or of 'the sufferings which some believe the soul must endure after dissolution, it is rare indeed that the last days or hours of life are passed in dread.

Oliver Wendell Holmes has recorded his protest against the custom of telling a person who does not actually ask to know that he cannot recover. As that loving observer of mankind asserts, so must every one who knows whereof he speaks assert, that people almost always come to understand that recovery is impossible; it is rarely needful to tell any one that this is the case. When nature gives the warning death appears to be as little feared as sleep.

Most sick persons are very, very tired; sleep—long, quiet sleep—is what they want. I have seen many people die. I have never seen one who seemed to fear death, except when it was, or seemed to be, rather far away. Even those who are constantly haunted, while strong and well with a dread of the end of life forget their fear when that end is at hand.—Selected.

Then Cometh the End (8).

We are going to be through this life before very long. The longest life is short when it is over; any time is short when it is done. The gates of time will swing to behind you before long; they will swing to behind some of us soon, but behind all of us before long. And then the important thing will be . . . not what men thought of us, but what He thought of us, and whether we were built into His kingdom. And if, at the end of it all, we emerge from life's work and discipline crowned souls, at home anywhere in God's universe, life will be a success.—Borden P. Bowne.

Familiarity With Death (10).

At one end of the city of Algiers is the large Arab cemetery. Every one goes to see it, and if the visitors are ladies they choose Friday as the time, as on that day—the Mohammedan Sabbath—the natives would flock to the cemetery in a body, dressed in their gayest and best, and unveiled, to picnic among the graves of their friends.

Death a Phase of Life (11).

The experience that comes when one who is nearest and dearest to us passes on into the unseen world is strangely significant. We at once realize that death is not the end of life, but merely one phase of experience in life, and its nature is to uplift and purify the friend left on this side, and to offer its absolute testimony to the persistence of the communion between the two—the one still an inhabitant of the visible world, the other of the unseen world. He who has gone on to the life just beyond is as real a personality as ever.—L. Whiting.

Death the End of Earth-life (12).

Mr. Ruskin, writing on the robin, says: "It takes a worm by one extremity in its beak, and beats it on the ground until the inner part comes away. Then seizing it in a similar manner by the other end, it entirely cleanses the outer part, which alone it eats. One's first impression is that this must be a singularly unpleasant operation for the worm, however fastidiously delicate and exemplary in the robin. But I suppose the real meaning is, that as a worm lives by passing earth through its body, the robin merely compels it to quit this—not ill-gotten, indeed, but now quite unnecessary—wealth. We human creatures who have lived the life of worms, collecting dust, are severed by death in exactly the same manner."

Illusions (13).

I know I am only repeating what we all believe—and all forget. It is never too late to preach commonplaces, until everybody acts on them as well as admits them—and this old familiar truth has not yet got so wrought into the structure of our lives that we can afford to say no more about it.

"Surely every man walketh in a shadow." Did you ever stand upon the shore on some day of that "uncertain weather, when gloom and glory meet together," and notice how swiftly there went, racing over miles of billows, a darkening that quenched all the play of colors in the waves, as if all suddenly the angel of the waters had spread his broad wings between sun and sea, and then how, in another moment, as swiftly it flits away, and with a burst the light blazes out again, and leagues of ocean flash into green and violet and blue. So fleeting, so utterly perishable are our lives for all their seeming solid permanency. "Shadows in a career," as George Herbert has it—breath going out of the nostrils. We think of ourselves as ever to continue in our present posture. We are deceived by illusions. Mental indolence, a secret dislike of the thought, and the impostures of sense, all conspire to make us blind to, or at least oblivious of, the plain fact which every beat of our pulses might preach, and the slow creeping hands of every parish clock confirm. How awful that silent, unceasing footfall of receding days is when once we begin to watch it! Inexorable, passionless.—Alexander Maclaren, D. D.

Death Not the End (14).

Our friends pass out of our sight, but they still are. The babe grows into the man, and the man grows into the saint, or may so grow. Imperfection may shade over into beautiful perfection. Partial knowledge may "know even as we are known." All rivers run to the sea. "To the sea of glass these mortal lives of ours do bend." These forerunners of the end,—the halting gait, the trembling voice, the whitening locks, why weep over them, when there cometh the beginning on the other side, "the end less beginning of the better chance?" We must not measure life by length of days. The soul is of more value than all the world. At the end the Christian falls to rise again. He is conqueror, though he die. He is kin to the ageless, deathless God. Is this a high hope? Be it so. It is the hope of the gospel of the Son of God. It is a hope that consecrates all present, perishing things, to the high purpose of the soul's enrichment, and its fadeless life in heaven. If the sailor adds the steel of heroic endurance to his tense muscles as he strains to reach the cottage where anxious hearts await his home-coming, shall not the Christian endure the discipline of all things if only he may reach his home in heaven?

A Christian poetess, writing on the thought if she knew that she were to die tomorrow, says:

"I might not sleep for awe; but peaceful, tender,
My soul would lie
All the night long; and when the morning splendor
Flushed o'er the sky,
I think that I could smile—could calmly say,
It is his day."

To such a soul, death is not the end, but the beginning.—W. E. Fischer, D. D.

Sober-minded (15).

Death is a subject which may at present be remote from our thoughts, but it is an experience in which we shall all one day or other be interested. To be frequently in the contemplation of death is perhaps the mark of a feeble rather than of a robust spirit, yet we ought not to refuse the calls which in God's providence invite us to consider death. And, if it be extravagant to demand that a large part of our life should be consumed in contemplating its end, we may, like Nelson, while fighting on deck yet keep our coffin in our cabin. For it is a grosser and more dangerous blindness entirely to ignore our latter end than even to be too much absorbed in it. And indeed it is a fact, although a humiliating one, that it is to death we owe much of our interest in religion. This one benefit at least we derive from the grand enemy, that it compels us to question it, what it hides, what it commits to, what it means; whereas if life were continuous on earth and in the flesh we should feel it impossible to resist the temptation to find all our contentment, here and now, in what appeals to sense. But as one by one men are irrevocably summoned from earth even the most worldly are compelled to follow them with inquiry. Each man knows that the day is coming when for himself and by himself he must make trial of the vast unimaginable beyond. Suspended over the dark abyss he cannot but question what it contains, what forms of life may there exist. Shall we find there fellowship with an all-powerful and loving Spirit? Shall we find there a life continuous with the present, governed by the same moral ideas, fulfilling similar purposes? Or shall we be launched into we know not what chaos of hostile influences, and adverse and calamitous conditions, or at any rate into a life for which the present is no preparation? Is our conscious connection with things and persons forever broken when we cease to take part in this visible world?—Marcus Dods, D. D.

Abolished Death (16).

A writer in Fortnightly, under his leading thought, "The Dying of Death," states as a general fact that death has ceased to act as a motive in life; and gives what he supposes to be the causes of a change in thought on the subject. The suggestion that death does not loom so largely in man's thoughts as apparently it once did agrees with every one's observation, and probably with nearly every one's experience. The pulpit, quite as fully as the press, perhaps more so, is a mirror of public sentiment. It is always seeking for the strongest motive toward the religious life, and employs the strongest considerations in its appeals. But there has come a change, the extent of which can only be realized by reading the religious books and the surviving sermons of a period so late as fifty years ago, and comparing them with the living sermons of today. One never now hears the once familiar descriptions of the terrors of physical death. On the contrary, both press and people seek to smooth over the great highway and beautify it with flowers. The funeral choir brings out its choicest voices. The officiating clergyman sums up the virtues of the departed. The press lends its aid, giving wings to the eulogium—and indeed there is nothing terror-inspiring left to the King of Terrors than can be eliminated. A funeral is now a beautiful spectacle, filled with tenderness, reverence and beauty, and this pleasing impression is left upon the memory.—The Interior.

The End of the Day (17).

It was said by a great Dutch painter, the teacher of many pupils, that "the end of the day is the proof of the picture." When all the little details are blotted out in the dusk, and you can see the perfect design of the artist, then you know whether he is an artist or not. And is it not the end of the day which is the proof of the picture in that painting at which we are all at work, the portrayal of our own personalities in our lifework?—D. Macfadyen.

The End Near. (18)—A Monk near his end was heard to exclaim, "I care little for earthly things now; soon I shall travel among the stars."

"Swift To Its Close" (19).

There is an hour, just after sunset, when all nature seems to be preparing for rest, when the heavens are telling, in the rich coloring of the dying day, the story of the great Light which never wanes! We watch the majesty of all this, and realize the swiftness with which our lives are ending. Then, oh then, the loved ones, absent from us, come into affectionate remembrance; and those, too, whom we have loved and lost awhile who rest in the peace of God, invoke our loving hopes and earnest prayers.—W. T. Parker, M. D.

A Fixed Time (20).

"I suppose you have your itinerary all mapped out, even to a day," I said to a friend about making a long tour abroad.

"No," he replied, "that would spoil it all for me. I do not tie myself down to either places or times. I shall go and stay, and go and stay again, as the mood takes me."

That, though, is something most tourists cannot do. There is a limit to the number of days they will have at their command. The sailing-dates are fixed for both going and coming. It is not from choice but from necessity that, having cut it short, what they take in and leave out, they "apply their hearts to the wisdom" of making the most they can of their sight-seeing days.—Ballard.

Death, the Revealer. (21)—Life—We shall not know what life is until we die! Death is not a descent, but a never-ending ascent into the larger spaces and the fuller delights!—J. Ossian Davies.

Does Death End All? (22).

We feel no serious sadness over the fading of the grass and the leaves in autumn, for we know they will soon return, and the earth will appear with renewed beauty in the opening spring. It is very different in regard to man. He dies, and his place knows him no more. The question before us is not primarily, What is the purpose of life? but, Has life any purpose? The question is vital, for the answer inevitably shapes a man's life. As we think in our heart, so we are. If the golf-player is startled to discover that the slightest mental distraction spoils his stroke, should it be hard to convince any man who is in earnest that it is necessary to think straight and reach conclusions if he will have his life run straight and true?—Stimson.

The Unknown Tomorrow (23).

There are the great changes which come to some one every day, which may come to any of us any day, which will come to all of us some day. Some of us will die this year; on a day in our new diaries some of us will make no entry, for we shall be gone. Some of us will be smitten down by illness; some of us will lose our dearest; some of us will lost fortune. Which of us it is to be, and where within these twelve months the blow is to fall, is mercifully hidden. The only thing that we certainly know is that these arrows will fly. The thing we do not know is whose heart they will pierce. This makes the gaze into the darkness grave and solemn. There is ever something of dread in Hope's blue eyes. True, the ministry of change is blessed and helpful; true, the darkness which hides the future is merciful, and needful if the present is not to be marred. But helpful and merciful as they are, they invest the unknown tomorrow with a solemn power which it is good, though sobering, for us to feel, and they silence on every lip but that of riot and fool-hardy debauchery the presumptuous words, "To-morrow shall be as this day, and much more abundant."—Alexander Maclaren.

Death's Estimate of Life (24).

When the great preacher, Massillon, preached the funeral sermon of Louis XIV., he made an immense impression with his first words. Slowly lifting his eyes, as he stood in the pulpit, he swept them in silence over all that magnificent funeral pomp. Then he fixed them on the lofty catafalque, where lay the body of the famous king. After a long silence he said, "My brethren, God alone is great." It is a simple and thrilling truth that when life is gone, nothing that life possessed is worth anything at all.

Death's Shadows Flee Before Eternity's Light (25).

To the lover of the Lord, the true morning comes when this tabernacle is laid down.

For when the last shadows gather, when our feet touch that cold dividing stream from which the bravest for the moment shrinks, when we stand on the verge of that darkness which to the unbeliever is dark indeed, it may affect us with a momentary shiver, though often there is not even that. Yet for us it will be only that deeper darkness which they say comes just before the dawn. A moment, and then there will be the glory shining on the hills of God, and the light which no more goes down. We shall know all that we have waited and hoped for, all that we have prayed and longed to know. The riddles of life will be solved. The darkest things will open out and show us Divine love at the center. The mystery of God will have no more hiding in it. We shall see Him as He sees us, and doubt and pain and fear will flee away.—Greenburgh.

Death's Swift Approach (26).

No man can look upon a field of corn, in its yellow ripeness, which he has passed weeks before when it was green, or a convolvulus withering as soon as plucked, without experiencing a chastened feeling of the fleetingness of all earthly things.

No man ever went through a night-watch in the bivouac when the distant hum of men and the random shot fired told of possible death on the morrow; or watched in a sick-room, when time was measured by the sufferer's breathing, or the intolerable ticking of the clock, without a firmer grasp on the realities of Life and Time.

So God walks His appointed rounds through the year: and every season and every sound has a special voice for the varying phases of our manifold existence. Spring comes, when earth unbosoms her mighty heart to God, and anthems of gratitude seem to ascend from every created thing. It is something deeper than an arbitrary connection which compels us to liken this to the thought of human youth.

And then comes Summer, with its full stationariness, its noontide heat, its dust, and toil, an emblem of ripe manhood. The interests of youth are gone by. The interest of a near grave has not yet come. Its duty is work. And afterwards Autumn, with its mournfulness, its pleasant melancholy, tells us of coming rest and quiet calm.

And now has come Winter again.

It is not a mere preacher's voice performing an allotted task. The call and correspondence are real. The young have felt the melancholy of the autumnal months. With a transient feeling—even amounting to a luxury—the prophetic soul within us anticipates with sentiment the real gloom of later life, and enables us to sympathize with what we have not yet experienced. The old have felt it as no mere romance—an awful fact—a correspondence between the world without and the world within. We have all felt it in the damp mist, in the slanting shadows, the dimmer skies.—F. W. Robertson.

Life Is Fleeting (27).

Bubbles are supposed to burst almost as suddenly as they are blown; but rosin bubbles are exceptional. Of a pleasing appearance, silvery luster, and reflecting different rays of light, they will remain for months, it is said, as perfect as when they were formed. Their permanency is ascribed to the sudden coagulation of the rosin, thus imprisoning the air by a thin film of solid matter and preventing its escape.

Among youth particularly, how much building of air-castles! John Quincy Adams speaks of "the vain and foolish exultation of the heart which the brighter prospects of life will sometimes excite." Some of these things, however, seem to have considerable substance in them, and hold their fascination during most or all of the natural life. Many great men otherwise have resembled rosin bubbles in their solid success, but in the failure to prepare for another existence it was only bubbles after all, however apparently substantial. The butterfly wing is gaudy and evanescent, though lasting through the long summer's day. Says Paul, "Seek those things which are above, not the things on the earth." (Col. 3:1.)—Homiletic Review.

The Entrance to a Richer Life (28).

Dying is only a process in which we pass into larger, fuller, richer life. This body (the flesh) which was assumed by our Lord Jesus Christ, dwelt in by His life, purified by His purity, transfigured with Him on the Mount of Transfiguration, consecrated forever in His sacrifice on the Cross, will then be viewed in all the blessedness and perfection of its divine character. This perfect work, attested in the resurrection of "Christ the first fruits," will be completed in those who are Christ's at His coming, when "death shall be swallowed up in victory." "And there shall be no more death, neither shall there be mourning, nor crying nor pain any more." "Thanks be to God who giveth us the victory through our Lord Jesus Christ." He is risen! Therefore all that He said is true. He is risen! Therefore He is the Son of God. He is risen! Therefore He lives to fulfill His promises. He is risen! Therefore the grave is robbed of its victory. He is risen! Therefore we shall rise again. We close our eyes in peace to open them without an interval or a break of what we can be aware, in the gladness and fullness of the everlasting morning. We shall find in the heavenly land the dear ones from whom we have been separated; we shall know them, they will know us, and we shall enter upon a life of service there, if we have had a life of service here.—The Christian Intelligence.

The Naturalness of Death (29).

When a man's work is done, death is as natural and as beautiful as the falling leaves of autumn. All of us are wise enough to see that. I sometimes think that no more merciful death could have been chosen for that noble brother of ours, Abraham Lincoln, than the swift bullet which brought instant oblivion to his deadly weariness. His work was done.

It had been a Titan's task. Strong and brave and tender and loving he had held himself through it all. Worn and weary, deadly weary, he was. Then, in an instant, the burden was dropped, rest came, the soul passed on to his God and our God to serve in what other spheres we know not, and the poor, tired, worn-out body was laid to rest. Is this condoning the deed of the assassin? By no means. It is recognizing that the purposes of the Eternal Goodness are worked out through the follies and mistakes of men.—Rev. E. G. Brown.

The Fact of Death (30).

It is a remarkable change, when we come to think of it, which at death passes at once on the material and the immaterial part of the nature of man. The soul is separated from its mortal tenement; and that spiritual existence, whose warm affections we vainly referred to the material heart, and whose thoughts and fancies we vainly referred to the material brain, now lives apart from both, and independent of either. But the soul was always a mystery; it was invisible before, and it is no more now; we cannot tell how it left the body, but we never knew how it lived in it, or where in this mortal framework was its home; and its departure is no more inexplicable than its existence. It is on the more familiar body, that the more palpable and the more affecting change is wrought. The contrast with that which a little before it was, strikes us painfully and harshly; and an undefined and mysterious awe comes over us, as we stand by the body from which the soul has gone. The heart is there, but it beats no longer; the eye, but it sees no more; and the kindliest and best-loved voice cannot arrest the attention of the dull, cold ear. The color of life has fled from the cheek, and the light of intellect from the brow; the multitudinous machinery of animal life is there, but the vital spark to set it in motion is wanting; and when weeping friends stand round the bed of death, that, which once could never see their grief without seeking to soothe and lighten it, is now wholly unresponsive.—Boyd.

ILLUSTRATIVE POETRY.

And Then Comes Night (31).

Life is a leaf of paper white
Whereon each one of us may write
His word or two, and then comes night.

—Lowell.

Two Views of Death (32).

While man is growing, life is in decrease,
And cradles rock us nearer to the tomb;
Our birth is nothing but our death begun.
As tapers waste, that instant they take fire.

* * *

While we are dying, life is on increase,
The sun is rising on sepulchral gloom,

Our death is nothing but our life begun;
The hour of birth is when the saints expire.
—Young's Night Thoughts.

The Veil (33).

"Slight as thou art, thou art enough to hide,
Like all created things, secrets from me,
And stand a barrier to eternity.
And I, how can I praise thee well and wide
From where I dwell upon the hither side,
Thou little veil for so great mystery?
When shall I penetrate all things and thee
And then look back? For this I must abide,
Till thou shalt grow and fold and be unfurled
Literally between me and the world.
Then I shall drink within beneath a spring
And from a poet's side shall read his book.
Oh! daisy mine, what will it be to look
From God's side even of such a simple thing?"
—Alice Meynell.

How Still He Lieth (34).

How still he lieth in his narrow bed!
    The marks of rugged toil are on his face
    And hands, folded so calmly in their place
Upon his quiet heart: the years have fled
And left a silver aureole on his head;
    The lines of age are smoothed away, and now
    The look of youth returning crowns his brow.
How peacefully he sleeps with naught of dread
That he must wake and hurry to his toil!
    No fears of coming ill disturb his rest,
    Nor tho'ts of sorrow o'er his spirit sweep.
They lay him tenderly beneath the soil
    And gently press the sods upon his breast,
    For lo! He giveth His beloved sleep!
—Frederick E. Snow.

Death (35).

I was ever a fighter, so—one fight more
    The best and the last!
I would hate that death bandaged my eyes, and forebore
    And bade me creep past.
No, let me taste the whole of it, fare like my peers,
    The heroes of old,
Bear the brunt, in a minute pay glad life's arrears
    Of pain, darkness and cold.
For sudden the worst turns the best to the brave,
    The black minute's at end,
And the elements rage, the fiend voices that rave,

Shall dwindle, shall blend,
Shall change, shall become first a peace out of pain,
Then a light, then thy breast,
O thou soul of my soul! I shall clasp thee again,
And with God be the rest.

—Browning.

When Baby Died (36).

How brief the stay, as beautiful as fleeting,
The time that baby came with us to dwell:
Just long enough to give a happy greeting,
Just long enough to bid us all farewell.
Death travels down the thickly settled highway,
At shining marks they say he loves to aim;
How did he find far down our lonely byway,
Our little girl who died without a name?

She seemed so like a tender bird whose winglets
Are broken by the stress of rain and storm,
With loving care we pressed the golden ringlets,
And wondered could there be so fair a form;
For death had chiseled without pause or falter
Each feature that the sunny tresses frame:
No change of scene nor length of time can alter
Our little girl who died without a name.

We do not know the fond endearment spoken
To which she listened when she fell asleep.
And so beside a column that was broken,
We laid her to her slumber calm and deep;
We traced upon the stone with loving fingers
These simple words, affection's tear to claim:
"In dreams, beyond all earthly sorrow, lingers
Our little girl who died without a name."

Close folded there within the Bible hidden,
A flower fades that withered on her breast,
Upon the page where such as she are bidden
To seek the circle of His arms for rest.
"Of such the kingdom," comes to us so sweetly,
Those little ones without a touch of blame;
We know He shelters in His love completely,
Our little girl who died without a name.

She sleeps serene where fragrant mossy willows
In sweet and wordless tunes forever wave,
And summer seas in long and grassy billows
Break into bloom around her lonely grave.
In memory's hall how many heroes slumber,

We gild their deeds upon the scroll of fame;
We treasure far above this mighty number,
Our little girl who died without a name.
—Alonzo Rice.

Death's Real Terror (37).

Could I have sung one song that should survive
  The singer's voice, and in my country's heart
  Find loving echo—evermore a part
Of all her sweetest memories; could I give
One great thought to the people, that should prove
  The spring of noble action in their hour
  Of darkness, or control their headlong power
With the firm reins of justice and of love;
Could I have traced one form that should express
  The sacred mystery that underlies
  All beauty, and through man's enraptured eyes
Teach him how beautiful is holiness,—
  I had not feared thee. But to yield my breath,
Life's purpose unfulfilled!—This is thy sting, O death!
—Sir Noel Paton.

Only a Few More Years (38)

A few more years shall roll,
  A few more seasons come,
And we shall be with those that
    rest,
  Asleep within the tomb;
  Then, O my lord, prepare
  My soul for that great day;
Oh, wash me in Thy precious
    Blood,
  And take my sins away.

A few more suns shall set
O'er these dark hills of time
And we shall be where suns are not,
  A far serener clime;
  Then, O my Lord, prepare
  My soul for that bright day;
Oh, wash me in Thy precious
    Blood,
  And take my sins away.

A few more storms shall beat
  On this wild rocky shore,
And we shall be where tempests
    cease,
  And surges swell no more:
  Then, O my Lord, prepare
  My soul for that calm day;
Oh, wash me in Thy precious
    Blood,
  And take my sins away.

A few more struggles here,
  A few more partings o'er,
A few more toils, a few more tears,
  And we shall weep no more:
  Then, O my Lord, prepare
  My soul for that blest day;
Oh, wash me in Thy precious Blood,
  And take my sins away.
—Bonar.

Time (39).

Forenoon and afternoon and night,
Forenoon and afternoon and night,
Forenoon and—what?
The empty song repeats itself.

Our Silences (40).

What silences we keep, year after year!
With those who are most near to us and dear!
We live beside each other day by day
And speak of myriad things, but seldom say
The full, sweet word that lies just in our reach
Beneath the commonplace of common speech.

Then out of sight and out of reach they go ·—
Those close, familiar friends who loved us so;
And sitting in the shadow they have left,
Alone with loneliness and sore bereft,
We think with vain regret of some fond word
That once we might have said and they have heard.

For weak and poor the love that we express
Now seems beside the vast, sweet unexpressed,
And slight the deed we did to those undone,
And small the service spent to treasures won,
And undeserved the praise for word and deed
That should have overflowed the simple need.

This is the cruel cross of life, to be
Full-visioned only when the ministry
Of death has been fulfilled, and in the place
Of some dear presence is but empty space.
What recollected service e'er can then
Give consolation for the might have been?
                              —Selected.

No Need For Fear (41).

Why be afraid of Death as though your life were breath!
Death but anoints your eyes with clay. O glad surprise!

Why should you be forlorn? Death only husks the corn.
Why should you fear to meet the thresher of the wheat?

Is sleep a thing to dread? Yet, sleeping, you are dead,
'Till you awake and rise, here or beyond the skies.

Why should it be a wrench to leave your wooden bench?
Why not with happy shout run home when school is out!

The dear ones left behind! O foolish one and blind.
A day and you will meet—a night, and you will greet!

This is the death of Death, to breathe away a breath
And know the end of strife, and taste the deathless life,

And joy without a fear, and smile without a tear,
And work, nor care, nor rest, and find the last the best.

—Selected.

The Conquest of Death (42).

The ship may sink and I may drink
  A hasty death in the bitter sea;
But all that I leave in the ocean grave
  Can be slipped and spared, and no loss to me.

What care I though falls the sky,
  And the shrivelling earth to a cinder turn?
No fires of doom can ever consume
  What never was made nor meant to burn.

Let go the breath! There is no death
  To the living soul, nor loss, nor harm.
Not of the clod is the life of God:
  Let it mount, as it will, from form to form.

Love (43).

A mystic shape did move
  Behind, and drew me backward by the hair,
And a voice said in mastery while I strove,
  "Guess now who holds thee!"—"Death," I said; but there
The silver answer rang, "Not Death, but Love."

The Thinning Ranks (44).

The day grows lonelier; the air
  Is chillier than it used to be.
We hear about us everywhere
  The haunting chords of memory.
Dear faces once that made our joy,
  Have vanished from the sweet home band;
Dear tasks that were our loved employ,
  Have dropped from out our loosened hand.

Familiar names in childhood given
  None call us by, save those in heaven.
We cannot talk with later friends
Of those old times to which love lends
Such mystic haze of soft regret;
We would not, if we could, forget
The sweetness of the bygone hours,
  So priceless are love's faded flowers;
But lonelier grows the waning day,
  And much we miss upon the way
Our comrades who have heard the call
  That soon or late must summon all.

Ah, well! the day grows lonelier here,
　Thank God, it doth not yet appear
What thrill of perfect bliss awaits
　Those who pass on within the gates;
O, dear ones who have left my side,
　And passed beyond the swelling tide,
I know that you will meet me when
　I too shall leave these ranks of men
And find the glorious company
Of saints from sin forever free,
　Of angels who do always see
The face of Christ, and ever stand
　Serene and strong at God's right hand.

The day grows lonelier, the air
　Hath waftings strangely keen and cold
But woven in, O glad, O rare
　What love notes from the hills of gold!
Dear crowding faces gathered there,
　Dear blessed tasks that wait our hand,
What joy, what pleasure shall we share
　Safe gathered in the one home-land!

Close up, O comrades, close the ranks;
　Press onward, waste no fleeing hours;
Beyond the outworks, lo! the banks
　Of that full tide where life hath power,
And Satan lieth underfoot,
And sin is killed, even at the root.
　Close up, close fast the wavering line,
　Ye who are led by One divine.
The day grows lonelier apace,
But heaven shall be our trysting place.
　　—Margaret E. Sangster in the Congregationalist.

Unreturning (45).

Strange, is it not, that of the myriads
Who before us passed the gate of darkness through,
Not one returned to tell us of the way,
Which to discover we must travel to.

Alone (46).

Alone to land and upon that shore,
Alone to begin to live forevermore;
With no one to put us at our ease
Or teach us the manner and the speech
Of that new life.
Oh, that we might die in pairs or companies!

The Hour of Death (47).

Leaves have their time to fall
And flowers to wither at the north-wind's breath
  And stars to set—but all,
Thou hast all seasons for thine own, O Death!

  Day is for mortal care,
Eve for glad meetings round the joyous hearth,
  Night for the dreams of sleep, the voice of prayer—
But all for thee, thou mightiest of the earth.

  The banquet hath its hour,
Its feverish hour of mirth, and song, and wine;
  There comes a day for grief's o'erwhelming power,
A time for softer tears—but all are thine.

  Youth and the opening rose
May look like things too glorious for decay,
  And smile at thee—but thou are not of those
That wait the ripened bloom to seize their prey.

  We know when moons shall wane,
When summer birds from far shall cross the sea,
  When autumn's hue shall tinge the golden grain—
But who shall teach us when to look for thee?

  Is it when spring's first gale
Comes forth to whisper where the violets lie?
  Is it when roses in our paths grow pale?
They have one season—all are ours to die!

  Thou art where billows foam,
Thou art where music melts upon the air;
  Thou art around us in our peaceful home,
And the world calls us forth—and thou art there.

  Thou art where friend meets friend,
Beneath the shadow of the elm to rest —
  Thou art where foe meets foe, and trumpets rend
The skies, and swords beat down the princely crest.

  Leaves have their time to fall,
And flowers to wither at the north-wind's breath,
  And stars to set—but all,
Thou hast all seasons for thine own, O Death!

—Felicia Hemans.

TEXTS AND TREATMENT HINTS.

Keeping the End in View.

Lord, make me to know mine end,
And the measure of my days, what it is;
Let me know how frail I am.
Behold, Thou hast made my days as handbreadths;
And mine age is as nothing before Thee;
Surely every man at his best estate is altogether vanity.

—Ps. 39:4.

1. Life is brief and death is near for all.

2. By ignoring this fact, multitudes lose one of the mightiest motives to right living here and preparation for the hereafter.

3. Our prayer should be that God would keep a keen realization of it ever before us.

The Transitoriness of Life (48)

"So teach us to number our days, that we may apply our hearts unto wisdom."—Ps. 90:12.

This is the key-note of the 90th Psalm. It numbers sadly the days and vicissitudes of human life; but it does this, not for the sake of mere sentiment, but rather for practical purposes, that it may furnish a motive for a wiser life of the heart. We know nothing of the Psalm except that it was the composition of "Moses, the man of God." It was written evidently in the wilderness, after years of apparently fruitless wandering; its tone is that of deep sadness,—retrospective; its images are borrowed from the circumstances of the pilgrimage,—the mountain-flood, the grass, the night-watch of an army on the march.

See here again what is meant by inspiration. Observe the peculiarly human character of this Psalm. Moses, "the man of God," is commissioned not to tell truths superhuman, but truths emphatically human. The utterances of this Psalm are true to nature. Moses felt as we feel, only God gave him a voice to interpret, and he felt more deeply than all, what all in their measure feel. His inspiration lay not in this, that he was gifted with legislative wisdom; but rather in this, that his bosom vibrated truly and healthfully to every note of the still sad music of humanity.

We will consider:

I. The feeling suggested by a retrospect of the past.

II. The right direction of those feelings.—Robertson.

HIS DAYS AS GRASS.

"As for man, his days are as grass; as a flower of the field, so he flourisheth. For the wind passeth over it, and it is gone; and the place thereof shall know it no more."—Ps. 103:15-16.

1. Our plans and expectations are all for permanency. We live and labor, and love and strive as though the years were endless.

2. The facts of experience are all against us. From infancy to old age, those about us are constantly receiving the final summons.

3. Wisdom would lead us to recognize-and act upon this fact.

THE FEAR OF DEATH CONQUERED.

Perfect Love Casteth Out Fear.—1 John 4:18 (49).

I. Is not the bondage to the fear of death the one heavy burden of life? I do not mean that the fear of our own individual death is a constantly present fear. It may but seldom occur consciously to the mind. But though the prospect and the thought be banished, the bondage abides still. The hunger of a soul is felt, though the attention be distracted from its existence. A life occupied only upon the things which perish feels resting heavily upon it a burden; and that burden is the bondage to the fear of death. The weariness of a worldly life is in part bodily and mental fatigue, but it is more than this: it is the protest of a spirit which was meant for other things. To have forgotten death, to have put it out of sight, out of our reckoning, is itself the completest death. The enemy is not to be conquered by closing the eyes upon him. He is the conqueror, who is only to be cast out by another conqueror.

II. St. John in our text declares that fear has a conqueror's power; it can inflict torment. It is a power which requires another stronger power to exorcise it. This power of grace is "perfect love." In this Epistle St. John does not speak vaguely and sentimentally about love. He connects it directly with God's goodness to us, and with our duties as children of the Father. And as love grows, fear, the fear that has torment—the fear, that is, of finding Him a God of hate in the next world whom we have found, by blessed experience, to be a God of love in this —becomes no longer tenable. It is forced out of the soul by the spreading roots of affection and trust, for while it abides it is the lingering shadow of unfaithfulness. Love is not the grace which has made obedience superfluous; it is a feeling which, like Aaron's serpent, has swallowed up all the rest, which has taken up into itself, absorbed, duty and obedience, as unconscious and spontaneous offerings of the will.—Rev. A. Ainger.

"We All Do Fade as a Leaf" (50).

"Probably not one person in a thousand knows why leaves change their color in the fall," an eminent botanist is quoted as saying. "The common and old-fashioned idea is that all this red and golden glory we see now is caused by frosts. A true and scientific explanation of the causes of the coloring of leaves would necessitate a long and intricate discussion. Stated briefly and in proper language, those causes are these: the green matter in the tissue of a leaf is composed of two colors, red and blue. When the sap ceases to flow in the fall, and the natural growth of the tree ceases, oxidation of the tissue takes place. Under certain conditions the green of the leaf changes to red; under different conditions it takes on a yellow or brown tint. The difference in color is due to the difference in combination of the original constituents of the green tissue and to the varying conditions of climate, exposure, and soil. A dry, cold climate produces more brilliant foliage than one that is damp and warm. This is the reason that American autumns are so much more gorgeous than those of England. There are several things about leaves that even science cannot explain. For instance, why one of two trees growing side by side, of the same age and having the same exposure, should take on a brilliant red in the fall and the other should turn yellow; or why one branch of a tree should be highly colored, and the rest of the tree have only a yellow tint, are questions that are as impossible to answer as why one member of a family should be perfectly healthy and another sickly. Maples and oaks have the brightest colors.—Selected.

"One Taken and the Other Left." (51).

The separation made by death is always a solemn thing. I. How it would sweeten the parting if each were assured of the other's faith! II. How different many a leave-taking would be, if both knew that it was only for a little while, and that the reunion would be everlasting! III. How blessed for mourners left in tears to know assuredly that those who are gone have only departed "to be with Christ!" and this bright assurance may be the comfort of all whose friends gave evidence, ere they fell asleep, that they had really been "living by faith in the Son of God, Who Loved them and gave Himself for them."—Knight.

"The Night Cometh."—John 9:4 (52).

When I turned my calendar to a new page, on the first of the month, I read this: "Life is but once. We shall never pass this way again. Drink the cup, wear the roses, live the verses." "Drink the cup,"—that means when hard experiences come to us, when we feel bowed down with the weight of cares and responsibilities, when we are crushed by a sense of our own inadequacy, accept it all sweetly as a part of the inevitable. Don't reluct at it; don't go off into a corner and think, "I am more unfortunate than ever anybody was;" don't entertain the thought of the hardness and somberness of life, but face what you must face, it may be with smiles or it may be with tears, but face it in a brave and lofty spirit. Face the clouds without forgetting the sunshine. Accept the darkness of the night without forgetting the eternal stars. So Socrates drank the fatal hemlock, so we shall drink the cup of experience put to our lips, in a way that shall bear witness to the superiority of the life within to the steady burning within of the fire of a courageous heart and a sweet and gentle soul. "Wear the roses," appreciate the good in life, seek the bright and the beautiful whether in outward nature or in human nature,—they are there waiting for us to catch the inspiration and the good cheer they bring. "Wear the roses,"—not only on our external persons and in our drawing-rooms, but in our minds and our hearts, in the daily conduct of our lives. Beauty wherever found should make us beautiful within. Sunshine and blue sky should find their reflection within. Truth and goodness, as personified in others, should touch us in the depth of our natures to make us clean, and pure and good, too. Cultivate an appreciation for what is helpful and inspiring in the world about us, in the people we meet every day, and let it have an uplifting and refining influence in our own lives. Take the joys of life holily. Wear all the roses of personal character in others, in character blossoming more beautifully in ourselves. What a wonderful thing life becomes when we can think of it as opportunity to seek and find what is best everywhere! We must cultivate our taste for what is best, and then, if we walk in the fields, we shall find it. If we wander up and down the streams, we shall find it. If we sail the seas, we shall find it. Wherever we cultivate the acquaintance of external nature, we shall find it. And the same thing is true of our association with people. Look for the good things, the happy things, the noble things, the roses of life in humanity; and, almost before you know it, they will have influenced you, and you will be wearing them in your inmost consciousness. "Live the verses,"—make life rhythmical, make it a harmony, make it a poem. Is that hard to do? All the same, try to do it, and keep on trying. Rhythm in life,—we know it in the soughing of the pines; we know it in the flag as it yields gently to the persuasion of the breeze; we know it in music, music composed by gifted souls, and interpreted to us by instrument and voice; we know it in the songs which poets have sung; we need to know it in ourselves. We are writing a poem, we are composing a symphony,—at least we are set to do that in our own characters. What a different thing it makes of this career of ours, in space and time if we can keep the fires of the poetic, the rhythmic and musical, the fires of the ideal, burning within. It is a great thing to write the verses, it is a great thing to sing them, it is a great thing to live them. Did it ever occur to you that this whole universe of ours is set to music? Did it ever occur to you that all human life ultimates in harmony,—discords everywhere, but finally the building up out of them of the universal human symphony from the hands of the Infinite Composer? Why should not you and I out of the discords of our own lives bring to pass the harmony of a rhythmic character? What Tennyson has done, what Browning and all the poets have done, what Beethoven and Wagner and their fellows have done in great ways, that we are to do in our little ways.—Rev. Frederick A. Hinckley in The Christian Register.

"God Took Him."—Gen. 5:24 (53).

There are many ways of passing from one state of existence to another. Look at the case of Enoch, concerning whom we simply read, "He was not, for God took him." We do not know how the process was conducted. Whoever saw the evaporation of a dewdrop? Whoever saw the exact moment when the flower came up into visibleness? Take the case of Elijah concerning who we read, "He was carried up." We think of the chariot of flame and of attendant angels. Imagination pictures a vivid scene of transport. In the case of Enoch there was simply abstraction, in the case of Elijah there was pompous, glorious visibility and triumph. Take the case of Paul, concerning whom we read that his life was "poured out." He was ready to be offered as a libation. His death was a kind of offering or sacrifice unto God. Take the case of Christ Himself, concerning whom we read that "He laid down His life." No man took the life from Him, else had His death been a mere murder; He laid it down of Himself, and thus His death became a sacrifice and an atonement. Group all these instances and see in what various ways

God takes His children to Himself: "God took him." "He was carried up;" "He was poured out;" "He laid down his life." As to the glorious Christ we simply read that "He rose" and that "He went away." Christ never asked to be prayed for. Christ worked with the resources of boundless power. Jesus gives, not receives; Jesus sends, but is not sent. In these distinctions, so exquisite, yet so palpable, I find the best illustrations of the deity of my Lord.—Joseph Parker.

"Then Shall the End Come."—Matt. 24:14 (54).

The Certain End.

It is not possible to rule these words out of life. They are perpetually recurring. You tell of any process, you trace out how it is going to work on from step to step, you see how cause opens into effect, and then effect, becoming cause, opens into still further effect beyond; but always, by-and-by, your thought comes to a stoppage and a change. The process is exhausted. "Then cometh the end." Your story has to round itself to that.

Let us think of this characteristic of life, and see what it means.

I. We may begin by noting this—which is the most striking thing about the whole matter—the way in which men's desire and men's dread are both called out by this constant coming of the end of things. Look (1) at man's desire of the end. It is, in the most superficial aspect of it, a part of his dread monotony. There is something very pathetic, it seems to me, in man's instinctive fear of being wearied with even the most delightful and satisfactory of all the experiences which he meets with in the world. Is it not a sign, one of the many signs, of man's sense that his nature is made for larger worlds than this, and only abides here temporarily and in education for destinies which shall be worthy of its capacities? "I would not live alway" has been a true cry of the human soul. (2) But this is the most superficial aspect of it. Very early in every experience there comes the sense of imperfection and failure in what we have already done, and the wish that it were possible to begin the game again. Already there are some things in life which the soul would fain get out of life. The first sketch has so marred the canvas that the perfect picture seems impossible. In many tones, yet all of them tones of satisfaction, men desire the end. (3) Turn now to the other side, and think of the dread with which men think of the coming of ends in life. There is (a) the sheer force of habit. It is the inertia of life. That this should cease to be is shocking and surprising. (b) Very often one shrinks from the announcement of the coming end of the condition in which he is now living, because, when he hears it, he becomes aware how far he is from having yet exhausted the condition in which he is now living. (c) There is the great uncertainty which envelops every experience which is untried.

II. The workman's voice has not to summon out of the east the shadows of the night in which no man can work. God sends it. And, if around the instability of human life is wrapped the great permanence of the life of God, then is there not light upon it all? All satisfaction with the temporariness comes only from its being enfolded and embraced within the eternity of the Eternal.—Phillips Brooks.

"For It Is Appointed Unto Men Once to Die."—Heb. 9:27 (55).

I. Our attitude toward death—death the inevitable—will have much to do with determining our experience in life.

II. Do we merely thrust it from our minds as an unwelcome intruder? Or do we think of it in spite of ourselves, and cower and cringe at the thought?

III. Or have we accepted Christ's glorious adjustment of the whole matter for us, and do we rest in His blessed promises?

"Your fathers, where are they? And the prophets, do they live forever?"—Zech. 1:5.

It is all but impossible to invest that well-known thought with any fresh force; but perhaps, if we look at it from the special angle from which the prophet here regards it, we may get some new impression of the old truth. That special angle is to bring into connection the eternal Word and the transient vehicles and hearers of it.

Did you ever stand in some roofless, ruined cathedral or abbey church, and try to gather round you the generations that had bowed and worshiped there? Did you ever step across the threshold of some ancient sanctuary, where the feet of vanished generations had worn down the sandstone steps at the entrance? It is solemn to think of the fleeting series of men; it is still more striking to bring them into connection with that everlasting Word which once they heard, and accepted or rejected.

But let me bring the thought a little closer. There is not a sitting in our churches that has not been sat in by dead people. As I stand here and look round, I can repeople almost every pew with faces that we shall see no more. Many of you, the older habitues of this place, can do the same, and can look and think, "Ah, he used to sit here; she used to be in that corner." And I can remember many mouldering lips that have stood in this place where I stand, of friends and brethren that are gone. "Your fathers, where are they?" "Graves under us, silent," is the only answer. "And the prophets, do they live forever?" No memories are shorter-lived than the memories of the preachers of God's word.—Alexander Maclaren, D. D.

II. THE DEATH OF LITTLE CHILDREN.

REFLECTIONS AND ILLUSTRATIONS.

The Loss of Little Lives (56).

On an average one-fourth of the population of the world die at, or before, the age of seven. One-half die before the seventeenth year. "The air is full of farewells to the dying." Hearts are breaking and homes being made desolate hourly. And the only ray of light that falls across the world's dark shadow, cast by the death of this multitude of little children, shines forth from the Book of Books, in the words of Him who has "brought life and immortality to light."

Drawing Power. (57)—A father whose only child was taken by death was noticed eagerly studying his Bible. On being asked what he was doing, replied, "I am trying to find out where my little boy has gone, for I want to go there too."

Jesus and the Children (58).

Jesus alone of all ancient religious teachers noticed children. From Him has come the tender love for children to-day. We must thank Him for our better homes. Not long since, we read of an incident that aptly illustrates this truth. A number of persons were looking at some missionary pictures with a friend who knew Chinese ways, and were puzzled by his quick remark, "These are Christians." They looked closely at the group. There was a Chinese father with a quaint Chinese baby in his arms, and a Chinese woman sitting beside him. "How do you know?" asked one of the number, failing to see anything in the picture to guide one as to the religion of the family. "Don't you see the father has the baby in his arms? No heathen Chinaman would think of that," was the reply. Christianity is the foundation of the sacred joys of home.

"In the Morning" (59).

Reginald John Campbell tells the story of a "little girl who had always been accustomed to bid her father good night in the same words. She was an only child and loved as only children are. She used to say 'Good night, I shall see you again in the morning.' The time came when Death's bright angel, bright to those who go,—dark to those who stay, summoned her to heaven. In her last moments she summoned her father to her side and putting up her little arms and clasped them around his neck and whispered with her rapidly dying strength, 'Good night, dear father, I shall see you again in the morning.' She was right, as the child always is right about the highest things. Sorrow endureth for a night, but joy cometh in the morning."

An Indelible Impress (60).

If you go into the mint, you will see them place a bit of metal on the die. With a touch as silent as a caress, but with the power of a mighty force, the stamp moves against it. And when that touch is over, there is an impression upon the coin which will abide when a thousand years are passed away. So our life moves up against another, filled with the power and stamped with the image of Christ's likeness; and when that touch of parent, or teacher, or friend is over, there are impressions that will remain when the sun is cold and the stars have forgotten to shine.—Bennett.

Lifting a Child up into Christ's Arms (61).

I remember a few years ago, a little child died, and just before his soul went home, he asked his father to lift him up, and the father put his hand under the head of the child and raised it up. But the child only said, "That is not enough; that is not what I want; lift me right up." The child was wasted all to skin and bones, but still his father complied, and lifted the dying child out of his bed. But the little fellow kept whispering, fainter and fainter, "Lift me higher, higher, higher!" And the father lifted higher and higher, till he lifted him as far as he could reach. Yet, still the barely audible whisper came, "Higher, father, higher," till at last his head fell back, and his spirit passed up to the eternal King—high at last.

Young Children in the Church (62).

At one time sixty per cent of the membership of a certain Denver church was under fifteen years of age. The rector for years declared that he was working for the next generation. He spent himself for the children. While the mature and stolid older folks were not neglected in the ministrations, yet the whole set of the church was in the interest of the young. To say nothing of the spiritual results, which were enormous, but simply as a business proposition, the rector's course is being abundantly justified. The children are now becoming the men and women of affairs, and the church is taking a place of unusual influence in the city. —Fouse.

A Baby's Smile (63).

A clergyman, on his way to church, passed by a window where a mother was holding a little baby. He smiled at the baby and the baby smiled at him. Another time he passed, and the baby was there again, and once more he smiled. Soon the baby was taken to the window at the hour when he usually passed. They did not know who the gentleman was, but one day two of the older children followed to see where he went on Sunday. They followed him into the church, and as he preached in a winning way, they told their father and mother, who felt interested enough in their baby's friend to wish to go. The whole family, who had previously neglected the worship of God, were brought to the Saviour by a smile.—Spurgeon.

Child Nurture (64).

Let it be understood by parents that the Christian doctrine of childhood as the subject of grace, with Christian youth and manhood as its fruit-bearing continuation, imposes strictest attention to the youngest and smallest. The nearer to infancy, all the more necessity of watchfulness and prayer, of godly example and precept, and the use of all means which the Christian parent may command for the sanctification of his offspring. First impressions are the most important, because they are not easily, if ever wholly effaced. They form the bias of the nature, and parents are bound to see that it is not contrary to religion by causing the first impressions to be in its favor. But to do this no time is to be lost. They must realize that not to begin in time may be to begin too late, that both the earthly and eternal destiny may be fixed, and must be in no slight measure affected, by the powerfully formative influences that operate from infancy on in the life of childhood. How much of loss to the child, extending into the years beyond, parental failure in its Christian nurture may mean only eternity can tell.—The Christian View of Childhood.

Bringing the Children to Christ (65)

A familiar story is that of a visitor to Coleridge who argued vehemently against the religious instructions of the young, and declared his own determination not to "prejudice" his children in favor of any form of religion, but to allow them at maturity to choose for themselves. The answer of Coleridge to the particular argument was pertinent and sound enough: "Why prejudice a garden in favor of flowers and fruit? Why not let the clods choose for themselves between cockleberries and strawberries?"—The Christian Advocate.

Saving All the Little Ones (66).

When I was a child, there was, in the readers, a story about Mr. Dustin, whose house was burned, and his wife captured by the Indians, and he attempted to flee with his little flock of children. He had decided to select one of the children out of the number, and, placing that child on the horse with himself, to fly to a place of safety. He rode up to the little group of children with that purpose in mind, and at first thought he would take the elder boy; for that boy was dear to his heart, and was the pride of his life. But he saw that that boy was holding by one hand the tiny little girl, only about two years of age; and holding the other hand was a larger girl, and the boy and the girl were dragging the little one along; and he said, "I cannot take the boy." Then he thought he would take the little one; and when he saw her sweet face turned up to him, he said, "She is my joy." But as he drew near the tiny child, the great hazel eyes of the elder girl were turned up to him, and he saw the face and eyes of his wife; and the man cried "Never! I will save the other children too." He then turned; and bidding the children fly for their lives, he became like a tiger at bay;—and turning toward the savages, under his unerring aim and steady and strong blows the savages went down; and all the other children were saved with the one he had purposed to save. In your work there is another child, and yet another child, and yet another child; and God's thought goes out for all these other children. The one thing for each one of us to say, is this: "I will stand between all the children of this earth and hell itself."—Rev. R. I Greene, D. D.

Child Religion (67).

We must distinctly recognize that there is such a thing as piety
in childhood, and parents are encouraged to hope for its appearance in
their offspring, provided they will use the means which God has authorized and appointed for its development. The Church is to increase by the
nurture of the children who are born within it, as well as by the conversion of those grown-up persons who have been long outside of its pale,
and the true idea of a Christian household is when all the children in it
grow up into the love and service of Christ as naturally as they do into
the likings and dislikings of their parents in other and less important
respects.—W. M. Taylor, D. D.

Christ Saves the Children (68).

A little boy and his sister were going through a narrow railway "cut"
one day. As they reached the middle of it they heard a train coming.
Picking the little fellow up his sister crowded him into a cleft in the
rock-wall and shrank up against him, crying, "Cling close to the rock;
cling close to the rock." He clung and they were safe. So Christ, the
Rock of our salvation, shelters our little ones from the perils of life and
the terrors of death.

A Heaven Full of Children (69).

"Holman Hunt's magnificent painting, 'The Triumph of the Innocents,' is to my mind the most important religious picture of the century. Breathing through every careful line and glowing color is the soul,
the spirit of the picture, which irradiates it with

> 'The light that never was on sea or land,
> The consecration and the poet's dream.'

"The spirits of the murdered children of Bethlehem—not a great
multitude, as they are often thoughtlessly depicted, but a little band such
as really played in that little village—have followed after Jesus on His
flight. . . . The Holy Child looks around, and seeing the spirits of
His playmates, welcomes them with the gladness of a divine sympathy.
These children are the first of His glorious band of martyrs, and as they
draw near to Him the meaning of their martyrdom flashes upon them, and
their sorrow is changed into joy. The last group of little ones have not
yet felt His presence, and the pain and terror of mortality are still heavy
upon them. Over the head of one of them the halo is just descending.
. . . One baby saint looks down amazed to see that the scar of the
sword has vanished from his breast. In front floats a trio of perfectly
happy spirits, one carrying a censer and singing, the others casting down
branches of the palm and the vine. At their feet rolls the river of life,
breaking into golden bubbles, in which the glories of the millennium are
reflected.

"All mystical, symbolical, visionary! But is it not also true? Think
for a moment. It is the religion of Jesus that has transfigured martyr-

dom and canonized innocence. It is the religion of Jesus that tells us of a heaven which is full of children."—Henry Van Dyke, The Christ-Child in Art.

"What a Waste of Life (70).

Some while ago, in a mood for such thoughts, our eye fell on the item that in one year the deaths in four Eastern cities amounted to 43,432; and of this number 24,767 were children under five years of age.

The last sentence fixed our attention—twenty-four thousand, seven hundred and sixty-seven children died during the year! This in four cities only! Of the rest of the forty-three thousand, four hundred and thirty-two, who can tell their eternal destiny? Some went to heaven, some went to hell. But concerning these little ones none can doubt. Taking the aggregate of other cities, villages, and the country at large, we comprehend a fact that finds expression at the Saviour's lips: "Of such is the kingdom of God." And in a sacred couplet:

> Millions of infant souls compose
> The family above.

The adults had worked out their mission or failed to do it. But these little ones! Had they no mission? Was their being a failure? Lived they and suffered and died, and is the world all the same as though they had not been? Nay, verily. Theirs was a precious ministry, and one that they only could fulfill.

"What a waste of life!" exclaims the worldly economist as he figures up the statistics of population. "They lived in vain" is the thought of the man ambitious of making his mark on the age. "Mere blanks, flowers that came to no fruit, broken off, fallen, faded" is the thought and feeling of many.

But Christian philosophy presents a more ennobling and comforting view. Cold and selfish would this world of ours be without these children. They preach the evangel of beauty and innocence; they break the incrustations of worldliness; they come to love and to be loved; they touch chords vibrating solemnly, sweetly, which are reserved only for their tiny hands; they stir in the heart hidden wells of feeling; they preserve human sympathy from utter ossification; they deeply subsoil our hard natures.

Children in a Chariot of Fire (71).

When the Lawrence Mills were on fire a number of years ago—I don't mean on fire, but when the mill fell in—the great mill fell in, and after it had fallen in, the ruins caught fire. There was only one room left entire, and in it were three Mission Sunday-school children imprisoned. The neighbors and all hands got their shovels and picks and crowbars, and were working to set the children free. It came on night and they had not yet reached the children. When they were near them, by some mischance a lantern broke, and the ruins caught fire. They tried to put it out, but could not succeed. They could talk with the children, and even pass them some coffee and some refreshments, and encourage them to keep up. But, alas, the flames drew nearer and nearer to this prison. Superhuman were the efforts made to rescue the children; the men bravely fought back the flames; but the fire gained fresh strength and returned to claim its victims. Then piercing shrieks arose when the spectators saw that the efforts of the firemen were hopeless. The children saw their fate. They then knelt down and commenced to sing the little hymn we have all been taught in our Sunday-school days, Oh! how sweet: —"Let others seek a home below which flames devour and waves overflow." The flames had now reached them; the stifling smoke began to pour into their little room, and they began to sink, one by one, upon the floor. A few moments more and the fire circled around them, and their souls were taken into the bosom of Christ.—Moody.

A New Interest in Heaven (72).

A minister who had lost his child asked another minister to come and preach for him. He came and he told how he lived on one side of a river and felt very little interest in the people on the other side, until his daughter was married and went over there to live, and then every morning he went to the window and looked over that river, and felt very much concerned about that town and all the people there. "Now," said he, "I think that as this child has crossed another river, heaven will be dearer to him than ever it has been before." Shall we not just let our hearts and affections be set on the other side of the river? It is but a step; it is but a vail; we shall soon be in the other world.

Christ's Enfolding Love (73).

"The best sermon I ever heard Mr. Spurgeon preach was in the Boys' Orphanage. There was an infirmary connected with the orphanage, and in it was a dying boy. Mr. Spurgeon sat down by the little cot, and in a voice full of tenderness, said to him, 'My dear, you have a great many precious promises all around this room, and do you know you are not going to stay with us long? Do you love Jesus?' 'Yes.' 'Jesus loves you better than you love Him, and He is going to take you to Himself. There will be no suffering there. Did you have a good night?' 'No, sir; I coughed all night.' 'Ah, my child, coughing all night and weary all day. Here, outside are the boys overflowing with health, and you coughing all night, weary all night—but Jesus loves you, and He is going to take you to Him, and then He will tell you all about it, and then you will be glad you waited here so patiently.'"—John B. Gough.

Following the Lambs (74).

A traveler in the Orient told of seeing a shepherd trying to get his sheep to come to him, across a stream. They refused to respond to his call until he took two little lambs over in his arms. The old ones followed readily then. Their lambs on the other side, drew them. So children in heaven often draw parents thither.

The Difference (75).

One of the missionary magazines gave a touching incident recently illustrating this difference between the tomb of hope and of despair: Two Korean women stood watching a funeral procession on its way to the foreign cemetery. "What sight is this?" said one. "The burying of the missionary's son," answered the other. "That is very, very sad," replied the first. In Korea a son is the most precious of all possessions. "It is not so bad for them as for us," said the other sadly. "They know something that makes them sure that they will get their children back some day. We know nothing about how to get ours back again."

We need the darkness of a heathen sky against which to see the glory of the resurrection hope, in order fully to appreciate it. How it takes the bitterest sting from the loss of dear ones, and how it cheers men as, one by one, they approach life's eventide.

Her Only Hope (76).

One who crossed the Atlantic some years ago related this pathetic incident of the voyage.

The saddest sight of life we ever witnessed was on an ocean voyage, in the death and the burial of the child of a lowly German mother. Her husband had been smitten by consumption, and with that longing so peculiar to this form of disease thought if he could only breathe the air of his own boyhood's Rhine cliffs he would be well again. But being poor he had to cross in February in the steerage. The cold winds, scanty fare, and hard beds were too much for him, and he had but scarcely reached his home when hemorrhages attacked him and he sent to St. Louis for his wife and only child, a son, that he might see them once again. The wife sold her scanty household outfit and taking her babe, set out to see her husband's face ere she should know what penniless widowhood and orphanage meant.

She wept night and day, and most of all because she knew not what would become of the fatherless child. But soon she learned God's purpose; the child wasted away; his mother's grief had robbed him of his nature's nurture, and she could secure no other. The poor people with her taxed themselves, and the little milk left from cabin use was procured, but the child closed its eyes in its mother's arms. She sat with it in her arms, bemoaning her sad fate until the ship's officers compelled its burial.

The ship carpenter prepared the rough box with the weights to sink it to the ocean's bed; tender hands clipped the golden locks from the little head, to be carried to the dying father, and what remained was parted over the pale brow. No wraps enfolded it but the faded calico gown. A poorer neighbor spread her white linen handkerchief over its face, and the carpenter filled up the space with clean pine shavings, and as he did his work he groaned and said: "God bless this poor mother, God be thanked the wee bairn is safe." The captain came down to read the committal service according to law. He was a hard-faced, swearing, blustering Englishman, but beneath had a manly heart. He said to the carpenter, "Screw down the lid."

"Oh, no, captain," said the heart-stricken mother, "let me look at my baby once more."

He turned away and waited. Again he said to the grief-stricken mother, "I am sorry to deprive you of any comfort. God knows you have few enough, but I must read the service."

She lifted herself, and the carpenter screwed down the lid, amid the sobs of the poor around her and the tears as well of those happier in this world's goods looking down from the upper deck. The captain read in plaintive tones the service, and he faltered as he read, "I am the resurrection and the life." Poor man! Why he faltered there at the anchor of human hope we could never tell. He took the box to be lowered into the billowy bed, the mother shrieked: "Oh captain," and laid hold once more of her treasure; the captain stood waiting for her to kiss that rough box, and then she said in broken English, "Fadder, Thy will be done," and the little casket dropped into the sea, which took it quickly to its bosom, and a little bubble rose, the sea's last messenger to tell us that all was well.

We Would Not Bring Them Back (77).

There is a beautiful story, says Dr. J. R. Miller, of a boy whose young sister was dying. He had heard that if he could secure but a single leaf from the tree of life that grew in the garden of God, the illness could be healed. He set out to find the garden, and implored the angel sentinel to let him have one leaf. The angel asked the boy if he could promise that his sister should never be sick any more if his request were granted, and that she should never be unhappy, nor do wrong, nor be cold or hungry, nor be treated harshly. The boy said he could not promise. Then the angel opened the gate a little way bidding the child to look into the garden for a moment, to have one glimpse of its beauty. "Then, if you still wish it," said the angel, "I will myself ask the King for a leaf from the tree of life to heal your sister." The child looked in; and, after seeing all the wondrous beauty and blessedness within the gates, he said softly to the angel, "I will not ask the leaf now. There is no place in all this world so beautiful as that. There is no friend so kind as the Angel of Death. I wish he would take me, too."

Plucked by the Gardener (78).

If a rosebud is plucked from the parent bush and placed in water, it will blossom into a beautiful rose, sooner than its equally developed sister that is left on the bush. Yet we mourn when God, the loving soulgardner, plucks from its earthly environment a life that is just beginning to unfold its possibilities. To our earthbound vision the life is nipt in the bud. We cover the little casket with cut flowers, and it is fitting that we do so, for they are the emblems of the life that is perfected by its changed environments. The gardener takes it away that it may the more quickly develop into the perfect blossom of eternity.—The Homiletic Review.

"Father, Father, Come This Way" (79).

I remember a number of years ago I went out of Chicago to try to preach. I went down to a little town where was being held a Sunday-school convention. I was a perfect stranger in the place and when I arrived a man stepped up to me and asked me if my name was Moody. I told him it was, and he invited me to his house. When I got there he said he had to go to the convention, and asked me to excuse his wife, as she, not having a servant, had to attend to her household duties. He put me into the parlor, and told me to amuse myself as best I could till he came back. I sat there, but the room was dark, and I could not read, and I got tired. So I thought I would try and get the children and play with them. I listened for some sound of childhood in the house, but could not hear a single evidence of the presence of little ones. When my friend came back I said: "Haven't you any children?" "Yes," he replied, "I have one, but she's in Heaven, and I am glad she is there, Moody." "Are you glad that your child's dead?" I inquired.

He went on to tell me how he had worshiped that child; how his whole life had been bound up in her to the neglect of his Saviour. One day he had come home and found her dying. Upon her death he accused God of being unjust. He saw some of his neighbors with their children around them. Why hadn't He taken some of them away? He was rebellious. After he came home from her funeral he said: "All at once I thought I heard her little voice calling me, but the truth came to my heart that she was gone. Then I thought I heard her feet upon the stairs; but I knew she was lying in the grave. The thought of her loss almost made me mad. I threw myself on my bed and wept bitterly. I fell asleep, and while I slept I had a dream, but it almost seemed to me like a vision.

"I thought I was going over a barren field, and I came to a river so dark and chill-looking that I was going to turn away, when all at once I saw on the opposite bank the most beautiful sight I ever looked at. I thought death and sorrow could never enter into that lovely region. Then I began to see beings all so happy looking, and among them I saw my little child. She waved her little angel hand to me and cried, 'Father, father, come this way.' I thought her voice sounded much sweeter than it did on earth. In my dream I thought I went to the water and tried to cross it, but found it deep and the current so rapid that I thought if I entered it would carry me away from her forever. I tried to find a boatman to take me over, but couldn't, and I walked up and down the river trying to find a crossing, and still she cried: 'Come this way.' All at once I heard a voice come rolling down, 'I am the way, the truth, and the life; no man cometh unto the Father but by Me.' The voice awoke me from my sleep and I knew it was my Saviour calling me, and pointing the way for me to reach my darling child. I am now a Sunday School superintendent, my wife has been converted, and we shall, through Jesus as the way, see our child some day."—Moody.

Not Afraid To Go (80).

A tiny child belonging to a primary class was very ill. Perhaps a shadow fell from the grave faces of the mother, nurse, and doctor. The little one looked into the dear mother's eyes and asked, "Am I going to die?" "You are very sick, darling," said the mother, steadying her heart and her voice for her child's sake. "Perhaps Jesus means to take you home to be with Him."

"Will I go to Jesus, mother?" "Yes, dear." "Is it that Jesus that Mrs. C. tells about in the class—just the same one?" "Yes, the very same Jesus." "Oh, then I'm not afraid to go to Him, for Mrs. C. keeps telling us how good He is, and how He loves the little children and says, 'Come unto me and forbid them not.' "—Julia H. Johnson.

Blossoms of Hope (81).

In the land in which Jesus once lived, they tell a beautiful legend. On the morning of that first Easter Day, it is said, as Jesus stepped forth from the grave, immediately flowers of the most fascinating beauty burst forth wherever His foot had touched the earth. His disciples, had they but looked with care, might have found Him by the beauties He left in His wake. Only a legend indeed, but in a spiritual sense it is absolutely true. From the grave that day, Christ brought us fair blossoms of promise and of hope; we still gather them and rejoice in their possession.

Merely Transplanted Flowers (82).

The children whom Christ has taken to Himself are just as truly alive as those which He has left on earth. As Dr. Maclaren well said: "The dead and the living are not names of two classes which exclude each other. Much rather, there are none who are dead. The dead are the living who have died. Whilst they were dying they lived, and after they were dead they lived more fully. Every one who has died is at this instant in the full possession of all his faculties, in the intensest exercise of all his capacities, standing somewhere in God's great universe ringed with the sense of God's presence, and feeling in every fibre of his being, that life which comes after death—that life which is not less but more real.

God Puts Out the Light (83).

The family group was broken, and the bereaved mother wept over her loss with a friend. "It's bad enough all the time," she sobbed, "but it's at bedtime that I miss Jimmie most. You see, he had always been rather delicate, and I took an extra look at him after he was in bed. Oh, dear! I can almost see him now, as he used to smile up at me after I'd tucked him in nicely and kissed him, and was ready to put out the light."

"God has done that for Jimmie now," said the friend, after a silent prayer for guidance in the choice of the right word.

"What do I mean?" as the mother started. "Just this, dear. God loved Jimmie even more than you did, and He saw that it was the dear little lad's time to rest. How many times, I wonder, have you gently insisted that Jimmie come to bed when he was all eagerness to stay up longer? How many times have you lovingly turned out the light while he was still anxious to talk and laugh with you? Well—the heavenly Father, knowing Jimmie's needs better than you could, saw that it was time for a longer rest, time to put out the earthly light.

"A greater light, we cannot doubt, now shines about Jimmie, but his tired little body no longer needs such light as we know. So God has extinguished it in His own good time and way."

The thought that so tenderly comforted the weeping mother is full of solace for us all, since to each and all must come, recurrently, the time when "God puts out the light" that has transfigured and transformed our working days. Not the light of life, perhaps, but the light of joy, of success, of just pride in some dearly loved one, of health, perhaps even of hope and faith. And in such times of darkness nothing can so uphold, so strengthen, so encourage us as the thought that the gloom and shadows come from God Himself; that we have but to wait His good time for the return of the normal sunshine. For, by the Father's own appointment, day follows night, gladness follows sorrow, peace follows trial, just as inevitably and surely as night is succeeded by day in the natural world.

Small need to more than suggest the seed-thought. In times of grief especially, it is well to seize a good thought and hold on to it firmly till we can realize its truth, believe it, feel it. And this comforting, helpful thought of our heavenly Father Himself for our own good, putting out the light which we, infantwise, would insist upon retaining—what does it mean but "Our times are in His hand?"—Ethel Colson in The Continent.

Cross Lots. (84)—An aged Christian was at first sad when he heard of the death of a little girl whom he greatly loved. Then suddenly his face grew bright, and he said: "Why, she's gone cross lots, while I am going all around this long distance. I am glad for her."—S. S. Times.

A Completed Life (85).

Sometimes God calls our children home to Himself for their good. He may do it because He would save them from a sad and sorrowful future. It is difficult to complete life righteously and grandly. Boyd, the famous "Country Parson," writes: "It comes back to me how Norman McLeod came into my father's house, the day after that best of all good men died. His words were: 'Now here is a completed life. He never can do anything to vex or disappoint you now, God knows what you and I may come to.' After a pause: 'No, nothing of that; by God's mercy we shall end well.'" The great Lord President Inglis, when it was proposed to set up some grand memorial of his career, wisely objected, replying, "Nobody could tell how he might besmirch his reputation ere he went." God knows the future of our children and may take them to save from a sad future.—Selected.

The Rustle of Angel Wings (86)

The twilight hour had come. The last lingering rays were fading beyond the western horizon. The stars had appeared on duty for their long night vigil. The soft southern zephyrs were fanning my tired brow. The fragrant aroma of the tall magnolia and the full-blown lilac were borne to me upon the evening breeze. The blessed Bible lay open before me. I had been reading the great apostle's letter to the Church at Corinth. Through them he had spoken to the ages and to me. I was ravished with his statement. The lesson of "the corn of wheat" stirred my heart as never before. It was an hour of sweet and holy meditation. My angel baby hovered near me. Listening love heard the rustle of her wings. How thin the veil! Just beyond the flesh that twilight air was filled with the disembodied dead. My loved and lost for a little while! Beyond the vale of tears, beyond the valley of sighs roamed my sainted child. Yes; we shall meet where the eye is fire and the heart is flame.

In that hour of reverie suddenly a merry child burst into my room. In a clear, flutelike tone it broke into a wild, ecstatic glee. The piano sat in the shadow of the opposite corner. Its keys were without the touch of human hand. The silver chords were dumb and silent. The moment the happy child uttered its cry of joy my ear caught the soft and distant sound of music. I listened intently. The child's voice had stirred the silent strings. The flutelike note had started its own sound wave. We do not need any dissertation on science here. Take your theory and pass on. The old silver chord in the very pitch and tone of that elf's voice began to vibrate. It created its own sweet harmony. The entire gamut felt the tremor of that voice.

Like phantoms, multitudes of thoughts passed before me in that twilight vision. The dying melody of those silver chords, whose silent tongues were set a-going, stirred me profoundly. I thought of Whittier's soliloquy in "My Soul and I."

> Like warp and woof, all destinies
>   Are woven fast,
> Linked in sympathy like the keys
>   Of an organ vast.
> Pluck one thread, and the web ye mar;
>   Break but one
> Of a thousand keys, and the paining jar
>   Through all will run.

Is not my heart like a harp of a thousand strings? Will not the touch of an almighty hand sweep every chord of the human soul? Will not the music be like that of same grand cathedral choir whose sound shall reach the distant shore? Ah! your soul may be silent now, but it must needs be kept in tune with the Infinite. In some twilight hour your ear will catch the sound of its softest melody and will feel the renewal of some vanished hand.

But there is a difference. If these chords are swept by spirits, the forces that live beyond the shadows, its music can never die. And there is a note whose harmony is soon gone; it soon fades away. For

> Time has laid his hand
> Upon my heart gently, not smiting it;
> But as a harper lays his open palm
> Upon his harp, to deaden its vibrations.
>   —Rev. J. Marvin Nichols.

The Little Children (87).

"When our little boy died" has been the beginning of a pilgrimage of many bereaved parents. The death and burial of the babe dates impressions on the whole family circle that have matured to godliness.

The old may outlive their friends, the middle-aged may make enemies who are glad to be rid of them, or, wandering off, they may die where none lament; but the babe is without prejudice in life and mighty in death. It is God's messenger of reconciliation, his flag of truce in this world of enmities, envies, wrath and strife. It has a strong hold on two hearts, if no more. The empty crib, the half-worn shoes, the soft locks of hair that few may see prolong the painful yet pleasing memory of the angel visitor that looked in upon us and smiled, and went to heaven, bidding us, amid care and sorrow, to follow on.

There is something so peculiarly affecting in the loss of a child that we sympathize with the parent who said that he believed no minister was prepared to bury another's child who had not buried one of his own.

"It was only a baby." Ah! they know not, who talk so slightingly, how deep and long a shadow that little form can cast. "In the death of children heaven is receiving large contributions from earth. Next to the conversion of a soul, the enemy of God and man may take least pleasure in the death of a child. His snares are prevented and his prey lost."

We bless God for our creation. The opening of a career of immortal existence is in itself a great event—a mission of life and glory which death cannot frustrate. Though the voice of praise swell as the sound of many waters, and the celestial harpers are numberless, yet His ear detects every new voice and joyful string, and the praise of these little ones glorifies Him. In this view the babe, even of a few days and sickly, that goeth from the cradle to the grave, is of more intrinsic importance than material worlds.

The mystery of pain is one of the hardest trials of faith. It is natural to associate suffering with guilt. But what have they done, the innocents? Even here there is a lesson and a consolation if our hearts can receive it. He who knew no sin was made perfect through suffering. May not our children, who cannot confess Him before men, be permitted at this one point to have fellowship with their Saviour and ours? May not this refining fire chasten and prepare for the eternal heaven the fallen nature which they, with us, inherit? A drop of this baptismal fire falls even on them. By a brief experience of pain in the mortal body, before they quit it for the immortal, even they come to some knowledge of the price of their redemption, and the contrast of a few painful hours may heighten the joys of eternity.

A Hindoo woman said to a missionary: "Surely your Bible was written by a woman." "Why?" "Because it says so many kind things for women. Our Shastas never refer to us but in reproach." "Parents, watching by the couch of suffering innocence and seeing the desire of their eyes taken away at a stroke, have found themselves busy running over the Scriptures for comfort and gathering up, as a stay of their hearts, what God has said about their little children." How full and precious and unequivocal are the passages of comfort! The conclusion is: Surely the Bible was written by a parent. And so it was. He knows the heart of a parent and works by it to the glory of His grace.

"O, prattling tongues, never formed to speech, and now still in death, how eloquently you preach to us! O, little pattering feet, leading the way, how many are following after you to heaven!" We thank God for your ministry. And if it be in vain, the fault and the loss will be all our own.—Bishop McTyeire.

A New Cradle. (88)—A little girl had a baby sister who died, and the little baby was put into a tiny coffin. When the little girl saw it, she said, "Mother, baby has got a new cradle!" That was a pretty name for it. Death is but being lulled to sleep in the arms of Infinite Love.—The Free Methodist.

The Universal Experience (89).

A Hindoo woman, the beautiful Eastern legend tells us, lost her only child. Wild with grief, she implored a prophet to give back her little one to her love. He looked at her for a long while tenderly, and said:

"Go, my daughter, bring me a handful of rice from a house into which Death has never entered, and I will do as thou desirest."

The woman at once began her search. She went from dwelling to dwelling, and had no difficulty in obtaining what the prophet specified; but when they had granted it, she inquired:

"Are you all here around the hearth—father, mother, children—none missing?"

The people invariably shook their heads, with sighs and looks of sadness. Far and wide as she wandered, there was always some vacant seat by the hearth. And gradually, as she passed on, the legend says, the waves of her grief subsided before the spectacle of sorrow everywhere; and her heart, ceasing to be occupied with its own selfish pang, flowing out in strong yearning of sympathy with the universal suffering, tears of anguish softened into tears of pity, passion melted away in compassion, she forgot herself in the general interest, and found redemption in redeeming.—Rev. F. B. Meyer.

Resignation (90).

There is no flock, however watched or tended,
  But one dead lamb is there!
There is no fireside, howsoe'er defended,
  But has one vacant chair.

The air is full of farewells to the dying,
  And mournings for the dead;
The heart of Rachel, for her children crying,
  Will not be comforted!

Let us be patient! These severe afflictions
  Not from the ground arise;
But oftentimes celestial benedictions
  Assume this dark disguise.

There is no death! What seems so is transition;
  This life of mortal breath
Is but the suburb of the life elysian,
  Whose portal we call death.

She is not dead—the child of our affection—
  But gone into that school
Where she no longer needs our poor protection
  And Christ himself doth rule.

Not as a child shall we again behold her,
  For when with raptures wild,
In our embraces we again enfold her,
  She will not be a child;

But a fair maiden in her Father's mansion,
  Clothed with celestial grace;
And beautiful with all the soul's expansion
  Shall we behold her face.

                              —Longfellow.

Safe in Heaven (91).

      "I spoke to my God
        As I knelt in prayer,
        And I said, "Thy care
      Is our guard and guide,
      Is she 'neath the sod
      Who they said has died?"

And the answer came as a trumpet calls,
"She abides with me in the heavenly halls."

That Immortal Sea (92).

      In a season of calm weather
Though inland far we be,
Our souls have sight of that immortal sea which
            brought us hither,
Can in a moment travel thither,
And see the children sport upon the shore,
And hear the mighty waters rolling evermore.
                              —Wordsworth.

They Would Not Wish Him Back (93).

The golden gates were open
And heavenly 'Angels' smiled
And with their tuneful harpstring
Welcomed the little child.

"They shouted 'high and holy,
A child hath entered in,
And safe from all temptation
A soul is sealed from sin.'

"They led him through the golden streets
On to the King of kings,
And a glory fell upon him
From the rustlings of their wings.

"The Saviour smiled upon him
As none on earth had smiled,
And Heaven's great glory shone around
The little earth-born child.

"On earth they missed the little one,
They sighed and wept and sighed,
And wondered if another such
As theirs had ever died.

"Oh! had they seen through those high gates
The welcome to him given,
They never would have wished their child
Back from his home in Heaven."

—Selected.

Legend of the Pitcher of Tears (94).

[The following poem was written by Mary Amsden Burroughs, to the painting, "The Pitcher of Tears" by Paul Thurman. The poem appeared in the Golden Rule.]

Many days a stricken mother,
  To her loss unreconciled,
Wept hot, bitter tears, complaining,
  "Cruel Death has stolen my child."

But one night as she was sleeping,
  To her soul there came a vision,
And she saw her little daughter
  In the blessed fields Elysian.

All alone the child was standing,
  And a heavy pitcher holding;
Swift the mother hastened to her
  Close around her arms infolding.

"Why so sad and lonely, darling?"
  Asked she, stroking soft her hair,
"See the many merry children
  Playing in the garden fair.

Look, they're beckoning and calling,

Go and help them pluck the flowers,
Put aside the heavy pitcher,
Dance away the sunny hours."

From the tender lips a-quiver
Fell the answer on her ears:
"On the earth my mother's weeping,
And this pitcher holds the tears.

Tears that touch the heavenly blossoms
Spoil the flowers where'er they fall;

So as long as she is weeping,
I must stand and catch them all."

"Wait no longer," cried the dreamer;
"Run and play, sweet child of mine;
Never more shall tears of sorrow
Spoil your happiness divine."

Like a bird released from bondage
Sped the happy maid away,
And the mother woke, her courage
Strengthened for each lonely day.

Once and Forever (95).

Our own are our own forever, God taketh not back His gift;
They may pass beyond our vision, but our souls shall find them out,
When the waiting is all accomplished, and the deathly shadows lift,
And glory is given for grieving, and the surety of God for doubt.

We may find the waiting bitter, and count the silence long:
God knoweth we are dust, and He pitieth our pain;
And when faith has grown to fulness, and the silence changed to song,
We shall eat the fruit of patience, and shall hunger not again.

So sorrowing hearts, who humbly in darkness and all alone
Sit missing a dear lost presence and the joy of a vanished day,
Be comforted with this message that our own are forever our own,
And God, who gave the gracious gift, He takes it never away.
—Susan Coolidge, in Sunday School Times.

Still With Us (96).

In that great cloister's stillness and seclusion,
By guardian angels led,
Safe from temptation, safe from sin's pollution,
She lives, whom we call dead.

Day after day, we think what she is doing
In those bright realms of air;
Year after year, her tender steps pursuing,
Behold her grown more fair.

Thus do we walk with her, and keep unbroken
The bond which nature gives,
Thinking that our remembrance, though unspoken,
May reach her where she lives.
—Longfellow.

The Reaper Death (97).

"There is a reaper, whose name is Death,
   And with his sickle keen
He reaps the bearded grain at a breath,
   And the flowers that grow between.

'Shall I have naught that is fair?' saith he;
   'Have naught but the bearded grain?
Though the breath of these flowers is sweet to me,
   I will give them all back again.' "

He gazed at the flowers with tearful eyes,
   He kissed their drooping leaves;
It was for the Lord of paradise
   He bound them in his sheaves.

'My Lord has need of these flowerets gay,'
   The reaper said, and smiled;
'Dear tokens of the earth are they,
   Where He was once a Child.

'They shall all bloom in fields of light,
   Transplanted by my care,
And saints upon their garments white
   These sacred blossoms wear.'

And the mother gave, in tears and pain,
   The flowers she most did love;
She knew she would find them all again
   In the fields of light above.

O, not in cruelty, not in wrath,
   The Reaper came that day;
'Twas an angel visited the green earth,
   And took the flowers away."
                                —Longfellow.

Glorified (98).

Not changed, but glorified! Oh beauteous language
   For those who weep,
Mourning the loss of some dear face departed.
   Fallen asleep.
Hushed into silence, never more to comfort
   The hearts of men,
Gone, like sunshine of another country,
   Beyond our ken.

We Shall Find Them (99).

I wonder, O, I wonder, where the little faces go,
That come and smile and stay awhile, and pass like flakes of snow—
The dear, wee baby faces that the world has never known,
But mothers hide, so tender-eyed, deep in their hearts alone.

"I love to think that somewhere, in the country we call heaven,
The land most fair of everywhere will unto them be given:
A land of little faces—very little, very fair—
And every one shall know her own and cleave unto it there.

"O grant it, loving Father, to the broken hearts that plead!
Thy way is best—yet O, to rest in perfect faith indeed!
To know that we shall find them—even them, the wee white dead—
At Thy right hand in Thy bright land, by living waters led!"

His Monument (100).

He built a house, time laid it in the dust;
He wrote a book, its title now forgot;
He ruled a city, but his name is not
On any tablet graven, or where rust
Can gather from disuse, or marble bust.

He took a child from out a wretched cot;
Who on the State dishonor might have brought;
And reared him in the Christian's hope and trust,
The boy to manhood grown, became a light
To many souls and preached to human need
The wondrous love of the Omnipotent.
The work has multiplied like stars at night
When darkness deepens; every noble deed
Lasts longer than a granite monument.
                              —Sarah Knowles Bolton.

Little Boy Blue's Toys (101).

Ay, faithful to Little Boy Blue they stand
  Each in the same old place—
Awaiting the touch of a little hand,
  The smile of a little face;
And they wonder, as waiting the long years through
  In the dust of that little chair,
What has become of our Little Boy Blue,
  Since he kissed them and put them there.
                              —Eugene Field.

Transplanted (102).

Ere sin could blight or sorrow fade
  Death came with friendly care;
The opening bud to heaven conveyed,
  And bade it blossom there.

"In the Heart of a Child" (104).

An angel paused in his onward flight
  With a seed of love and truth and right
And said, "O, where can this seed be sown
  Where 'twill yield most fruit when fully grown?"
The Saviour heard and said as He smiled,
  "Place it at once in the heart of a child."

Dear Little Hands (105).

Dear little hands, I miss them so!
All through the day, wherever I go—
All through the night, how lonely it seems,
For no little hands wake me out of my dreams
I miss them all through the weary hours,
I miss them as others miss sunshine and flowers;
Daytime or nighttime, wherever I go,
Dear little hands, I miss them so.

The Children On the Shore (106).

But for those first affections,
  Those shadowy recollections,
    Which, be they what they may,
Are yet the fountain light of all our day,
Are yet a master light of all our seeing;
  Uphold us—cherish us—and have power to make
Our noisy years seem moments in the being
Of the eternal silence; truths that wake,
      To perish never;
Which neither listlessness nor mad endeavor
      Nor man nor boy,
Nor all that is at enmity with joy,
Can utterly abolish or destroy!
  Hence, in a season of calm weather,
      Though inland far we be,
Our souls have sight of that immortal sea
      Which brought us hither,
        Can in a moment travel thither,
And see the children sport upon the shore,
And hear the mighty waters rolling evermore.
                              —Wordsworth.

The Maister and the Bairns (107).

The Maister sat in a wee cot hoose,
  Tae the Jordan's waters near,
An' the fisher folk crushed and crooded roun',
  The Maister's words tae hear.

An' even the bairns frae the near-han' streets
   Were mixin' in wi' the thrang—
Laddies and lassies, wi' wee bare feet,
   Jinkin' the crood amang.

An' ane o' the Twal' at the Maister's side,
   Rase up an' cried alood—
"Come, come, bairns, this is nae place for you,
   Rin awa' hame out the crood."

But the Maister said, as they turned awa'—
   "Let the wee bairns come tae Me!"
An' He gathered them roun' Him whar He sat,
   An' lifted ane up on His knee.

An' He gathered them roun' Him whar He sat,
   An' straikit their curly hair,
An' He said to the won'erin' fisher folk
   Wha crooded aroun' Him there—

"Sen na' the weans awa' frae me,
   But raither this lesson lairn—
That nane'll win in at heaven's yett
   That isna as pure as a bairn!"

An' He that wisna oor kith and kin,
   But a Prince o' the far awa',
Gethered the wee anes in His airms,
   An' blessed them ane an' a'.

O Thou who watchest the ways o' men,
   Keep our feet in the heavenly airt,
An' bring us at last tae Thy hame abune,
   As pure as the bairns in hairt.

                              —W. Thomson.

It Is Best (108).

Mothers, I see you with your nursery light,
Leading your babies all in white,
   To their sweet rest;
Christ, the Good Shepherd, carries mine tonight,
   And that is best!

I cannot help tears when I see them twine
Their fingers in yours, and their bright curls shine
   On your warm breast;
But the Saviour's is purer than yours or mine:
   He can love best!

You tremble each hour because your arms
Are weak; your heart is wrung with alarms,
   And sore oppressed;
My darlings are safe, out of reach of harm;
   And that is best.

You know over yours may hang even now
Pain and disease, whose fulfilling slow
   Naught can arrest;
Mine in God's gardens run to and fro,
   And that is best.

You know that of yours the feeblest one
And dearest may live long years alone,
   Unloved, unblest;
Mine are cherished of saints around God's throne,
   And that is best.

You must dread for years the crime that sears,
Dark guilt unwashed by repentant tears,
   And unconfessed;
Mine entered spotless on eternal years,
   Oh, how much the best!

But grief is selfish, and I cannot see
Always why I should so stricken be,
   More than the rest;
But I know that, as well as for them, for me
   God did the best!

                    —Helen Hunt.

TEXTS AND TREATMENT HINTS.

"Except Ye Be Converted and Become As Little Children."—Matt. 18:3 (109).

I. The first fact about childhood is its dependence, and the glorious appeal of the child spirit is felt when they act upon this dependence. They not only fly to our arms when distressed or afraid, they yield themselves willingly to our guidance and control. Strong and thoughtful minds feel this fact about children with keenness even unto poignancy. And this is the first and last and the deepest fact in our relations to God, the Father of all. He sees our unlimited dependence on Him. For life and breath and all things, alike in the earthly and the spiritual spheres, we have no source to draw on but His power, His wisdom, and His tender mercy. It is here we need to learn directness and simplicity. Our clouded faith, our sinful hearts, our proud independence, have separated us from Him by destroying this sense of dependence and the simple act of faith in which it is expressed. Here Jesus would have us become as little children, for in the kingdom of heaven it is this attitude of trust which is perfected, this sense of dependence upon God's fatherly grace for all things, which rules all thought and is the spring of all action. . . . .

II. The second fact about childhood is the simplicity of its motives. That, indeed, constitutes one of the great problems which parents and teachers meet in dealing with vigorous and happy young children. The one thing, the one disastrous skill they have not yet attained, is to conceal or to mix their motives. When they do begin to hide the reasons of conduct, or to act from a considered combination of impulses and motives, they have already begun to enter into the sin of the human race. They have been caught in the net of complex moral standards, and the unselfish and selfish elements of life have begun to be mixed up in their cup of experience.—Pres. W. D. Mackensie, D. D., in the S. S. Times.

"My Beloved Is Gone Down to His Garden . . . . to Gather Lilies."—
Song of Solomon 6:2 (110).

I. Children are tender plants committed to our care.
II. Christ is the head-gardener.
III. He gathers the blossoms when He will.
IV. Gathered by Him they are fadeless.
V, Shall we not permit Him to do what His love and wisdom deem best?

"He Shall Gather the Lambs in His Arm and Carry Them in His Bosom."
—Isa. 40:11 (111).

I. We mistakenly think of death as "ruthlessly snatching our little ones from us." An utterly false conception, like so many other notions we cherish concerning death.
II, The lessed truth is that Christ lovingly calls the children to Himself.
III. They are forever safely beyond the reach of pain and temptation.
IV. We may rejoin them by and by if we will.

"Suffer the Little Children to Come Unto Me"—Luke 18:16 (112).
Permit them to come to me:
I. In loving devotion; the personal approach of prayer.
II. In glad trust; and simple acts of service.
III. In answer to the final summons; when it becomes evident that human efforts to keep them no longer avail.

"And the Streets of the City Shall Be Full of Boys and Girls Playing in
the Streets Thereof."—Zech. 8:5 (113).

The religion of Christ makes full provision for children:
I. In the home. Christian nurture.
II. In the church. The emphasis given to child religion.
III. In heaven. Their salvation assured.

"The Lord Gave and the Lord Hath Taken Away; Blessed Be the Name
of the Lord."—Job. 1:21 (114).

I. Both we and our children belong to God.
II. While He has the right to dispose of us as He will, that right is always exercised in love and never arbitrarily.

III.   Believing this we should accept his will unquestioningly.

"They Shall Hunger No More, Neither Thirst any more; Neither Shall the Sun Strike Upon Them, Nor Any Heat."—Rev. 7:16 (115).

There is a "brighter side" to bereavement, when children are called home.

I.   There is no question as to their eternal safety.

II.   There is certainty of escape from many earthly perils and sorrows. "No hunger, thirst, etc."

III.   They are still ours though absent for a little while from the family circle.

"And Jesus Called to Him a Little Child."—Matt. 18:2 (116).

I.   Childhood has no immunity from death.
    One-fourth of the race die under eight years of age, and one-half under eighteen.

II.   All children who go out into the other life go out in answer to Jesus' call.

III.   And He stands waiting with open arms to receive them.

A Well-Conditioned Child Illustrates the Distinctive Features of Christian Character (117).

I.   Because he does not assert nor aggrandize himself.

II.   Because he has no memory for injuries.

III.   Because he has no pride of opinion; confesses ignorance.

IV.   Because he can imagine; and has the key to another world.— John Watson, M. A.

III. DEATH IN YOUTH.

REFLECTIONS AND ILLUSTRATIONS.

Two Sons Reunited in Death (118).

They are not lost, but simply in another clime awaiting our coming. Another writes: "My friend, who is the editor of a religious journal, lost a son by death only a few weeks before Easter. I could not keep back the tears when I opened his paper, a little later, and saw in the lines of the editorial page, the cry of the soul of the editor. These were the words: "Never before was our Easter hope brighter or more comforting. Never before had we greater reason to rejoice in the doctrine of the resurrection, nor to thank God for the evidences that it is true. The dead shall live again. We shall see them. We shall be with them. Our reunion shall be eternal." Going on to speak about his own personal loss, he said, "We wept for him. We are weeping still. We think of him as now with his brother, who died sixteen years before him. Surely the Master has brought them together. They are happier than we could make them, and we shall be happier, when restored to them, than we ever could have been had they not been given to us."

Hope in Blossom (119).

A traveler returned from Bermuda wrote, "I have before me a blossom that was picked in the bud in Bermuda more than a fortnight ago. It has opened to a full flower with petals more than nine inches long, and a spread of six inches. It is a sweet breath from the south in these bleak days of spring. It is a rarer delight to see these lilies where they grow. Last month, when the blizzard was howling about the steeples of our churches, I stood at the side of a field of lilies, perhaps twenty or thirty acres in extent. A hundred thousand flowers were in bloom in that single field. The air was heavy with their perfume and the bees were humming from flower to flower busy with their golden harvest; and beyond, over the edge of the field, stretched the silver sea." The writer goes on to say, "It was a picture filled with a sense of brightness and hope, faint image of that bright prospect which spread before the eyes of those disciples on their first Easter morning, when the glad message went hurrying from lip to lip—'The Lord is risen.'"

Make Your Son Your Companion (120).

My heart goes out in sincere pity to the man who cannot make a companion of his boys. Do you know, fathers, that you are unconsciously depriving yourself and your sons of the sweetest pleasures if you do not make them your companions?

Think what you are doing by allowing them to grow up without your protecting care. Some day, perhaps, you will realize what you miss by not associating with them more. Be with all your children just a much as possible while they are little, for by so doing you will become young yourself and will appreciate with keener zest the good things of this life.

The reason why many boys go on the wrong road is because their fathers maintain an indifferent attitude toward them from the time they are two years of age until they are eighteen or nineteen. You cannot reasonably expect a boy to turn out as you should like to have him if you take no personal interest in his welfare. I know of a father who has a son in whom he takes a genuine interest, and they are the closest chums it is possible to imagine. It is, of course, impossible for them to be together all the time, for the father works all day at his store and the boy goes to school, but at night they are together. The father does not monopolize the companionship of his son by any means, for he invites other boys to call at the house, and when you see them all together you can well imagine that there is no man about. The father enters into all the sports of the little fellows, who rightly aver that "he is great." That boy is now almost nineteen, but when he had passed the age of twelve the father said:

"My, oh, my! next year you'll be in your 'teens, and then what shall I do?"

"Same as you've always done," said the boy, while a dimple came in his cheek and a sly twinkle came to his eye. "You know we've pledged ourselves to stick together forever."

"So we have, so we have," said the father, "and no matter how big you get, you will always be my chum."

That's the way to treat your boys.—The Baptist Commonwealth.

Diminishing Chances (121).

The testimony of one thousand converted Sabbath-school scholars in the United States, Great Britain and Canada:

128 scholars converted at age of from 8 to 12 years.

392 scholars converted at age of from 13 to 16 years.

322 scholars converted at age of from 17 to 20 years.

118 scholars converted at age of from 21 to 24 years.

40 scholars converted at age of from 25 to 60 years.

52 per cent by age of 16.

84 per cent by age of 20.

96 per cent by age of 24.

4 per cent at older ages.

A Boy's Mistake—A Sad Reconciliation (122).

There was an Englishman who had an only son; and only sons are often petted, and humored, and ruined. This boy became very headstrong, and very often he and his father had trouble. One day they had a quarrel, and the father was very angry, and so was the son; and the father said he wished the boy would leave home and never come back. The boy said he would go, and would not come into his father's house again till he sent for him. The father said he would never send for him.

Well, away went the boy. But when a father gives up a boy, a mother does not. You mothers will understand that, but the fathers may not. You know there is no love on earth so strong as a mother's love. A great many things may separate a man and his wife; a great many things may separate a father from his son; but there is nothing in the wide world that can ever separate a true mother from her child. To be sure, there are some mothers that have drank so much liquor that they have drunk up all their affection. But I am talking about a true mother; and she would never cast off her boy.

Well, the mother began to write and plead with the boy to write to his father first, and he would forgive him; but the boy said, "I will never go home till father asks me." Then she plead with the father, but the father said, "No, I will never ask him." At last the mother came down to her sick-bed, broken-hearted, and when she was given up by the physician to die, the husband, anxious to gratify her last wish, wanted to know if there was something he could do for her before she died. The mother gave him a look; he well knew what it meant. Then she said, "Yes, there is one thing you can do. You can send for my boy. That is the only wish on earth you can gratify. If you do not pity him and love him when I am dead and gone, who will?" "Well," said the father, "I will send word to him that you want to see him." "No," she says, "you know he will not come for me. If ever I see him you must send for him."

At last the father went to his office and wrote a dispatch in his own name, asking the boy to come home. As soon as he got the invitation from his father he started off to see his dying mother. When he opened the door to go in he found his mother dying, and his father by the bedside. The father heard the door open, and saw the boy, but instead of going to meet him, he went to another part of the room, and refused to speak to him. His mother seized his hand—how she had longed to press it! She kissed him, and then said, "Now, my son, just speak to your father. You speak first, and it will all be over." But the boy said, "No, mother, I will not speak to him until he speaks to me." She took her husband's hand in one hand and the boy's in the other, and spent her dying moments in trying to bring about a reconciliation. Then just as she was expiring—she could not speak—so she put the hand of the wayward boy into the hand of the father, and passed away! The boy looked at the mother, and the father at the wife, and at last the father's heart broke, and he opened his arms, and took that boy to his bosom, and by that body they were reconciled. Sinner, that is only a faint type, a poor illustration, because God is not angry with you.

I bring you tonight to the dead body of Christ. I ask you to look at the wounds in his hands and feet, and the wound in his side. And I ask you, "Will you not be reconciled?"—Moody.

A Boy's Religion (123).

I was standing before the window of an art store, where a picture of the crucifixion of our Lord was on exhibition; as I gazed I was conscious of the approach of another, and turning beheld a little lad gazing intently at the picture also. Noticing that this mite of humanity was a sort of street Arab, I thought I would speak to him; so I asked, pointing to the picture, 'Do you know who it is?' 'Yes,' came the quick response. 'That's our Saviour,' with a mingled look of pity and surprise that I should not know. With an evident desire to enlighten me further, he continued, after a pause, 'Them's the soldiers, the Roman soldiers,' and with a long-drawn sigh. 'That woman crying there is His mother.' He waited, apparently for me to question him further, thrust his hands into his pockets, and with a reverent and subdued voice, added, 'They killed Him, Mister. Yes, sir, they killed Him!' I looked at the little ragged fellow and asked, 'Where did you learn this?' He replied, 'At the Mission Sunday-school.' Full of thought regarding the benefits of Mission Sunday-schools I turned away and resumed my walk, leaving the little lad looking at the picture. I had not walked a block when I heard his childish treble calling 'Mister! Say, mister!' I turned. He was running toward me, but paused; then up went his little hand and with triumphant sound in voice he said, 'I wanted to tell you He rose again! Yes, mister, He rose again.'"—Sel.

A Lofty Life Purpose (125).

A true, lofty life may be lived with a very small modicum. There is no proportion between wealth and happiness, nor between wealth and nobleness. The fairest life ever lived on earth was that of a poor man, and with all its beauty it moved within the limits of narrow resources. The loveliest blossoms do not grow on plants that plunge their greedy roots into the fattest soil. A little light earth in the crack of a hard rock will do. We need enough for the physical being to root itself in; we need no more.

Young men! especially you who are plunged into the busy life of our great commercial centres, and are tempted by everything you see, and by most that you hear, to believe that a prosperous trade and hard cash are the realities, and all else mist and dreams, fix this in your mind to begin life with—God is the reality, all else is shadow. Do not make it your ambition to get on; but to get up. Having food and raiment, let us be content. Seek for your life's delight and treasure, in thought, in truth, in pure affections, in moderate desires, in a spirit set on God. These are the realities of our possessions. As for all the rest, it is sham and show.—Alexander Maclaren, D. D.

Remember Thy Creator In Youth (126)

A lady came to Dr. Chalmers and said: "Doctor, I cannot bring my child to Christ. I've talked, and talked, but it's of no use." The Doctor thought she had not much skill, and said, "Now you be quiet and I will talk to her alone." When the Doctor got the Scotch lassie alone he said to her, "They are bothering you a good deal about this question; now suppose I just tell your mother you don't want to be talked to any more upon this subject for a year. How will that do?" Well, the Scotch lassie hesitated a little, and then said she "didn't think it would be safe to wait for a year. Something might turn up. She might die before then."

'Well, that's so," replied the doctor, "but suppose we say six months." She didn't think even this would be safe. "That's so," was the doctor's reply; "well, let us say three months." After a little hesitation, the girl finally said, "I don't think it would be safe to put it off for three months —don't think it would be safe to put it off at all," and they went down on their knees and found Christ.

Youth's Opportunities (127).

The young can come to Christ easily; for those whose youth is past it is frequently difficult. Dr. Wilton Merle Smith, in his recent book of sermons, aptly says: "The little ones come easily. Childhood is all defenseless against heaven, but it is harder for the growing boy, still harder for yonder man just crossing the threshold of manhood. With every added year the weight of sin increases, and harder is it for the grace of God to draw the soul to itself. By and by such may become the weight of sin that omnipotence cannot move it. Yes, my friends, it is vastly easier to come to the Master now, than by and by. Childhood is the open door, youth the closing gateway, manhood the barricaded entrance. Not long ago, in a company of Christians, where more than a hundred were gathered, we took a ballot. It was found that three-quarters of them had been converted before twenty-one years of age, and nine-tenths of them before twenty-five. It is a momentous truth that the chances for conversion in after life, young men, decrease inversely as the square of the years."

Youth's Need of Christ (128).

A company of hunters were eating their lunch up in the Scotch highlands when one of them spied, on the face of a great precipice opposite, a sheep on a narrow ledge of rock. He pointed it out to the rest, and one of the guides explained that the sheep had been tempted by the sight of green grass to jump down to some ledge a foot or two from the top of the cliff. Soon, having eaten all the grass there, and unable to get back, there was nothing else for it to do but scramble down to some lower ledge; there in turn it would finish what might be there and have to jump to some ledge yet lower.

"Now it has got to the last," said he, looking through the field glass and seeing that below it went the steep cliff without a break for two or three hundred feet.

"What will happen to it now?" asked the others eagerly. "Oh, now it will be lost! The eagles will see it and swoop down upon it, and, maddened with fright and hunger, it will leap over the cliff and be dashed to pieces on the rocks below."

Is it not just like that that a soul goes astray? A man is tempted to partake of the pleasures that are on the ledge just a little lower than the high tableland of moral life on which he has lived. Do some of you not know what it means? It is only a little way down, so you think, to that show of pleasure or seeming gain, attractive as the show of green grass was to the sheep, you expected to go right back, but it is easier to go **down**

to the next ledge than it is to get back, and so down you ko, like King
Saul and like the lost sheep. One year, two years pass away and your
heart becomes harder and more indifferent than you thought possible for
you.

Do not despair, even though you are on the last ledge, the Good
Shepherd is hunting for you. He has left the ninety and nine in the
wilderness and has come out over the bleak mountains of sin seeking for
you. If you will heed his voice, he will lift you again to the highlands
of peace and joy. He, and He alone, can save you.—Rev. Geo. B. Gray.

What To Live For (129).

To be a young man on the right side of the King; to be clothed in
the faultless righteousness of Christ, to get a commission straight from
the throne of God, to be crowned unto manhood's completeness by Jesus,
and thus to do life's work—that will be to make no failure. It will be
to have done some good here. It will be to find a welcome yonder.

"There's a fount about to stream,
There's a light about to gleam,
There's a midnight darkness changing into day;
Men of thought, and men of action, clear the way."
—The Young Man Fair-Squaw.

Dare to Be Religious (130).

Young men, dare to be religious, in the finest, loftiest, grandest
meaning of that word. Don't allow yourselves to be laughed out of your
reverence for the word of God and the piety of your father and mother.
Don't consider it a disgrace to be called "good." Don't be coaxed and
wheedled and seduced into forbidden sins. Have some courage. If you
can do no more, do as Luther did at the Diet of Worms, when he said,
"Here I stand, I can do naught else. God help me. Amen!"

The gospel is in sympathy with young men. That scene at the tomb
of Jesus settles that. Therefore have a stout heart, and dare to be
religious.

What sort of religion are you to strive for? There are many brands.
Let yours be a manly religion. Don't let it degenerate into cant. Don't
let it melt down into mushy sentimentalism. Don't let it die away into
a starveling rite, the naked bones of formalism and ritual. Don't let it
lapse into a moss-grown, mildewed theology. Let it be sincere and
straightforward. Let it be clear-cut and stalwart. Let it be sympathetic
and tender. Let it fine-grained and broad-brained. Let it be rich, full,
free, divine.—Rev. James E. Vance, D. D.

Christian Culture (131).

You are rich, and your children may inherit your riches. You are
talented, and your children may inherit your talents. But you cannot
convey to them by will your education, or your principles, or your religion. These are to be impressed upon them, not by one act, but by the

constant persevering efforts of your daily life. But under "the grace of God" they may become, and they will become, what you most desire them to be and in nine cases out of ten will be reprints of yourselves. Learn, then, to "show piety at home."

A Father's Tribute to His Son (132).

[Edward Leigh Pell, Jr., firstborn son of Dr. Edward Leigh Pell, of Richmond, Va., a youth of brilliant mind and rare promise, died on September 15, 1910. His father, confined to his bed by sickness, dictated the following tribute, which was read at the funeral by the officiating minister.]

The world has no room for a boy. He is too rough for its taste, and in his awkwardness he often rubs it the wrong way. We treasure our men, our women, and our girls, but we only tolerate our boys—tolerate them with the hope that they will soon cease to be boys.

But a boy is like a cocoanut brought to us fresh from the tree, enveloped in its great shaggy covering. The goodness is all within, and you must crack its very heart to find it. You never know what is in the heart of a boy until it has been cracked by some hard vicissitude of life.

When I was taken sick my boy squared his frail shoulders to bear his father's burdens. Day after day he went to the office and tried to take his father's place; and when they gave him business worries to bring home, he would often hide them in his pocket and meet his father with a smiling face. His father should not be worried.

One day he came home in pain and laid down his work. When they were about to take him away to the hospital, I went to him and said: "My boy, you know I have always loved you with all my heart."

"And I have loved you with all my heart too," he replied; "but papa, don't worry; I don't mind the operation. I am only afraid you will worry and it will make you worse. Don't worry, papa."

And day after day there came a message of love from the hospital with its admonition not to worry.

When at last he began to realize that he must go, he sent for me.

"God has been good to us," I said to him, "and we can trust Him."

"I am trusting Him," he said.

"We've had lots of good times together, my boy, and we are going to have many more; for I am coming to you, and we shall live together forever."

And he gave my hand a squeeze that broke my heart.

At the last moment, while talking to his mother, his brilliant mind as clear as it had ever been in all his life, he looked up suddenly and exclaimed: "They are coming."

"Who are coming, my child?" asked the mother.

"O, the angels, the angels! I see them!"

"And won't you come for me, my boy?" asked the mother.

"Yes, yes. Good-by, good-by, good-by."

And he passed within the veil as peacefully as a babe drops to sleep on its mother's breast.

This is what I found in the heart of my boy. Perhaps you will find it in the heart of your boy too—when it has been cracked.—Christian Advocate.

A Father's Mistake (133).

There is a little story that has gone the round of the American press that made a great impression upon me as a father. A father took his little child out into the field one Sabbath, and, it being a hot day, he lay down under a beautiful shady tree. The little child ran about gathering wild flowers and little blades of grass, and coming to its father and saying, "Pretty! pretty!" At last the father fell asleep, and while he was sleeping the little child wandered away. When he awoke, his first thought was, "Where is my child?" He looked all around, but he could not see him. He shouted at the top of his voice, but all he heard was the echo of his own voice. Running to a little hill, he looked around and shouted again. No response! Then going to a precipice at some distance, he looked down, and there, upon the rocks and briars, he saw the mangled form of his loved child. He rushed to the spot, took up the lifeless corpse, and hugged it to his bosom, and accused himself of being the murderer of his child. While he was sleeping the child had wandered over the precipice. I thought as I heard that, what a picture of the church of God!

How many fathers and mothers, how many Christian men, are sleeping now while their children wander over the terrible precipice right into the bottomless pit. Father, where is your boy to-night?"—Moody.

Just Away (134).

"I cannot say and I will not say
That he is dead, he is just away,
With a cheery smile and a wave of his hand
He has wandered into another land."

He himself had gone upon the journey of all days. Yet his things still lay about the house, his favorite tennis racket, the old red sweater, darned in several places with wool of a lighter shade, the leaky fountain pen on his desk, the bunch of keys fallen from a jacket pocket onto the closet floor, all these stung us like poisoned arrows. "If you can stand the first smart of seeing them around," said one who was wise in sorrow, "they will comfort you by and by." I believe the dear dumb things kept our grief wholesome and clean like the wound which the surgeon opens daily that it may heal better later on. We named him tremulously at first, but by and by we told over his jokes and pet sayings with a bitter-sweet mirth, we learned to smile bravely into the picture of the gay, boyish face and in our family plans to consider what he would have wished. In short, to act as if he was "just away."

We had taken scant interest in another land while our family circle was unbroken. Now we scanned eagerly every scrap of verse, sermon, or book which dealt with a "Beyond." We demanded immortality for our own, but learned as bitterly as weeping Eve, or sorrowing David of old that human knowledge has no key to the door of the Hereafter. Then when we had vainly explored all other paths, we found God upon the Hills of Prayer. We were comforted. There is no word tender or blessed enough in human speech to explain how. All that we can solemnly affirm is that the great majestic presence of the Father abides upon those everlasting hills.

We learned there that our beloved was safe in God's keeping. Wherever he may abide, it is well with him. Our fluttering hearts whisper that he still thinks and yearns for us, though among the heavenly mansions. He is "just away," a little nearer to God than we. We must walk worthily that we too may draw nearer. Sometimes we wonder in our blundering way if we have guessed the meaning of his swift departure from us? Perhaps it was because God desired to make Himself known unto us.—The Congregationalist.

The Next Room (135).

"Those who are gone from you, you have. Those who departed loving you, love you still, and you love them always. They are not really gone, those dear hearts and true, they are only gone into the next room and you will probably get up and follow them and yonder doors will close upon you and you will be no more seen."—Thackeray.

ILLUSTRATIVE VERSES.

They Wait For Us (136).

There are pictures in our river—
Pictures full of wondrous beauty—
Of the trees that bend above it,
Of the cloudlets floating o'er it,
Of the western sun and sky,
Of the mountains dark and high;
And our hearts are thrilled and
    glowing
As we stand and see it flowing—
Coming, going,
In its wondrous beauty flowing,
Flowing to the Inland Sea.
Standing on the bridge above it,
Gazing out upon the sea,

How our thoughts are with it flow-
    ing,
Going, flowing
Far beyond the Inland Sea,
Out into the world beyond us,
Where the dear ones who have
    loved us
Work and wait—
Work with us to "tell the story"
Of the love and power and glory
Of the mighty God above us
And the Christ who died to save
    us;
Wait with us the world's redemp-
    tion,
And the coming of our King.

A Buried Seed (137).

Two thousand years ago a flower
  Bloomed brightly in a far-off land;
Two thousand years ago its seed
  Was placed within a dead man's hand.

Suns rose and set, years came and went;
   That dead hand kept its treasure well;
Nations were born and turned to dust,
   While life was hidden in that shell.

The senseless hand is robbed at last;
   The seed is buried in the earth,
When, lo! the life long sleeping there
   Into a lovely flower burst forth.

And will not He who watched the seed,
   And kept the life within the shell,
When those He loves are laid to rest,
   Watch o'er His buried saints as well?

And will not He from 'neath the sod
   Cause something glorious to arise?
Ay, though it sleeps two thousand years,
   Yet all this slumbering dust shall rise.

Then will I lay me down in peace,
   When called to leave this vale of tears;
For "in my flesh shall I see God,"
   E'en though I sleep two thousand years.
                —Sarah H. Bradford

The Breaking Day (138).

We may hope with an undying hope
Since He who knows our need is just,
That somewhere, somehow, meet we must.
Alas for him who never sees
The stars shine through his cypress trees;
Who hopeless lays his dead away,
Nor looks to see the breaking day
Across the mournful marble play:
Who hath not learned in hours of faith
The truth to sight and sense unknown,
That life is ever lord of death,
And love can never lose its own.

New Life (139).

Only a little shriveled seed—
It might be a flower or grass or weed;
Only a box of dirt on the edge
Of a narrow, dusty window-ledge;
Only a few scant summer showers;
Only a few clear, shining hours—
That was all. Yet God could make
Out of these, for a sick child's sake,
A blossom-wonder as fair and sweet
As ever broke at an angel's feet.

Only a life of barren pain,
Wet with sorrowful tears for rain;
Warmed sometimes by a wandering gleam
Of joy that seemed but a happy dream.
A life as common and brown and bare
As the box of earth in the window there;
Yet it bore at last the precious bloom
Of a perfect soul in a narrow room—
Pure as the snowy leaves that fold
Over the flower's heart of gold.
                    —Henry Van Dyke.

Death Gaining an Entrance for Faith (140).

"Hearts that the preacher could not touch,
  By wayside graves are raised;
And lips cry, 'God be merciful!'
  That ne'er cried, 'God be praised!'"

He Lives (141).

"He lives—in all the past
He lives; nor to the last
  Of seeing him again will I despair,
In dreams I see him now,
And on his angel brow
  I see it written, 'Thou shalt see me there.'"

God Knows Why (142).

Gods knows why—
Alas! not we—that out of all this surging tide
        He stepped aside
Into quiet so profound before his time.
        Not a rhyme
Of the lyric, labor, ever shall he sing—
        Never bring
Any hard-won guerdon—rare reward of life—
        Out of strife.
Here he lies—we loved him—and we leave him here.
        Some bright sphere
Has made room, we know, to take our wanderer in.
        He shall win
Otherwhere what God had meant for him—and so
        While the snow
Beats and blows about his early grave, we'll say:
        "Far away
Safe and strong his life goes on at God's behest,
        And God knows best."
                    —Luella Clark.

Shall We Find Them at the Portals? (143).

Will they meet us, cheer and greet us,
　Those we've loved, who've gone before?
Shall we find them at the portals,
Find our beautified immortals,
　When we reach that radiant shore?

Hearts are broken for some token,
　That they live and love us yet;
And we ask, "Can those who've left us,
Of love's look and tone bereft us,
　Though in Heaven, can they forget?"

And we often, as days soften,
　And comes out the evening star,
Looking westward, sit and wonder
Whether when so far asunder,
　They still know how dear they are?

Past yon portals, our immortals,
　Those who walk with Him in white,
Do they, mid their bliss recall us,
Know they what events befall us,
　Will our coming wake delight?

They will meet us, cheer and greet us,
　Those we've loved who've gone before;
We shall find them at the portals,
Find our beautified immortals,
　When we reach that radiant shore.

Watching at the Gate (144).

The little hands are folded like white lilies on his breast,
The busy feet, so noisy once, are evermore at rest;
The snow drift of his little bed is stainless, smooth and still,
As if waiting for the laddie back, his cozy place to fill;
The hobby-horse is saddled, and gives forth a hearty neigh,
But the rider does not heed it, for he is far away.
He is dwelling with the angels, and, though I may be late,
I know he'll not forget me, but be watching at the gate.

His toys are laid upon the shelf, his clothes are put away,
The little rug is folded up, on which he knelt to pray;
His empty chair is by the hearth, as if expecting him,
And when I see that vacant chair my eyes with tears are dim.
I listen, wait, and listen for a voice that never calls,
For a step along the hallway, but the footstep never falls.
But this comfort I have always, that though I may be late,
I know he'll not forget me, but be watching at the gate.

His grave is on the prairie, where sweet clover blossoms grow,
Where the sky is clear and open, and the fragrant zephyrs blow;
Kind trees are bending o'er it, as if God had placed them there
To guard where he is sleeping with a never ceasing care.
Oh, my heart is aching, breaking, while I am waiting for the
　　bliss
Of the sweetness and the rapture of his gladsome smile and kiss.
But this thought cheers me always, that though I may be late,
I know he'll not forget me, but be watching at the gate.

—Rev. Campbell Coyle, D. D,

The Best Is Yet To Be (145).

The best is yet to be,
The last of life for which the first was made:
　　Our times are in His hand,
　　Who saith: "A whole I planned,
Youth shows but half: trust God; see all, nor be afraid.

Our Own (146).

Our own are our own forever; God taketh not back His gift;
　　They may pass beyond our vision, but our souls shall find them out
When the waiting is all accomplished, and the deathly shadows lift,
　　And glory is given for grieving, and the surety of God for doubt.

We may find the waiting bitter, and count the silence long;
　　God knoweth we are dust, and He pitieth our pain;
And when faith has grown to fulness, and the silence changed to song,
　　We shall eat the fruit of patience, and shall hunger not again.

So sorrowing hearts who humbly in darkness and all alone
　　Sit missing a dear lost presence and the joy of a vanished day,
Be comforted with this message, that our own are forever our own,
　　And God, who gave the gracious gift, He takes it never away.

—Susan Coolidge.

TEXTS AND TREATMENT HINTS.

"Remember Thy Creator in the Days of Thy Youth."—Ec. 12:1 (147).

1. God has a right to our entire and lifelong service.
2. God has a right to our constant love and gratitude.
3. God has a right to be glorified in us.
4. It is not a reasonable thing that we should give God the mere dregs of our life.—Rev. Tnos. H. Leale.

"Her Sun is Gone Down While It Is Yet Day."—Jer. 15:9 (148).

1. Nature has her fixed times and seasons.

2. Death has no seasons. It strikes down youth and age alike.

3. In the present instance this is illustrated. Youth, glowing in the flush of early promise is cut down.

4. Be ready, for in such hour as ye think not, the Bridegroom cometh.

"If Thou Hadst Been Here, My Brother Had Not Died."—John 11:21 (149).

We learn:

I. That the friends of Jesus are not exempted from affliction in the world. If such immunity might have been expected in any case, it surely would have been in that of the members of the Bethany family who so often received and entertained the Lord. In the highest sacrificial sense of the word, no one ever suffered for others as Christ did; but in a lower sense it is true that believers often do suffer for others; and when their benefit is secured thereby, the afflicted ones discover that their sickness has really been for the glory of God, so that they enter in a very real way into the fellowship of the Saviour's sufferings.

II. The friends of Jesus in their affliction turn directly and immediately to Him. In the day of prosperity it may be occasionally difficult to say whether a man is a Christian or not; but when, in time of trouble he makes straight for Christ, we know then most surely whose he is and whom he serves. Take a note of it then, and when affliction comes, observe to whom you flee for succor—for that will tell you whether you are, or are not, a friend of Jesus.

III. The response of the Lord comes often in such a way as seems to aggravate the evil. Christ loved the family at Bethany, therefore He did not come immediately at their call. "That looks like a non-sequitur, but it is the sober truth. He had in store for them a greater kindness than they could have dreamed of; and therefore He delayed till He could confer that upon them. There is nothing for us at such a time but to wait in patient, trustful expectation; but when we get to the end we shall see that there was love in the discipline.

IV. The friends of Jesus have different individualities but a common danger in their sorrow. In all our trials we are prone to lose sight of the universality of God's providence, and to torment ourselves with this unbelieving "if." It proceeds on the principle that the providence of God is not concerned in everything, and it gives to secondary causes a supremacy that does not belong to them. When calamity comes upon you, be sure that it is not because this or that accident prevented relief, nor because the Saviour was not with you, but because it was His will, and His will only, to bring about that which shall be better for you and others than your deliverance would have been.

V. The friends of Jesus have a blessed end to all their sorrows. "Rest in the Lord, therefore, and wait pa[iently for Him."—Rev. W. M. Taylor, D. D.

"Our Friend Lazarus Sleepeth."—John 11:11 (150).

Thoughts of death are suited to do us good. It is well that we should consider now, while yet life may be granted us, our latter end. It is well, when by any cause, either in the outward look of nature, or from what may happen within our homes, we are called off from taking thought only of present things—of what we shall eat, what we shall drink, wherewithal we shall be clothed—and constrained to face the most distant future; constrained to look into the darkness of the grave, and to question ourselves, each for himself, as to our preparation and as to our readiness to die.

I. "Our friend Lazarus sleepeth." That is the way in which Jesus spoke of death. He called it by no harsher word than sleep. Christ cannot mislead us, and He calls the death of His friend sleep. Let us not fear to lean upon His words for ourselves, for our companions; let this henceforth be the idea which we attach to death, "Our friend sleepeth." His toil is ended, his sorrows are ended, his pains are ended; he is out of the reach of the miseries of the sinful world. And when we say this, let us carry on our thoughts further. Death is sleep, but sleep implies an awakening. And this awakening, what is it to the Christian but the resurrection—the rising again of our body, the going back of the spirit; the fitting of the whole man to be an inheritor of everlasting life?

II. Note here a lesson (1) of warning, and that is, to be prepared for death and judgment—to live now, so that we may be ready at any moment to depart. Be no more putters off, but performers of your Lord's will. Think how any day, any hour, His words may be heard. Think how soon that night cometh in which no work may be done, in which to repent and amend will be no longer possible. (2) A lesson of comfort. At the appointed time Christ will come and awaken His friends, that where He is there also may His true servants be.—Rev. R. D. B. Raunsley.

"And Daniel Gave Thanks Before His God As He Did Aforetime."—Daniel 6:10 (151).

Dr. James Stalker described a "young man's religion" as:

I. Not merely a creed but an experience.

II. Not merely a restraint, but an inspiration.

III. Not merely an insurance for the next, but a program for this world.

"How Long Have I To Live?"—2 Sam. 19:34 (152).

This is a useful question for every man to put to himself. In the little time that remained to Barzillai he could find no enjoyment in eating and drinking, even at the king's table. There are many things in life which are not worth doing because the time is so short. If we could guarantee that our life should be continued for a century, we could arrange our affairs accordingly; but as our breath is in our nostrils, and as no man may boast of to-morrow, it is of infinite importance to regulate our plans in the light of that depressing fact. The meditation upon this text might run somewhat as follows: (1) How long have I to live that I may make the best of what remains? To make the best of an hour is to multiply its opportunities. (2) How long have I to live, that I may set my house in order? We should not leave the world in an unprepared state. Every man has some responsibilities which he should adjust whilst in comparative health. (3) How long have I to live, that I may do the most important things first? There is always an order of import' ance. To the husbandman it is of more importance at the proper 'eason that he should sow his seed rather than clean his windows. On a ship it is more important to have a qualified captain than a qualified cook. (4) How long have I to live, that I may pay all I owe? This inquiry does not relate to money only. We may be solvent in money and insolvent in character. What do we owe to those who love us? To our children? To the poor? To the whole cause of Christ? We are not to buy ourselves off by money; a subscription is not a soul.

What is it to live? It is not merely to exist. Men are not bodies only. A man may feed his body and starve his soul. When a man asks questions about his life he should bring them to bear upon his spiritual rather than upon his corporeal nature. There is a mockery of living. We may live without living, that is to say, our life may be only physical, or it may be shallow, or it may be selfish, or it may be running on false lines. The true life is in Christ alone. In every sense He is our life. Unless we are in Christ we have no life. He came to give us life. He complains, "Ye will not come unto me that ye might have life."

The question may be used in another and most thrilling sense. The question of the text relates only to earthly existence. The Christian preacher has a great answer to the inquiry, How long have I to live? The Christian preacher's answer is, forever!—Joseph Parker, D. D.

IV. DEATH OF THE MATURE. PARENTS, HUSBAND AND WIFE.

REFLECTIONS AND ILLUSTRATIONS.

His Mother's Bible (153).

A Bible class teacher was telling of the various translations of the Bible and their different excellences. The class was much interested, and one of the young men that evening was talking to a friend about it.

"I think I prefer the King James version for my part," he said; "though, of course, the revised is more scholarly."

His friend smiled. "I prefer my mother's translation of the Bible myself to any other version," he said.

"Your mother's?" cried the first young man, thinking his companion had suddenly gone crazy. "What do you mean, Fred?"

"I mean that my mother has translated the Bible into the language of daily life for me ever since I was old enough to understand it. She translates it straight, too, and gives its full meaning. There has never been any obscurity about her version. Whatever printed version of the Bible I may study, my mother's is always the one that clears up my difficulties."—Selected.

Our Mothers (154).

A little boy named Sydney presented a bill to his mother one morning. It was worded something like this: "Mother owes Sydney, for running errands, 4d.; for being good, 6d." Various other items brought the amount to a grand total of eighteen pence. The mother quietly took the bill, and on the following morning she placed it, with one-and-sixpence, on Sydney's plate. But with it was another bill: "Sydney owes mother, for the years of happiness, nothing; for nursing him through his last long illness, nothing; for being good to him, nothing." Other notes were added, and the grand account was nothing. The boy read the bill. Tears filled his eyes, and he rushed hastily to his mother, and flung himself into her arms, crying brokenly, "Oh, mother, let me love you, and do things for you for nothing."—Dr. R. F. Horton.

Remembering Our Dead (155)

Our dead do not die, until we kill them by forgetfulness. They live on in us and through us, even as we shall live in posterity. We are a heap of possibilities coming from the past, a mass of influence for the future. The continuous chain of good and evil knows no break, except we strengthen the latter and destroy the former. The immortal influence of example knows no interruption. The past is linked to the present; the future is prepared in the now. In this sense our loved ones never die, for they live in hearts and lives left behind. In moments of sacred joy, in hours of hallowed sorrow they beckon us on to love and duty. In times of trial and temptation, of success and failure, they stand out before our mental gaze. Once again we feel the pressure of the hand that gave childhood's blessing; once again their lips meet ours in the kiss of hope; once again we hear their voices uttering words of counsel or comfort, and by the purity of our lives, by the nobility of our deeds, by the honesty of our acts, we prove that, being dead, they yet speak.—Levy.

A Mother's Heart-sway (156).

But how the true mother holds her heart-sway even when the children are grown! Other loves and trusts and confidences come, but still the grown child sings:

> "Over my head in the days that are flown
> No love like mother-love ever was shown,
> No other worship abides and endures,
> Loving, unselfish and patient like yours.
> None like a mother can charm away pain
> From the sick brow and world weary brain.
> Slumber's soft calm o'er my heavy lids creep!
> Rock me to sleep, mother! Rock me to sleep!"

And there is this consolation for all who have known what it was to worship and find help at the shrine of a fond mother's heart: it was God in the mother's heart that drew the adoration. Her fond bosom was the inlet into which the great tide of divine love surged and kept it always full. "That he might be everywhere present, God made mothers."—Sel.

His Mother's Influence (157).

It was after a hush in the midweek meeting that one who was a stranger to the majority broke the stillness, as he arose to his feet, saying:

"If anyone had told me this morning that I would attend prayer meeting here to-night I would have questioned his sanity, but here I am, and right glad that I came."

Then, glancing over the congregation, he continued: "I see but two or three familiar faces, and that is not strange, for I was a youth when I worshiped here, and now I am past middle age. But this is the very pew where hundreds of times I sat beside my sainted mother."

From the pause that followed it was evident that the vivid memory of long gone days prevented speech, but when he had himself well in hand the stranger continued:

"Those of you who remember what a mother I had will, I am sure, bear me out in the statement that she lived so near her Lord that her influence was far-reaching. Anyhow, I have never been able to get away from it, although she was taken from me thirty years ago. To be sure, I had not honored my Lord as did she—far from it, but whenever during these motherless years, I have been tempted to stray from the path of rectitude I have been prevented by her restraining influence. And if you will bear with me, I will tell you why I am here to-night.

"Now, I do not give it as an excuse, for, somehow, in the pew where she stood so many times to testify for her Lord, I am not in a mood to excuse myself, but, like many another, I have allowed business cares to fully engross my time and thoughts of late, as to well-nigh crowd out preparations for the higher life.

"But this morning as I was sitting at my desk, puzzling over a discrepancy in accounts, I glanced outward and saw across the street the figure of a passing stranger who reminded me of mother. And then the memory of the best friend I ever had so overcame me that I saw the ledger through misty eyes, and soon my head was pillowed upon it."

There was another pause, and then, in a choked voice, he continued:

"Memory's curtains were drawn wide, as thus I sat, and among half-forgotten scenes I saw myself a child again, in this very pew, with mother at my side, and I felt—gray-headed man that I am—that such sweet memories were worth more to me than any amount of bank stock.

"Then, somehow, I felt as if mother wanted me to come here to-night and take a fresh start heavenward, and so I came thirty miles to attend this prayer meeting. Some of my hearers may take exceptions to the statement I am about to make, but, be that as it may, I confess that I came here to-night because I felt that mother would know it—and be glad!

"Yes," added he, "mother's influence brought me here, but I see now that it was only that I might catch so lasting a glimpse of the Father as to enable me in the future to be less absorbed in transitory things."

From the breathless silence that followed it was evident that all felt that the foregoing touching remarks were a fitting close to the meeting. And the pastor said, as he rose to offer a closing prayer:

"I am sure you will all feel like joining with me in thanking God, anew, for the influence of a Christian mother."—Helena H. Thomas in Endeavor World.

The God of the Fatherless (158).

That God is "the God of the widow and of the fatherless" is abundantly confirmed by even a brief biographical survey. There have been famous men who were sons of famous fathers, as, for instance, John Stuart Mill, son of James Mill; Thomas Babington Macaulay, son of Zachary Macaulay; William Pitt, son of Lord Chatham; John Quincy Adams, son of John Adams; Henry Ward Beecher, son of Lyman Beecher; and many more who might be mentioned, not to include in the list other famous men whose fathers played an important part in their heritage and education. But there is a world of comfort, suggestion and inspiration in the fact that so many "widows' sons" have played such a large part in the history of the world.—Robert Whitaker.

The Christian's Death. (159)—What Belfrage says of John is true of the departure of every believer. It is not like the evening star sinking into the darkness of the night, but like the morning star, lost to our view in the brightness of day.

Reunited Later On (160).

The wife of Charles Kingsley erected a marble cross on the grave of her husband, and on it she had these three words engraven: Amavimus, Amamus, Amabimus. We have loved, we love, we shall love. When Mrs. Browning died, her husband, taking from Dante these words, wrote them in her Testament: "Thus I believe, thus I affirm, thus I am certain of it, that from this life I shall pass to another better, there, where that holy lady lives, of whom my soul was enamored." Will God permit a hope like this to die? I do not have Christ's authority for the thought that we shall know each other beyond death, or that we shall be to each other what we were here, but to think otherwise would be contrary to the hope of millions. "Love never faileth," and Jesus Himself has said "If it were not so I would have told you."—Sel.

A Voice From the Tomb (161).

The other day I read of a mother who died, leaving her child alone and very poor. She used to pray earnestly for her boy, and left an impression upon his mind that she cared more for his soul than she cared for anything else in the world. He grew up to be a successful man in business, and became very well off. One day, not long ago, after his mother had been dead for twenty years, he thought he would remove her remains and put her into his own lot in the cemetery, and put up a little monument to her memory. As he came to remove them and to lay them away the thought came to him, that while his mother was alive she had prayed for him, and he wondered why her prayers were not answered. That very night that man was saved. After his mother had been buried so long a time, the act of removing her body to another resting place, brought up all recollections of his childhood, and he became a Christian. O, you mothers!—Moody.

The Joy Of It (162).

These words of comfort are from a little booklet by the sainted Dr. A. J. Gordon. Speaking to bereaved ones, he said:

"O you that have laid away your loved ones, has one of you been able to open the door to bring them back? How you have wished that some fair morning you could go out and turn the key and usher them back, and introduce them into the world again! But there is One that has the key: "Fear not; . . . I am He that liveth, and was dead; and, behold, I am alive forevermore, and have the keys of death and of the grave." Thou art the King of kings, O Christ, but Thou art also the King and Conqueror of death, and in a little while we shall hear Thy voice sounding down from heaven, "Awake and sing, ye that dwell in the dust." And we will sing as He calls us to Him. They that are alive and they that are in their graves instantly brought into one company, and then the consummating act, expressed in those words that we have not begun to fathom: "Caught up together with them in the clouds, to meet the Lord in the air: and so shall we be ever with the Lord. Wherefore comfort one another with these words."

Mother and Son (163).

Some of you, perhaps, have read that little story of "Laddie." A country boy wishing to make his fortune, comes to the great city of London. By and by he becomes a physician and gathers wealth and fame. His associations become most aristocratic and his handsome stone house becomes filled with the most artistic and beautiful things. For many years he made frequent visits to the old country home and his old country mother, but by and by the visits became more infrequent, and although he sent at regular intervals large sums of money to the old country mother, he at last never went to see her, and the mother's heart was breaking at her son's neglect. So one day she came to London and stood on the door-step of the great stone house. The servant admitting her, left her standing in the hall and told the doctor that a queer old woman from the country wished to see him. And he went into the hall to find his mother, and she said, "Laddie, I have come to stay with you, you are my boy, you know; I cannot bear the separation, I'll never leave you any more." The doctor took his mother into his private room and there they talked. He thought of his aristocratic friends, of the society in which he went, of the young girl whom he was so soon to marry, and then of his mother's strange country dress and stranger country manners, and he was ashamed of his old mother. And he said, "Mother, I don't think you had better stay here, you will be happier with your old friends. I will rebuild the country home for you; you shall have everything money will give you, but I don't think you will be happy here in this great city." And the poison of her son's infidelity entered her soul. The doctor went out and told the servants to prepare a room for an old nurse, and soon they retired for the night. After Laddie was in bed the door opened softly and in came the old mother. She came to the bedside and arranged the clothes and said, "Laddie I want to tuck you up again just as I used to do," and printing a kiss on his brow, turned and went away. Then there came a rush of noble, generous impulse to that doctor's heart. He said to himself, "Nay, she is my mother, I will not be ashamed of her. She shall live with me at my own house," and in the triumph of that noble resolution, he fell asleep. On the morning he dressed and went joyfully to his mother's room, but the bed had not been touched. He called his carriage, flew to the railway station, took the fastest train to the country town. She had not been there. He returned to the city, summoned detectives and put the police of the great city at work to find her. Month after month he continued the search until six months had passed, and then again with unremitting effort till a year had passed. Men as they passed him, said to one another, "What a change has come over that man." His form began to be bent, and his hair was sprinkled with gray, and his step had lost its spring. After eighteen long months had passed, one day in going through a hospital, an attendant asked him to come and see an old woman who had been run over by an omnibus, and was all the time talking about "tucking up Laddie in bed." He hastened to the little cot to find the almost lifeless and insensible form of his dying mother, all too late to find forgiveness.—Sel.

A Faithful Wife (164).

"What a shame for a big, strong man to be such a slave to an invalid wife!" were the words spoken a little too loudly by a girl in the saloon of an ocean steamer as a couple went down the stairway. An hour later the man in question took a seat beside the critic, who had formed and uttered her hasty judgment. "I think your remark, which I accidentally overheard, justifies me in telling you a little about my 'slavery' as you call it," he said. "It began thirty years ago, when my young bride nursed me through yellow-fever—alone—because everyone else had fled in panic. She did not have a sound hour's sleep for three weeks. Most of the time I was violently delirious, and how she managed to control me was a wonder. She brought me safely out of the disease before she fell ill with it herself. After she recovered she pulled me through a worse trial. I was in business with a man who proved a scoundrel, and for three years everybody except my wife believed that his villainy was mine. When I lost money and position, she did the work of three women. When sickness and death visited our home she met them with courage. For twenty-five years she did not spare herself. Five years ago her health gave way. She will never be well again. My 'slavery' is the slavery of a whole-hearted devotion to one of the noblest women ever given to earth. May you some day command as happy a 'slave'!"—Adapted from the Youth's Companion.

A Wife's Epitaph. (165)—In a Philadelphia cemetery is a husband's epitaph—tribute to his wife, which reads: "I thank my God upon every remembrance of thee."

Mother Love (166).

This command was preceded by the invitation, "Come thou and all thy house into the ark." "An aged mother lay on her death-bed. She was nearly one hundred years old, and the husband, who had taken the journey with her, sat by her side. She was just breathing faintly, but suddenly she opened her eyes and said, 'Why, it's dark.' 'Yes, Janet, it is dark.' 'Is it night?' 'Oh, yes, it is midnight.' 'Are all the children in?'" There was that aged mother living life over again. Her youngest child had been in the grave twenty years, but she was traveling back to the old days, and she fell asleep in Christ, asking, "Are all the children in?" Parents, are all the children in the ark of safety? God says, "Come thou, and all thy house."—Moody.

The Halo of Home (167).

Our higher and purer pleasures begin with the home, and these do not fade with the changing years, but sweeten and ripen to the end. Love is the first sweet gift of life, the first joy the infant feels when it nestles near the mother's heart, and the last joy to fade as, with the hand of a loved one in ours, we pass into the great unseen; nay, then it does not fade, but is only made immortal. How enriching and ennobling is the influence of spirit on spirit among—

"Those we love—
The dear religions of our heart."

A true marriage is not merely a matter of the flesh; it is a union of
souls, a blending of kindred natures made one forever. It is on this
union that the sanctities of home are built. There we are met in our
return from daily toil with—

"Those sunshine looks
Whose beams would dim a thousand days."

There our sorrows are divided and our joys are doubled. There our pathway has been strewn, as with spring flowers, by a thousand—

"Little, nameless, unremembered acts,
Of kindness and of love."

There we have heard our children's feet upon the stairs, and have
seen with a delight, not unmixed with awe, the angel of their birth and
path bending over their sleeping forms in holy supplication. There we
have become the "liegemen of love" until the tresses of gold faded into
the silver, which was as the dawn of another life. There, together, we have
seen our children grow up into manhood and womanhood, and, together,
blessed them as they went out into the battle of life. There, by tenderness, and gentleness, and loving counsel, and wise restraint, we have
laid up treasures of affection and devotion which enrich us now the twilight shadows fall. There, with the world of strife shut out, and the
world of love shut in, we have learned that life has no purer, deeper
happiness than that which dwells in the inglenook at home.

If wisdom and love have made our home something worthy of that
name—which is among the sweetest of our language—at its door all the
burdens drop off, as they will one day do at the gate of heaven. And
this happiness does not decay as we grow old, but is more sweetly real
ized in age, when the bark does not so often dare the sea but clings
to the haven—the haven of the household hearth. Truly, to the quiet and
loving spirit, next to the haven of heaven, is the haven of home. Safe-
sheltered here, we know they greatly err who say of the days of age that
we find no pleasure in them. And though we must needs confront that
tragedy, which our mutual love has deepened, that one must go first,
that same love teaches us that it is only for a little while.—From Life's
Eventide.

The Love of Home (168).

It is almost the universal custom in America, and seems to be growing in favor here, for great men to be buried in the place where they
have mostly lived, and among their own kith and kin. Washington lies
at Mount Vernon; Lincoln at Springfield; Emerson and Hawthorne under
the pines of New England; Irving on the banks of the Hudson; Clay in
Kentucky. They are laid to rest not in some central city or great struc-

ture, but where they have lived, and where their families and neighbors may accompany them in their long sleep.

Sympathy (169).

What is sympathy? It may be but a silent pressure of the hand. You will remember in the Greek myth how when brave Theseus entered the labyrinth with the purpose of slaying the Minotaur—the Cretan king's pet-monster, whose annual luncheon of fourteen Athenian youths and maidens was considered by Minos as a "matter of state policy"—Ariadne, the beautiful princess, put into the youth's left hand one end of a silken thread, she holding the other end. As he went on through the mizmaze, dizzy and perplexed, the moon hiding her face, the Minotaur's roar growing nearer and louder, every now and then, he would feel the sympathetic touch of the princess pulling the silken cord. Theseus was a very Hercules in strength and intrepidity; besides he had his father's magic gold-hilted sword. And yet he needed just that human sympathy to help him to victory, that silken cord to lead him back again after the victory.

> "A young wife stood beside a bier
>   Pale as a lily in her weeds,
> And prayed for death with every tear
>   As nuns drop Aves with their beads;
> A tiny hand stole into hers,
> A childish whisper checked her tears,
> I said, 'She is not all alone,
> The infant's grief will heal her own.'"

Most of all do we need the divine sympathy, substitutional, because the Christ was tempted in all points as we are. "And having had compassion on them," is repeated so many times in the New Testament that we do not hesitate to say that compassion is the leading attribute of Christ, and sympathy the very essence of Christianity.—Ide.

Filial Tenderness (170).

I recall a young man in his home—a very great and famous man whose name I must not mention. His was the case of a man of genius, born of parents who had no pretensions to genius at all, and who was incomparably in advance of his parents in culture and education. Many a young man so circumstanced has been tempted to give himself airs; to look down upon his parents as inferiors, to shudder when they drop their h's; to condole with himself as the offspring of bourgeois or plebian people, of whom he is obliged to be ashamed. Not so the young man of whom I speak. He had taken as his rule of life the highest of all ideals —the ideal of Him "who went down to His parents at Nazareth, and was subject unto them." I have sat at his table, and heard him pour forth the stores of his unexampled eloquence, and unroll the treasures of his large heart in lessons full of depth and beauty;—and then his dear old mother—a perfect type of English middle-class womanhood, with something of the holy Philistinism of a narrow creed which invests its humblest votaries with self-imagined infallibility—would lift up her monitory finger, before the assembled guests and say, "Now William"—we will call him "William," though that was not his name—"listen to me." Then while he and we respectfully listened, she would lay down the law with exquisite placidity, telling him how completely mistaken he was in these new-fangled notions—

> "Proving all wrong that hitherto was writ,
> And putting us to ignorance again."

"Yes, mother," he would say, when her little admonition ended; and then conversation would resume its flow quite undisturbed, and the dear old lady was more than satisfied. It was the greatness of her son's genius which made him so good a son. A smaller mind would have winced, or been contemptuous. "Men do not make their homes unhappy because they have genius," says Wordsworth, "but because they have not enough genius; a mind and sentiment of a higher order would render them capable of seeing and feeling all the beauty of domestic ties."—Dean Farrar.

A Mother's Sympathy (171).

The comfortings of mother-love are intelligent and comprehending. Let a mother alone for finding out what is the matter with a child. She is better than a doctor, for she knows what to do for a wounded spirit, a troubled heart. Her insight does not depend on words. She knows what he wants before he asks for it. Even if he cannot tell, she will read it in his look or his voice. And if he tries to tell, she will not misunderstand him. He goes to her, feeling sure she will understand. She comprehends him, and often knows what he wants better than he does. So God knows and comprehends us. Often in our vague longings, inarticulate distresses, and confused self-ignorance our appeal is like.—The Ripening Experience of Life.

The Change Death Works (172).

It is strange what a change is wrought in one hour of death. The moment our friend is gone from us forever, what sacredness invests him! Everything he ever said or did seems to return to us clothed in new significance. A thousand yearnings rise of things we would fain say to him —of questions unanswered and now unanswerable. All he wore or touched or looked have familiarly become sacred as relics. Yesterday these were homely articles, to be tossed to and fro, handled lightly, given away thoughtlessly: today we touch them softly, our tears drop on them; Death has laid his hand on them, and they have become holy in our eyes.

Those are sad hours when one has passed from our doors never to return, and we go back to set the place in order. There the room so familiar, the homely belongings of their daily life; each one seems to say to us, in its turn, "Neither shall their place know them any more."

Ah! Why does this bring a secret pang with it, when we know that they are where none shall any more say, "I am sick!" Could only one flutter of their immortal garments be visible in such moments, could their face, glorious with the light of heaven once smile on the deserted room, it might be better. One needs to lose friends to understand one's self truly. The death of a friend teaches things within that we never knew before. We may have expected it, prepared for it; it may have been hourly expected for weeks, yet when it comes, it falls on us sudnly and reveals in us emotions we could not dream. The opening of those heavenly gates for them startles and flutters our souls with strange mysterious thrills unfelt before. The glimpse of glories, the sweep of voices all startle and dazzle us, and the soul for many a day aches and longs with untold longings.—Harriet Beecher Stowe.

A Mother's Memory (173).

An old man sat on his veranda, one autumn evening, with the son of a former schoolmate. The visitor was a flippant young fellow, and talked much of his doubts about religion. The old man did not argue with him.

"It isn't worth while, Robert," he said; "you are only repeating what other men have suggested to you. You have not begun to think or feel for yourself."

Robert was insistent, and finally asserted that the doctrine of a future life was all a dream. "Death is death," he said. "When the breath goes out of the body, the soul comes to an end."

His aged host led him into his library, and showed him a portrait on the wall—a noble, saintly face. "Do you see her?" he said. "Can you guess what she was from her face—how high her intellect, how tender her nature, how near to God? I was her son. She was—and as I have never married, she always will be—the only woman in the world to me. Well, she is dead. And you say there is nothing of her left in the world—nothing? Why, look here, Bob, do you see that bush in the yard? A common weed with coarse leaves and colorless flowers, of no special use or beauty. But that weed grows in every country. It grew centuries ago; it grew before the flood. It is the same now it was then. It has come down through countless ages, seed after seed, the same growth, the same flower, the same thorns, unaltered. And if God," he said, rising in his earnestness, "if God has kept that little weed unaltered since the beginning of time, shall He extinguish the soul of my mother —the souls of all mothers—full of His truth and love, made of His likeness, who have done His work in the world? Shall the poor matter in its meanest type last, and the soul, which represents His intelligence, and His spirit, come to an end?"—Youth's Companion.

Love Of Home (174).

Abraham Lincoln, when a young man, joined a mounted volunteer regiment to resist the invasion of some Indian tribes. The danger over, he received his discharge; but his horse having been stolen he had to trudge the long weary distance to his home. His companion says: "As we drew nearer home the impulse became stronger, and urged us on amazingly. The long strides of Lincoln, often slipping back six inches in the loose sand, were just right for me, and he was greatly amused when he noticed me behind him, stepping along in his tracks to keep from slipping."

The Cure For Heartaches (175).

How many aching, breaking hearts there are in this world of ours, so full of death and separation from those we most dearly love? How many a woman there is who a few years ago, or a few months or a few weeks ago, had no care, no worry, for by her side was a Christian husband who was so wise and strong that the wife rested all responsibility upon him and she walked care-free through life and satisfied with his love and companionship? But one awful daw he was taken from her. She was left alone, and all the cares and responsibilities rested upon her. How empty that heart has been ever since; how empty the whole world has been. She has just dragged through her life and her duties as best she could with an aching and almost breaking heart. But there is One, if she only knew it, wiser and more loving than the tenderest husband, One willing to bear all the care and responsibilities of life for her, One who is able, if she will only let Him, to fill every nook and corner of her empty and aching heart.—Rev. R. A. Torrey.

Widows' Sons (176).

Schuyler Colfax, Vice-President during the first term of General Grant as President, was also a posthumous child. His mother married again when the boy was eleven years old. Henry Clay, like Andrew Johnson, was made fatherless at four. John Hancock of Revolutionary fame was only seven when his father died, and John Randolph "of Roanoke" was only two. Benjamin Rush, and John, Hugh and Edward Rutledge, notable men in the Revolutionary days, were all early left fatherless. Rush and Edward Rutledge were both signers of the Declaration of American Independence.

Other notable American statesmen and political or military leaders who were widows' sons were John C. Fremont, "the Pathfinder," bereaved of his father at five; Thomas H. Benton, father-in-law of Fremont, and a mighty statesman himself, left fatherless at eight; Edwin M. Stanton, the great War Secretary under Lincoln, and Salmon P. Chase, a rival with Lincoln for the Presidential nomination; Robert E. Lee, the great Southern Commander-in-Chief; George P. Meade, who commanded against him in the decisive battle of Gettysburg; and David Farragut, the naval hero of the Civil War. To these should be added Rufus Choate, the great senator, "in many respects the most scholarly of all American public men," John Fiske, the historian, Nathaniel Hawthorne, James T. Fields and Bret Harte.—Whitaker.

Sacred Are Sorrow's Tears (177)

There are few more bitter moments in life than those in which our tears fall as we look for the last time on the white face of our beloved dead; and God does not grudge us these tears. They are nature's relief, but they may be heaven's preparations too, sanctifying as well as soothing to the heart; "sacred are sorrow's tears, for Jesus wept."

In the touching story of the weeping sisters at Bethany we see death striking a home that seemed the unlikeliest on earth to be invaded by such a foe just then; for it had so long been the chosen retreat of Jesus, and its three inmates had been so long His dearest friends, that the keeping of it at least free from the desolation of death might have seemed essential to the comfort of the Lord Himself, to say nothing of the comfort of these close friends of His. Yet sorrow of the deepest kind came suddenly down, and over their loved brother's dead body the sisters were shedding bitter tears. Did Christ rebuke them? Nay, he added His own holy tears to theirs. The tenderest touch in the picture is that which shows how "Jesus wept." It was probably the first time they had seen their Lord in tears; at least it was the first time that He and they had wept together, and over the same thing, and He seemed in that dark hour to be more one with them than ever.

How intensely human these tears of His! He knew that Lazarus was not lost to them, and yet He wept. He knew that, in a few moments more, intensest joy would fill these mourning hearts, and yet He wept. He knew that almost immediately they would have garments of praise instead of the spirit of heaviness, and yet He wept. It was intensely human, intensely sympathetic, intensely beautiful, and intensely comforting as well; and it is a very suggestive fact that the Gospel by John —the gospel which more fully than any other shows us the real Godhead of Jesus—is the Gospel in which His perfect humanity also comes most clearly into view. It shows us that He who was Divine enough to raise the dead was human enough to weep with those that were mourning the dead; Divine enough to dry the mourner's tears, yet human enough to shed tears Himself.—Rev. G. H. Knight.

Home Religion (178).

The Gospel should be all powerful in the home. Horace Bushnell thought that the need of the world was "the out-populating power of a godly stock." When Christ becomes master of the home, it becomes possible to bless the world with a godly stock. Blessed are those homes where every member loves and obeys Christ. The following is a good motto to hang in the home: "Christ is the Head of this house; the Unseen Guest at every meal; the Silent Listener to every conversation." There is no other place where Christlike qualities shine so brightly. Obedience, love, reverence, patience, forbearance—such as these are household virtues. Let us invite Christ to come into our homes that He may teach us these things.—Daily Bible.

A Mother's Love (179).

I know a mother who lives down in the southern part of Indiana. Some years ago her boy came up to Chicago. He hadn't been in the city long before he was led astray. A neighbor happened to come up to Chicago, and found him one night in the streets drunk. When that neighbor went home, at first he thought he wouldn't say anything about it to the boy's father, but afterwards he thought it his duty to tell him. So in a crowd in the street of their little town he just took the father aside, and told him what he had seen in Chicago. It was a terrible blow. When the children had been put to bed that night he said to his wife, "Wife, I have bad news. I have heard from Chicago today." The mother dropped her work in an instant and said: "Tell me what it is." "Well, our son has been seen on the streets of Chicago drunk." Neither of them slept that night, but they took their burden to Christ, and about daylight the mother said: "I don't know how, when or where, but God has given me faith to believe that our son will be saved and will never come to a drunkard's grave. One week after, that boy left Chicago. He couldn't tell why—an unseen power seemed to lead him to his mother's home, and the first thing he said on coming over the threshold was, "Mother, I have come home to ask you to pray for me." And soon after he came back to Chicago a bright and shining light.—Moody.

Comfort in a Mother's Faith (180).

The comfort wherewith we ourselves are comforted of God is the perfect key to unlock all possible mysteries of human sorrow. It is a beautiful thing to have a theory that works out exactly in practice, and I know whereof I affirm.

My own dear mother was carried through terrible affliction buoyed up by this infinite, unfailing comfort. It was like charity—or "love"—it never failed. The strength of her unquestioning, abiding sense of God's love and of God's wisdom was like a tower of strength to the weaker souls around her. It was not an ecstatic, emotional faith; there was no denying of the existence of pain, nor of its definite sensation, but a beautiful willingness to endure hardness as a good soldier. The brave life has long been ended so far as it was of the earth, but the spirit of it is woven into the lives of all who knew her, and the whole community is richer for her patience and courage.

And if sorrow brings a soul nearer to the very heart of the God of all comfort and helps to bring other people too, it is a wonderful answer to our sad cries, "Why must this sorrow be?" The mystery of pain is solved. The great end of life is achieved if our souls are brought in unison with the Divine, if

"His completeness flows around our incompleteness;
Round our restlessness, His rest."

The way may be long, but the end is sure, and God is over all, blessed forever. And we can be partakers of the divine nature if we yield our wills to His.—The Congregationalist.

Somebody's Father (181).

I think that one of the saddest incidents of the war which I witnessed was after the battle of Gettysburg. Off on the outskirts, seated on the ground, with his back to a tree, was a soldier, dead. His eyes were riveted on some object held tightly clasped in his hands. As we drew nearer we saw that it was an ambrotype of two small children. Man though I was, hardened through those long years to carnage and bloodshed, the sight of that man who looked on his children for the last time in this world, who, away off in a secluded spot had rested himself against a tree, that he might feast his eyes on his little loves, brought tears to my eyes which I could not restrain had I wanted. There were six of us in the crowd, and we all found great lumps gathering in our throats, and mist coming before our eyes which almost blinded us. We stood looking at him for some time. I was thinking of the wife and baby I had left at home, and wondering how soon, in the mercy of God, she would be left a widow, and my baby boy fatherless. We looked at each other and instinctively seemed to understand our thoughts. Not a word spoken, but we dug a grave and laid the poor fellow to rest with his children's picture clasped over his heart. Over his grave, on the tree against which he was sitting I inscribed the words: "Somebody's Father, July 3, 1863."

Tell Mother I'll Be There (182).

Just before he left by special train to visit his dying mother, President McKinley wrote a telegram which probably has done more for the kingdom of God than any other single act of his life. The message read, "Tell mother I'll be there."

Rev. Charles M. Fillmore, Indianapolis, Ind., read this message and saw the possibilities that lay in it. He caught the phrase and wrote his world-famous hymn, "Tell mother I'll be there."

Charles M. Alexander took this song with him on an evangelistic tour around the world, and wherever he sang it the touching message reached the hearts of men. In the Welsh revival the only Alexander song carried by the Welsh singers was this song by Fillmore.

Writing of the Welsh revival, Mr. W. T. Stead, editor of The Review of Reviews, quoted the chorus of this song and told of its wonderful effects. Mr. Evan Roberts, the Welsh evangelist, remarked that the song touched more hearts and did more for Christ in the revival than any other song that was sung.

Numberless instances of conversion have followed the trail of this mother song. Strong men have heard it and have been broken. Prodigals have heard it and have come home. The song has been criticized and torn to shreds, but it does its work, and it has never yet been replaced by another that is better.

Mr. Fillmore is an Endeavorer through and through. He went to Peru, Ind., in 1904 to establish a church, beginning with thirteen members. When he left this place six years later there were six hundred members. While in Peru he was elected vice-president of the State Christian Endeavor union. He has written a number of other mother songs, touching and tender, that are sung with good effect in evangelistic work; among them are "Home and Mother," "My Good Old Mother's Religion," and "I'll Wear a White Flower for You, Mother, Dear."

The words of the famous song that have carried Mr. Fillmore's name and influence around the world are these:

When I was but a little child, how well I recollect,
How I would grieve my mother with my folly and neglect!
And now that she has gone to heaven, I miss her tender care;
O angels, tell my mother I'll be there.

Chorus:

Tell mother I'll be there, in answer to her prayer;
This message, guardian angels, to her bear;
Tell mother I'll be there, heaven's joys with her to share;
Yes, tell my darling mother I'll be there.

Though I was often wayward, she was always kind and good;
So patient, gentle, loving, when I acted rough and rude;
My childhood's griefs and trials she would gladly with me share!
O angels, tell my mother I'll be there.

When I became a prodigal and left the old rooftree,
She almost broke her loving heart in mourning after me,
And day and night she prayed to God to keep me in His care;
O angels, tell my mother I'll be there.

One day a message came to me; it bade me quickly come,
If I would see my mother ere the Saviour took her home;
I promised her before she died for heaven to prepare;
O angels, tell my mother I'll be there.

—Christian Endeavor World.

Looking Down from Heaven (183).

I remember in the exposition building in Dublin, while I was speaking about Heaven, I said something to the effect that "perhaps at this moment a mother is looking down from Heaven upon her daughter here tonight," and I pointed down to a young lady in the audience. Next morning I received this letter:

"On Wednesday, when you were speaking of Heaven, you said, 'It may be this moment there is a mother looking down from heaven expecting the salvation of her child who is here.' You were apparently looking at the very spot where my child was sitting. My heart said, 'that is my child. That is her mother.' Tears sprang to my eyes. I bowed my head and prayed, 'Lord, direct that word to my darling child's heart; Lord, save my child.' I was then anxious till the close of the meeting, when I went to her. She was bathed in tears. She rose, put her arms round me, and kissed me. When walking down to you she told me it was that same remark (about the mother looking down from heaven) that found the way home to her, and asked me, 'Papa, what can I do for Jesus?' "—Moody.

Home (184).

"Home is the child's birthright. The world should unfold to a child from the home-center; all experience and education should there begin, that center meaning love, protection, trust, honor, discipline.

"Home is the woman's kingdom. Her power radiates from the hearth, which is the natural focus of her highest strength, gifts, and ambitions. The farther from the hearth she goes, the weaker is her grasp of happiness, whether as giver or receiver.

"Home is the man's anchorage, his point of security, the harbor to which he returns after toil and weariness, after wandering; home, whether the man be in it or out of it, is his remedy against the roughness and incertitude of life; it shields him, repairs him, softens him, steadies him, holds him to his best.

"Home, in its highest aspects, is all this; and even when it falls short of the highest it retains a portion of its inevitable virtue and power. Beside the hearth we grow up, beside the hearth we must die.

"The backbone of a people is made of its homes, and the nation that would be a strong nation is bound to foster the home-instinct within itself."—The Englishwoman.

Self-Sacrificing Lives (185).

Above all, our sympathy and regard are due to the struggling wives among those whom Abraham Lincoln called the plain people, and whom he so loved and trusted; for the lives of these women are often led on the lonely heights of quiet, self-sacrificing heroism.—Theodore Roosevelt.

"Oh, Me" or "Oh, You"? (186).

Grandmother had suffered many weary months. Weighted with seventy-nine years, she was tired and wanted to be released. One afternoon I called, stepping in softly, and was told that she had just "gone home." I was glad, and I said so next day when reading and speaking the words of comfort.

The selfishness of sorrow. Crepe on the door, on the hats of the men, black dresses on the women, a slow-winding funeral train out to the grave, weeping, moaning, "Oh, me. She is gone; how can I live without her?"

Nearly all of the sorrow seems to be for self. My loss, my loneliness, my unhappiness. God has taken one of His children to Himself, has freed his body from all pain, his mind from all anxiety, has wiped all tears from his face, has taken him to a home of bliss, has crowned one of His saints. Is not our sorrow a protest against God's action?

Would we, if we could, restrain God from thus blessing His child? To go was gain for our dear one; would we withhold it from him for our gain? "Oh, me, I am so miserable," might well be changed to "Oh, you are so blessed."

There is a noble, an unselfish sorrow. Jesus was "a man of sorrows." But His sorrow was for others, not for Himself. And many of His disciples are acquainted with the same kind of sorrow, sorrow for others.

Just recently there came to my notice a touching tragedy, a man dying of sorrow. But the sorrow was intensely selfish, all for himself. When you cry, "Oh, me," analyze your sorrow; see if it is selfish. Selfishness, even in the form of sorrow, is not to be commended in one of the disciples of the "man of sorrows."—The Presbyterian Advance.

Death an Answer to Christ's Prayer (187).

We often speak of our sorrows as being God's strange answers to many of our prayers, prayers for greater holiness of heart and life, for more perfect detachment of spirit from the world, and for a deepening of faith. But do we ever think that in the death of our beloved who have gone home to heaven there has been only an answer to the greater prayer of Christ Himself? Why was it that that dear one was taken from your side, and from the love-grasp that would have held it longer if it could? Was it not because while you were praying, almost in agony,

'Father, let this dear one whom Thou hast given me be still with me where I am," Christ was praying, "Father, I will that this one whom Thou has given me be with me where I am;" and His prayer prevailed over yours, as it was right it should, for yours was ignorant but His was wise; yours was love, but His was love deeper still? Can you grudge your Lord that answer to a prayer of His?

> Our eyes behold Thee not,
> Yet hast Thou not forgot
> Those who have placed their hope, their trust, in Thee;
> Before Thy Father's face
> Thou hast prepared a place,
> That where Thou art there they may also be.
>
> —Selected.

A Glorious Death (188).

"Death is a glorious event to one going to Jesus," said David Livingstone.

Triumphant and glorious was the passing away from life of the famous evangelist, Dwight L. Moody. "He was not yearning to go; he loved his work"; said his son. "But suddenly he exclaimed, 'Earth recedes; heaven opens before me.' The first impulse was to try to arouse him from what appeared to be a dream. 'No, this is no dream, Will,' he replied. 'It is beautiful. It is like a trance. If this is death, it is sweet. There is no valley here. God is calling me, and I must go.'"

In the South Kensington Museum there hangs a picture of "The Death of Cromwell." The bed, the face of his daughter, the whole room are in shadows, but a bright light emanates from the Bible lying on his breast and flashes upward into his face a glory not of earth. The artist has pictured the secret of all glorious deaths. Thou wilt keep him in perfect peace whose mind is stayed on Thee.

> Men mourned about the Christian's couch, and said:
> "Alas! He leaveth home; this night he will be dead";
> While angels, smiling o'er the group forlorn,
> Whispered: "He cometh home, this night he will be born."
>
> —Tarbell.

Relics of the Departed (189).

We divide among ourselves the possessions of our lost ones. Each well-known thing comes to us with an almost supernatural power. The book we once read with them, the old Bible, the familiar hymn; then, perhaps, little pet articles of fancy, made dear to them by some peculiar taste—the picture, the vase—how costly are they now in our eyes! We value them not for their beauty or worth, but for the frequency with which we have seen them touched or used by them; and our eye runs over the collection, and perhaps lights most lovingly on the homeliest thing which may have been oftenest touched or worn by them.

But there are invisible relics of our lost ones more precious than the book, the picture, or the vase. Let us treasure them in our hearts. Let us bind to our hearts the patience which they will never need again, the fortitude in suffering which belonged only to this suffering state. Let us take from their dying hand that submission under affliction which they shall need no more in a world where affliction is unknown. Let us collect in our thoughts all those cheerful and hopeful sayings which they threw out from time to time as they walked with us, and string them as a rosary to be daily counted over. Let us test our own daily life by what must be their now perfected estimate; and as they once walked with us on earth, let us walk with them in heaven.

We may learn at the grave of our lost ones how to live with the living. It is a fearful thing to live so carelessly as we often do with those dearest to us, who may at any moment be gone forever. The life we are living, the words we are now saying will all be lived over in memory over some future grave. If we would know how to measure our words to living friends, let us see how we feel toward the dead. Let us walk softly, let us forbear and love. None ever repented of too much love to a departed friend; none ever regretted too much tenderness and indulgence; but many a tear has been shed for too much hardness and severity. Let our friends in heaven, then, teach us how to treat our friends on earth; thus, by no vain, fruitless sorrow, but by a deeper self-knowledge, a tender and more sacred estimate of life, may our heavenly friends prove to us ministering spirits.—Harriet Beecher Stowe.

ILLUSTRATIVE VERSES.

Guided Safely Home (190).

Out in the land of sky
There is a dazzling City, built of gold,
    Whose walls of jasper lie
Four-square beyond the stars. There we behold
    The risen Son of God.
No crown of thorns upon His brow are pressed,
    Nor marks of sorrow's rod
Upon His once-bruised back. He speaks of peace and rest
    To every struggling heart;
He bids us trust, and hope, and work, and pray—
    To do in faith the part
We have before us in life's little day.
    And so in His great love
We find our deepest joy, our life, our all;
    For He is there above
To guide us home, lest on the way we fall.

—Reichard.

A Noble Ambition (191).

Build thee more stately mansions, oh, my soul,
As the swift seasons roll!
Leave thy low-vaulted past
Let each new temple, nobler than the last,
Shut thee from heaven with a dome more vast,
Till thou at length art free,
Leaving thine outgrown shell by life's unresting sea.

—Oliver Wendell Holmes.

The Same Old Faces (192).

God does not send us strange flowers, every year,
When the soft winds blow o'er the pleasant places;
The same old forms look out from the same old faces,
The violet is here.

It all comes back, the odor, grace and hue,
Each fond relation of the life repeated;
Nothing is lost, no looking for is cheated
It is the thing we knew.

So after death's winter it shall be,
God will not put strange sights in heavenly places;
The same old love will look out from the same sweet faces,
And we shall cry, 'Beloved. I have thee!'

—From the German.

While We May (193).

The hands are such dear hands—
They are so full, they turn so oft,
    At our demands:
So often they reach out
With trifles scarcely thought about;
    So many times they do
    So many things for me, for you—
    If their fond wills mistake
    We may well bend, not break.
They are such fond, frail lips
That speak to us! Pray, if love strips
Them of discretion, many times,
Or if they speak too slow, or quick, such crimes
We may pass by; for we may see
Days not far off, when these small words may be
    Held not as slow or quick,
Or out of place, but dear—
Because the lips that spoke are no more here.

They are such dear, familiar feet that go
Along the path with ours—feet fast or slow,
    But trying to keep pace.
If they mistake,
Or tread upon some flower that we would take
    Upon our breast,
Or bruise some reed,
Or crush some hope until it bleed,
We may be mute,
Not turning quickly to impute
Grave fault; for they and we
Have such a little way to go—can be
Together such a little while along the way—
We will be patient while we may.

So many little faults we find!
We see them; for not blind
Is love. We see them; but if you and I
Perhaps remember them, some bye and bye
They will not be
Faults then, grave faults, to you and me;
But just odd ways, mistakes, or even less,
Remembrances to bless.
Days change so many things—yes, hours!
We see so differently in suns and showers!
Mistaken words tonight
May be so cherished by tomorrow's light!
We will be patient, for we know
There's such a little way to go.
                    —Author unknown.

Another Call (194).

Another hand is beckoning us,
　Another call is given;
And glows once more with angels
　　steps
　The path which reaches heaven.

Our dear and gentle friend, whose
　　smile
　Made brighter summer hours,
Amid the heat of summer time,
　Has left us with the flowers.

The light of her dear life went
　　down,
　As sinks behind the hill
The glory of a setting star,—
　Clear, suddenly, and still.

As pure and sweet, her fair brow
　　seemed
　Eternal as the sky;
And, like the brook's low song, her
　　voice—
　A sound which could not die.

And half we deemed she needed
　　not
　The changing of her sphere,
To give to heaven a shining one
　Who walked an angel here.

The blessing of her quiet life
　Fell on us like the dew;
And good thoughts where her foot-
　　steps pressed,
　Like fairy blossoms grew.

Sweet promptings unto kindest
　　deeds
　Were in her very look;

We read her face as one who
　　reads
　A true and holy book.

We miss her in her place of
　　prayer,
　And by the hearth-fire's light;
We pause beside her door to hear
　Once more her sweet "Good
　　Night!"

There seems a shadow on the day,
　Her smile no longer cheers;
A dimness on the stars of night,
　Like eyes that look through
　　tears.

Alone unto our Father's will
　One thought hath reconciled;
That He whose love exceedeth
　　ours
　Hath taken home His child.

Fold her, O Father! in Thine arms,
　And let her henceforth be
A messenger of love between
　Our human hearts and Thee.

Still let her mild rebuking stand
　Between us and the wrong,
And her dear memory serve to
　　make
　Our faith in goodness strong.

And grant that she, who, tremb-
　　ling here,
　Distrusted all her powers,
May welcome to her holier home
　The well-beloved of ours.
　　　　　　　　—Whittier.

Be Swift in Loving (194).

Be swift, dear heart, in loving,
　For time is brief,
And thou may'st soon along life's
　　highway
　Keep step with grief.

Be swift, dear heart, in saying
　The kindly word;
When ears are sealed, thy pas-
　　sionate pleading
　Will not be heard.

Be swift, dear heart, in doing
  The gracious deed,
Lest soon they whom thou holdest
    dearest
  Be past the need.

Be swift, dear heart, in giving
  The rare sweet flower,

Nor wait to heap with blossoms
  the casket
In some sad hour.

Dear heart, be swift in loving—
  Time speedeth on;
And all thy chance of blessed ser·
  vice
Will soon be gone.
          —British Weekly.

Sleep on, Beloved (195).

Sleep on, beloved, sleep, and take thy rest;
Lay down thy head upon thy Saviour's breast:
We love thee well; but Jesus loves thee best—
  Good-night! Good-night! Good-night!

Calm is thy slumber as an infant's sleep;
But thou shalt wake no more to toil and weep:
Thine is a perfect rest, secure and deep—
            Good-night!

Until the shadows from this earth are cast;
Until He gathers in His sheaves at last;
Until the twilight gloom is overpast—
            Good-night!

Until the Easter glory lights the skies;
Until the dead in Jesus shall arise,
And He shall come, but not in lowly guise—
            Good-night!

Until made beautiful by Love Divine,
Thou, in the likeness of Thy Lord shalt shine,
And He shall bring that golden crown of thine—
            Good-night!

Only "good-night," beloved—not "farewell!"
A little while, and all His saints shall dwell
In hallowed union, indivisible—
            Good-night!

Until we meet again before His throne,
Clothed in the spotless robe He gives His own,
Until we know even as we are known—
            Good-night!
            —Sarah Doudney.

Are Ye There, Janet? (196).

'Twas ilka nicht when John cam'
  hame,
An' pat his horses by,
He'd come up to the kitchen door
  An' keek in on the sly;
An' as he dichted clean his feet
  He aye had this bit cry—
"Are ye there, Janet?"
  An' I wad just say "Ay."

He hadna mony words, ye ken;
  He thocht mair than he said;
But aye I kent his heart was true
  As he earned oor daily bread.
I aye was glad to hear his step,
  An' syne his heartsome cry—
"Are ye there, Janet?"
  An' I wad just say "Ay."

He aye was prood, at kirk or fair,
  To hae me at his side;
'Twas just the same, year in, year
  oot,
  As when I was his bride,
He didna need to speak o' love—
  I kent it in his cry—
"Are ye there, Janet?"
  An' I wad answer "Ay."

The years cam roun', the years
  gaed by
Oor bairns were born and died:
Oor bonny lambs! Ah! sweir were
  we
To lay them side by side;
But ever at the gloamin' 'oor
  I'd hear the cheery cry—
"Are ye there, Janet?"
  An' I wad aye say "Ay."

It's ten years noo I've lived my
  lane—
  An' weary is the road—
Since my gudeman was ta'en frae
  me
  Up to the bricht abode,
Weel do I mind that last drear
  nicht!
  His last breath was the cry—
"Are ye there, Janet?"
  An' I could just say "Ay."

It'll no' be lang before I'll be
  Wi' my gudeman ance mair;
An' gladly I'll the summons hear
  To gang to him up there;
He's waitin' for me near the gate;
  When I win in he'll cry—
"Are ye there, Janet?"
  I'll smile an' just say "Ay."
        —A. B. Meldrum, D. D.

Heavenly Recognition (197).

We are quite sure
That He will give them back—bright, pure and beautiful.
We know He will but keep
Our own and His until we fall asleep.
We know He does not mean
To break the strands reaching between
    The Here and There.
He does not mean—though Heaven be fair—
To change the spirits entering there, that they forget
The eyes upraised and wet—
    The lips too still for prayer,
    The mute despair.
    He will not take
The spirits which He gave, and make

The glorified so new,
That they are lost to me and you.
        God never made
Spirit for spirit, answering shade for shade,
And placed them side by side—
So wrought in one, though separate, mystified—
And meant to break
The quivering threads between.

He and She (198).

"She is dead!" they said to him, "come away;
Kiss her and leave her—thy love is clay!"

They smoothed her tresses of dark brown hair;
On her forehead of stone they laid it fair.

Over her eyes that gazed too much
They drew the lids with a gentle touch;

With a tender touch they closed up well
The sweet thin lips, that had secrets to tell.

About her brows and her beautiful face
They tied her veil and her marriage lace,

And drew on her white feet her white silk shoes
Which were the whitest, no eye could choose.

And over her bosom crossed her hands;
"Come away," they said, "God understands."

And there was silence, and nothing there
But silence, and scents of eglantere,

And jasmine, and roses, and rosemary;
And they said, "As a lady should lie, lies she."

And they held their breath 'till they left the room
With a shudder, a glance at its stillness and gloom.

But he, who loved her too well to dread
The sweet, the stately, the beautiful dead,

He lit his lamp and took the key
And turned it—alone again—he and she.

He and she—but she would not speak,
Though he kissed, in the old place, the quiet cheek.

He and she: yet she would not smile
Though he called her the name she loved erstwhile.

He and she; still she did not move
To any passionate whisper of love.

Then he said, "Cold lips, and breast without breath
Is there no voice, no language of death,

"Dumb to the ear, and still to the sense
But to heart and soul distinct, intense?

"See now, I will listen with soul, not ear;
What was the secret of dying, dear?

"Was it the infinite wonder of all
That you ever could let life's flower fall?

"Or was it a greater marvel to feel
The perfect calm o'er the agony steal?

"Was the miracle greater to find how deep
Beyond all dreams sank downward that sleep?

"Did life roll back its record, dear,
And show, as they say it does, past things clear?

"And was it the innermost heart of the bliss
To find out so, what a wisdom love is?

"O, perfect dead!   O, dead most dear!
I hold the breath of my soul to hear.

"I listen as deep as to terrible hell,
As high as to heaven, and you do not tell.

"There must be pleasure in dying, sweet,
To make you so placid from head to feet!

"I would tell you, darling, if I were dead
And your hot tears on my brow were shed.

"I would say, tho' the angel of death had laid
His sword on my lips to keep it unsaid—

"You should not ask vainly with streaming eyes
Which of all deaths was the chiefest surprise,

"The very strangest and suddenest thing
Of all the surprise that dying must bring."

Ah, foolish world! O, most kind dead,
Though he told me, who will believe it was said.

Who will believe that he heard her say,
With the sweet, soft voice, in the dear old way,

"The utmost wonder is this—I hear
And see you, and love you, and kiss you, dear.

"I am your angel, who was your bride
And know that, though dead, I have never died."

                                    —Sir Edwin Arnold.

Sin Mither's Gane (199).

"It mak's change in a roon
    When mither's gane,
The cat has less contented croon,
The kettle has a dowie tune,
There's naething has sae blythe
        a soun,
    Sin mither's gane.

The father's there, but losh! puir
        man,
    Sin mither's gane,
Altho' he does the best he can,

He hasna sic a tender han'—
The bottom's oot o' nature's plan,
    When mither's gane.

Oh   lonely   house!   Oh   empty
        chair!—
    The mither's gane;
Yet fancy often sees her there,
Wi' a' the smiles she used to wear
Which brings our hearts maist to
        despair,
    To think she's gone."

Growing Old (200).

Softly, oh, softly, the years have swept by thee,
    Touching thee lightly with tenderest care;
Sorrows and death they have often brought nigh thee,
    Yet they have left thee but beauty to wear:
        Growing old gracefully,
        Gracefully fair.

Far from the storms that are lashing the ocean,
    Nearer each day to the pleasant home light;
Far from the waves that are big with commotion,
    Under full sail and the harbor in sight:
        Growing old gracefully,
        Cheerful and bright.

Past all the winds that were adverse and chilling,
    Past all the islands that lured thee to rest,
Past all the currents that lured thee unwilling
    Far from thy course, to the land of the blest:
        Growing old gracefully,
        Peaceful and blest.

Never a feeling of envy or sorrow
  When the bright faces of children are seen;
Never a year from the young wouldst thou borrow—
  Thou dost remember what lieth between:
    Growing old willingly,
    Thankful, serene.

Rich in experience that angels might covet,
  Rich in a faith that hath grown with the years,
Rich in a love that grew from and above it,
  Soothing thy sorrows and hushing thy fears.
    Growing old wealthily,
    Loving and dear.

Hearts at the sound of thy coming are lightened,
  Ready and willing thy hand to relieve;
Many a face at thy kind word has brightened;
  "It is more blessed to give than receive":
    Growing old happily,
    Ceasing to grieve.

Eyes that grow dim to earth and its glory
  Have a sweet recompense earth can not know;
Ears that grow dull to the world and its story
  Drink in the songs that from Paradise flow:
    Growing old gracefully,
    Purer than snow.

A Traveler (201).

Into the dusk and snow
  One fared on yesterday;
No man of us may know
  By what mysterious way.

He had been comrade long;
  We fain would hold him still;
But, though our will be strong,
  There is a stronger Will.

Beyond the solemn night
  He will find morning-dream,

The summer's kindly light
  Beyond the snow's chill gleam.

The clear, unfaltering eye,
  The inalienable soul,
The calm, high energy—
  They will not fail the goal!

Large will be our content
  If it be ours to go
One day the path he went
  Into the dusk and snow!
      —Clinton Scollard.

The Christian's "Good Night" (202).

The early Christians were accustomed to bid their dying friend "Good-night," so sure were they of their awakening on the Resurrection morning.

Sleep on, beloved, sleep, and take thy rest;
Lay down thy head upon thy Saviour's breast;
We love thee well, but Jesus loves thee best—
    Good-night!

Calm is thy slumber as an infant's sleep;
But thou shalt wake no more to toil and weep;
Thine is a perfect rest, secure and deep—
    Good-night!

Until the shadows from this earth are cast,
Until He gathers in His sheaves at last,
Until the twilight gloom be over-past —
    Good-night!

Until the Easter glory lights the skies,
Until the dead in Jesus shall arise,
And He shall come, but not in lowly guise—
    Good-night!

Until, made beautiful by love divine,
Thou in the likeness of thy Lord shall shine,
And He shall bring that golden crown of thine—
    Good-night!

Only "Good-night," beloved, not "Farewell!"
A little while and all his saints shall dwell,
In hallowed union indivisible—
    Good-night!

Until we meet again before His throne,
Clothed in the spotless robe He gives His own,
Until we know even as we are known—
    Good-night!

This hymn was sung by Mr. Sankey at the funeral of the Rev. Chas. Spurgeon.

Of One Departed (203).

She lingered on the shores of time a few short years, like one
Who seemed a stranger in a land whence all her kin had gone;
A far-away and plaintive look was on her sad young face—
A waif of adverse circumstance, she found no resting place.

But at the close of one dark day she softly fell asleep,
And we who stood around her couch could only look and weep;
Then to her face the smile returned, which had been gone for years—
A source of sacred joy to us, and yet a cause for tears.

The smile returned, unseen, till then, since fell disease had cast
A blight upon her buoyant youth in other days long past;
And when the trump of God shall sound, and all the dead shall rise,
That smile shall greet the Lord of Life descending from the skies.

     —Rev. J. R. Newell, Markdale, Ontario.

The Gladness of the Going (204).

O! the gladness of the going,
 When the faithful travel home;
O! the rapture of the welcome,
 Where their feet no more shall
  roam;
O! the beauty of the mansion,
 Which for them is all prepared,
And the bliss their souls inherit,
 Who in Jesus' love have
  shared:—
O! the joy 'neath heaven's dome
 When the faithful travel home!

Through the tempest and the sun-
 shine
 They have crossed life's vales
  and hills;
'Neath a changeful sky, their
 pathway
 Led them oft through many ills;
Now, before them lieth nothing
 Save the cloudless perfect day,
Shining o'er immortal beauty
 In an everlasting ray:—
O! the joy 'neath heaven's dome
 When the faithful travel home!

Unto this they've looked with
 longing,
 As their various paths they
  trod;
All have come through one dark
 valley
 As they've traveled home to God;
Some through years of long en-
 durance,
 In a moment some have passed.
But the hour of final testing
 Was of pain and woe their
  last:—
O! the joy 'neath heaven's dome
 When the faithful travel home!

From their trial to their triumph—
 Is a sure and high exchange;
All the secrets of the ages,
 Are the fields they swiftly
  range:
In the love of friends beloved—
 In the fellowship of Christ—
In the Father's gracious favor –
 Thus they keep the Spirit's
  tryst:—
Sweet the joy 'neath heaven's
 dome
 When the faithful travel home!
     —Lillian C. Nevin.

Recompense (205).

We are quite sure
That He will give them back—bright, pure and beautiful,
We know He will but keep
Our own and His until we fall asleep.
We know He does not mean
To break the strands reaching between
The here and there.
He does not mean—though Heaven be fair—

To change the spirits entering there, that they forget
The eyes upraised and wet,
The lips too still for prayer,
The mute despair,
He will not take
The spirits which He gave, and make
The glorified so new
That they are lost to me and you,
I do believe
They will receive
Us—you and me—and be so glad
To meet us, that when most I would grow sad
I just begin to think about that gladness, and the day
When they shall tell us all about the way
That they have learned to go—
Heaven's pathways show.

My lost, my own, and I
Shall have so much to see together by and by.
I do believe that just the same sweet face,
But glorified, is waiting in the place
Where we shall meet, if only I
Am counted worth in that by and by,
I do believe that God will give a sweet surprise
To tear-stained, saddened eyes,
And that His Heaven will be
Most glad, most tided through with joy for you and me,
As we have suffered most. God never made
Spirit for Spirit, answering shade for shade,
And placed them side by side—
So wrought in one, though separate, mystified—
And meant to break
The quivering threads between. When we shall wake,
I am quite sure we will be very glad
That for a little while we were so sad.

                                        —George Klingle.

O Happy Home (206).

O happy home, where thou art loved the dearest,
    Thou loving Friend and Saviour of our race,
And where among the guests there never cometh
    One who can hold such high and honored place.

O happy home, where each one serves thee, lowly,
    Whatever his appointed task may be,
Till every common task seems great and holy,
    When it is done, O Lord, as unto thee!

O happy home, where two in heart united
 In holy faith and blessed hope are one,
Whom death a little while alone divideth,
 And cannot end the union here begun.

O happy home, where thou are not forgotten
 When joy is overflowing, full, and free;
O happy home, where every wounded spirit
 Is brought, Physician, Comforter, to thee,—

Until at last, when earth's day's work is ended,
 All meet thee in the blessed home above,
From whence thou camest, where thou hast ascended,
 Thy everlasting home of peace and love.
        —Selected.

Sorrow Cheered By Hope (207).

There is many a heart that understands only too keenly the meaning of this moan:

"Oh, dearest one, we saw thy white soul shining
  Behind the face,
Bright with the beauty and celestial glory
  Of an immortal grace.
What wonder that we stumble, faint and weeping,
  And sick with fears,
Since thou has left us—all alone with sorrow
  And blind with tears?"

But it is also true—gloriously true—that many a one can enter just as fully into this song of a confident trust:

"The promise of the morrow
 Is glorious on that eve,
Dear as the holy sorrow
 When good men cease to live,
When brightening ere it die away
 Mounts up their altar flame,
Still tending with intenser ray
 To Heaven whence first it came.

Say not it dies, that glory,
 'Tis caught unquenched on high,
Those saint-like brows so hoary
 Shall wear it in the sky."

The Touch of a Vanished Hand (208).

We sigh for the touch of the vanished hand—
  The hand of a friend most dear,
Who has passed from our side to the shadowy land,
  But what of the hand that is near?

To the living's touch is the soul inert
  That weep's o'er the silent urn?
For the love that lives is our hand alert
  To make some sweet return?

Do we answer back in a fretful tone,
  When life's duties press us sore?
Is our praise as full as if they were gone,
  And could hear our praise no more?

As the days go by are our hands more swift
  For a trifle beyond their share,
Than to grasp for a kindly, helpful life—
  The burden some one must bear?

We sigh for the touch of a vanished hand,
  And we think ourselves sincere;
But what of the friends that about us stand,
  And the touch of the hand that is near?
          —British Weekly.

In the Presence of the King (209).

Under the cross of a mourner's pain
  Laid on the soul when you went to God,
We have walked a year, while the sun and rain
  Faded and freshened the grassy sod.

Have you ever missed us, walking alone
  By the beautiful shore of the jasper sea?
Have you kept the old place in your heart for your own,
  Wherever you linger—wherever we be?
In the harmonies that the holy sing
  Have you heard the voices we've missed so long?
Have you seen the light which their glad eyes bring
  Shining out from the heavenly throng!
Have you sat in the hush of some holy place
  When the heaven was flooded with God's own calms,
And kissed, for its mother, the angel face
  Of some little child that crept to your arms?
Are there any to comfort,—to cheer,—to bless?
  Is this the work to the freed soul given?
Does earth's most beautiful tenderness
  Find place in the blessed life of heaven?

Ah, vainly we question,—our pleading is vain
For words that the stilled lips cannot say,
Yet we feel your touch on our heart's sore pain,
Your eyes smile a welcome,—and yet we stay,
And clasping our crosses we'll try to wait,
No matter how many the summers be,
For whether our coming be soon or late
We know they are years with the King for thee,
They can add no shadow of pain or care
To dim the sweetness the dear face wore,
No lines of white to the silvery hair,—
For all that is beautiful entering there
Is beautiful evermore.
—Mary Lowe Dickinson.

The Christian's Home Going (211).

"A snow rim on my brow,
But summer in my heart,
My feet are weary now—
Soon earth and I must part.
But God has made my pathway bright;
And now at evening time there's light.

"A staff of easy grasp,
Supports my yielding limb;
He bids my faith to clasp
Its hold and trust on Him.
His will and care are my delight;
And lo, at evening time there's light.

"Like winter suns that shine
E'en through the cloudy rifts,
His love and favor now are mine.

Rich in my Father's gifts.
I may not fear, there is no night;
Behold at evening time there's light.

"My outward vision's dim,
My inward eye is clear;
My every thought of Him
Disperses every fear.
I know life's outcome will be right
For now at evening time there's light.

"Some night, or morn, or noon,
Life's journey will be done.
Nor do I fear if soon
My endless life's begun.
Then, oh the bliss of that first sight
When path and pillow flame with light!"

TEXT AND TREATMENT HINTS.

"She Goeth Unto the Grave to Weep There."—John 11:31 (212).

Comfort is not the only thing we need, if the graves of our beloved are to be made places of true blessing to our souls. Standing there, many solemn thoughts may well stir within us, many serious self-questionings, many deep heart-searchings may come. I. The life of the dead is sure to be reviewed, many half-forgotten incidents in it are sure to be recalled, and our own life in relation to the dead will be reviewed as well. II. Happy they who at such a time, will not have to weep over remembered harshnesses and bitternesses, over biting words that made a loving heart ache for days, over selfishness and sins that hastened the death so mourned at last, and made it a heavier sorrow than it would otherwise have been, because reparation is now an impossible thing!

III. Even where there is nothing of this, and the remembrances are only sweet, to stand at the grave is still a solemn thing. It brings us closer to eternal realities than almost anything else can do.—Selected.

"He Was Not For God Took Him."—Gen. 5:24 (213).

The death of an aged saint borders on a translation. So far as the Departed is concerned, there is nothing to mourn. He has, 1. Passed the ordinary limit of life; 2. Begun to feel the infirmities of age; 3. Life's mission is fulfilled; 4. Character ripened and matured; 5. Immediate translation to glory, with scarce any experience of dying. Mourning is occasioned in such instances simply by the wounded hearts of survivors. Ties cannot be sundered without pain. Must not confound the grief of nature with the hopeless and rebellious sorrow of despair, etc.—Sel.

"Thou Shalt Come to Thy Grave in a Full Age Like as a Shock of Corn Cometh in in Its Season."—Job 5:26 (214).

I. Religion preserves the body as well as saves the soul. Other things being equal piety prolongs life.

II. For the faithful Christian death crowns life. It is life's perfect rounding out and earthly completion.

"As One Whom His Mother Comforteth, So Will I Comfort You."—Isai. 66:13 (215).

A mother's business is to interpret God to her children by giving them such experience of maternal comfortings as shall help them to comprehend how deep and rich and dear a thing God means in that tenderest promise given to his earthly children, "As one whom his mother comforteth, so will I comfort you." Mrs. Browning's unpitying paternal parent did not help her to comprehend the meaning of the psalmist's words, "Like as a father pitieth his children, so the Lord pitieth them that fear Him," but that she was well mothered is indicated when she writes of God thus:

> I feel that His embrace slides down
> By thrills through all things made;
> As if my tender mother laid
> On my shut lids her kisses' pressure,
> Half waking me at night, and said,
> "Who kissed you through the dark?"

What sort of a mother Thomas Carlyle had is reflected in the fact that when he was aged and feeble, burdened with the weight of years, and left lonely by the death of his wife, talking one day with a friend about his weakness and desolation, the old man burst forth in a tremulous voice that was half humor and half sob, "It's a mother I want." One wishes somebody had been there to sing to him the quaint sweet words of the Scotch song:

> Like a bairn to its mither, a wee birdie to its nest,
> I wad fain be ganging noo unto my Saviour's breast;
> For He gathers in His bosom witless, worthless lambs like me,
> And He carries them Himsel' to His ain countree.

There is sanity, reason and the logic of common sense in the words of Mark Guy Pearse: "It is reasonable to trust the Power that has made a mother. To me a mother is the 'Fear Not' of nature, half a redeemer, a certificate and guarantee of God. I will trust the Power that makes a mother." He who creates mothers gives to us distincter and mort articulate reason for trusting Him in that tender promise in the pages of Isaiah, found in the heart of the austere Old Testament like honey in a cleft of the rock.—"The Ripening Experience of Life."

"When the Morning Was Now Come Jesus Stood on the Shore."—
John 21:4 (216).

He had been on the shore all the night, if they had but known it. We poor navigators and fishermen are tossed upon the nightly deep, the dark sea, the troubled waters, and we cannot even see the shore; but it is our joy to believe that He who makes the morning is standing yonder, and that we shall see Him by-and-by. What is this life of ours but a troubled lake, heaving and swelling and tossing, breaking into billows and dashing into foam, rising into storms, and occasionally falling into a beautiful calm! When our fishing is done, and we give it up, and want to get home, yonder the Saviour is standing on the shore and saying, "Children." Have you any Christ on your shore? Have you any hope that when your little fishing is done, and you have passed through "night" and caught "nothing," you will see Him on the shore who makes the "morning?" It will be a poor, wretched life for you if there be not in the midst of it, and round about it, this inspiring hope, this sure abiding and transporting confidence. But with such assurance all life will be a growing joy, all sorrow a strengthening and ennobling sacrament, and death itself shall be welcomed as a transformed enemy doing the work of the triumphant Master.—Joseph Parker, D. D.

"Blessed Are the Dead That Die In the Lord."—Rev. 14:13 (217).

I. The dead that die in the Lord. The term hardly needed much nice definition when to live in the Lord meant almost certainly persecution, and possibly martyrdom. To die in the Lord was the end of those who had lived in the Lord, and few were likely to make that profession who had not taken up the cross and followed Christ in the way. To die in the Lord is to die in possession of all that the Lord, by His incarnation and passion, has won for man; to die in the Lord is to pass up to live with Him. What life do you take through death to that world? Is it a fool's paradise which you are dreaming of there, or the Lord's? It is simply a question of at-homeness. Blessed are the dead that die in the Lord, who have lived with Him here, talked with Him, wrought for Him, and have pined for more perfect possession of all that makes the holy beauty of His character and glory of His life.

II. Wherein are they blessed who die in the Lord? What is it which transmutes man's great terror into an angel of benediction, and makes that which Nature shudders at a birth into a world of bliss? Here we rise into another region; a region of intense, conscious, joyous vitality; a region of intelligent, responsible, glorious activity, in which nothing that makes the dignity, the grandeur, of the burden of life is laid down, but only the pain. (1) Because death is birth to the believer, and birth is ever blessed. This is not the noon of life, but its struggling dawn; not its summer, but its bleak and wintry spring. Our high life is the seed in the ground which is growing, struggling into form. Blessed are the dead, for they are born, exiled from the body, at home with the Lord. (2) Born out of a life which is a long pain to a life which is a long bliss. "We that are in this tabernacle do groan, being burdened." (3) They pass out of relations and fellowships which are ever changing to those which abide and enlarge their ministries through eternity. (4) Blessed are they, for they are forever beyond the reach of all that may imperil the prize.—J. Baldwin Brown.

"Lazarus, Come Forth."—John 11:43 (218).

This is the sublime conclusion of the touching story of the raising of Lazarus. It presents the estimate the Saviour had of prayer. He knew His power and how all things were subject to Him; yet when He was about to perform this mighty work for the glory of God and the comfort of weeping hearts, He first prayed, and that prayer is full of confidence and trust. What a lesson to us to do everything with the same confident appeal to God (Phil. 4:6)!

The text again shows the mighty power of Jesus. The greatest, the mightiest conqueror of man is death. The most mysterious and irrevocable state is that of the dead. None can conquer in that war. None ever attempt to revoke the decree that bids all to enter the grave. We may sorrow over the outward tomb, and weep at our own losses; but none dream of changing the result. Now the mighty power of Jesus is manifest, in that, standing at the dark door of this dread mystery and these helpless sleepers, he says, "Come forth;" and there is nothing can resist His call. Death, the grave, the unknown sleep, all respond;

and he that was dead and buried stands again a living man, a loving brother. What joy and hope for those who trust in Jesus, not only for their loved ones gone before, but for their own glorious life beyond the death! "He has the keys of death and of hell."

"If In This Life Only We Have Hope In Christ, We Are Of All Men Most Miserable."—1 Cor. 15:19 (219).

What is the exact hope respecting the future that we owe to our risen Lord? Is it the hope that we shall exist forever? Is our continuous existence hereafter altogether dependent upon faith in communion with the risen Christ? No, this is not what the Apostle meant; our immortality is not a gift of the Redeemer, it is a gift of the Creator; and it is just as much a part of our being as any of the limbs of our body, or as reason, imagination, or any of the natural endowments of our mind.

I. We look forward as reasonable beings to immortality. But to what sort of immortality does this anticipation point? Is it, for instance, (1) the immortality of the race, and does the individual really perish at death? No, it is not this to which we men look forward. A race of beings does not really live apart from the individuals which compose it; only a person, only a feeling, thinking, and resolving, center and seat of life can be properly immortal. (2) Is it, then, an immortality of fame? How many in each generation could hope to share in such an immortality as this? (3) Is it an immortality of good deeds? No; the immortality of our actions is not an immortality which ever can satisfy the heart or the reason of man, since this yearning for immortality is above all things based on a sense of justice.

II. The hope in Christ is the hope of a blessed immortality. This He has won for us by His perfect and sufficient sacrifice on the cross, whereby our sins are blotted out; and His cross and His virtue is proved to us by His resurrection from the dead, that He lives in order that we may live also is the very basis of our hope in Him. Apart from this conviction, Christianity is indeed a dream; the efforts and sacrifices of Christian life are wasted; we are the victims of vain delusion, and are of all men most miserable.—H. P. Liddon.

"Jesus Wept."—John 11:35 (220).

I. Causes of Christ's sorrow.

II. Its peculiar character.

1. The possession of a soul.

When we speak of Deity joined to humanity, we do not mean joined to a body. Not a body inhabited by Deity, as our bodies are by soul. But we mean Deity joined to manhood—body and soul. With a body only, Jesus might have wept for hunger, but not wept for sorrow. That is neither the property of Deity nor of body, but of soul.

Humanity in Christ was perfect. The possession of a body enabled Him to weary; the possession of a soul capacitated Him to weep.

2. The spectacle of human sorrow. And this twofold:

Death of a friend: "Behold how He loved him."

Sorrow of two friends: "When Jesus therefore saw her weeping, . . . Jesus wept."

The death of His friend was a cause of the sorrow of Jesus.

Mysterious! Jesus knew that he could raise him. All-knowing wisdom: all-powerful strength. Yet "Jesus wept."

This is partly intelligible. Conceptions strongly presented produce effects like reality; e. g., we wake dreaming, our eyes suffused with tears—know it is a dream, yet tears flow on.

Conception of a parent's death. . . .

Solemn impression produced by the mock funeral of Charles V. . . .

To say that Jesus wept is only to say that His humanity was perfect; that His mind moved by the same laws as ours.

Moreover, it was only delay. One day Lazarus would die, and the mourning be real.

Now, observe, the sadness of Jesus for His friend is what is repeated with us all. The news comes—"He whom thou lovest is sick," and then, in two days—"Lazarus is dead." Startling! Somehow we twine our hearts round men we love as if forever. Death and they are not thought of in connection. He die! He die!

It is a shock to find the reality of this awful life; that we are swimming on a sea of appearances—floating on an eternity that gives way. These attachments, loves, etc., they don't hold; there is no firmness in them. We are, and then suddenly are not. Life and death, what are they?

Next, the sorrow of His two friends caused the tears of Jesus.

Look at this family. Three persons: a brother lost, two surviving sisters.

The sisters' characters were diverse. Martha found her life in the outer world of fact; Mary in the inner world of feeling. They are types of the practical and the contemplative.

Their way of manifesting feeling is different. Martha expressed herself outwardly in word, in action, in small acts of attention; she loved to discuss earnestly with the intellect the question of the resurrection—contended how things might have been otherwise. Mary did not express—felt herself inexpressible; reached truth by the heart, not by the mind; lived in contemplation. In manhood, one would have found life in the storm of the world; the other in retirement. As students, one would have studied the outward life of man in history; the other, philosophy, the causes of things, the world visible, and the stranger world within.

Two links bound these diverse characters together: love to Lazarus, attachment to the Redeemer. And this true union—similars in dissimilarity, worlds differing, spheres differing, yet no clashing—bound them together by one common pursuit.

Now one link was gone. Of him, Lazarus, we know little. Only he was one whom Jesus loved, and he had the strong attachment of such women as Martha and Mary.

His loss was not an isolated fact. The family was broken up; the sun of the system gone; the planets no longer revolving round a center harmoniously. The keystone is removed from the arch, and the stones are losing their cohesion; for the two minds held together only at points of contact. Points of repulsion, too, there were, manifest even in life. They could not understand one another's different modes of feeling: Martha complains of Mary at the feast. Lazarus gave them a common tie. That removed, the points of repulsion would daily become more sharp and salient.

Over the breaking up of a family Jesus wept.

And this is what makes death sad. Let him who calls death a trifle remember this—not that one man is gone, but that Bethany is no longer Bethany. A blight is there. You open a book, there is a name. A day comes, it is a birthday—the chair is vacant. In reverie you half rise up, but the name on your lips belongs to none on earth.

II. Character of Christ's sorrow:—Spirit in which Jesus saw this death.

Calmly: "Lazarus sleepeth." It is the world of repose where all is placid.

Struggling men have tried to forget this restless world, and slumber like a babe, tired—yea, tired at heart. Lazarus is stretched out to his Divine friend's imagination, but he lies calm. The long day's work is done—the hands are folded. Nothing to fret now but the "small cold" worm. Waves of shadow are flying over the long grass on his grave.

Friends are gathered to praise, enemies to slander. But praise and slander on his ear make no impression. Conscious he is, perhaps, elsewhere; but unconscious of earthly noise. Musketry over grave—requiem mass—minstrels making a noise. . . . All this is for the living; the dead hear not. But "he sleeps well." That is the tone of feeling with which to stand over the Christian's death-bed: "Our friend Lazarus sleepeth."

Next, sadly. Hence, observe, permitted sorrow.

Great Nature is wiser than we. We recommend weeping, or prate about submission, or say all must die; Nature, God, say, "Let nature rule, to weep or not."

Do you say tears imply selfishness—distrust? I answer: Weep. Let grief be law to herself. We infer that grief is no distrust of God—no selfishness. Sorrow is but love without its object.

Next, hopefully. "I go that I may awake him out of sleep; thy brother shall rise again." Not merely calmness, nor sadness, nor sorrow, nor despair, but hope.

Observe, the amount of hope depends on character and imaginative power.

Sanguine minds are elastic; it is very easy for them to blame deeper shadow, as if that which is natural spirits were all faith.

Allowance, too, must be made for imaginative power. That is the world of shadows; this the world of experience and recollection. Some persons live in the past more than in the future. Others there are who travel with the sun ever before them, keeping pace with the sun.

Hope will be small when imagination is scanty; but feebleness of hope is not feebleness of faith.

Lastly, in reserve—the reserve of sorrow.

On the first announcement, Jesus speaks not a word. When He met the mourners, He offered them no commonplace consolation. He is more anxious to exhibit feeling than to soothe. But Nature had her way at last. Yet even then by act more than by word the Jews inferred He loved him; "Jesus wept; then said the Jews, Behold how He loved him."

There is the reserve of nature and the reserve of grace.

We have our own English reserve: we do not give way to feeling. We respect grief when it does not make an exhibition. An Englishman is ashamed of his good feelings as much as of his bad. In sarcasm, sneer, and hummed tune, tears will be concealed. All this is neither good nor bad—it is nature.

But let it be sanctified; let reserve of nature pass into reserve of Christian delicacy.

Let us add a few words of application.

In this there is consolation for us. But consolation is not the privilege of all sorrow. Christ is at Lazarus's grave, because Christ had been at the sisters' home, sanctifying their joys and their very meals. They had anchored on the rock in sunshine, and in the storm the ship held to her moorings.

It is desolate when the heart is cut away by force, to seek a Saviour. He who has lived with Christ will find Christ near in death.

If you choose duty—God—it is not difficult to die.—Frederick W Robertson, **M. A.**

V. DEATH OF PERSONS OF PROMINENCE
MEMORIAL DAY.

REFLECTIONS AND ILLUSTRATIONS.

Bishop Vincent on Chaplain McCabe (221).

We come today to recall the career of one of our most brilliant and useful ministers—popular, well, and widely known, gifted—and now sorely lamented. His death is our loss. His life should be our lesson.

There has been but one McCabe—chaplain, singer, secretary, promoter, bishop. The mold was broken when he was cast. But he still lives in our memories and in the mansions Christ promised. Bishop McCabe had rare power both as orator and singer. He was a wizard in his way, a master magician in song and speech with his musical, flexible, and magnetic voice. His talk was music. In all the outgoings and outgivings of his personality there was a mystic power by which at will he moved and melted and mastered men. He knew how to open the most tightly clasped pocket book and the hardest and most firmly riveted heart. Men might resolve against his appeals as they enjoyed his eloquence but while they smiled he broke rivets and bands and the money came. He was a skillful and holy hypnotist. He was subject to currents of power from another world, tides that rolled in from the vast sea of influence carrying everything before them. He was most versatile and could do a great variety of things and do them well. Our noble chaplain-bishop was incarnated good will. But he could do cruel things on occasion but only under the play of impulse or in the interest of what he accounted "orthodoxy." He was what we call a "conservative." One sometimes wonders if such good and loyal souls are really acquainted with the theories of modern criticism and with the grounds of their defense as held by many thoughtful, scholarly, profound and saintly men in our times. The dear chaplain sang holy songs in a bewitching way, made brilliant appeals for gifts to many a worthy cause, preached royal sermons, he often jumped at conservative conclusions and put all the splendid energy of his personality into their defense as though he really understood both sides of the question. He was severe in his denunciations and turned humor into cruelty, pouring out his indignation in a fashion so extravagant and laughable that he himself almost forgot that he was in earnest—as he undoubtedly was all the time. It was not an unworthy motive that inspired such severities of speech. It was simple loyalty to God's Word as he understood God's Word. Really he was a fountain of love—love for God and love for man. He loved souls both as souls and as folks (and there is a difference)—and he won both love and admiration wherever he went. He captured people. Under the spell of his eloquence he became their master. They smiled when he smiled, shouted when he sang, and poured out all their loose change at his command.

I knew him first in the days of the war and heard one of his earliest reports of his experience in Libby Prison. He was even then thin and his face pale as a result of his confinement in Richmond. One can never forget the effect of his wonderful songs as he sang in those days. It was the treat of a lifetime to hear him sing Mrs. Howe's great "Battle hymn of the republic" and one could not hear him sing it without thinking of him and the occasion as the embodiment of the One Hundred and Twenty-sixth Psalm.

He must have had his dark hours. But nobody knew of them. Napoleon said, "Men in general are but great children." Our chaplain-secretary-bishop was always a rollicking, cheerful, impulsive, great-hearted and wise child—from first to last. He had his faults. When a man dies we never recall his weak points or his blunders. I am not sure that this omission is wise.

It is a splendid career—that of a gifted man in the service of man—thinking, planning, toiling, persisting—all in the interest of society, of the church, of the nation, of the race. Self may have something to do with it. Self must have something to do with it. We have no divine command to forget self, to repudiate self, to destroy self. We are to love our neighbor. But we are to love our neighbor as ourself. It is legitimate. It is divinely ordered—this normal, genuine love of self. And having this as the basis and bond of personality it is a royal thing to have as one's main life aim the helping of humanity through the church, through organized missionary and other philanthropic organizations, through political policies, through the everyday illustration of commercial and economic wisdom. In such a life nothing is secular. "Holiness unto the Lord" is stamped on all the activities of such a man. Bishop McCabe was a man of the world, treading the path that leads to the other world, singing as he went, dispensing benefits of every kind on the way, helping students, relieving poverty, paying debts for others. His face was lighted with smiles, his movement upward, onward, heavenward, drawing with the power of a magnet other people to follow him as he sought to follow Christ who all His earthly life "went about doing good."

Such a rare, genuine, ardent, useful, devout man was Bishop McCabe. And he is to be studied from many points of view. He was a manysided man. We might study "Charlie McCabe" as a boy, a son, a brother, a playmate, a student. What a genial, jolly, adventurous, aggressive boy he must have been!

We might study "Mr. McCabe" as a husband, a neighbor, a father, a citizen, a financier, a business man. No commercial obligations or interests, however, ever took the "boy" out of him!

We might study the "Rev. C. C. McCabe" as a Christian, a preacher, a pastor, a sweet singer of the songs of Zion, an orator—which in a sense he certainly was. It must have been a great thing to have him as a regular pastor!

A Significant Funeral Service (222).

The struggle between the Northern and Southern States of America closed forever at the funeral of General Grant. The armies of rebellion surrendered twenty years before: but the solemn and memorable pageant at the tomb of the great Union soldier, where the leading generals of the living Union and of the dead Confederacy stood shoulder to shoulder, and mingled their tears in a common grief, this historical event marked the absolute conclusion of sectional animosity in America.—Selected.

The Past an Index to the Future (223).

"And now that it is all over," said an old, wearied, and dying statesman, after a day of sad farewells, "it is not so bad, after all." The terror, the disquietude, is not in the thing suffered, but in our own faithless hearts. But if we look back at the past and see how portion after portion has become dear and beautiful, can we not look forward with a more steadfast tranquility and believe that the love and beauty are all there waiting for us, though the old light seems to have been withdrawn?—Great Thoughts.

Rufus Choate's Immortality (224).

Dr. Kerr said that when Rufus Choate, one of the greatest of New England's able statesmen, took ship for Europe in search of health, a friend said to him as he stepped on board the vessel, "You will be here a year hence;" thereby meaning that in a year's time his health would be restored and he would return to his work. "Sir," said the great lawyer, "I shall be here a hundred years hence, and a thousand years hence." In a few days Rufus Choate was dead, having landed in Halifax unable to continue his voyage. "He that liveth and believeth in me shall never die."

A Noted Preacher's Death (225).

God gathers His jewels out of the world, and they are souls. Christ came with His infinite power to help us, and the Holy Spirit daily labors with groanings unwordable to perfect individuals fit for the upper and better kingdom; and they do become fit for heaven. When the poor beggar, unclothed and sick and dying and starving, was to be transplanted, a convoy of angels came glistening from the interstellar spaces to take upon their snowy wings and snowy hearts the jewel out of earth's mire, and to bear it home: heaven gained something then, it gained much then. And so we repeat the word, "What an addition he is to heaven!" The sweet singer of Israel, the psalmist of old, giving the keynotes for all the ages and all hearts, so that the dying Christ and the dying Huss could take up his word, "Into thy hands I commit my spirit" —yes, this singer of old must welcome the singer of today. And what a singer he was! He knew the whole gamut of human nature—not one note merely, not one. He could break our hearts to tenderness with that song, "Those beautiful, beautiful hands, hardened with toil;" and how he stirred the heart of childhood with his trundle-bed song! With his far vision of the world and of time, he could lure us with his trumpet song, "Mine eyes have seen the glory of the coming of the Lord."

What a breadth! what a breadth! O that early singer that sang that
the Lord should triumph gloriously, and that later singer that foresaw
that every nation that would not serve him should perish, will find large
reinforcement in our singer when he comes to sing!

The first word that was said to me in the home, after the solemn
silence that followed the telegraphic news of our brother's departure,
was this, "What an addition he will be to heaven!" Is it possible that
we should take such a view as this, to see through our blinding tears
the rainbow glories that are around the throne? O, I think so. There
are two ways of looking at all things in this life. Yesterday a cloud of
unusual blackness hung over this part of Evanston, but above it was
bright. The cloud has passed away. It was only the burning of a tar
tank, it was not a world in consumption. When Christ descended into
the dark cloud of human grief, and saw not when again He should
emerge, it was said on one occasion that even in His circumstances He
rejoiced in spirit. Why? Because it had been demonstrated that the
gospel which He came to bring was suited to common men—the babes
could understand it! And so the great exultant joy welled up in the
midst of His grief, and for the joy that was set before Him He endured
the cross, despised the shame and came out to sit on the right hand of
God. So in our sorrow we may really accept the word, "What an addition he is to heaven!" Is it so? We heard recited here a moment since
all the lavish effort that God could make to magnify a human soul—
figure after figure, twenty or more of them, brief, sharp as musket
shots, in all possible endeavor to exalt the dignity and the worth and
the glory of the child of God who has passed through death. St. Paul,
knowing that we could not grasp these great possibilities with our present faculties, prayed that these faculties might be enlarged, quickened,
enlightened—"that the eyes of your understanding may be enlightened
that you may know the hope of your calling and the excellency of the
glory of God's inheritance in His saints." Yes it is possible that they
should add a great deal to heaven—a great deal!—Bishop Warren.

A Minister Estimated By His Successor (227).

I know of no more searching test for any ministerial career than
the test which that man can make who comes to a parish where his predecessor for an entire generation has stamped his personal and spiritual
characteristics upon his people. Friends, I do not know, I have sometimes wondered, how consciously you have realized the solemnity and
the responsibility of your position as guardians of the great reputation
of your ministers. What you are today largely determines the estimate
of what he was. Mt. Vernon Church is the principal witness, which can
neither be distorted no silenced, to this man's life. You yourselves, by
the lives you lead, by the things you have said, by the remembered
phrases you have spoken, by the types of mind and character you represent, have brought me into more close and vital contact with Dr. Herrick; have unconsciously revealed to me what must have been the motives, ideals and desires that lay behind his outward life, more certainly

and intimately than either you or he could have believed. He, being dead, yet speaketh, through you to me, and it is to some of those unconscious revelations that I would now turn.

First of all, as I have seen him in yourselves and listened to him in your conversation, I have perceived that he was pre-eminently a man of the Divine Spirit. It would be impossible for me to think of him except as unwordly, one whose soul was like a star that dwelt apart. I never heard him preach, but I have perceived that his sermons were distinguished by spiritual insight and prophetic fire—utterances of a life that was both pure and lofty, informed with a transcendant beauty. I have perceived that the power of his preaching did not lie in his accomplished delivery, his finished phrases, his accurate English, which fitted word to thought like hand to glove. It was not the truly admirable form; it was the undefiled substance, the subtle evidence of a present God which made him great. I have been told by many living lips how marvelously this manifested itself in his public prayers; I did not need that testimony; his own speech in you had told me long before..

There is a bitter experience which more than one minister has been called upon to endure when he has entered a new parish. The field has appeared fair for labor; has seemed to offer a rich opportunity for growth and service, but when he has seen it from within, he has found that it had a name that it lived and was dead. There was an imposing edifice and a fine equipment and large organization, but no vitality. It loomed large in the denominational Year-Book, but the heart of it was gone. There was no contact with the Source of Power. Tragic is the lot of him called to such a parish and inevitable his estimate of his predecessor. He places him among the large and dreary company of those who have degenerated from living voices into professional speakers.

But here, dear people, has been the entire reversal of this experience. One might almost transpose the words of Revelation, and say that this church had a name that it was dead, and behold it was alive! I am glad that the fitting public opportunity is now given to me to record that my first unmistakable impressions of this parish were those of its suppressed but profound vitality; its unusual spiritual power. I therefore perceived these many months ago that he who preceded me here was one who had made his ministry not a business, but a life. You have been the irrefutable witnesses to a lofty and devoted leader who walked with God as long as he walked with you. Your quiet earnestness; your unobtrusive devotion to a simple and real religion; your un usual and significant loyalty more to the office than to the man, more to the church than to him who for a time serves the church, all this is a great indorsement of the single-minded, self-effacing, finely-tempered ministry of Dr. Herrick.

It is meet, therefore, that we should do him honor, and that I, too, should have my especial and profound cause to join with you in honoring him whom we have lost. He has made ready our way and prepared our path. In these last two years, when this old church has been once more renewing her youth, enlarging her activities, ministering to an ever-increasing constituency; on this very day, when realizing her new found strength, she is shaking herself free from an encumbrance of the past and turning to the future with unhampered spirit, let us remember the ancient word: "Others have labored, and we have entered into the fruit of their labors." We are building the edifice for which he made provision; what we are doing now he, by the grace of God, made possible for us to do, and so we ought to pay him honor.

I hope the time will never come when the sense of his loss, to you who knew him, will grow less, or when the longing for that benign and gracious presence, wise with many years and tender through much experience, will have died away. Our affection and loyalty for him is one of the most precious, necessary and beautiful elements in our dear fellowship here. O let us keep poignant the consciousness of our great past and our great men; let us keep that consciousness as a precious inheritance and a powerful incentive.—Rev. Albert P. Fitch on Samuel E. Herrick, D. D.

Hungry For a Hope (228).

I have been told that on Sunday following the death of Lincoln, the American churches were crowded to the doors—all hungry to hear some word of assurance that though the great martyr had gone out into the mist and the mystery, that still somewhere he lived. The American people that day were willing to believe anything regarding that future save that he, who had led a nation through fire and war to the edge of the promised land of peace into which he was not permitted to enter, should find out in the unknown no path for his patient feet and no crown for his kingly head. Deep in every heart is an unsatisfied hunger which only eternity can explain and only an eternity can meet. The little girl with her arms full of flowers, which she has gathered, believes that just beyond the brook and over beyond the grassy knoll are larger and brighter ones than she has yet found; the young man, whatever be the success that has crowned his efforts, believes that over the blue range of mountains that lie on the horizon a larger success awaits him; and the old man comes down with tottering steps to the beach of an ebbing tide and believes beyond the waves is a land full of the victories and the love which this world denied. God has placed in our hearts a hunger which only eternity can satisfy.—Selected.

A Great Man's Death a Heavy Loss (229).

An extraordinary personality has gone out from our midst. It is impossible to measure his character and life by the ordinary standards which we use for measuring men. Our brother has left a vacancy of immense proportions—a vacancy which no other man in the denomination can fill. We could lose a great pulpiteer—one with magnetic eye, an eloquent tongue and natural oratorical power; one upon whose burning words thousands hang enraptured—but we could find another to take his place. We could surrender one of our executive leaders, and would mourn his going away, but we could find another of pre-eminent administrative ability who could quickly and successfully assume his duties. One of our chief educators might slip away—one who had profoundly impressed the intellectual life of the church, and who had been an inspiration to thousands of young men and women in our midst—but we could put our hands on another well qualified by natural endowment and training to take up the fallen scepter. We could lose one man with burning evangelistic consecration and zeal, and a tongue of flame—an irresistible pleader with unsaved men, an incarnation of convincing and persuasive speech—but could we not find another into whose hands this work might be committed? But a man has fallen in our midst who was so absolutely unique, so manysided, capable of so many kinds of leadership, so resourceful, so large of vision, so consecrated to his tasks, so inspirational in his leadership, and so tremendously devoted to his mission, that no man comes forward who is even willing to be considered a possible substitute.—Berry.

A Remarkable Tribute to a Remarkable Minister (230).

Like Abraham he went where he was called, and was faithful in all things.

Like Moses, he had led the people of God from doubts and fears to confidence for success in the face of any difficulties.

Like Joshua, he loved his country, and fought and suffered for its success.

Like Jonathan, he met many a discouraged brother, and cheered him by giving him strength from God.

Like David, he sang the church to victory, and shouted on the battle of blessed triumph.

Like Isaiah, he constantly pointed the church to brighter days and better things in the future.

Like Daniel, he was true through life to the teachings of his boyhood days.

Like Malachi, he believed in bringing all the tithes into the Lord's store house.

Like John the Baptist, he delighted to cry to the multitudes: "Behold the Lamb of God."

Like St. John, he believed with all his soul that Jesus Christ was the Son of God.

Like Peter, he honored the Holy Ghost by teaching the doctrine of the operation of the divine spirit upon the souls of men.

Like Paul, he rejoiced that Jesus died for all men, and he did his best to let the world know this blessed truth with pen, song, and sermon. He pled with the church to send the gospel to all the world.

Like Jesus, his Divine Master, whom he followed daily, "he went about doing good."

Like Enoch, "he walked with God, and he was not, for God took him."

Blessed man. Consecrated Christian, true to his God, his country, his church and his fellow man.

Enthusiastic for Methodism, he sought to inspire others to be of like enthusiasm, working to the very last moment of his busy life for the interest of the unsaved world.

The world is richer because he lived, worked, and died in the faith of the Lord Jesus Christ. When he died there was only one place he could go. That place was heaven. And there he is today. And it seems to me I hear him singing, "Worthy the Lamb that was slain for us." Amen and Amen.—Rev. Robert Stephens on Chaplain McCabe.

The Death of a Christian Lawyer (231).

This occasion is to me full of solemnity and also full of inspiration. It is full of solemnity in that it reminds us that, like Brother Weaver, we shall some day, perhaps not far away, be called on to close our law books for the last time, to write our last brief, to make our last plea in the courts of this world, and to stand ourselves for final judgment in the supreme court of the universe.

> "With equal step unpartial Fate
> Knocks at the palace and the cottage gate,"

calling lawyer and litigant to their last long home.

We are today reminded anew that all of us shall, one by one, be carried to the tomb by those who in their turn shall follow us.

Often amid the clash of conflict and the whirl of business we may be tempted to forget the gravity, if not the certainty, of this last great call. But we have met to pay tribute to a man who always kept upon his lips and in his heart a ready and a full and fearless answer to the last great summons. For Mr. Weaver carried in his bosom the deep assurance of his Master's guidance, love, and mercy. He carried it in his heart, and we saw it in his daily life. His face among us was the face of one who prayed in his closet to be a true brother to his fellowman.

Being a man of great faith, he was a man of great prayer. He walked and talked with the God of his fathers. He practiced law and read books; but better than that, he kept daily communion with the Great Spirit of all the good laws and all good books.

In his love of learning, in his honesty of dealing, in his purity of purpose, in his devotion to truth, and in his allegiance to virtue he was an ideal lawyer. He showed the world anew that a lawyer could and should be a Christian gentleman. Brother Weaver believed that a man's first allegiance was to his Creator, and that if a man be true to his God he cannot be false to his brother.

Now and then in modern times we read a long notice of the life and death of some prominent citizen, with never a word that he kept his hand in the hand of God. Fulsome words and fragrant flowers scattered over the grave of such a man make us doubly sad at the greatness of the failure. But here we meet to praise a lawyer who made the law of God the rule of his life. Mr. Weaver excelled in that pre-eminent and paramount virtue which keeps men close to God. Here we can strew sweet words and flowers, well knowing that they are no sweeter than the life and memory of our departed brother.

> "Howe'er it be, it seems to me
> 'Tis only noble to be good;
> Kind hearts are more than coronets,
> And simple faith than Norman blood."

We often hear, but seldom follow, the old Latin motto: Nil de mor-
tuis nisi bonum. Today we could discard the restrictions of that motto;
yet none could name Mr. Weaver but to praise him.

It is inspiring to remember the virtues of his life, and it is refresh-
ing and inspiring to witness this unusually large assemblage of lawyers
to pay tribute to the memory of a great Christian lawyer. It bespeaks
our love and reverence for truth and honor, for righteous living and true
fidelity to high ideals. It bespeaks our hope for an early day when
every lawyer will daily practice the supreme law of life and love.

I am glad that, though we cannot touch his hand, we still can feel
his life. His body rests in peace beneath the fading flowers, but he still
lives within our hearts. His spirit is in our midst, even as we wait to
speak anew his virtues; and I am quite sure and glad that the good influence of his life will never, never die.

The very presence here to-day of so many busy lawyers and citizens is another proof of the truth of the sweet words of the poet:

'There is no death! An angel form
Walks o'er the earth in silent tread,
And takes our best loved things away.
And then we call them dead.

But ever near us, though unseen,
The dear immortal spirits tread;
For all the boundless universe
Is life. There are no dead."—Selected.

A Distinguished Author (232).

Let us thank God that he printed so much and left so large a residue
of his wisdom in form for our permanent use. Let us thank God that
we have had him, and that we shall know where to find him hereafter.
One day a friend said to Dr. Horace Bushnell: "Dr. Bushnell, do you
know I think that when you come to heaven at last and are walking up
the streets of gold, that it is not unlikely that one of the archangels, or
someone else near the Master, will say to him, 'Master, there comes a
man you know';" and the great old man bowed his head and said, "I
trust so, but I trust also that when I come to see Him I shall be not
altogether unacquainted with Him, either." So may we not say of the
thing which has taken place this week, that someone may have said to
our loving Lord and Master, while our prince in Israel walked into His
presence, "There comes a man you know," and that he who had not
only written of the aspects of the Christian experience but experienced
the phases of the grace of Christ looked into the face of his loving Lord
with a consciousness that he knew Him also. "Let the beauty of the
Lord our God be upon us: and establish thou the work of our hands upon
us; yea, the work of our hands establish thou it." "So teach us to number our days (whether they reach four-score years or not) that we
(also) may apply our hearts unto wisdom."—Selected.

A Good Man a Revealer of God. (233)—"God alone is great!" exclaimed the eloquent French preacher pointing to the dead king. The saying is a true one, but the greatness and beauty of God are best revealed in his children.

An Influential Churchman (234).

What a superb transition from the highest range of official duty to the heavenly heights! Our beloved brother on Saturday morning last had his mind quickened and his heart warmed in loftiest thought; concerning these great interests which had engaged his attention from his childhood relating to the salvation of the world. On Sabbath morning he engaged in his beloved employment of preaching the gospel in one of the churches of this city, from a missionary point of view, and twelve hours later the weary pilgrim was walking the streets of gold. I think it glorious! The dark side of any such way intrudes itself upon our thought instead of the bright side. His stately form, his noble mien, his measured wise words, his bright sparkling eyes, these are gone from us and lie still and cold today and in a few days the solemn words will be said over him in his distant grave, "Ashes to ashes, dust to dust."

But there is another side to all this. We must gather some flowers to comfort this hour and gather them in very few words. I do not think, I cannot think of such an hour as this as an hour of sadness chiefly, and sorrow and regret. This is one of our brothers cut down and cut off as one of our coworkers, but exalted and crowned.

> "There is no death; what seems so is transition—
> This life of mortal is but the suburb of the life elysian,
> Whose portal we call death."

Did not our Lord say: "Whosoever liveth and believeth in me shall never die?" We might gather comfort from the thought of what he was, or what he is, of what we are, and of what we are to be.—Selected.

The Men Who Heed (235).

While sordid, self-seeking humanity is immersed in the things of gain and pleasure, noble souls devote themselves to the service of Christ and the alleviation of human needs. The cry of human need is the voice of God. How many there are who hear that voice and gather nothing. We see the rum traffic dragging its victims down to everlasting ruin, and we gather nothing. We see corruption in politics, graft in every place, as well as men in places of public trust, who fatten on the spoils of office, and we gather nothing. We see the poor herded like cattle in places which make virtue well nigh impossible, and we gather nothing. We see the growing tendency to lawlessness and the city overrun with thugs and thieves, and we gather nothing. A thousand needs with gaunt forms and heavy tread go trooping past, and we gather nothing, but go our way to make money, have a good time, bask in the sunshine of the goddess of pleasure and indulge ourselves in the delights of sensuous living.

Dominating Characteristics (236).

If I were asked to give in a word our brother's dominating characteristic I would say that it was his perennial optimism; in other words,
his unfaltering faith, for (the dictionary to the contrary, notwithstanding) faith and optimism are about the same thing. Our friend was a
magnificent believer. He was little troubled with doubts; he believed
in God; he believed in people; he believed in the church; he believed in
the Bible; he believed in the gospel; he believed in the conquering
power of Jesus and he looked confidently to his triumph all over the
world. He was as sure that the King is preparing to reign on the earth
tomorrow as he was that the sun would rise tomorrow—that is why he
was so sunny; faith works that way. Faith and hope are very near
neighbors; doubt and despair also live close together.

In all my acquaintance I never knew a more kindly man. His tenderness was beautiful. His sympathies went out toward multiplied objects of need. How charitable he was in his judgments of others! How
intensely he loved his friends! Will anyone attempt in this presence to
estimate the measure of his benefactions?—Selected.

Huxley and Spencer (237).

To Morley in 1883 (vol. II, 62), Huxley wrote: The great thing one
has to wish for as time goes on is vigor as long as one lives, and death
as soon as vigor dies. It is a curious thing that I find my dislike to the
thought of extinction increase as I get older and nearer the goal. It
flashes across me at all sorts of times with a sort of horror.

Men of Two Worlds (238).

The Pilgrims were open-minded. The windows of their souls were
flung wide to the sunrisings; and while, it may be, they saw no flaming
visions, yet in the radiance of the instreaming light they saw things
with their own eyes. They had attent ears, and notes of the old, but
ever new song of the morning stars were caught by them and turned into
music for the day's march. They had experiences in the Mount to
which their bronzed but shining faces bore testimony. They knew
Christ because they believed Him, and they believed Him with an increasing confidence and tenacity because they knew Him. The Spirit
witnessed with their spirits; and because of His indwelling they were
able to bear personal witness to the truth. Their contact with the
Father in all the leading ways in which He comes into manifestation to
His children was direct. Things divine were real to their apprehension.
They would not have made the statement with the same assurance; but
"We know" would have had just as much pertinency on the
lips of these men as on the lips of the great apostle. They
did not know so much; but what they did know they knew
with equal certainty. The gates of their souls turned easily
on their hinges; and it took but a touch of the unseen Hand to swing
them open and secure admission for thoughts from on high. In the dis-
closures of still hours, in earnest meditation, and through intercourse
with God and with one another, they were made rich in heavenly lore.
Still the Pilgrims were not mystics. They used all the faculties they

possessed in quest of the truth. Reason and feeling, faith and patience, activity and serene passiveness were all brought into requisition to secure a better understanding of the character and will of God. They searched the Scriptures. They meditated and prayed. They studied providences and compared opinions.—Frederick A. Noble, in "The Pilgrims."

Memorial Day (239).

Our heroes—how many and brave and self-sacrificing they were! Dr. Henry Clay Trumbull, late editor of the "Sunday School Times," tells of one of them:

It was before Richmond. He was Major Camp, of the 10th Connecticut, of which regiment Dr. Trumbull was the chaplain. The major and the chaplain were bosom friends. An assault had been ordered. Major Camp had been absent on other duty. But just before the assault he appeared, wiping from his face the perspiration caused by his exertions to join his regiment. As he came up the chaplain's face fell with disappointment. Reading his look—they were so intimate they called each other by their first names—Major Camp said quietly and tenderly, "What is the matter, Henry? Has anything happened?" "No, but I'm sorry you have returned for this assault," the chaplain answered. "Oh! don't say so, my dear fellow; I thank God I'm back." "But I'm afraid for you," said the chaplain. "Well, you wouldn't have the regiment go in with me behind, would you? No, no; in any event I thank God I am here," replied the major. Then the major went about with the cheerfulest face and tone encouraging the men. The ordered moment for the assault approached. The left of the second line was assigned to Major Camp. "May I not as well take the left of the front line, Colonel?" quietly asked Major Camp of the commanding officer. "Certainly, if you prefer it," was the colonel's reply. This more dangerous place Major Camp took because it gave him better chance to lead and encourage the men. The signal for the assault was given. The cheers of the men rang out. The friends clasped hands. "Goodby, Henry. Goodby," warmly said Major Camp. That "goodby" sent a chill to the chaplain's heart. Never before in a score and a half of battles had that word been said. The chaplain followed after the major; with great difficulty he caught up with him. "You do not doubt your Saviour?" the chaplain asked. "No, no, dear fellow, I do trust Jesus, fully, wholly," was the reply.

The chaplain went about his work among the wounded and the dying. Major Camp pressed on; stood a moment to reform a broken line; became thus a more easy mark for the enemy's bullet; the ball pierced his lungs; he fell—dead as by a lightning's flash.

Afterward Dr. Trumbull wrote his noble history under the title, "The Knightly Soldier." So that young life was gloriously finished for this world.

But do not let us forget the nameless heroes who never won such chronicle. Upon hundreds of thousands of unknown graves on this Memorial Day the flowers will be strewed. The names of them may not be told, but their deeds and the results of them remain. Major Camp is but a more evident specimen among a vast company. They labored in the awful clash of battle; their blood cemented the Union and rescued liberty. They labored and we have entered into their labors.

Certainly Decoration Day should make us hold in ever-enduring and grateful memory the patient, strong, loving, matchless President, the chief leader through those red years.—C. Wayland Hoyt, D. D.

Patriotism's Ideals (240).

Our country calls not for the life of ease, but for the life of strenuous endeavor. Let us, therefore, boldly face the life of strife, resolute to do our duty well and manfully; resolute to uphold righteousness by deed and by word; resolute to be both honest and brave, to serve high ideals, yet to use practical methods.—Theodore Roosevelt.

The Expansive Pressure of Life. (241)

Of the countless suggestions and witnesses which come trooping to our door when we open it to these questions, I wish to seize on one. I want to emphasize the fact that the widening consciousness of life as something ever beyond ourselves, at the same time deepens the consciousness and worth of life within ourselves. The more you get beyond your narrow and selfish individuality, the more of an individual you become. Life everywhere grows in dignity and worth as it ceases to be ephemeral. In proportion as life is projected upon a large scale does it acquire interest and value. As the stage is widened, it invites to a more dignified performance, just as the great stage at the Auditorium at once connects itself in our minds with a different spectacle and a different treatment from that which would be possible upon the tiny stage on wheels where the itinerant showman presents his puppet-shows at country fairs. When the theater in which the drama of life is enacted becomes great enough, it calls for greatness of action. If a man can share the purpose which shapes the world; if he can be raised up to think the thoughts of God; if he can dream of infinite excellence, and plan for deeds that live, then his own personal life begins to stretch out to compass that which he can see and dream and be. Putting on immortality is another way of putting on individuality. Eternal life is the necessary complement of an adequate and abundant personal life. It would seem as if the expansive pressure of new values and new ideals must push the door open on the further side of life.—Selected.

Our Place in the World. (242)

There is, no doubt, a touch of melancholy often in the moment when we realize that a large part of our work may not produce its harvest till after we are dead and gone. Fain would we see the outcome with our own eyes. Gladly would we take part in the gains as well as in the labor. But the magnanimous spirit rises eventually over such a natural weakness. The unselfish man will not suffer himself long to be depressed or paralyzed by narrow considerations of this kind, preferring to reflect, as Christ suggests, that God, the great Master of the world's harvests, couples him with the future as with the past, and that no life fails to be a cause as well as an effect, stretching forward into the mor row as it reaches back into the past. It is this outlook which, above all things, lends a certain grace and breadth to human life, investing it with something of the long farsight and patience that belong to God himself. It throws on our existence here a richer light than if we merely sought to explain it all from the dominating present that lies between the cradle and the grave. For as half of life's wisdom depends on the knowledge of how far our place and responsibility extend, and of the precise limits at which our function ceases to be of use, so the other half almost may be said to consist in the sight of a great, growing order in which each one of us has some part of his own to play, some duty to discharge.

> "My brothers, 'neath the eternal Eyes
> One human joy shall touch the just—
> To know their spirits' heirs arise,
> And lift their purpose from the dust:
> The father's passion arms the son,
> And the great deed goes on, goes on."

It is the sum of that continuous process which is meant to form a sober exhilaration for us men in our work—"That both sower and reaper may rejoice together."—Rev. James Moffatt.

The Tombs of the Great (243).

After I had wandered through the vast edifice, the verger asked me whether I would not like to see the crypt, and I readily assented. But I soon regretted that I had done so, for as he opened the doorway that led to the dark recesses of the vaults there met me a cold, chilly atmosphere, heavy laden with the mouldy smell of corruption and death. I was ashamed to show my reluctance after having asked to see the burial place of the nation's great men, and descended a winding staircase.

The darkness was so dense that I could not see a foot in front of me, but the verger called to me that I would find an iron railing at hand, and by following that I would be guided to the crypt. I descended, then, into the darkness of the tombs.

On reaching the bottom I was surrounded on all sides by black vaults, but in the distance I could discern a light, on approaching which I found that the crypt really opened upon the cloister gardens of the whole cathedral. There the glorious spring sunshine was bringing flowers into bloom, and in the midst of the garden there was a beautiful fountain playing, and then I realized how, through darkness, I had come to the bright glory of the spring sunshine.

And thus it was that Christ upon the cross, after descending step by step in His humility, passed into the gloom of darkness. I can imagine that as He reached out His hand in the darkness it rested upon the will of God; and as He descended into the grave His soul cried out, "Thou wilt not leave my soul in hell; neither wilt Thou suffer Thine holy one to see corruption. Thou wilt show me the path of life; in Thy presence is fulness of joy; at Thy right hand there are pleasures forevermore." Thus, through the darkness of the grave, Christ came into the light of the resurrection morning.—Rev. F. B. Meyer

True Patriotism. (244)—That patriotism is purest that disregards opportunities for personal honor, and falters not when called to do the difficult duty, though it must be done in obscurity, far from the blaze of public approval. Patriotism burns brightest in the unselfish heart. —Selected.

Our Heritage of Love and Sacrifice (245).

Who planted the elms which give their overarching glory to every New England village of the older day? Not those who now walk beneath their shadows, but far-seeing, kindly men who knew that they could never walk beneath their shadows, but that their children might.

Who founded the colleges and schools? Were they instituted by men who hoped to enter there as learners themselves? Nay, but by men who so far realized the value of sound learning that they were able at real sacrifice to lay the foundations of the future. They, too, were a part of the vast company of men who had faith and who greeted the promise from afar.

And I read the heroism of this faith also in the eyes of each generation, as it gathers its children to its heart and looks into their eyes with yearning and hope. There is something sublime and beautiful in this faith that lingers with us—the faith that our children will continue and complete the things which are so meager and so incomplete in us. I see mothers toiling in loving patience for their children, merging their own happiness in theirs. I see fathers carrying heavier burdens that their boys may be well equipped for life. I recall sacrifices that my own father made because of his great desire that his boys might start with a better equipment than himself; and I remember that it is only one of countless illustrations, where a better education for the children, or some added happiness for them, meant the diminution of something for those who were making the sacrifice. And when the meaning of it sweeps over me at times, it seems as though it would be the crime of patricide itself not to be loyal and faithful to the trust committed, and the heritage of love and sacrifice received.—Rev. Frederick E. Dewhurst.

The Choir Invisible. (246)

Around is decay and death casts its shadow over all. The days come and go and seem to carry with them almost all of life. We labor and see so little of results. If we accumulate of earthly good, we know how uncertain is our tenure of it. And so much of our labor never assumes tangible form. We seem to be throwing our strength into a flowing stream by which it is swept away. But it is not so. That which is beyond our horizon does not cease to be. Life's greatest powers are those which cannot be measured by visible and accumulated results; they belong to the sphere of the spiritual. Evil or good, they project themselves into the unseen, and do so with a power that never exhausts itself. The word spoken lives after the sound dies away. It has entered another life and lives in it. The touch of the hand, expressing warm sympathy, leaves an influence that remains long after the pressure has ceased. The kind act writes itself in the heart in letters that cannot be obliterated.

Herein is the great joy and the reward of a faithful minister of the Gospel. Weary and discouraged he returns from the pulpit to his study, feeling he has labored in vain, and yet at a later time, he meets that sermon, lifted up and glorified in the Christian life of a person of whom, it may be, he had no knowledge when the sermon was preached. He has his earnest longings, which may not be realized in himself, but they have quickened others to like aspirations and to better living. A minister may burn his sermons, but he cannot his ministry. No fire can consume the love he awakened. No change of time can obliterate what he has spoken in the name of Christ.—Selected.

The Immortality of Influence. (247)

Savonarola, when he was about to die at the stake, strengthened his brethren of St. Mark's with these words: "I am certain that if I must die, I shall be able to aid you in heaven more than I have been able to do on earth. The work of the Lord will ever go forward, and my death will only hasten it." And therein he uttered a large part of the philosophy of history. This appears most impressively when one thoughtfully asks, Who are today the mightiest men in the world's affairs? For in our answer we cannot name any of our contemporaries; we are bound to name others whom we call the dead; as Washington and Lincoln, who are more potent now in politics than any living politicians; Shakespeare, who is still the supreme schoolmaster wherever our English tongue is spoken, affecting the mentality of millions who never even read his works; John Wesley, whose influence is both perpetuated and multiplied in the largest of the Protestant sects; Martin Luther, whose name is significant not only of great theological distinctions, but whose career still accounts for the existing boundaries of the great European nations; and greater than these, a certain Jewish tentmaker, itinerant, fugitive, almost unheeded by his own generation, now in his grave these two thousand years, under whose spell the whole civilized world still worships and thinks, loves and longs, lives and dies, Saul of Tarsus, Paul the Apostle—these, and the One whose name is above every name, were not only the great of their times; they are the great of our times. To lack anything contributed by the living would not so far affect us as suddenly to lose out of life what we have received from these dead who are not dead.

And these "immortal dead who live again in lives made better by their presence"—these are not the few whose names we thus may call, but the millions now nameless from whom the world which has forgotten them has yet derived the greater part of its inheritance of blessing and truth. They wrought as humbly as we must do, but they wrought in the Holy Ghost, and our work, too, if wrought in Him, may be as potent as theirs, and like theirs, be prolonged into an immortal influence. So may we "join the choir invisible whose music is the gladness of the world."—William M. Balch, D. D.

Memorial Day (248).

Today all over this land many of our people are engaged as we are in a memorial service of the soldier dead, and they are scattering blossoms and flowers over their graves. It will do them no good, but it will do us good. There ought to be many lessons learned today, and much good result from it—lessons of love and devotion for the beautiful land God has given us, of respect, affection and honor for the survivors who are yet with us. There are voices, quiet voices that come to us from all over the land; from the grave of Revolutionary sire and all those who in after years followed them in battle, and all unite in bidding us to be devoted to the flag, true to country, valiant in her defense. Let us honor the volunteer soldier of our land! Let us reverently cover his grave today with tokens of our affection! Let us remember the living, too; those who, maimed in any way, are among us, and those, too, who may have suffered less in wounds amid the fortunes of war. Their number is lessening, not one by one only, but companies and regiments of the Boys in Blue are dropping out every year. They are growing old, too, those that remain. Their sons and daughters are beginning to take the places in life of the past generation. The war of the rebellion, like those of other years, is rapidly receding from our vision. A new generation is coming into action. May they prove as worthy of their trust as the past generations have been.

Thus, my friends, have thoughts come clustering to my mind as I pondered upon Memorial Day. It is the soldiers' day. How I honor them! What great men they were! May they never cease, in spirit at least, to exist in this fair land, so that when valor is required to preserve the land, our sons may ever be ready.

Strew the graves with flowers! Bring them on, and kindly, gently, lovingly, lay the chaplets here and there. And, as you see the folds of the beautiful flag that our boys followed—for which they died—swear by the God of your Fathers that never an act, never a word, never a thought shall come from you that shall sully its glory or that may tend to its disgrace.—J. M. Kendig, D. D.

Greatness and Goodness (249).

That moral excellence is a condition of efficacy in the highest things is a truth perceived in spheres outside the Church. Did not Milton assure us that the poet must first be a good man? In one of his letters to the Lady Harriet Don, Burns writes concerning his engagement in the Excise, "One advantage I have in this new business is the knowledge it gives me of the various shades of character in man—consequently assisting me in my trade as a poet." It was rather thus in the line of sensual indulgence that his finest senses were blurred and the poet degraded in the man. Ruskin steadily taught that the first qualification for great art was to look on foulness with horror. Professor Tyndall insisted that character, no less than mind of the highest order, must distinguish the successful researcher. After recounting the discoveries of Berzelius, Regnault, and Joule, he adds, "There is a morality brought to bear upon such matters, which, in point of severity, is probably without a parallel in any other domain of intellectual action." To the same effect Novalis wrote long before: "Let him, therefore, who would arrive at a knowledge of nature, train his moral sense; let him act and conceive in accordance with the noble essence of his soul; and, as if of herself, Nature will become open to him." Blessed are the pure, for they see deepest and surest, they see the best of everything, and give the best report of it; and thus being and doing best serve their race. What, then, intellectual observers see with more or less clearness and maintain with more or less emphasis, revelation discerns with open vision and affirms with absolute assurance, that the highest and most effective servants of humanity are the pure in heart, the good, the true, the loving, the spiritual and godly, in a word the Christlike. In such men God is revealed and glorified. Great men raise our conception of man; good men raise our conception of God, He is magnified in them.—Watkinson

He That Doeth the Will of God Abideth Forever (250).

At East Northfield, over the grave of the great Evangelist, there is an inscription fraught with the one invincible assurance of immortality: "He that doeth the will of God abideth forever." In these words the culminating evidences of the great fact culminate. It is the proof of proofs. Because the doing of the will of God must ever go one, the doer of it must go on in its doing.

It is an axiom of physics that a moving body will continue moving until stopped by some opposing force. Friction and gravitation quickly arrest the flight of the cannon-shot, but the planet flies for ages of ages through the frictionless ether. The spiritual world, no less than the physical, has its axiomatic law of motion. We see the conscious doing of God's will in active progress. Their is nothing in the nature of things to arrest it, for, as Augustine said, "God is the nature of things." It must simply go on, the doing, and so the doer. It is this axiom of spiritual progress which Christian faith asserts in the Apostolic formula, "He that doeth the will of God continueth forever."—The Outlook.

He Died a Brave Man (251).

In my original company, raised at the beginning of the war, was a man of wealth and influence, about forty-five years old. He was blessed with a devoted wife and eleven children. His eldest son enlisted with him, and when we marched away we passed by his plantation. There at the gate were his wife and the other ten children, each of them waving the flag, even the baby. In our first battle the young man fell, shot through the body. "Tom," said a comrade, "are you badly hurt?" "Yes," he said; "I am shot through the body. Give my love to my mother." As his gallant spirit fled, I could hear his father cheering on the men. He was only a quartermaster-sergeant, but he rallied and cheered the boys like a general. I went up to him and told him his son was dead. The word struck him like a bullet; he fell forward on his horse's neck, and a great sob burst from his heart. In a few moments he straightened himself in the saddle, and exclaimed, "Thank God, he died like a brave man!" and until the fight was over I could hear him encouraging the men. At ter the battle, I assisted him to prepare the body of his son for burial, and together we laid the brave youth in his grave, not far from the spot where he fell.—Gen. M. M. Trumbull.

"Lives of Great Men Oft Remind Us." (252).

It is rather for us to be here dedicated to the great task remaining before us, that from these honored dead we take increased devotion to that cause for which they gave the last full measure of devotion; that we here highly resolve that these dead shall not have died in vain; and this nation, under God, shall have a new birth of freedom and that the government of the people, by the people, and for the people, shall not perish from the earth.—Abraham Lincoln at Gettysburg.

ILLUSTRATIVE VERSES.

A Crowned Life (253).

Nobly thy course is run—
Splendor is round it:
Bravely thy fight is won—
Victory crowned it.
In thy warfare of heav'n,
Grown old and hoary,
Thou'rt like the summer's sun,
Shrouded in glory.

A Strong Man (254).

'O God, for a man with a heart, head, hand,
Like one of the simple great ones,
Gone forever and forever by—
One still strong man in a blatant land."

The Swan Song of a Great Soul (255).

The following verses were written by that man of profound schol-
arship and deep piety, Professor Noah K. Davis, of the University of
Virginia, as he was nearing his eightieth birthday. They were read at
his recent funeral:

"Nearly Eighty."

A call for me
Across the sea;
Come home! thy work is done;
The sky is clear,
But night draws near,
Embark at set of sun.

Into the night
With spirit flight
Leaving my cares behind
Hoping for day,
I'll waft away
The other shores to find.

It is not far,
The evening star
Marks where that land begins.
Whose every height
In endless light
With hallelujah rings.

My home is there,
His love to share
Who gave Himself for me.
I hear the word,
I come, dear Lord,
'Tis heaven to be with thee.
—Baltimore Christian Advocate.

Reward (256).

"Servant of God, well done,
Thy glorious warfare passed;
The battle fought, the victory won,
And thou art crowned at last."

Tennyson (257).

No moaning of the bar; sail forth, strong ship,
Into that gloom which has God's face for a far light.
Not a dirge, but a proud farewell from each fond lip,
And praise, abounding praise, and fame's faint star light.

Lamping thy tuneful soul to that large noon
Where thou shalt choir with angels. Words of woe
Are for the unfulfilled, not thee, whose moon
Of genius sinks full-orbed, glorious, aglow.

No moaning of the bar; musical drifting
Of Time's waves, turning to the eternal sea,
Death's soft wind all thy gallant canvas lifting,
And Christ thy Pilot to the peace to be.
—Sir Edwin Arnold, on The Death of Tennyson.

Waiting for the Bugle (258).

We wait for the bugle; the night dews are cold,
The limbs of the soldiers feel jaded and old,
The field of our bivouac is windy and bare,
There is lead in our joints, there is frost in our hair.
The future is veiled and its fortunes unknown,
As we lie with hushed breath till the bugle is blown.
At the sound of that bugle each comrade shall spring
Like an arrow released from the strain of the string;
The courage, the impulse of youth shall come back
To banish the chill of the drear bivouac.
And sorrows and losses and cares fade away
When the life-giving signal proclaims the new day.

Though the bivouac of age may put ice in our veins,
And no fibre of steel in our sinews remain;
Though the comrades of yesterday's march are not here,
And the sunlight seems pale and the branches are sere;
Though the sound of our cheering dies down to a moan;
We shall find our lost youth when the bugle is blown.
—Thomas Wentworth Higginson.

Memorial Day (259).

In memory of our soldier dead—
The strong, the brave, and true—

O skies of May, shine tenderly,
And wear your robes of blue!
O breezes, softly, gently waft
The fragrance of our flowers
Upon the air while thus we deck
These honored graves of ours.

How bravely marched our heroes forth
To battle and to strife!
How nobly, for "our country's sake,"
Was offered each brave life!
True men! true hearts! true comrades all!
Just side by side went they,
Beneath their country's flag to win—
Or perish in the fray.

Their battle cry was—"Freedom,"
and.
Their motto—"for the right!"
And God looked down upon them
there,
"All loyal in His sight"—
And saw that they were weary,
and
Had done their duty well.
And we know He crowned with
laurels
His soldier-boys who fell
Upon the field of duty and
He called them home to rest
In sweetest peace eternal, on
His tender loving breast.
And here we lay our offerings
sweet,
Above each quiet head,
And thus we honor loyally
Our loyal soldier dead.
                    —Mary D. Brine.

Our Deathless Dead (260).

No name of mortal is secure in stone:
    Hewn on the Parthenon, the name will waste;
    Carved on the Pyramid, 'twill be effaced;
In the heroic deed, and there alone,
Is man's one hold against the craft of Time,
That humbles into dust the shaft sublime—
That mixes sculptured Karnak with the sands;
Unannaled, blown about the Libyan lands.
And, for the high, heroic deeds of men,
There is no crown of praise but deed again.
Only the heart-quick praise, the praise of deed
Is faithful praise for the heroic breed.

How shall we honor them—our Deathless Dead?—
    How keep their mighty memories alive?
    In Him who feels their passion, they survive!
Flatter their souls with deed, and all is said!
In the heroic soul their souls create
Is raised remembrance past the reach of fate.
    The will to serve and bear,
    The will to love and dare,
And take, for God, unprofitable risk—
    These things, these things will utter praise and pean
    Louder than lyric thunders Aeschylean;
These things will build our dead unwasting obelisk.
                    —Edwin Markham.

Victory (261).

Once they were mourners here below,
    And poured out cries and tears.
They wrestled long as we do now
    With sins and doubts and fears.
We asked them whence their victory came,
    They with united breath
Ascribe their conquest to the Lamb.

Suspiria (262).

Take them, O Death; and bear away
  Whatever thou canst call thine own!
Thine image, stamped upon this clay,
  Doth give thee that, but that alone!

Take them, O Grave! and let them lie
  Folded upon thy narrow shelves,
As garments by the soul laid by,
  And precious only to ourselves!

Take them, O great Eternity!
  Our little life is but a gust,
That bends the branches of thy tree,
  And trails its blossoms in the dust.
                    —Longfellow.

Thro' Sorrow—Joy (263).

Oh saddest sweet bond! and can it be
That through His sorrow joy is come to me,
That thus His glorious beauty I shall see?
Oh eyes; for whom such vision is in store,
Keep ye to all things pure forevermore,
Till ye shall close beside death's shadowed door;
Be lighted from within by unseen guest,
Send out warm rays of love to all distressed,
And by your shining lure them into rest!

Pass On (264).

O, call him not back to earth's weariness now,
For glories immortal encircle his brow.
From glory to glory, forever ascending,
His soul with the soul of the Infinite blending.
Great, luminous truths on his pathway shall shine * * *
To nobler heights, pass on, pass on.

Strength (265).

  "One blast upon his bugle horn
Was worth a thousand men."

Lost Awhile (266).

And in the morn those angel faces smile,
Which I have loved long since,
And lost awhile."

Soldiers Immortal (267).

They sleep beneath the daisied sod,
  And over them we strew
White lilies with their hearts of gold
  And roses bright with dew.
They sleep beside their rusty swords,
  The blue coats and the gray,
Till Gabriel blows the reveille
  Upon the Judgment Day.

They live within the nation's heart,
  Each gallant soldier-son
Who fought with Lee the losing fight
  Or marched with Grant and won.
They live in every silver star
  That glitters in the flag,
From old Nantucket's light to cold
  Alaska's farthest crag.

For, lo! the dust of Dixie's dead
  And stern New England's slain
Have filled the cracks in Freedom's wall
  And made it sound again;
And every drop of blood they shed
  Before the cannon's mouth
Cements the ties of brotherhood
  Uniting North and South.
                    —Minna Irving, in Leslie's.

Post Mortem Recognition (268).

During our Civil War, Punch, London's comic paper, held Lincoln
up to ridicule for the English people could not imagine that a man
of so humble an origin and so limited an education could be a great
statesman, and one of earth's truest noblemen. But the English people
gradually learned to know him as he was, and when word of his assas-
sination came, there appeared a cartoon in Punch that astonished the
world; it was entitled "Brittanica sympathizes with Columbia," and
represented Great Britain laying a wreath on the dead President's bier.
The beautiful tribute from Tom Taylor, whose pen had so often held
Lincoln up to ridicule, began with these pathetic words:—

You lay a wreath on murdered Lincoln's bier!
  You, who with mocking pencil wont to trace,
Broad for the self-complacent British sneer,
  His length of shambling limb, his furrowed face,

His gaunt, gnarled hands, his unkempt, bristling hair,
  His garb uncouth, his bearing ill at ease,
His lack of all we prize as deboniar,
  Of power or will to shine, of art to please;

You, whose smart pen backed up the pencil's laugh,
  Judging each step, as though the way were plain;
Reckless, so it could point its paragraph,
  Of chief perplexity, or people's pain!

Beside this corpse, that bears for winding-sheet
  The stars and stripes he lived to rear anew,
Between the mourners at his head and feet,
  Say, scurrile jester, is there room for you?

Yes; he had liv'd to shame me from my sneer,
  To lame my pencil, and confute my pen,
To make me own this hind of princes peer,
  This rail-splitter a true-born king of men.

A Nation's Strength (269).

What builds the nation's pillars high
  And its foundations strong?
What makes it mighty to defy
  The foes that round it throng?

It is not gold. Its kingdoms grand
  Go down in battle's shock;
Its shafts are laid on sinking sand,
  Not on abiding rock.

Is it the sword? Ask the red dust
  Of empires passed away;
The blood has turned their stones to rust,
  Their glory to decay.

And is it pride? Ah! that bright crown
  Has seemed to nations sweet;
But God has struck its luster down
  In ashes at his feet.

Not gold, but only men can make
  A people great and strong;
Men who, for truth and honor's sake,
  Stand fast and suffer long.

Brave men who work while others sleep,
  Who dare while others fly—
They build a nation's pillars deep
  And lift them to the sky.
          —Ralph Waldo Emerson.

Sometime (270).

Some time, when all life's lessons have been learned
  And suns and stars forevermore have set,
The things which our weak judgments here have spurned—
  The things o'er which we grieved with lashes wet—
Will flash before us, and life's dark night,
  As stars shine most in deeper tints of blue,
And we shall see how all God's plans were right,
  And what most seemed reproof was love most true.

And we shall see how, while we frown and sigh,
  God's plans go on, as best for you and me;
How, when we called, He heeded not our cry,
  Because His wisdom to the end could see;

And e'en as prudent parents disallowed
   Too much of sweet to craving babyhood,
So God, perhaps, is keeping from us now
   Life's sweetest things, because it seemeth god

And if, sometimes, commingled with life's wine,
   We find the wormwood, and rebel and shrink,
Be sure a wiser hand than yours or mine
   Pours out this potion for our lips to drink;
And if some friend we love is lying low,
   Where human kisses cannot reach his face,
Oh, do not blame the loving Father so,
   But wear your sorrow with obedient grace.

And you shall shortly know that lengthened breath
   Is not the sweetest gift God sends His friend,
And that sometimes the sable pall of death
   Conceals the fairest boon His love can send.
If we push ajar the gates of life
   And stand within, and all God's working see,
We could interpret all this doubt and strife,
   And for each mystery could find a key.

But not today. Then be content, poor heart;
   God's plans, like lilies, pure and white unfold;
We must not tear the close-shut leaves apart—
   Time will reveal the calyxes of gold;
And if, through patient toil, we reach the land
   Where tired feet with sandals loosed may rest,
Where we shall clearly know and understand,
I think that we will say, "God knew the best."

God Knows Best (271).

   We shall work for an age at a sitting,
And never grow tired at all,
And no one shall work for money,
And no one shall work for fame,
But each for the joy of the working,
And each in his separate star,
Shall paint the things as he sees them,
For the God of things as they are."

"And when at last, through patient toil, we reach that land,
Where weary souls with sandals loosed may rest,
Where we shall fully know and understand,
I think that we shall say, "Well, God knew best."
                     —Kipling.

Love (272).

Yea, God is love, and love is might,
  Mighty as surely to keep as to make;
And the sleepers, sleeping in death's dark night,
  In the resurrection of life shall wake.
                      —Alice Carey.

Not Far They Dwell (273).

"O, so far," one saith, "so far
Lies that shadow-circled shore!
Who shall tell us where they are,
Since they come to us no more?
Farther than the arrow flies,
  Upward sped from swiftest
      string;
Farther than the cloud wreaths
      rise
  From the mountains where they
      cling;
Nor the wing of homing bird
  Bears our greeting to that
      strand,
Nor our grief-wrung sighs have
      stirred
Aught of answer from that land.
O, so far, so strange and far!
Out beyond the tideless bar,
Farther than the storm cloud
      lightens,
Farther than the sunset brightens;

Nor the eagle's loftiest soaring,
Nor love's uttermost imploring
Scales the lowest battlement
Of the city where they went"
O, not far they dwell, not far!
Near as faith and mercy are;
Star-sown heights nor depths can
      part
Friends who meet in Jesus's heart.
Ramparts of the sunrise sky,
Bastions of infinity,
Are but outworks of the home
Unto which we too shall come.
Here the gate is open wide;
  There the farthest courts of
      space
Center on one altar side,
  Lighted by one blessed Face.
We on earth, our own above,
Linked in hope and life and love—
For the city where they went
Is the home of heart content.
              —Christian Endeavor World.

How Did You Die? (274).

Did you tackle the trouble that came your way,
  With a resolute heart and cheerful,
Or hide your face from the light of day
  With a craven soul and fearful?
Oh! trouble's a ton, or trouble's an ounce,
  Or a trouble is what you make it,
And it isn't the fact that you're hurt that counts,
  But only how did you take it?

You're beaten to earth? Well, well, what's that?
  Come up with a smiling face.
It's nothing against you to fall down flat,
  But to lie there, that's disgrace.
The harder you're thrown, why the higher you bounce;
  Be fond of your blackened eye!
It isn't the fact that you're licked that counts,
  It's how did you fight and why.

And though you be down to the death, what then?
　If you battled the best you could,
If you played your part in the world of men,
　Why, the critic will call it good.
Death comes with a crawl, or comes with a pounce,
　And whether he's slow or spry,
It isn't the fact that you're dead that counts,
　But only how did you die.

—Edmund Vance Cook.

He Lives (275).

In works we do, in prayers, we pray,
Life of our life, He lives to-day.

—Whittier.

Strong Men (276).

"The East is East, and the West is West, and never the twain shall meet,
Till the earth and sky stand presently at God's great judgment seat."
So it seemed for long years, but listen
"But there is neither East nor West, border nor breed nor birth,
When two strong men stand face to face, tho' they come from the ends
　of the earth."—Kipling.

Just Away (277).

I cannot say, and I will not say
That he is dead. He is just away!

With a cheery smile and a wave of the hand
He has wandered into an unknown land.

Think of him faring on, as dear
In the love There as the love of Here.

—Riley.

Lincoln (278).

And so they buried Lincoln? Strange and vain.
Has any creature thought of Lincoln hid
In any vault 'neath any coffin lid,
In all years since that wild spring of pain?
'This false—he never in the grave hath lain,
You could not bury him, although you slid
Upon his clay, the Cheops Pyramids,
Or heaped it with the Rocky Mountain chain.
They slew themselves—they but set Lincoln free;
In all earth his great heart beats as strong,
Shall beat while pulses throb to chivalry,
And burn with hate of tyranny and wrong.
Whoever will may find him, anywhere
Save in the tomb. Not there—he is not there.

—James McKay.

A Ballad of Heroes (279).

"Now all your victories are in vain"
Because you passed, and now are not—
Because in some remoter day
Your sacred dust in doubtful spot
　　Was blown of ancient airs away—
Because you perished—must men say
Your deeds were naught, and so profane
　　Your lives with that cold burden? Nay,
The deeds you wrought are not in vain.

Though it may be, above the plot
　　That hid your once imperial clay,
No greener than o'er man forgot
　　The unregarding grasses sway;
　　Though there no sweeter is the lay
Of careless bird; though you remain
　　Without distinction of decay,
The deeds you wrought are not in vain.

No, for while yet in tower or cot
　　Your story stirs the pulses play,
And men forget the sordid lot—
　　The sordid cares—of cities gray;
　　While yet they grow for homelier fray
More strong from you, as reading plain
　　That Life may go, if Honor stay,
The deeds you wrought are not in vain.

Envoy.
Heroes of old! I humbly lay
　　The laurel on your graves again;
Whatever men have done, men may—
　　The deeds you wrought are not in vain.

Memorial (280).

"We are not many, we who stand
Beside our comrades' graves to-
　　day,
Yet, while we live, with reverent
　　hearts
We'll honor those who went be-
　　fore;
While as each brother called,
　　departs,
Is re-enlisted one name more.

We stand upon the river's verge
And see the Golden City shine
Dividing River, bright and cool,
O'er which we all must take our
　　way,
When to that Harbor Beautiful
We all shall sail some day—some
　　day.

Peace (281).

Peace to the warrior band,
To those who lie
Nameless in graves unknown,
While the years march by
With the spoil of sigh,
Tribute of tear
To the dead who live,
To the heroes, silent prone
Beneath the verdant sod, the stor-
    ied stone.
Vain, fugitive
Record in crumbling sand
Of deeds that cannot die.

Peace to the thinning line,
The remnant wan
With the wintry rime,
The blight, the ban
Of sullen-tempered time,
Braving the years of ruth,—
Fit guerdon of the pain
Of those who in the cause
Of Freedom, child of truth,—
Scorning the bootless gain
Of earth for heaven's applause,
Have won the prize of everlasting
    youth,
Lulled by war's after-chime,—
The crooning, peaceful prime

Of fruitful years,—
Forget the wounds, the fears,
The Nation's bitter tears,
The din, the glare, the grime,
Ye, the symbol and the sign
Of the God in man!

Peace!
Let the war-song cease!
Let the love-bird's note
From the cannon's throat
Proclaim the world's release
From the bloody scourge!
Let the dove nest
On the war-ship's prow;
And where now
The thorn is,
And the clutching brier,
Let the rose unfurl her fire
And the clematis
Climb and aspire.
Peace!
Let the soul emerge;
Let the world have rest;
Let the sword rust in the sheath,
And for the foeman's brow
Twine the olive wreath.
—Rev. Edward J. Spencer in The
    Christian Register.

TEXTS AND TREATMENT HINTS.

"Samuel Judged Israel All the Days of His Life."—1 Sam. 7:15. (282).

Think of being able to account for all the days of a whole human history! Think of being able to write your biography in one sentence! Think of being able to do without parentheses, foot-notes, reservations, apologies, and self-vindications! When some of us attempt to write our autobiography, we have seen great blank spaces—we do not know what we did then; we have seen blurred, blotched pages, with erasures and interlineations, and we have said, "This reminds us of the daily and terrible mistakes of our life." So our book becomes an anomalous, contradictory irreconcilable thing. Here is a man whose whole life was consecrated to a God-given task.—Parker.

"A Faithful Minister and Fellow-Servant In the Lord."—Col. 4:7 (283).

I. A splendid lifework.
II. An enviable record.
III. An undying influence.

Dead Yet Speaketh (284).

"Moreover, brethren, I declare unto you the gospel which I preached unto you, which also you have received, and wherein ye stand; by which also ye are saved, if ye keep in memory what I preached unto you, unless ye have believed in vain. For I delivered unto you first of all that which I also received, how that Christ died for our sins according to the Scriptures; and that He was buried and that He arose again the third day according to the Scriptures."—I Cor. 15:1-4.

I. A messenger dead yet speaking. The message survives.
II. We honor the messenger's memory when we are faithful to his message.

"I Thank My God Upon Every Remembrance of You."—Phil. 1:3. (285).

The abiding influence of a great life; perpetuating itself in other lives uplifted by its touch.

"I Have Fought a Good Fight."—2 Tim. 4:7.

1. A great soldier fallen.
2. His lifestory bears witness to his nobility.
3. Its memory is an inspiration.

"He Being Dead Yet Speaketh."—Heb. 11:4 (286).

I. A good life is a perpetual benediction.
2. The influence exerted by it persists.
3. What messages come back to us from the departed saint?

"After this I beheld, and lo, a great multitude, which no man could number, of all nations and kindreds, and people, and tongues, stood before the throne, and before the Lamb, clothed with white robes, and palms In their hands."—Rev. 7:9 (287).

I. The multitude. The sight of a multitude is, in its way, as attractive as a magnet; we run to see the object which has gathered it together, and this may very properly be done in the present instance.

(1) The vastness of the multitude is most remarkable; (2) the variety of the multitude is no less remarkable than the vastness of it: "of all nations, and kindreds, and peoples, and tongues."

II. Their position. Attaching to their position there is evidently (1) a transcendent honor; (2) a superlative happiness.

III. Their adornment. We notice—(1) the spotless purity of their adornment: "white robes;" (2) its triumphal character: "palms in their hands."

IV. Their worship. (1) The song of their worship is replete with interest, the subject of it is salvation, the object God Himself. (2) The service of their worship is full of interest; it is full of both fervor and harmony.—E. A. Thomson.

As a Good Soldier of Jesus Christ."—2 Tim. 2:3 (288).

The daily life of every one of us teems with occasions which will try the temper of our courage as searchingly, though not as terribly, as battlefield, or fire, or wreck; for we are born into a state of war, with falsehood, and disease, and wrong, and misery, in a thousand forms, lying all around us, and the voice within calling us to take our stand as men, in the eternal battle against these. And in this lifelong fight, to be waged by every one of us, single-handed, against a host of foes, the last requisite for a good fight—the last proof and test of our courage and manfulness must be loyalty to truth—the most rare and difficult of all human qualities. For such loyalty, as it grows in perfection, asks ever more and more of us, and sets before us a standard of manliness always rising higher and higher; and this great lesson we learn from Christ's life, the more earnestly and faithfully we study it.—Thomas Hughes.

VI. MYSTERIOUS PROVIDENCES.
SUDDEN DEATH, ACCIDENT, DISASTER.

REFLECTIONS AND ILLUSTRATIONS.

God's Inscrutable Dealings (289).

Our careful and costly preparations for doing some special work for the Master may turn out to have been utterly wasted. We find things to be quite the opposite of what we expected. Health gives out at the very moment of intended action; or, through unlooked-for reverses, the means fail just at the last for doing what we had set our hearts on accomplishing. The devoted Lowrie goes down in the Bay of Bengal with the ship which is nearing the land, to bless which with his missionary labors he had made long and expensive preparation.

A father has planned to give the best education he can to an only son; but the son dies on the very threshold of his educational career. The father's generous hands are stayed and held.

A mother makes a long and tedious journey to see a sick child, taking with her carefully-prepared gifts for her child's relief and comfort. But she has no sooner come than she is told that her child is no longer living. What now of the gifts, of which her loving hands are full? The dear one, on whom she is ready to bestow them, is no longer here to receive them. In what strange perplexities are we thus sometimes overwhelmingly plunged! How inscrutable God's dealings with us and ours! But not always, and not for long, does the Father mean that His children shall be kept in harrowing suspense, nor long be balked in the expression of their love. Men, in shining garments, appear to the baffled and wondering disciples with words of explanation, of promise and of larger hope.—Ballard.

Unexpected Sorrow (290-A).

The utter unexpectedness of many life-sorrows is one of their strangest characteristics. They come like a thunder-burst out of a clear sky. not only without any premonition of their coming, but without any apparent reason for it; and the crushed heart asks, either angrily or despairingly, why it has been sent. Many another sufferer besides Job has turned the face to heaven in amazed perplexity, and prayed "Show me wherefore Thou contendest with me;" and when no answer to that cry has come, has either looked upon the whole thing as an insoluble mystery, or coldly and half-rebelliously resigned himself to the worship of another god altogether whom he calls "inevitable fate." But surely we are often entirely wrong in talking of the "mysteriousness" of God's dealings with us. We may not know all His reasons for them, but some of His reasons are plain enough. In multitudes of cases they are plainly His sharp but merciful way of summoning a reckless, self-centered, self

indulgent, worldly heart to stop and think. They are meant to shake
it out of its foolish security, and out of that love of the world which is
so ruinous to our best and highest life.—Rev. G. H. Knight.

Be Still (290-B).

To be on our guard against either hasty utterance or act in time of
sudden distress or danger; to remember that, bad as things are, they
may not be nearly as bad as they seem; to bear in mind that the "unknown, being always the region of terror," discouragements took more
discouraging when seen through discouraged eyes; that things may be
just ready to brighten when they look the darkest; never to forget the
wrong of resorting to any rash, desperate, dishonest, doubtful or self-
harming expedient for obtaining relief; to know that "God will not have
us break into His councilhouse or spy out His hidden mysteries," but
that we must wait His time with watching and prayer—such are the
lessons we need to learn.—Ballard.

God's Secrets (290-C).

There are secrets hidden in every tiny flower and grain of sand, in
every throbbing nerve and aching heart, which our keenest wisdom
cannot discover. Every tear is a profound mystery, every sigh is a
world of unimaginable things. No one can tell us why we laugh or why
we cry. No one can read his brother's mind or understand his own. He
who has studied human nature most closely has but touched the surface
of it. Those who can tell us most about man can only prove that he is
fearfully and wonderfully made. Men who have been investigating for
a lifetime the sins, sorrows, and diseases of the world, find that these
are still the everlasting riddle; and he whose faith has given him the
clearest vision of God, knows that these are but "a portion of His ways,
and the thunders of His power none can understand." The highest philosophy still prattles and stammers and guesses like a child, and we all
have to kneel down humbly declaring that our wisdom is but dim-eyed
folly.—Greenbough.

God's Justice (290-D).

God is Love, but He is also the Absolutely Righteous One, and we
may be certain that upon any of His doings, however terrible they may
be, not the least shadow of injustice will be allowed to rest. By Him
as Judge, not only some but all the circumstances of each case will be
tenderly taken into account. All possible mitigations of blame will be
mercifully considered. The force of evil upbringing and evil environment, the power of inherited predisposition to sin, the subtlety of temptation, the ineffectual resistances of the heart to sin that enslaved it
notwithstanding, all these will be impartially allowed for. Even the
faintest signs of real repentance at the very last, signs distinguishable
only by Him, will receive their full value at His hands, and His verdict
will be "according to truth," so absolutely and so transparently just
when revealed to all, that it will command the assent of every conscience that hears it. The reply of every heart will then be like the

"great voice of much people in heaven saying Alleluia! glory and honour and power to the Lord our God, for true and righteous are His judgments."—Selected.

When the Mists Have Rolled Away (290-E).

But better than all those things, whatever those things may be, is this brief but comprehensive assurance, that we shall know as we are known—face to face, and not through a thick, discolored looking-glass. We shall know God, whom we have so often mistrusted, and with the perfect image of His beauty we shall be forever satisfied. We shall know our own poor hearts, of which we have been so ignorant, and understand the full meaning of our life's strange story. And we shall know each other. There is a sort of rapture in that thought; we never have known each other, no not even our dearest. We have always been reading each other wrongly in the dark; and even in praying together, and when our lips met, we have misjudged each other; and all that will pass away when the true light shines, and we shall understand what the perfect love means which has no torment of suspicion or fear.—Knight.

Trusting In the Dark (291-A).

To a man bereft at a stroke of property, children, and health, a foolish woman once said, tauntingly, "What of your God now? Curse him and then die and be done with it." The man did better. He gave to the world, instead, a world-old and much-needed lesson on the happiness of enduring. By reason of it all the generations since have heard of and seen two things which it would have been an unspeakable loss to have missed—"The patience of Job and the end of the Lord."—Selected.

The Inexplicable (291-B).

There are many things we cannot explain, for life reaches out into the infinite. We know but little and feel ourselves limited on every side, but, believing in God, we bow to His will in the assurance that in some way suffering is not only compatible with his sovereignty, but in the end works for good. Moral responsibility involves freedom of choice, and, therefore, the possibility of suffering and misery. With the revelation of God to us there comes also the knowledge of his righteous administration, and the consequent penalty for transgression.—Selected.

Lesser Calamities Averting Greater Ones (291-C).

God knows that for men themselves no other calamity is comparable to the calamity of forgetting God. Earthquake and fire and flood seem costly ministers, but in reality they are cheap, infinitely cheap, if only they bring back God to his place of sovereignty in the hearts of men.

Life's Mystery (291-D).

Pain in some form and in some measure is universal. We live in a world of beauty, but there is sadness in it. There are tender relations; there is love; there is hope; there is the possession of wonderful powers, but there is sorrow. From childhood to age there are tears; sighs and groans are mingled with the strains of music. There is life, but it ends in death. We cannot escape from this condition. We are capable of the highest happiness. We instinctively seek it and ever work for it, but the pain and the sadness continue.

All this becomes a greater mystery when we recognize God as the Creator and Lord of life. Without the belief of God there would be absolute darkness as to the future; we would be intelligent beings with possibilities of the greatest good floating helplessly in a current rushing into an unknown canon of darkness. But even with the belief of God, we often ask, Why? and cannot answer. How can we reconcile suffering with the infinite love and almighty power of God?

The question often presses upon the heart of faith. The heart goes out to God; it also cries to Him from the depths, "Has the Lord forgotten to be gracious? Is His mercy gone forever?" Faith may say, "Though He slay me, yet will I trust Him," but the mystery is still about and upon us.—United Presbyterian.

Man's Insufficiency and Dependency Upon God (291-E).

A calamity like that at San Francisco could have been averted. God might easily have done this. It was simply the jar of a slowly settling geological "fault," re-enforced probably by a light volcanic tremor. Divine power could have intervened to prevent both these. We ask God to protect our lives, and we are grateful when He does it. The request is a rational one, and is doubtless often granted. But men are prone to grow careless. They forget God. San Francisco was a child of plenty. Nowhere on earth are mere physical blessings so abundant as in California. Do we not all know how much danger of hardness of heart there is in this? Which city to-day has a keener consciousness of man's insufficiency, of his dependence upon God, San Francisco or Naples? Naples has just been preserved from destruction. In a year she will forget it. How long will it take to efface the impressions of April 18 from the mind of California?

Not all men are profited by such experiences, it is true. Some are but confirmed in their skepticism. Yet these are a minority. The heart of man turns to God in the hour of doom. It has ever done so; it ever will. Loving parents on earth chide and punish their children. It is a grievous thing, but it yieldeth the peaceable fruit of righteousness. It always has done so; it always will.—Northwestern Christian Advocate.

Heaven's Light on Earth's Clouds (292-A).

There are many things in nature and so many in our own experiences that we can not understand; they look hard; they are often bitter to us; and we should doubt whether God loves us at all, whether He has not left us standing amid the grinding of the vast forces, utterly helpless, if God had not in so many ways assured us that He does love us. We must turn from experience and turn from nature to the Word of God and to that larger experience of the nations that serve God, to be assured of this. But the testimony of the Word of God and the testimony of human history, as men have obeyed that Word, makes it certain that God loves us with a great love, despite the devastations of nature and despite the shocks of calamity that come to us in our individual lives. Yet there shall come a time when we shall not need to argue the question—we shall see. We shall yet stand in the revealing light of a better world. That light will not only reveal what is then about us, it will also stream back upon our past, and illumine every dark spot along the pathway over which we have come. There have been very many of them, these dark places. But the light of eternity shall stream on to them, and we shall see.—Selected.

Human Responsibility for Disaster (292-B).

It is very evident, from the facts as disclosed to the public, that the disaster to the steamer "Oregon," was not by the "act of God," in the sense of not being preventable by man. The weather was pleasant, the sea calm, and the night clear, and there was the most ample sea room for both the schooner and the steamer without any collision. There was no necessity for this collision, other than that which resulted from the failure of somebody seasonably to do his duty. Whether the officers of the steamer or those of the schooner are to blame, or both are to blame, certain it is that the disaster is the result of negligence, and might and would have been prevented by proper attention and watchfulness.

Here, then, is a moral lesson, very wide and varied in its application to the events of this life, which we choose in a few words to emphasize. The essential idea of negligence is the omission to act when and where we should act. The providence of God is so conducted in this world that such omission is often as serious as the most positive form of action. This is taught by experience in the stern and sometimes awful penalties that follow the omission. Human life is full of illustrations to this effect. The destruction of health and even untimely death of many a man are the natural consequences, not so much of what he actually does, as of what he omits to do. Disasters in business life are often due to a want of seasonable attention.—The Independent.

A Challenge to Sympathy (292-C).

When any great disaster occurs the charity of our people is poured out upon it from the length and breadth of the land, with a superb generosity which ennobles all humanity. This impulse to give, to hold out a helping hand to the fallen is common to almost all the people of the American race. We ought to thank God for such a trait of national character, and for the Christianity which has taught it to us, here, where man has first had a chance to learn and practice pure Christianity unfettered by sectarian power.—Rebecca Harding Davis.

Human Sympathy (292-D).

Perhaps the most immediate effect of the San Francisco disaster is the shock it has given to men's religious convictions. Good Christian people are asking the most startling questions. The event indeed seems to have no ascertainable connection with orthodoxy. Nature has here been acting with a savagery more brutal than that of the greatest savage we know. The Hottentot, the Australian bushman, has a heart and conscience of some sort, but people see no heart or conscience in this wreckage. Could there be any approximation to feeling, to love as we know it, in a Power which murdered and destroyed in such fashion? Moreover, could men continue to regard themselves as of any serious account in a universe which treated them thus; which paid seemingly as much attention to their tears and prayers as to the buzz of summer flies? In those hours of horror man rushed everywhere to help his brother, but there seemed no help outside man.

> The sky which noticed all makes no disclosure,
> And the earth keeps up her terrible composure.

This apparent cosmic indifference to human welfare is the feature of life which, perhaps, more than any other, has impressed itself on the modern consciousness. "There is no justice in the outside universe," says a modern writer; "justice exists only in the soul" A German poet of to-day echoes the sentiment:

> Das ganze Weltall zeigt nur Leid und Pein;
> Jedoch das Mitleid fuhlt der Mensch allein!

"The whole world shows but sorrow and pain, but compassion is felt by man alone."—J. Brierly.

Carelessness and Its Consequences (292-E).

The Johnstown horror is so appalling that it has for the moment blotted out all thoughts about it from the mind of the public, beyond pity and eager charity. But there are one or two ideas suggested by it of which we should take cognizance while yet the cloud of death is black over us. Who and what is to blame for this vast destruction of property and the lost, uncounted human lives? What but, as usual, the easy, careless good-humor for which the native American is now con-spicuous among all other men?

A railway train is burned from an overturned stove, and a hundred men and women are literally roasted to death. A feeble effort is made in one or two states to compel railway companies to heat their cars without stoves; but the companies neglect the law and the great, good-humored public take it for granted all is right, and seat themselves in the stove-heated cars, to be appalled and indignant again when the hor-ror is repeated.

A mill is burned or a theater, with a similar holocaust of human beings. There is a momentary spasm of popular rage in which managers and manufacturers are threatened with dire punishment if they fail to provide suitable escape from their buildings. But in six months the danger, the law and the penalty are all forgotten by the jolly, easy-going American, who takes it for granted all is right.—The Independent.

The Key to the Mystery of Pain and Death (293-A).

The New Testament speaks of God as, in Christ, "emptying Himself, taking on Him the form of a servant." It teaches a limitation of the di-vine, that it may draw near to, and ally itself with humanity. But the considerations we have been enumerating raise the question whether such a self-emptying, such a limitation, have not been carried farther; whether creation itself, the bringing into existence of beings like ourselves, dowered with intelligence and free will, is not itself a limitation; whether the Infinite One, in fathering such a world and in guiding it, is not Himself under a Kenosis; whether we have not here, in nature and history, to do immediately with a self-limited power and knowledge; a power and knowledge that work as we do by experiment and effort; by partial successes, by mistakes and failures even; working against an outer indifference and even opposition on the way to a final and victorious good? May it not be that there was no other way than this— of humiliation and self-abnegation—of bringing such as we are to the best that is possible for us; that only in His union with us in failure and disaster lay the road to the perfectibility of our spirits, to our final bliss in oneness with Himself? May it not be that here, by this way of silence and philosophy, we are coming to a greater doctrine of the Cross, as borne by our God from the beginning of His relations with us; the doctrine of the "Lamb, slain from the foundation of the world;" that we have here the key to the mystery of the ages, the mystery of pain and sin, and mistake and death; have it in the doctrine of One who has stooped from his height to share our imperfection, to travel with us till the end is reached and the limitation is over; till the Kingdom is finally delivered up to the Father, and God is all in All?—Jonathan Brierly.

Object of Disasters (293-B).

Some one has said that if all the stars ceased shining, and then after a hundred years shone out again, there is not an eye but would be lifted heavenward, and not a lip but would break forth in praise. But the stars were shining when we were little children, and they are there tonight, and will be there tomorrow, and we are so accustomed to that glory that we rarely give to it a single thought. What eyes we have when we travel on the Continent! Every river and hill and castle we observe. But in Glasgow, and by the banks of Clyde, a district rich in story and in beauty, there we are so accustomed to the scenery that we have eyes for nothing but the newspaper. "One good custom doth corrupt the world," and it does so, because it lulls to sleep. It is a bad thing to grow accustomed to the wrong. It may be worse to grow accustomed to the right. And that is why in the history of the church God sends the earthquake and the crash of storm, that men may be roused and startled to concern, and escape the fatal sway of inattention. —G. H. Morrison, D. D.

God Is Never Worsted (293-C).

It has been thought that God's work is His defeat. Final disaster, some have taught, and even yet teach, means that God's plans have failed. Not so. God is no experimenter. He knew the end from the beginning. He is never worsted. Man experiments and often fails. Man is often disappointed, but he need not be eternally beaten. History is proof that though revolutions come and go, they leave a deposit of good for the race. As one has put it, "the revolution of '76 was but an evolution, a new nation was the result." The Civil War, instead of destroying this republic, only cemented it more securely together. Though six centuries came and went in the building of the cathedral of Cologne it stands now as "a poem in stone." The end of things is not annihilation, the death of all things is not irreparable loss. Destruction is unto construction. There is to be a new heaven and a new earth. Old things pass away that a new order of things may be.—Selected.

Sin's Suffering and Cure (293-D).

It was a glorious summer afternoon. Outside the trees were bathed in sunshine and the birds were filled with song.

Inside, the scene was the surgical ward of a London hospital. Four times in succession, strong yet marvelously tender hands had wheeled a timid, shrinking woman, or perchance a young girl to the vestibule of the dreaded operating theatre and the touch of the surgeon's knife. Dreaded, yet neither seen nor felt. Four times in succession, unconscious under the merciful anaesthetic, had a still, death-like figure been returned to her bed.

To one eye, unaccustomed to such scenes, and the strange combination of sunshine and pain, of song and apparent death, a vision seemed to rise which filled the mind with thought. That was one ward out of several in the same hospital. One hospital out of the many in London alone. Before imagination arose all the hospitals in England, in Britain, in America, in New Zealand and all the hospitals in heathen lands.

The hospitals of the world! Alas! this was not all. There came a vision of the millions of sick and suffering folk in Western lands, and the teeming millions of sufferers of all ages in India and China and Africa, who ought to be in hospital and who are not medically relieved. Then, in a flash, which seemed to fill with heat which could be felt, came the thought, "Through one man sin entered into the world and death through sin." The thought was overwhelming, but outside there were still the sunshine and the song. "For if by the trespass of the one the many died, much more did the grace of God, and the gift by the grace of the one man, Jesus Christ, abound unto the many." "God so loved the world that He gave His only begotten Son." There is always the sunshine of His love; the glory of the natural world; and the song of the redeemed who have been brought to Him through suffering, perchance by way of the surgeon's knife.—The Christian (London).

The Clay and the Potter (293-E).

The Bible knows nothing of self-made men. Even where St. Paul hints that every one must work out his own salvation, one feels that it is a lapse on his part, or that he meant something a little different from what the words convey. For the great and insistent teaching of St. Paul is that we become real men through an impartation from God. A great American preacher used often to use the phrase "character through inspiration." This is the Bible view. The favorite imagery of the Old Testament is that of the potter molding clay. We are in God's hands.

He fashions us as He wills. Man's work is to fall in with and assist God's work. Thus God fashioned the great men of Israel. Thus he made even the nation. The Old Testament attributes every incident in Israel's making directly to God. This is not hard doctrine. The first thing any man realizes is that he is in the hands of a greater power than himself, whether that power be a good God or an evil fate or simply a blind mechanism. Here is the greatness of faith. For since some power has us in its hands, how much better that it should be a loving and intelligent Potter who will mold us into a fine vessel than a heartless mechanism that will only wreck us in the end. But we are made, we do not make ourselves.—Lynch.

The Messina Earthquake (294-A).

Perhaps the most remarkable, and the most pitiful of the ruins, are those of the Duomo or Cathedral, which has stood so many centuries, now to be overthrown. The monster monoliths of granite, with gilded capitals, which once were the columns of Neptune's Temple at Faro, lie half or wholly covered by the painted woodwork and debris of the roof, among which are fragments of marble tombs and inlaid altars, golden figures of angels and sculptured saints—a mountain of ruined masonry many feet high and open to the sky. The beautifully carved pulpit has been hurled to the ground, together with the pillar which supported it, with the mosaic and frescoes, with the arches and cornices, which made the Duomo so rich a treasure house of art.

One thing alone remains of the ancient glory—the colossal figure of Christ in mosaic in the dome of the apse at the east end. It is still there, with serene countenance and hand uplifted in the act of blessing, as for five hundred years or more it has remained, gazing benignly on the passing generations of worshippers. The calmness of that majestic, lifelike figure was startling. I turned from it resentfully. 'How can a blessing rest on such awful destruction as this?' I exclaimed involuntarily. Then it was suggested that that benediction might reach beyond the church, beyond the fallen walls of the ruined city, a message of peace and consolation in their hour of need to souls in sore anguish of mind and body; and I was glad that the apse had not been destroyed.—The Nineteenth Century.

The Titanic Disaster (294-B).

Even the most superficial and careless can hardly escape giving thought to the sober reflections awakened by the foundering of the mammoth liner with its precious human freight. How utterly at the mercy of forces outside ourselves we are in spite of all the safeguards of science and skill!

How little the things which we often value so extravagantly count for in the great crisis times of life. The multi-millionaire and the steerage passenger are on a level.

What folly it is for a man to regulate his life and leave the spiritual factor out of the reckoning. How utterly bereavement and sorrow obliterate the artificial social distinctions which wealth and station and culture are so ready to make at ordinary times.

It would be easy to multiply these reflections indefinitely. And such an awful disaster as this one is calculated to lead all to do so. A floating mass of ice rams a floating palace, and in a few hours a multitude of souls pass out from time into eternity, leaving behind them their wealth and honors and plans, and standing spiritually stripped before the everlasting realities of the life beyond.

And what is wrought here in a more spectacular way, is duplicated every day, as, in the ordinary course of nature, thousands of men go out from this life into the life to come.

After all, one thing alone counts. For the man who lives with Christ here, when and how death ushers him into Christ's heavenly presence matters little. Christlikeness means readiness and readiness means everlasting joy and rest.

"Mysterious Providences" (294-C).

Fifty years ago a great many moralizers would have described the terrible Titanic disaster as "an inscrutable providence" and let it go at that. We know better today, not because we are less reverent, but because we are less ignorant of the law of cause and effect.

Fighting shy of any metaphysical entanglement in the interminable divine-foreknowledge-and-human-free-will argument one fact stands out as clearly as the stars stood out over the glassy sea on that fateful Sunday night of April the fourteenth and that is that sixteen hundred and fifty-two—possibly more—helpless souls went down to death because someone had blundered. And it was not blind blundering either; but reckless and deliberate neglect of the most ordinary common-sense precautions which even stupidity could have suggested.

If the Titanic's officers—and they were brave, true men too—knowing, because warned, that icebergs were in their vicinity, had slowed down their speed from twenty-seven to eight or ten miles for a few hours until the danger zone was passed, there would have been no wreck.

And if there had been ample life-saving equipment—instead of only one-fifth enough boats and rafts—even if the collision had occurred, most of the sixteen hundred would have been saved.

There was no mysterious providence about the matter, but rank human carelessness, greed, ambition to make a record—and no doubt the owners and not the officers were responsible for the resultant taking of desperate chances and insufficient equipment.

"Desert Journeys" (294-D).

In one of these modern books of the desert there is given a bit of dialogue between a man and a woman:

" 'The desert is full of truth. Is that what you mean to ask?' the man says.

"The woman made no reply.

"The man stretched out his hand to the shining expanse of desert before them.

" 'The man who is afraid of prayer is unwise to set foot beyond the palm trees,' he said.

" 'Why unwise?' she asks.

"He answers, 'The Arabs have a saying, "The desert is a garden of Allah." ' "

Life Meant to Be Heroic (294-E).

Life is meant to be a heroic thing. God's best gift to His greatest servants and sons has not been immunity from suffering, the surprise of woe, the black face of death, but equanimity, heroism, uttermost trust. Paul's wages for his immeasurable service in his Master's kingdom was of two kinds. He was beheaded as a criminal outside the walls of Rome; he met this order of outrage and death in the calm might of an inspired life and a glorious hope.

Calamity is not new, nor has it come to an end with the latest disaster. Faith is equally needed in the brightness of day and the blackness of night; faith is our life because mere temporal existence is in jeopardy every hour. We must not count too much on its continuance; we must face daily the certainty of final universal bereavement and we must do it in the singing power of a heroic faith.

"For though the fig tree shall not blossom,
Neither shall fruit be in the vines;
The labor of the olive shall fail,
And the fields shall yield no meat;
The flock shall be cut off from the fold,
And there shall be no herd in the stalls:
Yet will I rejoice in the Lord,
I will joy in the God of my salvation."
—Rev. George A. Gordon, D. D.

Every Day Tragedy (295-A).

Some people will begin to arraign Divine Providence, and expatiate upon the cruelty and sinister dreadfulness of a tragedy. But, let me remind you, that tragedy all told is no greater in extent than what is taking place all around you every day you live. It is the element of the dramatic in it that makes it seem so, and that is all. Take that out, face the thing as it really is, and you are only confronted by an old, old fact, a fact of universal experience and which none of us can escape, namely, the fact of death. We have to die only once; we die alone, no matter how many more may die at the same time. More people are dying in the world at this moment than went down on the Titanic the other night, but each one will have to pass through the dread portals alone. It is curious how little we realize this. You may speak of twelve hundred dead in the sunken Titanic, but every one of those dead made the great transition separately from all the rest, and summed up in his or her experience all that the whole twelve hundred had to meet and know. If only one person had been drowned.

that one person would have covered the whole territory of the disaster
we are discussing, for no person has to die two deaths, though all
must die. Death is an individual matter after all; and therefore the
only reason why one dwells upon it specially this morning in connection with the wreck of the Titanic is that that terrible event makes us
think, whether we will or no, about what we all have one day to
encounter, whether it come soon or late.—Rev. R. J. Campbell.

ILLUSTRATIVE VERSES.

Leave Them With God (295-B).

O anguished heart, nigh breaking for the dead
  Who died and made no sign,
Leave them with God: perhaps, ere life had fled,
They saw, at last, the Saving Christ Who bled,
Found their atonement in the Blood He shed,
  And trusted Love Divine.

Leave All to God (295-C).

Leave all to God: thy vision cannot scan
  His ways of Righteousness, His depths of grace;
  But thou shalt know, when thou dost see His face,
How full of holy love His perfect plan.

Leave all to God: but hear Him speak to thee,
  "Cling thou the more to Me when clouds are dark,
  Make sure that thou thyself art in the Ark;
All else thou then wilt calmly leave to Me."

Out of Darkness Into Day (295-D).

Fair visions gleaming through the darkness beckoned
  My buoyant steps along the sunny way;
Sweet voices thrilled me, till I fondly reckoned
  That life would be one long blue summer day.

This was the way my feet had gladly taken,
  And, blindly lured by that deceitful gleam,
I would have wandered on, by God forsaken,
  Till death awoke me from my fatal dream.

My pleasant path in sudden darkness ended,
  My footsteps slipped, my hope was well-nigh gone;
I could but pray; and as my prayer ascended,
  Thy face, O Saviour, through the darkness shone.

I woke from dreams; and, cured of all my blindness,
  I saw Thy Hand had checked my downward way:
The pain was keen, but all in loving kindness,
  That led me out of darkness into Day.

—J. D. Burns.

Divine Providence (295-E).

With God, all things together work for good:
    Nor less through tears,
  Than through life's purest, sweetest joys, we learn
To love the way we had misunderstood.
    For through the years
  He finds at length, who for the truth doth yearn,
  And knows that Heaven answers in return.

I tread the path of mortals here below.
> But here and now

The thorns that hedge me in are made to bloom,
And flowers of hope on desert places grow,
> I know not how.

A light, moreover, lifts the distant gloom,
And what is now my aid, I thought my doom.

—Selected

Their Monument (296-A).

Peasant and merchant and millionaire,
> Soldier and scholar and man of the sea,

Mourned by the world, they are resting where
> No towering monument ever may be;

But the waves that go rolling above them there,
> Where the pitiless fogs hover over the tide,

Shall never efface and shall never impair
> The glory they gained when they manfully died.

With only an hour in which to pray
> Where Death had found them and would not wait,

They sent the young and the weak away,
> Intrusting them to the whims of Fate;

Robbed of hope, they had strength to stay
> While the helpless ones and the women went,

And the dark sea, rolling till Judgment Day,
> Is their ever-enduring monument.

Peasant and merchant and millionaire,
> Soldier and scholar and roustabout,

By the torch's fitful and feeble flare
> They manfully swung the lifeboats out;

Whispering hopes that they might not share,
> They claimed the right of the strong and brave,

And their fame shall live till the last men bear
> The last of all heroes to his grave.

Christian and Jew, and humble and high,
> Master and servant, they stood, at last,

Bound by a glorious, brotherly tie,
> When doubting was ended and hoping past!

They stayed to show how the brave could die,
> While their helpless ones and the woment went,

And the sea that covers them where they lie
> Is their ever-enduring monument.

—S. E. Kiser.

The Conquered (296-B).

One is surprised to find so little in the Bible about success. It does not say: "Well done, good and successful servant," but it does say: "Well done, good and faithful servant." Fidelity to duty, loyalty to principle are the conditions for true plaudits at the end.

"I sing the hymn of the conquered, who fell in the battle of life—
The hymn of the wounded, the beaten, who died overwhelmed in the
    strife:
Not the jubilant song of the victors, for whom the resounding acclaim
Of nations was lifted in chorus, whose brows wore the chaplet of fame—
But the hymn of the low and the humble, the weary, the broken in
    heart,
Who strove and who failed, acting bravely a silent and desperate part;
Whose youth bore no flower on its branches, whose hopes burned in
    ashes away:
From whose hands slipped the prize they had grasped at: who stood
    at the dying of day
With the work of their life around them, unpitied, unheeded, alone;
With death swooping down o'er their failure, and all but their faith
    overthrown."

—E. C. Schaeffer, D. D.

Rest (296-C).

These lines were written a little before the death of the gifted
authoress.

We are so tired, my heart and I,
Of all things here beneath the sky,
One only thing would please us best—
Endless, unfathomable rest.
We are so tired; we ask no more
Than just to slip out by life's door;
And leave behind the noisy rout
And everlasting turn about.
Once it seemed well to run on, too,
With her importunate, fevered crew,
And snatch amid the frantic strife
Some morsel from the board of life.

But we are tired; at life's crude hands
We ask no gift she understands;
But kneel to him she hates to crave
The absolution of the grave.

—Mathilde Blind.

Carpathia (296-D).

Ship of the widows, of sorrow, of doom—
Hail her home from the scene of gloom!
  Ship of the shadows of grief and tears!
  Welcome her home to the crowded piers!
Ship of the shattered and sundered lives—
Welcome her home with her stricken wives!
    Welcome her, wave to her.
      Over her head
    The shadowy wraith
      Of dauntless dead!

Ship of the widows, of youth turned gray
In the awful woe of a single day;
　　Ship of sorrow and shadow and care,
　　Home from the seas of the dark despair,
Flags half-masted and hearts a-weep,
Welcome her home from the heartless deep!
　　　Welcome her, only
　　　　With sobs, not cheers;
　　　Home to our sympathy,
　　　　Home to our tears!

　　　　　　　　　　　　　　—Baltimore Sun

God's Afterward (296-E).

God always has an "afterward"
　For every bitter thing.
The flowers may fall, but fruit abides;
　The butterfly's bright wing
Is painted in its long night's sleep;
　Each winter hath its spring.
How glorious is the afterward
　When Easter joy-bells ring!

God always has an "afterward":
　The patriarch Job, of old,
When in the fires was yet assured
　He should come forth as gold;
And Joseph found it thus, when he
　Was by his brethren sold—
A wealth of blessing God designed,
　Unfathomed and untold.

God always has an "afterward"—
　An afterward of bliss;
First night, then morning, formed the day,
　So must it end like this!
His purpose, higher than our thought,
　We should be sad to miss;
Though hidden, folded in his hand,
　Faith still that hand would kiss.

God has a shining "afterward"
　For every cloud of rain;
We may not see the meaning now
　Of sorrow and of pain,
But nothing God permits His child
　Can ever be in vain;
The seed here watered by our tears,
　Yields sheaves of ripened grain.

God always has an "afterward";
  He keeps the best in store,
And we shall see it hath been so
  When we reach yonder shore:
The cross, the shame, He once despised,
  For the joy set before,
And as we follow we shall find
  Death is Life's opening door!

A Mother's Love (297-A).

Last night, my darling, as you slept,
  I thought I heard you sigh,
And to your little crib I crept,
  And watched a space thereby;
And then I stooped and kissed your brow.
  For O, I love you so—
You are too young to know it now,
  But sometime you shall know.

Some time, when in a darkened place
  Where others come to weep,
Your eyes shall look upon a face
  Calm in eternal sleep;
The voiceless lips, the wrinkled brow,
  The patient smile shall show—
You are too young to know it now,
  But sometime you may know!

Look backward, then, into the years,
  And see me here tonight—
See, O my darling! how my tears
  Are falling as I write;
And feel once more upon your brow
  The kiss of long ago—
You are too young to know it now,
  But sometime you shall know.

                                —Eugene Field.

TEXTS AND TREATMENT HINTS.

"Shall Not the Judge of All the Earth Do Right?"—Gen. 18:25 (297-B).

I. He is perfectly holy and just.
II. He is infinitely loving.
III. We and our dear ones are entirely safe in His hands.

"I Shall Know."—1 Cor. 13:12 (297-C).

1. Now I am ignorant of much.
2. Then these mists will roll away.

"I Was Dumb, I Opened Not My Mouth, Because Thou Didst It"— Ps. 39:9 (297-D).

That is not an easy thing to say. It needs a strong faith to say it: and yet what else can the heart of faith say than that? Get nearer to God yourself, crushed heart; think of this sore grief as meant to draw yourself at least nearer to Him. Leave it to Him to explain His own Righteousness at last, as He assuredly will.—Selected.

"Clouds and Darkness Are Round About Him, But Righteousness and Justice Are the Foundation of His Throne."—Ps. 97:2. (297-E)— Get nearer to God yourself, and the waves of sorrow will break quietly at the foot of that high Throne, and there will be "a great calm."

"What I Do Thou Knowest Not Now; But Thou Shalt Know Hereafter."—John 13:7 (298-A).

1. Present ignorance with regard to many of God's dealings is inevitable.
2. God comforts us, in the dark, by promising a dawn.

"What Is That to Thee; Follow Thou Me."—John 21:22 (298-B)

1. God is under no obligation to reveal to us His wise purposes.
2. Whether He provides an explanation of life's happenings or not our duty is unquestioning obedience, unswerving following.

"When I Thought To Know This It Was Too Hard For Me."—Ps. 73:16 (298-C).

1. There is much in life that we cannot understand or explain.
2. There need be nothing concerning which we cannot trust God's love.

"Thy Will Be Done."—Matt. 6:10 (298-D).

1. It is a wise will, not an arbitrary one.
2. It is a loving will.
3. It is our Father's will.

"Though My House Be Not So With God, Yet Hath He Made With Me An Everlasting Covenant, Ordered In All Things and Sure."—2 Sam. 23:5 (298-E). A soul turning away from bitter special experiences to repose in the thought of God's unfailing goodness, and thus escaping despair.

"For Now We See Through a Glass, Darkly; But Then Face to Face: Now I Know In Part; But Then Shall I Know Even As Also I Am Known."—1 Cor. 13:12 (299-A).

1. Life is often marked by inscrutable experiences.
2. Earth utterly fails us as an interpreter of these things.
3. We may find comfort for the present in the thought that in the future, they shall all be made plain. "I shall know."

"Though He Slay Me Yet Will I Trust Him."—Job 13:15 (299-B).

1. To trust only in the sunshine is not to trust God at all.
2. Trusting God when appearances are against Him is the supreme test of a genuine trust.

THE MEANING AND MINISTRY OF SUFFERING
(The Galveston Disaster.)

"He Himself Hath Suffered."—Heb. 11:18 (299-C.)

Bowing today in the shadow of the most awful disaster which has ever fallen upon an American city, and as our hearts tremble in sympathy with the multitudes who have been rendered destitute and homeless, or have been stricken with death, we ask ourselves for any word of comfort or of explanation in this continued tragedy of life of which this is but a single example. No doubt the full meaning of these sufferings is "hid with God's foreknowledge in the clouds of Heaven;" but some hope of a possible good coming at last out of it all—

> "Light after darkness,
> Gain after loss,
> Strength after weakness,
> Crown after cross;"

must be found, or the heart of humanity would break. For we are all sufferers. We are all children of sorrow. Each heart knoweth its own bitterness.

> "There is no flock however watched and tended
> But one dead lamb is there.
> There is no home however well defended
> But has one vacant chair."

We can come then as fellow sufferers with our afflicted neighbors in the South as we attempt to consider this morning the meaning of this great mystery of pain. We have done well to begin our thought on this subject with prayer, for he who loses his hold on God in the time of great sorrow, loses the only clue by which the human spirit can walk through this valley of the shadow of death, which we call earth, and not fall into a bottomless pit of despair. This world has well been called a "slaughter house resounding with the cries of a ceaseless agony."

The first sound from the lips of the babe is a cry, and the last sound from the wrinkled lips of age, a groan. Every life is a tragedy, and every biography a history of sorrow.

And more than this; for struggle, and suffering, and death are now seen to be built into the fundamental structure of the world. The very foundations upon which we build our homes are composed of the skeletons of creatures which perished long millenniums ago.

Suffering cannot be ignored. It cannot be dreamed out of existence. One may shut his eyes and with clinched teeth cry out that there is no sickness, nor suffering, nor death; but even as he speaks his cry becomes a wail as his own body or heart is cut with some bitter pain. Even then he may perhaps sob out his belief that this misery of flesh and life is only an "appearance," a false "claim" of the senses; but this "claim" of sickness and decrepitude looks like the real thing, and acts like the real thing, and feels like the real thing, and often kills like the real thing. The claim and the reality are alike except in name. And even these earnest mystics who revolt against the despotism of fact and boldly dare to affirm that earth is heaven, even they cannot bolt their own doors against the undertaker. A man may cheat his own senses, but he cannot cheat the grave. The Isle of Galveston, strewn with the dead bodies of men and women, and children, is the world in epitome; for the waves must dash sooner or later over every home and leave wreck and ruin behind.

What shall we say then to all this? What can we say? If we cannot trust that, somehow, to all good people

> "good
> Will be the final goal of ill." . . . .
> "That not a worm is cloven in vain;
> That not a moth with vain desire
> Is shriveled in a fruitless fire,"

then there is nothing to be said; there is no hope for those who suffer, and no outcome or meaning in life.

The only salvation against absolute despair for the stricken sufferer, is faith in God, or at least enough faith to cry out, "Lord, help mine unbelief." Life and pain and death are all absolutely and equally inexplicable without the postulate of a good God and a future life.

But if we have a Father in Heaven who loves us, then we can believe with certainty that while we may not understand altogether the meaning of pain, it has a meaning, and a meaning of good.

Then, too, we dimly begin to see that everything points that way. Everything that is good in life now is due to struggle and has come to its perfection through suffering. All civilization is the child of suffering. The nations which have had to struggle most are the greatest nations. The tribes which have not had to struggle for existence against cold and hunger and enemies, have never even become nations. All progress has been born of pain.

A distinguished scientist has recently said, that when modern science first made it plain that man had climbed to his present position on a ladder, every round of which was stained with blood, it was an awful revelation which almost drove men insane, making of them pessimists and atheists; for it was found that all life was war—the song of the birds a war cry, and even the adornment of the butterfly merely war paint. But one further step changed this scientific gospel of despair into a gospel of hope. It was discovered that this suffering, against which we so revolted, was the cause of all progress towards perfection, and that pain was the mother of the highest forms of life and the highest forms of happiness.

Indeed, progress has been well defined as "increase in the capacity for suffering." The earliest animals were built to avoid suffering. They were as big as an animal could be and walk and their sensitive parts were protected by an almost impenetrable armor. But where are those animals now? They are gone, and science tells us they were beaten in the struggle of existence "by little animals with the nerves on the outside."

Man's chief endowment, as contrasted with other animals, so the scientists say, is his ability to suffer more. Several new kinds of suffering were invented expressly for him. It has been well said that he alone, of all the animals, suffers in anticipation of coming perils, and grieves over the errors of the past. It is this greater capacity for suffering that has made men what they are.

I. Now we begin to see the application of the text. "He, Himself, hath suffered." He, who is the highest of all and the best of all, has suffered most of all! There is no mistake stranger than that which imagines that sickness and suffering have some connection with lack of faith or lack of holiness, and testifies to God's displeasure.

II. "He, Himself, hath suffered!"—and where He has led we must follow if we would be like Him and grow into His likeness. The servant is not greater than His Lord. Whom God loved most, suffered most, and even of Him it was said, "He hath been made perfect through suffering."—(Hebrews 2:10.) There is no other way.

The Apostle Peter prays: "The God of all Grace, Who hath called us into His eternal glory by Christ Jesus, after that ye have suffered awhile, make ye perfect."—(1 Peter 3:10.) After that ye have suffered awhile! There is no other way. You cannot have perfection yonder or perfection here until "after that ye have suffered awhile."

We have already seen that the strength and growth of man, physically and intellectually, in all past ages, has been determined by the struggle which he had to endure. That is true equally of moral and spiritual character.

Lack of suffering is one of the greatest dangers physically and morally. When one ceases to feel pain he is in a dangerous condition. Pain is a protest against something which is wrong. As a great theologian has said, pain is a signal of danger—"the only signal in the moral world." Without it the danger would be equally great but would not be recognized, and man would have no impulse to flee from it. Hunger is the signal that something is wrong with the physical nature, and that food is needed for its health. Pain of conscience is simply spiritual hunger and a signal that something is wrong with the moral nature, and that man must have for his comfort, as well as health, spiritual food.

Pain, therefore, is a proof of God's love for us. The gospel proves, and our best thinking agrees, that life is a school in which sorrow is one of the most efficient teachers. I think it was Edward Payson upon whom a friend called in time of sickness and said, "I am sorry to see you lying upon your back," and he replied, "Do you know why God puts us on our back? It is because He wants us to look upward."—Rev. Dr. Camden M. Coburn.

VII. CHASTENING—AFFLICTION.

REFLECTIONS AND ILLUSTRATIONS.

The Meaning of Affliction (299-D).

The Meaning of Affliction.—The more one knows of the most afflicted lives, the more often the conviction flashes across us that the affliction is not a wanton outrage, but a delicately-adjusted treatment.

I remember that once to a friend of mine was sent a rare plant, which he set in a big flower pot close to a fountain basin. It never throve; it lived, indeed, putting out in the spring a delicate, stunted foliage, though my friend, who was a careful gardener, could never divine what ailed it. He was away for a few weeks, and the day after he was gone the flower pot was broken by a careless garden boy, who wheeled a barrow roughly past it. The plant, earth and all, fell into the water; the boy removed the broken pieces of the pot, and, seeing that the plant had sunk to the bottom of the little pool, never troubled his head to fish it out.

When my friend returned, he noticed one day in the fountain a new and luxuriant growth of some unknown plant. He made careful inquiries, and found out what had happened. It then came out that the plant was in reality a water plant, and that it had pined away in the stifling air for want of nourishment, perhaps dimly longing for the fresh bed of the pool.

Even so has it been times without number with some starving and thirsty soul that has gone on feebly trying to live a maimed life, shut up in itself, ailing, feeble. There has descended upon it what looks at first sight like a calamity, some affliction unaccountable, and then it proves that this was the one thing needed, that sorrow has brought out some latent unselfishness, or suffering energized some unused faculty of strength and patience.—A. C. Benson.

Afflictions Are Guide-Posts (299-E).

What do I know about afflictions? I know only what everybody else knows—that they are guide-posts along the way of the pilgrimage. If the pathway lies through struggle and pains and fears, patience and love, and foes and fightings, you're pretty sure to be on the right road. What is this mighty "sea of troubles"? That's the Red Sea. Go right ahead and see the glory of God. This is death in the desert? Speak to the rock, a-quiver with the heat glimmer, and see the fountains of life burst forth. That? That's a king wailing the sorrow of a broken heart in the chamber over the gate. You're on the right way. These? A long line of prison "finger-posts"—Peter and John and Paul and Silas—lots of prisons on the right road. This? A storm on Galilee. Good many storms on the "Jesus Way." This headless body? John the Baptist. That one? Paul. This shadowy garden where the starlight gleams softly on the crimson dew of agony falling on the grass blades? Gethsemane. You have to pass through Gethsemane. This fearful hill? Calvary. This burst of glory and splendor of life and joy?

Oh, Pilgrim, this is Easter morn! You've come the right way, and you're Home, Pilgrim, you're Home!

Now, suppose you had avoided all this? Turned back to Egypt? Worshiped Diana, and kept out of prison? Made a little money by the sale of your Christ, like Judas? Gone around Gethsemane? Bowed to Pilate and avoided the Cross?—Robert J. Burdette.

Joys Sweetened By Sorrows (300).

Our joy will sometimes be made sweeter and more wonderful by the very presence of the mourning and the grief. Just as the pillar of cloud, that glided before the Israelites through the wilderness, glowed into a pillar of fire as the darkness deepened, so, as the outlook around becomes less and less cheery and bright, and the night falls thicker and thicker, what seemed to be but a thin, grey, wavering column in the blaze of the sunlight will gather warmth and brightness at the heart of it when the midnight comes.

You cannot see the stars at twelve o'clock in the day; you have to watch for the dark hours ere heaven is filled with glory. And so sorrow is often the occasion for the full revelation of the joy of Christ's presence.—Alexander Maclaren.

Trial a Source of Blessing (301).

After a forest fire has raged furiously, it has been found that many pine-cones have had their seeds released by the heat, which ordinarily would have remained unsown. The future forest sprang from the ashes of the former. Some Christian graces, such as humility, patience, sympathy, have been evolved from the sufferings of the saints. The furnace has been used to fructify.

The Service of Sorrow (302).

"My son," said the wise man, "despise not the chastening of the Lord, for whom the Lord loveth He chasteneth, and every son whom He receiveth." Chastening is our seal of sonship. Pain brings many a man for the first time in his life to feel his imperfection and his sin, and his need of an abiding helper.

"Who hath trod the ways of pain
Hath not met Him in the gloom
Coming swiftly through the rain?"

Just as the sweetest melodies must include some discord through the sharp and flat, so the sweetest notes of human character are never sounded till suffering has entered into the life.

"The cry of man's anguish went up unto God:
'Lord, take away pain!
The shadow that darkens the world Thou hast made,
The close coiling chain

That strangles the heart, the burden that weighs
 On the wings that would soar—
Lord, take away pain from the world Thou hast made.
 That it love Thee the more!'

Then answered the Lord to the cry of His world:
 Shall I take away pain
And with it the power of the soul to endure,
 Made strong by the strain?
Shall I take away pity that knits heart to heart
 And sacrifice high?
Will ye lose all your heroes that lift from the fire
 White brows to the sky?
Shall I take away love that redeems with a price
 And smiles at its loss?
Can ye spare from your lives that would climb unto Mine
 The Christ on His cross?' "

To lose suffering out of the world would mean to lose out of it the ladder up which man has climbed to every great achievement of the past; the only ladder by which any man can reach greatness and saintliness.

There is a sweetness of sympathy, a mellowness of spirit, a peace, a spiritual power which can only come "through suffering." Whom God makes great, and whom God makes godly he first appoints to struggle. "All that will live godly in Christ Jesus shall suffer."—(2 Tim. 3:12.)

"I must suffer," said the One whose name is above every name, "and enter into my glory." That was the only way even He could enter into His glory. He gathered the thorns of humanity and wore them as His crown!

So, according to the Scriptures, the greatest honor that can come to a Christian is to be allowed to know "the fellowship of His sufferings" (Phil. 3:10), and to fill up "that which is lacking of the afflictions of Christ." (Col. 1:24.) "I will show him how great things he must suffer for My name's sake," said our Lord of the one He most delighted to honor among the Apostles. (Acts 9:16.) "For unto you," said Paul to the martyrs of the early Church, "Unto you it hath been granted in the behalf of Christ"—as the best answer by the Father of Christ's best prayer for them—"not only to believe on Him, but also to suffer in His behalf." (Phil. 1:29.)

Those who know not by experience what suffering means—suffering of body, possibly, suffering of soul, certainly—and have never know what it means to feel a "fellowship" with His sorrows,

 "Are not so much as worthy to stoop down
  And kiss the sacred footprints of our Lord
 Upon the feet of any such an one
  As lieth patient here beneath His hand;
 Whom Christ has bound on His own cross to lie
  Beside Him till Himself shall give release."

Only they who suffer with Christ here can reign with Him hereafter, and though the mystery of pain cannot yet be fully explained, as no mystery of life can be explained, nevertheless we have inspired testimony that all these afflictions of life may work out for us yonder "an exceeding abundant and eternal weight of glory."

Even in this life, as we have seen, pain is one of man's greatest blessings.

May every stricken one, whose faith lays hold on Jesus, this day remember that "all things"—even these afflictions which seem so heavy —"all things," even now, "work together for good to those who love God."

> "He chose this path for thee,
> Though well He knew sharp thorns would pierce thy feet,
> Knew how the brambles would obstruct the way,
> Knew all the hidden dangers thou shouldst meet,
> Knew that thy faith would falter day by day;
> And still the whisper echoed, 'Yes, I see
> This path is best for thee.' "

—Camden M. Coburn, D. D.

Suffering Rightly Borne Enriches Mankind (303).

Remember that somehow suffering rightly borne enriches and helps mankind.—The death of Hallam was the birthday of Tennyson's "In Memoriam." The cloud of insanity that brooded over Cowper gave us the hymn, "God Moves in a Mysterious Way." Milton's blunders taught him to sing of "Holy light, offspring of heaven's first-born." Rist used to say, "The cross has pressed many songs out of me." And it is probable that none rightly suffer anywhere without contributing something to the alleviation of human grief, to the triumph of good over evil, of love over hate, and of light over darkness.

If you believe this, could you not bear to suffer? Is not the chief misery of all suffering its loneliness, and perhaps its apparent aimlessness? Then dare to believe that no man dieth to himself. Fall into the ground, bravely and cheerfully, to die. If you refuse this, you will abide alone; but if you yield to it, you will bear fruit which will sweeten the lot and strengthen the life of others who, perhaps, will never know your name, or stop to thank you for your help.—F. B. Meyer.

The Discipline of Hardship (304).

In April the peach orchard lends a faint, pink flush to the distant hillside, and that stands for the moralities. In September the ripe fruit lends a golden blush of clustered food to the same hill. And such is the fruit of religion. Great is the importance of the root moralities, but roots and boughs imply the ripened fruit.

The rule of life is health, prosperity and sunshine. But God hath appointed wrestling, defeat and suffering as important members of his corps of teachers.

Ours is a universe where progress is secured in the fruits and grains through chemical reactions. Steel is iron plus fire; soil is rock plus fire billow and ice plow; statues are marble plus chisel and hammer strokes; linen is flax plus the bath that racks, the club that flails, the comb that separates, the acid that bleaches.

Manhood is birth-gift plus struggles, temptation, wrestling and refusals to go downward and determination to climb upward. The saint is a man who has been carried off the field on his shield, victorious over inbred sin and outside temptation. Men who drift are men who drown.—Newell Dwight Hillis.

Comfort In a Cloud (305.)

A friend of mine told me of a visit he had paid to a poor woman, overwhelmed with trouble in her little room; but she always seemed cheerful. She knew the Rock. "Why," said he, "Mary, you must have very dark days; they must overcome you with clouds sometimes." "Yes," she said, "but then I often find there's comfort in a cloud." "Comfort in a cloud, Mary?" "Yes," she said; "when I am very low and dark, I go to the window, and if I see a heavy cloud I think of those precious words, 'A cloud received Him out of their sight.' And I look up and see the cloud, sure enough, and then I think—well, that may be the cloud that hides Him, and so you see there is comfort in a cloud.—Selected.

God's Deliverance (306).

God delivers us out of evils by turning them into greater good. He chastens us in the world that we may not be condemned with the world. He turns the tears of sorrow into the pearls of a brighter crown. By weaning us from the transitory, He leads us to the eternal. By emptying us of the world, He fills us with Himself. He makes the via crucis the via lucis. He causes us, in the very fire, to thank Him that our light affliction, which is but for a moment, is working for us a far more exceeding and eternal weight of glory.—Dean Farrar.

Affliction. (307)—After a severe attack of pleurisy, George Moore wrote in his diary, "God often reads us the story of our lives. He sometimes shuts us up in a sick-room, and reads it to us there. I shall never forget all that I learned this time last year."

Our Loss Their Gain (308).

A young woman was mourning the death of her mother. Her grief was so vehement that her friends feared to let her be present at the services preceding the removal of the dear remains from the house. To their surprise, however, not only was she perfectly calm, but in her face shone a great light, a light that was not dimmed even by the tears that filled her eyes as she took the last long look at the beloved face. Later she told them that as she stood near the casket she saw her mother, not lying still and cold, but living, glorious and radiant, while near her was the form of One "like the Son of God." "I could not grieve," she said simply, "when I looked upon my mother's joy." So, to the eye of faith, does the risen Christ still reveal the glorious life into which the departed have entered.—S. S. Times.

Our True Friends (309).

If it is true that the river of the water of life, which flows from the throne of God, is the only draught that can ever satisfy the immortal thirst of a soul, then whatever drives me away from the cisterns and to the fountain is on my side. Better to dwell in a dry and thirsty land, where no water is, if it makes me long for the water that rises at the gate of the true Bethlehem, the house of bread, than to dwell in a land flowing with milk and honey, and well watered in every part. If the cup that I fain would lift to my lips has poison in it, or if its sweetness is making me lose my relish for the pure and tasteless water that flows from the throne of God, there can be no truer friend than that calamity, as men call it, which strikes the cup from my hands, and shivers the glass before I have raised it to my lips. Everything is my friend that helps me towards God. Everything is my friend that leads me to submission and obedience.—Alexander Maclaren.

Affliction's Fruitage. (310).

Schubert said that of all his compositions the best had been written in days when he had most suffering to endure. The same may be said of David's Psalms and Paul's Epistles. The best and most helpful of the Psalms were written in the heart's blood mingled with tears. The richest and most comforting of Paul's Epistles came from an underground dungeon in Rome. So, still, deep suffering may be giving to many not only a richer personal experience of Christ's infinite grace, and a truer sympathy with other sufferers, but also a larger power for service, and opportunities of usefulness which, perhaps, they would have altogether missed had their sufferings been less. Some who are in the fining-pot of trial are tempted to complain, and ask how a loving God can find it in His heart to make them suffer so; but they know not what their loss would be if the fire should be put out, or even be suffered to cool. We do not see how present sorrow can be blessing at the end. Trust God to make no mistakes. Let Him take His own way and His own wise time, and the completion of the work will justify the process, and fill the lips with song.—Knight.

God's Way (311).

Many have sorrows, sufferings, losses, and distresses in their common days. Some find life very hard. It may be sickness, with its pain and depression. It may be bereavement, which brings loneliness and sorrow. It may be the loss of money, which sweeps away the earnings of years and leaves want. It may be the failure of friendships which have not proved true, making the heart sore and empty. Some people ask why it is they must suffer so, if God really loves them. We shall not try to answer the question, for we may not attempt to speak for God. But we may always say, "God is making us." Michael Angelo, as he hewed away at his marble, would watch the clippings fly under the heavy strokes of his mallet, and would say, "As the marble wastes the image grows." In the making of men there is much to be cut away before the hidden beauty will appear. The marble must waste while

the image grows. We never need be afraid of the hard days and the
painful things. If the marble had a heart and could think and speak,
it might complain as the sculptor's cutting and hewing go on so un-
feelingly, but when at last the magnificent statue is finished, the mystery
of the hammer and chisel is made plain. This is what the artist was
doing all the while. God's ways with us in his providences are incom-
prehensible. But when the life stands at last before God, complete,
there will no longer be any amazement, any asking why. In all the
strange and hard experiences, God has been making men of us.—J. R.
Miller, D. D., in "The Gate Beautiful."

When God's children pass under the shadow of the Cross of Calvary, they know that through that shadow lies their passage to the
Great White Throne. For them Gethsemane is as Paradise. God fills it
with sacred presences; its solemn silence is broken by the music of
tender promises; its awful darkness softened and brightened by the
sunlight of heavenly faces and the music of angel wings.—F. W. Farrar.

The Function of Sorrow (312).

The simplest and most obvious use of sorrow is to remind of God.
Jairus and the woman, like many others, came to Christ from a sense
of want. It would seem that a certain shock is needed to bring us in
contact with reality. We are not conscious of our breathing till obstruction makes it felt. We are not aware of the possession of a heart
until some disease, some sudden joy or sorrow, rouses it into extraordinary action. And we are not conscious of the mighty cravings of our
half divine humanity, we are not aware of the God within us, till some
chasm yawns which must be filled.

The account of life which represents it as probation is inadequate.
The truest account of this mysterious existence seems to be that it is
intended for the development of the soul's life, for which sorrow is in-
dispensable. Every son of man who would attain the true end of his
being must be baptized with fire. It is the law of our humanity that
we must be perfected through suffering.—From "Select Thoughts."

"Those Who Suffer Well" (313)

How colorless and flat would be the record of mankind's life un-
adorned with the beautiful strength of those who suffer well.

And how cold and forbidding, too, would be the world whence pity
was eradicated because there lived none worthy to be pitied.

To perpetuate the world's record of heroism and to evoke anew the
world's fountains of humanizing and brother-making sympathy, may
not the sick man rejoice to know that these are the high uses to which
disease dedicates him?

A suffering earth, in truth, but what a gloriously brave old earth
since first weakness of man's body tested the unconquerable strength of
man's soul. A royal succession they who through the accumulating centuries have borne their pains with "heads bloody but unbowed."

The torch of the sufferer's courage has passed on from generation
to generation and the flame is yet in no wise dim.

You are fallen sick? Misfortune, indeed! Yet honor, too! You are chosen in your day to pass on the undimmed torch.

Will you let its light flicker? Men watch and God waits to see.—The Continent.

Only a Little While (314).

A Galilee whose sea is crystal, whose city walls are built of jasper, its streets of gold and every gate a pearl, with its thousand times ten thousand of white-robed angels who will throng to welcome you, lies a little further onward when you have passed Samaria. What matter the cares and troubles by the way? What recks it if with aching brow and troubled heart we journey, and with feet that are torn and bleeding from the stones along the way, if Galilee lies beyond us? Here is comfort, inspiration for our hearts. By this thought life's sorrows are comforted and the hard and dangerous road through this dark Samaria is illumined and made resplendent by this blessed hope of immortality. Let the strife be bitter if it will—let dangers gather and sorrows increase. It is a thought of blessed comfort that this short life will soon be over, that though the conflict be a bitter one 'tis not so very long.

"A little while for patient vigil-keeping,
To face the storm and wrestle with the strong."

And the rest and joy and peace beyond are for eternity. This thought of immortality, could we only grasp it, ought to make a Bethel out of the blackest wretchedness.

"Oh, for a faith to grasp heaven's bright forever.
Amid the shadows of earth's little while."
                                    —Wilton Merle Smith, D. D.

Sorrow a Gift From God (315).

How selfish, how narrow our life would be if we had never known sorrow, if life had gone on and on unruffled and untroubled! Sorrow clears the vision; it sweeps away the mist of carefulness and thought for earth which has arisen in our path, and gives a clearer vision of the Father. The deepest sorrow, if accepted and borne in His name, some way bears us nearer to the world of spirit, to the heaven of life. There is a Divine alchemy in the fiery touch which purifies and enlightens the soul, a peculiar power which opens the life to heavenly vision. Have you not felt the whisper of His love as you stood alone in a death-chamber after some precious life had passed through the portals; felt the wonderful illumination and word of power in the after-hour when you stand in the thick darkness and the voices of earth are hushed.—Selected.

All Meant for Our Making (316).

There is a purpose in circumstance. Nothing in our lives is for naught. All things which have been given us—even our chains—are meant for our making—meant for the working out of our goodly destiny.

Bunyan, in prison, apparently cursed by sunless hours of solitude and loneliness, was a greater Bunyan than if he had been free to roam afield, writes Richard Wightman in the Metropolitan Magazine. The

walls which shut his body in could not confine his soul; it escaped them
and went out into all the world to lift to higher levels the hope and
vision of mankind.

The log cabin in which Lincoln was born lent its ruggedness and
simplicity to the man himself, and has become a shrine which men
approach with reverent feet as to some holy place which love and
truth have glorified.

The hard lot is ever the school in which greatness is taught, and
the best scholars are those who perceive the purpose of difficulty and
do not grow bitter as they grapple with it. The very genius of progressive living consists in a capacity to appreciate the day and what
the day holds; to find in all seasons and events a divine conspiracy to
refine the soul and make it a greater soul; to hail hardship with grim
gladness and bless the hills which must be climbed; to look with kindly
eyes upon every human thing; to accept with complacence the small
circle of opportunity until it has been shown that we are worthy to
move in a wider one. Along no other path may we come to our best
and largest estate of being and serving.—Selected.

Suffering in Vain (317).

But the sorrow that is meant to bring us nearer to Him may be in
vain. The same circumstances may produce opposite effects. I dare
say there are people listening to me now who have been made hard
and sullen and bitter, and paralyzed for good work, because they have
some heavy burden or some wound that life can never heal, to be
carried or to ache. Ah, brethren, we are often like shipwrecked crews,
of whom some are driven by the danger to their knees, and some are
driven to the spirit casks. Take care that you do not waste
your sorrows; that you do not let the precious gifts of disappointment, pain, loss, loneliness, ill health, or similar afflictions
that come into your daily life mar you instead of mending you. See
that they send you nearer to God, and not that they drive you farther
from Him. See that they make you more anxious to have the durable
riches and righteousness which no man can take from you than to
grasp at what may yet remain of fleeting earthly joys.—Alexander Maclaren, D. D.

Suffering Broadens Sympathy (318).

Another blessing of bereavement is the preparation for sympathy
and helpfulness which comes through sorrow. We have to learn to be
gentle—most of us, at least. We are naturally selfish, self-centered,
and thoughtless. Other people's griefs do not touch us, save in a superficial way. Sympathy is not a natural grace of character, even in most
refined natures. Of course, we all feel a momentary tenderness when
a friend or a neighbor is in any trouble. We cannot pass a house with
crepe on the door, and not, for an instant, at least, experience a sub-
duing, quieting sentiment. But the power to enter really into sympathy with one in grief or pain, comes only through a schooling of our
own heart in some way. While a home is unbroken the sorrows of

other homes do not find responsive echoes in the love that dwells there. True, "love knows the secret of grief," but even love that has not suffered cannot fully understand the heart's pain. But when a home has been broken, its inmates have a new power of helpfulness. Crepe on a neighbor's door means more after that. Mrs. Paull never wrote any truer words than in her "Mater Dolorosa," written after she had laid her own baby away amid the white blossoms:

> "Because of one small low-laid head all crowned
>   With golden hair
> Forevermore all fair young brows to me
>   Are fair."

—S. S. Times.

Be Not Cast Down (319).

Christians are sometimes perplexed and discouraged because of their trials. They know not what God is doing with them. They fear that He is angry with them. But they are "His workmanship." He is preparing them for their destination in the temple of His grace. These trials are applied to qualify and advance them. They will only "perfect that which concerneth" them. Howard was taken by the enemy and confined in prison. There he learned the heart of the captive; and his experience, originating in his suffering, excited and directed his thoughts and led him into all his extraordinary course of usefulness and fame. "It is good for me" says David, "that I have been afflicted." "I know," says Paul, "that this shall turn to my salvation." "For our light affliction, which is but for a moment, worketh for us far more exceeding and eternal weight of glory."—William Jay.

The Ministry of Affliction (320).

All affliction is to the good man disciplinary, and will come to an end. It will end in good, in glory. "Though weeping endureth for a night, joy cometh in the morning." Is it poverty that afflicts? Is it the unkindness of the world that afflicts? Is it a disappointment of hopes that afflicts? Is it temptation that afflicts? Whatever it be, it will not continue forever; its work will end; its purpose will be accomplished, and it will pass away. The cloud forms, drops its rain, and passes away for the sun to shine and flowers to bloom. The storm gathers, purifies the air, and passes away for the fragrant and healthful calm to settle like a benediction on the land. Affliction comes, administers its discipline, and passes away for the peace, joy, and glory to appear. Consider, then, the temporal nature of affliction in contrast with the eternal nature of the good which affliction is sent to accomplish. The fires of the furnace long since went out from which came the refined gold that will shine for a thousand years as a jewel or a crown. The Apollo Belvedere stands today a miracle of beauty, two thousand years after the chisel perished which gave it its immortal grace. Cologne's great spires pierce the sky, and will for centuries to come; but the scaffolding beneath which they grew and the tools which piled the marble toward the clouds will vanish in a day. So affliction is but for the moment; it passes away, but leaves an eternal blessing; it may vanish more quickly than furnace fire or sculptor's chisel or builder's scaffolding; but the work it has done for the soul, or the work God has done by it, will be more lasting than jewels of gold or statues and temples of stone.—"The Religious Instinct of Man."

Dark Days (321).

It has been pointed out that Walter Scott became great as a man and realized the highest expression of his genius not until the wave of adversity swept over his life. Mr. Benson pointed out the commonplace character of Scott's personal journal up to the time before the failure of his publishers took place. But after that failure a new note became vocal in the great writer's journal, a new personality emerged. One remembers in this connection the letter which, upon the day succeeding the news of the disaster Scott wrote to an intimate friend: "I have walked for the last time in these halls which I have built, looked for the last time, in all probability, at the domain which I have planted, but death would have taken these things from me if misfortune had not." The letter concludes with the words: "Adversity is to me a tonic and a bracer." "Look at that manuscript," says Ruskin, referring to Scott's novel of "Woodstock" which was in course of writing at the time, "written in the very maelstrom of that adversity and not by the quiver of a hair stroke, not by the suggestion of a single tremor in the hand, not by an erasure or change, not by any falling off in the creative interest of the story could anyone detect that when Scott wrote the second part of that novel he did so under a cloud of bitter adversity."

And biography is full of such unmaskings of the reserve forces of character through the pressure of the dark days succeeding the bright days in life.—Selected.

Blessings From Sorrow (322).

A still nobler kind of relief from undue dwelling upon personal sorrow is found in sympathy and care for others. A loving regard for the welfare of those about us, and unselfish devotion to their comfort, the habit of ministering to their needs and of sympathizing with them in their trials, will greatly support us in seasons of severe disappointment or personal bereavement. Our unwillingness to burden others with our griefs will help us to bear them bravely and quietly. Self-sacrifice does not create insensibility to suffering, but it gives strength to endure it with fortitude and even with cheerfulness.

Strength for the victorious endurance of many of life's disasters and troubles is afforded by an understanding and appreciation of real values. The prime object of life is not pleasure, or ease, or personal promotion. Still less, is it wealth. It is not things, but spiritual substance. It is not happiness, but character. In the fires that purify one can be content if he has no love for dross. The sorrows of childhood are real, but transient. By becoming a man one outgrows them. Those whose aspirations are spiritual, who hunger and thirst for righteousness, are above many of life's storms. They do not feel them. They look down upon them. They see them from above and so behold them transfigured and glorified by eternal sunshine. A noble spiritual aim will subordinate all of life's events to itself, getting gain to character from adversity as well as prosperity. All things work together for the realization of the loftiest ideals of those who have spiritual vision and aspiration. All the events of our life, including our afflictions, are material out of which we may make what we will. The soul that yearns for completeness will win glorious gain from losses and crosses and heart-breaking bereavements.—"The Christian Intelligencer."

A Prayer for Patience Under Trials (323).

If we still fear the future and shrink from what it may bring, grant us so constant a belief in Thy government of all things, and in Thy wise and loving design, that we may be confident that the future will help and not hinder us in good, and that step by step Thou art leading us to the perfect experience of Thy love, and the fullest development of our own nature. Forbid that we should feel as if we had lost everything, or the best things, because we have lost many of this world's joys and satisfactions. May all calamity bring into our hearts a stronger faith, a more enduring patience, a tenderer sympathy. Thou hast made us so that we crave for joy; fill us with Thy joy. Keep us from shrinking or repining at the trials or disappointments of life. Help us at all times and in all circumstances to say: "Good is the will of the Lord concerning us." Whether Thou seest meet to send us joy or sorrow, may we have the assurance that both come from our Father, who knows what is best for us.—Marcus Dods, D. D.

God Tests Us By Trouble (324).

Even the great Captain of our salvation was made "perfect through suffering" and "learned obedience through the things which He suffered." If even He, the Perfect Man, reached his complete equipment for His work through a soldier's endurance of hardship, His followers should not be reluctant to undergo a similar training if they aspire to approximate, in any measure, a like result.

Rev. Howard W. Pope tells the story of a Christian blacksmith who had a good deal of affliction, and, being challenged by an unbeliever to account for it, gave this as his explanation: "I don't know that I can account for these things to your satisfaction, but I think I can to my own. I am a blacksmith. I often take a piece of iron and put it into the fire and bring it to a white heat. Then I put it on the anvil and strike it once or twice to see if it will take temper. If I think it will, I plunge it into the water and suddenly change the temperature. Then I put it into the fire again, and again I put it into the water. This I repeat several times. Then I put it on the anvil and hammer it, and bend it, and rasp and file it, and make some useful article which I put into a carriage, where it will do useful service for twenty-five years. If, however, when I first strike it on the anvil, I think it will not take temper, I throw it into the scrap heap and sell it at half a penny a pound.

"I believe my heavenly Father has been testing me to see if I will take temper. He has put me into the fire and into the water. I have tried to bear it as patiently as I could, and my daily prayer has been, 'Lord, put me into the fire if you will; put me into the water if you think I need it; do anything you please, O Lord, only, for Christ's sake, don't throw me into the scrap heap!"—A. T. Pierson, D. D.

Not a Disablement, But an Equipment (325).

You may make of your loss not a disablement, but an equipment. You have learned a new, great lesson. Henceforth you should be more competent for that finest, most delicate ministration, sympathy toward those in trouble. A new temptation has come to you, a drawing toward the self-absorption of sorrow. Resist it bravely; let your loss be not a barrier, but a tie with other lives. And, O, my sad-hearted friend, just so surely as behind yonder clouds the sun is shining, so certain will there issue out of this trial of yours, if only you will meet it as best you can, a good to yourself and to others greater than you now can think.—James F. Merriman.

God Understands (326).

Every man bears his own burden, fights his own battle, walks in the path which no other feet have trodden. God alone knows us through and through. And He loves us, as Keble says, better than He knows. He has isolated us from all besides that He alone may have our perfected confidence, and that we may acquire the habit of looking to Him alone for perfect sympathy. He will come into the solitude in which the soul dwells, and make the darkness bright with His presence, and break the monotonous silence with words of love. We have Him only to speak to; He alone can understand us. He will rejoice with us when we rejoice, and weep with us when we weep. The heart knoweth its own bitterness; Gods knows it, too; and though a stranger cannot intermeddle with its joy, He, whose temple and dwelling-place is the soul that loves Him, is no stranger, but the soul's most intimate and only friend.—R. W. Dale, D. D.

True Comforters (327).

When affliction comes into the home, it is then we learn the blessedness of companions who live close to Jesus. They can bind up our wounded hearts as no one else can. They can find the right word and get near to us with the prayer that comforts. It is not Gehazi that the heart-broken mother wants, nor even Elisha's staff, it is Elisha, the man of God.—Selected.

Life's Mingled Cup (328).

The other day one of my boys, pointing to a heavy piece of iron wedged on one side of the driving wheel of a locomotive, asked what it meant. I reminded him that the counterbalance, as the piece of metal is called, was placed there to offset the weight of the crank pin and driver which communicate the power to the wheel. And then the thought occurred to me how much the counterbalance plays its part in the activities of human life. Our bright days are counterbalanced by dark days. Our times of prosperity are offset by times of adversity. For every sorrow there is in the divine providence a corresponding gain, and at the heart of every defeat there is for the man of faith the prophecy of new victory. Go where we will in the great universe of love and we find everywhere the working of this divine law of counterpoise—the divine love compensating for every earthly loss. "Where sin abounds grace doth much more abound." Where death walks with insolent feet life triumphs in exultant song. When earthly joys wither heavenly hope blooms in eternal beauty. When time wears out its vesture into thread-bare decay eternity robes herself in immortal splendor.

We want to realize, of course, that these bright days and dark in life which alternate in such swift succession are all part of a divine plan. These fleeting changes of prosperity and adversity, joy and sorrow, life and death, are not haphazard. They are not the chance happenings of a cruel and heedless fate. Nor are they ebullitions of God's fickleness or forgetfulness of His children. Not to tantalize and tease the soul, not that we may take our joys with trembling and our sorrows with cringing does our Heavenly Father set the dark days over against the bright days in life. God sends these seasons for the growth of what is worthiest and best within us. The dark days and the bright days are as necessary to the poise of your character as the counterbalance is necessary to the equilibrium of the wheel. It needs no profound thinking to realize what a grinding monotony life would be if there were no shadows to offset its sunlight. What an insipid thing joy would become—a surfeit in the banquet of life—if there were no bitters to cleanse the palate of the soul.—The Northwestern Christian Advocate.

Shadows (329).

Railway engineers do not like the shadows which are cast across the rails ahead of them by trees and other objects along the way. Sometimes these weird specters of the night look like men. Now they take the form of horses and cattle. And well these men of the throttle know that if these shadowy visitants are what they look as if they might be, danger lies close ahead. But soon they see that it is only moonlight playing them tricks.

A good share of the trouble Christians have in this world comes from shadows. Life's way does not always run through meadow land and prairie. Winding along the side of high hills, dipping deep into leafy dells, following the course of moonlit streams, and often seeming to plunge straight into the heart of some mountain of trouble, grim objects appear to lie on every hand to frighten us, and make us think that there never will be peace again. Then suddenly the thing we feared has melted away, and we have seen only shadows. Does it seem to us we are walking alone? Shadows. Close by our side is the dear One who never forgets His own. Are we fearful that we are not living up to our best, but that at last we shall meet the Father's frown? Shadows. Trusting Him, we are ever coming a little nearer to the ideal we have set before us. Do we fancy that our prayers are never to be answered? Only shadows. He is ever better than our fears. Some day we will know that the faintest cry we sent up was heard and never forgotten.—Edgar L. Vincent.

Enrichment by Grief (330).

It may be that somewhere, in this daily path of yours, a great sorrow is lurking, a sorrow that will blot, for a season, the sun from the heavens, and will lie upon your heart like a great load. What are you going to do with it when it comes? Are you going to be crushed by it, to be embittered and hardened by it, to let it cast a baleful shadow over your life and the lives of all who come near you? If you meet it as fate, that is what it will do for you; your life will be blasted. But that is not what it ought to do for you. It ought to bring you the largest, the richest, the most precious of all the gains of life. For this it is appointed; if you use it as it ought to be used, this will be its fruit. True and deep is the poet's insight when he sings:

"Count each affliction, whether light or grave,
  God's messenger sent down to thee; do thou
  With courtesy receive him: rise and bow,
And, ere his shadow pass thy threshold, crave
Permission first His heavenly feet to lave;
  Then lay before Him all thou hast. Allow
  No cloud of passion to usurp thy brow
Or mar thy hospitality; no wave
Of mortal tumult to obliterate
  Thy soul's marmoreal calmness. Grief should be
Like joy, majestic, equable, sedate,
  Confirming, cleansing, raising, making free;
Strong to consume small troubles; to commend
Great thoughts, grave thoughts, thoughts lasting to the end."

Such is the ministry of sorrow; such are the great and beautiful gifts grief always bears in her hands to those who receive her as God's messenger. And if, when your trouble comes to you, instead of raging against it in complaints and deplorings, which, to say the best of them, are futile, you will but stop and ask how you best may use the opportunity that has come to you; how you may keep your load from crushing others; how you may find surcease from your own sorrow in bearing the burdens of others; how the purifying influence of this suffering may make you gentler, kindlier, more helpful, more sympathetic—then the Scripture will be fulfilled in you which says that tribulation worketh patience, and patience, experience, and experience, hope; and you will come to see that your great sorrow was your soul's great opportunity. Surely this has been the experience of multitudes in all the ages who have found their lives enriched and ennobled by their griefs.—Washington Gladden.

Trouble Relaxes the World's Hold (331).

All pain, sickness, weariness, distress, languor, agony of body or mind, whether in ourselves or others, is to be treated reverently, seeing in it our Maker's hand passing over us, fashioning by suffering the imperfect or decayed substance of our souls. Every sorrow is a billow on this world's troublesome sea, which we must pass over on the Cross to bear us nearer home. Each trouble is meant to relax the world's hold upon us, and our hold upon the world; each loss to make us seek our gain in heaven.—Dr. Pusey.

Prayers Answered by Trials (332).

It is evident now that some of our most unpleasant experiences are, in the wisdom and goodness of God, the means by which God answers prayer. We pray for patience—the quality of soul that endures: but how can there be patience without pain, drudgery, and deferred hope? Patience and pleasant ease are incompatible. We pray for a tender heart, for a sympathetic nature, for love; but could this beautiful spiritual grace exist in a world where pain, helplessness, and death never come? Our very bereavement may be the direct answer to a prayer for spiritual excellence. "Shall we receive good at the hand of God, and shall we not receive evil?" Can we not trust His spiritual purposes?—From "Unanswered Prayers."

Looking Back From Heaven (333).

When you get to heaven and look back you will see that the days which now appear draped in mourning have been your best days—the fullest of good. When the plow has cut deepest, tearing up your garden of happiness and destroying the flowers of gladness, you will find loveliness a thousand times more wonderful.

God never destroys—He only and always fulfills. Out of sadness He brings light. Out of pain He brings health. Out of disappointment He brings appointments of good. Every year is a harvest growing out of past years, each one better than the one left behind.

"Why do we worry about the nest?
  We only stay for a day,
Or a month, or a year, at the Lord's behest,
  In this habitat of clay.
"Why do we worry about the road,
  With its hill or deep ravine?
  a dismal path or a heavy load
We are helped by hands unseen."
—William T. Ellis.

Heaven's Compulsion (334).

Let us thank God for the changes which will not let the deepest and best part of our nature alone. They are heaven's compulsion. Without them our human life would be an unexplored country. We should never penetrate to its interior, never climb its heights of vision, never discover its hidden wealth, never reap its finest harvests, never know what we are, what we can be, what we can do.—John Hunter.

The Rich Fruitage of Trouble (335).

Lazarus' death seemed an irreparable calamity; but the chief mourners themselves must have thanked God for it when they saw the outcome. Some time ago a hurricane devastated the rubber plantations in a certain section of Central America. It seemed at the time an unmitigated evil, but lo! from the ruins sprang up young trees so much greater in number as to make the plantations several times more productive. The owners are now thanking God for the devastation which at first they thought meant ruin. Could we but see the end from the beginning we would praise Him for much at which we now bitterly rebel.—S. S. Times.

None Immune From Trouble (336).

Power is no insurance against trouble either. This friend of mine had the power that goes with a genial character; business capacity, and wealth. Troubles came while he possessed the foregoing; he could not withstand the trial and loss of his power. Job had the power that goes with a clear conscience and great wealth. But he lost his wealth, his family and his health. One may see the same thing illustrated among the crowned heads of Europe, the nobility of England and the wealthy of America. Domestic troubles seem to be unusually frequent and fatal among some of the best-known families in the United States. There are skeletons in almost every closet, no matter what our power may be.

Wealth is no insurance against trouble. Naaman, a captain in the Syrian army, could have commanded any amount of money, but all the physicians of Syria could not cure him, and he had to turn to the humble prophet of Jehovah in Israel. Mr. Harriman owned enough stock in twenty-five thousand miles of railways to absolutely control the whole. In one way and another he controlled some fifty thousand miles more in railways. He controlled steamships that traversed the Atlantic and Pacific of fifty thousand miles additional. He owned a castle at Arden, with an estate of thousands of acres, yet he had his troubles, and at last he was overcome by the Conqueror of all.

In the time of trouble, what is there left to encourage and to uphold and to anchor our faith upon except the God of Abraham, Isaac and Jacob?—Selected.

Compensation for Suffering (337).

Only the soul which has suffered can understand the heart of Christ. Has a fair-weather friend proved faithless in the hour of need? Then you may know something of the meaning of the sorrowful look upon the Master's face as He gazes through the open door at Peter, whom still He loves. Have you been misunderstood, vilified, falsely accused of selfish motives, persecuted for righteousness' sake? Then you may grasp somewhat of the significance of Jesus' struggle with the Pharisees. Have the very people whom you are trying to serve, those whom you love to the point of martyrdom, turned to destroy you? Then you may grasp one aspect of the tragedy of Calvary. Youth shrinking from pain craves to hear of the heroic Christ; but the grandmother, in whose soft eyes hides the tender light of sympathy, longs, rather, to behold the Man of Sorrows, for she has learned through submission to life that a crown of thorns is the noblest crown.—Zion's Herald.

The Fruitage of Suffering (338).

There is little attempt in the Bible to solve the problem either of the origin or meaning of pain and evil. Israel rarely philosophized. Even where there is the nearest approach to a philosophy, as in Job, Job refuses to question one way or the other. He falls back on faith. He trusts God. He will trust Him though God slay him. This is the burden of the Epistle to the Hebrews. The author is sure of two things; first, that God loves, so there is purpose in the pain He sends us, whether of soul or body. The only explanation of chastisement is not to know why it comes, but who administers it. We who are grown up enough to know our earthly father loved us, see now that the punishment was born out of love, not cruelty. We know the Heavenly Father's love is infinite, so while we cannot understand, we know that he chastises in love for our good. But our author went further. He was a wise observer of life. He saw that suffering made great and perfect souls.—Frederick Lynch.

When Sorrow Comes (339).

Now, when I read in the New Testament that "Jesus wept," I remember that those tears fell in sympathy with Martha and Mary when they told Him that their brother was dead, and, remembering that Jesus is the same yesterday and today and forever, I say to all earth's mourning and sorrowing ones: "When you baptize the graves of your dead with your tears, you shed not those tears alone; the heart of the Eternal beats in tenderest sympathy with you."

Jesus Christ is God's perfect revelation of Himself to the world, and He is the same in the past, the present, and the future. His teachings remain the law of life for all men everywhere. His forgiving Spirit still says: "Neither do I condemn thee. Go and sin no more." He still says: "Suffer the little children to come unto Me, and forbid them not," and He still gives His unfailing sympathy to earth's bereaved and sorrowing ones. In Him the sons of men may safely trust.—The Changeless Christ.

God Is Love (340).

We may be sure that under all our afflictions is God's tender and wise love. Not one of our sorrows can be spared, as we shall know hereafter. "One interested in entomology secured with much difficulty a fine specimen of the emperor moth in larvae state. With deep interest he watched the little creature as it wove about itself the cocoon, which in shape resembles a flask. At length the time drew near for it to emerge from its wrappings and spread its wings of exceeding beauty. Long and hard was its struggle to force its way through the neck of the flask. The watcher's pity was aroused and he cut the cords, thus making the passage easy. But, alas! his kindness was cruelty. This struggle was needed to develop the wings. This severe pressure was necessary to cause the flow of fluids which created the marvelous hues for which this species is noted. Spared this, its wings were small and weak, dull in color, and its whole development imperfect."—Selected.

Suffering (341).

Suffering is of two kinds: pain which we endure in our own persons —Christ was "a Man of Sorrows;" and pain which we know by familiarity with others' suffering—Christ was "acquainted with grief."

The Christian rejoices in tribulation—in God; but that in spite of, not because of, tribulation.

We are perfected through suffering. What worthy crown can any son of man wear upon this earth except a crown of thorns? A Christian's motto everywhere and always is victory.

A man's work is not done upon earth as long as God has anything for him to suffer; the greatest of our victories is to be won in passive endurance; in humbleness, in reliance, and in trust we are to learn to be still, and know that He is God.—F. W. Robertson.

His Healing and Consolation (341-A).

We all, in turn, must face our forlorn hours of saddest bereavement. For us all, sooner or later, our house must be left unto us desolate. But . . . these natural sorrows are, and are meant to be, full of blessedness; the light of God shining upon them transmutes them into heavenly gold. The wounds which God makes, God heals. The fire which kindles the grains of frankincense upon His altar, at the same time brings out their fragrancy. All that He sends, if borne submissively, becomes rich in mercy. Upon the troubled soul which seeks Him, His consolations increase "with the gentleness of a sea which caresses the shore it covers.—Dean Farrar.

Tribulation (342).

In the New Testament we read that "in the world we shall have tribulation," that "through much tribulation we shall enter into the kingdom of God;" that we "glory in tribulations also;" and that we shall be "patient in tribulation." (Rom. 12:12.) That is the genuine climax: to be patient in tribulation. These highest things are the reward of simple faithfulness. The true heart enters into all the fulness of this true life that is hid with Christ in God.

The Hebrew disciples were thus reminded by their faithful and ever vigilant apostle: "By faith Enoch was translated that he should not see death, and was not found, because God had translated him: for before his translation he had this testimony, that he pleased God." This testimony has never been withheld from any soul that pleased God by the exercise of the faith that works by love. It never will be withheld from any soul that is fighting this good fight of faith.

To the believers at Ephesus their spiritual father and guide wrote: "All things that are reproved are made manifest by the light; for whatsoever doth make manifest is light. Wherefore he saith, Awake, thou that sleepest, and arise from the dead, and Christ shall give thee light. See then that ye walk circumspectly, not as fools, but as wise, redeeming the time because the days are evil." (Eph. 5:13-16.) "Walk circumspectly," that is, look around you: see where you are going and who are with you.—Bishop Fitzgerald.

Crosses. (343).

We have need of all our crosses. When we suffer much, it is because we have strong ties that it is necessary to loosen. We resist, and
we thus retard the divine operation; we relieve the heavenly hand,
and it must come again. It would be wiser to yield ourselves at once to
God. That the operation of His providence which overthrows our self-
love should not be painful to us would require the intervention of a
miracle. Would it be less miraculous that a soul, absorbed in its own
concerns, should in a moment become dead to self than that a child
should go to sleep a child and wake up a man?—Fenelon.

Sorrow a Very Real Thing (344).

Sorrow is very real and very dark. No false philosophy can be-
guile us from this sad conviction. If any man should say there is no
reality in sorrow and pain, we could not argue with him. If he is sincere, his mental constitution is not capable of appreciating an argument;
and if he is insincere, he is not open to argument. We know from
experience and consciousness that sorrow and pain are real.

Sorrow may be shared. This is a mystery. Your friend may not
only stand by you in time of trouble and speak encouraging words, but
he may lay his heart down by the side of your stricken heart and feel
the same pain you feel. He may so share it as to make it easier for
you to bear. The mother shares the sufferings of her child. The wife
shares the troubles of her husband. Christians may, and often do, share
each other's sorrows.

And cannot our Heavenly Father share our sorrows? He is touched
with the feeling of our infirmities. Earthly friends are limited on every
side. But He is not limited. He is strong enough to bear every burden
we can put upon Him. He invites us to cast our burden on Him. He
careth for us.

As sorrow is lightened by being shared, so joy is increased when it
is shared. So also our Heavenly Father shares our joys. To every faithful soul He says: "Enter thou into the joy of thy Lord." And He enters into our joys, also. Jesus taught us to think of God as a Father,
and we know full well that a father takes delight in the happiness of
his children. He enters into their joys with all his heart. Nothing
pleases him more than to know that his children are happy and prosperous. God is like that. When our hearts sing for joy, He is pleased.
In the Word of the Lord we are taught to "rejoice with them that do rejoice," and nothing is more certain than that all our pure and innocent
joys are shared by Him who is the foundation of all holy joy.—Christian
Advocate.

The Sick-Bed Hero (345).

Where is the world's greatest scene of heroism? On the battlefield,
Aboard the fighting warship? In the locomotive cab with certain wreck
ahead? On the ocean liner's deck when water is pouring into the hold?
Down in the depths of the burning mine with escape cut off? Up aloft

amid the flames in some great building where dauntless firemen risk their own lives to save imprisoned inmates? Along the midnight streets where officers of the law brave the lurking assassin's pistol?

Yes, in all these places there is real heroism that "brightens human story" and proves the stalwart stature of the human soul.

But none of these pictures reflects the highest ascent of courage which the intrepid spirit of man achieves. There is a spot where less of grandeur hovers, but immeasurably more of superb and unquailing courage defies the direst that calamity can bring.

The world's greatest scene of heroism is the sick-room—the chamber and couch of the patient sufferer who fights alone and unweaponed with the armored enemy, Death.—The Continent.

Faith Tested (346).

A jeweler gives as one of the surest tests for diamonds, the "water test." He says: "An imitation diamond is never so brilliant as a genuine stone. If your eye is not experienced enough to detect the difference, a simple test is to place the stone under water. The imitation stone is practically extinguished, while a genuine diamond sparkles even under water and is distinctly visible. If you place a genuine stone beside an imitation under water, the contrast will be apparent to the least experienced eye." Many seem confident of their faith so long as they have no trials; but when the waters of sorrow overflow them, their faith loses all its brilliancy. It is then that true servants of God, like Job, shine forth as genuine jewels of the King.—Homiletic Review.

Vision From the Valley (347).

A well-known minister wished to ascend a tower that commanded a fine view of the surrounding country. "Come this way, sir," said the guide, leading him to some steps which looked as if they led into a vault. "But I want to ascend, not descend!" "This is the way up, sir." A few steps down led to many steps up. So his Guide led Joseph down that He might lead him up to those heights of vision and power prepared for those who honor Him."—Sunday School Chronicle.

The Wrong Side (348).

Dr. George F. Pentecost tells about going to see a parishioner who was in deep affliction. He found her embroidering a sofa pillow cover. He asked her to let him take it in his hand. He purposely turned it on the wrong side, and then remarked to her that it did not seem beautiful to him, and that he wondered why she should be wasting her time upon it. "Why, Mr. Pentecost," she replied, "you are looking at the wrong side! Turn it over." "That is just what you are doing," he replied, "you are looking at the wrong side of God's workings with you. Down here we are looking at the tangled side of God's providence; but He has a plan—here a stitch and there a movement of the shuttle— and in the end a beautiful work."—S. S. Times.

Songs in Sorrow (349).

A little seven-year-old boy fell into one of the deep excavations for the New York subway one day, and was taken, bruised and suffering to the nearest hospital. When the doctor began to examine his injuries little James drew a deep breath. "I wish I could sing," he said, looking up at the big doctor. "I think I'd feel weller then." "All right, you may sing," said the doctor; and James began. So brave and sweet was the childish voice that, after the first verse, there was a round of applause from the listeners. As the doctor went on with his examination the boy winced a little, but struck up his singing again. The nurse and attendants, hearing the sweet, clear soprano, gathered from all parts of the building, until he had an audience of nearly a hundred. Through all the pain of the examination the child never lost the tune; and everybody rejoiced when the doctor announced: "Well, I guess you're all right, little man; I can't find any broken bones." "I guess it was the singin' that fixed me," said James. "I always sing when I feel bad," he added simply.—Onward.

Why Afflictions Come (350).

"Why are afflictions sent upon the people of God?" That is one of the easy questions. I don't know. And yet I reckon I know as much about it as anybody. I don't know, for that matter, why afflictions are also sent upon wicked people. I don't know why innocent children suffer for the sins of their parents. But they do. I don't know why Abraham Lincoln was assassinated by an actor, vanity-inflated with overwhelming sense of his own importance. I don't know why Socrates was poisoned while his judges remained in office. I don't know why Jesus Christ was crucified while Pilate sat on the judgment seat and Herod continued to pollute a throne with iniquities. I don't know why, for three hundred years, God's people, sheep of His hand and people of His pasture, walked on burning plowshares under skies of brass, while storms of persecution rained upon them in every form of horrible torture and fearful death.

But I do know that that is the way the church conquered the world for Christ. I do know that not one god of its persecutors is left in the world today, save as a broken fragment in a temple of dust.

What do I know about pain, and sorrow, and trouble? I know only what everybody knows—I know what has grown out of the heart-soil scarred by the plow and torn by the harrow. I look at the receding storm and I see the splendor of the rainbow.—Robert J. Burdette, D. D.

Sorrow Develops Character (351).

The leaves of the aromatic plant shed but a faint odor as they wave in the air. The gold shines scarcely at all as it lies hid in the ore. The rugged crust of the pebble conceals from the eye its interior beauty. But let the aromatic leaf be crushed; let the ore be submitted to the furnace; let the pebble be cut and polished; and the fragrance, the splendor, the fair colors are then brought out:

"This leaf? This stone? It is Thy heart
It must be crushed by pain and smart,
It must be cleansed by sorrow's art—
Ere it will yield a fragrance sweet,
Ere it will shine, a jewel meet
To lay before thy dear Lord's feet."

The same law is observable in spiritual character, which rules the formation of natural. How often in a smooth and easy life do men, who have something far better beneath, appear selfish, effeminate, and trifling! Suddenly they are thrown into some position of high trust, great responsibility, or serious danger—are called upon to face an enemy, or submit to the hardships of the campaign—and lo! the character shows a stuff and a fiber—ay, and a tenderness for others—which no one ever gave it credit for. Resolute will, dauntless self-sacrifice, considerateness, show themselves, where before we could see nothing but what was pliant and self-indulgent. Trial has unmasked latent graces of character; and although spiritual character is a thing of a higher order than natural, yet it is developed according to the same laws of the mind. —Goulburn.

Sorrow's Revealing Power (352).

These bright days and dark days in life as they come and go, sometimes in rhythmic cadence and sometimes in bewildering confusion, are also part of a divine revelation. They are days of revealing as well as days of discipline. God sends these alternating seasons into your life to reveal certain qualities within you, to call into play certain capacities, to make vital certain possibilities in your nature which the monotony of an unbroken experience could never bring. The changing days of life unmask the reserves of character. It is, of course, a truism that a man never knows how much he can endure until the day of adversity comes.—Selected.

Death's Uplifting Influence (353).

There is a beautiful and uplifting influence in the presence of death which nothing else brings in quite the same degree. Many a woman has become a better wife and a better mother for weeping with those who weep. The little petty vexations of home life which come trooping up to torment, shrink back in the face of deep affliction, and leave one strengthened in the thought that love and kindness and gentleness— all that makes for happiness—alone count. Life is too short to be spent in fret and worry, and nothing but death can so impress that truth on the mind of the careful and troubled housewife. If it is a husband who is being carried from his home, she resolves to be more tender to her own; if a little child, in her mind she clasps her wee ones nearer her heart. All that is compassionate, all that is holy, all that is pure comes to the surface to help in the resolution to lead a broader, fuller life, and thus make herself more helpful to her human kind. To be able to comfort, to lift up, to encourage and to help those in distress repays every true woman for the pain she endures at sight of suffering she might avoid. A doll no doubt escapes much of sorrow by being a doll, but a flesh and blood woman who chooses to be a doll rather than a woman, simply to avoid the ministry of pain, has but a narrow and barren existence.—Hilda Richmond.

Suffering (354).

In the Old Testament, God is represented as a Destroyer with a plumb-line in his hand. Now, a plumb-line is usually employed for the purpose of building up, but God is represented as using it for the work of destruction. "But the cormorant and the bittern shall possess it; the owl also and the raven shall dwell in it; and he shall stretch out upon it the line of confusion, and the stones of emptiness." Jehovah is represented as using the plumb-line in pulling down, inasmuch as he carries out this reverse of building with the same rigorous exactness as that with which a builder carries out his well-considered plan. The grand idea pictured by the prophet is, that in judgment God accomplishes his purpose with extremest exactness and discrimination. The blizzard owns the same rule as the zephyr; the storm that scatters is measured as delicately as the sunshine that ripens; one gracious will fashions the flower, and points the thorn; the same curious wisdom that creates, ultimately dissolves the organism into the dust. Heaven destroys as it builds, with line and plummet. What a mighty comfort it is, then, to know that the seeming irrationality of pain is not real, and that all suffering is adjusted to capacity and need! Amid all the confusion, waste, ruin, sweats, tears, and blood of the groaning creation, God stands with the measuring-line, dealing to every man trial, as He assigns to every man duty, according to his several ability. "For He knoweth our frame; He remembereth that we are dust."—W. L. Watkinson, "The Transfigured Sackcloth."

The Sculptor's Chisel (355).

You are a block of rough marble. You may some time come to be a statue of splendid proportions, but must be chiseled and hammered before that consummation can be reached. Grief, struggle, disappointment, the whole range of sad experiences which fill life so full, are the tools with which the Great Artist will change your shape by slow degrees, and convert you from a mere block to a thing of beauty.—George H. Hepworth, D. D.

The Meaning of Sorrow (356).

How is it that a genuine Christian recuperates after being stricken down by a severe adversity or a sharp affliction? Simply because his graces survive the shock. For one thing, his faith is not destroyed. When a ship is drifting toward a rock coast, and cannot be kept off the shore by her sails, she still has her anchor left; but if the cable snaps she is swept hopeless on the rocks. So when your hold on God is gone, all is gone. The most fatal wreck that can overtake you in times of sorrow is the wreck of faith. But if in the darkest hour you can trust God, though He slay, and firmly believe that He chastens you for your profit, you are anchored to the very throne of love and will come off conqueror. Hope also is another grace that survives. Some Christians never shine so bright as in the midnight of sorrow. One might have thought that it was all over with John when he was exiled to Patmos, or with John Bunyan when he was locked up in Bedford jail. But they were all put in the place where they could be the most useful.

And that reminds me to say that your sorrows may be turned to the benefit of others. An eminent minister who was under a peculiarly severe trial, said to me, "If I could not study and preach the Word to the utmost, I should go crazy." Active operation is both a tonic and a soothing sedative to a troubled spirit. Turn your sorrows outward into currents of sympathy and deeds of kindness to others, and they will become a stream of blessings. Working is better than weeping; and if you work on till the last morning breaks, you will read in that clear light the meaning of many of your sorrows.—Dr. Theodore L. Cuyler.

None Are Exempt (357).

God has His chosen and peculiar people, but He never spares the rod to spoil His child. I had a visit from a friend the other day who was broken-hearted in unexpected grief. A little rivulet of life had made his meadow beautiful, when suddenly its music was no more. And "Oh," he said to me, "if I had been wicked—if I had been a rebel against God, I might have understood it; but it is hard to be dealt with thus when I have striven to serve Him, and tried to be true to Him in home and business." You see at the heart of his so bitter grief there was a thought that is common to us all. My friend was like Elijah at his stream, saying, "I am a prophet and it can never dry." And one of the hardest lessons we must learn is that the name and nature of our God is love, yet for the man who trusts and serves Him best, there is to be no exception from the scourge.—Mornson.

Perfect Through Suffering (358).

Consider therefore how God makes a man great. Now and then an emergency arises in society, through organized wrong and entrenched oppression. A million slaves groan by day and with bitter tears at night exclaim against the cruel taskmaster, crying, "How long, O God, how long!" Then God stretches forth his hand upon some child to make him brave. The angel of His presence draws near to some poor man's house, and takes a little babe in his arms. He calls to His side the angel of suffering and whispers, "Take thou this little child and rear him for Me and make him great. Plant his path with thorns and sharp rocks, until the slave can track his path of crimson; load his little back with burdens, and make him strong by carrying; break his heart with suffering and make him sensitive to the sighs of slaves. Lead him through the desert and its blinding heat, that he may bring the pilgrims gently to the water springs. Make his face more marred than the face of any man of his generation, that the poor and weak may follow a leader who was in all points broken-hearted as they were. Then, when suffering hath made him brave, and burden-bearing hath turned to a giant's strength, bring him back, and with him we will free slaves." In

this school of suffering Moses was reared to gianthood. In this university of pain, persecution, and obloquy Paul was nurtured to greatness.
Under this tutelage Jesus grew, going by way of Gethsemane and Calvary toward the world's throne and the universal crown. God Himself
is the great sufferer, the King of sorrows, toiling up the hills of time,
His locks wet with the dew of the night, His feet bare, His heart broken,
never sleeping and never slumbering in His ceaseless solicitude to recover his lost son Absalom. As men go toward greatness they go toward complexity of faculty, fulness and richness of gifts, sensitiveness
and therefore liability to suffering.—Newell Dwight Hillis, D. D.

Following Christ in the Furnace (359).

I believe that persecuted ones have more blessedness than any other
saints. There were never such sweet revelations of the love of Christ in
Scotland as when the Covenanters met in the mosses and on the hill-
sides. No sermons ever seemed to be so sweet as those which were
preached when Claverhouse's dragoons were out, and the minister read
his text by the lightning's flash. The saints never sang so sweetly as
when they let loose those wild-bird notes among the heather. The flock
of slaughter, the people of God that were hunted down by the foe, these
were they who saw the Lord. I warrant you that in Lambeth Palace
there were happier hearts in the Lollard's dungeon than there were in
the archbishop's hall. Down there where men have lain to rot, as did
Bunyan in Bedford jail, there have been more dreams of heaven and
more visions of celestial things than in the courts of princes. The Lord
Jesus loves to reveal Himself to those of His saints who dare take the
bleak side of the hill with Him. If you are willing to follow Him when
the wind blows in your teeth and the snowflakes come thickly till you
are almost blinded, and if you can say, "Through floods and flames, if
Jesus lead, I'll follow where He goes," you shall have such unveilings of
His love to your soul as shall make you forget the sneers of men and
the sufferings of the flesh. God shall make you triumph in all places.—
C. H. Spurgeon.

Facing Trouble in Faith (360).

Your thorn in the flesh is—what? Whatever it be that disorders,
annoys, grieves you, makes life dark, and your heart dumbly ache, or
wets your eyes with bitter tears—counseled Samuel Longfellow, brother
of our poet—look at it steadily, look at it deeply, look at it in the thought
of God and His purpose of good, and already the pain of it will begin to
brighten.—Selected.

Crowns For Victors (361).

There is no virtue in mere suffering. There is no goodness inherent
in pain. Had there been nothing on the Cross but the human figure of
the Son of God, writhing in mortal agony, the spectacle had been repulsive. The submission to the reality of the cross was its glory. The endurance of actual bodily pain, positive anguish of mind and soul,—this
set the brilliants, outshining the stars, in the crown of victory.—Burdette.

Sometime (362).

"Sometime, when all life's lessons have been iearned,
And suns and stars forevermore have set,
And we shall see how all God's plans are right,
The things o'er which we grieved with lashes wet,
Will flash before us out of life's dark night,
As stars shine most in deeper tints of blue;
And we shall see how all God's plans are right,
And how what seems reproof was love most true."

Grace Sufficient (363).

The way is long, my Father, and my soul
Longs for the rest and quiet of the goal:
  While yet I journey through this weary land
  Keep me from fainting, Father, take my hand,
  And safe and blest, lead up to rest
    Thy child.

The way is long, my child, but it shall be
Not one step longer than is best for thee;
  And thou shalt know when thou at last dost stand
  Safe at the goal, how I did take thy hand,
    And, safe and blest, with Me shall rest,
      My child.

  —The Changed Cross.

Pain's Furnace (364).

Pain's furnace-heat within me quivers;
  God's breath upon the flame doth blow;
And all my heart in anguish shivers,
  And trembles at the fiery glow:
    And yet I whisper, "As God will;"
    And in His hottest fire am still.

  —Julius Sturm.

The Tearless Morn (365).

O Joy that seekest me through pain,
I cannot close my heart to Thee,
I trace the rainbow through the rain,
And feel the promise is not vain
  That morn shall tearless be.

  —G. Matheson.

The Cry (366).

The mistakes of my life have been many,
  The sins of my heart have been more.
And I scarce can see for weeping;
  But I'll knock at the open door.

I am lowest of those that seek Him,
  I am weakest of those who pray;
But I come as the Saviour bids me,
  And He will not say me nay.
                    —U. L. Bailey.

The Answer.

Rest, weary heart!
The penalty is borne, the ransom paid,
For all thy sins full satisfaction made!
  Strive not to do thyself what Christ has done,
  Claim the free gift, and make the joy thine own;
No more by pangs of guilt and fear distrest,
    Rest! calmly rest!
                —H. L. L.

The Joys That Remain (367).

Nuggets and dust upon the surface lie,
  But not the true continuing vein of gold;
Melted in fire and prisoned in the rock
  Its boundless wealth deep treasure-chambers hold.

So life's chance pleasures shine, exhausted soon;
  But when man seeks the joys that shall remain,
He finds them gleam from fire and from rock,
  Prisoned by fate and purified by pain.
        —Priscilla Leonard, in the Outlook.

Love's Chastenings (368).

When thou hast thanked thy God for every blessing sent,
What time will then remain for murmurs or lament?
When God afflicts thee, think He hews a rugged stone,
Which must be shaped, or else aside as useless thrown.
        —Richard Chenevix Trench, D. D.

Songs in the Night (369).

"Our peace is in His will." So sing the saints
  Above, the happy, holy, shining throng
  Of sinless souls; in joyous endless song,
With gladness full and free from all restraints.

"Our peace is in His will." In earth's complaints,
  In exile, want and torture, under wrong.
  Great hearts have learned to suffer and be strong;
God's will makes firm the weakest soul that faints.

To all who love His will he doth impart
  Sweet peace that fills their loyal souls with praise,
  Songs in the night and strength for weary days.

Courage (370).

The hardest things to bear we never tell;
　We wear a mask to every human eye;
We smile, and bravely answer, "All is well!"
　But naught is hidden from the deity.

How good it is that One can surely know,
　And give the sympathy for which we yearn;
Strength in our weakness, patience in our woe,
　And cheer to meet the worst at every turn

Of life's most crooked pathway. It is best
　There are both hills and valleys on our way;
The level ground gives little for a test
　Of brave endurance, or a strenuous day.

Fight hard or no one wins. Tell Him, aside,
　Of all the disappointments, all the fears,
The wrecks of plans, the hopes unsatisfied;
　But show the world no sign of loss nor tears.
　　　　　　　　　　　　—Sarah K. Bolton.

A Single Gold Hair (371).

"'God lent him, and takes him,' you sigh.—
　Nay, there let me break with your pain:
God's generous in giving, say I,
　And the thing which he gives, I deny

　　．　．　．　．　．　．　．　．　．　．　．　．　．

"So look up, friends! You who indeed
　Have possessed in your house a sweet piece
Of the heaven which men strive for, must need
　Be more earnest than others are, speed
　Where they loiter, persist where they cease.

"You know how one angel smiles there.
　Then courage! 'Tis easy for you
To be drawn by a single gold hair
Of that curl, from earth's storm and despair
　To the safe place above us. Adieu!"

The Golden Lesson (372).

Do not cheat thy heart and tell her,
　"Grief will pass away,
Hope for fairer times in future
　And forget today."
Tell her, if you will, that sorrow
　Need not come in vain;
Tell her that the lesson taught her
　Far outweighs the pain.
　　　　　　　　　　　—Adelaide A. Proctor.

Light Beyond (373).

The way is dark, my Father: cloud on cloud
Is gathering thickly o'er my head, and loud
The thunder roars above me. See, I stand
Like one bewildered; Father, take my hand,
And through the gloom lead safely home
      Thy child.

The way is dark, my child, but leads to light;
I would not have thee always walk by sight.
My dealings now thou canst not understand?
I meant it so—but I will take thy hand,
And through the night lead up to light
      My child.
             —The Changed Cross.

The Bitter Cup (374).

I saw a cup sent down and come to her
  Brimful of loathing and of bitterness;
She drank with livid lips that seemed to stir
  The depth, not make it less:

But as she drank I spied a Hand distil
  New wine and virgin honey; making it
First bitter-sweet, then sweet indeed, until
  She tasted only sweet.
          —Christina Rossetti.

The Loom (375).

A blind boy stood beside a loom
  And wove a fabric; to and fro
Beneath his firm and steady touch
  He made the busy shuttle go

"How can you weave," we pityingly cried.
  The blind boy smiled, "I do my best;
I make the fabric good and strong,
  And one who sees does all the rest."

O happy thought! Beside life's loom,
  We blindly strive our best to do.
And He who marked the pattern out
  And hold the threads, will make it true.
          —Selected

Sweetened Waters (376).

She waited long on God,
  And He forsook not; through the gloomy vale
She leant upon His staff until His rod
  Brake forth in blossoms pale.

Then did her spirit bless
The gracious token; then she saw the rife
Salt-crusted standing pools of bitterness
Spring up as wells of life.
—Dora Greenwell.

A Friend In Trouble (377).

Lord! a whole long day of pain
Now at last is o'er;
Darkness bringing weary strain
Comes to me once more.

Round me falls the evening gloom,
Sights and sounds all cease;
But within this narrow room
Night will bring no peace.

Come then, Jesus! o'er me bend,
And my spirit cheer;
From all faithless thoughts defend,
Let me feel Thee near.

Then if I must wake or weep
All the long night through,
Thou the watch with me wilt keep,
Friend and Guardian true!
—Lyra Germanica.

Humble Under Chastening (378).

Though crooked seem the paths, yet are they straight
By which Thou draw'st Thy children up to Thee;
And passing wonders by the way they see,
And learn at last to own Thee wise and great.

Let not my proud heart dictate, Lord, to Thee,
But tame the wayward will that seeks its own,
And wake the love that clings to Thee alone,
And takes thy chastenings in humility.
—Lyra Germanica.

Nestle (379).

God never would send you the darkness,
If He felt you could bear the light;
But you would not cling to His guiding hand
If the way were always bright;
And you would not care to walk by faith
Could you always walk by sight.

So He sends you the blinding darkness,
And the furnace of sevenfold heat;
'Tis the only way, believe me,
To keep you close to His feet;
For 'tis always so easy to wander
When our lives are glad and sweet.

Then nestle your hand in your Father's,
And sing, if you can, as you go;
Your song may cheer someone behind you
Whose courage is sinking low.
—The Crisis.

God Knows (380).

So lies my journey—on into the dark;
Without my will I find myself alive,
And must go forward. Is it God that draws
Magnetic all the souls unto their Home,
Traveling, they know not how, but unto God?
It matters little what may come to me
Of outward circumstance. . . . . .
My life, my being, all that meaneth me,
Goes darkling forward into something—what?
O God, thou knowest. It is not my care.
. . . My God, take care of me.
Pardon and swathe me in an Infinite Love
Pervading and inspiring me, thy child.
And let thy own designs in me work on,
Unfolding the ideal man in me!

. . . .

Lead me, O Father, holding by thy hand;
I ask not whither, for it must be on.

—George MacDonald.

God's Answer to Man's Anguish (381).

"The cry of man's anguish went up unto God:
   'Lord, take away pain—
The shadow that darkens the world thou hast made,
   The close-coiling chain
That strangles the heart, the burden that weighs
   On the winds that would soar;
Lord, take away pain from the world thou hast made,
   That it love thee the more!'

"Then answered the Lord to the cry of His world:
   'Shall I take away pain
And with it the power of the soul to endure,
   Made strong by the strain?
Shall I take away pity that knits heart to heart,
   And sacrifice high?
Will ye lose all your heroes that lift from the fire
   White brows to the sky?
Shall I take away love that redeems with a price,
   And smiles at its loss?
Can ye spare from your lives that would climb unto mine
   The Christ on His Cross?'"

TEXT AND TREATMENT HINTS.

"He Rebuked the Winds and the Sea, and There Was a Great Calm."— Matt. 8:26 (382).

This Redeemer and Restorer is none other than the Great Creator. As such He is clothed with the same mighty power. As easily and as effectually as He said, Let light be, and light was, He calmed the waves of the sea. Jesus was a few moments before—fast asleep. A waking man in a shipwreck may be on the watch for some means of escape. But a man asleep in a boat rapidly filling with water and on the point of going down!—such and so helpless did Jesus seem the one moment; and the next! He stands and speaks to the elements, and they hear with the facility and readiness of well-trained servants. "What manner of man is this! for He commandeth even the winds and water, and they obey Him."—Laidlau.

"Man Is Born To Trouble."—Job. 5:7 (383).

Eliphaz the Temanite was only expressing an age-long experience when he said, "Though affliction cometh not from the dust, neither doth sorrow spring out of the ground, yet man is born unto trouble as the sparks fly upward." He was not a soured pessimist who said that. It was not the petulant wail of a disillusioned man with whom everything had gone wrong. It was the calm, sad verdict of one who looked the world in the face, and his words are as true to-day as they were three thousand years ago. Grief is a universal baptism—the only baptism that is universal. The cup is always going round; and, at some time or other, in some way or other, in some measure or other, every child of Adam has to drink of it, and many have to drain it to the bitter dregs. All the world over, the chalice passes from hand to hand, from lip to lip.—Knight.

"Whose I Am, and Whom I serve."—Acts 27:23 (384).

I. Calamity teaches God's ownership. There are other teachers of that lesson, but calamity is the great teacher, throwing one back upon first principles.

There are two shipwrecks in the Bible, those of Jonah and Paul. They are very unlike, but alike they emphasize God's ownership. Jonah is trying to run away from God, but it can not be done, and he gives up and bids the sailors throw him overboard. Paul is being carried a prisoner to Rome, but he is upheld by knowing that he belongs to God. Calamity which beats Jonah down into submission lifts Paul up into confidence in Him whose he is.

II. It is good to know that we are God's. Even Jonah, in his despair, rises to great dignity, confessing his sin and bidding the shipmen throw him into the sea. Paul rises to a noble mastery of the situation.

III. We need to add our own act of service to God's ownership.— Homiletic Review.

"A Refiner's Fire."—Malachi 3:2 (385).

I. It is He who permits the trial.—The evil thing may originate in the malignity of a Judas; but by the time it reaches us it has become the cup which our Father has given us to drink. The waster may purpose his own lawless and destructive work; but he cannot go an inch beyond the determinate counsel and foreknowledge of God. Satan himself must ask permission ere he touches a hair of the patriarch's head. (Job 1:8-12.) The point up to which we may be tested is fixed by consummate wisdom. The weapon may hurt and the fire sting; but they are in the hands which redeemed us. Nothing can befall us without God's permission, and His permissions are His appointments. We cannot be the sport of blind fate or chance; for in trial we are still in the hands of the living Saviour.

II. It is He who superintends the trial.—No earthly friend may be near; but in every furnace there is One like the Son of Man. In every flood of high waters He stands beside us—staying the heart with promises, instilling words of faith and hope, recalling the blessed past, pointing to the radiant future, hushing fear, as once He stilled the dismay of His disciples on the lake: such is the ministry of Jesus. And as the sufferer looks back on the trial, he says, "I never felt Him so near before; and if it had not been for what He was to me, I could never have lived through it."

III. It is He who watches the progress of the trial.—No mother bending over her suffering child is more solicitious than is He—suiting the trial to your strength—keeping his finger on your pulse so as to stay the flame when the heart begins to flutter—only too eager to see the scum pass off, and his own face reflected from the face of the molten metal.—Meyer.

"Let This Cup Pass From Me."—Matt. 26:39 (386).

Many prayers are heard which are answered, not by lightening the burden, but by strengthening the bearer. Every one is brought at some time to cry in an agony, "Anything but this. Can it be that good can come out of this? Is it possible that this should be the best thing that can happen to me—this calamity with its hopeless desolation, its crushing misery, its ruthless extinguishing of schemes of usefulness, its humiliating reminders of past sins? Can this be that which I am to enter into and pass through?" What can we do but take up the prayer of our Lord, and say, "Father, if it be possible, let this cup pass from Me?" But in Christ's case this prayer was heard by a love which could choose for Him the greater blessedness which came by drinking the cup. To have spared Christ the suffering would have been to answer His prayer in appearance, but to disregard the deeper cravings of His spirit. Can any one suppose that if Christ had received the actual exemption from suffering He prayed for, it would have been a greater kindness on God's part than the kindness He showed in allowing the suffering to continue, and to work its grand effect in the salvation of the world?

And so in a measure is it with ourselves. Our cry of agony is not coldly put by; our heartbroken prayer is not disregarded. Far from it. God knows what we suffer, and feels with us; our pains pain His fatherly heart; but He knows that these pains are passing ,and that, when meekly and hopefully borne, they work for us a deeper joy and a fuller life. It is dreadful, indeed, to see the thing we fear drawing nearer day by day, marching irresistibly onwards over all cryings and entreaties we make, trampling apparently on our bleeding heart, and leaving a track of desolated hopes and apparently disregarded prayers; but by the very anguish we suffer we may measure the greatness of the end to be wrought by it, and the intensity of the joy with which God will compensate us.—Marcus Dods.

"When I Bring a Cloud the Bow Shall Be Seen."—Gen. 9:14 (387).

The rainbow is one of the most beautiful things God ever made, and His causing it to shine out on Noah just when his apprehension of further judgment was filling him with fear was one of the most beautiful things God ever did. The tender thoughtfulness of that sign of mercy comforted Noah, and it has comforted thousands since. It was in a beautifully human way, too, that God spoke of it: "When I bring a cloud over the earth, the bow shall be seen in the cloud, and I will look upon it, and remember my covenant." God's eyes and our eyes looking on the same thing at the same moment—that is a beautiful thought; but there is a more comforting one still, that He sees the bow where our weak and blind eyes do not see it at all.—Knight.

Blessed Are They That Mourn; for They Shall Be Comforted."—Matt. 5:4 (388).

The Master, when He said this, was fulfilling the prophecy,—"He hath sent me to bind up the broken-hearted" (Isaiah 61:1). He was speaking in the same line as when he said, "Come unto me, all ye that labor and are heavy laden, and I will give you rest." (Matt. 11:28.)

The words reach beyond the mourners simply over sin. They indeed are blessed in their consciousness of pardon and safety, but there is more than that here. He, the infinite Saviour, came to bring the kingdom of heaven, God's reign in the soul. That is a kingdom of peace. The believer comes to Him and is blessed in the coming. He comes with his heart borne down with earthly sorrow. Where else, to whom else in all the world can he go? Earth cannot help him. He comes to a sympathizing Saviour (Heb. 4:15), and he is in a place of calm. He hardly knows why or how, but peace and rest are in his heart, and they are blessedness.

That is for to-day. But the "shall be" looks forward to a time when God shall wipe all tears away (Isaiah 25:8; Rev. 7:17; 21:4). The anticipation of future blessedness touches and lightens the present sorrow.—William Aikman, D. D.

"Ye Have Need of Patience, That After Ye Have Done the Will of God, Ye May Receive the Promise."—Heb. 10:36 (389).

I. The patience needed is patience to live. "If life be long," said Richard Baxter, "I will be glad, that I may long obey," though he added, "If life be short, can I be sad to soar to endless day?" That is the noblest Christian attitude. To take lengthened suffering as an extended opportunity of glorifying God by calm acceptance of His will is infinitely better than to long faint-heartedly for release.

II. There are always sufficient reasons, both on His side and on our own, for any postponement of the home-call. Some of His best-loved children have so hard a lot, and such a warfare too with their imperfectly-sanctified natures, that it seems as if the greatest blessing He could give them would be just immediate release from all the suffering and all the sin; and often the words are uttered in paroxysms of unbearable pain—have we not often heard them?—"Oh, come, Lord Jesus, come quickly!" But what if the last fine touches have yet to be put to God's great work of reproducing the Christlikeness in the soul?"—Knight.

Now for a little while, if need be, ye have been put to grief in manifold temptations, that the proof of your faith, being more precious than gold that perisheth, though it is proved by fire, might be found unto praise and glory and honour at the revelation of Jesus Christ.— I Pet. 1:6, 7 (390).

1. Worldly fortune is not the highest end of life. "Faith, being more precious than gold that perisheth." There is, then, something more precious than gold, and that something is faithful or noble character. We may attain wealth, renown, and whatever else is embraced in the worldly conception of success, yet miss the main prize. And thousands of successful men are conscious that they have missed it, missed the centre lily whilst they gained the chickweed round the fringe. Let us dare to maintain, and that in the face of all mockers, that the fine qualities of the Christian character outshine in worth all flowers of pleasure, stars of honour, or sheen of gold.

2. That the supreme end of life, the perfection of character, is sometimes best attained through vicissitude and tribulation. "Now for a little while, if need be, ye have been put to grief in manifold temptations," that ye might be perfected, as gold tried in the fire is purified; and so ultimately be found clothed with eternal beauty, fitted for high ministries, undimmed by shadow of failure. Few pains are keener than the sense of failure, and through this acutest of distresses duly sanctified our being reaches its finest attributes. A large part of the campos of Central Brazil is burnt every year at the end of the dry season; but as the vegetation is scanty the fires pass quickly onwards, and do not appear to injure the trees and plants. Indeed, botanists believe that the vegetation benefits by the burning. As soon as the rains come, the scorched plants produce foliage earlier than where there has been no

fire, and often produce flowers when unburnt trees or shrubs of the same species remain flowerless. How often in the vineyard of God, where the flame of calamity has left a trail of loss and blight, springs the very pride of the garden.—Waterman.

"A Very Present Help in Time of Trouble" (391).

You are passing through a time of deep sorrow. The love on which you were trusting has suddenly failed you, and dried up like a brook in the desert—now a dwindling stream, then shallow pools, and at last drought. You are always listening for footsteps that do not come, waiting for a word that is not spoken, pining for a reply that tarries overdue.

At such times life seems almost unsupportable. Will every day be as long as this? Will the slow-moving hours ever again quicken their pace? Will life ever array itself in another garb than the torn autumn remnants of past summer glory? Hath God forgotten to be gracious? Hath He in anger shut up His tender mercies? Is His mercy clean gone forever?

I. This road has been trodden by myriads.—When you think of the desolating wars which have swept through every country and devastated every land; of the expeditions of the Nimrods, the Nebuchadnezzars, the Timours, the Napoleons of history; of the merciless slave trade, which has never ceased to decimate Africa; and of all the tyranny, the oppression, the wrong which the weak and defenceless have suffered at the hands of their fellows; of the unutterable sorrows of women and children—surely you must see that by far the larger number of our race have passed through the same bitter griefs as those which rend your heart.

Jesus Christ Himself trod this difficult path, leaving traces of His blood on its flints; and apostles, prophets, confessors, and martyrs have passed by the same way. It is comforting to know that others have traversed the same dark valley, and that the great multitudes which stand before the Lamb, wearing palms of victory, came out of great tribulation. Where they were we are; and, by God's grace, where they are we shall be.

II. Sorrow is a refiner's crucible.—It may be caused by the neglect or cruelty of another, by circumstances over which the sufferer has no control, or as the direct result of some dark hour in the long past; but inasmuch as God has permitted it to come, it must be accepted as His appointment, and considered as the furnace by which He is searching, testing, probing, and purifying the soul. Suffering searches us as fire does metals. We think we are fully for God, until we are exposed to the cleansing fire of pain. Then we discover, as Job did, how much dross there is in us, and how little real patience, resignation, and faith. Nothing so detaches us from the things of this world.

III. But God always keeps the discipline of sorrow in His own hands. —Our Lord said, "My Father is the husbandman." His hand holds the pruning knife. His eye watches the crucible. His gentle touch is on the pulse while the operation is in progress. He will not allow even the devil to have his own way with us. As in the case of Job, so always. The moments are carefully allotted. The severity of the test is exactly determined by the reserves of grace and strength which are lying unrecognized within, but will be sought for and used beneath the severe pressure of pain. He holds the winds in His fist, and the waters in the hollow of His hand. He dare not risk the loss of that which has cost Him the blood of His son. "God is faithful, who will not suffer you to be tried above that you are able."

IV. In sorrow the Comforter is near.—"Very present in time of trouble." He sits by the crucible, as a Refiner of silver, regulating the heat, marking every change, waiting patiently for the scum to float away, and His own face to be mirrored in clear, translucent metal. No earthly friend may tread the winepress with you, but the Savior is there.—Rev. F. B. Meyer.

VIII. RESIGNATION—TRUST.

REFLECTIONS AND ILLUSTRATIONS.

A Ray of Light (392).

There pierces through the shadow of the great disaster in the St. Paul Mine, at Cherry, Ill., a ray of light which is full of inspiration—a tale of heroism and faith the world can pay much to have. In this day of disbelief, of iconoclastic fads and moral rebellion, we can read the story of Clelland, the simple Scotch Covenanter, and be the better for it.

He, with nineteen others, found themselves entombed in the deadly mine, the fire sweeping nearer and the poisonous gases becoming more and more impossible to endure. He never hesitated. Strong in the faith of his fathers, and trustful of the goodness and mercy of the Supreme Being he had been taught to worship, he took no thought of human aid, but said: "We are in God's hands. He only knows whether we shall ever see our wives and children again. Let us pray." There in that dark hole, from which there seemed to be no hope of exit, these twenty simple-minded men—among them Italians and Lithuanians—knelt while Clelland held his glowing torch in his hand, and repeated the words of David: "Out of the depths have I cried unto thee, O Lord. Lord, hear my voice: neither let not the deep swallow me up, and let not the pit shut her mouth upon me."

And when the prayer was ended, Clelland led them in song:

> "O God, our help in ages past,
> Our hope for years to come,
> Our shelter from the stormy blast,
> And our eternal home!
>
> "Under the shadow of thy throne
> Still may we dwell secure;
> Sufficient is thine arm alone,
> And our defense is sure."

Cheered even in the depth of their despair by the trusting faith of this one man, his prayers, his song, and assimilating in some mysterious way that faith, these men once more took thought for their safety, sure that God would aid them. For hours they toiled, their food gone, sustaining life merely by drinking the water which settled on the damp floor of the mine, building a barrier against the destruction which was sweeping toward them. The hours followed on one another with terrible slowness. Days passed; but in that living death and dark, dank hole, it was Clelland's cheerful voice, his supreme trust, that held their hearts attuned to the Infinite, and their courage undismayed. They sang, Clelland leading, until all had learned the words and the tune:

"Abide with me! Fast falls the eventide,
The darkness deepens—Lord, with me abide!
When other helpers fail, and comforts flee,
Help of the helpless, O abide with me!

"Swift to its close ebbs out life's little day;
Earth's joys grow dim, its glories pass away;
Change and decay in all around I see;
O thou, who changest not, abide with me!"

Their throats were parched, their tongues stiff, and their voices weak; but through the long hours they with Clelland, sang and prayed:

"Help of the helpless, O abide with me!"

Never, perhaps, had the words been so fraught with meaning; never had those uttering them clung so tenaciously to them.

"Abide with me! Fast falls the eventide."

Then through the wall of earth, the rocks and barricade went up the solemn prayers to that God in whom they trusted; and He, as in the days of old, heard and answered. Their perfect faith had made them whole again.—Selected.

God is Life. (393)--Take your life out of the body, and a dead thing lies upon a slab of marble. Take God out of our earth, and this earth is a corpse, laid out by sable night and eternity.

Lying at His Feet (394).

As soon as we lay ourselves entirely at His feet, we have enough light given us to guide our own steps; as the foot soldier, who hears nothing of the councils that determine the course of the great battle he is in, hears plainly enough the word of command which he must himself obey.—George Eliot.

Whom I Believe (395).

When Dr. Alexander, one of the professors of theology in Princeton University, was dying, he was visited by a former student. After briefly exchanging two or three questions as to health, the dying professor requested his old student to recite a verse of the Bible to be a comfort to him in his death-struggle. After a moment's reflection the student repeated from memory the verse of Paul to Timothy—"I know in whom I have believed, and that He is able to keep that which I have committed unto Him unto that day."

"No, no," replied the dying saint, "that is not the verse; it is not 'I know in whom I have believed,' but 'I know whom I have believed.' I cannot allow the little word 'in' to intervene between me and my Savior to-day I cannot allow the smallest word in the English language to go between me and my Savior in the floods of Jordan."—Banks.

"Turned Lessons" (396).

In suffering and sorrow God touches the minor chords, develops the passive virtues, and opens to view the treasures of darkness, the constellations of promise, the rainbow of hope, the silver light of the covenant. What is character without sympathy, submission, patience, trust, and hope that grips the unseen as an anchor? But these graces are only possible through sorrow. Sorrow is a garden, the trees of which are laden with the peaceable fruits of righteousness; do not leave it without bringing them with you. Sorrow is a mine, the walls of which glisten with precious stones; be sure and do not retrace your steps into daylight without some specimens. Sorrow is a school. You are sent to sit on its hard benches and learn from its black-lettered pages lessons which will make you wise forever; do not trifle away your chance of graduating there. Miss Havergal used to talk of "turned leassons."—Meyer.

He Feared the Gate (397).

Late one stormy evening the old doctor was summoned to see a man who had been attacked with a sudden illness. The patient proved to be "Squire" Joyce, whom the doctor slightly knew. He examined him carefully, and gave him medicine. Then he arose to go, smiling cheerfully down at the anxious face of the sufferer.

"You will find yourself better in the morning, I hope," he said.

"Yes. Stay a minute, doctor. I want you to be honest with me. I have had seizures like this before. Shall I have them again?"

"It is probable."

"I want the truth—all of it."

"Yes, they will return."

"I may die in one of them—to-morrow?"

"Yes. Or maybe, not for years. It is uncertain. Do not waste your life in anticipating them. We all must go through the same gate some day."

"The gate—yes! But beyond the gate—what is there?"

His eyes were on the doctor's face, full of doubt, almost pain.

The two men were silent a moment. "What is there?" Joyce repeated harshly. "You are a member of a church—a Christian. I have no religious belief. Tell me, for the love of God, what is there beyond? If I may go tomorrow, what shall I find?"

"I do not know."

Joyce did not speak for a while, and then gave a forced laugh. "I need your help more for this than for my disease. I'd rather talk to you than a clergyman. You are a shrewd man of the world, and a good man. Sometimes I am greatly depressed, thinking of the darkness into which I am going. For thousands of years men have gone into it, leaving loved ones behind, and not one has sent back a word to say how it fares with him—not one."

"You are an old man, doctor," said Joyce, turning to him. "You are not far from the gate yourself. Are you not afraid of what may be beyond?"

"No," said the doctor. "No, I am not afraid. Look here." He rose and opened the door. Outside, in the dark hall, lay a little fox-terrier, drenched with rain. He was crouched on the floor, his eyes fixed on the closed door.

"This is my dog. He has followed me through the storm, and has been lying outside the door, knowing that I was within this chamber. He never was here before. He did not know what was in this room. He did not care to know. I was in it, his master, whom he loves. He was not afraid."

Joyce looked at the doctor keenly a moment before he spoke—

"You mean—"

"I mean that I am like poor Punch. I am not afraid of the dark room to which I am going. I do not ask to know what is there. All these years He has cared for me. I have been assured that in my hours of trial He has never failed me here. I sincerely believe He will not fail me yonder."

"But—I do not know Him."

"He knows you. I am authorized by the declarations of the Bible to say that His hand is stretched out to you. You can accept Him as your Guide and Teacher if you will. That done in sincerity, you will not fear the gate nor all that lies beyond."—Selected.

The Song of Trust (398).

Like the bird, which after many days of darkness and many days of singing itself again into the light, finds its little voice grown strong and sure, we who sing on through our trials and burdening shall some morning find our own voices sweetened and greatened from the long practice. The wavering note becomes steady, the harsh tone gently clear. Then do we know, O men and women, that the shadows of this world are sent but to train the weak voices and fit them for their places in the choir invisible.

> "Of those immortal dead who live again
> In minds made better by their presence: live
> In pulses stirred to generosity,
> In deeds of daring rectitude, in scorn
> For miserable aims that end with self,
> In thoughts sublime that pierce the night like stars,
> And with their mild persistence urge man's search
> To vaster issues."—From "The Great Optimist."

Feeling or Willing Resignation (399).

To bear sorrow with dry eyes and stolid heart may befit a Stoic, but not a Christian. We have no need to rebuke fond nature crying for its mate, its lost joy, the touch of the vanished hand, the sound of the voice that is still, provided only that the will is resigned. This is the one consideration for those who suffer—Is the will right? If it isn't, God Himself cannot comfort. If it is, then the path will inevitably lead from the valley of the shadow of death to the banqueting table and the overflowing cup.

Many say: "I cannot feel resigned. It is bad enough to have my grief to bear, but I have this added trouble, that I cannot feel resigned."

My invariable reply is: "You probably never can feel resignation, but you can will it."

The Lord Jesus, in the Garden of Gethsemane, has shown us how to suffer. He chose His Father's will. Though Judas, prompted by Satan, was the instrument for mixing the cup and placing it to the Savior's lips, He looked right beyond him to the Father, who permitted him to work his cruel way, and said: "The cup that My Father giveth Me to drink, shall I not drink it?" And he said repeatedly, "If this cup may not pass from Me, except I drink it, Thy will be done." He gave up His own way and will, saying, "I will Thy will, O My Father. Thy will, and not Mine, be done."—Meyer.

Father Will Meet Me (400).

I left Cheyenne, Wyo., one morning on the "overland flyer," for Omaha. The ride as far as Kearney is through a dreary, desolate country of sand knolls, prairie dog towns, barren hills, waterless valleys and dry streams. In the seat ahead sat a little boy, intently gazing upon the monotonous landscape. Dinner was taken in the diner. A social chat enlivened the weary hours. Still this little fellow sat there peering through the window. About the middle of the afternoon I spoke to him.

"My little man," said I, "aren't you tired?"

"Not much," came the quiet reply.

"Well, aren't you hungry?" I asked. The little fellow, looking up at me with a smile, replied:

"Yes, a little; but you see, papa is going to meet me at Grand Island."

Friend, what a lesson there is there for you and me. We are being carried along through life's journey at sixty heartbeats a minute. Our ticket is purchased for the through train with no stopover privileges. Why should we sit and grumble if the way be dreary at times? Why should we be complaining because life at times may seem monotonous? Let us remember that a Father is waiting to welcome us at the other end. Lisp a short prayer for the day as you climb out of your sleeping berth. The whistle will soon blow for the terminal, where friends are waiting to meet you. You are going this way only once, go it right.

"I Am" (401).

Are you a disciple of the Lord Jesus? If so, he says to you, "I am with you alway." That overflows all the regrets of the past and all the possibilities of the future, and most certainly includes the present. Therefore, at this very moment, as surely as your eyes rest upon this page, so surely is the Lord Jesus with you. "I am" is neither "I was," nor "I will be." It is always abreast of our lives, always encompassing us with salvation. It is a splendid, perpetual "now."—Frances Ridley Havergal.

A Steadfast Trust (402).

A chain, a girder, a pillar are not calculated for ordinary but for exceptional strain. A great faith in God, a steadfast trust in Him who died for us and whose death is the price of our peace, a love that many waters cannot quench nor the floods drown, a hope that is practically infinite—in these great qualities, convictions and expectations lies the solution of the problem of life's desperate situations.—W. L. Watkinson.

Confidence in God (403).

The secret of a happy life is confidence in a gracious Heavenly Father. Two boys were talking together of Elijah's ascent in the chariot of fire. Said one: "Wouldn't you be afraid to ride in such a chariot?" "No," said the other, "not if God drove!" God drives the chariot of every human life. So fear not, but believe and hope, for His power and love are omnipotent.

Patience (404).

Let us only be patient; and let God our Father teach His own lesson in His own way. Let us try to learn it well and learn it quickly; but do not let us fancy that He will ring the school bell and send us to play before our lesson is learned.—Kingsley.

Faith's Anticipations (405).

The larva of the male stag-beetle, said Dr. Christlieb, when it becomes a chrysalis constructs a larger case than it needs to contain its curled-up body, in order that the horns which will presently grow, may find room. What does the larva know of its future form of existence? And yet it arranges its house with a view to it! Is it then to be supposed that the same Power which created both the beetle and the man instilled into the beetle a true instinct and into the man a lying faith?

Two Golden Days (406).

There are two days in the week upon which and about which I never worry. Two care-free days, kept sacredly free from fear and apprehension.

One of these days is yesterday. Yesterday, with all its cares and frets, with all its pains and aches, all its faults, its mistakes and blunders, has passed forever beyond the reach of my recall. I cannot undo an act that I wrought, I cannot unsay a word that I said on yesterday. All that it holds of my life, of wrong, regret, and sorrow is in the hand of the Mighty Love that can bring honey out of the rock and sweet waters out of the bitterest desert—the love that can make the wrong things right, that can turn weeping into laughter, that can give beauty for ashes, the garment of praise for the spirit of heaviness, joy of the morning for the woe of the night.

Save for the beautiful memories, sweet and tender, that linger like the perfume of roses in the heart of the day that is gone, I have nothing to do with yesterday. It was mine; it is God's.

And the other day I do not worry about is tomorrow. Tomorrow, with all its possible adversities, its burdens, its perils, its large promise and poor performance, its failures and mistakes, is as far beyond the reach of my mastery as its dead sister, yesterday. It is a day of God's. Its sun will rise in roseate splendor on a new day of grace. All else is in the safe keeping of the Infinite Love that holds for me the treasures of yesterday—the love that is higher than the stars, wider than the skies, deeper than the seas. To-morrow—it is God's day. It will be mine.

There is left for myself, then, but one day of the week—to-day. Any man can fight the battles of to-day. Any woman can carry the burdens of just one day. Any man can resist the temptations of to-day.

Thy Will Be Done (407).

A Christian lady was once explaining to a friend how impossible she found it to say, "Thy will be done," and how afraid she should be to do it. She was the mother of one little boy, who was the heir to a great fortune, and the idol of her heart. After she had stated her difficulties fully, her friend said: "Suppose your little Charley should come running to you to-morrow and say, 'Mother, I have made up my mind to let you have your own way with me from this time forward. I am always going to obey you, and I want you to do just whatever you think best with me. I will trust to your love.' How would you feel toward him? Would you say to yourself, 'Ah, now I shall have a chance to make Charley miserable. I will take away all his pleasures, and fill his life with every hard and disagreeable thing that I can find. I will compel him to do just the things that are the most difficult to do, and will give him all sorts of impossible commands.'" "Oh, no, no, no!" exclaimed the indignant mother. "You know I would not. You know I would hug him to my heart and cover him with kisses, and would hasten to fill his life with all the sweetest and best." "And are you more tender and more loving than God?" asked her friend. "Ah, no," was the reply, "I see my mistake, and I will not be any more afraid of saying, 'Thy will be done,' to my Heavenly Father than I would want my Charley to be of saying it to me."—The Christian's Secret of a Happy Life.

Be Patient (408).

Patience cannot be cultivated in a short time. It requires years for some of God's children to bring this grace to that perfection attainable in this life. "Let patience have her perfect work." The husbandman waiting for the precious fruit and grain, gives nature the opportunity to do her full work. "Add to your faith patience." "Run with patience the course set before us," if needs must be—willing to pass through "tribulation which worketh patience."

The Christian's life is especially planned and watched over by the Infinite One. Let us therefore be patient and wait. In the realm of Providence,

"God's plans like lilies pure and white unfold:
        We must not tear the close shut leaves apart,
    Time will reveal the calyxes of gold."
"Rest in the Lord and wait patiently for Him."

His Hope (409).

When John Knox lay dying, his friend asked him, "Hast thou hope?" He spoke nothing, but raised his finger and pointed upward, and so he died.

The Father's Grip (410).

There is a simple child's story which always seems to me to convey a profound and too often forgotten truth. It is the tale of the boy who, with his father, was climbing some steep and dangerous place, and to whom a voice from below suddenly called up: "Have you fast hold of your father?" "No!" was the immediate answer; "but he has fast hold of me." That is the first, the main thing—not the sense of our keeping hold of God—if that were all, how weak, how ready to fall we all should be—but rather the sense that our Heavenly Father has hold of us, and that because   is greater than all, no one is able to pluck us out of His hand.

        "And so I go on, not knowing.
            I would not, if I might.
        I would rather walk in the dark with God,
            Than walk alone in the light.
        I would rather walk with God by faith,
            Than walk alone by sight."

It is the Lord, who made heaven and earth, who will bless and keep us.—George Milligan, D. D.

Resignation (411).

May you never know the sorrow so crushing, the loss so charged with agony, that your devout will cannot make your own the will that governs the universe, and pray with the deepest fervor, from the midst of blinding tears, Thy will be done!

But the mistake is in supposing that it is the prayer for such times and such trials alone, in supposing, indeed, that this is first and chiefly a prayer in these experiences of affliction and loss. Consider the words of the petition as our Lord teaches them to us: Thy will be done, as in heaven, so on earth—as in heaven, where is no blight nor sorrow nor bitter grief, where there shall be pain and sighing no more, and where God shall wipe the tears from every eye. There, where there is no resignation and no submission, and no sad endurance of unavoidable ills because there is no trouble there—God's will is done, and our prayer is that it may be accomplished, as in heaven, so on earth. Let the tried and suffering heart pray this prayer in the depth of mortal pain, but also, let us pray it as devoutly when life runs riotously in our veins and all the joy of the world is coursing in our blood.—Aked.

No Unpermitted Showers (412).

All providences are doors to trials. Even our mercies, like roses, have their thorns. Our mountains are not too high, and our valleys are not too low, for temptations; trials lurk on all roads. Everywhere, above and beneath, we are beset and surrounded with dangers. Yet no shower falls unpermitted from the threatening cloud; every drop has its order ere it hastens to the earth. The trials which come from God are sent to prove and strengthen us.—C. H. Spurgeon.

"I'm All Right" (413).

A recent writer tells how there lived near him a fine old Scotchman. Time had shortened his steps. His hair was silvery white. His shoulders were bent, and he was sorely drawn out of shape by rheumatism. But when his friend hailed him with "How are you today, grandfather?" there came back the cheery words: "Oh! I am all right. My old body has gi'n oot, but I'm all right." The body was falling to pieces, like an old house, but the faithful old man was being preserved with all the beautiful graces of the Christian life blossoming with sweeter fragrance as he neared the heavenly climate.

> So long His power has blessed me, sure it still
>   Will lead me on
> O'er moor and fen, o'er crag and torrent, till
>   The night is gone.

At Eventide (414).

I love to connect our word "serene" with the Latin word for evening, as well as with its own mother-word "serenus"—clear, or bright.

Often, after a windy, stormy day, there comes at evening a clear, bright stillness, so that at evening time there is serenity as well as light. So often in life's evening there comes a lull, a time of peaceful waiting "between the lights," the burden-weighted heat of the day behind, the radiance of eternity before. Perhaps the day has been in truth "life's little day," swiftly ebbing to its close; perhaps the worn, tired pilgrim has lived even beyond the measure of three score years and ten. In either case it is in truth the evening.

The dear face reflects "eternity's wonderful beauty," the sweet, serene spirit is freshened by dew from the heavenly Hermon, the fragrance of evening flowers fills the air, the songs of birds come in tender, satisfied cadences, and even the clouds which remain are enriched and made radiant by rays from the Sun of righteousness.

We whose evening is not yet, are entranced with the exquisite blending of the warm human affection with the celestial flame kindled from the sacred altar. With hushed souls we minister and are ministered unto, until, too soon, the twilight time is past, and the evening and the morning have become the eternal day.—Christian Observer.

The Silver Lining (415).—"Get into the habit of looking for the silver lining of the cloud, and, when you have found it, continue to look at it rather than at the leaden gray in the middle. It will help you over many hard places."

The Dark Days (416).

It is so human to cry out in dismay when we are frightened by the blackness that settles over our lives as the clouds of trouble and of pain are pasing over them. Human to believe for a time that they are too dense ever to break away and let the sunshine through. So human to try to find somone else at fault and not our own mistakes, our sins, or our almost inexcusable ignorance. So human to forget that we have been Christ-warned again and again of the way that is pain-haunted, where the ghosts of our wrong thinking and careless living stand guard and will not allow us to forget how much we have lost of joy and gathered of sorrow, that need never have been.

These memories are so large a part of our everyday life that they cannot be separated from the "everyday sorrows," and the heaviest sorrows that have ever been borne by human hearts have not been because God willed them, but because somehow they grew out of sinfulness or ignorance, ·and instead of being classed as an unusual one, it belongs alone to the one soul and God, who sorrows with it.

There is always strength for what God puts in our way, always the "Comforter" to share the natural, unavoidable griefs of our everyday lives. God never wills us any condition that needs to crush out all joy in life. His compensations are commensurate to every trial that comes to us through unavoidable causes or natural processes. It is only when we pass away beyond, and defy His will by going our own foolish way, that we find the bottomless abyss of pain, the full meaning of uncomforted sorrow. We must keep close, with our eyes on Him while we walk the waves, or, like Peter, we will find ourselves sinking beyond our depth. But even on the stormiest sea we may always be safe if we are going toward the Christ's outstretched hand. Remember you need only to hold fast to that hand to bear your "everyday sorrow," for He knows all about it, wept with other mourners, then comforted them and helped them to bear, and so He will help you if you will give Him the chance Peter gave Him on the sea, but of how many of His doubting, distressed children He can say: "How often would I, but ye would not."

> "The way is long, my child, but it shall be
> Not one step longer than is best for thee,
> And thou shalt know at last, when thou shalt stand
> Close to the gate, how I did take thy hand,
> And quick and straight led thee to heaven's gate, my child!"
> —Burlington Hawkeye.

A Song in the Night (417).

Seven men were buried beneath thousands of tons of rock which fell without a moment's warning in a Cornish tin mine. Willing hands soon began the work of rescue, though all despaired of finding any one alive. Their worst fears were not quite realized. One man was found, and was removed from his comrades uninjured, the rocks having formed an arch over him.

After two days the men who were at work, having been greatly en-couraged by finding one man alive, called very loudly to ascertain whether others were alive and could speak. One man answered. He was an active Christian, a Sunday School superintendent.

"Are you alone?" asked some one.

No; Christ is with me," was the answer.

Are you injured?" was the next question.

Yes," replied the imprisoned man; "my legs are held fast by something." Then in a feeble voice he sang:

"Abide with me! Fast falls the eventide,
The darkness deepens—Lord, with me abide!
When other helpers fail, and comforts flee,
Help of the helpless, O abide with me!"

They heard no more from him. Two days later they found him with his legs crushed by a huge rock which rested on them, but it was known from his life and last words that he had gone to be "forever with the Lord."

When he was buried his funeral was attended by hundreds of people. According to the local custom, they carried the casket through the streets with their hands; and on the way to the cemetery and also at the graveside his favorite hymns were sung. All were weeping as they finally sang the hymn which was last upon his lips, "Abide with me;" and many felt the desire of their own hearts expressed in the words: "In life, in death, O Lord, abide with me."—Kind words.

The Source of Resignation (418).

The supreme source of resignation and comfort in suffering and sorrow is trust in the loving heavenly Father, the Father of mercies and God of all comfort, who is revealed in the Scriptures and especially in the character and the sufferings of Jesus the Christ. An inward assurance of filial relationship to God is an unfailing support in trouble of very sort and every degree. To know that God himself heals all our sorrows, and is the tender and sympathizing companion of our loneliness, and that He will cause all calamities as well as all blessings to work together for our good, makes us victorious in the hour of agony. —Selected.

My Heavenly Home (419).

There is no power in death, even though it come cruelly and harshly, to destroy this peace. Stephen in the hour of death had the face of an angel, and had comforting visions of his ascended Lord. The stones of the mob, and even the gnashing on him of their teeth, had no power to shut out the glories revealed to him.

On January 10th, 1860, the Pemberton mill, a large cotton factory at Lawrence, Mass., suddenly fell into ruins, burying the operatives in the debris. Some were rescued alive; others would have been, but a broken lantern set the ruins on fire and the rescuers were driven from their work. As they turned away, they distinctly heard some imprisoned girls who had been brought up in the Sunday School singing that precious hymn of William Hunter's—

"My heavenly home is bright and fair."

And up from the flaming jaws of death there came the brave chorus,—

"I'm going home to die no more."

—Banks.

Help to Bear (420).

In a short story in Harper's Magazine, entitled "An Angel in the House," Harriet Prescott Spofford has told about a woman who suddenly became blind in her old age. Quickly her prayer came, "Oh, our Heavenly Father, come to us with Thy Spirit. Help us to be willin'. Be with us in the dark:—oh, be with us in the dark!"

With her husband, whose heart is breaking under the affliction, she visits the oculist, who gently tells her that nothing but a miracle can bring back her lost sight, "And the days of miracles are gone," he adds.

"No," she said quietly, "it may not be worth while for me. But the Power that made this world must still be living in it,"

"And can transcend law? I wish it could and would."

"Perhaps not that way," she answered with a lovely dignity. "But by comin' to me—and helpin' me to bear. By comfortin' him," for he had dropped his head in her lap and was crying like a child. "Dear, it is the Lord's will;" she said, her hand resting on his head. "I would have liked to see the beautiful world again—but in the next life there will be so much to see, p'rhaps it is best to rest a little first. Dear, dear," as he shook her with his sobs, "I would let you have your will. Shan't the Lord have His will, too, when we love Him so?"

"There is no charge," said the doctor when the man drew out his ancient wallet. "She has done more for me that I could do for her."

Not Afraid (421).

It is well, then, to be assured that one of the purposes served by the mission of Christ was to dispel the fear of death by destroying that which gave it power to terrify. The fear of death is here represented as a bondage, a condition of slavery out of which every child of God must be emancipated. There is an old Talmudic legend that the dimple on every man's and woman's upper lip was impressed by the hand of God, who in creating all human flesh whispered, "It is well," but pressed His finger on our mouths to prevent us telling each other what we know. This legend aptly enough expresses the thought that every child of God should live with absolute fearlessness, however little he may be able to justify his confidence to those who challenge it. The freedom with which the truth makes free is rarely enjoyed, rarely even conceived. Men are content "to grunt and sweat" under the bondage of the world, its anxieties, its restraints, rather than live with God in perfect freedom.

A life here and now that is but the full expression of our own will and spirit, a life that verifies that "all things are ours," that everything is for the children of God, is the rarest kind of life.—Dods.

The Prepared Path (422).

The only serious matter is to discover the prepared path. We may do this by abiding fellowship with the spirit. Remember how when Paul essayed to turn aside from the prepared path of life, and to go first to the left to Ephesus, and then to the right unto Bithynia, in each case the spirit of Jesus suffered him not. For the most part the trend of daily circumstances will indicate the prepared path; but whenever we come to a standstill, puzzled to know which path to take of three or four that converge at a given point, let us stand still and consider the matter, asking God to speak to us through our judgments and to bar every path but the right. When once the decision is made, let us never look back. Let us never dare to suppose that God could fail them that trust Him, or permit them to make a mistake. If difficulties arise, they do not prove us to be wrong, and probably they are less by His path than they would have been by any other. Go forward. The way has been prepared; the mountains are a way; the rivers have fords; the lions are chained; the very waves shall yield a path; the desert shall be a highway to the land that flows with milk and honey.—F. B. Meyer.

Those Who Are Missed (423).

Mortal years take away those we love. How can we face a Merry Christmas and a Happy New Year when all the mirth and happiness of life is covered by the pall of grief? The holiday season is an ordeal— an almost insupportable one—to many suffering hearts. Who shall roll away the stone from the door of their sorrow? It is the old question, forever new. And the old answer is forever true—the answer of eternity to time. It is the angels that roll away the stone. Never is heaven nearer to us than when we celebrate the coming of Christ, the incarnation of the Eternal in our clay, and close upon it, the passing of the years of earth. Those who have left us for heaven are very near—and theirs is the Happy New Year, the immortal year, whose joys cannot fade or fail. The sense of loss abides with us. That we cannot change nor cease to feel. But the sense of the love of God, at this holy day time, can so be felt, too, that the thought of the little child taken up in His arms, the gentle saint gone home to Him, the strong souls whom He has called up higher, will lift our spirits up into the joy in which those loved ones stand transfigured, safe from all the chances and changes of the years.

Love is the immortal thing against which time and death cannot prevail; and God is love. To look from the earthly years upward to the heavenly is to rejoice, even through tears.—Harper's Bazar.

God's Bird (424).

There is a story of an Indian child who one day came in from the wheat-field with a hurt bird in her hand. Running to the old chief, she said: "See! This is my bird. I found it in the wheat. It is hurt." The old man looked at the wounded bird and replied slowly: "No, it is not your bird, my child—it is God's bird. Take it back and lay it down where you found it. If you keep it, it will die. If you give it back into God's hands, He will heal its hurt and it will live."

What the old Indian said of hurt birds is true of hearts hurt by sorrow. No human hand can heal them—the only safe thing to do in time of grief is to put our lives into God's hands, to commit them to Him. His hands are gentle and skillful. They will not break a bruised reed nor quench the smoking flax. He will give us just the help we need and just when we need it.—Selected.

Implicit Trust (425).

What a vast proportion of our lives is spent in anxious and useless forebodings concerning the future, either our own or that of our dear ones! Present joys, present blessings, slip by and we miss half their sweet flavor, and all for want of faith in Him who provides for the tiniest insect in the sunbeam. O, when shall we learn the sweet trust in God our little children teach us every day by their confiding faith in us? We who are so mutable, so faulty, so irritable, so unjust, and He who is so watchful, so pitiful, so loving, so forgiving! Why cannot we, slipping our hand into His each day, walk trustingly over that day's appointed path, thorny or flowery, crooked or straight, knowing that evening will bring us sleep, peace, and home?—Selected.

All Is Well (426).—The Christian with Tennyson exclaims: "I have felt:" in the darkness I hear the sentinel walking up and down, whispering "All is well!"

Fear Not For I Am With Thee (427).

In a sketch of his boyhood the Rev. John McNeil, a Scotch preacher and evangelist, tells this story of an experience with his father: "I remember one Saturday night it was nearly midnight when I started to tramp six or seven miles down through the lonely glen to get home. The road had a bad name. This particular night was very black, and two miles outside our little village the road gets blacker than ever. I was just entering the dark defile, when about one hundred yards ahead, in the densest of the darkness, there suddenly rang out a great, strong, cheery voice: 'Is that you, Johnny?' It was my father—the bravest, strongest man I ever knew. Many a time since, when things have been getting very black and gloomy about me, I have heard a voice greater than any earthly parent cry: 'Fear not; for I am with thee.' And lo! God's foot is rising and falling on the road before us as we tread the journey of life. Don't let us forget that."

Clouds Transformed (428).

In one of the German picture galleries is a painting called "Cloud-land." It hangs at the end of a long gallery, and at first sight it looks like a huge, repulsive daub of confused color, without form or comeliness. As you walk toward it, the picture begins to take shape; it proves to be a mass of exquisite little cherub faces like those at the head of the canvas in Raphael's "Madonna San Sisto." If you come close to the picture, you see only an innumerable company of little angels and cherubim.

How often the soul that is frightened by trial sees nothing but a confused and repulsive mass of broken expectations and crushed hopes! But if that soul, instead of fleeing away into unbelief and despair, will only draw up near to God, it will soon discover that the cloud is full of angels of mercy.—Theo. L. Cuyler.

For the Sake of the Living (429).

It is natural in the earliest sudden agony of bereavement to lead a life of torpor, except in one direction. Nerves, acute to the sense of suffering, are blunted to all other feelings. If there be any emotion, it is often one of profound wonder that anybody on God's earth can be happy when we are so sad, and of resentment at the rebound of others from the shock of sorrow. The first laughter in the house, the first gay whistle of a boy running in from school, the first interest shown in business or in politics by the head of the house seems forgetfulness of the one who has gone, and moves the heart still absorbed in grief to a sentiment akin to indignation.

Nevertheless, reaction must come, and it argues no lack of tenderness in memory, but only a natural and wholesome state of things when the song comes back to the lips which have been dumb and the talk around the table ripples on, unsubdued by the vacant chair. It is a happy thing, too, when the dear one is not dropped out of the talk, when reference is made to her as of old, to him as when he was going in and out among us. We treat our dead very coldly when we never mention their names, never allude to their wishes, act as if indeed they had ceased to belong to us and ours.

For the sake of the earthly living, let us always bear in our minds a thought of the heavenly living, our beloved in other worlds, as much ours when there as while here.—Margaret Sangster.

The Smile of the Pilot (430).

Robert Louis Stevenson's story of a storm that caught a vessel off a rocky coast and threatened to drive it and its passengers to destruction, is thrilling. In the midst of the terror one daring man, contrary to orders, went to the deck, made a dangerous passage to the pilot house, saw the steersman lashed fast at his post holding the wheel unwaveringly and inch by inch turning the ship out once more to sea. The pilot saw the watcher and smiled. Then the daring passenger went below and gave out a note of cheer. "I have seen the face of the pilot and he smiled. It is all well."

Blessed is he who in the midst of earthly stress and storm can say with equal assurance, "I have seen the face of my Pilot and he smiled."

Like As a Father (431).

A little incident which beautifully illustrated the words of David, spoken so long ago, came under my notice recently. It so impressed and comforted me that I want to pass it on.

We were seated around the tea table in my friend's pleasant home, when it seems the little daughter reached to help herself with undue haste. The father reproved her, and it must have been very gently, for there was not any interruption in the conversation. But a lady seated by the child's side told me afterward that Jennie's eyes filled with tears, and she slipped quietly away from the table. But I did notice Mr. H—— excusing himself and also leaving the room.

Immediately after tea I had occasion to visit the adjoining sitting room, where I found the little one nestled in her father's strong arms, the tears still falling from her blue eyes, but looking up trustfully into the brown ones bent above hers and glistening with sympathy, while the voice, tender and manly, was saying: "There, there, darling; papa would not hurt his little pet's feelings or spoil her supper if he could help it. See, papa could not eat any more when he knew you were feeling so badly. Now, sweetheart, let us go and see if there is anything left for us. Mother will attend to us herself."

For some time they talked softly; then I heard a little ripple of laughter, and they went to finish the meal, her hand clasped in her father's.

But I had my lesson. What a sweet remembrance for that child. Thank God for our Christian fathers, and while the tears dropped down my cheeks I cried silently, "Does God love me so?" And the answer came and stayed: "Like as a father pitieth his children, so the Lord pitieth them that fear Him." Psa. 103:13.—Christian Guardian.

The Master Close at Hand (432).

A woman who was not long ago in circumstances of extraordinary trial, said that she was lying awake at two o'clock in the morning. As every one knows, this is the hour of lowest vitality, and when the body is weak, the mind often shares the depression. She was in a place where she did not know what step to take next. One course seemed open to her, but it was a course that she much disliked to take. While she hesitated, balancing considerations in her thought, she said that she heard a voice speaking as distinctly as if it were that of a friend in the room, "O! thou of little faith: wherefore dost thou doubt?" Who spoke? No one was near. The moonlight lay in silver waves on the floor of the room. But she had heard the voice, she understood its gentle chiding, she asked for more faith, and fell asleep. When the full light of day came she rose and went on her way, reinforced and confident, for her faith was now great where it had been little. The result proved that God, as He always does, waited to keep His promise.

> "If Jesus came to earth again
> And walked and talked in field and street
> Who would not lay his human pain
> Low at those heavenly feet,

And leave the loom, and leave the lute,
  And leave the volume on the shelf,
To follow Him unquestioning, mute,
  If 'twere the Lord Himself?"

—Selected.

A Hopeless Death (433).

I want something better than the best disbeliever in Jesus Christ ever possessed. God forbid that I should ever say an untrue or an unkind word about any of the sons of men—least of all that I should seem to tear aside with ruthless hand the veil that hides the secret place of sorrow! But the occurrence to which I am about to refer was not done in a corner, and I only bring to your mind what you all know when I mention the time when Colonel Ingersoll endeavored to fulfill the promise made to his brother, who was also his boyhood's playmate, and pronounced his funeral address. It was in June, 1879. This brother had died in Washington, and Colonel Ingersoll stood by the coffin and tried to read his address. His voice became agitated, his form trembled, and his emotion overcame him. Finally he put down the paper, and, bowing himself upon the coffin, he gave vent to uncontrollable grief. When at last he was able to proceed he raised himself up, and among other words he said these: "Whether in mid-ocean or 'mid the breakers of the farther shore, a wreck must mark at last the end of each and all; and every life, no matter if its every hour be filled with love and every moment jeweled with a joy, will at the last become a tragedy as sad and dark and deep as can be woven of the warp and woof of mystery and death.. . . .Life is a dark and barren vale between the cold and iceclad peaks of two eternities. We strive in vain to look beyond the heights. We lift our wailing voices in the silence of the night, and hear no answer but the bitter echo of our cry." Could ever words more sadly hopeless have been uttered at a time like that? And then he added what to me were the most pathetic words of all—something about "hope trying to see a star, and listening for the rustle of an angel's wings."

Mrs. Browning most truly writes:

" 'There is no God,' the foolish saith,
    But none, 'There is no sorrow.'
  And nature oft in bitter need
    The cry of faith will borrow.
  Eyes which the preacher could not school,
    By wayside graves are raised;
  And lips cry, 'God be pitiful!'
    Which ne'er said, 'God be praised!' "

I think I should like greater comfort and a better hope than that.
—Mills.

Troubles Ahead (434).

Many have dreaded troubles which they thought must come; and while they went on ever expecting to make the turn in their path, which was to open out fully the evil, lo! they found that they had reached the journey's end, and were at the haven where they would be. Even **for** others it is not wise to indulge in overmuch looking forward in fearfulness. Come what may to the dearest ones we have on earth, God and His upholding grace will be there, and He cares for them more than even we can do. An earnest commendation to His love will avail them more than all our fretting.—H. L. Sidney Lear.

"Be Still" (435).

Do you know what Luther said? "Suffer and be still and tell no man thy sorrow; trust in God—His help will not fail thee." This is what Scripture calls keeping silence before God. To talk much of one's sorrows makes one weak, but to tell one's sorrows to Him who heareth in secret makes one strong and calm.—Tholuck.

"They Shall Not Be Afraid" (436).

Rev. Charles H. Spurgeon, of London, in his commentary on the ninety-first psalm, makes this interesting record: "Before expounding these verses I cannot refrain from recording a personal incident which illustrates their power to soothe the heart when they are applied by the Holy Spirit. In the year 1854, when I had scarcely been in London twelve months, the neighborhood in which I labored was visited by Asiatic cholera, and my congregation suffered from its inroads. Family after family summoned me to the bedside of the smitten, and almost every day I was called to visit the grave. I gave myself up with youthful ardor to the visitation of the sick, and was sent for from all corners of the district by persons of all ranks and religions. I became weary in body and sick at heart. My friends were falling one by one, and I felt, or fancied, that I was sickening like those around me. A little more work and weeping would have laid me low among the rest; I felt that my burden was heavier than I could bear and was ready to sink under it. As God would have it, I was returning mournfully from a funeral, when my curiosity led me to read a paper which was wafered up in a shoemaker's window in Dover Road. It did not look like a trade announcement, nor was it, for it bore, in good bold handwriting, these words, 'Because thou hast made the Lord, which is my refuge, even the Most High, thy habitation, there shall no evil befall thee, neither shall any plague come nigh thy dwelling.' The effect upon my heart was immediate. Faith appropriated the passage as her own. I felt secure, refreshed, girt with immortality. I went on with my visitings of the dying with a calm and peaceful spirit; I felt no fear of evil, and suffered no harm. The Providence which moved the tradesman to place those verses in his window I gratefully acknowledge, and in the remembrance of its marvelous power I adore the Lord my God."

We are not afraid of pestilence when there is no pestilence. We are not afraid of war when peace reigns. But are we not afraid of what men say or think of us? Are we not afraid of some loss or adversity? Why should we be afraid of anything? The Lord our God is round about us—what foe can make our souls afraid?—Selected.

His Angels Charge Over Thee (437).

A Christian woman had occasion to go across a ferry to New York late one night. On the boat she noticed a man watching her, who approached later and asked, "Are you alone?" "No, sir," said the lady. The man dropped behind, but the lady heard his step after her as she walked through the deserted street, and lifted her heart to God in prayer for protection. Presently the step quickened, and the man was walking beside her. "I thought you said you were not alone." "I am not, sir," was the lady's reply. There was a note of sarcasm in the man's voice as he remarked, "I do not see one—who is your company?" "The Lord Jesus and His holy angels," was the reply. With the briefest pause, the man responded, "Madam, you keep too good company for me. Good evening!" And he raised his hat and left her to her better companionship.—The Christian.

Cloudy Days' Trust (438).

A heart rejoicing in God delights in all His will and is surely provided with the most firm joy in all estates; for if nothing can come to pass beside or against His will, then cannot that soul be vexed which delights in Him and hath no will but His, but follows Him in all times, in all estates; not only when He shines bright on them, but when they are clouded. That flower which follows the sun doth so even in the dark and cloudy days: when it does not shine forth, yet it follows the hidden course and motion of it. So the soul that moves after God keeps that course when He hides His face; is content, yea, even glad at His will in all estates or conditions or events.—R. Leighton.

Resignation (439).

"I shall never believe in prayer again" said a broken-hearted girl, as the Youth's Companion tells us. "If ever any one prayed in faith, I prayed that my mother might recover. But she died. Oh, how could God be so cruel?"

Wisely her friend answered. "There are few deaths, thank God, where no one present prays that the dear one may live. Do you suppose that the gift of prayer was given us in order that no one may ever die? Do you think God intended men to live on in growing infirmity, till at last they pray for death to save them from despair? If God gave us all we ask for—gave it to all men—we should never dare to pray. Prayer is a blessing because God knows best how to answer. God knows when to say no.

"You prayed. Thank God that you could pray. You prayed in hope, and even now you would not have it otherwise. Pray still, but pray in trust. Pray that God will give you strength for your present burdens, and light enough to follow in the path of duty, one day at a time. You said you could never pray again, but you will.

"There are no unanswered prayers. Pray that you may know your duty; pray for rest and hope and trust. With those will come peace and new courage, but not absence of sorrow. The peace and courage will enable you to bear the sorrow. That will be the answer to your prayer."

So with calmness of spirit the sad young woman faced the world again, and daily prayer gave her daily strength. In the deepening of her life and the strengthening of her character her friends discovered the answer to her prayers, even those that had seemed unanswered.

Trusting Our Guide (440).

There is One only whose wisdom is infallible, whose advice never errs, and He would be our Guide. There is a little prayer in one of the Psalms which pleads: "Cause me to know the way wherein I should walk." This prayer, if sincere, will always be answered. We may see no hand leading us. We may hear no voice saying, as we walk in the darkness, "This is the way, walk ye in it." Yet if we seek divine guidance and accept it implicitly, we shall always have it. We have it in Browning:

> "I go to prove my soul!
> I see my way as birds their trackless way,
> I shall arrive! what time, what circuit first,
> I ask not: but unless God send his hail
> Or blinding fireballs, sleet or stifling snow,
> In some time, His good time, I shall arrive;
> He guides me and the bird. In His good time!"

Not only do we have keeping and guidance in Christ, but everything we need on the way, and then eternal blessedness.—J. R. Miller, D. D.

Holding Our Father's Hand (441).

A prominent business man had a Christian wife who died praying for his conversion. One night, while lying awake in the darkness of his room, he heard a voice from the little bed at his side, "Take my hand, papa, it's so dark." He reached forth his large strong hand and took the small trembling one in it until the frightened child fell asleep. Then that strong business man looked up through the darkness and said: "Father, take thou my hand as I have taken the hand of my child, and give rest of soul, for Jesus' sake." Then it was that he felt the comforting influence of the divine presence, and knew that God was nigh. —Theodore Cuyler, D. D.

Finding the Roses (442).

A German allegory tells of two little girls. They had been playing together in a strange garden, and soon one ran in to her mother full of disappointment. "The garden's a sad place, mother." "Why, my child?" "I've been all around, and every rose-tree has cruel, long thorns on it." Then the second child came in breathless. "O mother, the garden's a beautiful place!" "How so, my child?" "Why, I've been all around, and every thorn-bush has lovely roses growing on it." And the mother wondered at the difference in the two children.

Lives Rooted in God (443).

"Strangers with thee,"—then we may carry our thoughts forward to the time when we shall go to our true home, nor wander any longer in the land that is not ours. If even here we come into such blessed relationship with God, that fact is in itself a prophecy of a more perfect communion and a heavenly house. They who are strangers with Him will one day be at "home with the Lord." And in the light of that blessed hope the transiency of this life changes its whole aspect, loses the last trace of sadness, and becomes a solemn joy. Why should we be pensive and wistful when we think how near our end is? Is the sentry sad as the hour for relieving guard comes nigh? Is the wanderer in far off lands sad when he turns his face homewards? And why should we not rejoice at the thought that we, strangers and foreigners here, shall soon depart to the true metropolis, the mother-country of our souls? I do not know why a man should be either regretful or afraid, as he watches the hungry sea eating away this "bank and shoal of time" upon which he stands—even though the tide has all but reached his feet— if he knows that God's strong hand will be stretched forth to him at the moment when the sand dissolves from under him, and will draw him out of many waters, and place him high above the floods in that stable land where there is "no more sea."

Lives rooted in God through faith in Jesus Christ are not vanity. Let us lay hold of Him with a loving grasp—and "we shall live also" because He lives, as He lives, so long as He lives. The brief days of earth will be blessed while they last, and fruitful of what shall never pass. We shall have Him with us while we journey—and all our journeyings will lead to rest in Him. True, men walk in a vain show; true, the "world passeth away and the lust thereof,"—but, blessed be God! true, also, "He that doeth the will of God abideth forever."—Alexander Maclaren, D. D.

I Will Fear No Evil (444).

Even the shadow of death loses all its terrors when we are close to God. How confidently David sings in his Shepherd Psalm, "Though I walk through the valley of the shadow of death, I will fear no evil; for thou are with me; thy rod and thy staff they comfort me."

No man who has seen as much of the shadow of death as I have will ever make light of it. It is indeed a dark shadow. It fell over my house one day, and a noble boy, my firstborn son, the light and the gladness of the household, faded out of our sight. And though more than twenty years have passed since I stood under that shadow, a hundred times a year, when I am alone, my heart grows tender and my eyes fill with tears in memory of that day. But, thank God, the blackness of the shadow has long since passed away. The shadow has grown white, for now I feel and know that though out of my earthly presence that sweet song bird has flown, and sings there no more, still it sits in the Tree of Life and sings, and I shall hear it again.—Banks.

Look Up (445).

In the early days of Britain, when the Christian Cuthbert and his companions were driven from the bitter land to sea, and then were cast upon a dreary shore by a terrible storm, they cried, "No path is open for us; let us perish: we are driven from land to sea and from sea to land." And Cuthbert answered, "Have ye so little faith, my comrades?" and then lifting his eyes to heaven he prayed, "I thank thee, Lord, that the way to heaven is still open." When there is no other way to look for help, we may look up.—The Classmate.

Unbroken Connection with God (446).

I stood upon a bridge spanning a railroad in Boston, and reflected how those rails disappearing around yonder curve, stretched on, without a break, across three thousand miles of continent, till, beginning at the Atlantic, they stopped only at the Pacific Ocean. It would be a matter of faith ("not by sight") to commit myself to them, in order to make the overland journey. So of sending a message over the equally continuous wires. Yet more of seeking communication by "wireless," where, however, a continuous intervening medium is assumed—not seen. The return current of the telegraphic wire, in order to complete the circuit, has, in fact, long been entrusted to an invisible medium, and not in vain. "Call upon me, and I will answer thee" "From the secret place of thunder."—Homiletic Review.

Let Christ Bear It and You (447).

An aged, weary woman, carrying a heavy basket, got into a train with me the other day, and when she was seated she still kept the heavy burden upon her arm. "Lay your burden down, mum," said the kindly voice of a workingman. "Lay your burden down, mum; the train will carry both it and you."—Jowett.

Our Captain (448).

Some years ago, when Captain Dutton was commander of the "Sarmian," we had entered the River St. Lawrence on our homeward voyage, when suddenly a heavy fog arose which completely hid the shore and all objects from view. The ship, which was going at full speed, continued on her course without relaxing the least. The passengers became frightened, considering it extremely reckless on the part of the captain. Finally, one of them went and remonstrated with the mate, telling him of the fears of the passengers. He listened, then, replied with a smile: "Oh, don't be frightened; the passengers need not be the least uneasy; the fog extends only a certain height above the water, and the captain is at the masthead, and is up above the fog, and it is he who is directing the vessel!"—The Baptist Commonwealth.

Today and Tomorrow (449).

Today's wealth may be tomorrow's poverty, today's health, tomorrow's sickness, today's happy companionship of love, tomorrow's aching solitude of heart, but today's God will be tomorrow's God, today's Christ will be tomorrow's Christ. Other fountains may dry up in heat or freeze in winter, but this knows no change, "in summer and winter it shall be." Other fountains may sink low in their basins after much drawing, but this is ever full, and, after a thousand generations have drawn from its stream, is broad and deep as ever. Other fountains may be left behind on the march, and the wells and palm-trees of each Elim on our road be succeeded by a dry and thirsty land where no water is, but this spring follows us all through the wilderness, and makes music and spreads freshness ever by our path. We can forecast nothing beside. We can be sure of this, that God will be with us in all the days that lie before us. What may be round the next headland we know not; but this we know, that the same sunshine will make a broadening path across the waters right to where we rock on the unknown sea, and the same unmoving mighty star will burn for our guidance. So we may let the waves and currents roll as they list—or rather as He wills, and be little concerned about the incidents or the companions of our voyage, since He is with us.—Alexander Maclaren, D. D.

Childlike Trust (450).

A wild storm was raging around a prairie home one night. The windows were blown in, and no lights could be kept burning. It was only with difficulty that the doors could be braced against the blast. The father was absent from home, and the mother, grandmother, and three children sat in the darkness in a room on the sheltered side of the house, fearing that at any moment the house might be swept from the foundations by the force of the wind. Suddenly eleven-year-old Walter was missed. He had been holding a whispered conversation with his grandmother only a few minutes before. Frantic with fear, the mother called him at the top of her voice, and, receiving no reply, started to grope her way through the darkness and confusion of the house to find, if possible, the missing boy. She found him in his room sound asleep! And when she asked him how he could go to sleep when they were all in danger, he simply replied: "Why, mama, grandma told me God would take care of us, and I thought I might as well go to bed again."—New York Observer.

The Faces Loved Long Since and Lost Awhile (451).

If we love, we must lose. Where love is not, there is nothing to lose. Inasmuch as loss is inevitable, the wise man will ask whether it does not have a meaning deeper than any the reason of man has yet formulated, and he will try to have that attitude toward life and death which makes grief ennobling.

The tasks of some who have gone before seem to have been completed. After years of toil and triumph these workers have gone to their reward.

> "Fear no more the heat o' sun,
>   Nor the furious winter rages;
> Thou thy worldly task hast done,
>   Home hast gone and ta'en thy wages."

At the grave of the child and of the young man or the young woman there comes the feeling that earth has been robbed, that there are tasks and no one to do them. It is then that we need to recognize the imperfections of our knowledge and to believe—

> "That nothing wall·s with aimless feet;
>   That not one life shall be destroyed;
>   Or cast as rubbish to the void,
>   When God hath made the pile complete."

We do not lose those whom we love.

> "But in the sun they cast no shade,
>   No voice is heard, no sign is made,
>   No step is on the conscious floor!"

Yet they are ever with us. Our lives are poor in feeling and imagination if we cannot find the meaning of Tennyson's lines—

> "Thy voice is on the rolling air;
>   I hear thee where the waters run:
>   Thou standest in the rising sun,
>   And in the setting thou art fair.
> "Far off thou art, but ever nigh,
>   I have thee still, and I rejoice;
>   I prosper, circled with thy voice;
>   I shall not lose thee though I die."

In the hour of temptation and when duty is hard the memory of one who trusted us in our days of weakness and blindness saves us from cowardice and sin. There are those who say they are weak because father, mother, wife, husband, or friend is gone. Have not such persons learned very imperfectly the lessons of affection? Are they eye-servants who do nothing well when the master is absent? Is their affection so earthy that it cannot live upon memory and hope? If we have not been selfishly receiving, and giving in return nothing of value, ought we not to be stronger when those who have taught us what is worth while and have inspired us to put our best into our work are no longer with us to guide and cheer us? The patriot is stronger because he has before him the example of his country's heroes. The Christian rejoices in tribulation, for he believes he is continuing the work of the martyrs of his faith. Is the example of those whom we have known less powerful than that of those whom we have never seen?

We have lost our friends for a while. The Christian lives in hope. With Paul he says, "I am persuaded that neither death, nor life, nor angels, nor principalities, nor powers, nor things present, nor things to come, nor height, nor depth, nor any other creature shall be able to separate us from the love of God, which is in Christ Jesus our Lord." The love of God is the basis of hope. Those who have not the certainty of God's love may use the word hope, but they know not its meaning. The boundless ocean upon which our loved ones have embarked is the ocean of God's love. "That which drew from out the boundless deep" has turned again to its home.

"What is excellent
As God lives is permanent;
Hearts are dust, heart's loves remain:
Heart's love will meet thee again."
—The Christian Century.

ILLUSTRATIVE POETRY.

Come To My Help (452).

Come to my help, O Master!—once in sorrow
    My more than brother—King of Glory now;
Even in my tears a gleam of hope I borrow
    From the deep scars around Thy radiant brow.

Come to my help, as once God's angels hastened
    To cheer Thee in Thy midnight agony;
O Lord of angels! once by suff'ring chastened,
    Forget me not in mine infirmity.

Walk Thou the wave with me, the tempest stilling;
    Let me but feel the clasping of Thy strength—
Thy heavenly strength—through all my pulses thrilling,
    I shall not fear to reach the shore at length.

                                —Dr. Bethune.

Resigned (453).

As chiselled image unresisting lies
    In niche by its own Sculptor's hand designed,
So to my unemployed and silent life
    Let me in quiet meekness be resigned.

If works of faith and labours sweet of love
    May not be mine, yet patient hope may be
Within my heart like a bright censer's fire
    With incense of thanksgiving mounting free.

Thou art our Pattern to the end of time
    O Crucified! and perfect is Thy will;
The workers follow Thee in doing good,
    The helpless think of Calvary, and are still.

                                —Caroline M. Noel.

No Fear (454).

"To Thy beyond no fear I give:
    Because thou livest, I live,
Unsleeping Friend! why should I wake
    Troublesome thought to take
For any strange to-morrow? In thy hand,
Days and eternities like flowers expand.
"Odors from blossoming worlds unknown
    Across my path are blown;
Thy robes trail hither myrrh and spice
    From farthest paradise;
I walk through thy fair universe with thee,
And sun me in thine immortality."

My Hope (455).

For though from out our bourne of time and place
    The flood may bear me far,
I hope to see my Pilot face to face,
    When I have crossed the bar.

                —Tennyson.

The Lost Chord (456).

"I sat alone at the organ at the close of a troubled day,
When the sunset's crimson embers on the western altar lay;
I was weary with vain endeavor, and my heart was ill at ease,
And I sought to soothe my sadness with the voice of the sweet-toned
    keys.

But my hands were weak and trembling, and my fingers all unskilled,
To render the grand old anthem with which my soul was filled;
Thro' the long day's cares and worries I had dreamed of that glorious
    strain,
And I longed to hear the organ repeat it to me again;

But it fell from my untaught fingers discordant and incomplete,
I knew not how to express it, nor to make the discord sweet;
So I toiled with patient labor till the last bright gleams were gone,
And the evening's purple shadows were gathering one by one.

Then a master stood beside me and touched the noisy keys,
And lo! the discord vanished, and melted in perfect peace;
I hear the great organ pealing my tune that I could not play—
The strains of the glorious anthem that had filled my soul all day.

Down thro' the dim cathedral the tide of the music swept,
And among the shadowy arches the lingering echoes crept;
And I stood in the purple twilight and heard my tune again,
Not my feeble untaught rendering, but the master's perfect strain.

So I think perchance the Master, at the close of life's weary day,
Will take from our trembling fingers the tune that we cannot play;
He will hear thro' the jarring discords, the strains but half exprest,
He will blend them in perfect music, and add to them all the rest."

                —Mrs. Minnie Kinney.

The Sweet Refrain (457).

I hear it singing in the dawn—
    A world-old, sweet refrain—
I hear its notes insistent drawn
    In music of the rain;
It sings within the swaying corn,
    A canticle of cheer
That glorifies the golden morn:
    "He loves thee; do not fear."

I hear it singing in the noon
When aging summer grieves,
And fading maples sadly croon
    The farewell of the leaves;
I hear it when 'mid shrouding
      snows
The chanting winds intone
A threnody above the rose:
    "Will He not keep His own?"

I hear it singing in the night
 When out across the bar
The moonlight falls in shimmering white,
 And calls my bark afar;
It sings to me when vesper bells
 Steal out upon the deep,
And through all nature sings and swells;
 "He loves thee; rest and sleep."
 —Rose Trumbull in Sunday School Times.

A Little Way (458).

A little way—I know it is not far
To that dear home where my beloved are;
And yet my faith grows weaker, as I stand
A poor, lone pilgrim in a dreary land,
Where present pain the future bliss obscures;
And still my heart sits like a bird upon
The empty nest, and mourns its treasures gone;
 Plumed for their flight,
 And vanished quite.
Ah me! where is the comfort?—though I say
They have but journeyed on a little way!

A little way!—this sentence I repeat,
Hoping and longing to extract some sweet
To mingle with the bitter. From Thy hand
I take the cup I cannot understand,
And in my weakness give myself to Thee!
Although it seems so very, very far
To that dear home where my beloved are,
 I know, I know,
 It is not so;
Oh! give me faith to feel it when I say
That they are gone—gone but a little way!
 —Anon.

Thy Will (459).

One prayer I have—all prayers in one—
 Since I am wholly Thine;
Thy blessed will, O God be done,
 And let Thy will be mine!

Be Not Afraid (460).

When death is at hand, and the cottage of clay
 Is left with a tremulous sigh,
The gracious forerunner is smoothing the way
For its tenant to pass to unchangeable day,
 Saying, "Be not afraid, it is I."

When the waters are passed, and the glories unknown
  Burst forth on the wondering eye,
The compassionate "Lamb in the midst of the throne"
Shall welcome, encourage, and comfort His own,
  And say, "Be not afraid, it is I."
                              —Nathaniel Hawthorne.

Life's Lessons (461).

A child came close to his teacher's side,
  His book tight clasped in his little hand,
"Teacher," he said with wistful eyes,
  "We're coming to words that I don't understand;
I've turned the pages over and over,
  And the words are so big and they're all so new,
When we come to the lesson where they are put,
  Oh, teacher, I don't know what I'll do."

The teacher smiled at the troubled face,
  And tenderly stroked the curly head.
"Before we reach them I think you will learn
  The way to read them," she gently said;
"But if you shouldn't, I'll help you then.
  And don't you think that the wisest plan
Is to learn the lesson that comes today,
  And learn it the very best you can?"

And it seems to me it is so with us;
  We look at the days that are still ahead—
The days that perchance may never be ours—
  With a pitiful longing and nameless dread.
But surely the Teacher who gives the task
  Will lovingly watch as we try to read
With faltering tongue and tear-dimmed eyes,
  And will help His children in time of need.
                              —Christian Observer

The Rod (462).

O Thou whose sacred feet have trod
  The thorny path of woe,
Forbid that I should slight the rod,
  Or faint beneath the blow.

Give me the spirit of Thy trust,
  To suffer as a son;
To say, though lying in the dust,
  Father! Thy will be done!
                              —J. D. Burns.

Faith and I (463).

"We pace the deck together,
  Faith and I;
In stress of midnight weather,
  Faith and I;
And catch at times a vision
  Of the bright Eastern sky
Where waiteth God to tell us
  That we shall never die."

Trust (464).

Faith and hope
Will teach me how to bear my lot—
To think almighty wisdom best,
To bow my head and mumur not.
The chast'ning hand of One above
Falls heavy, but I kiss the rod;
It gives the wound, and I must trust
Its healing to the self-same God.

—Eliza Cook.

The Angels of Grief (465).

With silence only as their benediction,
  God's angels come
Where in the shadow of a great affliction,
  The soul sits dumb!

Yet, would I say what thy own heart approveth:
  Our Father's will,
Calling to Him the dear one whom He loveth,
  Is mercy still.

Not upon thee or thine the solemn angel
  Hath evil wrought;
The funeral anthem is a glad evangel—
  The good die not!

God calls our loved ones, but we lose not wholly
  What He hath given;
They live on earth, in thought and deed, as truly
  As in His heaven.

—John G. Whittier.

Compensation (466).

The graves grow thicker, and life's ways more bare
  As years on years go by:
Nay, thou hast more green gardens in thy care,
  And more stars in thy sky!

Behind, hopes turned to grief, and joys to memories,
   Are fading out of sight;
Before, pains changed to peace, and dreams to certainties,
   Are glowing in God's light.

Hither come backslidings, defeats, distresses,
   Vexing this mortal strife;
Thither go progress, victories, successes,
   Crowning immortal life.

Few jubilees, few gladsome, festive hours,
   Form landmarks for my way;
But heaven and earth, and saints and friends and flowers,
   Are keeping Easter Day!

               —Anon.

The Assurance of Faith (467).

So life stands, with a twilight world around;
   Faith turned serenely to the steadfast sky,
Still answering the heart that sweeps the ground,
   Sobbing in fear, and tossing restlessly—
Hush, hush! The dawn breaks o'er the eastern sea,
'Tis but thine own dim shadow troubling thee.
         —Edward Rowland Sill.

The Blessed Will (468).

"My God, my Father, while I stray
Far from my home on life's rough
    way,
O, teach me from my heart to say,
   Thy will be done!

"If Thou shouldst call me to re-
    sign
What most I prize—it ne'er was
    mine;
I only yield Thee what was Thine;
   Thy will be done!"

Resignation (469).

O thou Most High! from whose celestial dwelling
   Infinite radiance of virtue shines,
Let me behold, Thy richest mercy telling,
   The presence of Thy love in the confines
Of my own heart, reflection of Thy glory.
   Thou rulest not within without the striving
   Of ages old contention with sin;
The mastery of power is Thy devising:
   Eternal love the sway, doth my own fealty win.

How fierce the winds have blown that brought the blasting
   Of bud and flower, of fragrance and of song;
They mark the day that in its sacred passing
   Brought life and joy: and on the memories throng
Mysterious transports of life's fleeting story.

Like field of golden grain, in summer waving,
　O'er which the light and shade successive play,
Where clouds before the golden sun are chasing,
　Pierced through with rays,—so is life's fitful day.

If in our day like clouds must be the sorrow,
　Thy love provides the rays that pierce them through
The rosy hue, gives promise of tomorrow,
　Which cloud and sun at close of day renew;
Perchance the bow on cloud life's story telling.
The sky above looks clearest after showers,
　The earth below stands clad in brighter green;
While, after storm, the birds' song in its bowers
　Is sweetest heard: the flowers most beauteous seen.

Thus, God of love, I thank Thee for the cadence,
　The apparent discords of life's organ sound.
Thy master hands on keys, foretell the advance,
　That sweetest music strike when closest harmony found,
Of minors of life's song into the majors swelling.
Thou Artisan divine, play on! Thy theme unfolding,
　Till paean roll on paean o'er the soul;
Earth's sighing into heaven's new song swelling,
　If but our life Thy glory may extol.

—Rev. Floris Ferwerda.

My Pilot (470).

Sunset and evening star
　And one clear call for me
And may there be no moaning of
　the bar
When I put out to sea.

Twilight and evening bell
　And after that the dark!
And may there be no sadness of
　farewell
When I embark!

For tho' from out our bourne of time and place
　The flood may bear me far,
I hope to see my Pilot face to face
　When I have crossed the bar.

—Tennyson.

Patience (471).

Let us be patient! These severe afflictions
　Not from the ground arise;
But oftentimes celestial benedictions
　Assume this dark disguise.

We see but dimly through the mists and vapours,
　Amid these earthly damps,
What seem to us but sad, funereal tapers
　May be heaven's distant lamps.

There is no death! What seems so is transition;
    This life of mortal breath
Is but the suburb of the life elysian,
    Whose portals we call death.
                        —Longfellow.

Somebody Knows and Cares (472).

Somebody knows when your heart aches,
    And everything seems to go wrong;
Somebody knows when the shadows
    Need chasing away with a song.
Somebody knows when you're lonely,
    Tired, discouraged and blue;
Somebody wants you to know Him,
    And know that He dearly loves you.

Somebody cares when you're tempted,
    And the world grows dizzy and dim:
Somebody cares when you're weakest,
    And farthest away from Him.
Somebody grieves when you've fallen,
    Though you are not lost from His sight;
Somebody waits for your coming,
    Taking the gloom from your night.
                        —Fanny Edna Stafford.

Angel of Patience (473).

To weary hearts, to mourning homes,
God's meekest angel gently comes;
No power has he to banish pain,
Or give us back our lost again;
And yet in tenderest love, our dear
And heavenly Father sends him here.

There's quiet in that Angel's glance,
There's rest in his still countenance!
He mocks no grief with idle cheer,
Nor wounds with words the mourner's ear;
But ills and woes he may not cure
He kindly trains us to endure.

Angel of patience! sent to calm
Our feverish brows with cooling palm;
To lay the storms of hope and fear,
And reconcile life's smile and tear;
The throbs of wounded pride to still,
And make our own, our Father's will!

O thou who mournest on thy way,
With longings for the close of day;
He walks with thee, that Angel kind,
And gently whispers, "Be resigned;
Bear up, bear on, the end shall tell
The dear Lord ordereth all things well!"
—John G. Whittier

Surrender (474).

I said, "Let me walk in the fields."
  He said, "No, walk in the town;"
I said, "There are no flowers there."
  He said, "No flowers, but a crown."

I said, "But the skies are black,
  There is nothing but noise and din;"
And he wept as he sent me back,
  "There is more," he said, "there is sin."

I said, "But the air is thick,
  And fogs are veiling the sun;"
He answered, "Yet souls are sick,
  And souls in the dark undone."

I said, "I shall miss the light,
  And friends will miss me, they say;"
He answered, "Choose tonight,
  If I am to miss you, or they."

I pleaded for time to be given;
  He said, "Is it hard to decide?
It will not seem hard in heaven,
  To have followed the steps of your Guide."

I cast one look at the fields,
  Then set my face to the town,
He said, "My child, do you yield?
  Will you have the flowers or the crown?"

Then into his hand went mine,
  And into my heart came he,
And I walked in a light divine,
  The path I had feared to see.
—George Macdonald.

The Godward Path (475).

"It matters not which road I take,
  How dark or lone it be—
I know, O God, 'twill somewhere join
  The road that leads to thee.

I make mistakes, wrong turns I take—
  The right way do not see—
Tho long and hard I make my road
  'Twill join the road to thee.

Calm is my soul, my trusting heart
  From doubt and fear is free—
For soon or late all roads will join
  The road that leads to thee."
—Althea A. Ogden.

Patient Trust (476).

And though at times impetuous with emotion
  And anguish long suppressed,
The swelling heart heaves moaning like the ocean
  That cannot be at rest,—

We will be patient and assuage the feeling
  We may not wholly stay;
By silence sanctifying, not concealing,
  The grief that must have way.

              —Henry W. Longfellow.

The Tenant (477).

This body is my house—it is not I;
Herein I sojourn until, in some far sky,
I lease a fairer dwelling, built to last
Till all the carpentry of time is past.
When from my high place viewing this lone star,
What shall I care where those poor timbers are?
What though the crumbling walls turn dust and loam,
I shall have left them for a larger home.
What though the rafters break, the stanchions rot,
When earth has dwindled to a glimmering spot!
When thou, clay cottage, fallest, I'll immerse
My long-cramped spirit in the universe.
Through uncomputed silences of space
I shall yearn upward to the leaning Face
The ancient heavens will roll aside for me.
As Moses monarch'd the dividing sea,
This body is my house; It is not I,
Triumphant in this faith I live and die.

          —Frederic Lawrence Knowles.

To a Waterfowl (478).

There is a Power whose care
  Teaches thy way along that pathless coast,
The desert and illimitable air,
  Lone wandering, but not lost.

All day thy wings have fanned,
  At that far height, the cold, thin atmosphere,
Yet stoop not, weary, to the welcome land,
  Though the dark night is near.

And soon that toil shall end;
  Soon shalt thou find a summer home, and rest,
And scream among thy fellows; reeds shall bend,
  Soon, o'er thy sheltered nest.

Thou'rt gone, the abyss of heaven
  Hath swallowed up thy form; yet, on my heart
Deeply hath sunk the lesson thou hast given,
  And shall not soon depart.

He who, from zone to zone,
  Guides through the boundless sky thy certain flight,
In the long way that I must tread alone
  Will lead my steps aright.

—Bryant.

Faith (479).

If I could feel my hand, dear Lord, in Thine,
  And surely know
That I was walking in the light divine,
  Through weal or woe;

If I could hear Thy voice in accents sweet
  But plainly say,
To guide my trembling, groping, wandering feet,
  "This is the way."

I would so gladly walk therein, but now
  I cannot see.
Oh, give me, Lord, the faith humbly to bow—
  And trust in Thee!

There is no faith in seeing. Were we led
  Like children here,
And lifted over rock and river bed,
  No care, no fear,

We should be useless in the busy throng,
  Life's work undone,
Lord, make us brave and earnest, true and strong,
  Till heaven is won.

—S. K. Fulton.

TEXTS AND TREATMENT HINTS.

"Thy Will Be Done."—Matt. 6:10 (480).

When the heart has been wrung by anguish, when the waters have overwhelmed us, the proud waters have gone over our soul, when we have been beaten back and trampled down and when the sun has darkened in our sky and the stars forgot their shining, in the wreck of a career, in the blight of hope, when the unforeseen and the unlooked-for has made mock of our ambitions, when a lingering sickness has taken out of our life that which alone made life worth living, or death robbed us of that which has given us the best joy we have known on earth and left us, as it seemed, friendless, unpitied, homeless in the night, then we have tried to stay our faltering faith on God with this prayer of fathomless pain: Thy will be done.—Aked.

"Though He Slay Me Yet Will I Trust Him."—Job 13:15 (481).

Those who pray truly are usually tested severely. Once, while under great mental depression, a minister was reading a good book, when his eye fell upon this sentence, quoted from Luther: "I would run into the arms of Christ, though He stood with a drawn sword in His hand." The thought came bolting into his mind, "So will I too;" and those words of Job occurred immediately, "Though He slay me, yet will I trust in Him."—(Job 13:15) His burden slipped away, and his soul was filled with joy and peace in believing.

Comfort Texts (482).

"As thy days so shall thy strength be." (Deut. 33:25).
"The joy of the Lord is your strength" (Neh. 8:10).
"Seek the Lord and His strength" (Psa. 105:4).
"The Lord is my strength" (Hab. 3:19).
"In quietness and confidence shall be your strength" (Isa. 30:15).
"The Lord shall renew their strength" (Isa. 40:31).
"I will go in the strength of the Lord God" (Psa. 71:16).
"And He strengthened me" (Dan. 10:18).
"Be strong in the Lord, and in the power of His might" (Eph. 6:10).
"The Lord stood with me, and strengthened me" (2 Tim. 4:17).
"Strengthened with might by His Spirit" (Eph. 3:19).
"Through faith, out of weakness were made strong" (Heb. 11:34).
"My strength is made prfect in weakness" (2 Cor. 12:9).
"Their Redeemer is strong" (Jer. 50:34).
"I can do all things through Christ which strengtheneth me" (Phil. 4:13).—Sunday School Illustrator.

"The Lord Is My Shepherd, I Shall Not Want"—Ps. 23:1 (483).

After the fight at Chattanooga those who were sent to bury the slain are said to have come upon a dead Union boy in a sitting posture —his back against a tree and in his lap a pocket-Bible lying open at the twenty-third Psalm. How, on the instant, does this young man change for us the whole aspect of that battlefield! Before the battle we were thinking of the opposing armies only as two great wholes, as but two terribly destructive machines—the sole question at issue being which of the two were the more likely to out-match, out-fight, and out-destroy the other. But how completely is the whole struggling mass now resolved into distinct and rounded personalities; how flashed upon us the conviction that amid all the roar, confusion and carnage of battle, each soldier stands just as clearly apart to the All-seeing Eye as in the stillness and solitariness of the closet of secret prayer. How blessedly real it makes for us the fact of a close, personal relationship to Christ, and the possibility that this relationship may be for each and every soul a union of intimate confidence; of sweet and indissoluble affection. How it raises us above the dreary monotony of all commonest things, lifting each soul to the sacredness of individual fellowship with the one all-merciful Father, the ever-loving Saviour, the all-comforting Spirit. Instead of the noun of multitude, "mankind," so cheerless in its vagueness and generality, how it gives us, in its stead, the warm, loving personality, giving us to Christ by our names and giving Christ by all His appropriate names to us; inviting us whenever we will to turn away from all the neglects, injustices, envies and cruelties of the world, and with the upward glance of the loving child's confidence to say: "The Lord is my shepherd; I shall not want. He leadeth me by the still waters. He restoreth my soul. Thy rod and thy staff they comfort me."

The Bible is, in this respect, just such a book as we might expect it to be, if it be indeed a message from God to us His children.

It was the sad lament of one of the greatest of heathen philosophers that "God does not care for individual men." But we see everywhere in the Bible that God does care for individual men.—Selected.

"In Patience Possess Ye Your Souls."—Luke 21:19 (484).

Lives have been wrecked, homes made unhappy and desolate, because of the neglect to cultivate this important virtue. In every position and circumstance of life it is needed.

> "Ah! more than martyr's aureole,
> And more than hero's heart of fire,
> We need the humble strength of soul,
> That daily toils, and ills require."

We are told that our Heavenly Father is a "God of Patience." Of Him we can ask at all times power to be patient, assured that we will receive such. Aside from our Lord and Savior, there is no character who illustrates so fully the value and result of patience as that of Job. "Ye have heard of the patience of Job." . . . Abraham, after he had patiently endured, obtained the promise.

> "Not to him who rashly dares,
> But to him who nobly bears,
> Is the victor's garland sure."

In the revelation given to St. John, the divine, we find that to the angel or minister of the church of Thyatira is given the seal of approval for patience; and to the angel of the church of Philadelphia, a promise to keep from temptation, "because thou hast kept the word of my patience." "The patient in spirit is better than the proud in spirit." "Be patient toward all" is the exhortation given by the great apostle.—Selected.

"Then Shalt Thou Lift Up Thy Face Without Spot."—Job 11:15 (485)

"The clouds are always beautiful and clear, no matter what is in the house. Just look up, mamma!" said a little girl to her mother, as they stood on the doorstep of the dingy factory tenement. The mother looked up. There were the billowy white clouds, and as she looked at them she forgot the dirt and discomfort around her. It is a good thing to look up. God is in the heaven above us, and when we see the clouds let us remember that they are around about His throne.

There is a lesson in the Bible about the uplifted face. "Then shalt thou lift up thy face without spot." This phrase, found in the Book of Job, is extremely beautiful as a figure of speech, and at the same time very expressive of certain facts in religious experience. It expresses the attitude of a soul at peace with God according to the provisions and terms of the Gospel. Confidence is implied in this utterance, for a man without peace and confidence will hang his head with guilt and shame, not lift it up without spot. It would be well for us to cultivate more the grace of the uplifted face, the look of trust and confidence in our heavenly Father. He is good; His attitude towards us is loving; His acts are wise.

"I Will Bless the Lord at all Times"—Ps. 34:1 (486).

Who said that? Surely he must have been one remarkably exempt from the troubles of life? Not so. He was one whose life was fuller of strange vicissitudes, and more loaded with trials than that of almost any other at his side. Great mercies he had to speak of, great deliverances, great honors, great joys; but he could also tell of great sorrows, great calamities, great reverses of fortune, great punishments for his sins. And yet, with all these full in view, he could say, "I will bless the Lord at all times," in my darkest as well as in my brightest hours, in my weary wanderings as well as in my peaceful home, in my sorest chastenings as well as in my purest joys; and it was not simply "I will bless the Lord."—Knight.

"I Know Whom I Have Believed, and Am Persuaded that He Is Able to Keep that which I Have Committed unto Him against that day."—2 Timothy 1:12 (487).

The apostles did not, like some of their boasted successors, claim infallibility. It was enough for them that their Master could make no mistake. They never supposed that He had handed down to them His unerring vision and judgment. St. Paul often confessed, as all great men do, that his knowledge was woefully limited. He acknowledged that the highest inspiration gave a man only very partial vision, that in speaking of religious things he himself could not always trust his own judgment, and that he was often like one groping in the dark. He was not certain of everything or of a great many things. There were many rooms in his house of faith into which the light had never shined; things mysterious, things doubtful, things open to question. We know in part, and we see through a glass, darkly. His customary language was, "We walk by faith and not by sight," but here and there he found rock from which nothing could move him, and declared as he does here, "I know."—Selected.

"Let not Your Heart Be Troubled".—John 14:1 (488).

One form of sorrow mentioned by the New Testament is the sorrow occasioned by bereavement. Sin creates the one, and death is the cause of the other. The Lord annihilates the gulf that was created by guilt. What can He do with the awful vacancy created by death? His comfort is peculiarly immediate and strong and sweet. And how does He comfort us? First of all, I think He comforts us in the dark sorrow of bereavement by helping us to look out of the window of love.

I. Now, the window of love looks out upon the past, upon the days we lived together with the loved one before bereavement came. And the gracious ministry of the window of love is this—that it only reveals to us the lovely. All that was beautiful in the loved one shines out in the light. All the frailties and infirmities are seen in new views. Some beauties we have never noticed appear in this comforting retrospect. Every mourner in Christ Jesus knows the love-window and the gracious things that are unveiled for the comfort of the soul.

II. And there is a second window to which the Holy Spirit leads us in our grief. This is the window of faith, and it looks out upon the present. We gaze through this window upon our broken, desolate, lonely life, and we see footprints on the road—nay, we see the Lord Himself. There is given to us an intimate sense of Providential nearness and guidance. We are endowed with the assurance that God is awake and tenderly at work. When we look through the faith-window, life is seen not as chaos but as order, and its happenings are not the blind issues of chance, but the outcome of the graciously tender plan of our Father in heaven.

III. And there is a window to which the comforter takes the soul, unveiling to him prospects that bring exquisite comfort. This is the window of hope, and it looks out upon the morrow, and through that window we see our Father's house with the many mansions. We see the intimacy of its fellowship: "Where I am there ye shall be also." We see the gathering together of the scattered family to be "forever with the Lord." Through this window of hope we gaze "O'er moor and fen and crag and torrent," and beyond all these we see the fair dawning in which the angel faces smile "which we have loved long since and lost a while."

The comfort which I have mentioned is very real, and every sorrowing soul can obtain it in the treasury of grace. It is offered without money and without price. There is no other comfort for sorrows such as these. The one who sorrows for sin may see an opiate in the pleasure of the world, but he will awake again to the strained reality, and his grief will be more poignant than ever. And the one who sorrows in bereavement will exist in an ever-darkening prison unless there comes the comfort of the Light of life. Our Lord Jesus came "to comfort all that mourn." "Earth has no sorrow that heaven cannot heal."—Dr. J. H. Jowett in the Christian World of London.

"And if Christ Be Not Risen, Then Is Our Preaching Vain, and Your Faith Is Also Vain."—1 Cor. 15:14, 15 (489).

What Comes of a Dead Christ?

I. The first point the Apostle makes is this: that with the resurrection of Jesus Christ the whole gospel stands or falls.

II. Secondly, with the resurrection of Jesus Christ stands or falls the character of the witnesses.

III. Again, with the resurrection of Jesus Christ stands or falls the faith of the Christian.

IV. Lastly, with the resurrection of Christ stands or falls the heaven of His servants.—Alexander Maclaren, D. D.

"But When the Morning Was now Come, Jesus Stood on the Shore"—John 21:4 (490).

"Morning" and "Jesus." Write a poem on these words—"Morning" and "Jesus." Or put the two words, and just see the rapid variations of human life—"night" and "nothing," "morning" and "Jesus." That is the Christian life, and in as far as we are vitally Christian do we enter into the mystery of these apparent contradictions. Meet a Christian man under certain circumstances, and you will see as it were upon his countenance, "night" and "nothing." You say, "How gloomy he is, and how much depressed! There is no spring in him, no tunefulness, no inspiration; only 'night' and 'nothing.' " See him the next day, or month, or year, and his countenance glows like the morning, and his voice is tuneful, and he brings with him an atmosphere pure, and vital and vitalizing. That is Christian life—sometimes very low, but always in Christ and always on the rock. Dwell on these sweet and tuneful words a little longer. Look at them, because the eye will help the ear.—Joseph Parker, D. D.

"After that Ye Have Suffered a Little While." 1 Peter 5:10 (491).

Suffering is inevitable. Through much tribulation we must pass to our reward on high. No cross, no crown; no Gethsemane, no emptied grave; no cup of sorrow, no chalice of joy; no cry of forsakenness, no portion with the great, or spoil with the strong. All who suffer are not necessarily glorified; but none are glorified who have not somehow suffered. We must drink of His cup, and be baptized with His baptism, if we would sit right and left of the King. The comet that stands longest nearest to the sun must have plunged furthest into the abyss.

Let sufferers take heart! If only their sufferings are not self-inflicted; if they do not result froom their own mistakes and sins; if they arise from that necessary antagonism to sin and the present world into which close following of the Crucified must necessarily bring any one of us; if they are borne, not only submissively, but with the heart's choice, as of those that delight to do the will of God—then each pang is a milestone marking their way onwards to the goal of light and glory.

Suffering is necessary to our characters.—The Apostle does not for a moment wish his converts spared from the ordeal. Nothing short of necessity would ever lead God to expose us to the fire. But in no other way can our truest bliss be achieved. In no other school-house are the lessons of obedience so acquired as in that kept by sorrow. The Lord Himself was once a scholar there, and carved His name on the hard and comfortless boards. In no other ordeal can we lose so much dross; drop so much chaff, learn so much of our own nothingness; be drawn so close to His companionship; or be taught such true estimates of the comparative values of things, weighing the present against the future, till we feel that it is not worthy to be compared with the glory to be revealed.

Suffering is limited.—At the most, it is for but a little while. Remember how often the Lord Jesus repeated the words, it is only "a little while" (John 16:16-19). It was a note on which His fingers lingered, as if loth to leave it. Compared with all the future, the longest life of suffering is only for a moment; and, contrasted with the weight of glory, the heaviest trials are light. Let us not look at the things which are seen, but at those which are not seen. The hills which would daunt the traveller seem diminutive when they are seen lying about the feet of some soaring Alp. Weeping can only stay for the brief summer night, and in the early twilight must hasten veiled away; because joy cometh in the morning, bringing the herald-beam of the long, happy summer day, on which night can never fall or draw her dusky veil.—Rev. F. B. Meyer.

IX. PROBATION: READINESS FOR THE SUMMONS.

REFLECTIONS AND ILLUSTRATIONS.

Jonathan Edwards' Resolutions (492).

Resolved, To live with all my might while I do live;

Resolved, Never to lose one moment of time, but improve it in the most profitable way I possibly can;

Resolved, Never to do anything which I should despise or think meanly of in another.

Resolved, Never to do anything out of revenge;

Resolved, Never to do anything which I should be afraid to do if it were the last hour of my life.

The True Foundation (493).

It will not do for any man to build his hopes of heaven on anything but the foundation of an implicit faith in the atoning work of Jesus Christ. The story is told of a man who dreamed that he constructed a ladder from earth to heaven, and that, whenever he did a good deed, his ladder went up two feet. When he did a very good deed his ladder went higher, and when he gave away large sums of money to the poor, it went up further still. By-and-by, it went out of sight, and as years rolled on, it went up, he thought, past the clouds clear into heaven. The man expected that when he died he would step off his ladder into heaven, but he heard a voice thunder from Paradise, "He that climbeth up some other way, the same is a thief and a robber." Down the man came, ladder and all, and he awoke. He then realized that if he wanted to be saved he must obtain salvation in another way than by good deeds, and he took that other way, which leads past the atoning cross of Jesus Christ.—Selected.

Preparations (494).

This life is but a preparation for the eternal years. When we contemplate life after death from the life before death, a belief in immortality makes the present life more important.—E. F. Sanderson.

Ready (495).

A writer in a recent number of the British Weekly describes the last meeting of Principal Rainy and Dr. Alexander McLaren, in the spring of 1906. It was at the assembly of the United Free Church that they met, and sat for a while together. When they went out a bystander heard their farewell. "Good-by, Rainy," said the younger man. "Good-by," was the reply of Rainy as they shook hands. "It won't be long now," said McLaren. "No, it can't be long now. Good-by." The Jerusalem that is above was in their view, and the peace of it, then very attractive, now laps them round.

A Reminder (496).

The late Cardinal Vaughan wore an iron bracelet on his left arm during the latter part of his life. On the inside of the bracelet were sharp spikes. When the strange ornament was finally adjusted it was fastened by means of a pair of pliers so that it could not be taken off. After his death it was cut off the arm.

Farsightedness (497).

Farsightedness and nearsightedness are both defects in human eye-sight. The same rule obtains in daily living. The man who looks forever into the far future does not see his nearest duty; and the man who sees only the daily routine close about him cannot advance toward larger things. To see life steadily and "see it whole" should be each man's endeavor.—Selected.

Absorbed in Trifles (498).

Awhile ago the newspaper told that a skeleton had been found in the Alps. It proved to be the skeleton of a tourist who was anxious to secure that much-coveted Alpine flower, the edelweiss, but in the attempt to reach it the climber had slipped, with fatal consequences. The flower was evidently in his hand when he slipped. But what did it profit him to gain the flower and lose his life? What will it profit you to grasp your prize and lose your life?—W. L. Watkinson.

Travelers (499).

People who pass the Rothschild mansion in the fashionable quarter of London often notice that the end of one of the cornices is unfinished. One is likely to ask, "Could not the richest man in the world afford to pay for that cornice, or is the lack due simply to carelessness?" The explanation is a very simple yet suggestive one when it is known. Lord Rothschild is an orthodox Jew, and every pious Jew's house, tradition says, must have some part unfinished, to bear testimony to the world that its occupant is only, like Abraham, a pilgrim and a stranger upon the earth. The incomplete cornice on the mansion seems to say to all who hurry by in the streets, bent on amassing worldly wealth, or going along with the maddening crowd in the paths of folly: "This is not Lord Rothschild's home; he is traveling to eternity!" We too should remember that we are travelers. The good Dean Stanley left as an inscription to be placed on his tomb these words: "The end of a traveler on his way to Jerusalem!"—S. S. Times.

Eleventh Hour Repentance (500).

Let us not deceive ourselves about eleventh-hour repentance. For we do not die when and as we would arrange it. "Men think all men mortal but themselves." Men are everywhere arranging to live, not die. They are snatched away from the midst of their ordinary vocation, busy about everything except getting ready to die. Thousands die by accident. Thousands more lie so wrapped in unconsciousness or racked by delirium that no voice of exhortation can reach them. Thousands more cannot, in their last conscious hours, summon up their energies to think or pray, while others are terrorized beyond the capacity for repentance, and seem to be able to harbor no emotion except that of despair.

"The Central America," a huge vessel from California, foundered at sea some time in the fifties. A few survivors were picked up by the crew of a vessel which, stealing through the darkness, was startled to hear voices from the waves. These survivors told a strange tale. When all hope was gone the men rushed to drink. The vessel had on board many successful gold diggers. Of these some in despair flung their gold wildly about the deck, others as wildly scrambled for it. Others still loaded their belts and their pockets with it and went down like lead. The men were crazed; they did not know what they were doing. There was despair in every case; there was no thought of repentance.

Life's True Work and Motive (501).

The fireman who risks his life to save someone in a burning building, the member of the life-saving crew who battles with the waves to rescue a man from drowning, are not thinking of winning a medal from the government, but of saving a human being in peril. So the true servants of the Master, trying to reclaim and uplift the lost and helpless, are moved by pity for the souls of men instead of by any vision of a starry crown for themselves. "Upon His head are many diadems," writes John of the glorified Christ, but it was not seeking these that our Lord came to earth to be a brother to humanity.—Forward.

Christ or the World? (502).

A very frank young woman said: "I would like to belong to the world while I am young and can enjoy life, and then when I am old I would like to belong to the Lord."

An eccentric man once built his house on the extreme western coast of Ireland, because, he said, that he wished to reside next to an American town. He did, in a sense, live next to one, and yet the Atlantic Ocean stretched between. So if we think we are so near being a Christian that we shall be counted in, and yet are serving our idols, we may know that an ocean wider and deeper than the Atlantic rolls between us and our Lord. We must belong to one or the other.—J. M. Bingham.

Prepared to Die (503).

The peace that belongs to a Christian prepared to meet Jesus at a moment's notice, was strikingly shown at the recent railroad wreck on the New York Central at Batavia, N. Y. The people, who were trying to get the men from under the engine which was lying on its side upon the wrecked Pullman sleeper, heard calls for help, but could not find just where the man was lying until he waved a stick through a hole in the wreckage. As quickly as possible they raised him and lifted him out and carefully laid him upon an improvised cot. He said: "Telegraph my brother in Detroit," giving the name, street and number, "and tell him to tell my wife." A moment later he said, with a look of quiet peace: "I am a Christian and I am not afraid to die." They carried him to the hospital and a few hours later he had gone to meet the Judge of all the world.

No Oil In Their Lamps (504).

"They took no oil in their lamps." They made no provision for the time of need which was fast approaching. They permitted earthly pleasures or cares to quiet their fears for the future.

There is an old Eastern fable about a traveler in the Steppes who is attacked by a furious wild beast. To save himself the traveler gets into a dried-up well; but at the bottom of it he sees a dragon with its jaws wide open to devour him. The unhappy man dares not get out for fear of the wild beast, and dares not descend for fear of the dragon, so he catches hold of the branch of a wild plant growing in a crevice of the well. His arms soon grow tired, and he feels that he must soon perish, death waiting for him on either side. But he holds on still: and then he sees two mice, one black and one white, gnawing through the trunk of the wild plant, as they gradually and evenly make their way round it. The plant must soon give way, break off, and he must fall into the jaws of the dragon. The traveler sees this, and knows that he will inevitably perish; but, while still hanging on, he looks around him, and, finding some drops of honey on the leaves of the wild plant, he stretches out his tongue and licks them. After quoting this fable Tolstoy quotes the opening chapters of Ecclesiastes as an expression of this Epicurean escape from the terrible plight in which people find themselves as they awaken to the fact of existence. The issue "consists in recognizing the hopelessness of life, and yet taking advantage of every good in it, in avoiding the sight of the dragon and mice, and in seeking the honey as best we can, especially where there is most of it........"

Such is the way in which most people, who belong to the circle in which I move, reconcile themselves to their fate, and making living possible. They know more of the good than the evil of life from the circumstances of their position, and their blunted moral perceptions enable them to forget that all their advantages are accidental......The dullness of their imaginations enables these men to forget what destroyed the peace of Buddha, the inevitable sickness, old age, and death, which tomorrow if not today must be the end of all their pleasures.—Selected.

Life A Discipline (505).

Sooner or later we find out that life is not a holiday, but a discipline. Earlier or later we all discover that the world is not a playground; it is quite clear God means it for a school. The moment we forget that, the puzzle of life begins. We try to play in school; The Master does not mind that so much for its own sake, for He likes to see His children happy, but in our playing we neglect our lessons. We do not see how much there is to learn, and we do not care, but our Master cares. He has a perfectly overpowering and inexplicable solicitude for our education; and because He loves us, He comes into the school some-times and speaks to us. He may speak very softly and gently, or very loudly. Sometimes a look is enough, and we understand it, like Peter, and go out at once and weep bitterly. Sometimes the voice is like a thunder clap startling a summer night. But one thing we may be sure of—the task He sets us to is never measured by our delinquency. The discipline may seem far less than our desert, or even to our eye ten times more. But it is not measured by these; it is measured by God's love; measured solely that a scholar may be better educated when he arrives at his Father's. The discipline of life is a preparation for meet-ing the Father. When we arrive there to "behold His beauty" we must have the educated eye; and that must be trained here. We must needs much practice—that we shall "see God." That explains life—why God puts man in the crucible, and makes him pure by fire.—Herald & Presbyter.

Time Halts Not (506).

Time halts not! No; it bears thee with its ceaseless roll towards that eternity where hesitation will be forever ended. Death halts not, whose miserable tread is ever advancing alike upon the waiting saint and the poor sinner. Judgment halts not, but moves forward to the appointed day, close in the rear of the last enemy. What is to be the duration of your hesitation? You propose and expect to make the needed preparation for eternity sometime this side of death.—Palmer.

Missing Life's Best (507).

A story runs of a young man who picked up a golden coin lying in the road. Ever after, as he walked along he kept his eyes fastened on the ground in hope of finding another. In the course of a long life he picked up a good deal of gold and silver, but in all these years he never saw the lovely flowers by the wayside, or grassy dell, or mountain peak and silver stream. He caught no glimpse of the blue heaven above or snowy clouds, like angel pillows, telling of the purity beyond. God's stars came out and shone like gems of everlasting hope, but he kept his eyes upon the mud and filth in which he sought the treasure; and when he died, a rich old man, he knew this lovely earth only as a dirty road in which to pick up money as he walked along.

Be Ready For The Call (508).

Some years ago, when Mr. Moody was holding his great meetings in Glasgow, two miners from Coatbridge came into the Inquiry Room; one of them sincerely anxious for his soul's salvation, the other careless and disposed to scoff at his friend for his seriousness, yet accompany-ing him into the after meeting. The next day there was a terrible acci-dent in the mine where the friends were working in the same shift. The roof of the mine had fallen in, crushing into splinters the supporting timbers, and underneath a huge piece of coal one of the two miners lay fatally injured and dying. It was the serious and penitent one of the two. When it was seen that there was no hope of extricating him, he called a few of his mates who had been laboring to get him from under the fallen mass, and spoke to them about their souls.

"Mates, you know I have been a bad man and an irreligious one; but last night I gave my heart to the Lord Jesus Christ, who has forgiven all my sins. I am dying now, and I would to God that you were all as I am in this hour—at peace with God, with all my sins forgiven me." Then, turning to his friend who had been with him in the Inquiry Room, he said to him, especially, "Oh, Willum, a'm so glad I settled it a' last nicht Willum, man, it's gran' to be forgiven. Tak' it yoursel', man, and tak' it the noo'." And with this confession he went home to Christ. —Pentecost.

True Living (509).

Some one once asked a well known author to state, in a few words, his idea of what is the secret of a true life. He responded, "Inviting into it the best things." Could it be more happily expressed? Can there be anything more attractive than a life that maintains this attitude, of inviting and welcoming the best things? And may we not adapt this thought to the vocation of the preacher and the teacher? What is true teaching, if not an invitation to the best things? But it must be in the way of invitation, and not of command. The process of uprooting and destroying the weeds is entirely different from that of cultivating the plant. In the one case, violence, in the other, gentleness; in the one, severity, in the other, patience; in the one, condemnation to death, in the other, nourishment to life. Men are not coerced into being good. They must be shown the way, and invited, not driven, to walk in it.

The gospel of Jesus Christ is a gospel of invitation. "Come" is the keynote, and it is sounded over and over again. To be sure the Saviour could be severe when the occasion demanded. He could call a man a hypocrite and a whited sepulcher to his face if need be, and He could wield a whip of small cords very effectively; but in the most of His work and in the great body of His teaching there runs the sweet-toned chord of invitation. He is the leader, the sympathizer, the guide, but not the driver. This is not the only reason, but it is one of the reasons, why His gospel, which He did not even commit to writing, and which had such an obscure beginning, has so grown and widened in the hearts of men that it promises soon to fill the whole earth.—The Advance.

Opportunities (510).

The issues of life concentrate themselves into a few special points of opportunity. The success and failure of life depend upon whether these opportunities are grasped when they present themselves or whether they are neglected and permitted to pass. Life's greatest opportunities are not like the great ships which sail from the chief ports of the world, which sail and come again and sail at stated intervals from the same ports. The great chances touch once at the pier of our lives, throw out the planks of opportunity over which our feet may pass, ring their signal bells in our ears, and then sail out of the harbor and away into the eternal sea and never come again. The little chances linger and return, but the great chances come and go and never come again. . . . If with illumined sight we could look back over the lives of the people by whom we are surrounded, how many great and rich opportunities would we see that they have permitted to drift by them unimproved!—J. T. McFarland.

Heeding The Divine Voice (511).

We can't choose happiness either for ourselves or for another: we can't tell where that will lie. We can only choose whether we will indulge ourselves in the present moment or whether we will renounce that for the sake of obeying the divine voice within us—for the sake of being true to all the motives that sanctify our lives.—George Eliot.

Ready For The Summons (512).

Our ship was bound for Constantinople. About one hundred miles to the east of Malta the wind dropped, and for three days we experienced a dead calm. The sails idly flapped against the masts as the ship slowly rolled from side to side. I had gone below to dinner with my three fellow midshipmen. We had just commenced our pea-soup and salt pork when the captain's voice was heard, "All hands on deck. Furl sails." And looking down to our cabin he said, "Now youngsters, up on deck. Look alive!"

"What could this order mean? Why, there's no wind. Not a cloud to be seen. Wish there was." We soon had our wish. It was no use discussing the "why." We had to obey. My work was to furl the mainroyal sail. When up aloft, I saw a jet black cloud on the western horizon. It rose rapidly. Beneath it was a white line. We were evidently in for a white squall. Hurriedly the sails were furled. By this time one-third of the sky was clouded over. The captain and officers were looking anxious.

About half a mile astern of us was a brig. All her sails were set. Evidently the coming squall had not been noticed, and was unprepared for. Only a few minutes before the squall struck her, we saw the crew hurrying aloft to furl the sails. At that moment a flash of lightning struck the brig, and we heard afterwards that four of the crew, who were furling the foretopsail, were struck and fell to the deck, charred corpses. The next moment we lost sight of her and thought she had foundered. A minute more and the hurricane struck us.

How was it our captain had expected the tempest, when there was no cloud to be seen, and no wind to be felt? Passing the barometer in his cabin he noticed that the mercury was rapidly falling, and was sure a storm was coming, and hence the order, "All hands on deck. Furl all sails." Here were two vessels near each other, yet how differently commanded! If on a voyage, in which ship and under which of these captains would you like to be? Your reply at once is, "Under the captain on the lookout, and in the ship prepared for the storm."

Apply this true narrative to yourself. We are on a voyage from Time to Eternity. A greater tempest is nearing. Your sky may be just now unclouded. No storm in sight. You may be saying, "Take thine ease, eat, drink, and be merry" (Lk. 12:19). "Foolish one, this night thy soul (life) shall (or may) be required of thee."—Scottish Monthly Visitor.

Two Surprises (513).

There are two surprises, one may venture to think, which await us in the day when the Lord returns to make his reckoning with his servants. One the place of honor given to plain, simple men and women, who put a great spirit of service into humble opportunities; the other the tragic shame of multitudes of feeble, self-centered, respectable people who buried their talents in dull and complacent routine.—Cosmo Gordon Lang.

Observing The Tide (514).

At one of the big summer resorts on the west coast of England, where hundreds of bathers enjoy the surf, there is a watchman stationed in a tower on the roof of the hotel. His sole duty is to observe the tide. After the tide has turned, and is on the ebb, there comes a time when the undertow will sweep the strongest swimmers from their feet, carrying them beneath the surface and out to sea. The watchman knows when the dangerous time is at hand, and he rings a great bell to warn all concerned. Across the miles of sand beach the peal of the danger bell goes. When the bathers hear it, they turn at once to the shore. If one should say, "Just five minutes more of this fun, and then I will go out," he would be covenanting with death, for the bell demands instant obedience. There have been cases of disobedience, and always the result has been loss of life. Notices are placed in conspicuous positions calling attention to the importance of instantly leaving the water when the bell rings, and announcing that the refusal to do this clears the authorities of blame in case of accident.

In the moral life of all, the warning of conscience sounds the danger note. It bids us seek safety. The undertow of temptation is not to be trifled with. Security lies in avoiding it, under the warning of the voice of conscience. When we refuse to obey, disaster will follow, and the loss will be our own fault.—The Quiver.

"I Theekit Ma Hoosie In The Calm Weather" (515).

All day long the snow had fallen, as if with quiet, steady purpose. As the light faded, the wind rose, and rose till the night was one of the wildest. In each little house on the countryside the inmates knew that they were cut off from their neighbors, and that that night there could be neither coming nor going. Light after light in the little village went out, and all was dark. Yet, though it was now near midnight, there was one window—had there been any one but God to see it—in which still shone a light. It was in the farmhouse high on the hillside. For within an old man lies dying. Late in the evening he had taken a turn for the worse, and the daughter began to be afraid, knowing that on such a night she could send for no one, either doctor or minister, and feared she might have to face the Angel alone. Hour after hour she watched and waited. She looked on the gray locks that had once been black as the raven, on the pale cheeks once red as berries, on the strong, straight nose that still spoke to her of all his strength and uprightness. Never again, she murmured to herself, would she see him in the little church, bearing the vessels of the Lord—the tallest, dearest figure among all.

"Father," she said at length, "wull I read a chapter to ye?"

But the old man was in sore pain, and only moaned. She rose, however, and got the Book and opened it.

"Father," she said again, "what chapter wull I read to ye?"

"Na, na, lassie," he said, "the storm's up noo; I theekit (thatched) my hoosie in the calm weather."

And thereafter she waited without fear.—J. X. L., in the British Weekly.

High Standards (516).

No human being has ever attained to such high standards of living that there was nothing higher to work for. What a blessing this is! For there is no such joy in life as the reaching out after high standards and working toward them. Those who are content to live by any lower standard than the highest that they can conceive of, know nothing of the real zest and joy of life, of course. "Aren't your high standards sometimes a strain?" was asked of a man who was making an effort to move toward such standards. "No, indeed," was the instant reply; "it's low standards that make the strain." Those who are closest to God show the real strain in life is the tug of pulling away from God. The more nearly we get into oneness with Him and His will, the more completely we have God and the universe working with us, instead of against us. It is the way of the transgressor that is hard. Christ's yoke is the only strain-easing harness we can ever wear. But we can always discover ways of fitting our lives into it more perfectly, and this is His never-ceasing invitation to greater joy.—Examiner.

The Whole Matter Settled (517).—The child of God who has settled the question of salvation may well rest in quietness, knowing that all is well. The man whose future is a great uncertainty is guilty of folly if he lies down at ease and thrusts his peril from his mind.

No Difference (518).

To us all, under average conditions, come the same strength of youth, the same decay of old age. And after the usual span of years we are returned punctually to mother earth.

> Scepter and crown must tumble down;
> And in the dust be equal laid
> With the poor crooked scythe and spade.

While we are above ground, nature deals out a good deal of equality amongst us. The qualities of things are entirely democratic. If an emperor runs his head against a stone wall he will get from it precisely the same reception as if he were a laborer. A rope will hang you or water will drown you without the slightest reference to your social position. An orange will taste the same in the mouth of a millionaire as in that of a bootblack. If there is any difference it will be in favor of the bootblack. Sea-sickness will upset a duke in the same brutal way as a day-tripper. In the king's palace as in the shepherd's hut love and hate, fear and hope, the joy of achievement and the pang of disappointment are the same things, and make themselves felt just in the same way. We might trace the similarity in a thousand ways. This is the democracy, the equality of nature.—J. Brierly.

Caring For The Vineyard (519).

The story is told of a man of large wealth who lived most of the year in a country home among the hills of Vermont, in America. All his inheritance and surroundings were those of culture and luxury. All the temptations of wealth drew him toward ease and selfishness. But instead of that he was known in the little church of the place, and throughout the neighborhood, as a self-sacrificing, hard-working, consecrated Christian. One day a minister who visited the church asked him how he came to throw himself so heartily into Christian work. His answer was quaint but striking:

"When I became a Christian, and began to read my Bible with appreciation of its meaning, I read that I was called into the vineyard of the Lord; and I made up my mind at once that I was not called there to eat grapes, but to hoe, and I've been trying to hoe ever since!"

The man with the hoe is needed in every church. Those Christians who come into the Lord's vineyard and have no idea of doing anything, are usually in the majority. "I've joined the church," said such a man to his pastor, "and I feel that I am saved. But you'll have to excuse me from coming to prayer meetings, or taking up Sunday-school work. I'm too busy." All he wanted was the grapes. He let other members do the hoeing. How much blessing and strength does a Christian like that get? How much are we getting—and is the reason of our lack entirely unconnected with a lack of hoeing?—Selected.

Aim High (520).

Some men are afraid of being too religious. What we need today is men who believe deep down in their souls what they profess. The world is tired and sick of sham. Let your whole heart be given up to God's service. Aim high. God wants us all to be his ambassadors. It is a position higher than that of any monarch on earth to be a herald of the cross, but you must be filled with the Holy Spirit. A great many people are afraid to be filled with the Spirit of God— afraid of being called fanatics. You are not good for anything until the world considers you a fanatic. Fox said that every Quaker ought to shake the country ten miles around. What does the Scripture say? "One shall chase a thousand, and two shall put ten thousand to flight." It takes about a thousand to chase one now. Why? Because they are afraid of being too religious. What does this world want today? Men— men that are out and out for God and not half-hearted in their allegiance and service.—Moody.

Our Business Is To Live (521).

At a private meeting of friends, on one occasion, George Whitefield, after referring to the difficulties attending the gospel ministry, said he was weary of the burdens of the day, and was glad that in a short time his work would be done, and he should depart to be with Christ. All present owned to having the same feeling, with the exception of Mr. Tennant. On seeing this, Mr. Whitefield, tapping him on the knees, said, "Well, Brother Tennant, you are the oldest man among us; do you not rejoice to think that your time is so near at hand when you will be called home?" Mr. Tennant replied that he had no wish about it. Being pressed for something more definite, he added, "I have nothing to do with death. My business is to live as long as I can, and as well as I can, and serve my Master as faithfully as I can, until He shall think proper to call me home."—S. S. Times.

Change Revealing the Unchanging (522).

It is maddening to think of the sure decay and dissolution of all human strength, beauty, wisdom, unless that thought brings with it immediately, like a pair of coupled stars, of which the one is bright and the other dark, the corresponding thought of that which does not pass, and is unaffected by time and change. Just as reason requires some unalterable substratum, below all the fleeting phenomena of the changeful creation, a God who is the rock-basis of all, the staple to which all the links hang, so we are driven back and back and back, by the very fact of the transiency of the transient, to grasp, for a refuge and a stay, the permanency of the Permanent.

But that conception of the meaning of each event that befalls us carries with it the conception of the whole of this life as being an education towards another. I do not understand how any man can bear to live here, and to do all his painful work, unless he thinks that by it he is getting ready for the life beyond, and that "nothing can bereave him of the force he made his own, being here." The rough ore is turned into steel by being

> "Plunged in baths of hissing tears,
> And heated hot with hopes and fears,
> And battered with the shocks of doom."

And then—what then? Is an instrument thus fashioned and tempered and polished destined to be broken and "thrown as rubbish into the void?" Certainly not. If this life is education, as is obvious upon its very face, then there is a place where we shall exercise the facilities that we have acquired here, and manifest in loftier forms the characters which here we have made our own.—Alexander Maclaren, D. D.

Casting Out The Rubbish (523).

When we turn out our rooms, our libraries, we are continually astonished at the rubbish we have allowed to gather, rubbish that has crowded out so much better things. The life record often shows worse than that of the rooms. The supreme effort here should be to gather and find house room only for the best. It is thus we can make life interesting to the last moment. Some of the chief occupations today are occupations which store nothing. What inner accumulation comes from spending six nights in the week at bridge whist? A scientific ordering of life will be largely a science of accumulation. We shall settle with ourselves what things are to be sought and retained, and what treated as negligible.—J. Brierley, in Religion and Experience.

Dust To Dust (524).

In Schliemann's excavations among the ruins of Mycenae, he came upon a royal tomb. The noble rank of its inmate was betrayed by many infallible tokens, but chiefly by a golden mask, a rusted sword and a dented shield. He concluded that this was the grave of Agamemnon, who was known as the King of Men. The mask was here, but where was the face? The sword was here, but where was the hand that held it? The shield was here but where was Agamemnon's right arm? A handful of dust.

Lighting The Lamps (525).

A child riding with his mother on a railroad train noticed the porter lighting the lamps in the car in the middle of the day. "Why does he do that?" he asked his mother. "Wait a minute and you will see," she answered. Presently, with no warning, the train dashed into a long, black tunnel, threading the mountain-top. No time then for lighting the lamps, but great need for their light. In the dash and roar of our hurrying lives, some of us are too busy to enter this Word for its light. In the dark of the day that is coming to us all, what shall we do?"—Selected.

How Shall I Make the Most of Life? (526).

"To be or not to be, that is the question," quoted a young man who was utterly discouraged with life. The answer of his friend, was: "That is not the question at all. The question whether we are to be or not is a question we were not asked in the beginning, and have no right to raise. We can not discuss it with knowledge either of the joys that remain or the duties that are impending, nor yet the future shame that awaits us in some after life for the cowardly shirking of the burdens of this one.

" 'To be or not to be' is the question of the stage, propounded by a half-crazed character in a plot. The question of the real man on the stage of life, is, 'Being, how shall I make the most of life?' For we are, whether we like it or not; and we have no right but to be, and to be the most and best we can. Life is a discipline, it is not given us for our own pleasure alone, nor can any man live it or end it and affect himself alone. Life is the gift of God; and no man liveth unto himself, and no man dieth unto himself. Life is before you, long years of it, I hope. Duties are before you, earth is before you, with needs and hopes and sorrows, sorrows needing your strength and com-

fort. Whether you shall be or not is God's question, and for the pres
ent you know His answer. Your question is what you shall be, and
how."—The Youth's Companion.

Not Abusing the World (527).

Living in a perishing world, we are to use it, not abuse it. All
its forces we are to subdue, and to make them contribute to the comfort and general well-being of society. This involves struggle, but the
struggle is for man's betterment. Everything is to serve us, if we are
wise enough to see it so. Nothing is meaningless that God has made.
The end of all things, in our relation to them, is that they be made
subordinate to the opening-out of the soul's best life here and forever.—
The Lutheran Observer.

The Loom of Life (528).

It is a solemn thought, that every one of us carries about with
him a mystical loom, and we are always weaving—weave, weave, weaving—this robe which we wear, every thought a thread of the warp,
every action a thread of the weft. We weave it, as the spider does
its web, out of its own entrails, if I might so say. We weave it, and
we dye it, and we cut it, and we stitch it, and then we put it on and
wear it, and it sticks to us. . . . . . .   A man is known by the
company he keeps, and if your friends are picked out for other reasons,
and their religion is no part of their attraction, it is not an unfair conclusion that there are other things for which you care more than you do
for faith in Jesus Christ and love to Him. If you deeply feel the bond
that knits you to Christ, and really live near to Him, you will be near
your brethren. You will feel that "blood is thicker than water," and however like you may be to irreligious people in many things, you will feel
that the deepest bond of all knits you to the poorest, the most ignorant,
the most unlike you in social position;—aye! and the most unlike you in
theological opinion, that love the Lord Jesus Christ in sincerity.—Alexander Maclaren.

The Flight of Time (529).

He, who has found upon earth the city of his affections, and who
with every onward step is only advancing toward a mist, may well
look upon New Year's day as a day of sorrow. Well may it be a dark
and gloomy day to the man who, as a poor and humble pilgrim, is
journeying to some royal city where he has not a single friend to welcome his arrival or offer him the shelter of a roof. A poor and humble
pilgrim am I; but, God be thanked, I know of One who long ago prepared for me a place. Hence it is that as I pass the milestones, each
in succession becomes an altar, on which I present oblations of gratitude and praise. There are many, I am aware, to whom the thought
of flight of time is dispiriting. For me, I feel that He hath not given
the spirit of fear, but of power.—Tholuck.

Wasting Life (530).

I know an idiot boy who spent his life in spinning a top. No doubt that boy in his dim consciousness passed through all our mortal experiences. He had his good days and his bad days, and sometimes when he went home he had the experience of one who had won a battle, and sometimes the experience of one who had lost a battle. But there is something strangely incomplete and pathetic, spending the whole of life in spinning a top. But if there were no larger significance in life than "what shall we eat or what shall we drink, or wherewithal shall we be clothed," if it were not more than that, then that idiot boy with his top was a striking picture of the race. What are we all doing but spinning tops? The tops vary, some are big and some are small; some have more gilt than others. What is the whole universe, but a great scene of empty top-spinning? The whirling suns, the stars in their courses, the planets in their movements—what are they all but colossal tops driven by idiotic forces, through eternities, in aimless cycles? Ah, if there be no intelligence in the world, no spirituality in its government, no great issue to it all, then it is a scene of pathetic emptiness, failure and despair! Only a larger interpretation of life will satisfy you. Life is utterly disappointing and incomplete without spiritual ideals, principles, ideas, and hopes. Man without spiritual instincts is always asking, Is life worth while? The man who whips his top for seventy years and keeps it going with sweat and blood, until the hum of the top dies in the silence of the graves, ought to be discontented with such a life. Discontent is the only natural thing in the universe if there are in life no deep moral purposes and no spiritual consequences; but it is another thing if the spiritual note is brought into it. The Church if Christ does not ask, "Is life worth living?" Life in the hand of a spiritual man is linked in with a larger education. It is a discipline out of which you come kings, and it leads you into a larger and imperishable inheritance. To the worldly man life is a blunder, a jest, a tragedy; to the spiritual man a discipline, a science, a triumph. The spiritual life that lasts is the real life. The spiritual instincts survive all changes. Without the spiritual instincts life is an unsolvable problem. But given to you the love of God, the sense of His wise government, and the assurance that the afflictions of the present time will work out for you a far more exceeding and an eternal weight of glory, and you will find rest unto your soul.—Condensed from an article on "The Life Indeed," by Dr. W. L. Watkinson, in Homiletic Review.

Making the Most of Life (531).

If you asked yourself or anyone else, Is it a matter of absolute indifference to God what results from your life? you would be answered that it is impossible to conceive of God at all without supposing that He desires every human life to serve some good purpose. This, at all events, is Christ's view. This is what made His life what it was, influential to all time, and the unfailing source of the highest energy to all other lives. That is to say, He has given us the most cogent of all demonstrations that in proportion as we accept his view of the connection of our life with God shall we resemble Him in the utility and permanent result of all we do. It has become obvious that in the world of nature nothing is isolated and independent, that all nature is one whole, governed by one idea and fulfilling one purpose. Human lives are under the same law. No life is outside of the plan which comprehends the whole; every life contributes something to the fulfillment of the great purpose all are to serve. Our Lord tells us that this purpose is in the mind of God, and that He judges us by our fulfillment or nonfulfillment of His will. And that we should be reluctant to bring forth fruit to God or hesitate to live for Him has its root in the foolish idea that God and we have opposing interests, so that to help out God's idea of the world and to work with Him and toward His end is really not our best. Nothing seems enough to teach us that God is all on our side and that He has laid up for us abundant provision for feeling and thought and for spiritual strength and joy.— From "Footsteps in the Path of Life."

Ready for the Bridegroom (532).

Both the wise and the foolish virgins started out in readiness for the bridegroom's coming with their lamps trimmed and burning, but only the wise were found in the end with a supply of oil sufficient to last. The bridegroom came unexpectedly; there was no time after His coming was heralded to make preparations. What does the oil symbolize? In Old Testament times priests and kings were set apart for their office by having their heads anointed with oil. The word Messiah means the anointed One. "Zechariah saw in vision a golden lamp-stand with seven lamps, and on either side of it an olive tree, from which oil flowed through golden pipes to feed the flame. The interpretation of the vision was given by 'the angel that talked with' the prophet as being 'not by might nor by power, but by my spirit, saith the Lord.' So we follow the plainly marked road and Scripture use of the symbol when we take the oil in the parable to be the sum of the influences from Heaven which were bestowed through the spirit of the Lord. The lamp is the spiritual life of the individual, which is nourished and made visible to the world as light, by the continual communicating from God of these hallowing influences." This interpretation is from the pen of Doctor Maclaren, as also this lesson: "All spiritual emotions and vitality, like every other kind of emotion and vitality, die unless nourished. There is nothing in our religious emotions which have any guarantee of perpetuity in it, except upon certain conditions. We may live, and our life may ebb. We may trust, and our trust may tremble into unbelief. We may obey, and our obedience may be broken by the mutinous risings of self-will. We may walk in the 'paths of righteousness,' and our feet may falter and turn aside. There is certainty of the dying out of all communicated life, unless the channel of communication with the life from which it was first kindled, be kept constantly clear. The lamp may be 'a burning and a shining light,' but it will be light 'for a season' only, unless it is fed from that from which it was first set alight; and that is from God Himself."—Tarbell.

Keep the Fires Burning (533).

Dr John Robertson tells of a Scotch village where, years ago, all the hearthfires had gone out. It was before the days of matches. The only way to rekindle the fires was to find some hearth where the fire was yet aglow. Their search was fruitless until at last they found a flaming hearth away up on the hill. One by one they came to this hearth and lighted their peat, put it carefully in the pan, shielding it from the wind, and the fires were soon burning again throughout the community.

Are the fires getting low in your heart? Has the chill of worldliness settled down upon you? God has plenty of fire on the hill. Climb up into His presence through the path of surrender, and He will take the live coal from the altar and lay it upon your heart and upon your lips. This is the fullness of the Holy Ghost. This is the passion for souls.—The Standard.

Eternity in the Heart (534).

These things which, even in their time of beauty, are not enough for a man's soul—have all but a time to be beautiful in, and then they fade and die. A great botanist made what he called "a floral clock" to mark the hours of the day by the opening and closing of flowers. It was a graceful and yet a pathetic thought. One after another they spread their petals, and their varying colors glow in the light. But one after another they wearily shut their cups, and the night falls, and the latest of them folds itself together, and all are hidden away in the dark. So our joys and treasures, were they sufficient did they last, cannot last. After a summer's day comes a summer's night, and after a brief space of them comes winter, when all are killed and the leafless trees stand silent,

"Bare, ruined choirs, where late the sweet birds sang."

We cleave to these temporal possessions and joys, and the natural law of change sweeps them away from us one by one. Most of them do not last so long as we do, and they pain us when they pass away from us. Some of them last longer than we do, and they pain us when we pass away from them. Either way our hold of them is a transient hold, and one knows not whether is the sadder—the bare garden beds where all have done blowing, and nothing remains but a tangle of decay, or the blooming beauty from which a man is summoned away, leaving others to reap what he has sown. Tragic enough are both at the best—and certain to befall us all. We live and they fade; we die and they remain. We live again and they are far away. The facts are so. We may make them a joy or a sorrow as we will.—Alexander Maclaren, D. D.

ILLUSTRATIVE VERSES.

Ready (535).

The Master will knock at my door some night,
  And there in the silence hushed and dim
Will wait for my coming with lamp alight
  To open immediately to Him.

. . . . .

If this is the only thing foretold
  Of all my future, then I pray
That quietly watchful I may hold
  The key of a golden faith each day
Fast shut in my grasp, that, when I hear
  His step, be it at dawn or midnight dim,
Straightway may I rise without a fear,
  And open immediately to Him.

—Margaret J. Preston.

The Two Villages (536).

Over the river, on the hill
Lieth a village white and still;
All around it the forest trees
Shiver and whisper in the breeze;
Over it sailing shadows go
Of soaring hawk and screaming crow,
And mountain grasses, low and sweet,
Grow in the middle of every street.

Over the river, under the hill,
Another village lieth still;
There I see in the cloudy night
Twinkling stars of household light,
Fires that gleam from the smithy's door,
Mists that curl on the river's shore;
And in the road no grasses grow,
For the wheels that hasten to and fro.

In that village on the hill,
Never is sound of smithy or mill;
The houses are thatched with grass and flowers,
Never a clock to tell the hours;
The marble doors are always shut,
You may not enter at hall or hut;
All the village lie asleep;
Never again to sow or reap;
Never in dreams to moan or sigh,
Silent, and idle, and low they lie.

In that village under the hill,
When the night is starry and still,
Many a weary soul in prayer,
Looks to the other village there,
And weeping and sighing, longs to go
Up to that home from this below;
Longs to sleep by the forest wild,
Whither have vanished wife and child,
And heareth, praying, his answer fall,
"Patience! that village shall hold ye all!"

—Rose Terry Cook.

In His Steps (537).

Dear Master, in thy footsteps let us go,
Till with thy presence all our lives shall glow,
And souls through us thy resurrection know.
   Alleluia, Christ is arisen!

—Lucy Larcom.

Singing Cross-Bearers (538).

Not on the towering mountain-peak
  Crest-crowned with fiery glow
Do men the earth's rich harvests seek,
  But in deep vales below.

Not for some glaring high emprise
  Seek thou far-soaring wings;
That faith is noblest in God's eyes
  That bears a cross—and sings.

Girded Wayfarers (539).

Silent, like men in solemn haste,
Girded wayfarers of the waste,
We pass out at the world's wide gate,
Turning our back on all its state;
We press along the narrow road
That leads to life, to bliss, to God.

—Horatius Bonar.

Weaving (540).

Children of yesterday, heirs of tomorrow,
What are you weaving? Labor and sorrow?
Look to your looms again: Faster and faster
Fly the great shuttles prepared by the Master,
Life's in the loom: Room for it! Room!

Children of yesterday, heirs of tomorrow,
Lighten the labor and sweeten the sorrow;
Now, while the shuttles fly faster and faster,
Up, and be at it. At work with the Master.
He stands at your loom: Room for Him! Room!

Children of yesterday, heirs of tomorrow
Look at your fabric of labor and sorrow,
Seamy and dark with despair and disaster,
Turn it—and lo! The design of the Master.
The Lord's at the loom.
Room for Him! Room!

The Reaping (541).

The tissue of the life to be
We weave with colors all our own
And in the field of destiny
We reap as we have sown.

—Whittier.

A Prayer (542).

When on my day of life the night is falling,
And, by the winds from unsunned spaces blown,
I hear far voices out of darkness calling
My feet to paths unknown.

Thou who hast made my house of life so pleasant,
Leave not its tenant when its walls decay;
O Love Divine, O Helper ever present,
Be thou my strength and stay.

Be near me when all else is from me drifting,
Earth, sky, home's pictures, days of shade and shine,
And kindly faces to my own uplifting
The love which answers mine.

I have but thee, my Father! let thy spirit
Be with me then to comfort and uphold;
No gate of pearl, no branch of palm I merit,
Nor street of shining gold.

Suffice it if, my good and ill unreckoned,
And both forgiven through thy abounding grace,
I find myself by hands familiar beckoned
Unto my fitting place:

Some humble door among thy many mansions,
Some sheltering shade where sin and striving cease,
And flows forever through heaven's green expansions
The river of thy peace.

—John G. Whittier.

The Daily Praise (543).

O, what is life?
A toil, a strife,
Were it not lighted by thy love divine.
I ask not wealth,
I crave not health:
Living or dying, Lord, I would be thine!

O, what is death
When the poor breath
In parting can the soul to thee resign?
While patient love
Her trust doth prove,
Living or dying, Lord, I would be thine!

Throughout my days,
Be constant praise
Uplift to thee from out this heart of mine;
So shall I be
Brought nearer thee;
Living or dying, Lord, I would be thine!

—Fenelon.

As a Tale That Is Told (544).

Forenoon and afternoon and night, forenoon
And afternoon and night—
Forenoon and—what!
The empty song repeats itself.   No more
Yea, that is life: make this forenoon sublime,
This afternoon a psalm, this night a prayer,
And Time is conquered, and thy crown is won!

—E. R. Sill.

"Twilight and Evening Bell" (545).

We are growing old, brother, side by side.
Let us pray for one another, God will guide,
For the love that in the dawning,
Filled with glory all the morning,
Is the changeless love of Christ that will abide.

We are growing older, brother, time is short.
Let the work that we have willed to do be wrought,
Let the hand of help be given,
Speak the word of God and heaven,
Keep the spirit sweet and tender as we ought.

We are growing older, brother, but the way
Has been bright with grace, and glory, day by day,
And the storms of life that found us,
Put the strength of God around us,
Though our eyes were dimmed a little by the spray.

We are growing older, brother, closer press,
For the sunset heart must need the soft caress.
Often when the stars are burning,
Come the mem'ries and the yearning
For the high and holy hearts that used to bless.

We are growing older, brother, so they say.
Just a little wrinkled now, and getting gray,
  But the outward is the seeming,
  They who speak to us are dreaming,
Youth immortal crowns us in the perfect day.

We are growing older, brother; earth is dressed
In no colors like the country of the blest,
  And the one who walks beside us,
  Jesus Christ, the good, will guide us
Till we find the Father's face and there we rest.

We are growing older, brother, even so;
Though the twilight bells are ringing soft and low,
  Richest gifts of earth are given,
  And a welcome waits in heaven,
To the Father's friends and friendship do we go.

—Selected.

My Wish (546).

Let me but live my life from year to year
  With forward face and unreluctant soul,
  Not hastening to nor turning from the goal;
Not mourning for the things that disappear
In the dim past, nor holding back in fear
  From what the future veils; but with a whole
  And happy heart, that pays its toll
To Youth and Age, and travels on with cheer.

—Henry van Dyke

Be Ready (547).

"Be ready in the morning!"—
  This was thy voice, O Lord,
To Moses in the desert,
  First penman of thy word.
Thou badst him up the mountain
  To meet thee face to face,
There learn directly from thee
  What laws should rule our race.

"No man shall come up with thee;"
  Alone thou mad'st him climb
That rugged brow of Sinai,
  Majestic through all time.
What tongue can tell his trembling.
  When, leaving all behind,
Alone, alone, he ventured
  To meet the Eternal Mind!

"Be ready in the morning!"
  Teach us these words to hear,
For we must shortly face thee
  With triumph or with fear.
Prepare our hearts to meet thee
  As children of thy love;
Then step by step we'll journey
  To holier heights above.

"No man shall come up with thee!"
  Alone. O God, alone,
We know that we must travel
  Into the vast unknown.
Prepare us for that morning,
  To meet thee all alone;
Aid us to climb the future,
  Alone, great God, alone!

—selected.

Say Not "Another Day" (548).

There is a nest of thrushes in the glen;
  When we come back we'll see the glad young thmgs,"
He said. We came not by that way again;
  And time and thrushes fare on eager wings!

"Yon rose," she smiled. "But no; when we return,
  I'll pluck it then." 'Twas on a summer day.
The ashes of the rose in autumn's urn
  Lie hidden well. We came not back that way.

Thou traveler to the unknown ocean's brink,
  Through life's fair field, say not, "Another day
This joy I'll prove"; for never, as I think,
  Never shall we come this selfsame way.

Service (549).

Do something! Do it now! The work which lies
  Close to your hand this moment is the best—
His choice for you—the choice that must be wise;
  Then do your duty, and forget the rest.

—Edith Hickman Divall.

In God's Eyes (550).

One was a king they told me,
  And one was a common clod—
Stripped of their outward seeming,
  How will they look to God?

For one there was blare of trumpets,
  For the other no acclaim—
When God inscribes his records,
  How will he write each name?

Men praised the royal purple
  And scorned the common stole—
Does God in the life eternal
  See aught but the naked soul?

—Susie M. Best.

If I Should Meet the Lord Today (551).

I mind me what He said that day
  I, idling, met Him in the path,
  Not careless speaking, nor in wrath:
"Go, labor in My field today"—
I mind me what He said that day.

If I should meet the Lord today,
  Walking among His harvest sheaves,
  Would He ask, "Have you aught but leaves?"
And if He asked, what could I say,
If I should meet Him in the way?
The summer-time is gone today,
  The harvest-fields are sere and brown,
  Not light but heavy heads hang down—
Sheaves I have gathered, could I say,
If I should meet the Lord today?

—David H. Ela.

TEXTS AND TREATMENT HINTS.

What Is Your Life?—James 4:14 (552).

I. It is a gift. This means responsibility.

II. It is a preparation. It means getting ready for something.

III. It is a conflict.

IV. It is a test. A new ship has a trial trip. A boy has to go at first as an apprentice.

V. It is an uncertainty. How long will you live? Will you make a success of your life? You must decide what you will do. Your life can not be bought with money. What will you do with it? It is too precious for you alone to care for. Give it to Jesus. He will make it glorious.—Homiletic Review.

"Be Thou Faithful Unto Death, and I Will Give Thee a Crown of Life."— Rev. 2:10 (553).

Faithfulness is the main distinction of the noblest and best of all these angels of Christ's Church. The high moral excellence of honorably discharging the duties which were assigned to them is obviously made by our Lord the great principle and test of acceptable service. These words of the Master mean—

I. Faithfulness to the human heart. We sometimes make mistakes by not listening to what our hearts tell us about our fellow men.

II. Faithfulness to the conscience. The spirit that overcomes the world is the spirit of Christ. It is only when we arm the soul with the same mind that was in Him, only when we take up the cross to follow Him even to Calvary, and there to suffer with Him, that we can gain the victory. He has promised victory to him that overcometh.

III. Faithfulness to our Master and His word under all circumstances. We may be forgotten by our fellows, hidden from all eyes but His; we may have no sympathy from companions, no cheering words from comrades in the fight; we may even hear nothing further on this score from the great Captain of our salvation. But we must be faithful unto death in our spirit, our trust, our obedience, and our love.—H. R. Reynolds.

"To Him that Overcometh Will I Give a......New Name, Which No Man Knoweth Saving He that Receiveth it."—Rev. 2:17 (554).

I. Note the large hopes which gather round this promise of a new name. (1) The new name means new vision; (2) it means new activities; (3) it means new purity; (4) it means new joys.

II. Look at the connection between Christ's new name and ours. Our new name is Christ's new name stamped upon us. On the day of the bridal of the Lamb and the Church the bride takes her Husband's name.

III. Note the blessed secret of this new name. There is only one way to know the highest things of human experience, and that is by possessing them.

IV. Note the giving of the new name to the victors. The renovation of the being and efflorescence into new knowledge, activities, perfections, and joys, is only possible on condition of the earthly life of obedience, and service, and conquest.—A. Maclaren.

"I....Have the Keys of Hell and Death."—Rev. 1:18 (555).

The text shows—

I. That we must look higher than a natural agency for the account of the death of a single individual. Of course here, as in other departments of His administration, our Lord walks by second causes. Disease, violence, and natural decay are His instrumentality. But who calls the instrumentality into play? Who sets it at work? Who first touches the hidden spring? Undoubtedly the great Redeemer. Death is a solemn thing, a thing of vast moment, and cannot be decreed except immediately by Him. The key is in His hand exclusively.

II. Again, death is often regarded in the mass, and on a large scale, a view which derogates altogether from its awfulness and solemnity. Death is the transaction of an Individual with an individual, of Christ the Lord with one single member of the human family. For every individual the dark door turns afresh upon its hinges.

III. Death is in no way the result of chance. The death of each person is predestined and forearranged. Christ Himself trod the dark avenue of death; He Himself passed into the realm of the unseen. There are His footsteps all along the path, even where the shadows gather thickest round it, as there were the footsteps of the priests all along the deepest bed of Jordan. "Though I walk through the valley of the shadow of death, I will fear no evil, for Thou art with me."—Garlburn.

"Establish Thou the Work of our Hands."—Ps. 90:17 (556).

Feelings pass, thoughts and imaginations pass: Dreams pass: Work remains. Through eternity, what you have done, that you are. They tell us that not a sound has ever ceased to vibrate through space; that not a ripple has ever been lost upon the ocean. Much more is it true that not a true thought, nor a pure resolve, nor a loving act, has ever gone forth in vain.—Robertson.

"And They Heard a Great Voice from Heaven Saying Unto Them, Come up Hither."—Rev. 11:12 (557).

I. The voice of God comes to us from heaven and says to us, "Come up hither." The new voice of God speaks not to the ear, but to the heart. The whole Bible is a great voice from heaven. Revelation furnishes us with a continuous proof that it is the upward path which God would have us choose from the two that are before us.

II. A second voice that invites us up to heaven is that of our blessed Savior. What was the Redeemer's whole appearance on earth but one earnest, unceasing, lifelong entreaty that men would turn to God.

III. The blessed Spirit, too, adds His voice to that which invites us toward heaven. The whole scope and object of His working is to make us fit for heaven, is an indication of His design and His wish that we should go up thither. The Spirit, the Purifier, as He makes us holier and better, thus fitting us for a clearer atmosphere and a nobler company, is ever whispering within us that it must be a higher life in which virtue will be perfect, and another world in which hearts will be pure.

IV. The voice of our dear friends who have fallen asleep in Jesus invites us to "come up hither." Let us plant our feet on the rock, and take not one step further in the evil way, for tomorrow may end our path, and today is the accepted time.—Selected.

"Be ye also ready."—Matt. 24:44 (559).

I Within the margin of a few years you can definitely prophesy your death. The one certainty.

II. It is a species of insanity for a man to know this and refuse to act upon it.

III. Preparation is simply the whole-hearted acceptance of Christ.

IV. Having done this you can say: "I will fear no evil."

"And Be Ye Yourselves Like Unto Men Looking for their Lord."—Luke 12:36 (560).

I. Christ is coming.

II. Accounting day will be ushered in by His coming.

III. Anticipate and prepare for Him and it.

X. RESURRECTION—IMMORTALITY.

REFLECTIONS AND ILLUSTRATIONS.

A Contrast (562).

Two pictures have recently been described, in which Death appears as a destroyer and as a friend. In the first he comes into a scene of gaiety where revelry and pleasure are at their height. As a cowled and ghastly form he passes through and leaves bodies lying stark and lifeless, while the living flee from him. So he is a destroyer. In the other picture he has come to an aged saint in the church belfry, and has touched him lovingly so that a look of peace is on his face. The window is thrown open and a bird sings its song on the sill. Death has come as a friend to close the hard gates of life, and to open the gates of eternity. It makes all the difference to whom death comes, whether he is destroyer or friend. To him who treads the path to life with Jesus Christ, going toward the tomb with Him until the tomb closes, there is assurance of an opened tomb, and a path that stretches on upward where the foot marks lead away from the grave. There have always been dreams of that life beyond, which has mastered death, but no one save this Christ of the opened tomb has ever come back to bear news of it, and to promise entrance into it.—Selected.

Unanswerable. (563)—"I came from God," said the poet-preacher, George McDonald, "and I am going back to God, and I won't have any gaps of death in the middle of my life."

Homegoing (564).

The old images of death were the skull and cross-bones, the darkened house, the hearse, the black robes of darkness and plumes plucked from the wings of night and gloom. Then came Christ. With one blow He shattered these barbarous conceptions. Dying was homegoing. Death was the door into His Father's house. Here men burn with fever and shiver with cold; yonder is the soul's summerland. Here the tree ripens fruit once a year; there every month. Here men are starved, pinched, dwarfed; there they shall grow. Here reason is a spark; there it will be a flame. Here song has a single note; there it shall deepen into a symphony. Here a man feeds on a crust; there is the fruit of the tree of immortal life. Here he drinks at a broken cistern; there flows the river of the water of life. Shakespeare is the true man in intellect, and of his forty faculties, here starved and seminal, there men shall be Shakespearean, and more, in every one of his gifts, as if a hundred poets and sages and heroes were united into one full-orbed man. Therefore Paul's abandon of joy at the very thought of death.—Hillis.

The Gladness of Hope (565).

We read that in the cities of Russia at the beginning of every Easter day, when the sun is rising, men and women go about the streets greeting one another with the information: "Christ is risen!" Every man knows it; but this is an illustration of how a man, when his heart is full of a thing, wants to tell it to his brethren. He does not care if the brother does know it already; he goes and tells it to him again. And so when the truth of Christ's gospel shall come so home to each and every one of us that all men shall be filled with the glad intelligence, and tell the story of how men are living in the freedom of their heavenly Father, it shall not be needful to have a revival of religion.—Phillips Brooks.

A Mother's Anticipation (566).

I know a mother, who, fifty years ago, stood by the casket that held the body of her firstborn. It was the first great sorrow of life and it crushed her young heart. I looked into her face. I mentioned that fact which occurred fifty years ago. The whole expression changed immediately. There it lived just as it lived fifty years gone by. In the night she wakes up and remembers her darling and waits for the morning hour, and she turns over in the darkness of the night, stains the pillow with her tears and kisses the pillow in imagination as kissing her firstborn. That mother, after half a century, can not be separated from that great moment in life, and she is just living and waiting and chanting this tonight in her old age: "I wonder if she's changed! I wonder how she'll look! I wonder if she'll know me when she sees me! I wonder! I am getting sometimes overanxious to see her!"—Cortland Myers, D. D.

The Resurrection Hope (567).

The very same gospel which sets before the single believer the glorious issue of life, at the same time and by the same message binds up his hope with that of every other believer and, more than that, with destiny of the whole world. It is only by neglecting the resurrection that the Christian can be isolated.—Brooke Foss Westcott.

What's the Use (568).

Some one has put on the market a picture of a human skull, with the words underneath: "What's the Use?" You look into the empty eyesockets and the yawning chasms in what was once a human countenance, and realize that to this same material ruin is coming the physical frame in which we live. In such a mood as fits this thought there comes the querulous, hissing, pessimistic wail, "What's the Use?"

We answer the wail with the rejoinder that there is a great deal of use. We do not expect this body to last forever, but expect to live forever. As long as we live in this body we are called on to live well and wisely. We are to take as good care as possible of the body, so that it may serve its day and end. When it falls into decay and ruin, we shall be able to do without it if we have done in and with it just what we ought to have done.—Lutheran Observer.

Death's Blessings (569).

So under the prospect of the greatest of all farewells God has been pleased to make the world more kindly. Death has touched all relationships and hallowed them. It is the source and the spring of more than half life's gladness. In a father's care, in a mother's love, in the devotion of husband and wife and in the bond of friendship there is a sweet solicitude, a depth, a grasp, a hunger that the world would never have dreamed of but for death.—George H. Morrison.

Two Views of Death (571).

The best thought of the nineteenth century, at least so far as the English race is concerned, is summed up in the poetry of Tennyson and Browning. For each of them the art of poetry was the serious expression and perpetuation of great thoughts,—not the idle song of idle singers. One was the greater artist, the other the greater thinker: which was the greater poet it is perhaps too early to try to say. But the works of both are interesting equally for their resemblances and their contrasts. Both passed through doubt and struggle: both became poets of peace and faith. But how differently their struggles and their victories are expressed!

Perhaps the most interesting of these contrasts is that between the two poems which these men wrote as they looked forward to death,— not merely to death in the abstract, but to the individual poet's end, personally conceived and faced. In each case the poem was actually written near the end of life, and in each case it was intended to stand as the epilogue to the author's works. Tennyson's swan-song is known to everyone. For him death meant "sunset and evening star," a tide "too full for sound or foam," a gentle passing into the great sea, met by a Pilot perfectly trusted. Browning's is less familiar, but no less characteristic as it is no less noble. Passing by the moment of death altogether, he considers what he shall be to his friends when they think of him as departed. Shall they pity him, as imprisoned in darkness after so wide and vigorous a life?

> "No, at noonday in the bustle of man's worktime
>   Greet the unseen with a cheer!
> Bid him forward, breast and back as either should be,
> 'Strive and thrive!' cry 'Speed,—fight on, fare ever
>   There as here.'"

It would be idle to try to claim superiority for either attitude. One represents one mood, the other another. One will best console one man, the other another. For some death is friendliest when thought of as the calm voyage, with full sail spread at sunset, into a stormless though mysterious sea. For others it cannot possibly be welcomed except as giving hope for unstopped, or even freer and fuller, activity.

Guesswork and Proof (572).

Socrates, in the presence of death, exclaimed: "Would that we could more securely and less perilously sail upon a stronger vessel or some divine word!" As David Purves says: "There is no more pathetic utterance of antiquity than this." The true soul wistfully scanning the mysterious waste of waters and fancying that it discerned far away the golden isles, and yet not sufficiently sure as to weigh anchor and launch out into the deep! A syllogism is a frail vessel for so tremendous a venture; a metaphysical theory, a paper-boat to dare the dread abyss. The cry of Socrates was the cry of humanity before the advent, even when it could get as far as this.

The coming of the Lord has changed all this. We have found the stronger vessel in which to sail, the divine word has been spoken to assure our heart. The anchor is ours that will neither snap nor drag. The Pilot is ours who perpetrates no shipwreck, and whose face we shall see when "the tide which drew from out the boundless deep turns again home." The slippery raft of Socrates' conjecture has been exchanged for the Ark of God that cannot founder. The New Testament teaches with a positiveness and triumph all its own.—Watkinson.

W. J. Bryan's Argument (573).

If the Father deigns to touch with divine power the cold and pulseless heart of the buried acorn and make it burst forth from its prison walls, will He leave neglected the soul of man, who was made in the image of his Creator? If He so stoops to give the rosebush, whose withered blossoms float upon the autumn breeze, the sweet assurance of another springtime, will He withhold the words of hope from the souls of men when the frosts of winter come? If matter, mute and inanimate, is changed by force of nature into a multitude of forms that never die, will the spirit of man suffer annihilation after it has paid a brief visit like a royal guest to this tenement of clay?

Intimations of Immortality (574).

Two friends were driving along a country road, and as they went each kept calling the other's attention to some new charm in the scene. "How prettily the brook winds over there in the meadow," said one, pointing to a zigzag line of brilliant green, in vivid contrast with the hues of the surrounding landscape.

The girl strained her eyes. "Why, I can't see any water; can you?"

Her friend laughed. "No, I don't see the brook itself. But that strip of green tells me that the water is there."

I am the Resurrection (576).

Yes, it is true now, and it ever will be true, as Christ Himself said, "I am the resurrection and the life." It is He Himself that is the resurrection, and He Himself that is the life of the world. Of all persons who have ever been upon our earth, there is but one of whom the hearts of men never tire. "Every hero becomes a bore at last," said Emerson. But not so can any one say of the risen Christ. More and more He becomes an inspiration. More and more He grows in beauty. His power is ever on the increase. That power will never cease—because He, the risen Christ, is today and always, to every Christian disciple, Companion and Savior.

Tennyson and Hallam. (577)—Said the great Tennyson in a better moment: "It's the reality of life! Where's Arthur, my heart's love, the greatest genius of the literary world, going out in boyhood? Where's Arthur? He lives!" Then Tennyson turned away from all question and began to sing beautiful music.—Selected.

A Glorious Certainty (578).

We have all echoed those words of the noted divine:—"I want something more than a guess for my dying pillow!" Thank God we have it.

"Intimations of Immortality" are all well enough for poetry; they will do to interest an idle hour when I am well and strong, and my lease on life seems flawless.

But we want something more than felicitious expressions and esthetic fancies when the room is darkened and a white-capped nurse is taking our steadily rising temperature, and a baffled physician is compelled to suspect defeat. At such times we want something very definite, authoritative, beyond a peradventure. Nature is full of whispers, hints, suggestions, implications, pointing to the probability of a future life.

Reason can work out the problem almost to a final certainty. Cicero said, "There is, I know not how, in the minds of men a certain presage, as it were, of a future existence, and this takes deepest root and is most discoverable in the greatest geniuses and most exalted souls."

But neither poets, nor naturalists nor philosophers nor all combined, can give me what I want when death's shadow falls across my life.

Thank God Christ can! He does!

No wonder that, as the realization of this came upon the great Apostle afresh, he burst forth into that ecstatic, jubilant classic of Eternal optimism:

"O death where is thy sting?

O grave where is thy victory?

But thanks be to God who giveth us the victory through our Lord, Jesus Christ."

No wonder that Easter is a time of joy and gladness.

It celebrates the bringing of life and immortality to light; the scattering of the haze and mists of sweet fancies and beautiful guesses, and the shining forth in all its noonday brilliancy of the Sun of Righteousness; the enthronement in our hearts of a blessed certainty, which neither death, nor musty tombs, nor aught else can ever again dim.—The Christian World.

How Christ Changed Things (579).

The Roman orators exclaimed, "If there be a meeting place of the dead!" Then Christ entered the scene, whispering that God was fully equal to the emergency named "death." Passing through the grave, He exclaimed, "Because I live ye shall live also!" And from that hour death was clothed with sweet allurement. The falling statesman, the dying martyr and mother welcome the signs of death as signals hanged from the heavenly battlements. The iron mask of death fell off, and death stood forth a shining angel of God coming for welcome and convoy.

The dark river narrowed to a tiny ribbon. It seemed but a step to the immortal shore. The path of death became a path of living light. Striking hands with Jesus Christ, the little child, the sage, the statesman, and the seer alike went joyously toward death, and disappearing, passed on into an immortal summer.—N. D. Hillis, D. D.

Raised With Christ (580).

It is doubtless a glorious thing to have been created sinless and to have kept that blessed estate, but it is something sweeter far to have gone down with the Son of God into the darkness of the sepulcher unafraid, and to have come up to that new life as "children of the resurrection." When the oldtime fury broke out in 1870 in the streets of Paris, the most precious treasure in the Louvre, the Venus of Milo, disappeared. When shells were bursting in the Rue Rivoli and in the Place du Carousel and in the Gardens of the Tuilleries, the statue sunk out of sight. But when order was restored, and peace came back, the most beautiful form in all the world was recovered from her secret burial and returned to her sacred pedestal. For long, long months the statue slumbered in the earth only to rise to a second and more secure existence. Them that sleep in the dust will God care for, and raise "to die no more, being children of the resurrection."—Selected.

Immortality A Present Possession (581).

Set aside, if you have ever had it, the notion that immortal or eternal life is something to come by and by, after you have died and risen from the dead. Understand that immortality is a present possession. You are immortal, or you never will be........If you would have a right to the tree of life, if you would have the right to know that there is a tree of life, you must seek this immortal life here, and seek it from the God who is here, and seek it through the channels that He opens for you........We must have the immortal life here and now if we would have a rational hope to have it hereafter.—Lyman Abbott.

More Windows (582).

We seldom stop to think what a house without windows would be like. The gloomiest prison usually has at least some slits in the wall to let the light in, if not to let the sight out. The incoming light is but one thing, though very important. Windows are for outlook, with all which is meant by it.

There is a significant reminder of our limitations below from the pen of Alexander Maclaren: "Our house which is from heaven will have a great many more windows in it than the earthly house of this tabernacle, which was built for stormy weather." It will be well for us if we remember this double lesson. Let us not expect to have as broad an outlook here and now as we shall have hereafter and yonder. How can we see in all directions, and understand all things when we have only a limited number of windows? It is expecting too much. We are not supposed to know and to comprehend everything in the universe, or we would have the means at command. Let us not fret about it, but take on trust what we cannot see.

Then let us be jubilant over the hope set before us that by and by our house will have more windows. The infinite Builder has promised a wider outlook, a broader vision, a clearer view by and by. And what beautiful things He will provide for us to look upon!

Meanwhile, the narrowest house below, and the most restricted in outlook, has yet a window toward the sky. Through this enough may be seen of that fair expanse of blue to enlarge and also to quiet the heart and to keep one glad while waiting for the many windows of "the house which is from heaven," which is being prepared for us.

Victor Hugo's Argument for Immortality (583).

"I feel in myself the future life. I am rising, I know, toward the sky. The sunshine is over my head. Heaven lights me with the reflection of unknown worlds.

"You say the soul is nothing but the result of bodily powers: why then is my soul the more luminous when my bodily powers begin to fail? Winter is on my head and eternal spring is in my heart.

"The nearer I approach the end, the plainer I hear around me the immortal symphonies of the worlds which unite me. It is marvelous, yet simple. It is a fairy tale, and it is a history. For half a century I have been writing my thoughts in prose, verse, history, philosophy, drama, romance, tradition, satire, ode, song—I have tried all. But I feel that I have not said the thousandth part of what is in me. When I go down to the grave I can say, like so many others, 'I have finished my day's work,' but I cannot say, 'I have finished my life.' My day's work will begin the next morning. The tomb is not a blind alley, it is a thoroughfare. It closes in the twilight to open with the dawn. I improve every hour because I love this world as my fatherland. My work is only a beginning. My work is hardly above its foundation. I would be glad to see it mounting and mounting forever. The thirst for the infinite proves infinity."

Asleep in Jesus (584).

The Christian name for a burial ground is cemetery, "sleeping place."

> "Sleep is a death; oh, make me try,   20-1
> By sleeping, what is it to die!
> And as gently lay my head
> On my grave as now my bed."

"A man goes to bed willingly and cheerfully, because he believes he shall rise again the next morning, and be renewed in his strength. Confidence in the resurrection would make us go to the grave as cheerfully as we go to our beds."

Our Immortal Destiny (585).

There are the thousand intimations that man is destined for an immortality. If death is natural, what do you make of these? I had a friend who left for Canada the other day, and he took some of his luggage into the cabin with him; but the great boxes went down into the hold, and on each of them was written "Not wanted for the voyage." Every one of these chests was an absurdity if all was over when the ship reached Halifax—and man has a hundred things "Not wanted for the voyage"—things that are meaningless without a life beyond. Now remember that the New Testament knows nothing of a shadowy immortality of souls. It is man that is immortal, soul and body, each glorified to be the organ of the other. And if in the progress towards that immortality there comes a moment when these twain are sundered—a moment when soul and body, which make man, are torn apart by a relentless power—I say that that calls for an explanation which the death of bird or beast does not demand.—Rev. G. H. Morrison.

Victory Through Fellowship (586).

A father and a child were roaming through a wide country pasture. The little one prattled in the sunshine, now clinging to the father's hand in an ecstasy of confidence, and now flying as fast as his feet could carry him to a thicket where the wild flowers grew. When away from the immediate presence of the protector, the child would turn every now and again to be sure that the father was there, as though for the moment he had forgotten that he was not alone, and then, with the delightful certainty of being carefully watched, would roam still farther, intent on some new object. Suddenly danger appeared in the ominous bark of a dog. The child felt the instant need of guardianship, and with trembling haste rushed to the father's embrace, his cheeks blanched with fear, his eyes filled with tears. The strong arms, however, were no sooner around him than he grew calm again, and the old smile returned. The consciousness of absolute safety destroyed the terror of the dog's bark, because father and child were heart to heart. The relation between Enoch and God must have been like that when he walked with God, "and he was not, for God took him." Stephen's victory was like that when he bore insult and persecution with a face like an angel. If we walk with God, and have fellowship with our Lord Jesus Christ here, we shall have victory over death.—Selected.

The End is the Beginning (587).

There comes a day when every college class has its experience of disintegration. The annual reunions, at first so overflowing with mirth, become gradually saddened because one and another have dropped out, and finally there is only the last survivor, and when he is gone that class lives only in the college records. The same experience is true of families. The question naturally asked when a member of the household, long absent, returns to an old home is about the changes that have taken place. There are sure to be vacant chairs at the table.

and sure to be new mounds in the graveyard; but, if we are Christians who believe in the life everlasting, we know that for every life that ends here there is life begun in the home whence they go no more out. Just as we constantly close our eyes at night and pass into a state of restful unconsciousness, to waken in the morning ready to take up the tasks of another day, and enjoy another day's pleasure, so death closes our eyes on earth merely to open them upon the transcendant glory of an endless day.—Selected.

Despair and Hope (588).

A recent writer says that Rider Haggard suggests that life is a game of blind man's buff on a narrow mountain top, played in the mist. Players are constantly slipping over the precipice, but nobody notices because there are plenty more, and the game goes on. Left to ourselves, that is all there is to it. A man is here today and gone tomorrow. Where he is gone there is no sage wise enough to tell us. We call but he returns not. One did return. All our human sepulchers have footprints which lead down. There are no heel marks toward the grave. That is, there is only one pair of footprints with heel toward the grave, and the foot was nail-pierced. Christ has passed through the grave, and has shown that there is meaning and life beyond it.

The Instinct of Immortality (589).

There is within each of us an instinct of immortality. We do not need science to teach us that. The feeble efforts we put forth here to do good and to cultivate in our lives all that is best seems a prophecy of a more complete work and life in another sphere of existence. Do you think God will take the tools out of the workman's hands just when he has learned to use them properly, or that He will discharge His servants just when they are best able to serve Him? It may sometimes appear to me that my hope of a future life is all vain. That God does not care for me, and has not given to me an instinct of the immortal life, but when I think how He guides the birds of passage on their long and dreary way, I am led to ask, "Is not a man better than a bird?" and I find hope and cheer in the lines of the poet addressed to the waterfowl:

"He, who from zone to zone
 Guides through the boundless sky thy certain flight,
In the long way that I must tread alone
 Will lead my steps aright."

Men in all ages and in all spheres of life have had their thoughts turned to the future. In his old age Goethe said: "My own conviction of a continued existence springs from my consciousness of personal energy, for I work incessantly to the end. Nature is bound to assign to me another form of being as soon as my present one can no longer serve my spirit." Jean Paul Richter says: "We desire immortality, not as a reward of virtue, but as its continuance."—Herbruck.

Christ's Interpretation of Death (590).

Here is Christ's first great interpretation of the mystery of death: "The child is not dead (in your sense of that word, seeing only the grave), but sleepeth." Put this scene alone, and these words alone, over against the Old Testament reticence, and (if there were nothing more to the same purpose in the New Testament) even this interprets death and gives the believer a new hope.—C. I. Scofield, D. D.

"Resurgam" (591).

A singular fact in the history of St. Paul's Cathedral, London, is, that the first stone which the architect ordered the masons to bring from the rubbish of the former cathedral, destroyed by fire, was part of a sarcophagus, on which had been inscribed the single word "Resurgam," "I shall rise again." The prophecy was fulfilled, for out of the ruins of the old a veritable poem in marble has arisen.

Every soul born into this world has "resurgam" written upon it, "I shall rise again." God has filled all nations with emblems of this doctrine. If the little insect that is formed on the leaf in a few short days takes wings and soars into life, if the dry root that has lain motionless during the winter frosts sends its green life upward toward the tender smiling sky of the springtime, if the little grain of wheat holds in its bosom a potentiality that will produce its kind after ten millenniums have sped by, how much greater the possibility that lies in the life of man! The one sweet triumphant note which the soul of every man flings out as it passes on through the gates of the material realm is, "Resurgam."—Selected.

Shall He Live Again? (592).

In my home last night I looked at a picture which reminded me of that tragedy in the death of Thomas Chatterton, eighteen years of age. He wrote such marvelous poetry that he had to deceive the publishers in order to get them to believe it, in order for them to use it. He said he had dug it out of some of the old archives in some of the museums, and the publishers marveled at it! Some great genius had had his name put to it, and they printed it. He was such a genius that he couldn't make them believe that he wrote it and was forced to say that it was the work of somebody else. He wrote poems—oh, such startling poems—but he just wrote a few, and in his lone room in a London garret the greatest genius England ever saw, at that age, starved to death, and in his despair he helped it on with a dose of arsenic!

Where is Thomas Chatterton? He is making poetry somewhere! Great, universal God, I know many a young man or young woman in this world of our bright with the poetic gift, with the artistic touch, never having the possibility of any development, all their lives hedged up and imprisoned and compelled to live in that kind of environment without any opportunity or possibility! Here's a young man with splendid gifts, working seven days in the week and unable to come to church tonight. He has an ambition for an education. He talked it over with me. He writes most beautifully; father gone, mother—half dozen children, all younger than he! For six years he has been slaving his life for their support, and every possibility has gone from him. One of the saddest expressions in human life is this one: If I only had a chance!

If there is a just God in the heavens, sometime, somewhere, you will have a chance! I say it with all reverence, but with a deep conviction in my soul, that if this life is all, then this world is the worst possible world that even Almighty God Himself could make, that sin has done as much for this world as Almighty God could do in human conception.—Cortland Myers, D. D.

Implanted in the Race (593).

We can trace this belief in immortality in an unbroken chain from the earliest records of history to the present time. Cicero, who made the most exhaustive study of the subject that has come down to us from ancient times said: "The immortality of the soul is established by the consent of all nations." The Chaldean Tablets, written before the time of Abraham, contain prayers for the dead. The literature of all ancient nations is colored with the belief. The tombs of Egypt with inscriptions 4,000 years old, are witnesses to the belief of that ancient race. The literature and sculpture of the Phœnicians, the Assyrians, Greeks and Romans are eloquent with the hope of another life. It formed the basis of Homer's song; the rude Norseman built his mythology upon it. It is seen in the lamps which lighted the sepulchers of Greece and Rome. The Gallic warrior had his armor buried with him that in another world he might follow his favorite pastime, war. With the plumed and painted Indian, are buried his bow and arrow and wampum that in the "Happing Hunting Ground" he may pursue the chase. In India the widow was buried on the funeral pyre of her husband that she might serve him in the spirit world. In Persia the grave is often left partly open to facilitate the resurrection of the dead. The Japanese believe not only in the immortality of man but of animals. The lowest tribes of central Africa and even the degraded Patagonians, the lowest of the human family, teach a future existence.—James D. Rankin, D. D.

The Soul's Plea (594).

One of the apparently tragical phases of human life is that so many cherished plans are never completed, so many precious hopes never realized. Too often the evening comes when man's best work is only begun. It would seem that our noblest purposes are unfulfilled, our highest aspirations unsatisfied. True it is, as one has said, that "a broken column is the fit monument of our life."

It is related that Humboldt, the great German naturalist, who attained the age of ninety, exclaimed shortly before his death: "Oh, for another one hundred years!" How many an earnest, ambitious mortal has felt with sadness of heart that the term of life on earth is all too short. Death utters his summons and the impatient workman must leave his task unfinished. And the restless soul pleads for immortality.— McCulloch.

An Instinctive Craving (595).

We have an instinct for immortality. It is born with us and is woven into the very tissues of our life. Under spiritual cultivation it becomes stronger and more vital. Instinctive desire is met by corresponding reality; water for the thirsty, food for the hungry and paradise for the aspiring soul of man. How beautifully William Cullen Bryant illustrates this imperishable instinct for life eternal in his poem, "To a Waterfowl." He describes the flight of the bird toward the southland, its speeding onward, far up in the sky, led unerringly by a Power all-wise, all-loving:

"Thou'rt gone, the abyss of heaven   3
    Hath swallowed up thy form; yet on my heart
Deeply has sunk the lesson thou hast given,
    And shall not soon depart.

"He who, from zone to zone,
    Guides through the boundless sky thy certain flight,
In the long way that I must tread alone,
    Will lead my steps aright."

—Selected.

This Mortal Shall Put On Immortality (596).

We see death only from the outside. The body, which has been the means of expression and communication, ceases its work, and we say our friend is dead. But this only means that we have no further intercourse with him. There is no answering pressure of the hand, and the loving voice is still. Yet our friend lives, nevertheless; for all live unto God. Somewhere in God's Kingdom he is engaged in the activities and has the experiences which belong to that unseen realm. And all the while he and we are in the hands of our Father.

Love met us and prepared the way when we came into this life; similarly love meets us when we pass into the next life and prepares the way for us there. Death, then, is only an incident in the existence of an immortal spirit. It is a passage from a lower to a higher phase of our continuous life. In the great resurrection chapter which I read from St. Paul, the animal body is replaced by a spiritual body; the corruptible puts on incorruption, and the mortal puts on immortality. As Paul puts it in another chapter, the earthly house of our tabernacle is dissolved, but we are clothed upon with another habitation, a house not made with hands, eternal in the heavens. And all the successive phases of this life of ours are comprised in the divine thought, and are gathered up in one great plan of love and wisdom. The gloom and terror, then, with which the imagination has shrouded this subject are heathen, and not Christian, or they are borrowed from the outward appearance which masks the hidden spiritual fact. St. Paul, who was looking forward to a violent death, speaks of it with incidental ease as the time of his departure, or, as he put it, the time of his sailing. The term he used was a nautical one, and means an unmooring, as if Paul thought of raising the anchor or casting off the lines and sailing for another haven and another shore. And the writer of the fourth Gospel reports the Master as speaking of the many mansions in the Father's house, and of places prepared for many. Rightly, then, do we say that this event is no more an ending than it is a beginning. The earthly life has ceased, and the immortal life has begun. On this fact our thought should dwell today. To us the heartache, the tears, the loneliness, and the emblems of sorrow; to him the fullness of life immortal.—Dr. Borden P. Bowne.

The Lesson of Easter (597).

What manner of being is this who alone among all its millions of earth commands the supreme place in our thoughts and actions? His words, His deeds, His character, His sacrifice declare Him to be the Son of God. The Son of man, He called Himself the brother of us all, and yet in the most divine way, its fullest and final revelation of heaven to men. He it is with whom we have to do, and who has to do with us.

His pre-eminent claim is in the fact that He is the Redeemer of the world. "And I, if I be lifted up." Startling statement. Again and again He made the declaration: "The Son of man must be lifted up." And what did He mean by that lifting up of Himself? The magnifying of His wisdom, the beauty of His life? More than this. "For this He said signifying what death He should die."

O, what a lifting up was that upon the cross, outside the city walls! What a lifting up to pain and darkness and shame and death! This is the tragedy of the ages. "But He was wounded for our transgression, and the Lord laid on Him the iniquity of us all."

"The Son of man must be lifted up." What made that must? Wherein was the divine necessity of His death? First because of our sins and our helplessness in guilt. Second, because of His infinite love for men. O, it was not the nails, nor the power of the Roman soldier which held Him to the cross. Had He willed it He could have saved Himself. The power which chained the sufferer to the cruel tree was His infinite love for sinful man. "He must die because he would save, and He would save because He did love."

"And I will draw all men unto Me." The mightiest power in the world today is the cross of Christ. This is the magnet which rivets all eyes, dominates all hearts, more and more. It is transforming the lives of men and nations. O, thou wondrous cross! All other lights on earth grow dim before Thy Easter. "O Galilean, Thou hast conquered!"

> "Were this whole realm of nature mine,   7
>   That were a present far too small,
> Love so amazing, so divine,
>   Demands my soul, my life, my all."
>
> —Dr. Henry M. Curtis.

Risen With Christ (598).

The event of Christ's resurrection is glad tidings of greater joy to all people than was the event of His birth, great as that was. The good news that the annual return of the Easter festival brings fresh to our memories is, that if Christ be risen, then they that love Him and are in Him are risen with Him.

The present resurrection of Christians with Christ is a most precious truth, which, it may be safely assumed, does not enter as vividly and sensibly into their belief and life as it should. The resurrection that is to be, after their victory over death, engrosses their thought to the exclusion of a proper consideration of the resurrection that now is. The glory of the fondly anticipated second resurrection outshines so far as to eclipse the glory of the first, which is part of their present experience. While it is well for Christians not to be insensible to the joy that awaits them, it is not well for them to be oblivious to the joy that is possible to them now. For the joy that was set before Him, Jesus endured the Cross, despising the shame; and it is no discredit for the disciple to be as his suffering Lord was.

In the midst of life's vicissitudes and manifold tribulations, Christians have an indisputable right to all the comfort and strength which the prospect of a joyful resurrection, at the last day, can impart. This right they must not be denied. Of the consolation that springs from the deserted tomb in the garden they will not be deprived. Permit them to cherish their best and brightest hopes. It is not in the power of the most vivid imagination, exercised to its utmost tension, to exaggerate the ecstasies of that hour when they shall be caught up to forever participate in the glory of their risen and exalted Redeemer.—Selected.

eath But a Shadow (599).

Christ put Himself into the very power of death, that henceforth those who will only believe will find it but a shadow, and no longer the old dreadful reality. They will day by day so walk with God in heavenly fellowship that they will be among the first of those "caught up to be forever with the Lord." This makes a new heaven. It is within the heart. It makes a new earth; heaven is all about. It makes Calvary and the resurrection for the first time full of the richest meaning. Easter then is the great springtime of the new heart. We will then be living in the New Jerusalem already let down from heaven, where the Lamb is indeed the light thereof! May our prayer ever be: "O Lord, hasten the day when Easter shall mean this to the world; and may that meaning begin by faith in me!" Then can we say to the call, "He is risen," "He is risen, indeed."—Riale.

The Resurrection (600).

Massive stones and cathedral arches do not keep the remains of royalty more securely than the wide elements of nature are preserving the vestiges of every man that ever breathed. From ocean depths, from mountain-side; from the forest and from the desert; they shall come again!

And thus, the earth is more valuable than you would think it. God has far more to watch over in it than its living population. It rolls on its way, bearing in its bosom a vast freight of that which is yet to people heaven. Let us remember, that the quiet burying-place which we pass with scarce a glance, contains mines which in God's sight are richer by far than ever enriched Peru. Not merely the mouldering remains of organized matter; not something which has seen its day and done its work; but something whose day is only coming, and whose work is not yet well begun; something which rests less in memory than in hope; the "body still united to Christ!" The field of the world is a harvest-field. Not vainly did our fathers call the burying-place God's Acre. It is sown with the seeds of God's harvest; and the day of resurrection is God's reaping-day.

The places on earth that are quietest now will be most bustling on that day of resurrection! When the hum has ceased in the great city's streets, the sequestered walks of its burying-place will be trodden by many generations together. It is a strange thing to stand in the breathless stillness of some populous cemetery, and to think what a stirring amid its dust the voice of the last trump will make!—Boyd.

The Glorified Body (601).

The wisest people of antiquity exerted all their ingenuity to arrest the progress of decay in their beloved dead; and so successful was their skill, that we can even yet draw forth from the sepulchral pyramids of Egypt, forms that two thousand years since walked the streets of cities whose very ruins have disappeared before the touch of time. It was but the other day that I held in my hand the hand of a little Egyptian boy who died two thousand years since; and it was a strange thing as it were to touch that hand across that long waste of years. And though, when we look on the decaying features, which in all their fragility have outlived rocks and empires, we may smile at this earnest anxiety to preserve the least important part of man, we cannot but feel a thoughtful interest in the contemplation of that pious care which made men so anxiously seek to preserve the lips they had in childhood kissed, and the knees they had climbed. It was a praiseworthy, even though a futile task, for such as knew of no resurrection, to care for even the material part of man; and though we, in these modern days, may bury our dead from our sight, and yield the battle with decay, it is not because we feel no concern in even the decaying relics of a parent or a friend; it is because we know assuredly that this mortal shall put on immortality, and that God Himself will watch over it in the space which must elapse before it does so. Give, then, Christians, the body to the grave; and never seek to arrest its quiet progress to rejoin the elements. Let it decay like all things here, returning peacefully to the dust from whence it was taken; and rather cherish in your memory the pleasant recollection of its health and strength, than preserve in your dwelling the wasted image of its weakness and ruin. Lay it in the grave, in the certain hope of a joyful resurrection; and when you come to die, cling to the same blessed hope. Know that never pyramid

kept ancient king so carefully and well as earth and air and sea will
keep the mortal part of your friend and of yourself. And anticipate,
through Jesus, that coming day, when the blessed soul shall tenant
its glorified body, and the glorified body shall be rendered meet for
the dwelling of the blessed soul.—Boyd.

A Personal Resurrection Day (602).

There must be a personal resurrection day to every soul which
seeks salvation through the risen Saviour as truly as there was a resurrection day for Him. For it is written in the Word that those who
have trusted Him have passed from death unto life and are risen together with Him. And by a true parallel of the inner sense of spiritual
things the soul's resurrection day is as really a day of new understanding as was the resurrection day of Jesus. Not until the new man has
commenced to live by the birth from above does comprehension of
heavenly things become possible to the human soul. Only the living
disciple knows the living Christ. The world indeed is eager to claim
acquaintance with Him; it boasts its admiration for His philanthropy,
His gentleness, and His self-sacrifice. But that is only the acquaintance
of those whose judgment-day plea will be that He taught in their streets.
The brethren to whom He appeared alive for the space of forty days
would never have consented to say that mere idle hearing of His wayside teachings could have given anyone a conception of the divinity
of their Lord. And so it is even now, not the complacent reader of the
gospel story, but the sinner who has been forgiven by Him, who appre-
ciates the Christ. Nobody knows the Lord who has not heard the
voice that quickens the dead from their trespasses. But with that
quickening voice and crowding close upon it, what knowledge comes of
tenderness that soothes as a mother soothes, of grace that sustains
like the bulwarking of a mighty rock, of providence that delivers, of
joy that illuminates, and of love that transforms.—The Continent.

Many Witnesses (603).

Emerson said: "We are much better believers in immortality than
we can give grounds for." Max Mueller remarked: "Without a belief
in personal immortality religion surely is like an arch resting on one
pillar, like a bridge ending in an abyss.". A scientist like Sir Humphrey
Davy can say: "We know enough to hope for immortality, the individual immortality, of the better part of man." Southey said: "Faith
in a hereafter is as necessary for the intellectual as for the moral character." It is Wordsworth who speaks of "The faith that looks through
death." Longfellow was enraptured with the idea, "Thou glorious spirit
land! Oh, that I could behold thee as thou art the regiver of life, and
light, and love, and the dwelling-place of those beloved ones whose
being has flowed onward like a silver-clear stream into the solemn
sounding main into the ocean of eternity." Goethe once remarked to
a friend: "Setting, nevertheless, the soul is always the same sun. I
am fully convinced it is a being of a nature quite indestructible, and
that its activity continues from eternity." The great philosopher Kant
wrote: "The summum bonum then is practically only possible on the

supposition of the immortality of the soul." John Fisk, the evolutionist, gave utterance to his belief thus: "I believe in the immortality of the soul, not in the sense in which I accept the demonstrable truths of science, but as a supreme act of faith in the reasonableness of God's work." Again he says: "Each new discovery but places man upon a higher pinnacle than ever and lights the future with the radiant color of hope." Hugo says: "I feel in myself the future life." And what did Tom Paine write? "The belief in a future state is a rational belief founded on facts visible in creation. I hope for happiness beyond this life." The famous botanist, Asa Gray, said: "Not vitality, but personality, is our evidence for immortality." We know of no finer words on this subject than those spoken by Benjamin Franklin: "Life is a state of embryo, a preparation for life. A man is not completely born until he has passed through death."—Wiest.

Dying—Renewing (604).

The leaf falling from the tree is not lost, it is conserved by being converted into another form of life. The caterpillar encases itself in its chrysalis from which under the warming sun it breaks its shell and bursts forth into new life. In its hibernating state it still lived. Behold the bird's nest in the field with its treasure of eggs. After a little while the shell only is left behind, while the bird itself has flown. Nature speaks to us in a thousand tongues, it flashes forth truth in myraid forms. The river that flows past this city has done so for ages past. The Indian worshiped on its banks as we do now; not a particle of its waters is the same, and yet it is the same river and will go on forever. "I die daily." I am throwing off this body, but the soul, the organizing, vitalizing principle within me is renewing me day by day.— The Christian World.

"The Dead Are the Living" (605).

No one ever stated this blessed truth of immortality more clearly than did Dr. Alexander Maclaren in his memorable words: "The dead are the living. Every man that has died is at this instant in full possession of all his faculties, in the intensest exercise of all his capacities, standing somewhere in God's universe, ringed by a sense of God's presence, and feeling in every fiber of his being that life, which comes after death, is not less real, but more real, not less great, but more great, not less full or intense, but more full and intense, than the mingled life, which, lived here on earth, was a center of life surrounded with a crust and circumference of immortality. The dead are the living. They lived while they died; and after they die, they live on forever."

"The Dead Are" (606).

We do not speak of our departed friends as of those who "were" or "have been." No, we speak of those who are in better worlds. The range of death is but narrow and but momentary in duration. Death makes the entrance into fuller, perfect life possible. If it were not so, God would never permit death. He has a better sphere in store for us. This earth is a place for temporary sojourn; there is another sphere in which is the permanent home. Death is necessary only that we may pass from this temporal life into the eternal glory. That is the law universal. The seed dies that it may have a glorious resurrection in the full-grown stalk crowned with the rich grain, multiplied many times. Is there not here a picture of the resurrection glory of the believer? Is not Longfellow right? "The grave itself is but a covered bridge leading from light to light through a brief darkness." Yes, it is so. Why be afraid of the brief darkness? Are we not familiar enough with temporary darkness? We sleep. All is dark. There is no fear in us when we go to sleep. Death is going to sleep. We shall awake. What an awakening that must be for every soul. What a flood of light and love divine must burst upon him who falls asleep in Jesus!—E. F. Wiest, D. D.

"There Is No Death, What Seems So Is Transition" (607).

To Jesus Christ, death and the resurrection were not separable events, with a long interval between the two. They were simultaneous events; rather, they were synonymous words, signifying the same event. Death is the dropping of the body into the grave, where it mingles with the dust. Resurrection is the upspringing of the spirit from the body, when through accident, disease, or old age, it has ceased to be a tenable abode. Three times Jesus Christ raised the dead. Each time He assumed that the free spirit was close at hand, could hear His voice and would obey, each time the spirit which had escaped from its tenement returned to animate it again.

If I thought that life becomes extinct, it would be very difficult to persuade me that it is revived again after a long and dreary sleep. But I do not believe that life ever becomes extinct. I might be said to believe in resurrection because I do not believe in death. When my skeptical friend asks me for proof of immortality, I reply by asking him for proof of mortality. That after the organ has been reduced to ashes it can be reconstructed seems to me incredible. But I see no reason for thinking that the organist is dead because the organ has been burned.—Lyman Abbott.

Death the Gate of Life (608).

It is one of the most wonderful provisions of redemption that by divine wisdom and power, death, than which there is nothing more dreaded among men, has been transformed into a medium by which the soul of the believer makes its exit from a world of death into a world of endless life. If the choice had been left to us, we would have selected any other medium.

I have looked upon a sunset sky, when the cloud strata have taken the form of stairway of burnished gold reaching into infinite space; and it seemed as if I could almost discern the forms of descending angels and ascending saints, and I said, "Surely, this is the ladder Jacob saw—this is the gate of heaven." Then the vision changed, as the scene took on still greater brilliancy, and pencils of light seemed to trace the glowing vision of the Apocalypse, until there appeared walls of jasper, and gates of pearl, and a thousand flashing domes and towers, and I said: "Surely, this a scene fit to gild with glory the last earthly hour of a child of God." But instead of choosing one of the brightest and most attractive objects, God has chosen one of the darkest and most repulsive, and made it a medium of the soul's transition from earth to heaven.—Anonymous.

White Funerals (609).

The last interment in the cemetery is another scene where the noise of the shout of joy strangely mingles with the weeping of the people. The godly life which is a series of progressive enhancements ends with a triumph which explains all that has gone before, which crowns all that has gone before. The Master had a white funeral. "And entering into the tomb, they saw a young man sitting on the right side, arrayed in a white robe." And that robe "white as snow" was a figure of the mighty radiant elements which lighted the tragedy of Calvary. The blessed dead who die in the Lord share with Him in the glory and hope of the resurrection unto life eternal. Very often, as we have seen, do the sweet and bitter mingle perplexingly; but in the churchyard this ambiguous experience becomes most acute and baffling. Travelers tell us of fruits of the wilderness "which taste bitter and sweet, a strange concentrated essence of the tropics," and so after years of acquaintance with commingling sweets and bitters, we come to the graveyard, the borderland, where we taste the concentrated essence of the contrasted problems of sin and redemption, the anguish of death and the rapture of immortality, the consciousness that all is won in the very event and moment in which all is lost.

George Sand writes, "I felt twenty years younger on the day that I buried my youth." She felt no sadness in the transition; only the sense of a truer wisdom, a serener peace, a completer liberty, an expanding horizon. But if the burial of one's youth may become such an emancipation, how much younger shall we feel on the day that we bury our age! What shall be the glory and joy of the final emancipation when our friends bury us, and this corruptible puts on incorruption, this mortal immortality! Our Master dared not to tell us more, lest we should have been overweighted with the vision. All golden weddings and diamond jubilees only faintly foreshadow the sweet release, the full felicity. Do we believe our creed? The very magnificence of the Christian hope is sometimes felt by us as a difficulty, we are tempted to think it too grand to be true. Rather is it too grand to be false. Think of our hope in the light of creation! If the evolution of ages culminates in humanity, nothing except a great destiny for the race will justify the mighty expense. Think of our hope in the light of redemption! Only as a splendid destiny awaits those for whom Christ died is the cross justified. Let us confidently believe, looking for the coming of the Lord Jesus unto eternal life. If all through life we proceed from grace to grace, we surely have nothing to fear in its ending. Transfiguring gleams from the opening heavens will gild that last funeral, palms hide the willows, and joy break through the swimming eyes of the mourners; it shall be the whitest of white funerals as it is in sure and certain hope of resurrection to eternal life.

And when grim Death doth take me by the throat,
  Thou wilt have pity on Thy handiwork;
Thou wilt not let him on my suffering gloat,
  But draw my soul out—gladder than man or boy,
When Thy saved creatures from the narrow ark
  Rushed out, and leaped and laughed and cried for joy,
And the great rainbow strode across the dark.

                              —W. L. Watkinson, D. D.

ILLUSTRATIVE VERSES.

The Resurrection Hope (610).

Paulinus preached the gospel in Northumbria, England, in the early ages to King Edwin and his warriors. Edwin was silent, but one of his aged warrior-sages arose and said, "Around us lies the black land of Night." Then,

"Athwart the room a sparrow
Darts from the open door:
Within the happy hearth-light
One red flash and no more!
We see it come from darkness,
And into darkness go:—
So is our life, King Edwin!
Alas that it is so!
"But if this pale Paulinus
Have somewhat more to tell;
Some news of Whence and Whither,
And where the soul will dwell:—
If on that outer darkness
The sun of hope may shine,
He makes life worth the living:
I take his God for mine."

He Is Not Dead (611).

He is not dead, this friend. Not dead,
But in the path we mortals tread;
God some few trifling steps ahead,
And nearer to the end.
So that we, too, once past the bend,
Shall meet again, as face to face, this friend
We fancy dead.

—Robert Louis Stevenson.

God's Springtime (612).

Dr. Archibald Hodge once gave rein to his imagination in a lecture on theology. He drew for his hearers a picture of Laura Bridgman, blind and deaf and dumb, on a day of mighty restoration. What wealth of knowledge poured in upon her sensibilities! What revelations dawned like planets swimming into the astronomer's ken, upon her astonished mind! What wonders of vision and of love enriched her receptive soul! God's springtime will come. Oh, the surprise of immortality! "God giveth it a body."

"A body wearing out,
A crumbling house of clay!
O agony of doubt
And darkness and dismay!

Trust God and see
What I shall be,—
His best surprise
Before your eyes!"

Soul and Body (613).

The body says , "I am thirsty,"   And for its thirst there is water,
The body says, "I am cold,"   And shelter warm in the blast,
The body says, "I am weary,"   And for its ache there is slumber;
And last of all, "I am old."   But it dies, it dies at last.

But I am a soul, please Heaven,
And though I freeze in my cage,
Or burn in a sleepless fever,
I shall live untouched of age.

—Ethelwyn Wetherald.

Rise To Immortality (614).

Son of God, tne grave defying,
Raise us also into life;
Help us, on Thy power relying,
Sin to conquer in the strife;
Crucified with Christ, may we
Rise to immortality.

Hope On (615).

Have faith in a third-day morning,
In a resurrection hour;
For what ye sow in weakness
He can raise again in power.

.   .   .   .

And the hopes that never on earth shall bloom,
The sorrows forever new,
Lay silently down at the feet of Him
Who died and is risen for you.

—Harriet Beecher Stowe.

The Haven (616).

I have made a voyage upon a golden river,
'Neath clouds of opal and of amethyst.
Along its banks bright shapes were moving ever,
And threatening shadows melted into mist.

My journey nears its close: in some still haven
My bark shall find its anchorage of rest,
When the kind Hand, which every good has given,
Opening with wider grace, shall give the best.

"Auf Wiedersehen" (617).

We walk along life's rugged road together
Such a little way.
We face the sunshine or the stormy weather
So brief a day.
Then paths diverge, from sorrow so appalling
We shrink with pain,
Yet, parted far and farther, still keep calling,
"Auf Wiedersehen."

Despair not! See, through tear dimmed eyes, before us
    Such a little way,
Lies God's dear garden, and His sun shines o'er us
    A long, long day.
There all paths end, long parted loved ones, meeting,
    Clasp hands again,
The past, the pain forgot in rapturous greeting,
    "Auf Wiedersehen."

                       —Susie E. Abbey.

Love's Dream (618).

"Yet love will dream and faith will trust
(Since He knows our need is just),
That somehow, somewhere meet we must.
   "The truth to flesh and sense unknown,
That life is ever Lord of death,
   And love can never lose its own."

                       —Whittier.

A Fuller Life (619).

"And they shall be mine, they as on earth we knew them,
The lips we kissed, the hands we loved to press,
Only a fuller life is circling through them,
Unfailing bliss, unchanging loveliness."

The Song of Faith (620).

Day will return with a fresher boon;
   God will remember the world!
Night will come with a newer moon;
   God will remember the world!

Evil is only the slave of good,
   Sorrow the servant of joy,
And the soul is mad that refuses food
   Of the meanest in God's employ.

The fountain of joy is fed by tears,
   And love is lit by the breath of sighs;
The deepest griefs and wildest fears
   Have holiest ministries.

Strong grows the oak in the sweeping storm,
   Safely the flower sleeps under the snow,
And the farmer's hearth is never warm
   Till the cold wind starts to blow.

Day will return with a fresher boon;
   God will remember the world!
Night will come with a newer moon;
   God will remember the world!

The World a Tent (621).

When my bier is borne to the grave,
And its burden is laid in the ground,
Cry not like the mourners around,
"He is gone"—"All is over"—"Farewell!"
But go on your ways again,
And, forgetting your own petty loss,
Remember his infinite gain;
For know that this world is a tent
And life but a dream in the night,
Till Death plucks the curtains apart
And awakens the sleeper with light!

Immortality (622).

O Christ, whose cross began to bloom
    With peaceful lilies long ago,
Each year above Thy empty tomb
    More thick the Easter garlands glow.
O'er all the wounds of that sad strife
Bright wreaths the new, immortal life.

The Morn (623).

So long Thy power has blest me, sure it still
    Will lead me on
O'er moor and fen, o'er crag and torrent, till
    The night is gone,
And with the morn those angel faces smile
Which I have loved long since, and lost awhile!
                                    —J. H. Newman.

We Shall Meet (624).

God is not cruel, stern though His decree;
Joys He took from us He has still in store!
He cannot mean that we should meet no more:
Come back for me!

The Lamb the Light (625).

The bride eyes not her garments,
But her dear bridegroom's face;
I will not look on glory,   12
But on the King of Grace.

Not on the crown He giveth,
But on His pierced hands;
The Lamb is all the glory
Of Immanuel's land.

The Heavenly Home (626).

There is a calm beyond life's fitful fever,
    A sweet repose, a never-failing rest,
Where white-robed angels welcome the believer,
    Among the blest, among the blest.
There is a home where all the soul's deep yearnings,
    And silent prayers shall be at last fulfilled;
Where strife, sorrow, murmurings and heart-burnings
    At last are stilled, at last are stilled."

Face to Face (627).

Face to face with Christ, my Saviour;
Face to face what will it be,
When with rapture I behold Him,
Jesus Christ Who died for me?

The Beyond (628).

They talk about the fading hopes, that mock the years to be,
But write me down as saying there's hope enough for me,
Over the old world's wailing the sweetest music swells,
In the stormiest night I listen and hear the bells—the bells!

Revealer and Revealed (629).

From glory unto glory that ever lies before,
Still widening, adoring, rejoicing more and more,
Still following where He leadeth from shining field to field,
Himself our goal of glory, Revealer and revealed.

The Easter Dawn (630).

My heart that many a weary day
Went sighing cn its way,
  With the clear light the morning brings
  Exults again and sings,
As one who in a dreary night
  Lies tossing and distraught,
Welcomes the earliest gleams of light
  On the cloud curtains wrought.

"The Lord is risen!" His ransomed sing,
And bells of gladness ring.
  "The Lord is risen!" my heart replies;
  And hope with Him shall rise.
No more beside an empty tomb
  I wait, where love is cold.
The light of morning breaks the gloom;
  The words of promise hold.

The welcome, Faith, that faltered long,
To thine own happy song;
  And hope and love, with visions sweet,
  Where dawn and shadow meet.
Out of the night of doubt and fear
  God makes His morning shine.
The fulness of the day is near—
  Its light forever mine.

—Rev. Isaac Ogden Rankin.

˙Resurgam (631).

The fool asks, "With what flesh? in joy or pain?
Helped or unhelped? and lonely, or again
Surrounded by our earthly friends?"
I know not; and I glory that I do
Not know; that for eternity's great ends
God counted me as worthy of such trust
That I need not be told.
Out to the earthward brink
Of that great tideless sea,
Light from Christ's garments streams.
Believing thus, I joy, although I lie in dust,
I joy, not that I ask or choose,
But simply that I must.
I love, and fear not; and I cannot lose,
One instant, this great certainty of peace.
Long as God ceases not, I cannot cease;
I must arise.

—Helen Hunt Jackson.

Teachers (632).

The grasses and the sod,
　　They are my preachers. Hear them preach
When they forget the shroud, and God
　　Lifts up these blades of grass to teach
The resurrection! Who shall say
What infidel can speak as they?

—Joaquin Miller.

Easter's Answer (633).

Does death end all?
Does earth complete the story?
Is there no sequel to life's broken tale?
　　Sounds there no call,
　　Fraught with the hope of glory,
From out the gloomy shadows of the vale?

　　Lives there no seer,
　　Whose eye has pierced the gloaming,
And won from it, reluctant, visions bright?
　　Can we but fear,
　　That after weary roaming,
Death has no recompense?—the tomb but night?

　　The countless host,
　　For which death's gates keep swinging;
The loved ones, for whom other loved ones weep;
　　Are these all lost?
　　And is affection clinging
To friends embraced in an eternal sleep?

If this is all—
If when the heart stops throbbing,
And all the wheels of being cease to roll
If this is all,
And life ends with earth's sobbing,
And "dust to dust" was "spoken of the soul."

Then must we loathe
The powers that make known,
The soul's capacity for higher joy;
Then must we loathe
The heart's affections sown
But for the frosts of winter to destroy.

No!—Death is life,
And parting is but meeting
Beyond the cloudland shadowing the grave.
No!—Death is life
And, as earth's years are fleeting,
We grasp the immortality we crave.

The empty tomb—
Blest prophecy of glory—
Is vanquished by the great all-conquering One.
Its scattered gloom
Confirms inspired story:
Time sees the youth of being just begun.

—J. H. B.

Risen In Christ

Christ is risen! We are risen!
Shed upon us heavenly grace,
Rain and dew and gleams of glory
From the brightness of Thy face!
So that we, with hearts in heaven,
Here on earth may fruitful be;
And by angel-hands be gathered,
And be ever, Lord, with Thee!

—C. Wordsworth.

Weeps No More (635).

Thus said the Lord, "Thy days of health are over,"
And, like the mist, my vigor fled away,
Till but a feeble shadow was remaining,
A fragile form fast hasting to decay.

The May of life, with all its blooming flowers,
The joy of life, in colors bright arrayed,
The hopes of life, in all their airy promise—
I saw them in the distance slowly fade.

Then sighs of sorrow in my heart would rise,
And silent tears would overflow my eyes;
But a warm sunbeam from a higher sphere
Stole through the gloom, and dried up every tear.

"Is this Thy will, Good Lord? the strife is o'er;—
Thy servants weeps no more."

—Mowes, H. L. L.

The Call of God (636).

Beneath the cover of the sod
The lily heard the call of God;
Within its bulb so strangely sweet
Answering pulse began to beat.
The earth lay darkly damp and cold,
And held the smell of grave and mold,
But never did the lily say,
"O who shall roll the stone away?"
It heard the call, the call of God,
And up through prison-house of sod
It came from burial-place of gloom
To find its perfect life in bloom.

—Author Unknown.

The Love That Will Not Let Me Go! (637).

Love, that will not let me go,
I rest my weary soul on thee;
give thee back the life I owe,
That in thine ocean depths its flow
May richer, fuller be.

O Light, that followed all my way,
I yield my flickering torch to thee;
My heart restores its borrowed ray
That in thy sunshine's blaze its day
May brighter, fairer be.

O Joy, that seekest me through pain,
I can not close my heart to thee;
I trace the rainbow through the rain,
And feel the promise is not vain
That morn shall tearless be.

O Love, that lifted up thy head,
I dare not ask to fly from thee;
I lay in dust life's glory dead,
And from the ground there blossoms red
Life that shall endless be.

—George Matheson.

Repose (638).

O! soft are the breezes that play round the tomb,
And sweet, with the violet's wafted perfume,
  With lilies and jessamine fair.

The pilgrim, who reaches this valley of tears,
Would fain hurry by; and, with trembling and fears,
  He is launched on the wreck-covered river.

Here, the traveler, worn with life's pilgrimage dreary,
Lays down his rude staff, like one that is weary,
  And sweetly reposes forever.

—Karamisin.

No Death (639).

"There is no death; the stars go down
  To rise upon some fairer shore,
And bright in heaven's jeweled crown
  To shine forevermore."

The Living Lord (640).

The Lord is risen indeed,
He is here for your love, for your need—
Not in the grave, nor the sky,
But here where men live and die.

—Gilder.

My Guide (641).

There is no path in this desert waste,
  For the winds have swept the shifting sands;
The trail is blind where the storms have raced,
  And a stranger, I, in these fearsome lands.
But I journey on with a lightsome tread;
  I do not falter nor turn aside;
For I see His figure, just ahead—
  He knows the way I take—My Guide.

There is no path in this trackless sea;
  No map is limned on the restless waves;
The ocean snares are strange to me
  Where the unseen wind in its fury raves;
But it matters naught; my sails are set;
  And my swift prow tosses the seas aside;
For the changeless stars are steadfast yet,
  And I sail by His star-blazed trail—My Guide.

There is no way in this starless night;
  There is naught but cloud in the inky skies;
The black night smothers me, left and right,
  I stare with a blind man's straining eyes;
But my steps are firm, for I cannot stray;
  The path to my feet seems light and wide;
For I hear His voice—"I am the way!"
  And I sing as I follow Him on—My Guide.
                              —Robert J. Burdette.

Outcome of Peace (642).

          I cannot lose
One instant, this great certainty of peace:
Long as God ceases not, I cannot cease;
I must arise.
                    —Helen Hunt Jackson.

Love Crowned With Immortality (643).

The comfort of the Easter day
Comes not alone to those who lay
Their loved ones down with sealed eyes
To sleep beneath the bending skies,
But to those hearts whose restless moan
Tells of sweet hopes too swiftly flown.
Of friends who tossed love's costly flower
Aside—the bauble of an hour,
And left us, while they yet remain,
A legacy of ceaseless pain.
By these sad graves through darkened days,
A tender, white-robed angel stays,
To roll the stone, that we may see
Love crowned with immortality.
                    —Helen Stroug Thompson.

TEXTS AND TREATMENT HINTS.

"He Has Risen"—Luke 24:6 (644).

I. The Resurrection of Jesus is the pledge of the Resurrection of each believer.

"Because I live ye shall live also," He said. It is the voice of the Risen Christ that calls the dead to life.

II. The Resurrection of Jesus is the pledge of His Kingship and of the Last Judgment.

"The Son of man shall come in His glory and all the angels with Him and shall sit on the throne of His glory and shall judge the world."

III. The Resurrection of Jesus is the seal of His Atonement for the sins of man.—Selected.

"And He That Was Dead Came Forth"—John 11:44 (645).

I. Light on the problem of death and the clouds of sorrow which gather around it, on the Valley of the Shadow of Death, on the Dark River all must cross, is one great need of humanity. These are typified by the trial, the death, and the burial of Christ.

II. The feelings of Jesus in the presence of death His disciples also should have:—

a. A deep indignation at sin, which brings death, and adds its poison, and sting, and bitterness to death.

b. Sympathy with the afflicted.

When the noted Father Taylor, of Boston, was at the point of death some one suggested to him that he would soon be with the angels. He spoke up quickly, "I don't want angels, I want folks."

III. Jesus is the resurrection and the life; the giver of eternal life which lasts beyond the grave, and makes the resurrection possible and blessed. He proved His assertion and promise by raising Lazarus from the dead.

IV. The raising of Lazarus proved that the soul has an existence independent of the body, that death does not end all.—Peloubet's Notes.

"Blessed Are the Dead That Die in the Lord"—Rev. 14:13 (646).

A voice from heaven explicitly directed the holy apostle to write: "Blessed are the dead which die in the Lord from henceforth: Yea, saith the Spirit, that they may rest from their labors; and their works do follow them." Gracious are these words. Unbroken existence, rest from all burdens and troubles, and a reward for all the service and the fruition of all the hopes that belong to Christian discipleship on earth—surely this message covers all the possibilities of spiritual blessedness and answers the inquiries that will be made by receptive and responsive souls.—Bishop Fitzgerald.

The Things Which Are Seen Are Temporal; but the Things Which Are Not Seen Are Eternal—2 Cor. 4:18 (647).

Paul is not speaking of bodily sight only, for he tells of "craftiness, and hidden things of shame" which shall perish, as empty prayers will fall short; and one of the lasting things is the face of a good man which clings in memory.

But Paul at Ephesus had been looking at things that ought to perish, however men valued them; and he contrasted them with what God looks at and holds worth preserving.

I. What are the perishables? 1. A house made with hands. A real home must shelter love, and self-denial, and the nurture of character. 2. Troubles. Affliction is meant to be "but for a moment."

II. What are the eternal things? 1. Honest character. 2. "The face of Jesus Christ" (2 Cor. 4:6). We have seen it only in thought but it includes the revelation of God's holiness and patient, hopeful love. 3. Heaven.—Homiletic Review.

"He is Risen"—Luke 24:6 (648).

The fact of Christ's resurrection is viewed in three aspects in Scripture; and these three emerge upon the consciousness of the early church successively. It was, first, a fact affecting Him, a testimony concerning Him, carrying with it necessarily some great truths with regard to Him, His character, His nature and His work. Later it came to be to them a pattern, and a pledge, and a prophecy of their own resurrection. And finally it came to be a symbol of the spiritual resurrection and newness of life into which all they were born who participated in His death. They knew Him first by His resurrection; they then knew the power of His resurrection as a witness of their own; and they knew it as being the pattern to which they were to be conformed even whilst here on earth.

"But Thou Shalt Know Hereafter."—John 13:7 (649).

The day of resurrection into the life beyond shall be more than all other days a day of understanding. That will be the fulfillment to us of that infinitely solacing promise: "But thou shalt understand hereafter." That will be the hour when the apostle's saying shall come true for us each: "Then shall I know fully even as also I was fully known." Even when the disciples least understood their Lord, there was never a time when He did not understand them perfectly. So it is blessed to remember that now our little and poor knowledge of Christ does not imply any defect in His knowledge of us. He does not see in a mirror darkly. He knows us fully. And the precious promise of Easter is that in like manner we shall fully know Him.—Selected.

"Thanks Be to God Which Gives Us the Victory."—1 Cor. 15:57 (550).

1. The victory over sin.
2. The victory over earthly trials.
3. The victory over death.

"O Death Where Is Thy Sting?"—1 Cor. 15:55 (651).

1. Out of Christ death is so bitter in prospect and in experience that men have questioned if life, which at last inevitably leads to it, is worth having.

2. Christ has transformed death from a foe into a friend.

3. With what glad gratitude this should fill our hearts.

"Death Is Swallowed Up In Victory."—1 Cor. 15:54 (652).

Through Christ the Christian is enabled so to triumph over death that

1. The fear of it is banished.

2. The actual experience becomes radiant.

3. And death itself becomes merely a door opening into glory.

Our Friend Lazarus Sleepeth; But I Go, That I May Awake Him Out Of Sleep.—John 9:11 (653).

Jesus called Lazarus His friend,—blessed title, glorious privilege, friend of Jesus! Am I His friend? He gives us the test,—"Ye are my friends if ye do whatsoever I command you." His command is, trust Me, love Me, serve Me. Do I obey this? Then I am Jesus' friend, and what is more, He is my friend. This friendship is a treasure neither time nor chance, men nor devils, life nor death can take away. Let us not imagine Christ is not our friend because we suffer. He allowed Lazarus to die, yet we are told Jesus loved Martha and her sister and Lazarus. Jesus' friends now upon earth may all die, may all sleep; but He has not forgotten them, one day He will say to the angels "My friends sleep, but I go to awake them." Then the Lord Himself shall descend with a shout, with the voice of the archangel and with the trump of God. And the dead in Christ shall rise first; then we which are alive and remain shall be caught up together with them in the clouds to meet the Lord in the air, and so shall we ever be with the Lord.—Rev. R. H. Hardening.

For As The Father Raiseth Up The Dead, and Quickeneth Them; even So The Son Quickeneth Whom He Will.—John 5:21 (654).

Life is the prerogative and gift of God, alike of Father and Son. So declare these words of Saint John; and all life is essentially one. But to the conscious recipient is there not a difference in the gift suggested by these same words corresponding to the person of the giver? Surely to such a recipient a gift carries with it the personality, the touch, of the hand from which it comes. And it is this personality which gives it most often its highest value and influence. "The gift without the giver is bare." But what is true of our smaller earthly tokens is vastly truer of the high gifts of heaven, and this highest gift of all. Grateful, happy, is it to the devout soul, to recognize in every heart throb, every function, physical or spiritual, the Father's forethought and provision for His children. But an element of even deeper tenderness and love, as well as responsibility, is added to the gift, as coming from the wounded human hand of Jesus. It glows and breathes with the very spirit of His life and redeeming work.

And this is the gift, this life, which He gives to every earnest seek-ing heart; for "whom He will," is after all only another expression, according to the gospel, for "whosoever will."—R. U. McVickar, D. D.

"If a Man Die Shall He Live Again?"—Job 14:14 (655).

The only reasonable argument against the immortality of the soul is the death of the body.

The body dies, and, so far as we can see, all individual existence ceases. There is no response. There is no manifestation of continued life. . . . The ordinary evidence of our senses denies the doctrine of the immortality of man.

To this denial an obvious reply is that death is one of the oldest of all facts.

From the beginning of time, death has confronted life. So far as the death of the body constitutes an argument against the immor-tality of the soul, it was as valid a contradiction a hundred thousand years ago as it is today. But it has never prevailed. The argument is plain enough, and makes its appeal to the reason of every man, but it has never been effective. . . .

Nothing happens to show that the argument of death is invalid in any particular. There it is, and we can not gainsay it. But we do gainsay it. The primitive man, contemporary with the glaciers, buries in the grave of his dead the symbols of his faith in immortality. Confronting the unanswerable facts, he cries, "My friend is dead, but he shall live again!" And this cry of hope, of confidence, of victory, has been repeated every day since life and death began. It is evident that something is the matter with an argument which is at the same time so plain and so everlastingly unconvincing.—"Everyman's Religion," by George Hodges.

"If a Man Die Shall He Live Again?"—Job 14:14 (656).

This is a question as old as the tragic fact of death. "There is hope of a tree, if it be cut down, that it will sprout again, and that the tender branch thereof will not cease. But man dieth, and wasteth away, yea, man giveth up the ghost, and where is he?" This question has been asked by multitudes, before and since the time of Job. We stand by the side of the wasting forms of loved ones, we see their pallid faces, parched lips, fluttering temples and finally that awful some-thing that tells us that they have known the mystery, and in death's presence we weep and instinctively ask again the question asked by the perfect and upright man in the land of Uz so many ages ago: "If a man die shall he live again?" To this question our race, with few exceptions, has instinctively answered "Yes." All religions, both true and false, are based on this assumption. "Without such a belief," says Max Muller, "religion is like an arch resting on one pillar, like a bridge ending in an abyss." The burial customs of the most primitive peoples reveal the fact that they believe that this mortal must put on immortality. The most ancient literature of the Hindus and the Chinese reveals this same hope, and with this same hope the ancient Egyptians seemed to be filled. Sages and philosophers of every land and age, as well as common people like ourselves, have not been satisfied with any other thought. Something within us seems to demand it and something without us seems to assume it.—Hilsther.

"To Depart and Be With Christ."—Phil. 1:23 (657).

I. Christ calls death falling asleep. He is using one of the phrases which daring and trustful men had coined, and He is giving it proof and reality. When He stands beside the bed of Jairus' little daughter He softly says, "Talitha cumi," "My little lambie, arise." He is awaking a child from sleep. When He stops the bier of the widow of Nain's son He calls, "Young man, I say unto thee, Arise." He is calling one who is at rest back to active life again. When He stands at the tomb of Lazarus, dead four days ago, He cries, "Lazarus, come forth." He is calling one who is lying in the rest chamber to the light of the day and its duties. As a little child will come in from its play when the shadows fall; as a man seeks his rest when his day's toil is done; as a traveler weary and footsore will lie down to renew himself at his journey's end; so, said Jesus, when we die, we sleep. But we sleep to wake.

II. He calls it a going to the Father. This is the word which remained unspoken until the end, but it was His most cherished thought. When He gathers His disciples together in the upper room, and He is upon the eve of His dying, then the word is like a refrain in a song, a recurring note of music in His addresses. Again and again He repeats, "I go to My Father." He is like an emigrant who has been for years in another hemisphere and in the land of strangers. He has been busy with its life and its industries. He has endured its hardships and isolation. Now the time of His sojourn is over and the hour of His return is come. He is going to the Father. He is going home.

III. He calls it, in this conversation, by a singular word. "They spake of His decease." In the literal and significant meaning of the word it was His "exodus." We cannot doubt why the word was chosen. It is the thought of death from the point of view of one who is about to go out by it as by a door. How full of light is this word. Death is an exodus, a going out from the land of the stranger, from the house of bondage, from affliction and thankless toil, from the state of the slave. Death is a deliverance and a boon. It is a going through a wilderness, with its loneliness and its pain and privation, but it is a going through a wilderness upon a journey which is to end in the land which is the promise of God.—J. H. Clough, D. D.

"Because I Live, Ye Shall Live Also."—John 14:19 (658).

He lives who once was dead. He did not go through the valley of death and come out on the other side to prove to Himself that there is life on the other side. He knew it. But He went through and

came out to show us that death does not end all. He will conduct
us into the valley, through the valley, and out of the valley. Rejoice,
for He lives. Rejoice, because death shall have no more dominion over
us. We are not going into a blind alley, but into a grand thoroughfare.—Selected.

"But Some Will Say: How Are The Dead Raised Up, And With What Body Do They Come?" I. Corinthians, 15:44, replies: "It Is Sown a Natural Body; It Is Raised a Spiritual Body" (659).

A body bearing no relation to the one that was buried would make
void the resurrection. "He that raised up Jesus from the dead shall
quicken your mortal body for His spirit that dwelleth in you." This
resurrection body will be fashioned like unto His glorious body. "When
Christ our life shall appear we shall be like Him."

Our Lord, after His resurrection, was not an unclothed spirit.
"Handle me and see, for a spirit hath not flesh and bones as ye see
Me have." This same Jesus will return to earth to raise from the
dead His sleeping saints (for believers do not enter into glory until the
resurrection), and translate the living believer. "For the Lord Himself shall descend from heaven with a shout . . . and the dead in
Christ shall rise first, and we who are living and remain shall be caught
up together with them to meet the Lord in the air; and so shall we
ever be with the Lord." "Then shall be brought to pass the saying,
Death is swallowed up in victory." This will be the first resurrection—
"they that are Christ's at His coming." It will be a triumphant and
glorious resurrection—"every man in his own order."

The day is fast approaching when the archangel will trumpet the
"assembly" call of God, and they that "sleep in Jesus" shall come forth
and take up the heavenward march to glory. "Christ the first-fruits,
afterward they that are Christ's at His coming." Then will be fulfilled
the words "Because I live, ye shall live also."—Selected.

"God Is Not the God of the Dead, But of the Living."—Matt. 22:32 (660).

There has been in all ages a vast amount of speculation as to the
state of the soul, after the death of the body, before the day of the
resurrection, and many very widely different opinions have been and
are still held even by good and Christian people.

It is a question which can only be settled, if at all, by a study of
the teachings of the Bible. The refined and fine-spun arguments which
reason can furnish on the probabilities in the case throw very little
light on the subject and have never yet so satisfied a single soul as to
cause it to have any well grounded belief or trust in the conclusions
which reason has come to on the tremendous subject. If we would
know anything about the matter it will be found in the revelation which
God has been pleased to make to us, and especially in the teachings
of Christ. It is a matter which we are all interested in, and I do not
consider the time wasted, even if after earnest research we are not
able to come to as definite a conclusion about it as about some other
points of revelation.

If the Savior had not intended us to know something about it He would have remained silent on the subject, which I do not think He has done. My research leads me to two conclusions as follows:

First. That the soul does subsist after death and in some place of abode suited to its altered condition.

Second. That this state is not, in all probability, a state of insensibility, but of thought, consciousness, content and happiness.—H. N. Conry, D. D.

"Dust Thou Art, And To Dust Thou Shalt Return."—Gen. 3:19 (661).

It was a quaint but solemn fancy of the poet, to apostrophize a molehill in a churchyard, as containing part, perhaps, of a great company of human beings. It is strange, indeed, to think how many mortals may meet in that small hillock; how winds and rains may there have brought together in death those who never met in life; how the warm blood once ran through that crumbling mould; how every atom of it claims closest kindred with ourselves! And we remember, too, how science tells us, not as a striking fancy, but as a certain fact, that the whole material world is pervaded by the atoms which entered into the material frames of generations that are gone. There is something of them in the yellow autumn harvests, and in the leafy summer trees; something in the dust which our footsteps stir, and which the breeze wafts in play. There is but one generation of humankind alive at once; but there are a hundred slumbering in the dust together. "All that tread the globe, are but a handful to the tribes that slumber in its bosom." No wonder that men, upon any authority less certain than that of the Almighty God Himself, should have failed to believe that what was so widely dispersed and so completely assimilated, should ever be separated, assembled, quickened again.—Boyd.

"If Christ Hath Not Been Raised, Then Is Our Preaching Vain, Your Faith Is Also Vain . . . Ye Are Yet In Your Sins. Then Also They That Are Fallen Asleep In Christ Have Perished."—1 Cor. 15:17, 18 (662).

I. If this is the final word about Him, there is not a shadow of hope.

"Eat, drink and die, for we are souls bereaved.
Of all the creatures under heaven's wide cope,
We are the most hopeless who had once most hope,
And most beliefless that had most believed.
Ashes to ashes, dust to dust,
As of the unjust, also of the just,
Yea, of that Just One, too!
It is the one sad gospel that is true,—
Christ is not risen."

II. But this is not the last word. Rather, it is this,—"Christ hath been raised. He is alive forevermore." The story of Christianity is the story of the risen Christ. All that has been done He has done. His last promise to His disciples, as He sent them out, was, "Lo, I am with you always, even unto the end of the world."—J. R. Miller, D. D.

And They Departed Quickly From The Sepulcher With Fear And Great Joy; And Did Run To Bring His Disciples Word.—Matt. 28:8 (663).

On their way to the sepulcher the two Marys are walking together in the same dark shadow that from the beginning has shrouded the hearts of mourners visiting the last resting-places of their dead. They go, looking to find all at the tomb as they saw it left by Joseph and Nicodemus on the preceding Friday afternoon. It is as quiet as it was then, but in all else how changed! The stone lying at a distance away and, where it had stood, a black open doorway instead. The accustomed signs of death are gone. Can it be that they had missed the way; that they have come to the wrong spot, as is not unfrequently the case amid the intricate windings of a modern city cemetery? No, they cannot have mistaken either the path or the place. The path from Jerusalem is both short and plain. The sepulcher is by itself, in a private garden. The place and its surroundings are recognized as soon as seen; the same stone-hewn vault, the same rocky shelf on which they saw tenderly laid the lifeless body of their Lord. Here lay His head, and there His feet. But there where lay His feet are now only the linen bandages in which the body was wound, and here wrapped together in a place by itself is the napkin that was about His head. Even the silence is changed; more profound and painful than it would be were the body still here.

At this so strangely altered appearance the two friends are most deeply and painfully perplexed—the perplexity soon turns to affright as close beside them is suddenly seen standing, with lightning-like countenance and snow-white apparel, an angel of the Lord. Falling upon their knees they lean forward, bowing their faces in terror to the ground.

From this terrified suspense they are quickly relieved, however, by the loving tones of the angel's voice which is as fear-dispelling as his words: "You seek Jesus who was crucified. He is not here. He is risen. Come see the place where the Lord lay."—"From Text to Talk."

"Now Are We The Sons of God, And It Doth Not Yet Appear What We Shall Be."—1 John 3:2 (664).

The fact of sonship is a fact with an unmeasured sequence. In a hollow of the hills sleeps a stagnant pool; no prophet am I, nor need be, to foretell its history. Yonder is a silver ribbon on the hillside, a streamlet beginning its journey to the sea. Dare I, who am so confident about the future of the pool, venture prophecy of the stream? Can I guess what forces it will gather to itself as it winds through the valleys, what manifold purposes of men it may come to serve, what wealth of cities and of nations it may come to carry on its bosom to its home in the ocean? Stagnant pool! I know its tale; but "living water"—"it doth not yet appear" what they shall be. And these things are an allegory of the life that is life indeed.

Let us get back into the antecedents of this fact of sonship. Out of what has it emerged? Look into the heart of man, with its sin, hate, rebellion, and uncleanness, until the spirit sinks at the baseness of it. It was fairly photographed, this unregenerate heart of man, by One who knew "what was in man." "From within, out of the heart of man proceed evil thoughts, adulteries, fornications, murders, thefts, covetousness, wickedness, deceit, luxuriousness, an evil eye, blasphemy, pride, foolishness." What, then, is this marvel of grace? This darkness enlightened, this stubbornness broken, this foulness cleansed, and the heart of a man, photographed thus by One who saw and knew, becoming the Bethlehem of a new incarnation of the Son of God! If that is done out of such material—and it is done, is it not?—what may we not expect the love of God, by whose power such a wonder is wrought, will still do? If "from death to life" is thus possible, from life to more life, and yet more, must be possible also.—Sculptors of Life.

"The Sting of Death Is Sin, And The Strength of Sin Is The Law. But Thanks Be To God Which Giveth Us The Victory Through Our Lord Jesus Christ."—1 Cor. 15:56, 57 (665).

We shall take up these two points to dwell upon.

I. The awfulness which hangs round the dying hour.

II. Faith conquering in death.

I. That which makes it peculiarly terrible to die is asserted in this passage to be guilt. We lay a stress upon this expression,—the sting. It is not said that sin is the only bitterness; but it is the sting which contains in it the venom of a most exquisite torture. And, in truth, brethren, it is no mark of courage to speak lightly of human dying. We may do it in bravado, or in wantonness; but no man who thinks can call it a trifling thing to die. True thoughtfulness must shrink from death without Christ.

1. Now, the first cause which makes it a solemn thing to die is the instinctive cleaving of everything that lives to its own existence. That unutterable thing which we call our being—the idea of parting with it is agony.

2. The second reason is not one of imagination at all, but most sober reality. It is a solemn thing to die, because it is the parting with all round which the heart's best affections, have twined themselves.

II. We pass to our second subject—Faith conquering in death.

Let us understand what really is the victory over fear. It may be rapture, or it may not. All that depends very much on temperament; and, after all, the broken words of a dying man are a very poor index of his real state before God. Rapturous hope has been granted to martyrs in peculiar moments.

1. In the first place, brethren, if we would be conquerors, we must realize God's love in Christ. Take care not to be under the law. Constraint never yet made a conqueror; the utmost it can do is to make

either a rebel or a slave. Believe that God loves you. He gave a triumphant demonstration of it in the Cross. Never shall we conquer self till we have learned to love. My Christian brethren, let us remember our high privilege. Christian life, so far as it deserves the name, is victory.

There is need of encouragement for those of us whose faith is not of the conquering, but the timid kind. There are some whose hearts will reply to all this, Surely victory is not always a Christian's portion. Is there no cold, dark watching in Christian life; no struggle when victory seems a mockery to speak of—no times when life and light seem feeble, and Christ is to us but a name, and death a reality? "Perfect love casteth out fear."—Frederick A. Robertson.

"So Also Is The Resurrection of The Dead. It Is Sown In Corruption; It Is Raised in Incorruption; It Is Sown in Dishonor; It Is Raised In Glory."—1 Cor. 14:42-44 (666).

I. This body of ours is a body that, whenever and however sown, is sown in corruption, in dishonor, and in weakness. These are the three capital faults of our present mortal bodies. And the three faults are intimately connected and mutually related. They grow into one another; they flow from one another; first corruption, then dishonor, lastly weakness. (1) Corruption is liability to dissolution and decay. The body that is to be sown in corruption is a body capable, or susceptible, of decomposition. It may be broken up. And when it is broken up, its fragments, or fragmentary remains, may be resolved into the constituent elements, or component particles, of which they consist. (2) But dishonor also belongs to what is sown: to the bare grain, to the mortal frame. Under the rich and rare clothing of joyous health, of radiant and smiling bloom, we watch the slow and secret gnawing of the insidious element of corruption that is too surely to undermine it all. The honor that is so perishable is scarcely honor at all. (3) As corruptibility implies dishonor, so it occasions, or causes, weakness. It paralyzes physical strength. It paralyzes both strength of endurance and strength for action and performance.

II. None of these defects will be found in the resurrection body. That body is incorruptible, indestructible, a meet companion for the immaterial and immortal soul. It is to be no clog or restraint, through its impotency, on the free soul; but apt and able, as its minister, strong to do its pleasure.—Rev. R. S. Candlish.

"If a Man Die Shall He Live Again?"—Job 14:14 (667).

God has answered the question very clearly for us. Most of the secret things of God and of man are mysteries only because our eyes are holden. Lord, open our eyes that we may see. God has written the truth of immortality large in several volumes. First is the book of nature. Through the laws of the natural world God first spoke to man. "Howbeit that was not first which is spiritual, but that which is natural." Nature preaches the Gospel of life, the conservation of its forces. "Let nothing be lost" is its imperial command. The seed is sown into the ground, it dies, decays, but ere long it bursts forth into new life. In the furrows of the field God has written the fact of resurrection.

Second, the Bible. Now things are not necessarily true because they are in the Bible, but they are in the Bible because they are true. The Bible is a book of life. Through it runs, like a scarlet line, their idea of life. The patriarchs were buried with their fathers. There was the dim idea of a reunion beyond. Job, down in the depths of despair raises the question, but in the same breath answers "I wait till my change comes." Psalms and prophecies alike are colored by this thought and inspired by their hope. The New Testament throbs with it. The apostolic teaching was that of the resurrection.

Third, the personal Jesus. It was a hope in His own heart and He inspired it in the hearts of His followers. "Because I live, ye shall live also." "I go to prepare a place for you." In His own personal life He won the victory over death and the grave and conclusively demonstrated the fact of immortality, so that men might no longer doubt.

Fourth. But God has written this truth in our own personal lives and experiences. We have certain instincts, certain longings and desires, certain unrest, unfulfilled yearnings, these will find their answer, their corresponding element elsewhere. These undeveloped powers of our being will come to fruition, to completion yonder. The incomplete life demands a future life.—C. E. Schaeffer, D. D.

"In My Father's House Are Many Mansions."—John 14:2 (668).

I. How much the presence with us of this realized immortality— the alert awareness of the reality and proximity of the other world— would do to keep earth from becoming too prominent, too predominant, in our thinking.

The sounds and sights of sense press in upon us with such insistency; they are so clamorous in their efforts to gain and hold and monopolize our attention, that these things which though more real, and infinitely more important, are unseen, are ever in danger of being thrust aside or obscured.

It is so much easier to see than to perceive; to hear than to reflect, to sense things than to spiritually discern them, that the former is apt to shoulder the more subtle method aside. We permit earth's songs to silence heaven's melodies, and earth's spectacles to eclipse heaven's visions.

But he who has come under the spell of this "power of an endless life;" who has cultivated the habit of bi-worldliness as a permanent heart attitude—for him first things are kept first, and earth is a continual reminder of heaven.

II. What a difference the keen realization of these great truths as vividly present facts would make in us when bereavement comes into our lives.

We suffer not merely because of our loss of some dear one. The fact of temporary separation is not sufficient to account for the poignancy of our grief. But it is rather the dimness and vagueness of our apprehension of their continued existence that intensifies our sorrow. It is so hard to get away from the graveyard thought which persistently clings to us, and in spite of our better knowledge we think of them as captives in a tomb.

III. And then, as a crowning experience, how this distinct realization of the other life robs the thought of death—the fuller entrance into that other life—of all dread.—J. H. B.

"God took him."—Gen. 5:24 (669).

I. Early in the Bible record, in the fifth chapter of Genesis, we read of the first translation. "And Enoch walked with God: and he was not; for God took him." Beautifully has Dr. J. T. McFarland expressed all that we know about Enoch:

> They talked and walked, down many years—
> The way was called The Vale of Tears;
> But he who walked with God received
> Such comfort that he little grieved.
> And walking thus, and talking so,
> The Man and God fared onward slow,
> Until they reach a secret spot—
> God took him, and the man was not.

II. And it came to pass many centuries later, that Jehovah would take up Elijah by a whirlwind into heaven. He, too, had walked and talked with God; God took him and he was not. The rushing whirlwind was a fitting accompaniment for the departure of the stormy prophet.

III. But no man ever walked and talked with God as did His Son Jesus Christ. Forty days after His resurrection He and His disciples were on the Mount of Olives over against Bethany. And He lifted up His hands, and blessed them. And it came to pass, while He blessed them, He parted from them, and was carried up into heaven.—Tarbell.

XI. HEAVEN.

REFLECTIONS AND ILLUSTRATIONS.

Heaven Anticipated (670).

I heard the other day of an old man who was dying of an excruciating trouble. And his minister, doing his poor best to comfort him, said, "Courage, friend, you will soon be in heaven." "Why, sir," said the old saint, "what do you mean? I've been in heaven for twenty years." That was the secret of the heroic courage that amazed the world in the early Christian martyrs. That was why tender women and fond mothers could sacrifice everything they loved for Christ. It was not that they were stronger than the heathen; but it was that they saw more than the heathen—they saw through the veil into another kingdom, where Christ was enthroned at the right hand of God. I stood a few months ago in one of those amphitheatres where the Christian martyrs used to be put to death. It was a little worn by the storms of countless years, but so perfect that bullfights are still held in it. And as I pictured the thousands who once filled these seats, and gazed on the battle with the wild beasts below, I thought how perfectly they could see everything, except the one thing that made all the difference. The crowds saw not the vision of the opened heaven.—G. H. Morrison, D. D.

The Many Mansions (671).

It is all one house—it is all the Father's home—and we and the dead but dwell in different rooms. Not into any far country do we travel in the awful moment when this life is done—not through a shadowy and undiscovered land has the soul to journey that it may be with God—it is only a passing from one room to the other; a step through the veil into a brighter chamber—there is no facing of the storm or of the night, for we never are beyond our Father's roof. I can understand a country child being afraid when it is sent out in the darkness on some errand. For it goes out alone into the night, and the road is lonely, and every shadow awesome. But when a child is called into the dining room that it may be with its father and its mother; when it leaves the schoolroom with its weary tasks, and goes to the room where its father and mother are—that moment, if childhood and fatherhood be real, is one of the brightest moments of its day. Brethren, in our Father's house are many rooms, and death is but the leaving of the schoolroom. Not on some perilous journey are we sent, out of the home, into the stormy night. 'Tis but a step, and lo! another room—brighter and larger than the one we left—for our task is over and our school days done, and we shall be glad with God for evermore.—Morrison.

The True Sight (672).

There is much sorrow which would instantly be turned to joy if those who weep could see things as they really are. The loss of a friend is grieved over; but if we could follow the friend into the glory of heaven, we should rejoice. The things we think are calamities and causes for sorrow, if we could see them as God sees them, would appear to be blessings. If Mary had found the body of Jesus in the tomb, as she expected to do, it would have been cause for grief. The empty tomb at which she grieved was the reason for the world's hope. Mary did not recognize Jesus. How needless her sorrow was! For if she had known Him, joy would have filled her heart. Is it otherwise with us in our times of fear? Jesus is beside us, even speaking to us; but we do not know it is He, nor do we hear His words of comfort. We grieve and let ourselves be crushed by our sorrows, not knowing that the sorrow is only the shadow of a great joy, and that what seems to us emptiness and loss is really the blessedness of heaven.—From "Evening Thoughts."

Merely Going Home (673).

The hospital tents had been filled up as fast as the wounded men had been brought to the rear. Among the number was a young man mortally wounded and not able to speak. It was near midnight, and many a loved one from our homes lay sleeping on the battlefield—that sleep that knows no waking until Jesus shall call for them. The surgeons had been their round of duty, and for a moment all was quiet. Suddenly this young man, before speechless, called in a clear, distinct voice, "Here!" The surgeon hastened to his side and asked what he wished. "Nothing," he said. "They were calling the roll in heaven, and I was answering to my name." He turned his head and was gone to join the army whose uniforms were washed white in the blood of the lamb.—Selected.

Released (674).

A friend in Ireland once met a little Irish boy who had caught a sparrow. The poor little bird was trembling in his hand, and seemed very anxious to escape. The gentleman begged the boy to let it go, as the bird could not do him any good; but the boy said he would not, for he had chased it three hours before he could catch it. He tried to reason it out of the boy, but in vain. At last he offered to buy the bird; the boy agreed to the price, and it was paid. Then the gentleman took the poor little thing and held it out on his hand. The boy had been holding it very fast, for the boy was stronger than the bird, just as Satan is stronger than we, and there it sat for a time, scarcely able to realize the fact that it had got liberty; but in a little while it flew away, chirping, as if to say to the gentleman, "Thank you! thank you! you have redeemed me." That is what redemption is—buying back and setting free. So Christ came back to break the fetters of sin, to open the prison doors and set the sinner free. This is the good news the gospel of Christ—"Ye are not redeemed with corruptible things as silver and gold, but with the precious blood of Christ."

Other Worldliness (675).

There are few things that the average Christianity of this day needs more than that note of unworldliness, of belonging to another community than that in which our lot in the present is cast, which my text prescribes for us. We must speak the language of the land in which we dwell, but we should speak it with a foreign accent. There should be something about us, even when we are doing the same things as other people do, and which we must to a large extent do, that tells that the same things are by us done from such different motives that they become different from themselves when done by the men whose cares and interests and hopes are "cribbed, cabined, and confined" by the triviality of the transient present.

And that wholesome detachment will enfeeble no work, will darken no joy; but it will take the poison out of many a sorrow, and it will make small things great, and to be greatly done. He that stands above his work can come down upon it with more efficient blows, and the man that is lifted above the things seen and temporal will be able to draw all the sweetness out of them, to recognize all the nobleness in them, and to work nobly upon them. You are the citizens of another community; therefore you are to work here worthily thereof.—Alexander Maclaren, D. D.

Going Home (676).

It was evening, and a woman with the sunset light in her face was nearing home. The journey had been long and hard and the sky overcast with clouds. But now she was almost home and the gold and crimson lights of sunset were just ahead. It had been a journey full of toil and there had been many troubles. She had not minded the hardships so much, for she had early learned that they were to be expected by all who traveled that way. But there had been bitterness and cruel hurts.

The shadows were lowering behind her, but the sunset light gleamed before. Seh thought of those whom she had helped and who yet needed even greater help; she knew, but they did not; she hesitated to go on, though rest and home were just ahead. But perhaps it was not given her to help any more, for she was very, very tired.

So many things had hurt. She had not been ready of speech or action in defense against cruelty and wrong when the shafts had come her way; and besides she had been so busy there had not been time to return like for like. Or perhaps, and she had not been quite sure about that, perhaps it had been best and right for her to endure in silence. She was not sure. And if she were to send forth winged shafts of bitterness, perhaps they might go astray, striking some who already had overmuch of pain. What would God have her do? That had always been the question. Her philosophy and her faith were plain and simple: "We ought to try to do what God wants us to do, no matter what people do or say; for pleasing God is all that counts in the long run, anyway." Such had been her summing up in her own homely phrasing.

But simple and plain as were this faith and philosophy, they had cost much. And now, when she was so near home, she did not regret, but was glad, as glad as one so weary could be. For the simple faith that had not questioned the commands did not now question the promises

Often she thought of what seemed to her the little accomplished; but she had tried faithfully always to do her best. And she remembered God's mercy.

Home was almost in sight. There were rest and peace and joy without shadow of pain or sorrow. There was something wonderful about this homegoing. For as the light faded in the sunset a new day would dawn, a day made glorious by the light which filled it, the light of the glory of God. This day would never end. In place of sorrow and pain and partings, there would be peace and gladness and meetings wonderful in their joy. There would be glory and joy unspeakable.

And so the weary traveler journeyed on to the sunset.—Herald and Presbyter.

Mothers are Looking Down from Heaven (676).

I remember in the Exposition building in Dublin, while I was speaking about heaven, I said something to the effect that at this moment a mother is looking down from heaven expecting the salvation of her daughter here tonight, and I pointed down to a young lady in the audience. Next morning I received this letter:

"On Wednesday, when you were speaking of heaven, you said, 'It may be this moment there is a mother looking down from heaven expecting the salvation of her child who is here.' You were apparently looking at the very spot where my child was sitting. My heart said, 'That is my child. That is her mother.' Tears sprang to my eyes. I bowed my head and prayed, 'Lord, direct that word to my darling child's heart; Lord save my child.' I was then anxious till the close of the meeting, when I went to her. She was bathed in tears. She rose, put her arms around me, and kissed me. When walking down to you she told me, it was that same remark—about the mother looking down from heaven—that found the way home to her, and asked me, 'Papa, what can I do for Jesus?' "—Moody.

Where Heaven Is (677).

"You forgot to mention where heaven is," said a good lady to her pastor after a sermon on the better land. "On yonder hilltop stands a cottage, madame," replied the man of God; "a widow lives there in want; she has no bread, no fuel, no medicine, and her child is at the point of death. If you will carry to her this afternoon some little cup of cold water in the name of Him who went about doing good, you will find the answer to your inquiry."—Heavenly Harmonies.

Earth's Best. (678)—Do not make heaven attractive merely by deposing earth. A cheap expedient! Make earth its richest and best, and then be able to make heaven still higher.—Phillips Brooks.

The Heavenly Hope (679).

Such a hope of the life to come is filled with blessing. The rich and learned and powerful, who have faith, may know that what they have is but a hint as to what they are to have; and the poor and weak may know that some day they will be heirs, with the rich, of the riches of the Father's glory. This is God's gift to the poor man, and not man's efforts to pay off earth's debts with checks on the bank of heaven. This hope of immortality is a blessing rare to the sick and persecuted and tempted and neglected and suffering of our race. Through their sufferings and tears they may discern the meaning of the cross and receive its promise of a life when temptations shall no more torment, when there shall be no more tears, when rest shall be theirs, and sorrow and sighing shall flee away. This same blessing comforts those whose forms are bending low with the weight of years. While the snows of winter are gathering upon their heads they may have eternal springtime in the heart, awaiting that life with Christ, which is "far better." Immortality gives the hope that comforts the heart of the one who sits in sorrow because

> "A reaper whose name is Death
> Hath with his sickle keen
> Reaped the bearded grain at a breath
> And the flowers that grew between,"

and like Israel's king when his little boy lay dead, we may rise up, and putting off the garments of grief may say, "I shall go to him, he shall not return to me."

Thus the hope of immortality through the living Christ becomes a blessing in every condition of life.—S. S. Hilscher, D. D.

The Open Gates (680).

The gospel is the offer to all who will have it of eternal life. Christ is His own gospel. A mighty change must be wrought in men. On this side of the grave they are urged to receive this gospel and to share its benefits. That which is born of the flesh is flesh; we must be born again through faith in Christ. If a man die he shall live again, but only through faith in Christ will his life be one of fellowship with God. This faith swings heaven's gate wide open and makes the child of time in the fullest sense the child of eternity.

Longings For Heaven. (681)—Should longings for heaven fill much of our thought and time? Not to such an extent as to prevent the devotion of all our energies to the work assigned us by the Master. Surely not to the breeding of the slightest discontent with the duration of our tarrying here. Saint Paul's position about it (Phil. 1:23) would seem to be ideal.

Sounds From Home (682).

On the shores of the Adriatic it is said that the wives of the fishermen are in the habit, at eventide, of going down to the seashore and singing a stanza of a familiar hymn. After they have sung it they listen till they hear, borne by the winds across the sea, another stanza of the same hymn, sung by their husbands as they are tossed by the gale upon the waves. From the shore of heaven the Father calls down to His beloved, tossed on the waves of passionate humanity, a word of affection and approval.—S. S. Times.

Death a Genial Angel (683).

Death should be thought of as a gentle, genial angel, God's kindly messenger sent to convey His permission for our release from earth tasks, so that we may with shouting hail the fact that school is out and we are going home. "Not of the clod is the life of God; let it mount as it will from form to form." How strange, when we come to think of it, to speak of ourselves or our friends as "in danger" when we or they draw near the moment of looking into the face of our Redeemer. Too many of these phrases, born of blind unbelief and saturated with the sludge of the senses, are found on the lips of those who should give testimony to another way of beholding matters.—The Riches of His Grace.

Home (684).

Heaven is a beautiful home. It is a prepared place for a prepared people. It is sure for those who love God. And all who love or trust Him will be brought there safely. He is able to keep them from falling, and to present them faultless before the presence of His glory with exceeding joy, and he will do it for all who trust Him. He is the only wise God. He is our Saviour. Glory and majesty, dominion and power are His now and forever, and He will keep us all along the way until He brings us into the home of eternal holiness and happiness and glory.

Compensation In Heaven (685).

It will not take long for God to make up to you in the next world for all you have suffered in this. As you enter heaven He may say: "Give this man one of those towered and colannaded palaces on that ridge of gold overlooking the Sea of Glass. Give this woman a home among those amaranthine blooms and between those fountains tossing the everlasting sunlight. Give her a couch canopied with rainbows to pay her for all the fatigues of wifehood and motherhood, and house-keeping, from which she had no rest for forty years. Give these newly-arrived souls from earth the costliest things and roll to their door the grandest chariots, and hang on their walls the sweetest harps that ever responded to singers seraphic. Give to them rapture on rapture, cele-bration on celebration, jubilee on jubilee, heaven on heaven. They had a hard time on earth earning a livelihood, or nursing sick children, or waiting on querulous old age, or battling falsehoods that were told about them, or were compelled to work after they had got short-breathed, and rheumatic, and dim-sighted. Chamberlains of heaven, keepers of the King's robe, banqueters of eternal royalty, make up to them a hundred-fold, a thousandfold, a millionfold for all they suffered from waddling clothes to shroud, and let all those who, whether on the hills or in the temples, or on the thrones or on Jasper wall, were helped and sanctified and prepared for this heavenly realm by trial and pain, stand up and wave their scepters!" And I looked, and behold! nine-tenths of the ransomed rose to their feet, and nine-tenths of the scepters swayed to and fro in the light of the sun that never sets, and then I understood better than before that trouble comes for beneficent purposes, and that on the coldest nights the aurora is brightest in the northern heavens.— T. DeWitt Talmage.

"Meet For The Inheritance" (686).

Heaven would be an uninteresting realm, and, in some respects, a dangerous one if we were not educated for it by means of trials which bring out nobility of character. Only after the friction of time is it safe to promise a frictionless eternity.—William T. Herridge.

Heaven Is Christ (687).

Beautiful are these words of Phillips Brooks: "Heaven is not only real because His humanity is there, not merely glorious because His greatness is there. It is dear because His love is there." And beautiful, too, are the dying words of Charles Kingsley: "It is not darkness I am going to, for God is light. It is not lonely, for Christ is with me. It is not an unknown country, for Christ is there."—Selected.

Compensation in Eternity (689).

It is not possible for us to have in this life any grief or misfortune that will not find in eternity such alleviation and compensation that we shall forget it absolutely, or cease, at any rate, to remember it with any pain. Is it some physical defect, like deafness? Our ears will hear such wonderful things there that in the first hour we shall almost forget that we ever were deaf. Is it lameness? We shall speed there with a wish over spaces that stagger our belief. And thus every one of earth's handicaps will be removed in heaven.—Amos R. Wells.

Identification (690).

At one time when David Livingstone was engaged in work connected with his great mission in dark Africa, he was attacked by a huge lion of the jungle. The ferocious beast grasped the arm of the missionary in his powerful jaws and broke the bone. Livingstone was rescued by two friends who had accompanied him, but for a long time he was obliged to keep his arm in a sling. He carried the scar of the wound as long as he lived. When the faithful natives brought back his dead body to his native land, this scar on the arm once broken was one of the means by which the remains of the missionary were identified by his friends.

"The Lord knoweth them that are His." When the final day of judgment comes, the Lord will separate His faithful ones from the numberless multitude, from the kindreds of all nations. He will know His own by the scars they have received for Him in the fight of faith. He will know them by their likeness to Jesus Christ.—Homiletic Review.

The Great White Throne (691).

A great white throne . . . its occupant the carpenter of Nazareth, robed in the majesty of the Ancient of Days. . . . His retinue of angels stretch in surging, shimmering ranks beyond the stars, far upward to the gate of heaven. Before Him are gathered all nations:

Adam from his grave hard by the gates of the lost Paradise; patriarchs and prophets, whose eminent ashes long since mingled with common clay; the great, from marble sarcophagi and carven shrine; the beggar, from his unmarked wayside grave; the child that breathed but once and shuddered and expired—all sweep upward at the voice of the archangel. But more important than the scene is the procedure of the Judge. He makes a distinct line of separation between the resurrected dead. "He shall separate them one from another, as a shepherd divideth his sheep from the goats." Criterion: Past treatment of Himself. He came to earth a stranger. Acceptance or rejection of the Stranger the basis of judgment.—Rev. S. G. Nelson.

The Cheerfulness of Heaven (692).

Cheerfulness has its consummation in heaven. To some minds, however, the conception of heaven is not attractive. They have a fellow feeling with the youngster who said to his mother, "Mamma, if I should die, and go to heaven, do you think Jesus would let me come down to earth on Saturdays and play with the boys if I was real good the rest of the week?" Heaven, in the imagination of some, is desired as an escapement from hell. It is simply selected as the alternative of a direr evil. Should such souls pass, unregenerate, into paradise, they would come far short of cheerfulness, and would gladly avail themselves of a prompt exit to the place prepared for the devil and his angels.

Heaven is the happy home of multitudinous ransomed ones, who have come out of "the great tribulation, and have washed their robes, and made them white in the blood of the Lamb." They have entered the beautiful Zion above "with songs and everlasting joy." There are no tears in heaven save those wept by saints on earth; and these sparkle like gems in the bottle where God preserves them. The "sweet fields beyond the swelling flood" are upheaved by no graves, for death is a total stranger there, and the bells of the New Jerusalem clang forth no funeral knell. "All bitterness, and wrath, and anger, and clamor, and evil speaking," are banished from heaven; and every member of the glorious company is "kind one to another, tender hearted," and helpfully loving. At the marriage of Cana the wine ran short, and Christ miraculously provided for the guests enough to fill six water pots. His guests in heaven drink of the river of unsullied pleasures, and are abundantly satisfied with the fatness of the Father's house. At His right hand there is fullness of joy; and every saint is satisfied when he awaketh in the likeness of Christ. He is satisfied then, and his capacity for satisfaction increaseth wondrously. The law of heaven is a law of lordly growth; of growth "from glory to glory."—Rev. Henry T. Scholl.

Future Recognition (693).

The subject of future recognition is one that occupies the mind of thoughtful people as much or more than any other living question. While it is a general belief that we shall know each other in heaven, as David said in regard to his boy that had died, "I shall go to him but he shall not return to me;" and yet how faint is our conception of the immediate state of the departed. How many heart-broken mothers have mourned and wept beside the cold grave as the body of their darlings are being placed in the seeming resting place, until the resurrection morn, while really the angels have already escorted their spirits to the home of the soul, and have introduced them to kindred spirits above.

While there is but little said in the Scriptures in regard to the immediate state of God's departed ones, yet Jesus left on record His statement, assuring us that the soul of the departed does not sleep in the grave until the general judgment. In Luke 16 we have Christ's account of the rich man and Lazarus. Christ says, "And it came to pass that the beggar died, and was carried by the angels into Abraham's bosom." We learn by this narrative that Christ taught His disciples that as soon as the soul of the righteous leaves the body, it is carried by angels to a resting place in the paradise of God. It seems so reasonable that Christ should have some statement concerning the immediate abode of those who die in the Lord. If in this life it is to us "a heaven below our Redeemer to know," then how reasonable it seems that heaven is composed of two apartments, one here and one over there, and that there is just a step between the two. It seems reasonable that Christ intended to teach us that when we leave our friends here we join our friends who have gone before. How comforting it must seem to the poor, afflicted, suffering saint of God to know that death is only a sweet messenger come to "deliver them from all their troubles," and to introduce them to their loved ones who have preceded them. Not until we know God's plans and purposes will we understand how much He has done to make us happy here and hereafter.—The Christian Advocate.

Heaven's Occupations (694).

It is true the labors which are now laid on us for food, raiment, outward interests, cease at the grave. But far deeper wants than those of the body are developed in heaven. There it is that the spirit first becomes truly conscious of its capacities; that truth opens before us in its infinity; that the universe is seen to be a boundless sphere for discovery, for science, for the sense of beauty, for beneficence and for adoration. There new objects to live for, which reduce to nothingness present interests, are constantly unfolded. We must not think of heaven as a stationary community. I think of it as a world of stupendous plans and efforts for its own improvement. I think of it as a society passing through successive stages of development, virtue, knowledge, power, by the energy of its own members. Celestial genius is always active to explore the great laws of the creation and the everlasting principles of the mind, to disclose the beautiful in the universe and to discover the means by which every soul may be carried forward. In that world, as in this, there are diversities of intellect; and the highest minds find their happiness and progress in elevating the less improved. There the work of education, which began here, goes on without end; and a diviner philosophy than is taught on earth reveals the spirit to itself, and awakens it to earnest, joyful effort for its own perfection.—Emerson.

Future Life Hidden (695).

The mother hangs over the cradle wondering whether the child will be worker or thinker or dreamer, but nature will not answer. The youth spreads the sail, puts out to sea to make his fortune, but even his best beloved can not tell whether he shall strike a hidden rock, and the craft go down, or whether with weather-beaten sails and laden with treasure he shall return in victory from a world-round voyage. Gold and gems lie in the earth, but man must uncover them; medicines and balms are in the trees for fevers, but man must find them; the brain and nerve make up a mental harp, but man must tune the strings; a purple flood courses through man's veins and arteries, but a scholar must solve the secret; an unseen continent lies hidden beyond the western clouds, but the voyager must discover the new world. Somewhere are islands of peace "that lift their fronded palms in air," but the vista opens step by step, scene by scene, in orderly sequence. And therefore this silence about the life beyond the tomb is natural and normal, and to be expected. When we are at the end of our life voyage as spiritual discoverers, like the Genoese captain, we, too, shall behold perfumed boughs floating in the current, and discern afar off in the morning twilight a fire kindled on the beach, while the perfume of a sweetness hitherto unknown shall greet the traveler. Out of the deep of God's mind and purpose we came; into the deep of God's heart and will we go; therefore all is well for those who seek the land beyond the sea. There is nothing hidden that shall not be revealed, and nothing revealed that man can find out for himself.—N. D. Hillis, D. D.

Looking Forward (696).

Run familiarly through the streets of the heavenly Jerusalem; visit the patriarchs and prophets, salute the apostles and admire the armies of martyrs; lead on the heart from street to street, bring it into the palace of the great King; lead it, as it were, from chamber to chamber. Say to it: "Here must I lodge, here must I die, here must I praise, here must I love and be loved. My tears will then be wiped away, my groans be turned to another tune, my cottage of clay be changed to this palace, my prison rags to these splendid robes; 'for the former things are passed away.'"—Richard Baxter.

God's Palace. (697)—It comes to this, that when God would build a palace for Himself to dwell in with His children, He does not want His scaffold so constructed that they shall be able to make a house of it for themselves, and live like apes instead of angels.—MacDonald.

The Way to Heaven. (698)—"Take the first turn to the right, and go straight forward."—Bp. Wilberforce.

"That Better Country" (699).

But it has the same meaning for our own future as for that of our friends. When death shall come to us at last, it will not mean extinction, but, if we are hid with Christ in God, merely transfer. "That better country" will be the new home in which our souls, no longer clogged by earth's limitations, will expand and develop with naught to retard their progress. How this scatters the fears which clutched our hearts in the night of our ignorance.

Friends In Heaven (700).

Are we not richer for their being there? Are we not made nearer to heaven by thinking of them there? They have known us so intimately, they have known our history, our individuality, our soul wants, our aspirations, our trials. We have wandered with them hand in hand through the tangled wood of life. We have lost our way together. We have hungered and thirsted together, and looked out with weary and perplexed star-gazing, now trying this path and now that; and we have rejoiced together when our way has been made plain before us. We have seen them wrestle and strive with life, as we still must. We have seen their heart fail and their hand fall slack, as our full oft may do. We have seen them bear the wrench and strain, the cruel agony which life forces inexorably upon all, in one or other of its phases; and last of all, we have seen them at the river of death. We have seen the heaven opening and the angels descending, and they have been borne from our sight, and as they rose they were transfigured and became as the sons of God.—Harriet Beecher Stowe.

Our Loved Ones There (701).

Heaven will be sweeter and more beautiful, more to be desired because of the entrance through its shining portals of our loved ones. It will be easy for us some day to let go of this life and go to be with the multitude of the redeemed who have "washed their robes and made them white in the blood of the Lamb." Let us think of the last and sweetest home coming in the Father's house of many mansions, where our dear ones are waiting for us, and some night, God knows how soon it may come, they will meet us with outstretched hands. May the blessed Christ come into our hearts more completely, and may we rest our weary souls on Him.—Christian Work.

The Heavenly Company (702).

One of the very greatest attractions of heaven will be its company. There the wicked cease from troubling; for all are holy. What a world ours would be if there were none but godly people in it, even with the imperfections of the present state! But there will be none but the children of God there; and everyone of them will be better than the best are here. If we have ever enjoyed the company of our fellow-believers on earth, when our lips have been unsealed to speak out what lies nearest the heart, what will our enjoyment of their fellowship be when both they and we are perfect?—Stalker.

Eastern Windows. (703)—Someone has beautifully said that the saints and prophets—the ones who even here see more clearly than their fellows—are those who lie sleeping with faces toward the uncurtained eastern windows, whose thin eyelids permit something of the glory of the other world to glimmer through.

Eternity and Loneliness (704).

When you are feeling lonely, think of the hosts of friends you will make during the endless ages you are to live in the spirit world. Think of the great men and women you will meet there, the beautiful ones with whose lives your life will be entwined, the joys of unbroken friendship and exalted communion. Can we not endure a little loneliness, if necessary, during these brief years of preparation?—Wells.

"I Live There." (705)

—A devout Scotchman being asked if he ever expected to go to heaven gave the quaint reply: "Why, mon, I live there!" All the way to heaven is heaven begun to the Christian who walks near enough to God to hear the secrets He has to impart.—Epworth Herald.

Drummond's Illustration (708).

Suppose I hold in one hand a beautiful quartz crystal, and in the other an acorn. There is no comparison between the two as regards beauty. My crystal is many times more beautiful than the dull and shapeless acorn, and yet if I put the crystal through all the processes in my laboratory, I can make nothing else out of it. It returns at last to the same six-sided prism. But if I put my acorn in the ground, by and by there arises the majestic oak. The crystal has reached its highest development. There is nothing beyond for it to attain to, but the acorn is only the germ of what it may be. Now this is the difference between morality and real vital spirituality. Morality has reached its best development upon earth and oftentimes is far more beautiful than spirituality. Ah, but it doth not yet appear what spirituality shall be. It is only in the germ here. By and by in the world to come, compared to what it is now, it shall be as the majestic oak is to the dull and shapeless acorn. Do you compare morality with spirituality? Remember you are comparing the dead crystal with the living seed—the one is dead, the other has life abiding in it. "He that hath the Son hath life."—Selected.

"His Guest" (709).

If we make Jesus the guest of our hearts in this world, he will admit us to be His guest in the celestial mansion. When we return home from a long journey, it is not the house, the furniture or the fireside that gives us joy; it is the sight of the loved ones there. So in our Father's house it will not be the pearl-gate or the golden streets; we shall be glad when we see our Lord! In the language of Bonar's sweet hymn—which I heard sung at his funeral—

"Christ will be the living splendor,
Christ the sunlight mild and tender,
Praises to the Lamb we render,
   Ah, 'tis heaven at last!

"Broken death's dread bands that bound us,
Life and victory around us,
Christ the King Himself hath crowned us,
   Ah, 'tis heaven at last!"
                        —Rev. Theodore L. Cuyler, D. D.

Heaven's Estimate of Values (710).

The deeds that stand highest on the records in heaven are not those
which we vulgarly call great. Many "a cup of cold water only" will
be found to have been rated higher than jeweled golden chalices brimming with rare wines. God's treasuries, where He keeps His children's
gifts, will be like many a mother's secret store of relics of her children,
full of things of no value, what the world calls "trash," but precious
in His eyes for the love's sake that was in them.

All service which is done from the same motive in the same force
is of the same worth in His eyes. It does not matter whether you
have the gospel in a penny Testament printed on thin paper with black
ink, and done up in cloth, or in an illuminated missal glowing in gold
and color, painted with loving care on fair parchment, and bound in
jeweled ivory. And so it matters little about the material or the scale
on which we express our devotion and our aspirations; all depends on
what we copy, not on the size of the canvas on which, or on the material in which, we copy it. "Small service is true service while it
lasts," and the unnoticed insignificant servants may do work every
whit as good and noble as the most widely known, to whom have been
intrusted by Christ tasks that mould the ages.—Maclaren.

The Influence of Heaven on Earth (711).

Henry Ward Beecher once received a letter begging him to preach
the next Sunday on hell that the writer might be kept from commit-
ting a great sin to which he was tempted. Mr. Beecher chose as his
text for that day "In my Father's house are many mansions," and said
in his sermon that if that verse would not save the man, nothing would.

An Incorruptible Inheritance (712).

Incorruptible, i. e., as to its substance. It is not liable to decay.
Nature looks her best in the days of early autumn. The golden corn-
sheaves; the gorgeous tints of the fading leaves; the berries of the
wild rose and the rowan; the undiminished foliage of the forest trees;
the ruddy wealth of the orchard: but, amid all, our enjoyment is tinged
with sadness, for we know that decay lies beneath, eagerly at work;
and that ere long the woodland glade will be strewn with the dying
leaves, falling in myriads before the gale, and rotting in drenched heaps.
So, too, mid our happiest converse with beloved ones, a sad foreboding
sometimes invades our hearts, suggesting that it will not last: the art-

less child must leave the mother's embrace; the brother will choose another confidante than the sister whom he dearly loved. But the knowledge of God, like our treasure in heaven, cannot corrupt, nor can it be stolen from us by any thieving hand. It cannot pass from us; nor we from it. It cannot share the fate of any earthly possession. Nay, when we are stripped of all things else, and sit like another Job amid the wreck of former wealth, then we begin as never before to take measure of our eternal treasure; and there arises before us such a conception of the magnificence of our inheritance in God that we cry, "Give what Thou wilt! without Thee I am poor; and with Thee rich; take what Thou wilt away!"—Meyer.

The Influence of Heaven on Earth (713).

All history shows that if men do not first look up they will not look out; if they do not look ahead into the great tomorrow, they will grow hard and cynical and careless as to the people who are around them today. God save us from a world untouched, uncleansed and uninspired by the influence of a future life.—Robert Francis Coyle, D. D.

Our Father's House (714).

It is all one house—it is all the Father's home—and we and the dead but dwell in different rooms. Not into any far country do we travel in the awful moment when this life is done—not through a shadowy and undiscovered land has the soul to journey that it may be with God—it is only a passing from one room to the other; a step through the veil into a brighter chamber—there is no facing of the storm or of the night, for we never are beyond our Father's roof. I can understand a country child being afraid when it is sent out in the darkness on some errand. For it goes out alone into the night, and the road is lonely, and every shadow awesome. But when a child is called into the dining-room that it may be with its father and its mother; when it leaves the schoolroom with its weary tasks, and goes to the room where its father and mother are; that moment, if childhood and fatherhood be real, is one of the brightest moments of its day. Brethren, in our Father's house are many rooms, and death is but the leaving of the schoolroom. Not on some perilous journey are we sent, out of the home, into the stormy night. 'Tis but a step, and lo! another room—brighter and larger than the one we left—for our task is over, and our schooldays done, and we shall be glad with God for evermore.—George H. Morrison.

(715.)

Bright as is the sun and the sky and the clouds, green as are the leaves and the fields, sweet as is the singing of birds, we know they are not all, and we will not take up with a part for the whole. They proceed from a center of love, which is God, but they are not His fulness: they speak of heaven, but they are not heaven; they are but as stray beams and dim reflections of His image—crumbs from his table.—John Henry Newman.

Dr. Van Dyke's Picture of Heaven (716).

Heaven is like the life of Jesus with all the conflict of human sin left out. Heaven is like the feeding of the multitude in the wilderness with everybody sure to get ample to eat. Heaven is like the woman sinner from the street who bathed the feet of Jesus in her tears and wiped them with her hair. I do not want to know more than that. It is peace, joy, victory, triumph. It is life. It is love. It is tireless work, faithful and unselfish service going on forever. The way to achieve all this is to try to follow Christ today, tomorrow, and the day after through prayer and right living.—Henry Van Dyke, D. D.

The Two Awakings (717).

The truth which corresponds to this metaphor, and which David felt when he said, "I shall be satisfied when I awake," is that the spirit, because emancipated from the body, shall spring into greater intensity of action, shall put forth powers that have been held down here, and shall come into contact with an order of things which here it has but indirectly known. To our true selves and to God we shall wake. Here we are like men asleep in some chamber that looks toward the eastern sky. Morning by morning comes the sunrise, with the tender glory of its rosy light and blushing heavens, and the heavy eyes are closed to it all. Here and there some lighter sleeper, with thinner eyelids or face turned to the sun, is half conscious of a vague brightness, and feels the light, though he does not see the colors of the sky nor the forms of the filmy clouds. Such souls are our saints and prophets, but most of us sleep on unconscious. To us all the moment comes when we shall wake, and see for ourselves the bright and terrible world which we have so often forgotten, and so often been tempted to think was itself a dream. Brethren, see to it that that awakening be for you the beholding of what you have loved, the finding, in the sober certainty of waking bliss, of all the objects which have been your visions of delight in the sleep of earth!—Alexander Maclaren, D. D.

(718.)

We are willing to depart and be with Christ if we are joined to Him, indissolubly, in body and soul; and the great secret of not being afraid to die is to have Christ in the heart, and to be working for Him. If we live for Him, we know that we shall live with Him hereafter. Death loses its terrors; we shall be willing to go hence. Care, anxiety, sin, suffering, we must have here, and we shall be willing to be released from them—to depart. The word "depart" signifies to set out, to sail, to let go. It is as if a vessel were fastened to the dock; the cable is firmly bound to the shore. Just loose the cable, unfurl the sails, set the vessel free; the winds are bearing it out into the open sea. Here we are now, working, toiling, but, if God will let the cable unloose, we shall sail out into the wide sea of eternity.—Bishop Matthew Simpson.

Heaven's Interests (719).

What we regard the greatest events of earth are not those which most interest celestial beings. We are jubilant over the advance of science, the progress of art, the achievements of statesmanship, the triumphs of war, the reform of old abuse. No doubt God and the angels rejoice in many of these. Whenever goodness triumphs, or a noble cause gains a victory, their shout answers earth's fidelity and progress. But how often does this world rejoice over smaller things than these? We hold jubilee over the pretty triumphs of selfishness, and sing over poor plans while heaven weeps. And are we not all too indifferent to that which is the beatitude of the skies?—Selected.

A Crown of Life (720).

In general, religion was to her a matter of course, not to be distinguished from life itself. At least, she gave no sign of inward conflict or struggle. The Beauty and Joy of the Lord set themselves to the music which pervaded her being.

What a long, rich, happy life! And what an afterglow follows the setting of her earthly sun!

> "Twelve long, sunny hours bright to the edge of darkness,
> . . . Then . . . a crown of stars." 3
> —Rev. Dr. Ames on Julia Ward Howe.

Other Sheep (721).

That little Japanese woman who told the story of her going out as a child into the garden in Japan to pray to the unknown God for the restoration of her sick mother to health, and who in gratitude because of that restoration had loved Him, though unknown, and carried His love in her heart, when she came to America and heard in a mission church the story of Jesus, and remained after the service and said to the leader, "Tell me of Him, for I have loved Him, and have worshiped Him, though I never knew His name," is but the picture of others whom God alone can know, who will at last be seen in that great multitude out of every kindred, and nation, and clime, who shall sing the song of the redeemed and cry, "Worthy is the Lamb that was slain; for He has redeemed us unto Himself!"—Behind the World and Beyond.

A Glorious Hope (722).

Harriet Martineau once said to a Christian: "If I believed in immortality, as you believe in it, as you profess to do, I should live a far better life than you appear to live. I should strive more earnestly and bear more patiently. I do not think I should ever be troubled with a fear, or worried with an earthly burden. I think it would be all sunlight and joy if I believed as you do in eternal things—in resurrection and a life beyond in which all things will be made right."

The Scholar's Heaven (723).

For the scholar, the thinker, the lover of truth there is a heaven no less than for the ignorant and the erring; and an expansion of knowledge, endless and ever growing, is one element in the prize presented to our ambition when we are urged to "lay hold on eternal life." For learned and unlearned, nevertheless, there is only one way of attaining the goal. The only way to lay hold on eternal life is to lay a hand of faith on Him Who says: "I am the resurrection and the life; if a man believe on me, though he were dead, yet shall he live; and whosoever liveth and believeth on me shall never die."—Stalker.

Treasures In Heaven (724).

Christ's word about treasure laid up in heaven was illuminated and transfigured for me when I passed through my first great sorrow. What other treasure is there like some one whom we tenderly love, a darling child for instance? And when such a treasure is laid up for us in heaven it is that our hearts may follow and be where our treasure is. Our hearts in heaven! There is no experience like some such transfer of treasure from earth to heaven to give heaven reality to our faith. "My little one is there," the mother heart cries. "I would be there with my precious child." And thereafter as never before heaven is real and the attraction of the life.

The passage of the spirit across the chasm death makes impassable to our bodies is like the flight of an arrow carrying the first slender thread to the other bank of some stream seen to be spanned by the suspension bridge. The first thread is such an one as the arrow can carry, but to that is attached one larger and heavier and to that still another, until the mighty cable to be the foundation of the bridge is safely across the chasm. Then it is only a question of time and faithfulness in work until the bridge is built and life's traffic has its highway. So the faith which follows the flight of the loved one's spirit across the abyss of death draws ever stronger faith and a more confident thought after it, until the soul has a highway for itself, a strong thoroughfare of faith by which it goes between earth and heaven securely. Heaven is joined to earth as the heart's familiar home.—Rev. Judson Titsworth.

"The Bonnie Hills" (725).

Some one illustrates the saint's anticipation of heaven by the case of "a young Scotch girl, who when taken ill in this country, knowing that she must die, begged to be taken back to her native land. On the homeward voyage she kept repeating, 'O, for a glimpse o' the hills o' Scotland!' Before the voyage was half over it was evident to those who were caring for her that she could not live to see her native land. One evening, just at the sun-setting, they brought her on deck. The west was all aglow with glory, and for a few minutes she seemed to enjoy the scene. Someone said to her, 'Is it not beautiful?' 'Yes, but I'd rather see the hills o' Scotland.' For a little while she closed her eyes, and then opening them again, and with a look of unspeakable gladness on her face, she exclaimed, 'I see them noo, and aye they're bonnie.' Then, with a surprised look, she added, 'I never kenned before that it was the hills o' Scotland where the prophet saw the horseman and the chariots, but I see them all, and we are almost there.' Then, closing her eyes, she was soon within the vale. Those beside

her know that it was not the hills of Scotland, but the hills of glory
that she saw. Perhaps there are some fair hills toward which you are
now looking, and for which you are now longing, and you may be
thinking that life will be incomplete unless you reach them. What
will it matter if, while you are eagerly looking, there shall burst upon
your vision the King's country, and the King Himself comes forth to
meet you and to take you into that life where forever you shall walk
with Him in white because you are found worthy? 'For the sufferings
of this present time are not worthy to be compared with the glory which
shall be revealed to usward.' "

ILLUSTRATIVE POETRY.

The Last Turn the Best (726).

So let the way wind up the hill or down,
O'er rough or smooth, the journey will be joy.
Still seeking what I sought when but a boy.
New friendship, high adventure, and a crown.
My heart will keep the courage of the quest,
And hope the road's last turn will be the best.

—Henry van Dyke.

Death Heaven's Gate (727).

Why do we worry about the nest?
  We only stay for a day,
Or a month, or a year, at the Lord's behest,
  In this habitat of clay.

The best will come in the great "to be";
  It is ours to serve and wait;
And the wonderful future we soon shall see,
  For death is but the gate.

—Sarah K. Bolton.

The Eternal Gate (728).

Far off and faint as echoes of a dream,
The songs of boyhood seem,
Yet on our autumn boughs, unflown with spring,
The evening thrushes sing.

The hour draws near, howe'er delayed and late,
When at the Eternal Gate
We leave the words and works we call our own.
And lift void hands alone

For love to fill. Our nakedness of soul
Brings to that gate no toll;
Giftless we come to Him who all things gives
And live because He lives.—Whittier.

It Yet Shall Be (729).

A sweeter song my soul has heard
Than angel anthem, lay of bird.

It cheers my heart in storm and night,
And makes both storms and darkness bright.

The sweetest song that comes to me—
The song of hope—it may yet be!

Is winter here? Have song-birds fled?
They have but flown; they are not dead!

The snows will melt, and with the spring
The birds return on joyous wing.

And flowers that faded long ago
Will bloom again in summer's glow.

Though skies be black, and dark the night,
The day draws near with blessed light.

So faces that have vanished here
In heaven's bright morn will reappear.

Sweet voices that are hushed and still
Will there again our spirits thrill.

Hopes may have flown, but not for aye,
True hope will live a deathless day.

Above the clouds, beyond the night,
Faith soars and sings in living light.

Thence comes the sweetest song to me,
The song of Hope—It yet shall be!
—H. H. Van Meter.

Pure Delight (730).

"There is a land of pure delight
Where saints immortal reign,
Infinite day excludes the night,
And pleasures banish pain."

The Future Life (731).

How shall I know thee in the sphere which keeps
The disembodied spirits of the dead,
When all of thee that time could wither sleeps
And perishes among the dust we tread?

For I shall feel the sting of ceaseless pain
If there I meet thy gentle presence not;
Nor hear the voice I love, nor read again
In thy serenest eyes the tender thought.

Will not thy own meek heart demand me there?
That heart whose fondest throbs to me were given;
My name on earth was ever in thy prayer,
And wilt thou never utter it in heaven?

In meadows fanned by heaven's life-breathing wind,
In the resplendence of that glorious sphere,
And larger movements of the unfettered mind,
Wilt thou forget the love that joined us here?

The love that lived through all the stormy past,
   And meekly with my harsher nature bore,
And deeper grew and tenderer to the last,
   Shall it expire with life and be no more?

A happier lot than mine, and larger light,
   Await thee there; for thou hast bowed thy will
In cheerful homage to the rule of right,
   And lovest all and renderest good for ill.

For me, the sordid cares in which I dwell,
   Shrink and consume my heart, as heat the scroll;
And wrath has left it scar—that fire of hell
   Has left its frightful scar upon my soul.

Yet though thou wear'st the glory of the sky,
   Wilt thou not keep the same beloved name,
The same fair thoughtful brow, and gentle eye,
   Lovelier in heaven's sweet climate, yet the same?

Shalt thou not teach me in that calmer home
   The wisdom that I learned so ill in this—
The wisdom which is love—till I become
   Thy fit companion in that land of bliss?

             —William Cullen Bryant.

She Rests (732).

"She resteth now. No more her breast
   Heaves with its weary breath;
Pain sits no longer on the brow
   Where lies the calm of death.
Sunk to her rest like tired child,
   She lies in slumber deep,
Soft folded in the arms of Him
   Who 'giveth His beloved sleep.'

"Nay, doth she rest? No: day nor night
   She resteth not from praise;
Her spirit, wing'd with rapture, knows
   No more earth's weary ways;
But ever toward the Infinite
   Her flight on, upward, does she keep,
For He gives active tirelessness
   Who 'giveth His beloved sleep.'"

The Wondrous Morn (733).

Dark streams are still dividing
   Between my Lord and me;
Time's midnight hills are hiding
   The land I fain would see

But oh! the wondrous morrow!
   Life without pain or loss—
The Saints without their Sorrow,
   And Christ without the Cross!

O Lord, recall Thy banished,
 And home Thy weary bring,
To view, where night has vanished,
 Their Country and their King!

—A. R. Cousin

"And That Shore Heaven!" (734).

O Joy! one step ashore, and that shore heaven!
 To clasp a Hand outstretched, and that Hand His
Who waits my coming, all earth's fetters riven,
 To share the glory of His saints in bliss!

To pass, by one short breath, from storm and stress,
 To breathe new air in one unbroken calm!
To sleep, and wake in undreamt blessedness,
 With conqueror's crown, white robe, and victor's palm!

"But Then We Rest Forever" (735).

Light is our sorrow, for it ends tomorrow,
 Light is our death which cannot hold us fast;
So brief a sorrow can be scarcely sorrow,
 Or death be death so quickly past.

One night, no more, of pain that turns to pleasure,
 One night, no more, of weeping, weeping sore;
And then the heaped-up measure beyond measure,
 In quietness for evermore.

Our sails are set to cross the tossing river,
 Our face is set to reach Jerusalem;
We toil awhile, but then we rest forever,
 Sing with all saints and rest above with them.

—Christina Rossetti.

Beckoned To My Fitting Place (736).

"I have but Thee, my Father! let Thy Spirit
 Be near me, then, to comfort and uphold;
No gate of pearl, no branch of palm I merit,
 Nor street of shining gold.

"Suffice it if—my good and ill unreckoned,
 And both forgiven through Thy abounding grace,
I find myself by hands familiar beckoned
 Unto my fitting place.

"Some humble door among Thy many mansions,
 Some sheltering shade where sin and striving cease,
And flows forever through Heaven's green expansion
 The river of Thy peace."

—Whittier.

Heaven's Nearness (737).

It seemeth such a little way to me,
　　Across to that strange country, the Beyond;
And yet not strange, for it has grown to be
　　The home of those of whom I am so fond;
They make it seem familiar and more dear,
As journeying friends bring distant countries near.

Over the River (738).

"Over the River"—the old, sweet song!
　The road to the rest there is not so long:
A song and a sigh and a brief good-by,
And we meet with the dreams 'neath a stormless sky!

"Over the River"—the song that thrills
　Its music down from the heavenly hills;
The pain and peril of life's time past,
And the rest that is given of God at last!

"Over the River"—so sweet it seems
　To drift away to the starlit dreams!
To fear no more the fall o' night
"Over the River," where "love is light!"

　　　　　　　　　　　　　—Atlanta Constitution.

Far Better (739)

Oh, safe at home! where the dark tempter roams not
　How have I envied thy far happier lot,
Already resting where the evil comes not,
　The tear, the toil, the woe, the sin forgot.

Oh, safe in port where the rough billow breaks not,
　Where the wild sea moan saddens thee no more,
Where the remorseless stroke of tempest shakes not,
　When, when shall I too gain that tranquil shore?

Oh, bright amid the brightness all eternal,
　When shall I breathe with thee the purer air,
Air of a land whose clime is ever vernal,
　A land without a serpent or a snare?

Away above these scenes of guilt and folly,
　Beyond this desert's heat and dreariness,
Safe in the city of the ever holy,
　Let me make haste to join thy earlier bliss.

Another battle fought and, oh! not lost,
　Tells of the ending of this fight and thrall,
Another ridge of time's lone mooreland crossed
　Gives nearer prospect of the jasper wall.

Just gone within the veil where I shall follow,
  Not far beyond me, hardly out of sight,
I down beneath thee in this cloudy hollow,
  And now above me in yon sunny light;

Gone to begin a new and happier story,
  Thy bitter tale of earth now told and done;
These outer shadows for that inner glory
  Exchanged forever, oh, thrice blessed One!

Oh, freed from fetters of this lonesome prison,
  How shall I greet thee in that day of days
When He who died, yea, rather who has risen,
  Shall these frail frames from dust and darkness raise!

              —Horatius Bonar.

Face to Face (740).

Brief life is here our portion;
  Brief sorrow, short-lived care;
The life that knows no ending,
  The tearless life is there.

O happy retribution;
  Short toil, eternal rest;
For mortals and for sinners,
  A mansion with the blest.

And now we fight the battle,
  And then we wear the crown
Of full and everlasting
  And passionless renown.

The morning shall awaken,
  The shadows shall decay
And each true-hearted servant
  Shall shine as doth the day.

    There God our King and portion,
      In fulness of His grace,
    Shall we behold forever,
      And worship face to face.

              —Selected.

Tears (741).

When I consider life and its few years,—
A wisp of fog betwixt us and the sun;
A call to battle, and the battle done
Ere the last echo dies within our ears;
A rose choked in the grass; an hour of fears;
The gusts that past a darkening shore do beat;
The burst of music down an unlistening street,—
I wonder at the idleness of tears.

Ye old, old dead, and ye of yesternight,
Chieftains and bards and keepers of the sheep,
By every cup of sorrow that you had,
Loose me from tears, and make me see aright
How each hath back what once he stayed to weep;
Homer his sight, David his little lad.

              —Lizette Reese.

"Worth Them All" (742).

"So wing thy flight from star to star,
From world to luminous world, as far
  As the universe spreads its flaming wall;
Take all the pleasures of all the spheres,
And multiply them all through the endless years—
  One moment of heaven is worth them all."

The Many Mansions (743).

So death has lost its terrors;
  How can we fear it now?
Its face, once grim, now leads to Him
  At Whose command we bow.

His presence makes us happy,
  His service our delight,
The many mansions gleam and glow,
  The saints our souls invite.

At The Dawn (744).

"As from my window, at first glimpse of dawn,
  I watch the rising mist that heralds day,
And see by God's strong hand the curtain drawn
  That through the night has hid the world away,
So I, through windows of my soul, shall see,
  One day, Death's fingers with resistless might
Draw back the curtained gloom that shadows Life,
  And in the darkness of Time's deepest might
Let in the perfect Day—Eternity."

The World Beyond (745).

A solemn murmur of the soul
  Tells of the world to be,
As travelers hear the billows roll
  Before they reach the sea.

When I Go Home (746).

When I go home may quiet reign,
  And nothing will I say or do.
To cause regret or needless pain
  In those I love when I go home.

When I go home, be it with me,
  As one that fully knows the way,
From dark confusion wholly free;
  May light o'erspread when I go home.

When I go home from world like this,
  May thoughts of rest and joy outweigh
All worldly good and transient bliss,
  While God approves, when I go home.

When I go home may naught remain,
  To show that heart or brain or hand.
Had willed or moved in wicked vein;
  Well done be said when I go home.

When I go home may royal guide,
  My last great journey shield and cheer;
No fear nor evil shall betide,
  No good-bye pangs, when I go home.

When I go home, welcome to me,
  May joy of life supreme impart,
Sweet shall the peace forever be,
  A victory won, when I go home.

When I go home, may stars that shine,
  In diadems of fadeless light,
(For winning souls a pledge divine)
  Inspire my song when I go home.

When I go home, shall I not find,
  My loved and lost in sweet repose,
Who passed the gate on Christ reclined
  To dwell with Him, when I go home?

When I go home, my glory crown
  Will be that Christ is there enthroned;
Where heaven's host to Him bow down,
  I shall have place, when I go home.
—Rev. T. J. Joslin, in Michigan Christian Advocate.

Yearning for the Homeland (747).

I am longing for the homeland
  And its rest from sin and strife;
I am yearning for the welcome
  With its warmth of light and life;
And the days seem long and weary
'Mid the earth scenes dark and dreary
While I wait till my Redeemer comes
  With angel guards for me.

O, I long to speed the story
    Of the coming of my King,
Until all who love my Saviour
    Hear with joy the welkin ring!
Though the waiting-time is weary,
And the midnight darkness dreary,
I rejoice; for soon the morning dawns
    To all eternity.

O the homeland, blessed homeland,
    With its bliss beyond compare!
How our ardent souls are yearning
    For the joys that wait us there!
And we haste to barge our treasure
On the river of Thy pleasure
For the home where joy shall wake our song
    Throughout eternity.

                              —Worthie Harris Holden.

The City Beautiful—"Precious in the Sight of the Lord is the Death of His Saints."—Psa. 116:15 (748).

Sometimes when the day is ended
    And its round of duties done,
I watch at the western windows
    The gleam of the setting sun.
When my heart has been unquiet
    And its longings unbeguiled
By the day's vexatious trials
    And cannot be reconciled,
I look on the slope of the mountains
    And o'er the restless sea,
And I think of the beautiful city
    That lieth not far from me.

And my spirit is hushed in a moment
    As the twilight falls tender and sweet,
And I cross in fancy the river,
    And kneel at the Master's feet.
And I rest in the shade that there falleth
    From the trees that with healing are rife—
That shadow the banks of the river—
    The river of water of life.

And some time, when the day is ended.
And the duties He gave me are done.
I shall watch at life's western windows
The gleam of the setting sun.
I shall fall asleep in the twilight
As I never have slept before,
To dream of the beautiful city,
Till I waken to sleep no more.
There will fall on my restless spirit
A hush, oh, so wondrously sweet,
And I shall cross over the river
To rest at the Master's feet.

—Boston Globe.

Perils O'er (749).

"Safe home, safe home in port,
Rent cordage, shattered deck!
Torn sails, provisions short!
And only not a wreck.
But, O, the joy upon the shore,
To tell our voyage perils o'er."

Do They Think of Me In Heaven? (750).

I am thinking of a city, with its streets of shining gold,
Gates of pearl and walls of jasper, with their glories manifold;
Of the house of many mansions where the ransomed spirits dwell,
And the glad, exultant chorus which their joyous voices swell.
O! I seem almost to hear them as their songs of praise they sing
To the Saviour who redeemed them, hailing him their Lord and King!
And I wonder if among that throng beside the glassy sea,
With their crowns and palms of victory, there are some who think
of me.

In that choir are souls translated who on earth to me were dear,
Friends to whom my heart clung fondly as we walked together here,
And the light of day seemed darkened as they said their last good-bys
And from earthly habitations passed to mansions in the skies.
Ay, I know they reached their haven in the city of their God,
For their trust was stayed on Jesus and His saving, cleansing blood;
But if only some least message might be wafted o'er the sea
From that mystic shore to tell me that they sometimes think of me!

Oft it seems when worn and weary with the burden and the heat,
Still I toil while hope seems waning, face to face with grim defeat
When my fainting soul is longing for a word of love or cheer
To sustain its failing courage and to banish grief and fear,
That the gloomy way would brighten all its dreary length along,
And my mouth be filled with laughter and my tongue with happy song,
That my heart would bound with gladness and my toil a joy would be,
Could I know that up in heaven there are souls who think of me.

Hush, my soul; the Master speaketh: "Keep thy garments undefiled;
Doubt not; fear not; can a mother e'er forget her helpless child?
Yea, she may forget, yet will not I forget, but still be true;
Thou shalt prove my love unfailing and my mercies ever new."
I will take the strength He giveth, lift the burden, tread the way
He appointeth, till it brighten to His perfect, cloudless day;
And whatever lot await me, this my sweetest thought shall be,
That the tend'rest Heart in heaven truly, kindly thinks of me.

—Ida M. Budd.

The Children Up in Heaven—"And the Streets of the City Shall Be Full
of Boys and Girls Playing in the Streets Thereof."—Zech. 8:5 (751).

"Oh, what do you think the angels say?"
   Said the children up in heaven;
"There's a dear little girl coming home today,
  She's almost ready to fly away
    From the earth we used to live in;
  Let's go and open the gates of pearl,
  Open them wide for the new little girl,"
   Said the children up in heaven.

"God wanted her here where His little ones meet,"
   Said the children up in heaven;
"She shall play with us in the golden street;
  She has grown too fair, she has grown too sweet
    For the earth we used to live in;
  She needed the sunshine, this dear little girl,
  That gilds this side of the gates of pearl,"
   Said the children up in heaven.

"So the King called down from the angels' dome,"
   Said the children up in heaven;
" 'My little darling, arise and come
  To the place prepared in the Father's home,
   The home the children live in.'
  Let's go and watch the gates of pearl,
  Ready to welcome the new little girl,"
   Said the children up in heaven.

"Far down on the earth do you hear them weep?"
   Said the children up in heaven;
"For the dear little girl has gone to sleep!
  The shadows fall, and the night clouds sweep
   O'er the earth we used to live in;
  But we'll go and open the gates of pearl!
  Oh, why do they weep for their dear little girl?"
   Said the children up in heaven.

"Fly with her quickly, O angels, dear!"
  Said the children up in heaven;
"See—she is coming! look there! look there!
At the jasper light on her sunny hair,
  Where the veiling clouds are riven!"
Ah! hush, hush, hush! All the swift wings furl!
For the King Himself, at the gates of pearl,
Is taking her hand, dear, tired little girl,
  And is leading her into heaven.
              —Edith Gilling Cherry.

Enraptured Thought (752).

"There is a land mine eye hath seen,
  In visions of enraptured thought,
So bright that all which spreads between
  Is with its radiant glories fraught."

Beyond (753).

It seemeth such a little way to me
  Across to that strange country—The Beyond;
And yet, not strange, for it has grown to be
  The home of those whom I am so fond,
They make it seem familiar and most dear,
As journeying friends bring distant regions near.

So close it lies, that when my sight is clear
  I think I almost see the gleaming strand.
I know I feel those who have gone from here
  Come near enough sometimes to touch my hand.
I often think, but for our veiled eyes
We should find heaven right around about us lies.

I cannot make it seem a day to dread,
  When from this dear earth I shall journey out
To that still dearer country of the dead,
  And join the lost ones, so long dreamed about.
I love this world, yet shall I love to go
And meet the friends who wait for me, I know.

I never stand above a bier and see
  The seal of death set on some well-loved face
But that I think, "One more to welcome me,
  When I shall cross the intervening space
Between this land and that one 'over there';
One more to make the strange Beyond seem fair."

And so for me me there is no sting to death,
  And so the grave has lost its victory.
It is but the crossing—with a bated breath,
  And white, set face—a little strip of sea,
To find the loved ones waiting on the shore,
More beautiful, more precious, than before.

—Ella Wheeler Wilcox.

Our Thought of Heaven (754).

Life changes all our thoughts of heaven;
At first we think of streets of gold,
Of gates of pearl and dazzling light,
Of shining wings and robes of white,
And things all strange to mortal sight.
But in the afterward of years
It is a more familiar place—
A home unhurt by sighs or tears,
Where waiteth many a well-known face.
With passing month it comes more near,
It grows more real day by day;
Not strange or cold, but very dear—
The glad homeland not far away,
Where none are sick, or poor, or lone,
The place where we shall find our own.
And as we think of all we knew,
Who there have met to part no more,
Our longing hearts desire home, too,
With all the strife and trouble o'er.

"Pass Over to Thy Rest" (755).

From this bleak hill of storms,
To yon, warm, sunny heights,
Where love forever shines,
  Pass over to thy rest,
  The rest of God!

From hunger and from thirst,
From toil and weariness,
From shadows and from dreams,
  Fass over to thy rest,
  The rest of God!

From weakness and from pain,
From trembling and from strife,
From watching and from fear,
  Pass over to thy rest,
  The rest of God!

From vanity and from lies,
From mockery and from snares,
From disappointed hopes,
  Pass over to thy rest,
  The rest of God!

From unrealities,
From hollow scenes and change,
From ache and emptiness,
  Pass over to thy rest,
  The rest of God!

From this unanchored world,
Whose morrow none can tell,
From all things restless here,
  Pass over to thy rest,
  The rest of God!

—H. Bonar.

Brief Life Is Here Our Portion (756).

Brief life is here our portion,
  Brief sorrow, short-lived care:
The life that knows no ending,
  The tearless life, is there.
O happy retribution!
  Short toil, eternal rest;
For mortals and for sinners
  A mansion with the blest!

There grief is turned to pleasure,
  Such pleasure, as below
No human voice can utter,
  No human heart can know.
And now we fight the battle,
  But then shall wear the crown
Of full and everlasting
  And passionless renown.

And now we watch and struggle,
  And now we live in hope,
And Sion, in her anguish,
  With Babylon must cope.
But He whom now we trust in
  Shall then be seen and known,
And they that know and see Him
  Shall have Him for their own.

The morning shall awaken,
  The shadows shall decay,
And each true-hearted servant
  Shall shine as doth the day:
Yes; God, our King and Portion,
  In fulness of His grace,
We then shall see for ever,
  And worship face to face.

O sweet and blessed country,
  The home of God's elect!
O sweet and blessed country,
  That eager hearts expect!
Jesus, in mercy bring us
  To that dear land of rest;
Who art, with God the Father,
  And Spirit, ever blest.

—Bernard of Cluny.

From Glory Unto Glory (757).

"From glory unto glory" of loveliness and light,
  Of music and of rapture, of power and of sight,
"From glory unto glory" of knowledge and of love,
  Shall be the joy of progress awaiting us above.

"From glory unto glory," with no limit and no veil,
  With wings that cannot weary, and hearts that cannot fail;
Within, without, no hindrance, no barrier, as we soar,
  And never interruption to the endless "more and more."

For the infinite outpourings of Jehovah's love and grace,
  And infinite unveilings of the brightness of His face,
And infinite unfoldings of the splendor of His will,
  Meet the mightiest expansions of the finite spirit still.

"Far Frae Hame" (759).

I am far frae my hame, an' I'm weary aftenwhiles,
  For the langed-for hame-bringing, an' my Father's welcome smiles,
I'll ne'er be fu' content until my een do see
  The gowden gates of heaven, an' my ain countrie.

The earth is flecked wi' flowers, many-tinted, fresh and gay;
The birdies warble blithely, for my Father made them sae;
But these sichts an' these soun's will as naething be to me
When I hear the angels singing in my ain countrie.

I've his gude word of promise that some gladsome day the King
To His ain royal palace His banished hame will bring
Wi' een and wi' heart running owre we shall see
The King in His beauty an' our ain countrie.

He's gratefu' that hath promised, He'll surely come again,
He'll keep His tryst wi' me, at what hour I dinna ken;
But He bids me still to wait, an' ready aye to be
To gang at ony moment to my ain countrie.

—Scotch Song.

Journey's End (760).

No way so long but find its goal.
No path so steep for struggling soul
But gains at last the mountain's crest
With vision bright and well-earned rest.
And when life's race is nobly run;
It's battle fought; its victory won,
God will make up its cost to me
Throughout a blest eternity.

—J. H. B.

Yours and Mine (761).

Where bide they all?
Dear friends of yesterday, last year and long ago,
Who walked with us when life was all aglow
And rainbows spanned the gloom.
Not far away we know—
They're only gone we trow,
Into the next room.

How sweet and strange!
We hear their tender voices as in olden days,
While we drift backward into sunny bays
With lilies all abloom—
In murmurs low they say:
"Love lights the mystic way
Into the next room."

Years wear apace.
Days dark with heavy mist now deep'ning into rain,
Close down upon us, and we view with pain
The spectral shadows loom,—
A mournful gleam! and lo,
We too lift latch and go
Into the next room.

—Etta M. Gardner.

TEXTS AND TREATMENT HINTS.

"In My Father's House Are Many Mansions; If It Were Not So, I Would Have Told You; For I Go To Prepare a Place For You. And If I Go and Prepare a Place For You, I Come Again, and Will Receive You Unto Myself; That Where I Am, There Ye May Be Also."— John 14:2, 3 (762).

For some reason, nowadays, we are not much concerned about heaven. The life we know is full, absorbing, and brief. It is a man's work. Heaven as pictured by winged cherubs and diaphonous angels does not appeal to us; it does not suggest a man's work.

In one experience we all are alike—we all were born. Another inevitable experience awaits us all—we all shall surely die. We ought to be concerned about what is beyond. It is certain that we cannot come back and try life again.

The question, On what condition is heaven to be attained? divides itself into two parts, Where and what is heaven? and, How can we get there? When we have answered the one we can quickly settle the other.—Stimson.

The Privileges of Heaven—Rev. 22:1-11 (763).

(1) The Throne of God and of the Lamb (v. 3). Their presence, guiding providence. (2) They shall see his face (v. 4), which only the pure in heart can see. The power and joy of intimate personal communion with God and Christ. (3) His name, representing all that God is in character, shall be in (on) their foreheads (v. 4), marking them as His children, and showing in their very appearance the heavenly character. (4) The Lord God giveth them light (v. 5). Direct inspiration, the illumination of the Spirit. The light is for all without distinction, doing for us spiritually all that light does for us in nature. (5) The water of life, freely. (6) The fruits of the tree of life. (7) The kings of the earth shall bring their glory into it; all that is good and desirable in this world shall belong to the perfect state. Nothing good shall be excluded, nothing banned. He shall inherit all things. (8) And they shall reign for ever and ever. He shall reign over himself, no longer "a heritage of woe," but "crowned and mitred o'er thyself reign thou." He shall reign over all things so that everything on earth and in heaven shall minister to His service in the kingdom of heaven.— Peloubet.

Our High Privilege. (764)—"Eye hath not seen, nor ear heard, neither have entered into the heart of man, the things which God hath prepared for them that love Him. But God hath revealed them unto us by His Spirit."—1 Cor. 2:9, 10.

"Blessed Are the Dead That Die In the Lord"—Rev. 14:13 (765).

I. Death is a curse. My text says, "Blessed are the dead." Still death is a curse. Separate and apart from the consolations of Christian faith, death is a tremendous evil. Nature shrinks from it shuddering. In most cases death presents the unmistakable features of a tremendous curse, being attended with sufferings which, however unpleasant to think of, it is well to anticipate, that we may be prepared for the worst, and, fortified by faith, may withstand the rude shocks of dissolution.

II. Death is a blessing. The union which is formed between Christ and His people being one of incorporation, and not merely one of co-operation, what the one is, the other is; and where the one is, the other is; and as the one feels, the other feels: and as our bodies and their limbs have all things in common, or the branches and trunk of a tree have sap in common, so Jesus and His people have all things in common. To be in Christ, then, to be in the Lord, implies that we shall infallibly enjoy all the blessings, temporal, spiritual, and eternal, which He shed His blood to purchase, these being secured to us by the great oath of God and the bonds of a covenant which is well ordered in all things and sure.

III. Death is a blessing as introducing us into a state of rest. (1) At death the believer rests from the toils of life. (2) At death the believer rests from the cares of life. Faith is often weak, and man is fearful; and so our life has many a troubled dream, that fills those with fears and terrors who are all the time safely folded in a Father's arms. (3) At death the believer rests from the griefs of life. "Many are the afflictions of the righteous, but the Lord will deliver him out of them," if never before, at death. Death cures all griefs; and his own best physic and physician, he applies the most healing balm to the wounds his own hands have made. No more true or beautiful way of announcing a good man's death than the old-fashioned phrase, "He is at rest."—Dr. Guthrie.

"I Will See You Again"—Jno. 16:22 (766).

Jesus implies that we are to be together and know one another in that world, even as we are together and know one another here. He said to His disciples: "Ye also shall sit upon twelve thrones, judging the twelve tribes of Israel"; and again those wonderful words: "I will see you again, and your heart shall rejoice, and your joy no man taketh from you." And yet again those dear words: "Rejoice not, that the spirits are subject unto you; but rather rejoice, because your names are written in heaven." These are only suggestions of the many words which our Lord spoke, proving that His children are to know each other even as they are to know Him in the life beyond.—Tompkins.

"Things That Are Above"—Col. 3:2 (767).

What are the things that are above? (1) The perfect standard. In the sanctuary above are the golden scales and weights. The ideal of righteousness is in the heavens; we must not compare ourselves with ourselves; we must be measured by the standard that is on high. Morality may be a mere attitude or posture, a calculated and mechanized conduct. Judged by the standard that is above, morality may be one of the calculations and tricks of hypocrisy. (2) The fountain of grace.

earthly wells cannot satisfy our thirst. The whole conception of redemption begins in heaven and returns to the glory of heaven. The
law is a fact which science might have discovered, which indeed prides
itself on discovering; but grace is divine revelation. We have come
to see that grace may be the higher law. It is an error to suppose that
grace is a mere sentiment. Grace is the pity of righteousness. (3) The
brightest hope. "If in this life only we have hope, we are of all men
most miserable." The lights are well above. It is impossible for the
earth to be anywhere but under our feet; the noonday sun is always
above our heads. The lights we strike are always perishing in the very
use. As the perfect standard is above, so, of course, is the perfect
discipline. "He that hath this hope purifieth himself." The hope does
not lull us into criminal slumber, it awakens and quickens us into the
highest activity of self-culture and social service. To know the full
meaning of "things that are above" we must pass through the gate of
death. We die to live. "It doth not yet appear what we shall be."
Our earthly house of this tabernacle is doomed, a doom in which we
acquiesce, because we have a house not made with hands. The pursuit
of "things that are above" elevates the whole range of human thought,
and unites in the true socialism all the interests of the world. In all
spheres of life a man bears the impress of his own ideals. How noble
then and how glorious should be the life of him who draws his whole
motive and encouragement not from the things that perish, but from
the "things that are above?" Do not let us talk about these things;
in God's name and strength let us try to live them.—Parker.

"Let Not Your Heart Be Troubled"—John 14:3 (768).

Why? Because you will soon follow Me through death, and death
will bring us together again? Not so. "I will come again and receive
you unto Myself." "Ye men of Galilee," said the angels, "why stand
ye gazing up into heaven? this same Jesus shall"—what? Soon take
you away from sorrow by death? Not so. "Snall so come in like manner as ye have seen Him go." "The Lord shall descend from heaven
with a shout, with the voice of the archangel and the trump of God"—
so says Paul to the sorrowful of his day. "The dead in Christ shall
rise first, then we who are alive and remain shall be caught up together with them in the clouds to meet the Lord in the air; wherefore comfort one another with these words." So it always is. Not our
going to the Lord in death, but the Lord's coming for us in glory is
the grand consolation and hope. The early Christians were described
as those who "love His appearing," who "wait for God's Son from
heaven." Could most Christians now be so described? Has not this
joyous hope, this eager longing for the Lord's personal return, almost
died out of the Church? We lose immensely by this. Both for the
quickening of zeal and for victory over sorrow and despair, we need
to have this blessed hope a far more constant inmate of the breast.
Sorrow and sighing would far more quickly fly away, if we but listened
more joyfully to the sweet words, "I will see you again, and your

heart shall rejoice, and your joy no man taketh from you." **If He** who so intensely loves us says, "Surely I come quickly," well may every heart that loves Him say, "Amen, even so, Come, Lord Jesus."—Knight.

All Tears Wiped Away (769).

"And God shall wipe away all tears from their eyes; and there shall be no more death, neither sorrow, nor crying, neither shall there be any more pain: for the former things are passed away."—Rev. 21:4. God wiping away all Tears.

The subject teaches—

I. A lesson of resignation.

II. A lesson of gratitude. The same Hand which chastises will one day wipe away our tears. It will not be long that we must wait before the faithfulness of God's word will be established.—J. N. Norton.

"In My Father's House Are Many Mansions: If It Were Not So I Would Have Told You. I Go To Prepare a Place For You. And If I Go And Prepare a Place For You, I Will Come Again, And Receive You Unto Myself; That Where I Am, There Ye May Be Also. And Whither I Go Ye Know, And The Way Ye Know."—John 14:2-4 (770).

How clear and satisfying a view of the life to come is presented in these words of our Saviour's! So positive an affirmation of its reality from the lips of one who came forth from God puts to silence the denials of unbelief. All speculations respecting the future state are valueless to those who have looked upon this picture of home life beyond the grave. How cheering in view of earthly conflicts, and what a stimulus to untiring activity in Christian work!

Into this land of many mansions, or abiding places, the Lord has gone as the head and representative of ransomed humanity. Our hope, as an anchor of the soul, is sure and steadfast, entering into that which is within the veil, whither the forerunner has for us entered, even Jesus. There He reigns for the overthrow of sin; and when He has accomplished His purpose of mercy in the hearts and through the agency of His faithful followers, He receives them to Himself that they may share His glory.

Nor need any one go astray. Christ is the way. Trustful reliance upon Him and His finished work will secure all the blessings that are wrapped up in the terms, Home and Father.—Sommerville.

"Where I Am There Ye May Be Also"—John 14:3 (771).

I. This dreadful strangeness of death is two-fold: It is first an unknown journey.

II. It is finally an unknown destination. Our souls are to be hurled away by an unknown storm; they are to be hurled at last upon an unknown shore.

III. And yet for millions, yea, for millions multiplied, all this dreadfulness has been done away. They have heard and believed these words of Christ, the twofold contradiction of our twofold fears; the last journey will not be desolate nor lonely, for He "will come again and receive you"; the eternal destination is no longer strange and dreadful, for He is gone "to prepare a place for you," sweetly saying, "Where I am there ye may be also." We are not to be swept away by a strange storm, but to drift gently out on summer sea.

"Then Shall I Know Even As Also I Am Known"—1 Cor. 13:12 (772).

The First Five Minutes after Death.

I. At our entrance on another state of existence we shall know what it is to exist under entirely new conditions. What will it be to find ourselves with the old self—divested of that body which has clothed it since its first moment of existence—able to achieve, it may be, so much,—it may be, so little; living on, but under conditions which are so entirely new. This experience alone will add no little to our existing knowledge, and the addition will have been made during the first five minutes after death.

II. And the entrance on the next world must bring with it a knowledge of God such as is quite impossible in this life. His vast, His illimitable life, will present itself to the apprehension of our spirits as a clearly consistent whole—not as a complex problem to be painfully mastered by the efforts of our understandings, but as a present, living, encompassing Being who is inflecting Himself upon the very sight, whether they will it or not, of His adoring creatures. "Thine eyes shall see the King in His beauty"—They were words of warning as well as words of promise.

III. At our entrance on another world we shall know ourselves as never before. The past will be spread out before it, and we shall take a comprehensive survey of it. One Being there is Who knows us now, Who knows each of us perfectly, Who has always known us. Then, for the first time, we shall know ourselves even as also we are known. We shall not have to await the Judge's sentence; we shall read it at a glance, whatever it be, in this new apprehension of what we are.—H. P. Liddon.

"Sorrow And Sighing Shall Flee Away"—Is. 25:10 (773).

They shall become obsolete words, having first become obsolete facts. Explain the meaning of the word "obsolete." Show how some words have passed out of use. Show that the time is coming when such words as "pain," "sorrow," "jealousy," "sighing," "sin," will be absolutely lost to human memory. New words will supersede old terms. Instead of such words as we have now given, there shall come up such words as "love," "holiness," "peace," "joy," "hope."

Construct a sentence made up of obsolete English words. By this illustration show that there shall be a similar obsolescence in religious or spiritual phraseology. Construct a sentence full of such words as "pain," "sin," "misery," "heart-break," and take that sentence to men who have been in heaven for a century and ask them to read it. They could not! The things signified having passed away, the signs which represented them have also perished.—Joseph Parker, D. D.

"That Where I Am There Ye May Be Also"—John 14:2 (774).

If you ask what shall be the nature of that life we are to live after death, we can answer that it will not be so very different from our present life. Eternal life is a present possession. It is the Christ-life within us. The essential elements will remain the same, the incidental, the accidental things will be done away.

It will be a sensuous life, not a sensual life, but a life in which we shall still have use for the senses. These will then just come to their fullest and higher degree and acuteness. Here we see through a glass darkly, there face to face. Here we must adjust our lenses, there we shall see eye to eye. We shall hear the new song and shall touch and handle the things of God.

It will be an intellectual life. Our faculties of knowledge shall be heightened, and we shall know as we are known. Our knowledge shall no longer be partial but complete.

It will be a spiritual life, it is the home of the soul. We shall not be less human but more really and ideally such. Three things we shall take with us from this life into the next: Our thoughts, our feelings, our will. What the character of that life shall be depends very largely upon what the character of my present life has been.

An Alpine traveler fell down into a stream of water that carried him beneath a tunnel of rocks until the stream flowed forth into the beautiful Rhine. So at death we plunge into the deep, dark river, but its waters flow on until they join that crystal sea just below the throne. Therefore I do not fear death. "In the night of death hope sees a star and listening love can hear the rustle of a wing."—C. E. Schaeffer, D. D.

"And The Books Were Opened"—Rev. 20:12 (775).

What are the books to be read? We are not told their title, but I think we may make some conjecture.

I. The first book will be the book of the law of God. Just as in our courts of justice the laws of the realm are always near at hand, that in any doubtful case they may be appealed to, so, I think, the first book will be the book of the revealed will of the holy and just God, a record of the laws and measures by which men will be tried.

II. The next book will be the book of the Gospel. Side by side with the volume of the law will stand the volume of God's love contained in the Gospel, the wondrous record of all that is done by God for man.

III. The third book will be the book of the dealings of God's Holy Spirit with the fallen family of man. Some of us may have already lost sight of the striving of the Holy Spirit with us; but God does not forget it: God does not lose sight of it.

IV. The book of God's providence will be opened. In it is kept, without any possibility of mistake, a record of all God's dealings with us externally. God is ever seeking by His providential dealings to bring us to Him.

V. The book of our life will be opened. Every one of us is writing a book; we are every one of us authors, although we may never have written a book, not even a line, in our lives. Though we may never have dreamt of printing a book, yet we are dictating to the recording angel the whole of our life from moment to moment, from hour to hour.

VI. The book of life. Jesus Christ is the Author of it. From beginning to end it is His. From the first page to the end, it is life all through: life as it first entered the soul; life as it grew and was fed and nourished and sustained, and the glorious results of life, the glorious harvest reaped by the soul; life which triumphs over our dead selves, which brings the dry bones together out of the gloomy sepulchre—the book of life, written by the Lord of life, Jesus Christ Himself.—W. Hay Aitken.

XII. OTHER WORLDLINESS.
CONSERVATION. AN EARNEST LIFE.

REFLECTIONS AND ILLUSTRATIONS.

She Gave Herself (776).

One of the missionaries at the Nashville Students' Volunteer Convention related the following pathetic incident of devotion to the Lord:

"Over on the west coast of Africa somebody carried the Gospel to a young savage girl sixteen years of age, and she came into the house of God on Christmas day to bring her offering, for they have a very beautiful custom of giving their best gifts to Christ on Christmas. They are poor, with a poverty which you and I know nothing about. Most of them could not bring anything save a handful of vegetables, but this girl, just saved out of heathenism, brought a silver coin worth eighty-five cents, and handed that to the missionary as her gift to God. He was astonished at the magnitude of it that he thought that surely the girl must have stolen this money, and for a moment he was about to refuse to accept it, but thought he had better take it, to save confusion.

"At the conclusion of the service, he called her aside, and asked her where she got that money, for it was really a fortune to one in her condition. She explained to him very simply, that in order to give to Christ an offering which satisfied her own heart, she had gone to a neighboring planter, and bound herself out to him as a slave for the rest of her life for this eighty-five cents, and had brought the whole financial equivalent of her life of pledged service, and laid it down in a single gift at the feet of her Lord."—Pittsburg Christian Advocate.

"Follow Me" (777).

"Follow me" is the sound of a trumpet. It is an appeal to those who are capable of great actions. Who are brave enough, honest enough, earnest enough, to renounce everything, to pierce through everything, that they may win Christ. If they can find it in their hearts to count the cost and pay, they enter into the life which is life indeed. . . . But the price has to be paid by everyone. . . . It will vary in different men, but it would be very extraordinary if it were not, in many, connected with money. There is nothing with which so many spiritual perils are associated. There is nothing to the advantages of which we are so keenly alive, to the risks of which we are naturally so blind. Does anyone realize the deceitfulness of the heart implied in a remark of St. Francis of Sales, that in all his experience as a confessor no one had ever confessed to him the sin of covetousness?— James Denney.

The Temple of God (778).

Slowly throughout all the universe that temple of God is being built. Wherever in any world a soul by free-willed obedience catches the fire of God's likeness, it is set into the growing walls, a living stone. When, in your hard fight, in your tiresome drudgery, or in your terrible temptation, you catch the purpose of your being and give yourself to God and so give Him the chance to give Himself to you, your life, a living stone, is taken up and set into that growing wall. Wherever souls are being tried and ripened in whatever commonplace and homely ways, there God is hewing out the pillars for His temple. O, if the stone can only have some vision of the temple of which it is to be a part forever, what patience must fill it as it feels the blows of the hammer and knows that success for it is simply to let itself be wrought into what shape the Master wills!—Phillips Brooks.

Dauntless Determination (779).

When General Grant was informed that his illness was sure to terminate fatally, he was engaged upon his life's memoirs. He had an intense desire to see it completed. His fame was secure, but he wanted to ensure a competence for his family. If the book were to be completed by any other hand than his own, its market value would be greatly depreciated. This was the consideration that strengthened the sinking soldier, that gave him courage to contend with fate and despair, and, stricken as he was by the most terrible of maladies, to check the advance of Death himself, while he made his preparations under the very shadow of the wing and the glare of the scythe of the destroyer. The spectacle of the hero who had earned and worn the highest national honors, working amid the miseries of a sick chamber to glean the gains that he knew he could never enjoy—the fainting warrior propped up on that mountain-top to stammer out utterances to sell for the benefit of his children—is a picture which can find few parallels in the whole of history.

Seeing the True Riches (780).

You will have very resolutely to look away from something else, if, amid all the dazzling gauds of earth, you are to see the far-off luster of that heavenly love. Just as timorous people in a thunder-storm will light a candle that they may not see the lightning, so many Christians have their hearts filled with the twinkling light of some miserable tapers of earthly care and pursuits, which, though they be dim and smoky, are bright enough to make it hard to see the silent depths of Heaven, though it blaze with a myriad of stars. If you hold a sixpence close enough up to the pupil of your eye, it will keep you from seeing the sun. And if you hold the world close to mind and heart, as many of you do, you will only see, round the rim of it, the least tiny ring of the overlapping love of God. What the world lets you see you will see, and the world will take care that it will let you see very little—not enough to do **you any good**, not enough to deliver you from its chains. Wrench yourselves away, my brethren, from the absorbing contemplation of Birmingham jewelery and paste, and look at the true riches.—Alexander Maclaren, D. D.

Service (781).

A woman living a few years ago in a miserable little village planted in front of her house a flower garden. When her neighbors crowded round to admire it she persuaded them to go and do likewise. She gave them seeds, she helped them to dig and weed, she kept up the work until they achieved success and were able to send flowers to the county fair. The poor-spirited women in other villages became wise in seeds and bulbs instead of scandalous gossip. The men, for shame, cleaned and drained the streets. The little woman is dead and forgotten, but her work will be a help to many generations.

An Eton boy, Quinton Hogg, appalled by the misery of a mighty dreadful London, got a barrel and a board, a couple of candles and some old books, and started a school at night, under London Bridge. He had two wharf rats as first scholars. When he died hundreds of thousands of poor men put a black band on their arms. They had been trained in the many polytechnic schools which had grown out of the barrel and boards—not only in Great Britain but in her colonies as well.

In short, we may be sure, when we waken each morning, that God has filled our hands with good seeds, which, if we plant them, will go on yielding fruit throughout the ages.

Whoever you are—wise or foolish, rich or poor—God sent you into this world, as He has sent every other human being, to help the men and women in it, to make them better and happier. If you don't do that, no matter what your powers may be, you are mere lumber, a worthless bit of the world's furniture. A Stradivarius, if it hangs dusty and dumb upon the wall, is not of as much real value as a kitchen poker which is used.—Selected.

The Secret of Victory (782).

Sir Walter Scott tells us that the battle of Bannockburn was the greatest ever lost by England or won by Scotland in the many wars between England, France and the Scotch. It was on the eve of this battle that the good abbot passed between the lines of the Scotch soldiery barefooted, exhorting them to fight for their freedom. They dropped upon their knees as he passed by and audibly prayed for victory. King Edward, the Second, who in person was commanding the English army, mistaking this act of devotion for one of supplication, called out to his men: "They kneel down—they ask forgiveness." "Yes," said a celebrated English baron, "but they ask it from God, not from us—these men will conquer or die upon the field," and they did conquer.—Selected.

The Rich Young Ruler (783).

His soul was like a boat tied fast, but tied with a long rope. It was able to struggle up the channel, past headland and light and buoy that marked the way; but always something held it back from perfectly laying itself at rest beside the golden shore. "What lack I yet?" And then said Jesus, "Go and sell all that thou hast, and thou shalt have treasure in heaven; and come and follow Me." He did not say, "You do not deserve wealth." He did not say, "It is wicked to be rich." He only said, "You will be free if you are poor, and then I can lead you to the Father, in whom you shall find yourself." He went back, past the buoys and headlands, down the bay to where the rope was tied, and cut the boat loose from its anchorage.—Phillips Brooks.

Life Means Opportunity (784).

It is always sad to see people throw away their opportunities. Opportunities come to every person offering their blessings and hopes— opportunities of improvement, opportunities of making friends, opportunities of doing good, opportunities of knowing God—and only too often they are allowed to pass to return no more. It is the tragedy of youth.

An artist has tried to teach this in a picture. Time is there with his inverted hour-glass. A young man is lying at his ease on a luxurious couch. Beside him is a table spread with delicacies. Passing by toward an open door are certain figures which represent opportunities; they come to invite the young man to activity, to manliness, to honor. First is a ragged sunbrowned form, carrying a flail. This is Labor. He has already passed unheeded. Next is a philosopher with an open book, inviting the young man to study. But this opportunity, too, is disregarded. The youth has no desire for Learning. Close behind the philosopher comes a woman with bowed head. She is carrying a child, and her dress is torn. She is a widow, and was begging alms, but her plea was in vain. Still another figure passes, endeavoring to woo him from his idle ease. It is a beautiful girl, who seeks, by love, to awaken in him noble purposes, to inspire him with an ambition worthy of his life. One by one these opportunities have passed, with their calls unheeded. At last he is rousing to seize them; but it is too late.

Bonds. (785)—Only the selfish and useless are ever free. Those who are worth anything in this world are bound by a hundred claims upon them. They must either stay caught in the meshes of love and duty, or wrench themselves free.—From The Inner Shrine.

Life's Heroism (786).

Living is usually harder than dying. It lasts longer, and it costs more. Yet merely to live on, day after day, and year after year, in the service of one's fellows, is not nearly so spectacular a thing as to die suddenly for a fellow being; therefore the heroes whose heroism consists in living do not get so much notice as the heroes whose heroism consists in dying. The "Jim Bludso" type of man, whose big heart and grim determination to keep his steamer's nose on the bank until all are saved are the cause of his death, is worshiped with an adulation entirely lacking for another whose grim determination to stand by his fellows lasts a lifetime instead of an hour, and who dies a common-place death in bed. Men do not always see things as God sees them. To "lay down his life for his friend" may mean to die, but it oftener means to live; and "greater love hath no man than this, that a man lay down (in life, not merely in death) his life for his friends."—Sunday School Times.

Fidelity (787).

We should be scrupulously zealous to fulfill our pledge to Christ in all particulars. Love should impel us to this. George Cary Eggleston has told of Mr. Chastian Cocke, a Virginia planter whose honorable dealings were known far and wide. "Never in all his life did he fail in an obligation or delay its fulfilment one hour beyond the appointed time, no matter how free he might be to delay, or how much trouble it might cost him to meet the obligation on time." Once a note fell due during a severe winter storm. He was in frail health, so sent his nephew, in his stead, on a sixty-mile ride over bad roads. When the messenger returned, he said, "All my life I have made it a rule to pay every dollar I owed on the precise day it was due, no matter if it cost me two dollars for every one dollar owed. The result is that my name is good in every bank in Richmond for any sum I may happen to want. Let me commend the rule to you. No man need undertake an obligation unless he wishes to do so. But, having undertaken it, he is in honor bound to fulfill it, no matter what happens. I know you had to swim a swollen river twice today. If I had not had you as a substitute, I should have made the journey myself, swimming the river as a necessary part of the proceedings."

Consecration (788).

A life fully consecrated to the service of Christ never counted for as much as today. The special call of the hour in which we live grows out of the very nature of things, out of life as we know it today with its manifold complexities, its multiplied opportunities, and hence its increased responsibilities for service in the kingdom of God. Today, as never before,

> "The common deeds of the common day
> Are ringing bells in the far-away."

Just as there are great crisis hours in the life of the individual and the nation, so there are crisis hours in the history of the Church. I am convinced that we are now facing a crisis hour, and it becomes us to take the situation seriously. We can think of great crisis hours through which the Church has already passed. It was a great hour when Luther and Zwingli led in that movement which resulted in the birth of the Protestant Reformation.—Selected.

Is Your Armor On? (789).

Every day we struggle with giants in the spiritual region; they are called principalities, and powers, and the rulers of the darkness of this world—invisible but mighty, nameless but strong because of fury. We can only overcome by the grace and power of the God of David.

Wherefore, take unto you the whole armor of God, that having with-
stood in the evil day you may stand firm and strong evermore. There
is a provided panoply, every part of which has been prepared and appointed by the Captain of heaven. In vain do we take swords of our
own manufacture, and adopt plans of our own feeble and perverse ingenuity. Stand in the old paths; demand to know the old ways; resolutely refuse to adopt any answer to satanic assault that is not included
in the replies of Jesus Christ Himself to the great foe; and constantly
pursuing this course, the course can have but one end—victory in the
name of the Lord, and heaven for evermore.—Joseph Parker.

Self-Sacrifice (790).

It is said that when Dr. Temple was Bishop of London he sent a
young man to a position involving much hardship. The young man's
friends tried to dissuade him from accepting it, and he went to the
Bishop and told him that he believed he would not live two years if
he accepted the appointment. Dr. Temple listened, and replied somewhat in this way: "But you and I do not mind a little thing like that,
do we?"—Miller.

Devoted Lives (791).

A young girl in New York worked for years without a vacation to
support a dependent old mother. Another young girl left her splendid
home in Philadelphia to be a missionary to the lepers and as I passed
the island where she had labored, said the speaker, a short distance from
Honolulu I was told to turn my glass in that direction, that I might
catch a glimpse of the inhabitants. As I did so I seemed to catch also
the fragrance of which Christ spoke in Korea. I met a missionary,
the daughter of a Presbyterian minister in this country, and she had
given up luxury, social position, everything to do her work there. Once
again I caught the fragrance of which Christ spoke, for "Wherever the
Gospel is preached, this shall be told as a memorial." "It is not the
big thing, not the conspicuous service, but the living at home as a true
father and a true mother, surrounding the homes with an atmosphere
of heaven, that, and being like Jesus, that counts." Tears were in the
eyes of hundreds in that great audience and many were heard to say,
"Oh! what comfort that talk brought to me." An old lady sitting near
the front was heard to say, "I couldn't give much money to foreign
missions, but I gave a son and a daughter."—Dr. Chapman.

Surrendered Souls (792).

When Henry Martyn reached the shores of India he made this entry
in his journal: "I desire to burn out for my God." "I refuse to be disappointed," exclaimed Hannington, in the darkest hour; "I will only
praise." James Chalmers, of heroic mold, once said: "Recall the
twenty-one years, give me back all its experience, give me its shipwrecks, give me its standings in the face of death, give it me surrounded with savages with spears and clubs, give it me back again with
spears flying about me, with the club knocking me to the ground—

give it me back, and I will still be your missionary." A short time after this was said, I read in an obscure corner of a daily newspaper words something like this: "A missionary eaten by cannibals"; and the death of this modern Paul was announced to the world. Are we still in the succession?

Zeal (793).

When the monks gathered round Wicliff's bed, which they hoped was his death-bed, and adjured him to recant, he replied, "I shall not die, but live and declare the works of the Friars." And he seemed to gain new inspiration, his health greatly reviving; and his words were ultimately fulfilled to the very letter.

"Not Worth While" (794).

John Stuart Mill, with all his learning and success in life, succumbed at last to what he called "the disastrous feeling of 'not worth while.'" He found that he had no clue to the meaning of life. And he thought the game not worth the candle. Cardinal Newman poured out his heart in the "Apologia:" "To consider the world in its length and breadth, its various history, the many races of men, their stories, their fortunes, their mutual alienations, their conflicts, their aimless courses, their random achievements and acquirements, . . . the greatness and littleness of man, his far-reaching aims, his short duration, the curtain hung over his futurity, the disappointments of life, the defeat of good, the success of evil, physical pain, mental anguish, the prevalence and intensity of sin, the prevailing idolatries, the dreary, hopeless irreligion; that condition of the whole race so fearfully yet so exactly described by the apostle, as 'having no hope and without God in the world,'"—All this is a vision to dizzy and appall, and inflicts upon the mind the sense of a profound misery which is absolutely beyond human solution.—Selected.

The Currency of Heaven (795).

When a traveler enters a foreign land, one of the first things he does is to get his money changed into the currency of that land. We can take none of earth's coin to heaven with us, but we can change it here by distributing liberally, thus "laying up in store." This is the exchange of currency Christ advised the young man of great possessions to make. No one of wealth is following Christ without this exchange, neither has he any foundation for the treasures of heaven.

All For Christ (796).

In one of our homes a few days ago I was told the story of a young missionary coming home on furlough. He invited his sister one day to take a walk with him. They followed the road leading to the schoolhouse on the pike, whither he had so often gone as a lad. He said to her, "I am tempted to stay at home and not go back again to India." "You had a call from God to go, did you not?" "Certainly I did," was the reply. "Have you the same kind of a call to stay, flattering as the offers are to do so?" "I do not think so," answered the young missionary, and the sister answered, "Much as we should love to have you with us, you would better follow the divine leading." Later this same sister was called to the mission field. Her noble work for and with the women of India is well known.—Selected.

Faithful Unto Death (797).

When a member of the Chinese mission force in the Hawaiian Islands, I knew a Chinese preacher who had already proved in South China the heroic fiber of his character. While assisting in opening a new mission at Sam Kong, Mr. Wong and others were attacked by a mob. The soldiers sent to give protection arrested Mr. Wong, who was later beaten with bamboo sticks because he was a Christian. As soon as possible his release was secured, and his wounds tenderly cared for. All through his suffering he was as happy and cheerful as ever, and when he recovered, he asked permission to go back and preach to the people among whom he had been beaten.—S. S. Times.

Unselfish Service (798).

Contrasting Savonarola with Lorenzo de Medici, Mr. Howells says: "Now that both have been dust for four hundred years, why do we cling tenderly, devoutly, to the strange frenzied apostle of the Impossible, and turn abhorring from that gay, accomplished, wise, and erudite statesman, who knew what men were so much better? There is nothing of Savonarola now but the memory of his purpose, nothing of Lorenzo but the memory of his: and now we see far more clearly than it that the frate had founded his free state upon the ruins of magnifico's tyranny; that the one willed only good to others, and the other willed it only to himself."

Enduring to the End (799).

In 1838, Father Sarrai, of the Soledad Mission in Mexico, refused to leave his work, though famine threatened and the people were too poor to help support him. He and his handful of Indians remained, though growing poorer and poorer every day. One Sunday morning, when saying mass at the crumbling altar, he fainted, fell forward, and died in their arms, of starvation.

Faithfulness (800).

When the battle of Coriole was being won through the stimulus given to the soldiers by the impassioned vigor of Caius Marcius, they mourned to see their leader covered with wounds and blood. They begged him to retire to the camp, but with characteristic bravery he exclaimed, "It is not for conquerors to be tired!" and joined them in prosecuting the victory to its brilliant end. "The crown of life" is promised to those who are "faithful unto death."—Australian S. S. Teacher.

Living to do God's Will (801).

God's will may daily be done by those whose place is obscure and whose gifts are humble. Angels in heaven live to do God's will. To do it perfectly and constantly is their supreme endeavor, and their endeavor is not frustrated. Christ came to earth to do the Father's will. At Jacob's well he said to His disciples, "I have meat to eat that ye know not of"; and when they wondered what this saying might mean, He said unto them, "My meat is to do the will of Him that sent Me, and to finish His work." The will of God is the harmony of the universe, the peace and joy of heaven. It is the perfect law of liberty of angels and of men. "Thy will be done" is the heart of all real prayer. The doing of God's will is our supreme privilege. That we may do it even imperfectly is the badge of our vital relationship to our Saviour. To do it perfectly everywhere and always is the Christian aim. When with all his heart one consecrates himself to the doing of the will of God, he possesses the peace that is power.

The Story of an Ear of Corn (802).

In the church tower of a town in Germany, we are told, there hangs a bell, and on this bell there is the image of a six-eared stalk of corn with the date, October 15, 1729, engraved upon it.

The first bell that was hung in this tower was so small that its tones could not be heard at the end of the village. A second bell was wanted, but the village was poor and there was not the needed money. Every one gave what he could, but the united offerings did not amount to enough.

One Sunday, the schoolmaster noticed growing out of the church wall a green stalk of corn, the seed of which must have been dropped by a passing bird.

The idea struck him that this stalk of corn could be made to produce the second bell. He waited till the corn was ripe, and then plucked the six ears on it, and sowed them in his garden.

The next year he gathered the little crop and sowed it again till he had not enough room in his garden for the crop, so he divided it among the farmers, who sowed the ears until the eighth year the crop was so large that when it was sold there was money enough to buy a beautiful bell with its story and birthday engraved upon it, and a cast of the stalk to which it owes its existence.

We may not be able to speak great words, but we can speak kind and true words; we may not be able to do great deeds, but we can do helpful and loving deeds. And these, with the blessing of the power of God's Spirit in our lives, will result in untold good and our reward will be sure.—Apples of Gold.

Aggressive Piety (803).

A French military critic at San Juan, during the Spanish-American War said the principal difference between an American soldier and a

French soldier was the initiative. The American soldier without any instructions from his captain or commander would initiate a movement that would produce great results.

This grows out of the fact that the American boy is a boy that is accustomed to think for himself and to grapple with new problems. Outside of military circles there is a hint in the principle that is of value. A minister, a district superintendent, a bishop, a Sunday School superintendent must have the initiative or fail to accomplish great results—initiate an advance at every strategic point. Soldiers in winter quarters and encampments are restless and enfeebled; lead them out against the enemy and they become an all-conquering force.

It was the "all-quiet-along-the-Potomac" spirit that was the grave of General George B. McClellan's hopes and aspirations. It was the initiative spirit that made Grant, Sherman, Sheridan, and McPherson heroes on every field of battle. "All quiet along the Potomac" is not a good motto for a minister of Christ or a church official. Sin is entrenched around us in many forms. Initiate a movement for its overthrow. The Church may be cold and putting forth feeble efforts for the redemption of the community. Plan a movement that will rally all the moral force of the community. Attack entrenched evil with the courage and daring of Stonewall Jackson and you will find that the stars in their courses will fight for you.—J. C. Gowan, in the California Independent.

Enduring Fidelity (804).

On the banks of the Kuruman, in the density of African heathenism, Robert and Mary Moffat toiled on for ten years without a single convert. Four hundred miles beyond the frontier of civilization, alone in the midst of savages, their faith never faltered. At a time when there was "no glimmer of the dawn" a letter was received from a friend in far-off England, asking if there was anything of use which could be sent. The significant answer of Mary Moffat was: "Send us a communion service; we shall want it some day." It came three years later, the day before the first converts were baptized. That faith was "assurance of things hoped."—Josiah Strong, D. D.

No Neutrality (805).

If God be intensely and passionately earnest that the right should conquer and the wrong be slain, then to be neutral is to disgrace that image in which I, and all the human race, were made. The epicureans of the old world, as you know, pictured the gods as utterly indifferent. They thought that they feasted and loved and lived for ever in an unruffled and ungodly ease. No echo of human sorrow ever reached them. No cry of a breaking heart ever distressed them. The shouting of voices in the world's dim struggle never flecked the sunshine of elysium. You cannot wonder that a neutral heaven that fostered in the citizens of Rome a neutral character. As a man's god is, so will a man become. Give him an indifferent heaven, and he becomes indiiferent. Hence history, with that wisdom of selection which laughs at the definitions of philosophy, looks at the self-pleasing and indifferent man, and calls him to this day epicurean.—G. H. Morrison, D. D.

The Prayer Life (806).

John Fox said, "The time we spend with God in secret is the sweetest time, and the best improved. Therefore, if thou lovest thy life, be in love with prayer." The devout Mr. Hervey resolved, on the bed of sickness, "If God shall spare my life, I will read less and pray more." John Cooke, of Maidenhead, wrote: "The business, the pleasure, the honor, and advantage of prayer press on my spirit with increasing force every day." A deceased pastor when drawing near his end, ex-claimed, "I wish I had prayed more."—Spurgeon.

Quenchless Zeal (807).

Gazzoli, the Italian soldier, fighting under Garibaldi, was lamed in both legs, and henceforth could only render hospital service. When reports of defeats and victories came in, Gazzoli's eyes would fill with tears, and then glisten triumphantly. "But I still can scrape lint for the doctor," he would say.—The S. S. Chronicle.

Lamps Out (808).

Lamps, but no oil! There was preparation to meet the bridegroom, and confidence, but a vain confidence, in an insufficient preparation. When the bridegroom came, the foolish virgins were left behind and the door was shut. We who call ourselves Christians have made our preparation and are waiting for Christ to come. We all have lamps, which represent what is external in our Christianity, whether it be rites, or creed, or works of charity, or morality, or zeal for our church. But have we oil, that true spiritual consecration of the soul which alone can fill outward acts with light and life?

The lamps may be of various shapes and patterns, but the oil must be the same in all. Whether, in burning, it shines out as repentance or faith or good works or worship, its essence is love, pure unselfish love to God and man. Where this love is wanting, there is no true spiritual life and no sufficient preparation to meet our Lord when He comes.— George Washburn.

An Earnest Life (809).

After I had spoken last Sunday to Hon. J. J. Maclaren's famous men's class, numbering four hundred, at the Metropolitan Church in Toronto, Canada, my theme being "Sacrifice and Service," Sir George Smith, of England, who sat by me on the platform, handed me this epitaph from the bronze monument in St. Paul's, London, to the memory of Major-General Charles George Gordon, commonly known as "Chinese" Gordon, because of the noble name he won as a Christian soldier in China:

> To the memory of General Gordon,
> Who, everywhere and at all times,
> Gave his strength to the weak,
> His sympathy to the suffering,
> His help to the oppressed,
> And his heart to God.

This is an exquisite and pathetic tribute to the greatest and best soldier that England ever produced. He was treacherously slain at Khartoum, Africa, which he had held against a long siege, until he was the last white man in the doomed city.

His last letter, written to his sister in England, said: "I am quite happy, thank God! And, like Samuel, 'I have tried to do my duty.'" His last day's diary ended with the words: "I have done the best for the honor of my country. Good-by." The outburst of popular grief in England and in all her colonies, when the news of Gordon's death became known, has not been paralleled in any land. In Westminster and St. Paul's the royal family and the court held memorial services, and all over Great Britain monuments have arisen to this great soldier, whose greatness was because of his gentleness and loyalty at all times to Jesus Christ. Lord Tennyson expressed the sorrow of the nation's heart in these beautiful words:

> Warrior of God, man's friend, not here below,
> But somewhere dead far in the waste Soudan;
> Thou livest in all hearts, for all men know
> This earth hath borne no simpler, nobler man.
>
> —H. M. Hamill, D. D.

A Swan Song (810).

In a little fishing village of England a clergyman labored for more than twenty-five years. His labor was not in vain, for he wrought a marvelous change in the sailors and fishermen of the village. At length he found his health far from good, and on consulting an eminent physician he was told that unless he cast anchor for a while his voyage of life would soon be over. In four years he was forced to stop and seek the milder climate of Italy. He never regained his strength, and returned to England for short visits only.

Before leaving home, in September of 1847, Henry F. Lyte announced that he intended to preach once more to his people. To the surprise and alarm of his family, he did preach, and in addition helped to administer the Lord's Supper. That same evening he handed to a relative the words and music of his great hymn, "Abide with Me." In a few hours he left his home for Southern France.

The last verse of one of his poems reads thus:

> "O Thou whose touch can lend
> Life to the dead, Thy quickening grace supply,
> And grant me, swanlike, my last breath to spend
> In song that may not die."

And, "swanlike" he spent his last breath; for in less than two months
after writing "Abide with Me," the hymn that has been for many
years a favorite one for funerals, the hymn writer died; and a marble
cross in the English cemetery at Nice marks his last resting place.—
Cora Lowe Watkins, in The Christian Advocate.

The Path of Sacrifice (811).

There is the path of sacrifice. They who tread that way receive no
outward crown. Am I a sinner because I have brought home no fleshly
reward? There is a path where the rewards are all unseen; and only
the highest walk in it; its name is love. Those who travel by it get
nothing in return; they bring back no sheaves. Is it because of their
sin they bring back no sheaves? Nay, but because of their holiness—
their love. Their joy is what they give, not what they get. They do
not prey upon others; they are preyed upon. That is their glory, that
is their recompense—to empty themselves, to lavish themselves, to be,
not the vulture, but the voluntary victim of the vulture. Their heaven
is the worldling's hell—unselfishness."

O Thou who hast trod the path unknown to the vulture and the
bird of prey, I bow this day to Thee! Thou, too, didst bring nothing
home after the flesh. No visible crown rewarded Thee. No outward
plaudits greeted Thee. No material kingdom owned Thy sway. Thine
was the cross from dawn to dark, the dying from morn to even. Men
said, "He must be a great sinner since He is so unprosperous; let Him
come down from the cross and we will believe in Him." They did not
see Thy hidden joy, Thy real unprosperity. They did not see that the
path of love is itself the path of self-surrender, that Thy cross made
Thy crown. But I see it, and I come to Thee. The world will wonder;
the vulture will marvel; the bird of prey will be astonished. They see
only the outside, and therefore they see nothing. But my heart knows
its own joy, and it is Thy joy—love emptying, love surrendering, love
gathering flowers from out the thorns with bleeding hand to strew another's way. Thy path may be wet with tears, but they are the tears
of the rainbow; show me Thy path, O Lord.—Matheson.

Investing In Eternity (812).

The true idea of a Christian life. It is a great venture, a stake upon
the eternal future. The Christian's reward is to be the product of an
investment in the future. Each man must ask himself this question:
Is my reward being had now? Is any left to be given by and by at
the hands of Christ?

But it does not necessarily follow that all good works done pub-
licly forfeit God's approval hereafter. We are to let our light shine,
etc. Christ's words come to this—a good intention to serve God is the
very soul of a good action, whatever be its outward form.

We should think of our work now as we shall think of it when
dying. We should live for a reward which shall not then appear to be
worthless.—Selected.

Heart Music (813).

A company of monks in the olden time lived together in a monastery, working, busily tilling the land and caring for the sick and poor, yet ever hallowing their work with prayer. Every evening they sang the beautiful hymn, "Magnificat," at their vesper service; but as they grew old their voices became harsh and broken, and they almost lost all tune, but they still sang on.

One evening a strange youth came in to see them. He was strong and beautiful; and when they began the "Magnificat" his lovely, clear voice soared upward, as if to sing at the very gate of heaven. The poor old monks listened, enraptured.

That night an angel appeared to the eldest monk and asked: "Why did not the old hymn ascend to heaven at evensong as before?" The monk, astonished, replied: "O, blessed angel, surely it did ascend. Heard you not in heaven those almost angelic strains from the voice of our gifted young brother? So sweetly he sang that our poor voices were hushed, lest we should mar the music." But the angel answered: "Beautiful it may have been, but no note of it reached heaven. Into those gates only music of the heart can enter."—The Christian Advocate.

Living Heaven On Earth (814).

O Christian men and women, do not deceive yourselves! Remember that God sees through shams, remember that God does not care for anything except the heart. He will not in the least value you for your professions or for your observance: but, "as he who hath called you holy, so be ye holy in all manner of conversation." If you want to make religion lovable, you must make it lovely; if you want men to accept your opinions, enable them, if you can, to respect your character; let men see in you a purer standard than their own, a loftier stature, a kindlier sympathy. The centuries do homage to real goodness: fairer than the morning or the evening star; it is the reflection of the life of Christ; it is as "a city set on a hill;" it is a pillar of fire moving over a wilderness of graves.—Canon Farrar.

The Pure In Heart. (815)

—"Blessed are the pure in heart." I am glad that it does not read, "Blessed are the great in intellect," or "Blessed are the rich in this world's goods," but "Blessed are the pure in heart." This brings the vision of God within the reach of all; for if all may not be rich or great, all can be pure.—Rev. Robert Forbes, D. D.

Livingstone's Devotion To His Work (816).

When Stanley went out to Africa and found Livingstone, he tried in vain to persuade him to return to England, as he was so utterly worn and exhausted by his many trials. Stanley writes of him: "He has been baffled and worried, even almost to the grave, yet he will not desert the charge imposed upon him by his friend, Sir Roderick Murchison. To the stern dictates of duty, alone, has he sacrificed his home and ease, the pleasures, refinements, and luxuries of civilized life. His is the Spartan heroism, the inflexibility of the Roman, the enduring resolution of the Anglo-Saxon—never to relinquish his work, though his heart yearns for home; never to surrender his obligations until he can write FINIS to his work."

Livingstone's biographer continues:—In December, 1872, Livingstone wrote, "If the good Lord permits me to put a stop to the enormous evils of the inland slavetrade, I shall not grudge my hunger and toils. I shall bless His name with all my heart." In the following March, he wrote, "Nothing earthly will make me give up my work in despair. I encourage myself in the Lord my God, and go forward."

The Worth Of It All (817).

A missionary once went out to India. He left a comfortable home and wealthy friends. He had to work hard and endure many trials. Some of his friends at home thought that perhaps he was sorry for having gone and would be glad to come back. So they wrote to know how he felt about it. Here is an extract from a letter which he wrote in reply:

"Our work is hard. It taxes both body and mind. What our reward will be hereafter, we know not. But one thing we do know. If we receive no other reward than what is given us here every day there is no other work on earth that pays so well. In all the pursuits of this world, even in my childhood hours, I never have found so much real pleasure as in preaching Christ, the Way, the Truth, and the Life, to these perishing heathen. It is a work that perfectly satisfies the cravings of my soul; and as I pursue it I can cheerfully sing:

> " 'Go, then, earthly fame and treasure,
> Come disaster, scorn, and pain;
> In Christ's service pain is pleasure,
> With His favor loss is gain.' "
> —From Rev. Richard Newton's "Best Things."

Living Epistles (818).

One of the ablest and most useful Christians in a certain city, on being asked, "What was it that led you to become a Christian?" replied, "A halfpound pressure on my coatbutton for five minutes." By this he referred to the fact that after consulting his lawyer, who was a Christian man, upon some matter of business, the lawyer gently laid hold on his coat-button and kindly asked him about his soul, and persuasively commended Christ to him. Can you not find opportunity to reason and persuade for some soul's salvation?

ILLUSTRATIVE POETRY.

I Know That My Redeemer Lives (819).

I know that my Redeemer lives;
  He that hath died hath con-
    quered death;
And ever living He forgives,
  As when He prayed with dying
    breath.
Thou bleeding Lamb! I trust in
    Thee;
  I know that Thou didst die for
    me.

Full oft with all my guilt in view,
  I fear there is no hope for me;
My sins that holy Sufferer slew;
  I pierced Him hanging on the
    tree.
His look of love my faith revives,
  And tells me my Redeemer
    lives.

Alas! since first I saw the Lord,
  Oft have I wandered from His
    side;
Slighted how oft His gracious
    word;
  Nay more—His precious name
    denied.
Yet those sweet accents, "Lov'st
    thou me?"
Recall my roving heart to Thee.

When sorrow its dark shadow
    flings,
  When sinks my soul in deepest
    woe,
This joy in tribulation spring,
Hope in despair, I know—I
    know—
And, Oh, what peace the know-
    ledge gives;
I know that my Redeemer lives.

Poor the world's noblest diadem,
  Faint is each bauble's bright-
    est ray;
One pearl exceeds earth's purest
    gem,
  One crown alone fades not away.
That pearl, that crown, my faith
    receives;
I know that my Redeemer lives.

Yes! I shall see Him as He is,
  Shall know Him e'en as I am
    known;
This weak, vile heart grow pure
    like His;
  His lovely image be my own.
Take—take, faint heart! the hope
    He gives,
And know that my Redeemer lives.
           —Unknown.

Ready (820).

Beware, my soul, take thou good heed lest thou in slumber lie,
And, like the five, remain without, and knock, and vainly cry;
But watch and bear thy lamp undimmed, and Christ shall gird thee on
His own bright wedding-robe of light, the glory of the Son.—G. Moultrie

God Gathers The Fragments (821).

A broken song, it fell apart
Just as it left the singer's heart,
A broken prayer hardly half said
By a tired child at its trundle bed;
A broken life hardly half told
When it dropped the burden it scarce could hold;
Of these songs and prayers and lives undone,
God gathers the fragments, every one.
           —Selected.

Keep Right With God (822).

When night comes, list thy deeds: make plain the way
'Twixt heaven and thee; block it not with delays;
But perfect all before thou sleep'st; then say
There's one sun more strung on my bead of days,
What's good score up for joy: the bad well scann'd,
Wash off with tears, and get thy Master's hand.

—Selected.

"Thou Art Near" (823).

O Love Divine, that stooped to share
Our deepest pang, our bitterest tear,
On Thee we cast each earth-born care,
We smile at pain while Thou art near.

Though long the weary way we tread,
And sorrow crown each lingering year
No path we shun, no darkness dread,
Our heart still whispering "Thou art near."

—O. W. Holmes.

A Call (824).

To the comforting, beautiful churchyard, to be with my dead and to pray,
World-weary and lonely and longing, I slipped in the gloaming today.
The face of sweet heaven bent o'er me, alight with the tenderest glow,
And something—the smile of the angels—fell soft on the sleepers below.

Their harps were enmeshed in the tree tops, light fingers were sweeping the strings,
I drank in the music seraphic, and marked the soft flutter of wings.
Those wings fanned invisible censers, so perfect the perfume they shed,
It seemed like a mantle of sweetness, descending to cover the dead.

I looked on the couches of velvet, embroidered with aster and rose,
And garnished with handpainted lilies—God's hand—where the sleepers repose;
I thought on the things they had toiled for, had longed for and ventured to pray,
And knew that up yonder in heaven they enjoyed the fruition today.

I wept—for my own destitution—then lifted my face to the skies,
The smile of the angels had faded, they looked down with pitying eyes.
Soft, soft fell their tears in the twilight, I felt that for me they were shed,
Compassionate tears for the living, but smiles for the fortunate dead.

Then lo! from the east came a brilliance, a glory illumined the air,
And I, in admiring wonder, forgot all my grief and despair.
Hope flashed through my trembling heartstrings, a something spoke low to my soul,
It fluttered its quivering white wings in yearnings that baffled control.

And then to my spirit lethargic a wonderful miracle came,
A hunger and thirst for achievement, for battle, in Victory's name.
A longing to fill up the breaches, to man all the guns in the strife,
To scatter the perfume of lilies like yon, in the pathway of life.

To play upon harps that are human, with fingers so vibrant with love
That, raptured, the listening angels would pause in the music above.
I rose in the golden effulgence that flooded the world with its light,
And knew that the God of the living had smiled on His servant tonight
                    —May Elliott Hutson, in the Christian Observer

Victory (825).

It is not life's tenure that I moan,
    Its many tears, its vanishing delights,
Nor all the bitterness my heart hath known
    In the grim silences of wakeful nights.

Nor doth my spirit in the battle quail,
    Dreaming of pleasure and inglorious ease;
My arm would answer mighty flail with flail,
    And try results with mortal destinies.

But this my prayer, and this my one request:
    That when my wrestle with the foe is done,
It be not said of me, "He did his best"—
    Not that alone, but let them add, "He won."
                    —Herbert Muller Hopkins in the Outlook.

"Not With Them When Jesus Came" (826).

Not with them, Thomas, on that Easter night
        When Jesus came
To bless His own, establishing by sight
        His wondrous claim?

Nay, blame me not; I paid the price in ruth—
        A week of doubt;
The ten rejoicing in the glorious truth,
        And I, left out.

Not with them when He breathed the Holy Ghost?
        How could you miss,
O Thomas, leader of a doubting host,
        That heavenly kiss?

Deride me not. For evermore I must
        This stigma bear—
Among the blessed who not seeing trust—
        I was not there.

Ah, Thomas, teach me by thy loss to be
        With those who pray
in full expectancy their Lord to see
        On Easter day!
                By Ella Gilbert Ives

His Vision (827).

This man, this blinded man, could not see things
A-near. He could not see the spoils of trade,
Or rolls of bills, or stocks, or dividends
That heap and heap. Nor could he see great piles
Of stones or rows of brick or tons and tons
Of steel or unmined wealth, or yet rich lands
That stretch and stretch.
        O blinded, blinded man!

But he could see afar. He could see the spoils
Of grace. He could see the dazzling trail of glory,
And he could see bright, glittering souls in earth's
Black night. He saw them; he gathered them
And reached them back to God. Behold this man,
Miser-like, bent to his task, hoarding wealth,
Most precious wealth, in a place unknown by moth
Or thief. Behold this man, this man who toiled
As one would toil who could see beyond the mists;
As one who could see the wondrous dawn, the morning
The brighter day, the noon, the everlasting
Zenith in far domains unlit by star
Or moon or sun; as one would toil who could see
The King in all His beauty; as one could see
The Christ waiting to receive His own redeemed.
        O visioned, visioned man.

TEXTS AND TREATMENT HINTS.

"Present Your Bodies a Living Sacrifice."—Rom. 12:1 (828).

I. We have in the text a very remarkable way of putting what I may call the sum of Christian service. The main leading idea is the gathering together of all Christian duty into the one mighty word—sacrifice. Sacrifice, to begin with, means giving up everything to God. And how do I give up to God? When in heart and will and thought I am conscious of His presence, and do all the actions of the inner man in dependence on, and in obedience to, Him. That is the true sacrifice when I think as in His sight, and will and love and act as in obedience to Him. To consecrate oneself is the way to secure a higher and nobler life than ever before. If you want to go all to rack and ruin, live according to your own fancy and taste. If you want to be strong, and grow stronger and more and more blessed, put the brake on, and keep a tight hand upon yourself, and offer your whole being upon His altar.

II. We have here likewise the great motive of Christian service: "I beseech you, therefore, by the mercies of God." In the Apostle's mind this is no vague expression for the whole of the diffused blessings with which God floods the world, but he means thereby the definite specific thing, the great scheme of mercy, set forth in the previous chapters, that is to say, His great work in saving the world through Jesus Christ. That is "the mercies" with which he makes his appeal. The diffused and wide-shining mercies, which stream from the Father's heart, are all, as it were, focussed as through a burning-glass into one strong beam, which can kindle the greenest wood and melt the thick-ribbed ice. Only on the footing of that sacrifice can we offer ours. He has offered the one sacrifice, of which His death is the essential part, in order that we may offer the sacrifice of which our life is the essential part.

III. Note the gentle enforcement of this great motive for Christian service: "I beseech you." Law commands, the gospel entreats. Paul's beseeching is only a less tender echo of the Master's entreaty.—Alexander Maclaren, D. D.

"To Keep Himself Unspotted From the World."—James 1:27 (829).

St. James specifies a distinct form of evil, the world; not other forms of evil.

Let me define what the world is. It is not this beautiful world, which weaves for God the living garment in which the Invisible has robed His mysterious loveliness. Drink in beauty and heaven as much as you will from that. Yet a narrow mind has sometimes been tormented with a scruple about the lawfulness of enjoying the world, even in this sense.

Nor, again, does the world mean domestic affections. Let us guard against a common mistake. Men tell us when we love our children they will be taken from us. Awful picture of a tyrant God! When we weep, they bid us dry our tears; they forget that Jesus wept. We love little enough; let us bring in no cold, desolating, stoical theory to make that little less. Desecrate not the sacred home of love by the name of the forbidden world.

The world that spots is the spirit of evil around us. Wherever men congregate for pleasure, business, or amusement, there is evil. It belongs to the town rather than to the country; to large societies rather than to small. A mixed, strange, many-headed monster is it. It is like the miasma of a marsh. Each single pleasure is harmless in itself till the noxious juices are drawn out. It differs in different ages; persecuting and soft, money-making, infidel and superstitious—a torrent which we must stem.

Observe, distinct effort is required in a man to "keep himself unspotted from the world." You are spottable; the world can spot you— "keep" yourself.

Moreover, we may not decline the danger. We must go right through. Christians must be soldiers, tradesmen, citizens. There can be no luxurious shutting ourselves up with our devotional books. The snow-river flows through the lake without imbibing its warmth. We must transmute the evil.

Out of the innumerable influences of that multiform evil we select only three.

I. The world's tainting influence upon delicacy of heart.

This tendency is universal. There are manufactories where the evil and the well-disposed mix in dangerous proximity for hours together; bold vice and modest virtue. Go higher still. Enter gay society; look at young persons at the end of two seasons. Observe the influence upon them of newspapers, novels, and conversation in producing familiarity with evil. They have tasted of the "tree of knowledge," and have gained knowingness. Oh, the degradation and agony of a heart which feels itself naked! When the drapery is torn from life, we know what lies beneath.

All this comes from the world; not from your own heart only, but from the miasma of many hearts. In a marsh each single plant is harmless; the festering, noxious juices come out of the many. The retired life is safe; in the crowd danger straightway rises.

This is the natural tendency, unless it be counteracted by the effort here spoken of—"Keep yourself unspotted from the world."

II. The world's power to make artificial.

Define the world as the not-natural. Picture the man of the world seeming to be what he is not—a well-bred person with every emotion under control, with features immovable. We are as sure of meeting consideration from him as if he were influenced by the Gospel. Yet all this bland courtesy is on the outside; it is the smoothness of coin caused by friction in the purse. The edges, the corners, the salient points, all individuality rubbed away. This species of worldliness begins early. The boy at school dares not speak of his mother and sisters; at last he becomes brutalized enough to ridicule his home. It is an unnatural control, as well as an unnatural affectation of feeling.

So in after-life. The world honors riches; we are feverishly afraid of being detected in poverty. If our fortune be diminished, we adopt meanness and artifices at home, that we may seem the same abroad.

The world honors politeness; hence compliments and flattery. Oh, the crushing sense of degradation that comes from it!

The world honors feeling; hence sentimentality.

The world honors high birth; hence the attempt to seem familiar with good society.

This is the world. Men and women who have not kept themselves unspotted from the world are not what they seem. Hollow and unreal, their affectation appears everywhere in accent, motion, and sentiment.

And, do what we will, we imbibe this. Dikes intended to keep out salt water still admit some. The precept to be natural makes us unnatural; we affect nature.

Now, there is no remedy for this but what St. James gives. Firstly, some familiarity with suffering; and, secondly, intercourse with God. We must live "before God the Father"; live in the splendors of the next world till this world is dim. The man living in sunshine is not dazzled by the oil-lamp. One who hears in his inmost soul the harmonies of everlasting harps will not mistake the discord of this world for music. One looking out for death and judgment to come will not heed the judgments of this world. Feel the powers of the world to come; that is the secret of keeping one's self unspotted from this world.

III. The power of the world to destroy feeling.

It is a common expression to speak of the heartlessness of the world. Let us trace the history of the decay of feeling. We passionately crave a more lively life. Life generally is a dull, vegetating existence. There are times when we get out of this; when the blood runs fast, and thoughts and imaginations crowd and hurry and precipitate, as if we had gigantic energy. It is the delightfulness of animal exhilaration. There are the different excitements of conversation, society, music, or of the stimulant of wine; all those things which the world offers; "all that is in the world, the lust of the flesh, and the lust of the eyes, and the pride of life, is not of the Father, but is of the world." There is the craving of the drunkard. Life would be robbed of its exhilaration, so he cannot give up drink. Now, this is the consequence: unsettlement and deadening of feelings.

So in the body. In the tropics man is matured early and decays early. He is old at thirty; the sensations of life are all felt early.

Similarly in the heart. Early maturity of feeling is premature decay of heart. Existence does not depend on time. One man at twenty-five has lived longer than another at fifty.

Observe, all God's pleasures are simple ones; health, the rapture of a May morning, sunshine, the stream blue and green, kind words, benevolent acts, the glow of good-humor. It is the time when you need nothing stronger than bread and water to be intoxicated with happiness.

But look at other excitements. The great calm presence and beauty of creation does not come forth to the sorceries of artificial excitement. Stimulate the jaded senses with town life, and then there is no radiant wisdom left in the simplicities of life.

This is the lesson we press upon the young. Keep unspotted from the world. The keenness of wonder is by degrees lost early, and is followed by exhaustion of feeling; and men become blase of life.

Oh that the young would learn from the experience of those who know it. Remember Solomon's state. Is there anything whereof it may be said, "See, this is new?" Ye that live in pleasure, to this you are coming!

There are peculiar features in the present time. The world is moving fast, and we with it. There are a multiplicity of pleasures; a cheapness in their purchase, and change in their variety. Thousands see foreign lands now. There are the excitements of railways, speculation, and literature. These produce exhaustion of feeling and of interest. Compare the patriarchal times, and we find the man of one hundred and fifty had not lived so much as the man of forty now. Let Christians, therefore, be on their guard. They have need of calmness. They have the power of the Gospel and duty to soothe them. Remember the Cana feast. Would you have your best last? Avoid stimulus; live plainly. You will drink the rich body of heavenly wine, and feel the refreshment of its sacred joy.

And now a word of application.

St. James gives a distinct view of religion. It is practical charity and purity. God's sovereignty and eternity are nothing without this. You are no favorite of Heaven to be exempt.

And, observe, both charity and purity are joined together, not kept separate. There is a difficulty in their union; but observance of the one cannot excuse neglect of the other.

The active must be worldly.

The strict, pure, quiet, dreamy, must be active.

External benevolence and inward purity go hand in hand.—Frederick W. Robertson, M. D.

"There Is But a Step Between Me And Death."—1 Sam. 20:3 (830).

It is true that just off there, two hours—ten steps—away, there is a spiritual world—into which at any moment we may be ushered; into which, before long, we shall, most certainly, all be ushered. A multitude on that ill-fated Atlantic liner, who at one o'clock in the morning still believed that their tenure of earthlift would be of years duration, at two o'clock—just about an hour later—crossed the boundary line between the seen and fleeting and the unseen and eternal, and they are living somewhere in that other world.

I. What fools we often are!

To know, to believe, to be ready to cite a long list of proofs of the existence of that other world, and yet to live for hours, days, years, with hardly a thought of it. To plan, and think, and toil and strive as if it was all an empty myth, a poet's idle dream.

II. Could any experience have a more ennobling influence upon the life than the keen realization of the nearness of the unseen world!

What a spur it proves to tireless zeal in the cause of Christ. What a blessed inspiration it provides when earth's storms threaten to extinguish the gleaming lights of hope and joy.

What an antidote it offers for neutralizing the baneful power of the hurtful things of this life over the soul.

Training ourselves to cherish this thought of its nearness does not shadow our lives, while it does rob death of its dread.

> "It seemeth such a little way to me,
> Across to that strange country, the Beyond;
> And yet not strange, for it has grown to be
> The home of those of whom I am so fond;
> They make it seem familiar and more dear,
> As journeying friends bring distant countries near."

III. It is our privilege and duty to cherish this alert awareness of the unseen world.

And it is a privilege which we cannot afford to forego. How many sorrows it would turn into joys. If, when dear friends are taken from us, instead of having "holden eyes," faith's vision would but follow the soul's flight into the realms of bliss, our gladness in their gain would almost extinguish our grief over our loss.

And how much the ever-present thought of it would do not only thus to mitigate sorrow, but weaken the grip of sordid earthiness and reinforce the soul in its conflict with sin.—J. H. B.

XIII. FRAGRANT LIVES—OUR INFLUENCE.

REFLECTIONS AND ILLUSTRATIONS.

A Treasure Which Endures (831).

Of all beautiful things a beautiful character is the most beautiful. That is not a thing that you can prove. It needs no proving. It is what we all acknowledge in our hearts. And if it is the most beautiful thing in the world, it is also the most useful. It is character that tells more than anything else in the long run, and that secures for mankind the wealth that is most worth coveting. There is not very much, perhaps, that we can do for our fellow men in what we call practical ways, but we can help them enormously by being just good men. It is more useful to be a great saint than to be a great inventor. Moreover, this is a treasure which endures. Many of the things that we build up with so much labor and care disappear and are forgotten like the towers we built with bricks when we were children, or the brave structures by the seashore that were swept away by the incoming tide. Our riches take wings and fly away, and we too fly away and are forgotten, and it seems as if all the toil of our life were for nothing. We go out of the world and carry nothing with us. But there is something that we carry with us. We take ourselves. We do not lose the character that we have been building up with so much patience and self-denial. That is ours to keep and ours to keep forever.

There is this to remember, too—that there is nothing that gives so much interest to the closing years of our life in this world, when much of our work has necessarily to be abandoned, as the belief that through those years of sadness, and weakness, and loneliness, it may be, God is still carrying on His own great purpose in us, and preparing us for the better things that await us beyond the grave.

As to the means by which the work may be done, I think we know pretty well what are the "means of grace," to use the old phrase. We know that we can do something, and we know what we can do if we are so inclined. We know that we can "pray in the Holy Ghost," and that we can "keep ourselves in the love of God," and that we can be "looking to the mercy of our Lord Jesus Christ," and so coming under the power of the endless life. We know that there is a certain attitude that we can assume, and certain habits that we can fall into, by the help of which we may ever be growing in all goodness and wisdom. There are many little things we could do if we would. We know how, in the ordinary business of life, we can get into the way of doing things. We do a thing once, and then we do it a second time, and a third time, and thus we get into the way of doing it. It becomes a habit and is done unconsciously and habit determines character.—The Home Messenger.

Springtime Lives (832).

Let the life be filled with the spirit of the springtime. Let the voice in its heart always keep saying to it, "You are to go on filling yourself with vitality and joy, day after day, month after month, and then cometh the end;" and then it is not a cessation of life, but fuller life which the heart expects. The end which comes to the promise of springtime shall be the luxuriance of summer! —Phillips Brooks.

Jenny Lind and the Lily (833).

When that queen of singers, Jenny Lind, was once singing at Cincinnati, there was a poor woman dying of consumption in the great city, of course an utter stranger to the former. She had two little children, who had a strangely longing desire to hear the "Swedish nightingale." Their mother's poverty utterly prevented her granting their wish. But the little ones thought if they could "only see her," it would be some consolation, and they resolved to carry her as a gift the greatest treasure they had—a beautiful lily they had reared. Their request to see her at the hotel was somewhat roughly refused; but still they urged their plea, until the childish voices attracted the attention of Jenny Lind, who was in an adjoining room. Opening the door, she inquired their errand, and, learning of their wish to see and hear her, she placed in their hands a "family" ticket for four people, and accepted the lily with loving words of thanks. That evening the audience noticed that in lieu of the costly floral offerings sent her that day, the piano simply bore a pot containing a lily, and they saw also that as she left the platform she looked down on the front row, and threw a kiss to two happy children seated there. Little marvel is it that all of us who recall Jenny Lind and her marvelous singing love even better to remember her beautiful Christian life and the numberless merciful and loving deeds that so adorned it.—C. E. World.

Heavenly Arithmetic (834).

Heaven's arithmetic has some principles that seem paradoxical. One of them is contained in Christ's estimate of the widow's pennies. How can a copper cent be worth more than a gold eagle? His rule for getting rich is equally strange: "Sell and give, and thou shalt have treasure." Does it make the treasure less desirable that it is to be in heaven's bank? His get-rich-quick plan may seem strange, but it is practical. Getting comes of giving. We get mercy by showing mercy; we get forgiveness by forgiving; we get honor by yielding the place of honor to others; we become princes by making ourselves servants; we become priests by making ourselves the friends and companions of sinners.—Christian Advocate.

Shedding Blessing (835).

Let the weakest, let the humblest, remember that in his daily course he can, if he will, shed around him almost a heaven. Kindly words, sympathizing attentions, watchfulness against wounding men's sensitiveness—these cost very little, but they are priceless in their value. Are they not almost the staple of our daily happiness? From hour to hour, from moment to moment we are supported, blest, by small kindnesses."—F. W. Robertson.

Mark Twain's Tender Tribute to His Daughter (836).

We take from Harper's Magazine the last thing that Mark Twain wrote—a touching and beautiful tribute to his daughter, Jean, who died just one year ago. It was written on the day of her death. He says:

"Jean's dog has been wandering about the grounds today, comrade-less and forlorn. I have seen him from the windows. She got him from Germany. He has tall ears, and looks exactly like a wolf. He was educated in Germany, and knows no language but the German. Jean gave him no orders save in that tongue. And so when the burglar alarm made a fierce clamor at midnight a fortnight ago, the butler, who is French and knows no German, tried in vain to interest the dog in the supposed burglar. Jean wrote me, to Bermuda, about the incident. It was the last letter I was ever to receive from her bright head and her competent hand. The dog will not be neglected.

"There was never a kinder heart than Jean's. From her childhood up she always spent the most of her allowance on charities of one kind and another. After she became secretary and had her income doubled she spent her money upon these things with a free hand. Mine, too, I am glad and grateful to say.

"She was a loyal friend to all animals, and she loved them all—birds, beasts, and everything—even snakes—an inheritance from me. She knew all the birds; she was high up in that lore. She became a member of various humane societies when she was still a little girl—both here and abroad—and she remained an active member to the last. She founded two or three societies for the protection of animals, here and in Europe.

"She was an embarrassing secretary, for she fished my correspondence out of the waste basket and answered the letters. She thought all letters deserved the courtesy of an answer. Her mother brought her up in that kindly error."

Hearts Like the Mown Grass (837).

When the summer heat is severe nothing looks more woeful than the mown grass. Whether it is the hayfield which has been left mere stubble by the mowing machine, or the front yard that has been cut close by the lawn mower, it turns brown as the scorching rays of the sun beat down upon it fiercely all day and for many days. But when the rain comes the trees brighten up, the vines are refreshed, droop-ing flowers lift up their heads, but no one rejoices so much and no plant is so blessed as is the mown grass. That is why one passage in the psalms speaks of God, when he comes to bless his people, as rain upon the mown grass.

It is a beautiful act when a boy or girl can quench thirst. For-tunate are those whose summer task is to sprinkle the lawn, the spray falling like rain upon the roots of the mown grass. I saw recently a man with such a spirit who built and filled with water a cement basin for the thirsty birds. Jesus Himself said that whoever gave a cup of cold water in the name of a disciple should not be without his reward.

But there are hearts also that are like the mown grass. You can tell them sometimes by the sadness of their countenances. The next time you see a troubled face, plan at once to be like a fine summer shower. Whoever, by some smile and cheery word or by some helpful deed, refreshes a weary heart and brightens a sad countenance is like rain upon the mown grass.—Rev. E. H. Byington in The Congregationalist.

A Dream (838).

A good Christian lady, we are told, once opened a home for crippled children. Among those who were received was a little boy three years old, who was a most frightful and disagreeable-looking child. The good lady did her best for him, but the child was so unpleasant in his ways that she could not bring herself to like him.

One day she was sitting on the veranda steps with the child in her arms. The sun was shining warm; the scent of the flowers, the chirping of the birds, and the buzzing of the insects lulled her into drowsiness. So, in a half-waking, half-dreaming state, the lady dreamed of herself as having changed places with the child, only she was, if possible, more foul and more disagreeable than he was. Over her she saw the Lord Jesus bending, looking intently and lovingly into her face, and yet with a sort of rebuke in it, as if he meant to say: "If I can love you, who are so full of sin, surely you ought for My sake to love that suffering child."

Just then the lady awoke with a start and looked into the face of the little boy who lay on her lap. He had waked up, too, and she expected to hear him begin to cry; but he looked at her—poor little mite—very quietly and earnestly for a long time, and then she bent her face to his and kissed his forehead more tenderly than she had ever done before.

With a startled look in his eyes and a flush on his cheeks, the little boy, instead of crying, gave her back a sweeter smile than she had ever seen on his face before.

From that day forth a complete change came over the child. Young as he was, he had hitherto read the feeling of dislike and disgust in the faces of all who had approached him; but the touch of human love which now came into his life swept all the peevishness and ill nature away and woke him to a happier life.

Do you know that there is no power in this world so strong as the power of love? As some one has truly said, "love is the greatest thing in the world."—Evangelical Messenger.

Just a Word Helps (839).

A young girl was passing an aged aunt one day when she suddenly stopped, laid her hand gently on the white head, and said: "How pretty your hair is, Aunt Mary!"

The simple words brought a quick flush of pleasure to the wrinkled face, and there was a joyous quiver in the brief acknowledgement of the spontaneous little courtesy.

A young man once said to his mother: "You ought to have seen Aunt Esther today when I remarked, 'What a pretty dress you have on, and how nice you look in it!' She almost cried, she was so pleased. I hadn't thought before that such a little thing would please her so."

"I never expect to eat any cookies as good as those you used to make, mother," said a bearded man one day, and he was shocked when he saw her evident delight in his words; for he remembered that he had not thought to speak before for years of any of the thousand comforts and pleasures with which her skill and love had filled his boyhood.—The Young Evangelist.

Noble Ideals.

Every man is subject to the overlordship of some ideal. It may be high. It may be low. It may be indifferent. But the ideal determines the life. As a man "thinketh in his heart, so is he." The ideal influencing heart, soul, imagination, thought, expresses itself in activity, character, life. The low ideal produces the base life, with all its attendant distresses, disappointments, and disasters. The high ideal produces the noble life, rich with graces, services, benedictions that bless mankind and bring contentment to the heart of the individual who is under its mystic and benignant sway.

Clearly it is the duty of the individual to yield to the dominance of the highest ideal. Not only because from its influence emerges the largest measure of personal contentment, but, rather, because it enables him to live at the maximum of efficiency for the benefit of humanity. It does not need to be demonstrated in these days that "none of us liveth to himself, and no man dieth to himself." The influence of the ideal goes far beyond the individual in whose life it is manifested.

The highest ideal is that which makes the highest and best life. And it must be, therefore, that this ideal has its source of inspiration in the best life. If it reaches the best it must come from the best. And it is so, for we find the highest ideal and the best life centering in Jesus Christ. President Hyde, in his book, The College Man and the College Woman, appeals to students in behalf of Jesus Christ in these words: "Start where you will in the moral world, if you follow principles to their conclusions they always lead you up to Christ. He touched life so deeply, so broadly, and so truly that all brave, generous living is summed up in Him. Starting with the code you have here worked out for yourselves, translating it into positive terms, and enlarging it to the dimensions of the world you are about to enter, your code becomes simply a fresh interpretation of the meaning of the Christian life. All that we have been saying has its counterpart in that great life of His. He gave His best; and how good and beneficent it was!"—The Ripening Years.

The Mud-Covered Saint (840).

Service is a great word. It cannot be overemphasized, for it is at the basis of the right kind of character. We are saved to serve.

There is a legend in the Greek Church that well illustrates the greatness of service. It is Dean Farrar who draws attention to it in some of his writings. The legend is about two favored saints, St. Cassianus—the type of monastic asceticism, individual character, which "bids for cloistered cell its neighbor and its work farewell"—and St. Nicholas, the type of generous, active, unselfish, laborious Christianity.

St. Cassianus enters heaven, and Christ says to him: "What hast thou seen on earth, Cassianus?" "I saw," he answered, "a peasant floundering with his wagon in the marsh." "Didst thou help him?" "No!" "Why not?" "I was coming before Thee," said St. Cassianus, "and I was afraid of soiling my white robes."

Then St. Nicholas enters heaven, all covered with mud and mire. "Why so stained and soiled, St. Nicholas?" said the Lord. "I saw a peasant floundering in the marsh," said St. Nicholas, "and I put my shoulder to the wheel and helped him out." "Blessed art thou," answered the Lord; "thou didst well; thou didst better than Cassianus."

And he blessed St. Nicholas with fourfold approval.

It is only a legend, but it proclaims a mighty lesson.—The Epworth Herald.

The Sympathy That Binds (841).

A Christian lady was pleading with a poor, sinful girl, who had gone far away from her mother's God, to come to Jesus for pardon and peace. Suddenly the girl turned upon her.

"And you have been to Him?" she asked.

"Yes, indeed, I have," was the reply.

"And has He given you rest?"

"He has. O, thank God, He has. He is my Saviour and Friend."

"Then put your arms about me and try to take me with you to Him," murmered the girl. "It would be easier to go with one who has been before."

It was the secret of success. Many will resent an attempt to draw them out of evil courses who will be won by that "touch of nature which makes the whole world kin." Let it be rather, "Come thou with us and we will do thee good." Another was rescued as she exclaimed, "I don't care what becomes of me!" by a gentle touch on the arm and the loving words of a stranger, who overheard and understood, "But I do."

It will be well to remember that Christ Himself was "touched with a feeling of our infirmities"—the word used in the original meaning sympathy.—Christian Work.

Sympathy (842).

"Don't give me any advice yet," begged a brave, uncomplaining person to one who was trying to offer too many suggestions in a time of trouble. "Just sit there and let me tell you all about it, and I'll

lave my courage back again soon. Just plain sympathy is all I can
ɔear." "Plain sympathy" is often the hardest thing to give, the comfort that it takes years of experience to learn how to bestow.—Zion's
Herald.

Life's Threads of Gold (843).

Little self-denials, little honesties, little passing words of sympathy, little nameless acts of kindness, little silent victories over favorite temptations—these are the silent threads of gold which, when
woven together, gleam out so brightly in the pattern of life that God
approves.—Dean Farrar.

Our Epitaphs (844).

We are all very busy—busy writing epitaphs. We do not let a
day pass without doing something in this line, and we are all busy, not
in writing epitaphs for others, but in writing our own. And we are making it very sure that people will read what we have written when we are
gone. Shall we not be remembered? If not by many, we certainly shall
by a few, and that remembrance we are making sure of by the tenor of
our lives. Our characters are the inscriptions we are making on the
hearts of those we know, and who will survive us. We do not leave this
office to others. We are doing it ourselves. Others might falsify and
deceive by what they might say of us. But we are telling the truth.
The actions of our passing life are facts visible, plain, undeniable.   We
engrave them on the minds of all observers.   How interesting the
question, What kind of epitaphs are we writing?   Will they be read
with joy or sorrow?   Remember the epitaphs we write are not for the
marble that tells where we lie, but for the memory of everyone that
knew us.—Great Thc

Not Wanted In Heaven (845).

When the plague came to London, King Charles fled to Hampton
Court.   He took with him all the ship money for his treasures.   His
people were dying like flies in the streets, and corpses were being burned
on the street corners.   But Charles left no copper penny, no silver
shilling, no golden guinea for the relief fund.   His people would not forgive him for his unspeakable cruelty.   One day he returned to London
with his outriders blowing their trumpets.   Then the people refused him
welcome.   Every man went into his house and shut the door.   A herald
brought word to Charles that he was entering a dead city.   Shame man-
tled the monarch's cheek.   This would never do, so the king turned
aside.   That night like a whipped dog, the monarch crept into town,
hidden in the darkness.   And many a man at death will go home to God,
and the judgment, with no one to come out to meet and greet him.   Oh,
it is a thought to blanch the cheek and turn it white as marble, that
many a man who is pursuing his ease, who never did a brave deed in
his life, who sacrificed nothing, will find that Livingstone and Luther
and Lincoln will turn their backs on him, and that he is neither waited
for in heaven, nor expected, nor desired!—Homiletic Review.

The Tug That Stood By (846).

Two vessels collided just outside the capes. One was a powerful liner on her way to port, the other a wooden freighter, bound Heaven knows where.

The steel bow of the liner tore a great hole in the other's side, and there was no chance of saving her. The commander of the liner, in immaculate uniform and brass buttons, very gallant and grave, gave orders that the crew of the miserable freighter should be transferred at once to his own vessel, to be taken to port in safety.

Only the captain of the little tramp freighter remained with the doomed craft. That grim tradition of the sea which demands that the captain shall remain until the ship is about to go down held him there, stern-faced and immovable.

"Lively now," shouted the commander of the liner. "No use staying there, man. It's only a matter of an hour or two. Come aboard quick if you're coming at all."

The captain of the freighter turned but a second toward the other. "Go to thunder!" he shouted back.

The commander of the liner, grinning good-naturedly, told the ship-news reporters of the incident, when he reached the dock next day. "Had his nerve with him," he said. "Knew he couldn't save the boat, but he stayed any way. He's the right sort. I'd be sorry if he lost out. But he's safe, I guess. We had to get into port, but when we left him a tug stood by, ready to take him off before his boat went down."

In the great life-tragedy of the universal sea, while the night lasts, and later, when the first gray streaks of dawn appear, disclosing with terrible exactness the wreck that the night has wrought, I want to be the captain of the tug that stood by.

Perhaps my vigil shall be wasted. Perhaps some great ocean liner, sweeping majestically after her mate to port, will stop her giant screw and take off the captain of the tramp freighter.

Perhaps when he reaches the deck he will turn and wave me farewell. More likely he will swoon with weariness and relief, and will not even see the face of the man on the tug that stood by. It matters not.

I do not want to be the commander of either of those great liners. Nor do I crave the pitiful glory of the man who was willing to go down with his ship. I want only to cast anchor again and disappear from the scene of the wreck, where no man knows and no man cares.

For I shall know—and none else need know—that through the night, his back to the mast and his burning eyes turned to the stars, the derelict knew I was there. Consciously or subconsciously, he knew I was waiting in the darkness for his call.

He did not call. He never learned my name. But when the sunlight of another day shall dispel the fearsome shadows of his night, he will remember. He will give thanks to the Master of the Waters for the tug that stood by.

Lights in the World (847).

Faithful Christians, those who are the real children of God, are reminded by St. Paul, in his letter to the Philippians, that they "shine as lights in the world holding forth the word of life." Not all lights are of the same magnitude, but the nature of light is always the same. There are places where the smallest light may be of essential service. Lighthouses are good illustrations of this fact. Of the lights on the coasts and rivers of the United States there are some fourteen hundred, but only forty-five are of the first order. Some of the smallest show the path of safety through very narrow, intricate and perilous channels. We can not be all lights of the first order like St. Paul and Martin Luther, or John Wesley, but we can all share to the measure of our ability in the sphere of influence which God gives us. By our fidelity, our purity, our love, our joy, our courage under the most trying circumstances, we can constantly hold forth the word of life. The light of life must be made manifest in homes and workshops, in stores, in factories and mines, on battlefields and in hospitals, and to the multitudes that throng the streets, or the world will be in darkness. The feeblest saint may cheer many and save at least a soul or two by letting his light shine. A candle in a cottage may be a more blessed luminary than a star in the sky.—Northwestern Christian Advocate.

Made in One Image (848).

I saw the other day a composite photograph of a group of physicians, eighteen in all, and all taken on the same plate and each one on the same spot. It was a beautiful face that was the resultant, full of refinement and sympathy. I have read that an artist-photographer once tried that same thing with a lot of people picked up on the street, and the result was a composite whose likeness seemed very much like the face of the Christ. I can believe this latter story since seeing actually the reproduction mentioned in the first-named similar incident. There is more of good in humanity than evil. The human spirit: what is it after all but the divine spirit? Among all the races there is the mark of their creation after the pattern of the Divine Original. The future American will be the superman made up of the best of all the races.—R. DeW. Mallary, D. D., in Immigration.

A Life of Service (849).

The biographer of Alice Freeman Palmer says of her service for others: "There was in her a wastefulness like that of the blossoming tree. It sometimes disturbed me, and for it I occasionally took her to task. 'Why will you,' I said, 'give all this time to speaking before uninstructed audiences, to discussions in endless committees with people too dull to know whether they are talking to the point, and to anxious interviews with tired and tiresome women? You would exhaust yourself less in writing books of lasting consequence. At present you are building no monument. When you are gone good people will ask who you were, and nobody will be able to say.' But I always received the same indifferent answer: 'Well, why should they say? I am trying to make girls wiser and happier. Books don't help much toward that. They are really dead things. Why should I make more of them? It is people that count. You want to put yourself into people. They touch other people, these others still, and so you go on working forever.' "—Ballard.

Just a Bit of Kindness (850).

Did you ever stop to think how beautiful kindness really is? In your walks have you ever met a young woman gently supporting on her arm an old, old man? He is blind. Time has brought silver to his hair. His steps are slow and feeble. With a cane he picks his way on, all the way guided and directed by the one who is so good to him. At the crossing of a street she says, "Here is a step up. Careful now! Step up!" Or, "Now down! Carefully!" So on they go, chatting all the way, the old man seeing things on every side through the eyes of his companion. And how your heart was stirred by the sight.

Or a young man is watching the steps of his wee brother. Boys do not always have the patience to do that. But see how carefully this one guards his brother from everything that would harm him! The world has no sweeter sight than real, true, manly kindness toward one who is weak and needs help on life's way.

On a stage coach one day a number of passengers rode many miles together. One man drew into his shell, settled down on the seat and never spoke a single word from one end of the journey to the other. Do you think that man looked beautiful to those who were his companions that day?

A little bit of steel struck by a mallet will chip away the hardest granite. Unkindness is the keenest steel in all the world for the chiseling away of beauty in face, life, and character. No matter how lovely the face might be in the beginning, if the one who possesses it gives way often enough to harsh and unkind words, the beauty will surely fade out of her face.

Do you want to be beautiful? Then be kind. Kindness costs something; it would be worth nothing if it did not.—Selected.

"Put Up Your Hand" (851).

On the twenty-fifth floor of the new La Salle Hotel, of Chicago, three workmen were busy on the girders. A platform which supported them fell. One man went down to the basement. The second caught a rope and a beam and held himself suspended over space. The third man got astride a girder. He looked down to his comrade and yelled at him: "Put up your hand!" The second man did so, and was slowly but surely drawn into safety. The hand from above rescued him.

None are so strong in this life that they can stand alone. One can often help, one often must be helped. It is the height of folly to be so arrogant in self-conceit as to imagine that never will the hour come when the help of another may be needed.

In the world's history a street sweeper saved a king, a peasant changed the history of Europe through Wellington, a Sepoy gunner made India English, a farmer's message led Washington over the Delaware, a newsboy's quick wit saved a hundred lives in a great New York fire.

Our individual work is different, but our interdependence on and with each other—to help and to be helped—is unchangeable.

Sometime, somewhere, we are certain to be on the twenty-fifth story of a mighty temptation. That temptation has a basement at the bottom, but we cannot see it. But far above us a voice shouts: "Put up your hand!" It may be the voice of conscience or the call of a helping fellow-being.

Put up your hand and rejoice, as you are drawn into safety, that true men stand together in helping each other. None can stand alone and keep out of the basement.—Exchange.

Gathering Life's Roseleaves (852).

In some parts of Italy, as soon as a peasant girl is married she makes a fine muslin bag. In this bag she gathers rose leaves; and year after year other rose leaves are added until, perhaps, she is an old woman. Then when she dies, that bag of rose leaves is the beautiful, fragrant pillow that her head lies on in the coffin.

It is possible for us, year after year, to gather the rose leaves of tender ministries, unselfish sacrifices, brave actions, loving deeds for Christ's sake. We cannot do this if we let the opportunities of our early years slip by. Little time will be left us, if we do, to find the pillow on which our dying head shall rest. We shall lose the desire to gather good deeds, and our hearts become selfish and unresponsive to our Lord.

Let us be watchful to crowd into our lives the lovely, unselfish, and helpful things, that we may show our love to Christ. And then at the last, our heads shall rest on something more fragrant than rose leaves—the fragrant memories of good deeds, sweet to ourselves, sweet to others, and approved by our Lord.—Selected.

Narrow Lives. (853)—It may be thou dost not love thy neighbor; it may be thou thinkest only how to get from him, how to gain by him. How lonely, then, must thou be! how shut up in thy poverty-stricken room, with the bare walls of thy selfishness and the hard couch of thy unsatisfaction!—George MacDonald.

The Old Clock On The Mantle (854).

Not long ago we made the lucky purchase of a somewhat venerable clock which the dealer—an old German—had kept in his store for over sixty years. It was of the "Seth Thomas" make, and there is something about its whole appearance which does us good. It has the look of thorough sincerity to it. Its upright mahogany case is soiled and substantial—nothing fancy or gew-gawish—and the big dial-plate and plain, Quaker-like, uncompromising figures; the long pendulum swinging patiently from side to side; the sober, work-a-day tick-tock, which keeps up so steadily and drowsily, and which seems to belong to an age less hurried and convulsive than ours; the striker hammering out the hours slowly, loudly, and unmusically, but quite unmistakably; the demure weights, descending little by little without flustration—all combining in giving us remarkably accurate time—make up a most restful and comfortable article of furniture to look at. The old clock resembles, to our mind, some rugged, homespun farmer of a former day on the New England hills, or some "old salt" just landing from his fishing smack. As we open the door of this respectable timepiece, stamped all over with upright and downright honesty, we notice the brief, homely, but very satisfactory placard: "Warranted Good;" and it somehow braces us up and makes us have more confidence in our fellow men. No scamp work there, but just conscientious, honorable workmanship, without lying or fraud! Would that every article turned out from our Yankee manufactories might have borne, without misrepresentation, such a label!

Now we don't want to preach a sermon or draw a moral. Yet it won't hurt us if we allow the old clock to preach to us—rebuking all shams and pretentiousness in us, and suggesting, as it looks at us with its open, trustful countenance, that if "warranted good" could be inscribed on our lives, without mental reservation or deceit, it would be a good certificate for the Day of Judgment.—W. C. Advocate.

Singing From The Heart (855).

A company of monks in the olden time lived together in a monastery, working, busily tilling the land and caring for the sick and poor, yet ever hallowing their work with prayer. Every evening they sang the beautiful hymn, "Magnificat," at their vesper service, but as they grew old their voices became harsh and broken, and they almost lost all tune, but they still sang on.

One evening a strange youth came in to see them; he was strong and beautiful, and when they began the "Magnificat" his lovely, clear voice soared upward, as if to sing at the very gate fo heaven. The poor old monks listened, enraptured.

That night an angel appeared to the eldest monk, and asked, "Why did not the old hymn ascend to heaven at evensong as before?" and the monk, astonished, replied: "Oh, blessed angel, surely it did ascend! Heard you not in heaven those almost angelic strains from the voice of our gifted young brother? So sweetly he sang that our poor voices were hushed, lest we should mar the music." But the angel answered: "Beautiful it may have been, but no note of it reached heaven. Into those gates only music of the heart can enter."—Selected.

Unseen Influences (856).

The writer recently made a journey, carrying a pocket-compass; placing this on the window-sill on the right hand side of the car, he was able not only to note the changes in the direction taken by the train, but also the frequent interruption of unsuspected forces tending to deflect the needle. When an extra track was passed, the needle turned uneasily; in passing a train, and more particularly a locomotive, it was disturbed; in going over an iron bridge it was violently agitated. At other points it wavered, possibly because of concealed magnetic currents in the soil; and in one spot it turned completely around and so persisted for some seconds, before righting itself. There are spiritual forces at work all the time, none the less real though hidden, which, on the one hand, account for much deflection of the soul from truth and right, and, on the other, make it necessary that the soul should be on its guard, since "Ten thousand foes arise and hosts of sin are pressing hard." —Homiletic Review.

Scatter Sunshine (857).

Be generous with smiles and kindly words, if with nothing else. That which costs the least is often most valuable in this strange world. And kind words and gentle acts of sympathy have a way of reflecting that many and many a time has rewarded the giver a thousand-fold. It is a great thing to remember peacefully at eventide that some burdened heart has blessed you during the day for a timely word of cheer or glint of encouragement.—Christian Work.

Marsh Lives (858).

Much of human character is pictured in the marsh. It is a symbol of a really selfish life: the life that is forever receiving, but never giving; the life that is surfeited with wealth, prestige, and power, and yet spends it upon its own hurtful lusts; the life that knows no lack save the lack of sympathy and helpfulness and love. Indeed, the marsh is a likeness of much that is nominally Christian life. Too few churches and too few individual Christian lives have sufficient religious outlet. The river of God is full of water, and all partake of an abundance of grace. The danger is in the choking of the outlets. When these are kept open by constant and helpful charities, life is both healthful and fruitful. No true life was ever hurt by its giving. Every blessing is to be handed on to others, and can hurt only when it ceases to flow.

Christian selfishness is beyond cure. The grace of God can do nothing for it. That grace is always flowing like the river. Like the manna, it is new every morning. When a man hoards it, be that grace what it may, it breeds corruption and death. "I will bless thee....and thou shalt be a blessing" is God's dual promise, and one is not possible without the other. The marsh that only receives, though it constantly receives, does not contradict, but only illustrates the truth. Its blessing is a curse. The one thing it needs is a sufficient outlet. The lack of that means death to it. There is more hope for the desert than for the marsh. The irrigating streams that are sent into the desert make it a fruitful garden; it blossoms like the rose, and the barren places become glad because of the coming of the lifegiving streams. But the same waters make the marsh only the more of a marsh. The ancient prophet saw in his vision the desert of Judah transformed into a paradise by the river of life that flowed from the threshold of the temple, and the waters of the Dead Sea quickened into life by the same power of God; for every-thing shall live whither the river cometh," save this only, "the miry places and the marshes thereof shall not be healed."—Rev. J. B. Henry.

What We Get Out Of Life (859).

of us seem to suspect, but we come into touch with them only when we "Human kindness and sympathy are more common virtues than many have made our lives open to them, when we are looking for them. The matter. does not stop here, however, for one of the most effective ways of cultivating these desirable traits in others, especially the young, is to act as if we expected to find them there," writes one who is studying humanity in a scientific search for facts. He has found the new, old truth that is repeated again and again in scripture, history, and ex-perience, and yet which each one of us must learn for himself or never know it at all. The world is a land of echoes, and the message we call to it comes back to us from every side. In very truth we get out of life what we put into it.—Selected.

Her Gift Saved Livingstone (860).

Rev. F. B. Meyer, in showing how life is linked with life in influence for good in work for the world, said: "When Livingstone went to Af-rica, there was a Scotch woman named Mrs. MacRobert, quite advanced in life, who had saved up thirty pounds, which she gave to the great missionary, saying: 'When you go to Africa, I want you to spare your-self exposure and needless toil by hiring some competent body-servant who will go with you wherever you go, and share your sacrifices and exposures.' With that money he hired his faithful servant known as Sebalwe. When the lion had thrown Livingstone down and crushed the bones of his left arm, and was about to destroy him, this man, seeing his critical condition, drew off the attention of the lion to himself, thinking that he would save his master at the cost of his own life. The lion sprang at him, but just at that moment the guns of other com-panions brought him down, and Livingstone's life was prolonged for thirty years. Surely that noble Scotch woman, as well as the servant, should be credited with some, at least, of the results of the noble de-votion of that great missionary."—Selected.

The Help Of Love (861).

Miss Fidelia Fiske, the missionary, was at one time almost utterly discouraged, nothing but defeat in her work seemed possible, and her burdens were almost heavier than could be borne. A native convert sat on the mat beside her, a poor, ignorant woman who could do nothing to help her, so she thought, but that woman straightened her back up against her and said, "Lean on me; lean on me; if you love me, lean hard." "No one can know what that expression of love did for me," said Miss Fiske; "it gave me strength, because love makes us strong."

It is the loneliness, the lack of comradeship with other Christians, that makes life so hard for missionaries in remote places. Said Mr. Waggoner, a missionary in Alaska: "I have been six years in Klanock, and only one Christian white man has come into the place during that time—a sea captain who came in on a boat. Our little girl was taken from us three years ago. The only one who came in to have a word of prayer was my native interpreter; he prayed in his own language. The work is not hard, the climate is not hard, the lack of food is not hard; we have no time to think about these things. It is the isolation of the field that is the hardship."

"At one station which I visited last February," said Mr. Waggoner, "one of the Alaskan natives who is trying to carry on the work, said, 'We have held all our meetings, but now I have preached all I know.' He can't read, and for months he had preached the sermons he had learned from our missionaries, and he had preached himself out. Of course we gave him fresh instruction. We are all hungry for spiritual food, and how can a man renew his strength without food?"—Tarbell.

Friends (862).

It is not the seeing of one's friends, the having them within reach, the hearing of and from them, which makes them ours. Many a one has all that, and yet has nothing. It is the believing in them, the depending on them, assured that they are true and good to the core, and therefore could not but be good and true toward everybody else—ourselves included. Ay, whether we deserve it or not. It is not our deserts which are in question but their goodness, which once settled, the rest follows as a matter of course. They would be untrue to themselves if they were insincere or untrue to us.—Miss Mulock.

For Those He Loved (863).

Down out of the big woods near a Pennsylvania town a log train was trundling homeward. In the engine with the man at the throttle were a number of little folks enjoying the trip. How happy they were to be permitted to sit near the stout handed engineer! They laughed and joked, and had the happiest time of their lives until all at once Mr. Miller (that was the engineer's name) made a discovery that caused his heart to almost stand still. The brakes would not work!

They were now on a heavy grade. Knowing that the cars on behind would crowd him hard, the engineer pulled the air brake. Then it was that he found out that the brakes would not hold.

Faster and faster the wheels rattled. Many who were riding in the cars jumped and saved their lives. The old engineer might have done the same. Did he do it? Bravely he stood at his post. "I will do all I can to save the children!" he said, and never flinched in the face of this terrible danger.

On a sharp curve the engine left the rails and went plowing down the steep embankment. Over on its side the great locomotive toppled, carrying down the brave man of the throttle, never to rise again. He had given the best he had for those he loved. He died at his post just as surely as any soldier on the field of battle.

Would you have been as true as that? You think you would. As you look at it now you feel sure that nothing could tempt you to leave the place of duty, be the peril what it might. And it may be that you would not. But the only way to be sure of that is to be faithful in every time of testing that may come. In most men's lives there sooner or later comes a time of great trial. All along the way before that supreme testing time there are decisions to be made, and made very quickly. How will you do when those come to you?

If you are true in the smaller things it may be taken for granted that when the time of greater stress comes, you will also meet the crisis like a man. Otherwise there is no certainty of it. For we are made ready for the hours of greatest stress by the little decisions we make along from day to day.

Be faithful every time. That is what gives strength. The man who says, "I think I will skip duty this time," weakens himself for the next time he is called on to face a hard thing.

If you can say, "I will stand up like a true soldier every time I come to a hard thing," then you may be safe in saying, "I would not show the white feather if my life were in the balance for what I believed to be the right!"—Baltimore Methodist.

Happiness. (864)—Phillips Brooks used to say: "If you are acquainted with happiness, introduce him to your neighbor."

The Immorality of Service for Christ (865).

"Verily I say unto you, wheresoever this gospel shall be preached in the whole world, that also which this woman hath done shall be spoken of for a memorial of her."—This is the gracious testimony of Jesus Christ to a kindly deed done by one of His humble ones to Himself. He glorifies it and makes it a gospel for the world. And this is the immortality of sincere godly service for the Master. Has our thought of merit in our doing perhaps led us to put too low an estimate on sincere service for Christ? Let us the rather be inspired by the thought that while we should not glory in our doing, Jesus does put immortal honor upon it.

Seen at its true eminence, here is one of the most beautiful scenes in the life of our Lord. Beautiful is the deed itself and as beautiful is the spirit and purpose of her who did it. The act was alike strong and courageous. See what the woman had to face. The venture of an unbidden intrusion, the presence of men, disciples at that, with a limited sense of courtesy; not only this, but she goes right on under the fire of their reproach. In all that company she seems to have but one friend, but what a friend! Who can be alone, or really miss any one with Him? Then see what she gave. It was only a box of ointment, but it was very precious, usually the gift of the wealthy, and she probably a poor woman. The occasion, the person, the spirit, the purpose, of the service, all these added to the preciousness of the offering. This bestowal of generous love was more fragrant than the costly nard itself.

We may detain the woman and gaze upon her amid all these unique surroundings; let the scene burn into the soul, "and point her out as one of the most touching spectacles in all the wide compass of history." Her heart has been arranging for that splendid service perhaps for days, she has wondered how it should be accomplished and where, scarce dreaming maybe of the singular and fitting occasion that would offer itself. At last it is accomplished, and so done, with such choice of the subject, and with such unselfish devotion, that all the waste has been swept out of her past life, and she stands complete in Him who loved her and gave Himself for her. Such is grace, wondrous grace! It was on the Christ she bestowed her offering, "on the only Human Head that had not lost its crown."—M. Rhodes, D. D.

Do Not Wait (866).—Never, never wait for post-mortem praise. Speak the kind words which love prompts, and remember that words of loving-kindness are the best possible tonic which can be given even to the happiest of mortals.—Kate Tannatt Woods.

"Well Done" (867).

Kind words count. Speak them often. Allow no one to speak disparagingly of the minister in your presence. Give the faithful man a lift with your kind tongue. Talk him up in the church, in the home, in society, in the street and everywhere. He will take courage, will preach better sermons, and will put increased enthusiasm into all his multiplied duties. He will win all along the line and you will have the joy of knowing that your bracing words proved a real tonic, and helped him to conquests he never would have achieved while struggling alone. Mr. Spurgeon once told of a faithful old servant who one day gave his master notice. "What, John, are you going to leave me?" said the master. "Yes, sir," said John, "I am going to leave." "But, John," replied the master, "don't I pay you enough wages?" "Yes, sir, the money you give me is all right." "Then why leave me?" "Well," answered John, "I have made up my mind to go." "But, John, you have been all around the world with me." "Yes, I have, sir, and you never once said, 'Well done, John.'" Ministers, as well as servants and wives, need the inspiration of a kind word, not flattery, but a word of honest appreciation. Flowers on the coffin lid cast no fragrance on the hard and stony road which has been traversed, and eulogy's blandest note falls silent on the ear of the departed. A kind word will put fresh heart into the fainting warrior, and he wins triumphs which will fill all heaven with joy.—Selected.

The Smoothers of the Way (868).

"She always made things easier," was the tribute given a little while ago to a quiet woman not much known outside the four walls of her household and in a charity or two, but who left an aching void behind her when she passed on into large life. No one who knew her could help recognizing the simple completeness of the statement. From her husband to her house maid, every one in the family felt his or her daily way smoothed and straightened by her tact and system and gentleness. She was a living example of George Eliot's saying: "What do we live for if it is not to make life less difficult for one another?"

To some girls and women perhaps this seems a small end to live for. Yet that it is so often approached makes the hope and the happiness of home. Life is increasingly difficult, increasingly complex in many communities today. The husband, the children, the friends of the woman who "makes things easier" more and more rise up and call her blessed. Her work is worth living for, because it continually makes every life within its influence seem better worth living. And when she is gone— how rugged the way, how heavy the burden without her gentle ministry! We hear a great deal nowadays about the "superfluous" woman. Some branches of woman's work may be overcrowded; but never, never, surely, the high vocation of the smoother of the way.—Harper's Bazar.

"I'll Stand the Pain" (869).

Every one remembers the awful Park avenue collision in New York city. One of the sufferers was a young man named Peter Murphy. His feet and legs were caught beneath the engine which had telescoped the car. He had worked one leg free and was about to pull the other loose when the roof of the car fell on both legs. While he hung there in agony Battalion Chief Farrel of the fire department came along, and Murphy begged him to lift the timbers off his legs. "If I do that," said Farrel, "the roof will fall on the other side. There are women there." "I didn't think of that," said Murphy. "Let it stay. I'll stand the pain." Heard you ever anything more Christlike? So he waited a long, terrible half hour, till his fellow-sufferers were dragged from under the ruins. Himself he could not save. No wonder that on March 9 following (this was in January) two thousand people escorted the crippled hero from Bellevue hospital to his home in New Rochelle. It was a tribute to something far finer than courage.—Pilgrim Teacher.

The Spent Life (870).

The life which gives multiplies itself. The life which absorbs destroys itself and others. All nature is built upon the plan of giving. The sun gives its light and its heat, the bird its song, the heliotrope its odor, The orchard yields its fruit for the good of man, the field its grain for the same purpose, and the mines give of their treasure.

If man is not a giver he is out of harmony with his surroundings. If he makes a Dead Sea of himself, he becomes fatal to everything that seeks life from him. No one comes back from Palestine and tells of the fish he caught in the Dead Sea. No one speaks of the beneficent influences coming from a Dead Sea life. It is all receiving, receiving. It gives out nothing, absolutely nothing, which it can retain. If perchance it makes a gift, it is poisonous.

Jesus knew what He was talking about when He said: "Except a corn of wheat fall into the ground and die, it abideth alone: but if it die, it bringeth forth much fruit." He had reference to Himself, and to the result of His vicarious death. If a man does not give of himself, he also abides alone until he withers and blows away. That any man may live the second life, the sowing of that life is required. If any one has worthy traits of character, these should be inculcated into the lives of associates.

Indeed, no one can live worthily and not place his spirit into the lives of those with whom he comes in contact. In this lies the value of friendship. When a great man becomes the friend of another, that other partakes of his greatness, and when the first man dies he is the disciple. This greatness is then passed on to another, and so on from generation to generation.

Life is more than meat, and the body more than raiment. God never intended for any man to shut himself up in the circle of what he eats and wears. If one's influence cannot penetrate these material things, the quicker he dies and makes room for something valuable, the greater the blessing to the world.—Selected.

The Secret of Influence (871).

Who shall tell us the secret of influence? Why does a leader lead? It is by the magnetism of a rich soul. And that is a secret, even to himself. A clean heart is the greatest power in the world. Its force is felt, not only in humanity, but above and below it. Above, for it knows how to pray; below, for even the brute beasts know and yield to it. The legend of St. Francis, how he tamed the wolf that was devastating Umbria, has its root of truth. It is akin with what Emerson records of Thoreau: "Snakes coiled round his leg; the fishes swam into his hand, and he took them out of the water; he took the woodchuck out of its hole by the tail, and took the foxes under his protection from the hunters." A man's character, as he enters a room, without a word spoken, tells upon the whole social temperature. We raise it or lower it, diffuse winter chills or summer warmth by the currents that prevail in our soul. It is recorded of Sir John Lawrence that he seemed never entirely at ease unless his wife was in the room. That gracious presence, to which he had been so long accustomed, seemed necessary to his atmosphere. Deeper than all deeds, all words, are these emanations from the heart's secret life. Herein lies the highest benediction of a sweet nature: that without conscious action, by simply being what it is, it acts as food and medicine to other souls.—W. J. Brierly.

Lost Chances (872).

Life is made up of golden chances—opportunities to do good. One lost is lost forever. If we miss doing a kindness to a playmate, we can never do that kindness again. If we might speak a pleasant word and we do not, we can never have just that word to speak again. Every opportunity that passes is past forever, and takes with it something that cannot be called back. Our character is either better or worse for every chance of good we take or neglect; and when we are grown, we will find that we cannot make ourselves over, try as we will. For this reason we should watch for and carefully utilize every opportunity to do good.—The Advocate.

Our Japanese Girl (873).

A young girl came to the missionary school in Tokyo, Japan, some years ago, for a few months. She was the daughter of a high official, one of the emperor's counselors, and she did not come to the school because she wanted an education, but in order to be near one of the teachers, who had formerly been her governess, and whom she loved very dearly. She was not only far higher in social rank than the other students, but older, and did not care to live with the others in the school buildings. So she had a room in a cottage among the officers and teachers, and was very happy there.

She was of a very kind and gentle nature, and soon teachers and pupils alike loved her. She, on her part, became deeply interested in Bible study. She was not allowed by her parents to stay very long at the school, and at the end of five months went home again. But before she went, she asked permission to be allowed to profess her faith in Christ.

She came to the school a heathen; she left it a Christian, and she took her Bible with her. At home in Tokyo she told all her friends what she had learned; and though she was a very quiet and gentle girl, she spoke so persuasively that several of them began to read the Bible at her request.

Four of her friends became Christians in this way. Then the girl became the wife of the governor of one of the neighboring provinces. She left Tokyo, but she carried her Bible with her. Today, in her new home, she is not only still leading others quietly to Christ, but has a Christian service in her home every Sabbath afternoon, thus witnessing openly for the gospel before the entire province.

This true story of what one young Japanese girl has done shows the value of an earnest, consecrated life. It shows the good that the missionary schools are doing in foreign lands. And it also suggests the thought that there are many American girls, who could do much to help forward the progress of the Kingdom of our Lord and Saviour Jesus Christ, if they would only live a Christian life and thus show to others the beauty of our Christian faith.—Apples of Gold.

Our Talents (874).

Your ability is the measure of your responsibility. To "whom much is given, much will be required." I passed a home where a gentleman was sprinkling the lawn. His little girl, a child of about six years, was helping papa as her childish fancy prompted. She would bring her toy watering pot to the father, and he, reducing the force of the stream, would fill it from the hose.

It mattered little to the grass and flowers whether the water which they needed was given through the large sprinkler or the child's toy watering pot. So it matters little to the world whether you are a man of one, two, five or ten talents, so you give it the best you have. The one-talent man giving his best is better than the ten-talent man giving his worst. It is not how much you give to the world, but what you give to it. There are a great many more little things to be done than big ones, but the things that are done for Christ are immortal.—New York Observer.

The Path That Leads to Yesterday (875).

I once saw a play advertised with the above title. If a man is growing worse day by day, the path that leads to yesterday, if he could but travel it, would take him back to the purity of life that he once possessed; but, if he is becoming better continually, the path to yesterday would lead him back into the ways of sin. But yesterday's path is trodden its last time. We may look back upon it with pride or with regret, still, the past is past. With regard to the opportunities of life, they are all "yesterdays" after they have past, and there is no road leading back to them. —Selected.

Truth in the Heart (876).

I have been reading this last week the biography of George Fox, the founder of the Society of Friends. Time and again this old Quaker was imprisoned because of his refusal to take an oath. The oath was in Fox's mind too sacred and solemn a thing for man to take upon his lips, but Cromwell's soldiers, and the Royalists under Charles, found alike that the word of the Quaker was better than the solemn oaths of other men; that when Fox and his followers gave their word, they signed in their honor, their character, their very life, and this world might pass away, but their word never. This is what the word needs, the splendid might and power of truth in the heart which distinguished the Friends of old.—Wilton Merle Smith, D. D.

A Beautiful Life (877).

There is, I think, no one thing in the life of Frances Burney (afterward Madame D'Arblay) more attractive than the beautiful attachment she formed for the aged Mrs. Delaney; a young lady of genius and fame, who would gladly at any time forego the brilliant assemblies of wit, learning and fashion where her praises were on every lip, that she might share the ripe wisdom, while she cheered the widowed loneliness, of her beloved friend of fourscore years.—Ballard.

Thinking of Others (878).

Dr. Guthrie used to tell an incident of a vessel that came upon a wreck. They went on board and found the emaciated form of a young man lying among a bundle of canvas. He was at the last extremity, and they thought he was all that was left of the sinking wreck. They saw that the poor dying man was making an effort to speak; they listened and heard him say, "There's another man on board." It was all that he could say, but it was enough: he had done what he could to save his fellow creature. And that is what God expects of you and me. Will you do it?—Selected.

Embodying Nobility (879).

The thing that appeals to men and women is the living spectacle of one who has really achieved a notable thing and who walks before us himself the embodiment of his own achievement? You know perfectly well that when Lord Roberts, "Bobs," comes back from India or from South Africa or from anywhere, and goes into certain circles, every young Englishman who sees him wants to be a soldier. You know perfectly well that when certain physicians, like William McClure, the "country doctor of the old school," move in certain circles, every worthy youth in the community, interpreting the medical profession in the light of its highest example, wants to go into medicine. I cannot imagine myself how anybody who ever heard Phillips Brooks preach could keep out of the ministry.—Bishop Thoburn.

The Signboard That Says "Be Kind" (880).

"If I can't make people feel better, I certainly am not going to make them feel worse," remarked a lady, recently. I thought: "What a fine motto to live by!" I know a young woman who is a positive terror to her best friends because of her sharp tongue. She believes in "speaking her mind." She says caustic things about her best friends, and then wonders why she has not more friends. She complains that she is not popular, but does not realize that she alone is the cause of her lack of popularity. She "drives tacks," so to speak, into everybody she meets, her sharp tongue being the hammer.—Selected.

Radiating Blessing (881).

A tourist spending his vacation among the rocks and wooded ravines of Muskoka in his ramblings one day came across a small stream of pure spring water. Heated by his walk, he improvised a drinking cup out of the crown of his panama hat and took a long satisfying draught of the sparkling water. Then he followed the winding stream up the valley until he came to its source. Hidden deep in the recesses of the forest, the water bubbled up from its mossy bed and sparkled like purest diamonds in the sunlight. He covered the spot with his hand, so small was the spring; but he could not stop the flow. The water oozed through his fingers and made its way down the valley, singing gayly as it went on its journey of mercy to carry blessing to bird and beast and leave everything green and beautiful behind it. The life that is clean and pure cannot but be full of blessing to others. Unconsciously it pours its blessings forth and, like the mountain spring, nothing can stop its flow.—Onward.

The Quiet Worker (882).

No public note is sounded over much of the best work that is done in the world. Many of the most valuable workers and thinkers have no advertisement in the public press. The spectacular or the dramatic element is lacking, and there is nothing in the good deed done to appeal to the curious eye or the itching ear of the present time. There is no public recognition of their value to society. Urged on simply by a conscientious desire to discharge their obligation to the generation in which they live, they toil contentedly on with intrepid faith. Not stimulated simply by the hope of reward here or the praise of men, they plod persistently forward, believing that the inscrutable future holds for them compensation which will be eminently satisfactory. It is satisfactory now, for they are men of faith, subsisting on the things hoped for and encouraged by the sight of things unseen. Of such the world is not worthy. Their conversation is in heaven. They are citizens in the commonwealth of the ages. They live not for a day. They can afford to abide their time for recognition. Ages upon ages after they shall have been known for their true worth to the world they will be enjoying the fruits of their unselfish labors. They are builders for eternity, and eternity alone can disclose the fine finish of their workmanship. Unknown to the columns of the public press, and uninfluenced largely by the compliments or criticisms of their contemporaries, they are content to be known on high and to live in expectation of the highest approval that the universe holds: "Well done, thou good and faithful servant."—Selected.

Investing Our Lives (883)

The following touching incident is related by a pastor, who, on visiting a family from a former parish, missed from it an afflicted son, a young man of twenty-five years, who never had walked. This young man's body was developed properly, but his limbs were shriveled and undeveloped. All these years his father had given him the greatest care and attention. Each day he carried him from from his room to the table and back again. On the occasion of this visit the minister did not see the helpless young man and inquired after his health. The father replied, "Did you not know that he had passed away?" Assuring the father that he did not, he expressed himself by saying, "It is well that it should be so." The father's reply was most touching and pathetic. "What you say may be very true, but I have put so much of my life into his that I cannot tell you how much I loved him and now miss him."—Selected.

The Heroic (884).

Sweet temper, the influence of right thought, the drawing power of a great religious wave, the reclining in self-satisfaction—call you that warfare? The religion of our day has come to be too largely a religion with the comfortable as its essence. This is really the only kind that about two out of three have to show to their fellow men. It is not the existence of doubt and criticism that keeps our young men out of the ministry so much as the lack of appeal to the heroic.

Wrestling, fighting, running a race, these are figures the Scriptures employ to represent the attitude of the church. These illustrations illustrate. Everybody can understand them. The world as well as the church see clearly their meaning. Is the church wrestling? No! Where are its struggles for the faith once delivered to the saints? The heroic in its life can scarcely be found. It is conducting no deal in earnest campaigns against oppositions of science falsely so-called, against antagonisms of skepticism, and oppositions of the world, the flesh and the devil. It is laughable and preposterous—a most ludicrous use of words—to talk of our services so formal, at times merely sentimental, at others as cold as they are beautiful, when even these, such as they are, engage us only if the sky is sunny and everything is fair, and we are not too sorely tempted to go visiting or on an automobile ride. Are we fighters, wrestlers, runners on the course, all intent upon the goal?—Selected.

Investments of Thoughtfulness (885).

My own money investments have generally brought me little but trouble and worry. But the investments of thoughtfulness which I happen to have made are increasing joys to me. Just try it. Think up some jolly word which you will say to the blind man you pass on the way to the office. Write a tender, strong little note to the mother who has lost her baby. Remember to congratulate Tom Brownson on his promotion. Give your sister Lucy a lift with that abominable third conjugation. Kiss grandma as you pass her, and whisper to her that she is the light of your home. Thank the minister for the comforting sermon he preached last Sunday, and borrow it for the benefit of bedridden Mr. Folsom. Put a blossoming geranium on a plate and set it in the middle of the dining-table. Oh, these investments of thoughtfulness are endless, and when you once begin with them there is absolutely no stopping.—The C. E. World.

Secret of Inner Life (886).

Doing nothing for others is the undoing of ourselves. We must be purposely kind and generous, or we miss the best part of existence. The heart which goes out of itself gets large and full. This is the great secret of the inner life. We do ourselves the most good doing something for others.—Horace Mann.

To Save Your Life (887).

The rule of the world is to "Look out for number one." Nothing could be more antagonistic than this to the teachings of Christ. His greatest dctrine, the underlying principles of all his works and deeds, was that of self-sacrifice, looking out for number two. Therefore he has given the plain message that to save our lives we must sacrifice them. —Selected.

The Work of the World (888).

To every man is given his particular work in life to do. Nobody has any right to stand idle in the market-place. As a matter of fact, there are many idlers, while a minority toils overtime to make up for their laziness. Someone has thus stated the case metrically:

> The work of the world is done by few;
> God asks that a part be done by you.
> > —Selected.

A Prayer (889).

Thou Lord and Giver of the earthly and the eternal life, we thank Thee that both are one for us in faith, as both shall be one in the experience of Thy children. Thou hast enriched our lives with friendship and with household ties. We bless Thee for all true-hearted fellowship of faith and love. Still are they ours whom Thou hast taken from us for still they live to Thee although we see them not. We thank Thee for their ministries of faithful affection and self-sacrifice. Make us, like them, a blessing to the world. And may their memory bring us strength to lead the joyful life of faith. Grant to us also help to overcome and bring us in Thine own good time into the dear companionship of love and joy where they have gone before. In the name of Christ. Amen.—The Congregationalist.

, A Dream (890).

A good Christian lady, we are told, once opened a home for crippled children. Among those who were received was a little boy three years old, who was a most frightful and disagreeable looking child.

The good lady did her best for him, but the child was so unpleasant in his ways that she could not bring herself to like him.

One day she was sitting on the veranda steps with the child in her arms. The sun was shining warm; the scent of the flowers, the chirping of the birds and the buzzing of the insects lulled her into drowsiness.

So in a half-waking, half-dreaming state, the lady dreamed of herself as having changed places with the child, only she was, if possible, more foul and more disagreeable than he was. Over her she saw the Lord Jesus bending, looking intently and lovingly into her face, and yet with a sort of rebuke in it, as if He meant to say, "If I can love you, who are so full of sin, surely you ought, for My sake, to love that suffering child."

Just then the lady awoke with a start and looked in the face of the little boy who lay on her lap. He had waked up, too, and she expected to hear him begin to cry; but he looked at her—poor little mite—very quietly and earnestly for a long time, and then she bent her face to his, and kissed his forehead more tenderly than she had ever done before.

With a startled look in his eyes and a flush on his cheeks, the little boy, instead of crying, gave her back a sweeter smile than she had ever seen before.

From that day forth a perfect change came over the child. Young as he was, he had hitherto read the feeling of dislike and disgust in the faces of all who had approached him, but the touch of human love which now came into his life swept all the peevishness and ill-nature away, and woke him up to a happier life.

Do you know that there is no power in this world so strong as the power of love? As some one has truly said, love is the greatest thing in the world.—Apples of Gold.

A Girl's Song (891).

At the time of the terrible accident a year or two ago at the coal mines near Scranton, Pa., several men were buried for three days, and all efforts to rescue them proved unsuccessful.

The majority of the miners were Germans. They were in a state of intense excitement, caused by sympathy for the wives and children of the buried men and despair at their own balked efforts.

A great mob of ignorant men and women assembled at the mouth of the mine on the evening of the third day in a condition of high nervous tension which fitted them for any mad act. A sullen murmur arose that it was folly to dig farther—that the men were dead. And this was followed by cries of rage at the rich mine owners.

A hasty word or gesture might have produced an outbreak of fury. Standing near me was a little German girl, perhaps eleven years old. Her pale face and frightened glances from side to side showed that she fully understood the danger of the moment. Suddenly, with a great effort, she began to sing in a horse whisper which could not be heard. Then she gained courage, and her sweet, childish voice rang out in Luther's grand old hymn, familiar to every German from his cradle, "A Mighty Fortress is Our God."

There was silence like death. Then one voice joined the girl's and presently another and another until from the whole great multitude rose the solemn cry:

> With force of arms we nothing can,
> Full soon are we o'erridden,
> But for us fights the godly Man,
> Whom God Himself hath bidden.
> Ask ye His Name?
> Christ Jesus is His name.

A great quiet seemed to fall upon their hearts. They resumed their work with fresh zeal, and before morning the joyful cry came up from the pit that the men were found—alive. Never was a word more in season than that child's hymn. In this same way many a noble life sings a song of cheer and inspiration which holds others steadfast to hard duty and arms them against temptation.—Selected.

The Inspiration of Noble Lives (892).

We cannot add to our knowledge an acquaintance with the life and character of any man or woman who has done well upon the earth, seeking for truth and doing righteousness, without adding something to our force of righteous will, something to our ability to resist the solicitations of our low ambitions and impure desires—Selected.

ILLUSTRATIVE POETRY.

To Give Is To Live (893).

"For whosoever will save his life shall lose it, and whosoever shall lose his life for my sake shall find it."

"Forever the sun is pouring its gold
On a hundred worlds that beg and borrow;
His warmth he squanders on summits cold,
His wealth on homes of want and sorrow;
To withhold his largeness of precious light
Is to bury himself in eternal night.
    To give
    Is to live.

"The flower blooms not for itself at all,
Its joy is the joy that diffuses;
Of beauty and balm it is prodigal,
And it lives in the life it loses.
No choice for the rose but glory or doom,
To exhale or smother, to wither or bloom.
    To deny
    Is to die."
        —Selected.

How Long? (894).

"Go break to the needy sweet charity's bread,
For giving is living," the angel said.
"And I must be giving again and again?"
My peevish and pitiless answer ran.
"Oh, no!" said the angel, piercing me through,
"Just give till the Master stops giving to you."
        —Selected.

Making The Most of Life (895).

We live not in our moments or our years:
The present we fling from us like the rind
Of some sweet future, which we after find
Bitter to taste, or bind that in with fears,
And water it beforehand with our tears—
Vain tears for that which never may arrive:
Meanwhile the joy whereby we ought to live,
Neglected or unheeded, disappears.
Wiser it were to welcome and make ours
Whate'er of good, though small, the present brings—
Kind greetings, sunshine, song of birds, and flowers,
With a child's pure delight in little things;
And of the griefs unborn to rest secure,
Knowing that mercy ever will endure.
        —Trench.

God's Greathearted (896).

God be thanked for His great-hearted,
From this mortal life departed,
Whom the angels gather in
From the hurt of pain and sin.

They shall tread no pathway dreary,
They shall never more be weary;
They have reached the fair home-place
And have seen the Father's face.

Gone for them are tears and sadness;
Who can measure their great gladness?
They may well rejoice and sing
For so rich replenishing.

God be thanked for our departed;
And God make us, too, brave-hearted.
In that land of "no more pain"
We shall find our own again.

—Selected.

L'Envoi (897).

When earth's last picture is painted and the tubes are twisted and dried,
When the oldest colors have faded and the youngest critic has died,
We shall rest, and, faith, we shall need it—lie down for an aeon or two,
Till the Master of All Good Workmen shall put us to work anew!

And those that were good shall be happy; they shall sit in a golden chair;
They shall splash at a ten-league canvas with brushes of comet's hair;
They shall find real saints to draw from—Magdalene, Peter and Paul;
They shall work for an age at a sitting and never be tired at all!

—Rudyard Kipling.

The Rose Beyond The Wall (898).

Near shady wall a rose once grew,
 Budded and blossomed in God's free light,
Watered and fed by morning dew,
 Shedding its sweetness day and night.

As it grew and blossomed fair and tall,
 Slowly rising to loftier height,
It came to a crevice in the wall,
 Through which there shone a beam of light.

Onward it crept with added strength,
 With never a thought of fear or pride,
And it followed the light through the crevice length,
 And unfolded itself on the other side.

The light, the dew, the broadening view,
  Were found the same as they were before.
It lost itself in beauties new,
  Breathing its fragrance more and more.

Shall claim of death cause us to grieve,
  And make our courage faint or fall?
Nay, let us faith and hope receive—
  The rose still grows beyond the wall,

Scattering fragrance far and wide,
  Just as it did in days of yore;
Just as it did on the other side;
  Just as it will forevermore.

—Selected.

"She Yet Speaketh" (899).

And still her silent ministry
  Within my heart hath place,
As when on earth she walked with me,
  And met me face to face.
Her life is forever mine:
  What she to me has been
Hath left henceforth its seal and sign
  Engraven deep within.

Goodness Outlasting Death (900).

I sing not Death. Death is too great a thing
For me to dare to sing.
I chant the human goodness, human worth,
Which are not lost, but sweeten still the earth;
The things that flee not with the upyielded breath,
But, housed in sanctuary of simple hearts,
Live undethroned when Death
Comes to the Chamber of a mighty King,
And sheds abroad the silence of his wing,
Then shakes his raven plumage, and departs.

—William Watson.

Sow Flowers (901).

Sow flowers, and flowers will blossom
Around you wherever you go;
Sow weeds, and of weeds reap the harvest,
You will reap whatsoever you sow.

Sow blessings, and blessings will ripen,
Sow hatred, and hatred will grow;
Sow mercy, and reap sweet compassion,
You will reap whatsoever you sow.

Sow love, and its sweetness uprising,
Shall fill all your heart with its glow;
Sow hope, and receive its fruition,
You will reap whatsoever you sow.

Preach Christ in His wonderful fulness,
That all His salvation may know;
Reap life through ages eternal,
You will reap whatsoever you sow.

—Ella Lander.

If We Understood (902).

If we knew the cares and trials,
    Knew the efforts all in vain,
And the bitter disappointment,
    Understood the loss and gain—
Would the grim eternal roughness
    Seem—I wonder—just the same?
Should we help where now we hinder?
    Should we pity where we blame?

Ah! we judge each other harshly,
    Knowing not life's hidden force;
Knowing not the fount of action
    Is less turbid at its source;
Seeing not amid the evil
    All the golden grains of good;
And we'd love each other better
    If we only understood.

Could we judge all deeds by motives
    That surround each other's lives,
See the naked heart and spirit,
    Know what spur the action gives,
Often we should find it better,
    Purer than we judge we should,
We should love each other better
    If we only understood.

Could we judge all deeds by motives,
    See the good and bad within,
Often we should love the sinner
    All the while we loathe the sin.
Could we know the powers working
    To overthrow integrity,
We should judge each other's errors
    With more patient charity.

—Rudyard Kipling.

The Heart Of a Friend (903).

A heart that is glad when your heart is gay,
　　And true in the time of cares;
That halves the trials of a fretful day
　　And doubles the joys that it shares.

A heart than can cheer your heart with its song,
　　And comfort your hour of need
A heart that is brave and faithful and strong,
　　Wherever misfortune may lead.

A heart that is yours when the way seems dark,
　　And yours in sunshine, too;
A heart that cares not for rank or mark,
　　But only the heart of you.

A heart that will shield when others abuse
　　The name that it knows is fair,
That would rather miss fortune and fame than lose
　　The love of a friend that is dear.

A heart that will hear no ill of you,
　　But is ever quick to defend,
A heart that is always true, steel true
　　Such is the heart of a friend.

　　　　　　　　　—Cornelia Seyle.

Love (904).

There grew a little flower once,
　　That blossomed in a day,
And some said it would ever bloom,
　　And some 'twould fade away;
And some said it was Happiness,
　　And some said it was Spring,
And some said it was Grief and Tears,
　　And many such a thing;
But still the little flower bloomed,
　　And still it lived and throve,
And men do call it "Summer Growth,"
　　But angels call it love!—Thomas Hood.

Obedient To The Vision (905).

Calvin lived within sight of Mount Blanc, but there is not a line in his writing which indicates that he ever saw it. We live within sight of exalted ideals, the visions of nobleness and duty that come to us; but do our lives indicate that we give heed to them? This purpose so beautifully expressed by Professor H. L. Koopman let us make our own:

When I am dead,
May this with truth be said,
On the rude stone that marks my lowly head,
That, spite of doubt and indecision,
In spite of weakness, lameness, blindness,
Heart's trickery and fate's unkindness,
Neglect of friends and scorn of foes,
Stark poverty and all its woes,
The body's ills that cloud the mind
And the bold spirit bind,
Still through my earthly course I went,
Not disobedient
Unto the Heavenly Vision.

—Tarbell.

Friendship (906).

O who will walk a mile with me
  Along life's weary way?
A friend whose heart has eyes to see
The stars shine out o'er the darkening lea,
  And the quiet rest at the end o' the day,—
  A friend who knows, and dares to say,
  The brave, sweet words that cheer the way
Where he walks a mile with me.

—Henry van Dyke.

If I Should Die Tonight (907).

If I should die tonight,
My friends would look upon my quiet face,
Before they laid it in its resting place,
And deem that death had left it almost fair;
And, laying snow-white flowers against my hair,
Would smooth it down with tearful tenderness,
And fold my hands with lingering caress—
  Poor hands, so empty and so cold tonight!

If I should die tonight,
My friends would call to mind, with loving thought,
Some kindly deed the icy hands had wrought;
Some gentle word the frozen lips had said;
Errands on which the willing feet had sped;
The memory of my selfishness and pride,
My hasty words, would all be put aside,
  And so I should be loved and mourned tonight.

If I should die tonight,
Even hearts estranged would turn once more to me,
Recalling other days remorsefully;
The eyes that chill me with averted glance

Would look upon me as of yore, perchance,
And soften in the old familiar way;
For who would war with dumb, unconscious clay?
So I might rest, forgiven of all, tonight.

Oh, friends, I pray tonight,
Keep not your kisses for my dead, cold brow—
The way is lonely; let me feel them now.
Think gently of me; I am travel worn;
My faltering feet are pierced with many a thorn.
Forgive, oh, hearts estranged, forgive, I plead!
When dreamless rest is mine I shall not need
The tenderness for which I long tonight.
—Belle E. Smith

The Shining Face (908).

O friend of mine, whom I shall see no more,
How little have the white sails borne to sea!
All that love wrought still lingers here with me,
Still, still we stand together by the shore.

Men say of travelers, "They are far away;"
And of the dead they say, "Their souls are gone;"
Yet now I know we keep the soul alone.
Bodies may travel, die—the spirits stay.

Now hath God blessed me as the blind are blessed,
Who, losing sight, have lost one sense alone;
For all the powers of my soul are grown.
The vision vanished, memory keeps the rest.

And I have but to hark to hear thy song;
Be still to feel thy presence, cheer and grace;
And in my dreams I see thy shining face,
Angel of God, to bid me still "Be strong!"
—Charles P. Cleaves, in Youth's Companion

Service (909).

Let me be the author of a little kindly deed
Of sacrifice and service for a fellow heart in need.
Let me live a poem of the self-denying will
To lend a hand of helping to a comrade up the hill.
Let me be an artist of the sunlight on the flowers,
To fill some brother's darkness with the dream of golden hours
Let me be a master of the music that the birds
Have set to artless measures with the most unstudied words!

Let me be a captain of the little hosts of joy
That lead us back in memory to the days of barefoot boy.
Let me be a ruler in the land of lost delight,
With power to keep a comrade from the darkness of the night.
And if I serve but lamely, and if my song be poor,
Ah! may it bear the blossom of green beauty to thy door,
From lane and hill and hollow, until the city street
Grows like a dream of Eden with the bright blooms round its feet!
—Baltimore Sun.

"Thou Shalt Be Missed."—1 Sam. 20:18 (910).

Your place is empty. You have gone away.
Oh, how we miss you every day.
Tears fill our eyes to see your empty chair,
And, folded carefully away, the clothes you used to wear.
How empty seems the house; our hearts so sore;
For oh! the place that knew you will know you nevermore.
Your place is empty. How our sad hearts yearn—
If that could only be—for your return.
God give us grace and strength, our faith and hope renew.
For you will not return to us, but we will go to you!

Your place is empty here, for so God willed;
But there, in heaven, your place is filled!
Your place is empty! God calls us, one by one,
To homes prepared by Him, when earthly work is done.
We would not have you leave that world of bliss,
E'en if we could, beloved, bring you back again to this;
Back to this world of sorrow, of suffering, again,
To long days, full of weariness, to nights of ceaseless pain.
Although we sorely miss you, the time will not be long
When we will hear your voice in heaven's glad song.

Your place is empty here, as soon my place will be;
When my home there is ready, then God will send for me.
My thoughts keep turning heavenward, but if it be God's will
To leave me here a little while, where dear ones need me still.
The days are swiftly passing and life will soon be done—
For me it is life's evening, and the low setting sun.
I am wearying for my loved ones, for, oh, I miss them so;
And when God sends for me I'll be ready then to go.
To that blest land of happiness from which none ever roam.
Then my place will be empty, when God hath called me home.
—R. M. Moody.

Remembered Smiles (911).

When in the dusk of some calm eventime,
They softly pass, the treasure-laden years,
Slow rainswept hours, amid the echoing chime
Of festive peal, or knell tolled out with tears;

What stirs the heart? A wraith from Memory's land
  Of some brave splendor? Nay, but rather this—
Remembered smiles, a heartease from the hand
  Of one who loved us, and a child's pure kiss.

—Mary M. Wilshere

TEXTS AND TREATMENT HINTS.

"He Went About Doing Good."—Acts 10:38 (912).

I. It was preeminently true of Christ.

II. It may be true of us.

III. We should live to make it true of us. This is the ideal life. Its influence lingers on after death has claimed the man.

IV. It is an epitaph which may be truthfully written over many a good man.

"This, That This Woman Hath Done (Shall) Be Told for a Memorial of Her."—Matt. 26:13 (913).

I. It was a deed of loving service.

II. It was done to Christ.

III. Lives rich in generous ministries rendered for Christ's sake write their own best records.

IV. Those records are the brightest page of the world's history.

"And All the Widows Stood by Him Weeping, and Showing the Coats and Garments Which Dorcas Made, While She Was With Them." —Acts 9:39 (914).

I. The noblest life is the life of tender sympathy which finds expression in kindly deeds.

II. Such lives are enshrined in the grateful memories of multitudes. They join the "choir invisible."

III. Let us find an immortality in the thankful remembrance of those whom we have helped as well as in heaven.

XIV. THE DEATH BED.

REFLECTIONS AND ILLUSTRATIONS.

Experiences and Last Words (915).

One of the sweet consolations of the weary pilgrim as he nears the end of the way is that then he often gets his clearest visions of the Celestial City beyond. Bunyan calls this stage "the land of Beulah, where the air is very sweet and pleasant and the sun shineth night and day, for this is beyond the valley of the shadow of death, and also out of the reach of Giant Despair; neither could they so much as see Doubting Castle from this place. Here, too, they met with some of the inhabitants of the land they were going to, for here the shining ones often walked, because it is on the very borders of heaven."

It is sometimes so. Many of God's pilgrims have these hours of vision in the closing stage of the journey, just as Moses got a sublime vision of Canaan from Pisgah's top. There are Pisgahs everywhere to the heart of faith. A mountain-solitude, the chamber of prayer, the sacramental feast, have often seemed to open all heaven to the wondering eye. But the chief mount of vision is just on this side of the river of death. The seers who see most of the glory are those who are appointed to die. There is a light sometimes upon a dying face that reflects a hidden sun, and murmurs are heard on dying lips that seem snatches of the songs of heaven. From meanest beds, in poorest garrets, God's dying saints have sometimes had visions of the coming glory far transcending anything of which poet ever dreamed.—Rev. J. H. Knight.

Perfect Peace in Death (916).—In the shipwreck of earthly hope we can have perfect peace; in the swellings of Jordan, too, we ought to have the same perfect peace, peace as perfect as in the heavenly home itself.—Selected.

The Life's Utterance (917).

The meaning of a sentence cannot be gathered into its last word; the last word takes significance from what has gone before. So with life. Dying utterances and even thoughts may not be taken into account Every dying man would be a saint. A great Southern statesman said to those who asked if some one should pray for him, as his pulse was failing: "No; my life must be my prayer. This solemn moment is not so significant as the solemn years that are gone. Let them stand."

Grotius (918).—Grotius, an eminent expounder of the law, and one of the greatest scholars of his age, said on his death-bed: "Heu! vitam perdidi operose, nihil agendo." "I have trifled away life laboriously, doing nothing."

Bunsen (919).

The dying Bunsen, looking into the eyes of his wife bending over him, said. "In thy face I have seen the eternal!" There are natures so rare and pure that they serve as mirrors of the heavenly. The influence of such transparent characters on society for good is immeasurable. Blessed are the pure in heart, for they shall see God—and blessed are they who commune with the pure heart, for through them is God revealed even now to the awed gaze of men.

The Pilot Found (920).

The other night I was called out to see a man who was dying, and, arriving at the house, I found it was an old pilot who had steered a well-known steamer up and down the Hudson river for years. He was a brave soul, but never did he prove himself braver than when the storm of death was beating down upon him. He was in fearful agony, but, pilot-like, he was perfectly calm and self-possessed. I talked to him of the Saviour's love and power, and he listened to me with intensest interest; but it was not until I presented Jesus to him as the pilot's Pilot, reminding him that he was now in the fog, beating up against the swift current of death, and that just as his old vessel needed someone with a clear eye and a strong hand to steer it when the tempest was on, so did his soul need a pilot to take him up the stream of death into port, and Jesus was the only one who could do that, did his face light up and the shadow of distress that had lain across it disappear. Then I asked him if he would take the Divine Pilot on board, and commit his soul into His keeping, and he uttered a glad and strong "I will" that touched all our hearts, and drew us instinctively closer to his bedside; and while we stood there, brightened and warmed by the sunlight on the old man's brawny face, we sang to the dying pilot that most appropriate hymn:

> "Jesus, Saviour, pilot me
> Over life's tempestuous sea.
> Unknown waves before me roll,
> Hiding rock and treacherous shoal;
> Chart and compass come from Thee;
> Jesus, Saviour, pilot me."

He died shortly after, and the look upon his face as it lay set in death was so peaceful, so trustful, so triumphant, that it seemed to say to all who looked upon it—certainly to us who were present when he took the Saviour aboard his bark—"I met my Pilot, and through His help have made the port!"

My brother, you will need that same Pilot some day. As a wise captain does, take Him on before you get near port. Without Him, what wilt thou do in the swellings of Jordan? If you have been on a bar at night, and felt that everything depended upon the man at the helm, you can appreciate what it would mean to come up to the inlet of death without a pilot, and be driven before its awful tide out upon the dark and trackless waters that lie beyond. God save you and me from such a fate!—Rev. John Balcolm Shaw, D. D.

Journey's End (921).

The fact of death has always presented much of mystery to us. We feel in the presence of the dead a sense of defeat. The face of our friend shows no recognition of our presence. The eyes are closed. The voice is hushed. The heart is still. Our friend has gone. This form we see was his. But it has been discarded. And as we miss the old-time light in the eye and the cordial greeting we say, "Surely an enemy hath done this." And we think of death as a despoiler. We name him "Terror"—"King of Terrors"—"The Last Enemy"—"Our Greatest Enemy."

And yet this view of death cannot be true. When we think of it in such terms as this we are looking at the facts purely from the fleshly side, from the side of physical activities. When we think of God we know this view of death is error. Our God is in control of the world. He has created us. He has constituted us as we are. Mortality is a universal fact. The preceding generations of men with their numberless throngs have all gone. There is no survivor of these past years who by any means, any skill, any subterfuge, has evaded the inevitable fact. Death is part of a universal plan of God. And He is a good God. We believe in His benevolence. We trust Him to be a God of love. He is righteous. "Shall not the Judge of all the earth do right?" He is a God of love. "Like as a father pitieth his children so the Lord pitieth those that fear Him." Hence a fact which He permits to be universal must be a beneficent one. Death, being universal, cannot be a fact to be feared. It cannot be an evil. It is part of an infinite plan—the plan of an Omnipotent goodness. The poet is true to fact and faith when he says:

> "And so beside the silent sea
> I wait the muffled oar—
> No harm from Him can come to me
> On ocean or on shore."

We are much wiser in our figures of speech with which we refer to death than we are in our usual attitude toward it.

We speak of life as a "journey" and we picture ourselves as pilgrims, staff in hand, measuring out the miles along a roadway sometimes smooth and pleasant, sometimes steep and narrow and strewn with stones; making our way at times in sunlight and skies of glory, and at other times in nights of storm and darkness, beset with dangers seen and unseen.—Rev. Herbert S. Wilkinson.

A Convincing Argument (922).

One strong argument for a future life, says the Homiletic Review, is found in the unfinished nature of the earthly career. Reason remains unsatisfied, and we know of no explanation for this life if it is not to be filled out. President William R. Harper just before he died, in January, 1906, said:

"I am going before my work is finished. I do not know where I am going, but I hope my work will go on. I expect to continue work in the future state, for this is only a small part of the glorious whole."

Evarts (923).—Evarts died like a rich, luxuriant tree broken down and killed by the weight of its own fruit.

Gelimer and Saladin (925).

Gelimer was king of the Vandals, and for years was a powerful sovereign. All that wealth, pomp and ambition could do failed to satisfy, and when led a captive, afterward, through the streets of Constantinople, at the chariot wheels of his conqueror, Belisarius, he too cried: "Vanity of vanities." The magnanimous Saladin, the opponent of the chivalrous Richard, England's lion-hearted king, lay dying surrounded by prince, peer and warrior. He bade them take his shroud and fasten it to his victorious banner-staff, and bid the heralds cry through the city streets: "This is all that is left, of all his greatness, to the mighty Saladin!"

Happy In Death (926).

Charles N. Crittenton, who devoted his life and ample fortune to the establishment of homes for unfortunate women in over seventy cities, died as he lived, a happy Christian. Not only his last words, but all that he said during the closing hours was recorded. Here are things he said:

"It is God's will—He knows best."

"I have tried to be a friend to these poor girls—always their friend."

"There will be no dark river when Jesus comes."

The entire chapter of Isaiah 53, word for word.

The Lord's Prayer.

Many passages of Scripture.

The Apostles' Creed.

"Thank God for the victory."

Tried to sing the "Glory Song."

"Jesus, blessed Jesus."

"Florence, my baby—my baby."

"Good-bye, Jesus is coming."

"Beautiful—all is beautiful."

"Jesus is here."

"Glory—glory."

The Lord Holds the Lines (927).

A Southern Christian woman, while dying, imagined in her delirium that she was riding in her carriage with her faithful servant on the driver's seat. "Is David driving?" she asked. "There is no danger if David is driving." "No, no, Missus," replied the weeping negro at her side. "Poor Dave can't drive now. De Lord has hold of de lines." And the humble servant spoke the truth for all ages. The Lord of life holds the lines and guides his children safely through the gate of death into the Paradise of God.

Sailing Away (928).

I am standing upon the seashore. A ship at my side spreads her white sails to the morning breeze and starts for the blue ocean. She is an object of beauty and strength and I stand and watch her until at length she hangs like a speck of white cloud just where the sea and sky come down to meet and mingle with each other. Then some one at my side says: "There! She's gone!" Gone where? Gone from my sight, that is all. She is just as large in the mast and hull and spar as she was when she left my side, and just as able to bear her load of living freight to the place of her destination. Her diminished size is in me, and not in her. And just at that moment when some one at my side says, "There! She's gone!" there are other eyes that are watching for her coming and other voices ready to take up the glad shout, "There she comes." And that is—dying.—Evangel.

Dying Words (929).

"I do things that other men-at-arms do," quaintly confessed Etienne de Vignolles, called La Hire, and contemporary of Jeanne d'Arc, daring death at the swordpoint. "O God, do Thou to me in this day of battles as I would do to Thee, if Thou were La Hire and I were God." "Thank God, I have done my duty," rejoiced Lord Nelson, his earthly triumphs over. "A king should die standing," remarked Louis XVIII, making a final effort toward royal dignity. Many centuries earlier the Emperor Vespasian had died saying the same thing. "It is a great consolation to me in my last hour," was the last speech of Frederick V of Denmark, "that I have never willfully offended anyone, and that there is not a drop of blood on my hands."

The End of the Journey (930).

We are wise when we think of death as the journey's end. The pilgrim has reached the place of rest and joy. The miles were weary, perhaps, but worth while for that which lay beyond.

The voyage was stormy, but the vessel has come safely to port. Behind are all the dangerous deeps, the tumultuous leagues. Here is quiet harbor, and harbor gladness, and congratulation.

The day's work is over. The evening recompense is here. Safely passed the hours of heat and toil. Finished the work which was set to be done.

And our hearts can chord with the words of the angel, "Blessed are the dead who die in the Lord." And with the apostle's declaration: "For to me to live is Christ, but to die is gain."

When we think of death with aversion it is because of conscience. It is because we know we are not at peace with the God of goodness whom we shall meet just beyond the fact of death. We know we have not done the things He wished us to do. We have not been careful of the trusts He committed to our care. We shrink from telling Him what we have done with the trusts He gave us. "The sting of death is sin."

But Christ comes to take away our fear of death because He comes to take away from us the burden of sin. He comes to free us from this condemnation. He comes to assure of the Father's deathless love. He becomes the propitiation for our sins and "not for ours only but for the sins of the whole world." Hence, we have "the victory through our Lord Jesus Christ," and we say in the beautiful words of the dying Frances Willard what it is God's plan that everyone dying should feel, "How beautiful to be with God." Or what John Wesley felt when, dying, he said, "The best of all is God is with us."

Christ also takes away any fear that death should end all. He rose to demonstrate the reality of the resurrection life. He brought life and immortality to light in the person of Himself. He that was dead, known to be dead, proved to be dead, showed Himself alive and alive forevermore. He became the first fruits of them that slept. And we with Him can say, henceforth, "O death, where is thy sting? O grave, where is thy victory?"—Selected.

P. T. Barnum (931).

Mr. P. T. Barnum said, after recovering from a severe illness, speaking of his feelings and thoughts when confined to his bed: "I looked back and could hardly recall a benefit I had rendered to my fellow-men in all my life. The folly, the stupidity of fooling away the few years given us here in childish strifes, bickerings and differences, occurred to me so strongly that I resolved that the sun would never go down on me cherishing malice in my heart against a single fellow-being."

Horace Bushnell (932).

When Horace Bushnell was dying, he murmured one day slowly, and in great weakness, to those around his bed: "Well, now, we are all going home together: and I say, the Lord be with you, and in grace, and peace, and love—and that is the way I have come along home."

It is the only way for us all—the way we must all tread—if from amidst the temptations and the trials and the sorrows of earth, we hope to find our way home together.—Martin.

Strauss (933).

At Ludwigsburg—where Strauss was born, and where also he died and is buried—a gentleman, one of his personal friends and admirers, told the following, of which he claimed to have been an eye and ear witness: Strauss had a daughter, whom he had, strangely, sent to a pietistic school, while he was separated from her mother. She was educated a pious girl, and subsequently married a physician. She was called home when her father was about to die, and was deeply affected. When he saw her weeping, he took her hand in his and said: "My daughter, your father has finished his course. You know his principles and views. He cannot comfort you with the assurance of seeing you again. What your father has done will live forever, but his personality will forever cease to be. He must bow to the unchangeable law of the universe, and to that law he reverently says, 'Thy will be done!'"

Theodore Monod (934).—Theodore Monod said that he would like the epitaph on his tombstone to be, "Here endest the first lesson!"

Last Words (935).

"Think more of death than me," said Marcus Aurelius Antoninus. "I have taught men how to live," was the dying boast of Confucius. "I have not so behaved myself that I should be ashamed to live; nor am I afraid to die, because I have so good a Master," said Ambrose, saint and Latin father. "I shall gladly obey His call; yet I should also feel grateful if He would grant me a little longer time with you, and if I could be permitted to solve a question—the origin of the soul." This was the closing utterance of Anselm,, eleventh century bishop of Canterbury. "For the name of Jesus and the defense of the church I am willing to die," said Thomas a Becket.—Advocate.

Cowper, the Poet (936).

I thank God is sometimes the case, I do not take my view of it from the top of my own works and deservings; though God is witness that the labor of my life is to keep a conscience void of offense toward Him. Death is always formidable to me, save when I see him disarmed of his sting by having sheathed it in the body of Jesus Christ."

(937.)

For some there is no rapture, only a sweet expectancy. In weakness of body and weariness of mind hardly a word is uttered, and all around the bed are falling tears.

Some, indeed, have even less than this. They die amid the shadows, trembling lest they should be castaways. Still, God's redeemed and loved are just as safe in the chariot of cloud as in the chariot of fire. The victory is real, though the song of victory is reserved for the other side, to burst forth in the first moment of entry within the veil. "I have no raptures," said a dying saint, "but I have perfect peace." That is enough. The song will come when the harp of heaven is in the hand, and the perfect voice can sing it as no voice can sing it here.

What gives this perfect peace? The cross and victory of a Redeeming Lord who gives to all believing souls the comfort of His own assurance, "Because I live, ye shall live also." It was the custom, of old, for the king's cup-bearer to taste the wine before putting the cup to the royal lips. If there was poison in it, the death of the cup-bearer would reveal the fact: the continued life of the wine-taster would be an assurance that the king might safely drink. So Christ "by the grace of God, tasted death." He drank of the cup, and showed that there was no poison in it for Him, for "behold, He is alive for evermore;" and therefore, Christian, there is no poison in it for you. He makes you a sharer in His own perfect life. Through the very lowest of your experiences Jesus went, that into the very highest of His experiences you might go. —Knight.

A Singular Request (938).

Mrs. L——, who died not long ago in College avenue, New York, made a singular request on her death-bed. She was passionately fond of dancing, and her death was hastened by an over-indulgence in that amusement. When she realized that she was about to die, she requested that her remains might be laid out on a board intead of in a coffin, and that she should be dressed in her new ball dress of flesh-colored satin, with white slippers. She also asked that a fashionable hair-dresser should be employed to dress her hair in the latest style, and that her head should be turned to one side after death, to show the hair to advantage. Her desire was complied with, excepting that a basket was substituted for the board. After the remains were arrayed for the grave, the corpse was placed in a chair, the head turned to one side in a life-like position, and the picture was perpetuated in a photograph. The circumstances of her making such a request of course drew a large number of curiosity-seekers to the funeral.—Pierson.

Right.—"I was right," said the dying Hensterberg.

"Farewell." (939)—When the Rev. C. Wolf lay dying, he whispered to his sister. "Close this eye, the other is closed already, and now farewell."

"All Is Over." (940)—"Drop the curtain, the farce is played out," sneered Rabelais, who previously had spoken of "going to the great perhaps." Demorax, second century Greek philosopher, indulged in a kindred expression, "You may go home. The show is over."

"A Last Look." (941)—When Dr. Belfrage lay dying, he expressed himself as longing to be conscious in his last moments, so as to have "a last look at this wonderful world."

Edmund Burke, the Statesman (942).

Edmund Burke, when his rival at the election in Bristol died, in the midst of a hot and exciting chase for honor and promotion, said: "He who has been snatched from us in the middle of the contest, whilst his desires were as warm and his hopes as eager as ours, has feelingly told us what shadows we are and what shadows we pursue."

Voyage and Haven (943).

We speak of life as a voyage and we picture ourselves upon the vast deep, sailing sometimes upon peaceful seas, and often amid tempests, avoiding as best we may the reefs of danger, meeting with what skill we have and what courage we can muster, the adverse currents and the buffetings of angry winds.—Selected.

Ready for the Summons. (994)—Richard Baxter spoke of the coming of his death-day as the coming of his "third birthday," and looked forward to it with the same joy as a child looks forward to a birthday feast: and good Rowland Hill used often to be heard singing softly to himself:

And when I'm to die,
To Jesus I'll fly.
Because He has loved me—I cannot tell why—
But this I do find,
We two are so joined,
He'll not be in glory and leave me behind.

The Future Life (945).

During my sickness my flesh was taken off me and flung aside like any other worn out and unseasonable garment; and, after shivering awhile in my skeleton, I began to be clothed anew and much more satisfactorily than in my previous suit. In literal and physical truth I was another man. I had a lively sense of the exaltation with which the spirit will enter on the next stage of its eternal progress after leaving the heavy burden of its mortality in an earthly grave, with as little concern for what may become of it as now affected me for the flesh I had lost.— Hawthorne.

Light From the Tomb (946).

The great artists of the world, when they have tried to picture the empty tomb of Jesus, have generally represented it with a great light bursting out from its somber depths. It is a fit representation. Easter is a glad and heartsome, and an illuminating day. The fact of the resurrection throws a great light upon some of the most perplexing questions raised by these curious, doubting souls of ours. It brings some clear knowledge as to the conditions of life after death. For we remember that great word which declares that Jesus in His resurrection life is "the first-fruits of them that are asleep." Which means, we imagine, that He is not only the pledge and assurance of the resurrection harvest by and by, but that He is a sample and illustration of what life after death is like.

Let him who is eager to know what life in the yonder world is like study the words, the conduct, the employments and enjoyments of the risen Jesus. There is definite information there.—Selected.

At Eventide (947).

I love to connect our word "serene" with the Latin word for evening, as well as with its own mother-word serenus—clear or bright.

Often, after a windy, stormy day, there comes at evening a clear, bright stillness, so that at evening time there is serenity as well as light. So often in life's evening there comes a lull, a time of peaceful waiting "between the lights," the burden-weighted heat of the day behind, the radiance of eternity before. Perhaps the day has been in truth "life's little day," swiftly ebbing to its close; perhaps the worn, tired pilgrim has lived even beyond the measure of three-score years and ten. In either case it is in truth the evening.

The dear face reflects "eternity's wonderful beauty," the sweet serene spirit is freshened by dew from the heavenly Hermon, the fragrance of evening flowers fills the air, the songs of birds come in tender satisfied cadences, and even the clouds which remain are enriched and made radiant by rays from the Sun of Righteousness.

We whose evening is not yet are entranced with the exquisite blending of the warm human affection with the celestial flame kindled from the sacred altar. With hushed souls we minister and are ministered unto, until, too soon, the twilight time is past, and the evening and the morning have become the eternal day.—Selected.

Deathbed Joy (948).

"There has been a joy in prisons and at stakes, it has been said, far exceeding the joy of harvest. 'Pray for me,' said a poor boy of fifteen, who was being burned at Smithfield in the fierce days of Mary Tudor. 'I would as soon pray for a dog as for a heretic like thee,' answered one of the spectators. 'Then, Son of God, shine Thou upon me!' cried the boy martyr; and instantly, upon a dull and cloudy day, the sun shone out, and bathed his young face in glory; whereat, says the martyrologist, men greatly marveled. But is there one deathbed of saint on which that glory hath not shone?" Recall Stephen, seeing Christ as he was about to die. —Selected.

Christ Versus Paganism (949).

The Chinese when dying are generally terrified by the evil spirits they fancy they hear and see. A miserly merchant on his deathbed shouted out: "Don't you see the evil spirits? They are calling for money. Get them money or they will have me!" His wife had to unlock the box and bring out strings of cash with which to appease the evil spirits. Contrast this with the death of a Chinese Christian child of which I have heard. She surprised the neighbors by saying she had not seen any evil spirits. She said: "There are no evil spirits near me; Christ is with me, waiting to take me, and why should I be afraid?"— Rev. E. J. Hardy.

"He Died Climbing" (950).

Like all life's lessons, the personal significance of the resurrection is one which we increasingly apprehend. At no point can we say, "I have fully understood or attained." Our reach is greater than our grasp and there is continual fresh light glowing from the risen Christ to guide us in our upward search. "Excelsior" is the descriptive life-motto of the man who realizes himself as one "risen with Christ;" and while he is never aught but fully satisfied with the perfections of his great Ideal, he never for one moment pauses to be satisfied in himself. Such pause, indeed, would be fatal to his true progress, and would defeat the God-formed purpose of his life. There is in a little churchyard in Switzerland a simple inscription of the tomb of one who perished in an Alpine accident, which has always appealed to me with singular force: "He died climbing." He had heard the call of the mountains, and lost his life endeavoring to respond. We have heard the call of the risen Christ, but, unlike the climber, we gain our lives in our sustained attempt to respond worthily. "Seek those things that are above" is a call to enjoy the largest possible life, for the very struggle develops latent possibilities and capacities, and each step upward is into fuller liberty and more perfect manhood.—Redeeming Vision.

No Fear (951).

A little child played in a large and beautiful garden with sunny lawns; but there was one part of it, a long and winding path over-shadowed by trees, down which he never ventured; indeed he dreaded to go near it, because a foolish nurse had told him that ogres and hobgob-lins dwelt within its darksome gloom. At last his eldest brother heard of this fear, and after playing one day with him, took him to the entrance of the grove, and leaving him there terror-stricken, went sing-ing throughout its length, then returning and taking the little fellow's hand, they went through it together. And from that moment the fear had fled. So Jesus, having passed through the valley of death, gives courage to His people. "Yea, though I walk through the valley of the shadow of death, I will fear no evil; for Thou art with me."—The Expositor.

Prepared (952).

I went to see a man the other day who was sick unto death. The friends told me before I saw him that the doctor gave no hope. I went in and sat by his side, and I asked him if the Lord was with him in his sickness and gave him peace, and with a glad smile he said: "Oh, yes, all the time. I suppose I shall only last a few days at the longest, but it is all right; I have been getting ready for this for fifty years, and it is all right now." God grant that you may so live, may so hear the voice of Jesus calling you to follow Him, and may follow Him so closely that in that hour of hours He shall come to receive you in peace.—Banks.

The Gift of Death (953).

God's messengers are ever on the wing. In silence they cross the threshold, and when they go away they leave a footprint named a grave. God's plans are not interrupted. There are no accidents, no catastrophes unto God. His wisdom and love are fully equal to every emergency—even to a grave digged in the grass. When the life-work has been done, when the harvest of influence has been sown and reaped, then He sends His messenger for release, guidance and convoy homeward. His latest, richest and crowning gift is the gift of death. At the summit of the desert palm is a single flowering bud. When the fullness of time comes the flower falls, the fruit swells, the seed drops. The flower dies and disappears, but the tree goes on. And it is the epic of man's life that disappears but does not die. Our best beloved disappears, but out of the darkness comes the voice, saying: "I still live."—Hillis.

"I Know Whom I Have Believed" (954).

There are to be found today men and women to whom Christ is as real as though they held His fleshly hand and looked into His sweet human face. They are as sure that heaven is around them as that their hearts beat within them. They know that God loves them as certainly as if He awoke them each morning with a kiss.

Some time ago I met with a picture representing two women in great sorrow. Standing behind the chairs on which they were sitting there appeared the figure of Christ stretching out His hand over them. They could not see Him, because their eyes were dim, but He was none the less present with them. He was near in all His effulgent brightness, with all His helpful power. At the foot of the picture this verse was written:

"Unheard, because our ears are dull;
Unseen, because our eyes are dim;
He walks on earth—the Wonderful—
And all great deeds are done for Him."

What we need is the power to see—to see chariots and horses on the mountains; to see God all about us; to see the strong right arm of the Almighty stretched out to help us; to see that the darkest clouds and most threatening surroundings are under the all-controlling power of the everlasting Father. And seeing this, we shall have the prophet's hope and the prophet's faith and the prophet's trust that they who are with us are more than they who are against us. The prayer, then, which befits our lips day and night continually is: "Lord, we pray Thee, open our eyes that we may see."—Christian Advocate.

A King (955).

A consumptive disease seized the eldest son and heir of the Duke of Hamilton, which ended in his death. A little before his departure from the world he took his Bible from under his pillow and read several comforting passages. As death approached, he called his younger brother to his bedside, and after talking affectionately and seriously to him, closed with these words: "And now, Douglas, in a little while you'll be a duke, but I shall be a king."—The S. S. Chronicle.

We Judge Ourselves (956).

Slowly and painlessly consciousness returned. He looked about him and remembered. It seemed but a moment, and yet the life he had lived on earth was as far from him as if he had died a century ago. In the stillness and measureless quiet which enfolded him after those last agonizing hours he knew that he had already entered into rest. So deep was the peace which fell softly as if from the vast heights above him that he felt no curiosity and was without fear. He was in a new life and he must find his place in it, but he was content to wait; and while he waited his thought went swiftly back to the days when, a little child, he looked up at the sky and wondered if the stars were the lights in the streets of heaven. One by one the years rose out of the depths of his memory and he recalled, step by step, all the way he had come: childhood, youth, manhood and age. He read with deepening interest the story of his life, all his thoughts, his words, the things he had done and left undone. And as he read he knew what was good and what was ill; everything was clear, not only in his unbroken record of what he had been, but in a sudden perception of what he was. At last he knew himself. And while he pondered, one stood beside him, grave and calm and sweet with the purity that is perfect strength. Into the face which turned toward him, touched with the light of immortal joy, he looked up and asked, "When shall I be judged?" And the answer came: "You have judged yourself. You may go where you will."—Hamilton W. Mabie, in Parables of Life.

Mozart. (957)—"Did I now say I was writing the requiem for myself?"

Living Well and Dying Well (958).

The list of striking and picturesque "last sayings" might be extended indefinitely, but to what further purpose? Enough have been given to prove the intrinsic oneness of all dying—as all living—humanity, to show that all sorts and conditions of the children of men can face the Great Adventure bravely and with good spirit, and to remind us that in death as in life "it is character that counts," and that makes all the difference between supreme if quiet courage and the coward shrinking which anticipates by "a hundred deaths" the single world transition arranged by an allwise Creator.

He who for our sakes traversed the Lonely Road in pain and sorrow went down to death loving and forgiving His enemies, caring for His friends, and shedding upon both past and future phases of existence the transcendent glow of His great heart and pure, did it because He had lived in this manner. And only those will exchange worlds with true dignity, hope, and sweetness who have trained for this final test, this wonderful experience, this Surprising Adventure, in the lesser, perpetual trials and vicissitudes of simple daily life.—The Christian Advocate.

The Sustaining Arm (959).

A serious surgical operation lying before me, with the certain knowledge that I was too weak to live through it save by God's help, knowing also the alternative of death, and with a large family of young children who needed me, I laid my case before the Lord.

Down into the death valley I must needs go and, thinking of the children, the way was dark and exceedingly bitter. The struggle was long and hard and I seemed to have no courage—the heavens were as brass. Always timid, I was afraid, wretchedly afraid, and homesick, too, for we were in a strange land and the speech was not mine own.

At last the night before the operation—dreaded unspeakably—came; the dear ones had gone, the nurse also. I turned the pages of my Bible to find comfort, but found none. And then suddenly, as I lay later with the soft moonlight in the room and wonderful on the distant mountains so serene and majestic in snowy beauty, the help came. Words of divine promise began to steal into my heart and mind with infinite comfort. "For the mountains may depart....but my loving kindness

shall not depart from thee, neither shall my covenant of peace be removed, said Jehovah that hath mercy on thee."

"Thy faithfulness reacheth unto the skies, thy righteousness is like
the mountains of God." "I the Lord will hold thy right hand saying
unto thee, Fear not."

Crowding, thronging, they came; not alone the dear familiar promises, mine in many a storm of sorrow, and come now with a new and
forceful message, but words I was not conscious of knowing at all, wonderful words, great promises, spoken as with the voice of One who
comforts as a mother comforteth. And in that hour of utter weakness,
a sense of my Father's love all about me brought peace, perfect peace.
I felt an indescribable joy and blessing such as I had never known. I
fell asleep to rest all the night, unafraid.

Of the weeks and months that followed when I slowly but surely
climbed back to life and ministry I need not tell, though God was with me
as never before and has been nearer and dearer through the year/
since.—The Congregationalist.

Almost Home (960).

Those who are familiar with John Bunyan's immortal allegory will
remember how he brings his Pilgrims, in the closing days of their homeward journey, into the Land of Beulah. They had left far behind them
the valley of the death shadow and the horrible Doubting Castle in
which Giant Despair imprisoned and tortured his hapless victims. In
this delightful Beulah land they found the atmosphere very sweet and
balmy. They heard continually the singing of birds and saw an abundance of flowers blooming by the wayside. The sun shone by night as
well as by day.

Glorious visions of heaven broke upon them, for they were in sight
of the Celestial City, and in their walks they encountered several groups
of the shining ones. Here they were not in want of the fruits of the
field or the yield of the vintage, for the King fed them with an abundance
of all the good things which they had sought for in all their pilgrimage.
As they walked to and fro in this goodly land they had more rejoicing
than when traveling in regions more remote from their Father's house.
Beside their path were open gates inviting them into orchards and vineyards, and gardens filled with flowers and fruits delicious to their taste.
In answer to their questions, the gardener informed Christian and Hopeful that these were the King's gardens, planted by Him for His own
delight as well as for the solace of the Pilgrims. The gardener invited
them to make free of all the orchards and the vineyards, and bade them
refresh themselves with the dainties. They were drawing near to the
end of their long journey, and beyond the river that has no bridge was
the New Jerusalem in all its flashing splendors. They were almost
home!—Cuyler.

A Fortune For You (961).

Many years ago, over here in Plymouth Church, Henry Ward Beecher
painted a picture like this: You are a poor man and ignorant. There is
a written document lying in a chest in your room. You cannot read the

writing, and you do not know what that document contains, but you have a suspicion that by it you might become the inheritor of great fortune. You take it out sometimes and look at it, and vainly wish that you could read it; but you put it back without gaining any knowledge of its purport. By and by some kind friend, learned in the language in which it is written, comes to your home, and the document is taken out, and he examines it for you. He reads, and as he reads grows more and more attentive. He stops to ask you, "Who is your father? What was his father's name?" You are full of interest and impatience to know what its contents are, until, unable to control yourself, you cry out, "Tell me what it is. Do not hold me in suspense. What is the news?" At length he says, "Why, sir, do you know that whole estate is yours? Here is your title. This is a will. The evidence is unquestionable. You are a millionaire. Your poverty is gone." "Read it again!" you exclaim. "Read it aloud, so that I can hear the words! Can it really be so?" Until at last you are convinced and enter into the sweet comfort of the knowledge.

So the world had heard whispers of immortality. There had been clouds and flaming chariots and vague, uncertain visions. But at last Christ came and opened to us God's will as it is revealed in the New Testament, and made known the wondrous treasures of our inheritance. He read it aloud to listening ears—"In my Father's house are many mansions. I go to prepare a place for you. And if I go, I will come again, and receive you unto Myself; that where I am, you may be also,"— until men caught up the refrain and have been preaching in every graveyard of earth that forever and ever man shall live. So long as the lifeboat will attract the sailor battling for his life amid the waves, just so long the glorious hope of immortality through Jesus Christ will charm men from their fears to His resurrected side.—Banks.

Show Him Your Hands (962).

Bishop Woodcock of Kentucky has told a touching story about a little heroine whom he knew. She was left motherless at the age of eight. Her father was poor, and there were four children younger than she. She tried to care for them all and for the home. To do it all, she had to be up very early in the morning and to work very late at night. No wonder that at the age of thirteen her strength was all exhausted. As she lay dying a neighbor talked with her. The little face was troubled. "It isn't that I'm afraid to die," she said, "for I am not. But I'm so ashamed." "Ashamed of what?" the neighbor asked in surprise. "Why it's this way," she exclaimed. "You know how it's been with us since mama died. I've been so busy, I've never done anything for Jesus, and when I get to heaven and meet Him, I shall be so ashamed! Oh, what can I tell Him?" With difficulty the neighbor kept back her sobs. Taking the little calloused, workscarred hands in her own, she answered. "I wouldn't tell Him anything, dear. Just show Him your hands.' —Selected.

Safe (963).

There is a beautiful legend told about a little girl who was the first-born of a family in Egypt, when the destroying angel swept through that land, and consequently who would have been a victim on that night if the protecting blood were not sprinkled on the doorposts of her father's house. The order was that the firstborn should be struck by death all through Egypt. This little girl was sick and she knew that death would take her, and she might be a victim of the order. She asked her father if the blood was sprinkled on the doorposts. He said it was, that he had ordered it to be done. She asked him if he had seen it there. He said no, but he had no doubt that it was done. He had seen the lamb killed, and had told the servant to attend to it. But she was not satisfied, and asked her father to go and see, and urged him to take her in his arms and carry her to the door to see. They found that the servant had neglected to put the blood upon the posts. There the child was exposed to death until they found the blood and sprinkled it on the posts and then it was safe. See to it that you are safe in Christ.—Moody.

Deathbed Repentance (964).

What, after all, is the evangelical doctrine of salvation? No man is ever accepted of God because of years of Christian experience and fidelity. When at last I come to the end of my service and life—either by lingering illness or, may God grant it! by sudden translation, I shall have to use these words when I come into the presence of the King:

"Nothing in my hand I bring,
Simply to Thy Cross I cling."

I shall not be received there because I have been a minister, or because I have struggled after righteousness. Salvation is not the reward of fidelity. I shall stand at the last accepted in the Beloved. This is the light that flashes over these dark hours in the mid-Atlantic, when the 1,500 passengers of the Titanic were waiting their doom. There were amongst them men who had neglected religion—men of godless, perhaps corrupted, lives. I am not thinking of any individuals, nor do I know the state of heart of any. Can we doubt that in these last hours they awakened to the consciousness of sin, and cast themselves upon the infinite mercy of God, and were accepted by Him? Remember the story of the malefactor on the cross. We have only this one story in the gospels, that none may presume, but we have this one story, to show that no human heart need despair. We shall find one day that multitudes of unexpected guests have found their way to the light and peace of the homeland.—Rev. Campbell Morgan.

Are You Ready? (965).

One of the best men I ever knew was for a long time a pastor, and then, for a short time before his stepping over the threshold into heaven, a theological professor. He was one of those rare men who lived above the petty things of sense, of whom one might think and say without any irreverence, "Ah, the Master must have been something like that!" He was asked once what he would do and say if he met Jesus Himself suddenly, some day, on the street. Quietly and simply he said: "I'd like to say to Him: 'Dear Master, I greet Thee. Long have I been waiting for Thee. I love Thee. What can I do for Thee now?" Greeting, watching, and waiting, loving, serving—are you ready just now if He come? Am I? "Let us not sleep—let us watch."—Troxell.

ILLUSTRATIVE VERSES.

The Valley of Sorrow (966).

I came to the valley of sorrow,
  And dreary it looked to my view,
But Jesus was walking beside me,
  And sweetly we journeyed it through.
And now I look back to that valley
  As the fairest that ever I trod,
For I learned there the love of my Father,
  I leaned on the arm of my God.

Yes, as I look back to the valley
  From the crest of its glory-crowned hill;
I call it my Valley of Blessing,
  So peaceful it lieth—so still;
And sweeter its calm to my spirit,
  Than the chorus of jubilant song;
'Tis there that the mourners find comfort;
  'Tis there that the weak are made strong.

O fair is the valley of sorrow!
  God's tenderest angels are there;
Its shadows are lighted by Patience,
  And sweet with the fragrance of Prayer;
Tired hearts gather strength in the valley,
  And burdens once heavy grow light;
Ah, sweet are the "songs of the sunshine,"
  But sweeter the "songs of the night."

O beautiful Valley of Sorrow!
  So holy, so calm, and so blest!
Thy ways are the fairest I travel
  This side of the Land of my Rest.
And if some day the Father should ask me
  Which was best of the paths that I trod,
How quickly my heart shall make answer:
  "The Valley of Sorrow, O God!"
                              —Author Unknown.

In Sorrow's Mists (967).

"Mary!"
In the gray dusk of morn she stands,
The spikenard fragrant in her hands;
She sees a dim form through the mists,
A foot-fall coming near she lists.
No strange, sweet thrill of holy fear
Foretells her heart of faith's reward:
"He comes, the gardener," she says;
And lo, it is the Lord!

"Mary!"
We stand amid the mists like thee!
The close at hand we cannot see;
Not knowing what they bring, we greet
Each day, and every soul, we meet;
But what seems sorrow's darkest hour
May bring us faith's reward,
And when we say "the gardener,"
Behold it is the Lord!

Marion Douglas.

The Home Light (968).

Whether the road be steep or whether the sky be gray,
You can sing and smile, o'er each lagging mile,
If only you know, that after awhile
There's a tryst to keep, and a tear to stay
And a hand to greet you, though long away.

Whether the task be hard or whether the hand be weak,
You can laugh and jest, if the hours for rest
Bring peace and calm to your troubled breast,
The flush of joy on a dear one's cheek,
And home the haven you joyful seek.

Whether the night be dark, or whether the toil be vain,
You can lift your voice and at heart rejoice,
Though lost the effort and ill the choice,
If the courage lost you can find again
In a light Love sets in the windowpane.

—Lalia Mitchell in Boston Magazine.

The Stars Shining (969).

Alas for him who never sees
The stars shine through his cypress trees!
Who hopeless lays his dead away,
Nor hopes to see the breaking day
Across the mournful marbles play;
Who has not felt, in hours of grief,
The truth, to flesh and sense unknown,
That life is ever lord of death,
And love can never lose its own!

—Whittier.

Answering The Call (970).

Beneath the cover of the sod
The lily heard the call of God;
Within its bulb so strangely sweet
Answering pulse began to beat.
The earth lay darkly damp and cold.
And held the smell of grave and mold,

But never did the lily say,
"O who shall roll the stone away?"
It heard the call, the call of God,
And up through prison house of sod
It came from burial place of gloom
To find its perfect life in bloom.

Emancipation (971).

Why be afraid of death as though your life were breath?
Death but anoints your eyes with clay, O glad surprise!
Why should you be forlorn? Death only husks the corn.
Why should you fear to meet the Thrasher of the wheat?

Is sleep a thing to dread? Yet, sleeping, you are dead
Till you awake and rise, here or beyond the skies.

Why should it be a wrench to leave your wooden bench?
Why not, with happy shout, run home when school is out?

The dear ones left behind! O foolish one and blind,
A day, and you will meet; a night, and you will greet!

This is the death of Death: to breathe away a breath,
And now the end of strife, and taste the deathless life;

And joy without a fear, and smile without a tear,
And work, not care nor rest, and find the last the best.
                              —Maltbie D. Babcock.

Into the Forever (972).

What may we take unto the vast forever?
    That marble door
Admits no fruit of all our long endeavor;
    No fawn-wreathed crown we wore,
    No garnered lore.

What can we bear beyond the unknown portal?
    No gold, no gains
Of all our toiling; in the life immortal
    No hoarded wealth remains,
    Nor guilt nor stains.

Naked from out the far abyss behind us
    We entered here;
No word came with our coming to remind us
    What wondrous world was near,
    No hope, no fear.

In to the silent, starless night before us,
  Naked we glide;
No hand has mapped the constellations o'er us,
  No comrade at our side,
  No chart, no guide.

Yet fearless toward the midnight black and hollow
  Our footsteps fare;
The beckoning of a Father's hand we follow—
  His love alone is there;
  No curse, no care.

—E. R. Sill

Gone Before (973).

Though he that ever kind and true
Kept stoutly step by step with you,
Your whole long, gusty lifetime through,
Be gone awhile before,
Be now a moment gone before;
Yet doubt not; know the seasons shall restore
    Your friend to you.

He has but turned a corner—still
He pushes on with right good will
Through mire and maish, by heugh and hill,
That self-same arduous way—
That self-same upland, hopeful way
That he and you through many a doubtful day
    Attempted still.

He is not dead, this friend—not dead,
But in the path we mortals tread,
Got some few, trifling steps ahead
And nearer to the end,
So that you, too, once past the bend,
Shall meet again, as face to face, this friend
    You fancy dead.

Push gaily on, strong heart! the while
You travel forward mile by mile,
He loiters with a backward smile
Till you can overtake,
And strains his eyes to search his wake,
Or whistling as he sees you through the brake,
    Waits on a stile.

—Robert Louis Stevenson.

When I Have Gone Away (974).

When I have gone away, dear heart,
  And left the scenes of earth behind,
Each link that forms of life a part,
  The higher, larger life to find,
Bring springtime flowers fresh and fair
  To lay above my place of rest,
And let them whisper to me there—
  The flowers that I love the best.

I know not now, dear heart, the ways
  Of that fair land of mystery;
How souls through the eternal days
  Grow sweet, and strong, and glad, and free;
But this I know—that love will last,
  Nor ever unresponsive grow,
And precious memories of the past,
  Will bind me to the hearts below.

Bring flowers for sweet memory's sake,
  And lay them low where grasses wave;
And they a deathless chain shall make,
  That reaches on beyond the grave.
And past the touch of blight or chill,
  'n fields where fadeless flowers grow.
Living and learning, loving still,
  Believe, dear heart, that I shall know.
                —Julia E. Abbott, in Zion's Herald.

Christ Has Risen (975).

Christ has risen—else in vain
All the sunshine, all the rain,
All the warmth and quickening,
And renewal of the spring.
Vain they were to charm our eyes,
Greening earth and gracious skies,
Growth and beauty, bud or bloom,
If within their fast-sealed tomb
All our dearer dead must dwell,
Sharing not the miracle.

Crocus tips in shining row,
Welcome, for your sign we know.
Every bud on every bough
Has its message for us now,
Since the Lord on Easter Day
Burst the bonds of prisoning clay;
All the springtime has a voice,
Every heart may dare rejoice,
Every grave, no more a prison,
Join the chorus, "Christ is risen."

—Susan Coolidge.

The Two Mysteries (976).

We know not what it is, dear, this sleep so deep and still;
The folded hands, the awful calm, the cheek so pale and chill;
The lids that will not lift again, though we may call and call;
The strange white solitude of peace that settles over all.

We know not what it means, dear, this desolate heart-pain;
This dread to take our daily way, and walk in it again;
We know not to what other sphere the loved who leave us go,
Nor why we're left to wonder still, nor why we do not know.

But this we know: Our loved and dead, if they should come this day—
Should come and ask us, "What is life?" not one of us could say.
Life is a mystery, as deep as ever death can be;
Yet oh, how dear it is to us, this life we live and see!

Then might they say—these vanished ones—and blessed is the thought,
"So death is sweet to us, beloved! though we may show you nought;
We may not to the quick reveal the mystery of death—
Ye cannot tell us, if ye would, the mystery of breath."

The child who enters life comes not with knowledge or intent,
So those who enter death must go as little children sent,
Nothing is known. But I believe that God is overhead;
And as life is to the living, so death is to the dead.

—Mary Mapes Dodge.

Comfort (977).

Thy comfort comes through pain,
Thy tender hand the burden lifts,
And hope shines through the cloud in golden rifts.
And unto those who trust Thee come again
Courage and peace and all such kindred gifts
"Clear shining after rain."

—C. J. G.

Easter Hope (978).

Carry the flowers of Easter
  To the darkened house of woe,
With their message of strength and comfort
  Let the lilies of Easter go;
Scatter the Easter blossoms
  In the little children's way;
Let want and pain and weakness
  Be cheered on our Easter day.

TEXTS AND TREATMENT HINTS.

I Will Not Leave You Comfortless: I Will Come to You—John 14:18 (979).

Our blessed Lord will have His people to be a joyful people. He would not have them of sad countenances and heavy hearts, but wishes them to rejoice in Him always, for the joy of the Lord is their strength. He was going away to prepare a place for them; He was coming to receive them to Himself into those heavenly mansions in His Father's house especially fitted for their occupancy, and in the mean time He would not leave them without "another Comforter," even the Spirit of truth, who should not only bring to remembrance all that He had spoken to them, but mediate His perpetual presence and guide them into truth not yet revealed because they were not now able to bear it. Thus associated with and dwelling in them they would not be comfortless (Gr. orphans), but children of God, joint-heirs with Christ, and members of the blessed family of which Christ is the head.

All these precious assurances of Christ to be with His own are made to His people today. We need not wait for His coming for us, or rather our going to Him, at death, or for His visible and personal appearance at the last day for the fulfillment of His promise, "I will come to you." We are sure He comes to all who will receive Him here and now. He comes through the office and influence of the Comforter, the Spirit of truth, who takes the things of Christ and shows them unto us. May we open our hearts to receive Him, and become fit temples for His holy indwelling!—Joel Schwartz, D. D.

Well Done, Thou Good and Faithful Servant: Thou Hast Been Faithful Over a Few Things, I Will Make Thee Ruler Over Many Things: Enter Thou Into the Joy of Thy Lord.—Matt. 25:21 (980).

God has the highest possible claim to our services, and His claim is universal and constant. No peculiarity of natural endowment, great or small, nor diversity of opportunity or means of doing good, works any change in the matter of personal responsibility. All power and means of doing good are the gift of God, and to meet our obligations all must be consecrated to His services.

Christ teaches us that the grandest possibilities are wrapped up in every human life; that by the right improvement of the talents given, be they ten or one, we shall by and by become rulers over many things and enter into the joy of our Lord; that constant devotion to God is the true philosophy of a successful life: "For what shall it profit a man if he gain the whole world and lose his own soul?" Happy then the man who recognizes the will of God as the rule of his every-day life. It may, it will, require sacrifice, possible suffering, and failure in many worldly enterprises and prospects, but fidelity to God is assured success. To the faithful servant of God triumph is not far off. Today improve the talents given; tomorrow the Master will say, "Well done," for the "Judge standeth at the door."—Selected.

He That Overcometh, the Same Shall Be Clothed in White Raiment; and I Will Not Blot Out His Name Out of the Book of Life, but I Will Confess His Name Before My Father, and Before His Angels.— Rev. 3:5 (981).

What earnestness there must be in the life of a Christian if we either look upon how much he has to overcome, or how much he is in danger of losing! We, as Christians, have before us difficulties and temptations, enemies within and without, especially that dreadful and deadly disease, self-confidence, when we are pleased with what we are and therefore do not press on toward the goal unto the prize of the high calling of God in Christ Jesus. But no matter what is in our way it ought not to discourage, still less deject us, as if it would be almost hopeless to think of overcoming. The last words in our text not only show us the glorious things we may lose, but they at the same time hold up before our eyes what we will gain by continuing the fight till the last enemy is overcome; yea, they are properly promises that ought to give us courage and strength to hold out to the end. Then what a victory,—white raiment, having our names in the book of life as members of the heavenly commonwealth, and confessed by our Saviour as being His before God and the world!

"Lord, if It Be Thou, Bid Me Come. And He Said, Come."
—Matt. 14:28 (982).

How different is the departure of a Christian from an apostate! James Hervey the English divine, died on Christmas, 1758. Having thanked his physician for his kind attentions, he exclaimed with holy exultation, "Lord, now lettest Thou Thy servant depart in peace, for mine eyes have seen Thy salvation!" And turning to his attendant, he said, "Here, doctor, is my cordial."

XV. GENERAL REFLECTIONS ON LIFE AND DEATH.

REFLECTIONS AND ILLUSTRATIONS.

Belief and Life. (983)—Your life cannot be good if your teaching is bad. Doctrine lies at the basis of life. You may profess to believe a good many things, but in reality what you believe is the very substance and inspiration of your character.—Selected.

Watch the Moves (984).

A long time ago, in 1565, when Elizabeth, Queen of England, was playing chess, the French ambassador entered her room, and while watching the progress of the game, he said to her: "Madam, you have set before you the game of life. You lose a pawn. It seems a small matter; but with the pawn you may lose the game." The queen understood his meaning, and saw the moral—that her progress in life as a queen depended upon prompt and right action in little things; that a pawn in the game of life must not be lost; that its value in the problem of life is incalculable. The lesson taught the queen is a good lesson for all thoughtful readers. Small mistakes in life are often serious in their results. If you would win the game of life, you must move your pawns with caution and skill. Small leakings will sink a ship. Little foxes spoil the vines. A single word is not much, but it may separate fast friends. One glass of ardent spirits is a little thing; but when it is drunk, the pawn may be lost that loses the game of life. A step may be a short one, and in itself of but little value; but if it is taken in the wrong direction, it will affect your destiny and turn you away from the pathway of success and honor.—Selected.

The Upward Trend (985).

If you are looking for that which is best in the men and women with whom you come in contact; if you are seeking also to give them that which is best in yourself; if you are looking for friendship which shall help you to know yourself as you are and to fulfill yourself as you ought to be; if you are looking for a love which shall not be a flattering dream and a madness of desire, but a true comradeship and a mutual inspiration to all nobility of living, then you are surely on the ascending path.—Henry van Dyke.

The Great Companion (986).

Professor James, in his book, "Varieties of Religious Experience," tells of a man of forty-nine who said: "God is more real to me than any thought or thing or person. I feel His presence positively, and the more as I live in closer harmony with His laws as written in my body and mind, I feel Him in the sunshine or rain; and all mingled with a delicious restfulness most nearly describes my feeling. I talk to Him as to a companion in prayer and praise, and our communion is delightful. He answers me again and again, often in words so clearly spoken that it seems my outer ear must have carried the tone, but generally in strong mental impressions. Usually a text of Scripture, unfolding some new view of Him and His love for me, and care for my safety......That He is mine and I am His never leaves me; it is an abiding joy. Without it life would be a blank, a desert, a shoreless, trackless waste."—Forward.

The Rounds on Which We Climb (987).

Every low desire, every bad habit, all longings for ignoble things, all wrong feelings that we conquer and trample down, become ladder-rounds for our feet, on which we climb upward out of groveling and sinfulness into nobler, grander life. If we are not living victoriously these little common days, we are not making any progress in true living. Only those who climb are getting toward the stars. Heaven at last, and the heavenly life here, are for those who overcome.—Scottish Reformer.

Now in Eternity (988.)

No man can pass into eternity, for he is already in it. The dead are no more in eternity now than they always were, or than every one of us is at this moment. We may ignore the things eternal; shut our eyes hard to them; live as though they had no existence,—nevertheless, Eternity is around us here, now, at this moment, at all moments; and it will have been around us every day of our ignorant, sinful, selfish lives. Its stars are ever over our heads, while we are so diligent in the dust of our worldliness, or in the tainted stream of our desires. The dull brute globe moves through its ether and knows it not; even so our souls are bathed in eternity and are never conscious of it. —Canon Farrar.

The Ministry of Christ's Truth (989).

Comfort—no other word expresses so well the ministry of Christ's truth to my life. To be uncomforted is to be filled with despair. The soul trusting in itself may be brave, but only the soul that finds itself in God is comforted.

From a happy childhood and a care-free girlhood I came to the stern responsibilities and cares of more mature life, only to find myself unprepared to meet them.

Life had been to me a lovely dream-filled thing, and when I found myself face to face with Reality, I cried out in bitterness and rebellion. This hard, rough path was surely not for me; my path had been a beautiful shining path. I had started out with glowing purpose to follow the Gleam, and in the path at my feet every ray of light had darkened. If I had been called to a great sacrifice I could have risen to its heights; it was the very common character of my lot that humiliated me and robbed me of my strength.

At this time there came to me a dark period of doubt. I did not want to be a doubter and struggled against its unhappy influence. With doubt came a distrust of God's care of my life. It seemed as if it were of no concern to the Heavenly Father that I suffered. I was a constant prey to the sense of the futility of life.

There remained of my wreck of faith and dreams a sense of God and a great desire to find the light. This sense of God comforted me even when I was unconscious of it, and always in the darkness I could hear His voice saying, "This way, my child, this way toward the Light," even as I had heard my mother's voice when as a little child I lost my way in the darkness of my room.

That Voice in the dark—what infinite tenderness and patience in its call! Following it I found light and the comforting enfolding sense of eternal love and care. All the feeling that life was unkind and that my obvious duties were unworthy my best effort was lost. Strength and courage came as I learned to accept all as the fulfillment of God's purpose in my life.

Not only do those who suffer a great bereavement need the consolations of the assurance of immortality. In my own life, in the hard daily duty, the truth symbolized by Easter floods my way with light. Life triumphant in all the universe—this is the larger faith that banished my sense of the shortness and vanity of life.

Good that dies not, Love that lives and blesses, even though He who called it forth has passed beyond our vision. These are the lessons of this Easter season when all nature is awakening to life and beauty. No longer baffled by a sense of the futility of life, but comforted with a great and abiding faith, knowing that I can never "drift beyond His love and care," I am still following the path that once seemed so dark. It has been a way of privilege and blessing.—Mrs. John Mason Turner, in the Congregationalist

Growing Toward Christ (990).

The Christian ideal is Christ. Development toward Him is self-realization. We become more individual as we become Christian. Personality is perfected by completeness of consecration to Christ. The process of becoming Christlike depends upon both the contemplation of His character and the receiving of His Spirit. Superficial and false standards of Christian character will continue to prevail unless the character of Christ be carefully and constantly studied and imitated. Beholding Him we become transformed into His likeness. But the process of transformation is not a formal copying, not an external imitation. It is a vital process in the heart by the agency of His Spirit. We cannot copy Him unless He quickens us; He will not quicken us unless it be our aim to copy Him. His outward life is the power that transforms us into His image, from glory to glory. A consistent, beautiful, powerful Christian life is possible to all who will study His character that they may copy it, and who seek to be anointed with His Spirit that by it they may be inwardly transformed.—Selected.

Life What You Make It (991).

On the walls of an old temple was found this picture: a king forging from his crown a chain, and near by a slave making of his chain a crown; and underneath was written, "Life is what one makes it, no matter of what it is made."

Noble-minded Men (992).

High-minded, manly, duty-doing men are the chiefest need of any state or nation; for, without such men, no nation ever achieved distinction or attained to greatness. Whatever else a nation may produce, if it does not produce high-minded, manly, moral men, it is well on its way to decadence and death.—Selected.

The Time for Tenderness (993).

Do not keep the alabaster boxes of your love and tenderness sealed up until your friends are dead. Fill their lives with sweetness. Speak approving, cheering words while their hearts can be thrilled and made happy by them; the kind things you mean to say when they are gone, say before they go. The flowers you mean to send for their coffins, send to brighten and sweeten their homes before they leave them. If my friends have alabaster boxes laid away, full of fragrant perfumes of sympathy and affection, which they intend to break over my dead body, I would rather they would bring them out in my weary and troubled hours, and open them, that I may be refreshed and cheered by them while I need them. I would rather have a plain coffin without a flower, a funeral without an eulogy, than a life without the sweetness of love and sympathy. Let us learn to anoint our friends beforehand for their burial. Post mortem kindness does not cheer the burdened spirit. Flowers on the coffin cast no fragrance backward over the weary way.—Hon. Tom Ochiltree, of Texas.

The Traveler (994)

The way is rough, and sometimes hard to tread; dust and mire are everywhere, the sun concentrates its oppressive rays, and the chill of winter adds its discomfiture; the traveler presses on; and, at last, reaches the summit of life's achievement which lies on the border toward the setting of the sun; and from this vantage, if his steps have been guided by looking well to the hills of God, he is permitted a vision of his triumphal and glorious conquest—a fitly finished journey.—Christian Evangelist.

Living Epistles (995).

The world has been burdened with abstract forms of belief. The demand has become imperative for the unselfish, the pure, the consecrated life. The world, "amid all the resources of modern science and art" and profuseness, still bends and breaks beneath the burden of its "vanity and vexation of spirit." Never in all the ages have the restless multitudes sent out so pathetic a cry for those who are "the shadow of a great rock in a weary land, and rivers of water in a dry place." If ever water is poured upon him that is thirsty, it will be done by those who are rooted and grounded in Christ. This is the true life and this is the great and noble creed. Our Lord said to Peter three times: "Do you love me?" And three times the Lord said: "Go and prove it." Formulas stand like statues, still and cold. With eager, longing eyes we still look for the blossoms and fruits of righteousness and true holiness of the individual life of the Christian. Our Christianity wields a general influence, the effect of which is to produce beautiful models of refinement, persons attractive and polite. Our schools have given us outstanding examples of good manners and lucid conceptions of the claims of propriety and common sense. Mere civilization, the "gilded trappings of wealth," the luster of learning, of the achievements of philosophy have nothing of which to boast in the matter of which we speak. The lizard may wiggle his way to the top of the tallest tree in this sunny land; but he is a lizard still, and must come down or die there. We read in the Bible of some who wait on the Lord, and that they mount up with wings as eagles. They do not grow weary; they do not faint. Their love is a "living fire, pure, warm, and changeless." They are the keepers of God's lighthouse, the dispensers of His truth. This life is the great and noble creed which none can analyze or answer or deny.

"Think truly and thy thoughts
  Shall the world's famine feed;
Speak t.uly and each word of thine
  Shall be a fruitful seed;
Live truly and thy life shall be
  A great and noble creed."

—Selected.

A Serene Old Age (996).

Said one reverend in years and sanctified by much suffering borne with sublime serenity: "Wait! The clouds always break—the sun never ceases to shine behind them. I am past fearing storms of any sort; they always do good somewhere."

If any of us should attain fourscore, would that we might attain the rare beauty of her calm, pale face in which the large, gentle gray eyes shone with the constant light of content and peace. Lovely pictures have been made of such aged people, sitting where the setting sun shone upon them with its glorifying rays. In this case she who knew that the storms were "doing good somewhere," seemed not to need Nature's illumination. An inward light seemed to brighten her dear face, as you may have seen some fine bit of transparent porcelain lighted by an unseen flame.

To grow more serene, more gentle, more confident of all ultimate good as years accumulate the evidences that the world is not a place of disordered misery in which suffering is the chief element and unavoidable pain the destined end and way of those who dwell in it, is the most beautiful phase of human existence.

Such as these have learned the potent charm of borrowed happiness and reflect the joy they see shining in your faces and gladdening your lives. The aroma of the flowers that do not bloom in their own gardens, perfumes their dwelling through the open casements which their generous hearts fling wide open to catch all the light and perfume the sun and air can bring. They do not talk of what they have lost, they tell you of what is flowing into other lives.

It is not rare for a lame man to enjoy the sure swiftness of another's speed; it is not unusual for the blind to sit and smile while others tell them how blue the sky is and how the swallows skim across the meadows and the sea. Here is again a part of the whole; the speaker grows eloquent because of his brother's lost sense and gains what is not his by nature in his effort to help him.

It is hard in the grip of overmastering fear or in dumb astonishment at evidences of wrongdoing among his fellows or in the face of appalling disasters to be still and wait in certainty that there can be no failure in the plan of our Creator, regarding that which is to complete the development of our race. Yet our finiteness has a narrow boundary and our vision is neither as keen nor as sure as a bird's.

Blessed are they who can wait and hope and take every drop of joy they can wrest from life in and about them, until they can see how the beautiful action and reaction of the great machinery brings out the best of this world and strengthens our hope of the life beyond.—New York Evening Post.

Unseen Angels (997).

Dr. Doddridge dreamed that he died, and, clad in seraphic form, was borne by an angelic attendant to a glorious palace in one of the rooms of which he left him, saying: "Rest here. The Lord of the mansion will soon be here with you; meanwhile, study the apartment." The next morning he was alone; and, upon casting his eyes round the room, he saw that the walls were adorned with a series of pictures. To his great astonishment, he found that it was his past life delineated there. From the moment when he had come into the world a helpless infant, and God had breathed into him the breath of life, until the present hour when he dreamed he died, his whole existence was marked down there; every event which had happened to him shone conspicuously on the walls. Some he remembered as perfectly as though they had occurred but yesterday; others had passed from memory into oblivion, until thus recalled. Things obscure in life, which had caused him pain, doubt, perplexity, uneasiness, were rendered clear now. The perils of his life were there—the accidents which had overtaken him in his mortal state, from all of which he had escaped untouched or but slightly hurt. One in particular caught his attention—a fall from his horse—for he recollected the circumstances well; it had been a perilous fall, and his escape was marvelous. But scattered in every picture, all along his whole career, he saw merciful, guiding, shielding angels, who had been with him unsuspected throughout his life, never quitting him, always watching over him to guard him from danger. He continued to gaze on these wonderful pictures; and the more he gazed, the greater grew his awe, his reverence, his admiration of the unbounded goodness of God. Not a turn did his life take, but it rested on some merciful act of interposition for him. Love, gratitude, joy, filled his heart to overflowing.—Selected.

With Faces Toward the West (998).

The Christian life is the ever ascending life. Eternal, it nowhere reaches its zenith. Its golden age is never in the past. No true interpreter of Christian life harks back wistfully to some experience along the way, but like Paul, aged, battle-scarred and bound, forgetting the things behind he reaches forward to the future crown. And, like Rabbi Ben Ezra, each soul that has found Christ's secret sings:

> "Grow old along with me,
> The best is yet to be,
> The last of life, for which
> The first was made."

There are, broadly speaking, three stages through which each life normally passes, and each of these stages contains its characteristic and proper satisfaction.

The proper satisfaction of childhood is sheer gladness. The child is care-free, innocent, abounding with vitality and satisfied just to be in action. He is easily pleased. His spirit is akin to the birds and flowers and needs no cause, nothing save a chance, to express the gladness that is in him.

The proper satisfaction of a grown man is happiness. His life is a network of conscious purposes. His satisfaction is found in the accomplishment of these purposes. He is ever setting up goals and striving for them—in business, in love, in the social relation, in personal morality, in human service. The feeling of worth which his life will have for him depends upon his success in reaching these goals. If he fails in love or in business or in service he is unhappy. If he succeeds he is happy. His purposes are his life and all things have meaning for him according as they help or mar these purposes.

But to old age these conditions and their satisfactions are denied. The bounding pulse of youth is gone and with it the thirst for play. Lacking strength and time, age has no heart to undertake new ventures in the realm of deeds. What satisfaction, then, has age? Must the soul live henceforth in memory only, the memory of past deeds done or foiled?

Not if somewhere on the way of life the soul has met with Christ! For Christ has that to give which transforms gladness and happiness into blessedness, and blessedness is a satisfaction the world cannot give and the world cannot take away.

The passing years cannot rob the soul of blessedness. It does not depend upon the strength of pulse or limb. It is not conditioned by the success or failure of the soul's purposes. Fortune comes and goes, but the blessedness Christ gives abides. Plans may tumble like a child's toy tower, tears may fall, the heart be broken, but through sorrow and ill-fortune the soul's faith may put forth leaves and blossoms as in perpetual spring.

Now blessedness is the inalienable and proper satisfaction of old age. Empty, indeed, and full of pathos is the aged soul in whom this flower has not begun to grow. The gladness that ripples on the surface of youth soon passes. The happiness that attends the success of life's enterprises will fade when the currents of energy cease to flow, But in the still depths of experience if the soul have blessedness it has a peace that passeth understanding.

And the reason why blessedness may abide with old age when other satisfactions have passed away is because it is a gift of God, depending, therefore, not upon the success of the fitful and finite purposes of man, but upon the constant and gracious purpose of the Father.

Gladness registers the soul's sense of its place in the world of nature. Happiness registers the soul's sense of its value in the world of human life. But blessedness registers the soul's sense of its worth to God.—From The Christian Century.

The Value of Life (999).

There are circumstances so afflicting and straitened, so tormenting and hampering, that we are apt to think we do well if only we do not cry out and let all the world know how we suffer; but there is a better thing to do always, and that is to set ourselves with patience and self-crucifixion to think of others and do our best for them. In the worst circumstances, in circumstances so perplexing we know not how to act, there remains a something to be done which we could in no other circumstances do, a good fruit to be borne which needs these grievous circumstances as its soil, and which, when it is borne, will be more sweet to our taste eternally than all the happiness which success and pleasure in this world can give. The fact that our Lord thought human life—a life in this very world that we have to live through—worth living, and the most capable life for spending a divine fullness of wisdom and goodness in, shows us that there are objects on which we may liberally spend ourselves in the persuasion that they will not disappoint us.—Marcus Dods, D. D.

"Once to Every Man" (1000).

"I can only pass this way once," somebody thoughtfully said concerning life. Have you ever thought how that note of oneness strikes through everybody's life in this world? In a moment—once a babe—once a child—once a youth; once becoming a young man or woman; once in the vigor of maturity; once in old age, should we live so long; once dying. All the stages we pass through only once. Really, when we come to think of it, our chance in this world is pretty narrow. If twiceness or thriceness were the note of our life here, a failure once or twice would not be so great a matter. But that grim fact of oneness makes living a mightily serious matter, doesn't it? So the question—how to make this one life of ours in this world nobly effective—is a very practical question for each one of us, is it not?—Wayland Hoyt, D. D.

In, But Not Of (1001).

Learn to be as the angel, who could descend among the miseries of Bethesda without losing his heavenly purity or his perfect happiness. Gain healing from troubled waters. Make up your mind to the prospect of sustaining a certain measure of pain and trouble in your passage through life. By the blessing of God this will prepare you for it; it will make you thoughtful and resigned, without interfering with your cheerfulness.

Be prayerful and you will be happy and innocent, and noble, too. Oh, my brethren, with deep earnestness would I urge you to pray, habitually, reverently, trustfully to pray to your heavenly Father, and never to rise from your knees until you feel that you rise victorious, and that you have been saying to God in the heartfelt purpose which gave might to the olden patriarch: "I will not let thee go, except thou bless me."—Frederic W. Farrar.

With God. (1002)—The heaven I desired was a heaven of holiness; to be with God and to spend my eternity in divine love and holy communion with Christ.—Jonathan Edwards.

The Only Unfading Crown. (1003)—Crowns and diadems are loseable things; it is only in the other world that there is a crown of glory that fadeth not away.—Matthew Henry.

"What Shall It Profit?" (1004).

What did Judas gain? The scorn of men, remorse, the death of a suicide. He lost his soul. "At Aix-la-Chapelle is the tomb of the great Emperor Charlemagne. He was buried in the central space beneath the dome; but the manner of his burial is one of the most impressive sermons ever preached. In the death chamber beneath the floor he sat on a marble chair—the chair on which kings had been crowned—and wrapped in his imperial robes, a book of the gospel lay open in his lap; and, as he sat there, silent, cold, motionless, the finger of a dead man's hand pointed to the words of Jesus, 'What shall it profit a man if he gain the whole world and lose his own soul?' "

A Beautiful Life (1006).

In one of the English cathedrals there is a monument to one of England's great and self-sacrificing bishops, Selwyn. Above the sarcophagus, which is of white marble, there is the recumbent figure of the great missionary, with a beautiful, placid countenance and the hands folded crosswise on the breast. A window, cross-shaped, filled with crimson glass, is so placed that when the noontide sun falls upon it, it throws the shadow of a blood-stained cross on the breast and face of the noble bishop beneath. It tells the secret of his beautiful life and of his peace. His life was made complete when he lived it under the cross. He walked humbly with Christ. And he did justly and loved mercy and was God's child.

Empty Lives (1007).

Think of the result of existence in the man or woman who has lived chiefly to gratify the physical appetites—think of its real emptiness, its real repulsiveness when old age comes and the senses are dulled and the roses have faded and the lamps at the banquet are smoking and expiring and desire fails, and all that remains is the fierce, insatiable, ugly craving for delights which have fled for evermore; think of the bitter, burning vacancy of such an end, and you must see that pleasure is not a good haven to seek in the voyage of life.—Henry van Dyke.

Spiritual Vision (1008).

Men see what they want to see. Mozart and a friend were walking when a lark soared toward the heavens singing as it went. "What a shot," said the friend. "What would I give to be able to catch that trill," said Mozart. A breeze arose. "It will startle a hare," said the friend. "What a diapason from God's great organ," said Mozart. Noah's raven found carrion and returned not; but the dove came back with an olive leaf. A man sees what he wants to see, and what he wants to see is the measure of the man. Jesus saw a vast and hungry crowd and was moved with compassion for them and fed them. The disciples a thronging concourse of tresspassers upon their privacy and asked that they be sent away. No doubt there is great need today for a change in conditions of life, but there is a far greater need for a change in us that we may come to see the conditions as they really are, and not as we with imperfect spiritual vision think them to be. Let us pray God to anoint our eyes that we may see as He sees.—Selected.

Souls With Bodies (1009).

I heard a gentleman say recently, and it seemed to me to contain fine thought-suggestion: "We are not these bodies of ours possessing a soul. We are living souls possessing these bodies." It makes quite a difference which view we take. In the one case we shall make looking after the bodily things, the food, the raiment, the housing, primary; in the other case, we shall make them secondary. I do not mean that we ought to neglect a reasonable care of the body, but that we should value that for its ministry to the real life, the life of mind, heart, conscience, soul; and that we should never allow it to take the place of this higher and deeper and better life. This means that we do not live to eat and drink and sleep: we eat and drink and sleep to live. This means that we do not live for pleasure and recreation, but that we have pleasure and recreation in order the better to live. The human mind is naturally hungry for knowledge, it wants to know. The human heart is naturally hungry for companionship, it wants to love. The human conscience, in its best estate today, is hungry for justice and equity, for uprightness and progress in personal character; it wants to see fair play; it wants to find itself advancing with every new day toward an ever-unfolding ideal. The soul of the man expressing itself through spiritual sensibility is hungry for the realities of the spiritual life: it wants to begin that life, or, if already begun, it wants to develop it right where it is and in the hour that now is. It is all these things taken together—the affairs of mind, heart, conscience, soul—that make real living, make manhood and womanhood, make the trend toward unending improvement, the climbing after the better and the best. It is in service of all these that we want to "drink the cup and wear the roses and live the verses." Whatever else we do, we cannot afford to "quench the fires" which keep the intellect, the affections, the moral purposes, the spiritual sensibilities alive. And, if there are those in our time, and in this great country of ours, so badly off in material conditions that these fires will not burn in and for them, then it is your duty and mine, and the duty of every fortunate man and woman, to help make those conditions better. What wrong can be so great as that which shuts off from men and women and little children the opportunities of growth along the lines of mind, heart, conscience, and soul? We must not quench these fires in ourselves, we must do what we can to make it possible for them to burn for the least fortunate of our brothers and sisters.—Rev. F. A. Hinckley, in the Christian Register.

Our Work a Divine Calling (1010).

There are hours in which work is transfigured—in which it does not appear drudgery, but a mission; in which every duty is attractive. All work then becomes a divine calling; and we see that men are not only called to be apostles, but also called to be carpenters, called to be merchants, soldiers, sailors, called to be artists, inventors; and that one can sweep a room for the sake of God, and be happy in doing it. Until our work is thus transfigured, and we see religion in it, it must be often a burden and a drudgery.—James Freeman Clarke.

A Crowned Soul (1011).

Any one that sets out in this life for the purpose of being happy will have a pretty tough time of it. There is not happiness enough in the world to go around, and the kind of which there is enough is not worth having. No one can ever be built up into a crowned soul by being favored with happiness. But when you go in for the best things, the fundamental things, and keep on doing so, somehow or other you will be likely to have a good deal of trouble and pain; but it will be pain which will have something divine in it, and something you would not exchange for any so-called happiness under the sun.

We are going to be through with this life before very long. The longest life is short when it is over; any time is short when it is done. The gates of time will swing to behind you before long. They will swing to behind some of us soon, but behind all of us before long. And then the important thing will not be what appointments we had, or what rank in the conference, or anything of that sort; not what men thought of us, but whether we were built into His kingdom. And if at the end of it all, we emerge from life's work and discipline crowned souls, at home anywhere in God's universe, life will be a success.—Borden P. Bowne.

Truth and Right Immortal (1012).

To us, limited by the environments of our earthly existence, seeing "as through a glass, darkly." this is the supreme lesson of Eastertide; that there is no death for truth and right. We cannot turn in any direction but we see re-enacted the tragedy of the Nazarene and the Cross. "Truth forever on the scaffold, wrong forever on the throne." For wrong, in its absolute sense, includes all the folly, the ignorance, the weakness of the race. Truth, honor, and virtue are ever on trial before the courts of earth, ever being condemned to the cross. And we, like the faithful women at the tomb, weep over our fallen idols, "not knowing the power of the resurrection." Like them, we bring our sweet spices to anoint the dead body, thinking that nothing is to be done; that the three days have become the type of all the days to follow. "But the three days pass, and then, joy of all joys, comes the resurrection morn! Hopes renewed, promises fulfilled, joy succeeding sorrow, victory following defeat! 'Peace be unto you,' is the salutation of the risen Christ."

Working Toward the Same Goal (1013).

No man has ever done his best; no man has shown fully what there is in him; no man has really made himself known; the tragedy of life is its solitudes. We walk alone. No one understands. We cannot reveal ourselves even to those most with us. The tragedy of life is its loneliness.

> "Yes! in the sea of life enisled,
>   With echoing straits between us thrown,
> Dotting the shoreless watery wild,
>   We mortal millions live alone."

> "The irresponsive silence of the land,
>   The irresponsive sounding of the sea,
> Speak both one message of one sense to me:
>   Aloof, aloof, we stand aloof."

Is that forever to be so? Will the unfolding, the self-disclosure, never come? We may think, indeed, that to great souls this is given in the present world—that Dante and Milton and Shakespeare and Raphael and Angelo and Solon and Plato and Beethoven did reveal themselves fully. What fatuity! It is said of Ole Bull that he was found on the wet rocks at night, drawing the bow over his violin. He said he was trying to put into his violin the anguish of the sea. He could not, nor could any Beethoven or Handel, Milton or Raphael unfold what they felt —in their own souls. Think of what they heard and saw and felt! The picture was larger than the canvas. "It is not lawful for a man to utter," said the apostle of his own vision when he had his glimpse of heaven; not unlawful because it was forbidden, but because it was beyond his powers. It is no less true of the visions of Dante and Beethoven and Fra Angelico. It was not possible, not "lawful." It is always so. Man cannot express himself here. Hence the need for heaven, that there may yet be another opportunity.

And if so concerning majestic souls which from their urns still rule the world, if they could not utter in speech or chisel or brush the things they felt, what shall we say of common humanity, those who never have been even awakened to their powers, but are like those who sleep beneath the yews of the ancient English churchyard, who, had they been awakened,

"The rod of empire might have swayed,
Or waked to ecstasy the living lyre?"

The tragedy of this world is its incompleteness. Therefore heaven is a necessity. Life must be more than a broken arch.

There is a piece of sculpture by French. It is of a youth chiseling with passionate haste and enthusiasm the marble, and already the form of a sphinx appearing. But as he works, making haste to produce his masterpiece, a dark form stands beside him, sable-clad, silent. She touches the uplifted hand holding the mallet. It is all over. The sable figure is Death. The artist is falling dead, and his lifework? It is incomplete beside him.

Now we make a point that the Power which has endued us with life can make life go on if He wants to. He who has brought before the universe a being like man, a being that loves Him, worships Him, that feels and suffers like a god, has not so impoverished Himself in power that He cannot cause that being forever to continue and to grow and mature, if He wants him to do so. God is not a bankrupt in His own universe. He has not set in motion a scheme of things which ends, as far as man is concerned, in a mockery; that is, he has not if he is a Christlike God. That artist is entitled to finish his masterpiece. It is in him. He has a right to make himself known.

Sometime, somewhere, in the ample ages and the boundless creation I shall attain to what I have dreamed. I shall see the Pilot's face when I have crossed the bar. I hear the Pilot saying now, "Rejoice, be glad, your great, your real reward shall not fail you. Your great reward is in heaven." The supreme reality is heaven.—From "Easter Reflections."

The Surrendered Life. (1014)—No man has ever lived in perfect surrender to the will of God unless he had made a free surrender of his life to the world.—Rev. R. J. Campbell, M. A.

Too Busy to Tell About Jesus (1015).

While evangelistic tent meetings were in progress in a certain section in New York City, a little girl in an Italian center came to her mother and asked her to tell about Jesus. "I am too busy," was the weary mother's reply. "Go to the tent, and the people there will tell you about Him."

Good mothers, with family cares and labors to fill the days and nights, are very busy women. They find very little time for anything else. Some find no time for needed rest, and are worn down into invalidism or early death.

But however busy, no good mother can ever be too busy to tell her children about Jesus, about the supremely important things that concern the life and eternal destiny of the children for whom she labors and cares.

Oh, what an opportunity lost, when a child's heart is hungrily open for a mother's teaching, and she turns the child away! How many there are who forego their sacred privilege and neglect their most precious opportunities for service?—Selected.

Reliability (1017).

"One cold morning in February we stood looking out upon a world encased in an icy armor which sparkled with unrivaled beauty in the sunshine. 'Beautiful!' said one. 'Yes, it is very beautiful, but it will all be gone before noon.' The little restless maiden, quiet for once as she gazed upon the glory, looked up and brightly said: 'Never mind. There'll be something else beautiful tomorrow.' The Lord who hath done great things for us, whereof we are glad, is doing, and will continue to do, great things for us, whereof we shall be glad. 'Jesus Christ is the same yesterday and today, yea and for ever.' "—Record of Christian Work.

Peace Amid Tumult (1018).

The olive leaf is bitter but it is a sign of peace. However much the deluge may welter around us, that holy, heavenly dove of peace is ready to descend into our hearts and rest therein; and if the plucked leaf which she bears to us from God in heaven seems bitter to us, yet none the less it is a leaf of the tree of life, a green leaf from that tree whose leaves are for the healing of the nations.—F. W. Farrar.

Flee From Death (1019).—Senor Castelar was once strongly opposed to the death penalty in the army, but later in his life he urged it, because, he said, "The soldier would not face death unless certain death were behind him if he recoiled."

Loving Words Unuttered (1020).

You remember how Tom Brown was off on a fishing excursion when he heard of the death of his old school master, Arnold of Rugby, how he started back at once and sat down alone in the chapel where the Doctor had already been buried under the altar, and how he turned to the pulpit and leaning forward with his head in his hands, groaned aloud. "If he could only have seen the doctor again for one five minutes; have told him all that was in his heart, what he owed to him, how he loved and reverenced him, and would by God's help follow his steps in life and death, he could have borne it all without a murmur. But that he should have gone away forever without knowing it all, was too much to bear."

Such sorrow as Tom Brown's has been the portion of countless mourners throughout the ages. What kind words are said of the dead, and how often his friends say, "If he only could have known how others regarded him!" "Oh, the anguish of the thought," writes George Eliot, "that we can never atone to our dead for the stinted affection we gave them, for the little reverence we showed to that sacred human soul that lived so close to us, and was the divinest thing God had given us to know." Anguish was Mary of Bethany's portion when her Lord was crucified, but there was no bitter self-reproach mingled with it. She had shown Him her love, she had anointed Him while living.—Tarbell.

The Riper Life (1021).

As year by year we grow older, from childhood into youth, from youth into manhood, then on into middle age, we find the other spiritual world growing ever larger. The circle of human forms that live around us lessens in number, but the memories that constitute this other world fasten themselves upon us and cling with an undying hold. By every lasting separation, with every new and final good-by, we are just so much more enriched within ourselves. Our life is no longer merely what we see around us; it consists not simply of the friends we meet, whose hands we shake, whose voices we hear, whose homes we share; for there is ever growing this other and larger sphere within. Nature on the outside does not change. The sunlight continues the same, the sky is a blue overhead, the grass may be just as green, or the snow be just as white and pure; and yet for us it is not the same. When we were young we lived in this blue sky and sunlight and snowfall and raindrop; it was all the life we had. Now, as we grow and ripen, we have so much more life within, so many other lives are added to our own that nature and its beauties fall into the background, and the world for us seems to be, above everything else, a world of souls. It is like an invisible host of feelings and memories that are to us for a possession everlasting.— Walter L. Sheldon.

Life's Best Prize. (1022)—Far away the best prize that life offers is the chance to work at work worth doing.—Theodore Roosevelt.

The New Morning (1023).

O that our new-born piety every morning might match with our new-born "mercies!" O that we could perceive, each morning, all the dear faces that meet us—the familiar affections, and all that nature paints, and all the happiness which bestrews our path—and all God's forgiveness, and all God's favors, and promises, and God's presence— as "new" things, to be taken, to be studied, to be admired, to be echoed back in praises and homage—just as a star new created! A creation! a creation for me! We shall best take our reflection of God, and be like Him, if we are always trying to go on, every day, to some "new" thing; some "new" attainment in the divine life; some "new" work done, and dedicated to Him; each "new" morning finding its echo in a "new" trait of holiness! And O, what a standard we should set! to what heights we should reach, before the year is over.—J. Vaughan.

The Gift of Life (1024).

Life is beautiful. Life is welcome. The spring is welcome because it comes bringing life. The fields rejoice, the trees of the wood clap their hands, and all nature sings. Welcome spring! Welcome life! When children look into the nest of a little bird and see the shell broken and the young bird bursting its sepulcher and coming forth alive, they leap for joy. When one who has been almost drowned is resuscitated and begins to breathe, there is joy and gladness. When the father takes his little child in his arms and realizes that she is his own living child, his heart throbs with joy. There is not gold enough in all the world to pay for the life of that little child.—Selected.

Make Friend of Trials. (1025)—Make friends with your trials, as though you were always to live together, and you will find that when you cease to take thought for your own deliverance, God will take thought for you.—Francis de Sales.

Sovereign Power. (1026)—Self-reverence, self-knowledge, self-control —these three alone lead life to sovereign power.—Tennyson.

A Noble Career (1027).

Here is a possible career for every one. Demonstrate the truth in your own living.

It will cost something. Again and again it will confront you with the hard choice between worldly prosperity and Christ's approval; between earthly ease and comfort and adherence to the right. But it's a noble choice if you choose the better part.

Anyone can pursue this career. All that it requires is a talent for fidelity. "Let him who will be 'great,' do thou be noble." Whatever other qualifications you may lack, you possess those requisite for this course.

"If you cannot write the story you can live it;
    If you may not make the music, be the song;
If you cannot paint the picture you can give it,
    Heart and soul the glowing canvas for the throng.

Sightless eyes shall see the colors in your action,
    Ears grown deaf shall hear the anthem in your deed.
Hearts unlearned shall find and count the holy pages,
    And the record of a life of beauty read."

No, it's not an easy path to tread. But they that wear soft raiment dwell in king's houses, and you are a soldier on the battle line; a toiler amid the tempest! And when the warfare is ended, when at last the tempest lulls, there's a crown, a port, a haven, and everlasting guerdon. And what does a little buffeting here amount to compared with what awaits those, who simply live the truth here, over there.—B.

The Deeds We Do (1028).

There are few who would be willing to be judged by the acts of their daily life, the manner of dealing with others, and the results that so often follow. We have a comfortable way of excusing ourselves for our mistakes and even for clearly defined injustice, as well as for our careless indifference to the plainest of duty calls, when something else seems more attractive—by offering "the will for the deed," declaring that we "meant well." We got sidetracked, that was all, and therefore those whom we have wronged, by what we have done, or left undone, have no real cause for a complaint.

Life would be an easy problem, were it so adjusted that days and hours filled with questionable deeds, with unworthy acts, which must react in injury to all concerned, could be atoned for by a weak declaration of a weaker remorse, and an assurance that our "intent" so pitifully worthless it failed to control our deeds should still figure great enough in God's sight to blot out the result of the loss sustained.

Even the sublime patience of the Master was strained by the professions, that meant so little, when the test was made of the real worth of those professions. "Why call ye me Lord, Lord, and do not the things I say?" He was taking into account their daily living, the things they did not, the things they claimed to believe. Words are but a painful mockery when they are not set as jewels in the deed that proves their worth. Broken promises hurt more because of the fact that someone knew how glad their fulfillment would make us, and promise only to go away and forget to be true to a careless vow too lightly made to keep its place in the memory. Something precious dies with the touch of an inexcusable neglect to do the promised "deed" of love, simply because it proved of too little importance to make itself felt at the right time.

When we have done battle with the insistent pain that follows in the wake of meaningless words, we can understand something of how the Master felt when those who cried one day, "Hosanna in the highest," so soon forgot, and cried "Crucify Him." They had called Him "Lord and Master" until it served them better to forget their promises of allegiance. And they were judged by what they did, not by what they had pretended to be.

If it be true that the foundation of our faith is laid in the acts of our everyday life, then surely if our words are to be considered, they must be the forerunners of our deeds, or they are meaningless. Let us be honest with God, honest with each other in "word and deed," remembering it is better to give the smaller pain of a refusal to do the things we care too little for, to hold them too sacred to be forgotten, than to give the far greater one of a disappointment to a love that trusted and believed beyond the mere words in which we clothed our promise.

> "The faith we hold is built on deeds we do,
>   As lofty temples rest on solid ground,
>   As through the earth-roots the flower is glory-crowned,
> And when our life is high, our creed is too."
>
> —Burlington Hawkeye.

Deeds Become Character (1029).

Transient deeds consolidate into permanent character. Beds of sandstone rock, thousands of feet thick, are the sediment dropped from vanished seas, or borne down by long-dried-up rivers. The actions which we so often unthinkingly perform, whatever may be the width and the permanency of their effects external to us, react upon ourselves, and tend to make our permanent bent or twist or character. The chalk cliffs at Dover are the skeletons of millions upon millions of tiny organisms, and our little lives are built up by the recurrence of transient deeds, which leave their permanent marks upon us. They make character, and character determines position yonder.

As said the apostle, with tender sparingness, and yet with profound truth, "he went to his own place," wherever that was. The surroundings that he was fitted for came about him, and the company that he was fit for associated themselves with him. So, in another part of this book, where the same solemn expression, "the second death," is employed, we read, "These shall have their part in . . . the second death," the lot that belongs to them. Character and conduct determine position.

However small the lives here, they settle the far greater ones hereafter, just as a tiny wheel in a machine may, by cogs and other mechanical devices, transmit its motion to another wheel at a distance many times its diameter. You move this end of a lever through an arc of an inch, and the other end will move through an arc of yards. The little life here determines the sweep of the great one that is lived yonder. The victor wears his past conduct and character, if I may say so, as a fireproof garment; and, if he entered the very furnace, heated seven times hotter than before, there would be no smell of fire upon him. "He that overcometh shall not be hurt of the second death."—Alexander Maclaren.

The Loom of Life. (1030)—We sleep, but the loom of life never stops; and the pattern which was weaving when the sun went down is weaving when it comes up tomorrow.—Beecher.

All Seeds Germinate. (1031)—Sow the seeds of life—humbleness, pure-heartedness, love; and in the long eternity which lies before the soul every minutest grain will come up again with an increase of thirty, sixty, or an hundredfold.—Rev. F. W. Robertson.

It is a glorious thing just to be alive. But ah! how much more glorious it is when we know that the life in which we rejoice will go on and not die; that when this house of clay, beautifully and wonderfully made, shall have been taken down; when it shall have become too fragile and weather-beaten by the storms of earth to hold us any more, we shall not be cast out to perish, but shall simply move on into some better and roomier house which the Eternal Love that holds us fast has provided for us! It is sweet and good to live, but how much sweeter and better when we know that what we call death will be merely a letting go of what which we can no longer hold, a casting off of that which can no longer serve us; a going out from that which is but a prison door, and when everything that is mortal about us will be swallowed up in the more abundant life!—David H. Greer.

Teach Me to Live (1032).

Instead therefore of calling the long time of weariness a "lingering here," we might better call it, as Job did, "a patient waiting all the days of our appointed time till our change come." If patience is to "have its perfect work that we may be perfect and entire, wanting nothing," we must let God take His own time as well as His own way for bringing the great release.

> Teach me to live! 'tis easier far to die,
> Gently and silently to pass away;
> On earth's long night to close the heavy eye,
> And waken in the realm of glorious day.

> Teach me that harder lesson, how to live
> And serve Thee in the darkest paths of life;
> Arm me to conflict, strength and patience give,
> And make me more than conqueror in the strife.
> —Voices of Comfort.

A Crowned Soul (1033).

Any one that sets out in this life for the purpose of being happy will have a pretty tough time of it. There is not happiness to go round, and the kind of which there is enough is not worth having. No one can ever be built up into a crowned soul by being favored with happiness. But when you go in for the best things, the fundamental things, and keep on doing so, somehow or other you will be likely to have a good deal of trouble and pain, but it will be pain which will have something divine in it, and something you would not exchange for any so-called happiness under the sun.

We are going to be through with this life before very long. The longest life is short when it is over; any time is short when it is done. The gates of time will swing to behind you before very long. They will swing to behind some of us soon, but behind all of us before very long. And then the important thing will not be what appointments we had, or what rank in the conference, or anything of that sort; not what men thought of us, and whether we were built into His kingdom. And if, at the end of it all, we emerge from life's work and discipline crowned souls, at home anywhere in God's universe, life will be a success.—Selec'

Life's Conflict (1034).

Life is meant to be one long conflict. The condition under which we work in this world is that everything worth while has to be done at the cost of opposition and antagonism, and that no noble service or building is possible without brave, continuous conflict. Even upon the lower levels of life that is so. No man learns a science or a trade without having to fight for it. But high above these lower levels there is the one on which we are called to walk, the high level of duty, and no man does what his conscience tells him or refrains from that which his conscience sternly forbids without having to fight for it. We are in the lists and compelled to draw the sword, and if we do not realize this, that all nobility, all greatness, all wisdom, all success, even of the lowest and most vulpine kind, are won by conflict, we shall never struggle for lower purposes, for bread and cheese, or wealth or fame, or love, or the like, with a comparatively light heart; but if there once has dawned upon a young soul the whole majestic sweep of possibilities in its opening life, then the battle assumes an aspect of solemnity and greatness that silences all boasting.

There is no room for boasting, but there is room for absolute confidence. You, young men and women, standing at the entrance of the amphitheatre where the gladiators fight, may dash into the arena with the most perfect confidence that you will come out with your shield preserved and your sword unbroken.

There is one way of doing it. "Be of good cheer! I have overcome the world." That is not the boast of a man putting on the harness, but the calm utterance of the conquering Christ when He was putting it off. He has conquered that you may conquer. Distrust yourselves utterly, and trust Jesus Christ absolutely, and give yourselves to Him, to be His servants and soldiers till your lives' end. He was no self-righteous braggart, but a very rigid judge of himself, who, close by the headsman's block that ended his life, said: "I have fought a good fight; I have finished my course; I have kept the faith." "Put on the whole armor of God," and when the time comes to put it off, you will have a peaceful assurance as far removed from despair as it is from boasting.—Alexander Maclaren.

Life's Meanings (1035).

Who knows all the meaning of his own word? Who can explain all the issue and ultimate relationship of the simplest things which he does, in the church or in the harvest field, or in any sphere of life? We know not what part we are taking in the building up of God's fabric. Sometimes when we little suppose we are doing anything at all towards building the temple of God, we are working most industriously in that direction . . . Sometimes life's monotony wearies us. . . . Let us look back into history that our cheerfulness may be revived. Men do not know . . . The barley harvest may be as a sacrament, the open field an unroofed church, the gracious words spoken to strangers may come back again in prophecy and its sublimest fulfillment.—Joseph Parker.

Thank God for Work (1037).

Thank God every morning when you get up that you have something to do that day which must be done whether you like it or not. Being forced to work and forced to do your best will breed in you temperance, self-control, diligence, strength of will, content and a hundred virtues which the idle will never know.—Charles Kingsley.

Tangled Webs (1038).

The want which we vainly proposed to relieve, soon looks up at us with reproachful face from the still graves. The tears we failed to wipe away, dry upon the cheek, and leave us in the presence of the averted features of distrust, instead of the eye of sweet reliance. The just expectation which we have disappointed cannot be recovered; there must be a long undoing, before you can weave again, in even lines and pattern fair, the tangled web of life.—James Martineau.

ILLUSTRATIVE POETRY.

My Guide (1039).

There is no path in this desert waste;
  For the winds have swept the shifting sands,
The trail is blind where the storms have raced,
  And a stranger, I, in these fearsome lands.
But I journey on with a lightsome tread;
  I do not falter nor turn aside,
For I see His figure just ahead—
  He knows the way—my Guide.

There is no path in this trackless sea;
  No map is lined on the restless waves;
The ocean snares are strange to me
  Where the unseen wind in its fury raves.
But it matters naught; my sails are set,
  And my swift prow tosses the seas aside,
For the changeless stars are steadfast yet,
  And I sail by His star-blazed trail—my Guide.

There is no way in this starless night;
  There is naught but cloud in the inky skies;
The black night smothers me, left and right,
  I stare with a blind man's straining eyes.
But my steps are firm, for I cannot stray;
  The path to my feet seems light and wide;
For I hear His voice—"I am the Way!"
  And I sing as I follow Him on—my Guide.
                              —Robert J. Burdette.

Day by Day (1040).

If thou but diest day by day
To sins that clog thy homeward way,

Each night shall be a grave of care,
And morn a resurrection fair.

And daily be thy strength restored
By the dear Presence of thy Lord.
                        —Author unknown.

Separation Transient (1041).

When the weary ones we love
Enter on their rest above,
When the words of love and cheer
Fall no longer on our ear,
Hush! be every murmur dumb!
It is only "Till He come."
                        —Bickersteth.

The Years (1042).

Sunrise, and noon, and sunset,
  And day slips into day;
Twilight, and dark, and daylight—
  The years have rolled away.
Days that have brought their honors,
  And days that left their scars—
Over it all the marvel
  Of each night with its stars.

Sunrise, and noon, and sunset,
  Day will slip into day;
Twilight, and dark, and daylight,
  The years will roll away;
Sunshine, and song, and gladness,
  Fair dreams that come in sleep,
Bird song, and nodding blossoms—
  These are we fain to keep.

Darkness, and light, and shadows,
  Sorrow, and golden cheer,
Blend into God's completeness,
  Into the finished year,
Into a memory fabric
  Woven of shade and shine—
These are the years unfolding
  In lives like yours and mine.

          —Wilbur D. Nesbit.

Gems From Browning (1043).

I am a wanderer! I remember well
One journey, how I feared the track was missed,
So long the city I desired to reach
Lay hid; when suddenly its spires afar
Flashed through the the circling clouds. You may conceive
My transport; soon the vapors closed again,
But I had seen the city, and one such glance
No darkness could obscure.

          —From "Paracelsus."

    Ah, but a man's reach should exceed his grasp,
Or what's a heaven for?

Butterflies may dread extinction, you'll not die, it cannot be!

From the gift looking to the Giver,
And from the cistern to the river,
And from the finite to infinity,
And from man's dust to God's divinity.

Oh world, as God has made it! All is beauty!
And knowing this is love, and love is duty.
—From "A Guardian Angel."

We are in God's hand,
How strange now looks the life He makes us lead;
So free we seem, so fettered fast we are,
I feel He laid the fetter! Let it lie.
—From "Anarea del Sarto."

The common problem, yours, mine, every one's,
Is not to fancy what were fair in life
Provided it could be, but, finding first
What may be, then, find how to make it fair
Up to our means, a very different thing!
My business is not to remake myself,
But make the absolute best of what God made.

The Soul's Sunrise (1044)

Our lives have oft been darkened by the shadows of the years.
Our eyes ofttimes been blinded with a brimming flood of tears.
Anguish wrung the hearts within us with its iron grip of care,
And the loads 'neath which we staggered, our souls were loath to bear.

Life's ways stretched on before us under skies with storms o'ercast;
And our frail bark was driven hard before the bitter blast.
We have loved—and lost our loved ones. We reaped earth's golden field
But to have time's raging torrents sweep off the garnered yield.

We saw the sun in splendor to its flaming zenith rise;
To meet with sombre setting, and to walk 'neath leaden skies.
Often hope has died within us; and faith been slain by fear,
And life's dull and wintry landscape was overcast and drear.

And then! Life's starless darkness was all flooded o'er with light!
The dawn of an immortal day vanquished the gloom of night,
From out the riven sepulcher heaven's radiant sunlight shone.
Christ conquered death; won endless life, and shares it with His own.

All hail! blest Easter morning! with thy message bright with cheer.
All hail! faith's cloudless dawning breaks, dispelling mists of fear.
Our hearts now thrill with gladness as before they sank in gloom;
All the birds are set asinging, and all the flow'rs abloom.
—L. M. H.

Ashes (1045).

These ashes, too, this little dust,
  Our Father's care shall keep,
Till the last angel rise and break
  The long and dreary sleep.

Then love's soft dew o'er every eye
Shall shed its mildest rays.
And the long-silent dust shall burst
With shouts of endless praise.

—Selected.

The Pilgrim Soul (1046).

"March on, my soul, nor like a laggard stay!
March swiftly on. Yet err not from the way
Where all the nobly wise of old have trod—
The path of faith made by the sons of God.

"Something to learn, and something to forget:
Hold fast the good, and seek the better yet;
Press on, and prove the pilgrim hope of youth—
That creeds are milestones on the road to truth."

—Henry van Dyke.

The Good Shepherd (1047).

(From the Spanish of Lope de Vega.)
Shepherd! that with thine amorous, sylvan song
Hast broken the slumber which encompassed me,—
That mad'st Thy crook from the accursed tree,
On which Thy powerful arms were stretched so long!
Lead me to mercy's ever-flowing fountains;
For Thou my shepherd, guard and guide shalt be;
I will obey Thy voice, and wait to see
Thy feet all beautiful upon the mountains.
Hear, Shepherd!—Thou who for Thy flock art dying,
O, wash away these scarlet sins, for Thou
Rejoicest at the contrite sinner's vow.

O, wait!—to Thee my weary soul is crying,—
Wait for me!—Yet why ask it, when I see,
With feet nailed to the cross, Thou'rt waiting still for me!

—Henry W. Longfellow.

Responsibility (1050).

God has crammed both thy palms with living seed;
    Let not a miser's clutch keep both hands tight
But scatter on the desert's barren need
    That fragrant blossoms may reward God's sight.

God has dipped deep thy cup into His spring,
    Which drippeth over, it is so well filled;
Lend it to some parched life, and let it bring
    Laughter and song to voices drought has stilled.

God gave to thee His only well-loved Christ,
    Whose steps have smoothed the road that leads thee home,
Tell those whose road is rough, whose way is missed,
    That He has called all weary ones to come.

So shall thy giving set for thee God's smile,
And thine own soul drink deep draughts of His love;
Earth's shadows shall grow bright as heaven, the while
A web of glory round thy life is wove.

—British Congregationalist.

Work (1051).

No man is born into the world whose work
Is not born with him; there is always work
And tools to work withal, for those who will;
And blessed are the horny hands of toil!

—Lowell.

Builders (1052).

We are building every day,
In a good or evil way.
And the structure, as it grows,
Will our inmost self disclose.

Till in every arch and line
All our faults and failings shine;
It may grow a castle grand,
Or a wreck upon the sand.

Build it well, whate'er you do;
Build it straight, and strong, and true;
Build it clean, and high, and broad;
Build it for the eye of God!

—I. E. Diekenga.

What Does It Matter? (1053).

It matters little where I was born,
    Or if my parents were rich or poor;
Whether they shrank at the cold world's scorn,
    Or walked in the pride of wealth secure.
But whether I live an honest man,
    And hold my integrity firm in my clutch,
I tell you, brother, as plain as I can,
        It matters much.

It matters little how long I stay
    In a world of sorrow, sin and care;
Whether in youth I am called away,
    Or live till my bones and pate are bare.
But whether I do the best I can
    To soften the weight of adversity's touch
On the fading cheek of my fellow men,
        It matters much.

It matters little where be my grave,
  Or on the land or in the sea,
By purling brook or 'neath stormy wave,
  It matters little or naught to me
But whether the Angel Death comes down
  And marks my brow with his loving touch
As one that shall wear the victor's crown,
        It matters much.
                            —Noah Barker.

A Scotch Epitaph.

Our life is but a winter's day.
Some only breakfast, and away;
Others to dinner stay
  And are full-fed;
The oldest man but sups
  And goes to bed.
Long is his debt
  That lingers out the day;
He that goes soonest
  Has the least to pay.

TEXTS AND TREATMENT HINTS.

The Illusiveness of Life (1054).

By faith Abraham, when he was called to go out into a place which he should after receive for an inheritance, obeyed; and he went out, not knowing whither he went. By faith he sojourned in the land of promise, as in a strange country, dwelling in tabernacles with Isaac and Jacob, the heirs with him of the same promise: for he looked for a city which hath foundations, whose builder and maker is God.—Heb. 11:8-10.

I. The deception of life's promise.

II. The meaning of that deception.

Let it be clearly understood, in the first place, the promise never was fulfilled. I do not say the fulfillment was delayed. I say it never was fulfiled. Abraham had a few feet of earth, obtained by purchase,—beyond that, nothing; he died a stranger and a pilgrim in the land. Isaac had a little. So small was Jacob's hold upon his country, that the last years of his life were spent in Egypt, and he died a foreigner in a strange land. His descendants came into the land of Canaan, expecting to find it a land flowing with milk and honey; they found hard work to do—war and unrest, instead of rest.

And such is life's disappointment. Its promise is, you shall have a Canaan; it turns out to be a baseless, airy dream—toil and warfare—nothing that we can call our own; not the land of rest, by any means. But we will examine this in particulars.

1. Our senses deceive us; we begin life with delusion. Our senses deceive us with respect to distance, shape, and color. That which afar off seems oval turns out to be circular, modified by the perspective of distance; that which appears a speck, upon nearer approach becomes a vast body. To the earlier ages the stars presented the delusion of small lamps hung in space. The beautiful berry proves to be bitter and poisonous; that which apparently moves is really at rest; that which seems to be stationary is in perpetual motion: the earth moves—the sun is still. All experience is a correction of life's delusions—a modification, a reversal of the judgment of the senses; and all life is a lesson on the falsehood of appearances.

II. Our natural anticipations deceive us—I say natural in contradistinction to extravagant expectations.

"Whatsoever a Man Soweth, That Shall He Also Reap."—Gal. 6:7 (1055).

All these experiences were undergone by the same man: the persecutor was persecuted; he who shut up others in prison was shut up in prison himself; he who breathed out threatenings and slaughter against the saints was himself stoned, beaten with rods, and pursued by the vengeance of furious men. What are we taught by such facts?

I. That a man's life comes back upon him.—"Whatsoever a man soweth, that shall he also reap." One feels in reading such experience that the sense of justice is satisfied. Suppose that Saul had after his conversion settled down into a state of Christian comfort and enjoyment; in such a case there would have been a want of moral completeness. Paul himself would have been injured. To have allowed him to wash the blood of the saints off his hands, and to enter upon a course of personal luxury would have been to demoralize human nature. He must reap what he himself had sown! Such is the severe but beneficent law! This law keeps things equal. If any man could mingle bitter cups for others, and never be compelled to drain their dregs himself, he would soon become a devil. God shows him that his turn is coming. Every blow he strikes will be re-delivered upon himself; every pain he inflicts upon others will sting his own heart: every harsh word will come back to torment him.

II. That a man's Christian experience must be affected by the un-Christian life he has lived.—This is the most remarkable thing in connection with the subject. One would suppose that after conversion all the former life would be done away. Such is not the case. Physically it is not so; why should it be so spiritually? The man who has physically abused himself will feel the effects of his sin after conversion; old age will come upon him swiftly; his energies will decay before their time; his memory will betray him; and even trivial difficulties will fill him with dismay.

In reviewing these statements in the light of history and revelation we see:

First—That the distribution of penalties is God's work, and not man's. "Vengeance is mine," etc.

Second—That under all the apparent confusion of human life there is a principle of justice.

Third—That the greatest sufferings may be borne with patience and hopefulness. When did Paul complain of his lot? When did he say that he had suffered more than his share? From him let us learn "how good a thing it is to suffer and be strong."—Joseph Parker, D. D.

(1065.)—But ye, beloved, building up yourself on your most holy faith, praying in the Holy Spirit, keep yourselves in the love of God, looking for the mercy of our Lord Jesus Christ unto eternal life.—Jude 20:21.

I. Life is a building contract.

II. We are co-builders with God.

III. We are building for Eternity.

IV. Build well!

"No Man Liveth to Himself" Rev. 14:7 (1056).

I. Look at the text as it is interpreted for us by the section of the Epistle to the Romans in which it is found. That section is devoted to an elucidation of the principles by which the early Christians were to be guided as to their observance or nonobservance of particular festival days and as to their abstinence or nonabstinence from certain kinds of meats and drinks. "None of us," says the Apostle, "liveth to himself." However it may be with others, none of us Christians liveth unto himself. Each of us has accepted Christ as his Redeemer and Lord and is seeking in all things to serve Him, so if one eateth unto the

Lord, and if another eateth not, he eateth not unto the Lord. Because we are seeking to live to Christ, there is, in reference to all matters indifferent, perfect liberty to the individual conscience, and no one has a right to judge or set at nought another for doing that of which he is fully persuaded in his own mind, and which he is seeking to do as unto the Lord. Not our own pleasure, but rather the glory of Christ and the edification and peace and progress of the brotherhood, is to be made the rule of our lives.

II. Consider the text as an inevitable condition of human evistence. No man's life terminates on himself alone, but each of us exerts an influence through his character and conduct upon all with whom he comes in contact. Make haste, then, and see whether the effect of your life on others is good or evil; and if evil, seek for goodness and renewal at the hand of Christ.

III. Read the text as it expresses the deliberate purpose of every genuine Christian. The true believer forswears self. From the moment of his conversion his whole being runs Christward. The volume of the river may be small at first, but, small as it is, its direction is decided, and it gathers magnitude as it flows, for it drains the valley of his life. He keeps himself for Christ, because he owes everything to Christ. —W. M. Taylor, D. D.

Our Use of the Materials (1057).

A well known modern artist, having visited Italy last winter, was asked which of the great masterpieces of art he had seen there impressed him most. He answered, "Fra Angelico's painted slab. It proved the sincerity of his devotion to art. The man who could paint angels was as faithful and zealous when it became his duty to paint a stone, as though his subject had been one of transcendent merit."

The power of a great artist is proved, not by the size or loftiness of his subject, but by the way he treats it, however small it may be. Giotto showed more skill in drawing a single letter than many painters have displayed upon huge, crowded canvasses.

God puts materials into the hands of every human being for one great work, and that is the highest development of His own life. Each of us would like to make life illustrious in deeds that declare their importance to men, but the materials with which we have to do seem meager and mean. A dull brain, inherited disease, vulgar surroundings, what, we think, can the longing soul do with these? It may be that the dull stone is given to us to paint, not the face of an archangel.

God will not blame us for the materials which He Himself has given. He will take account only of the way they are used. It was the Great Teacher who declared that it was He who had been faithful over a few things who was made ruler over many things.—Youth's Companion.

Life (1058).

Every human life is a fresh one, bright with hopes that will never be realized. There may be differences of character in these hopes; finer spirits may look on life as the arena of successful deeds, the more selfish as a place of personal enjoyment.

With man the turning point of life may be a profession—with woman, marriage; the one gilding the future with the triumphs of intellect, the other with the dreams of affection; but, in every case, life is not what any of them expects, but something else.

3. Our expectations, resting on revelation, deceive us. The world's history has turned round two points of hope; one, the first—the other, the second coming of the Messiah. The magnificent imagery of Hebrew prophecy had described the advent of the Conqueror; He came—"a root out of a dry ground, with no form or comeliness; and when they saw Him there was no beauty in Him that they should desire Him."

II. The second inquiry, therefore, is the meaning of this delusiveness.

1. It serves to allure us on. Suppose that a spiritual promise had been made at first to Israel; imagine that they had been informed at the outset that God's rest is inward; that the promised land is only found in the Jerusalem which is above—not material, but immaterial; that rude, gross people, yearning after the fleshpots of Egypt—willing to go back into slavery, so as only they might have enough to eat and drink —would they have quitted Egypt on such terms? Would they have begun one single step of that pilgrimage, which was to find its meaning in the discipline of ages?

2. This non-fulfillment of promise fulfills it in a deeper way. The account we have given already, were it to end there, would be insufficient to excuse the failure of life's promise; by saying that it allures us, would be really to charge God with deception. Now, life is not deception, but illusion. We distinguish between illusion and delusion. We may paint wood so as to be taken for stone, iron, or marble—this is delusion; but you may paint a picture, in which rocks, trees, and sky, are never mistaken for what they seem, yet produce all the emotion which real rocks, trees, and sky, would produce. This is illusion, and this is the painter's art; never for one moment to deceive by attempted imitation, but to produce a mental state in which the feelings are suggested which the natural objects themselves would create.—Frederick W. Robertson.

"Every Man That Hath This Hope Purifieth Himself."—1 John 3:3
(1059).

Performance must not make a mock of possibility.

> Here faith is ours, and heavenly hope,
>   And grace to lead us higher,
> And there are perfectness and peace,
>   Beyond our best desire.
> Oh, by Thy love and anguish, Lord,
>   Oh, by Thy life laid down,
> Grant that we fall not from this grace,
>   Nor cast away our crown.

This word of the apostle brings a wind from the high places of God and Eternity to cleanse and freshen into health our common life. Do you remember Shelley's cry to the west wind that swept his island home?

He felt there was life in it, and, perhaps, life for him; he saw how it sent the swift clouds before it, tipped the sea waves with silver, lifted even the dead leaves into semblance of life, and he longed to share the impulse of its strength.

> Oh, lift me as a wave, a leaf, a cloud!
> I fall upon the thorns of life! I bleed!
> A heavy weight of hours hath chained and bowed
> One too like thee, tameless and swift and proud.

What he needed was not the wild west wind, but the Spirit of God to sweep over his wondrous faculties; and, wizard of song as he was, what mightier music the world might have had! And what we need also to touch our powers to finer endeavors, and our lives to nobler issues, is the free play upon our spirits of the wind from the hills of God; "the powers of the world to come."—"Sculptors of Life."

"Seek Those Things Which Are Above."—Col. 3:1 (1060).

The call that comes to us today is more imperious and immediate. This mortal must put on immortality. Life and character and all that makes life worth having are not a gift, but a conquest and an achievement. "If ye are risen with Christ, seek the things that are above where Christ is"—not above in the heavens, which no hand has yet charted, but above in the timeless relations of the ideal life where we may always look for him, however high we ascend.

This mortal must put on immortality—not as when one changes the soiled working-garb for holiday dress, but rather as when one gears the machinery of his present task into the wheels of eternity. Do not think that you can get through these transient earthly things, and put them out of sight, and be done with them. Rather must the habits, the characteristics, the hopes of yesterday, be carried forward into the work of tomorrow. So that what we need, is to acquire the thoroughness, the composure, the self-restraint, the perspective which shall help us do the work of tomorrow, whether that tomorrow find us working there or here. —Selected.

"Therefore, My Beloved Brethren, Be Ye Stedfast, Unmoveable."— 1 Cor. 15:58 (1061).

I. The duty which is connected with our being steadfast and unmovable in the faith of the resurrection, and of the resurrection life, is (1) to be about the work of the Lord; (2) to abound in it; (3) to abound in it always.

II. The motive—your labor is not in vain. It is in the Lord that your labor is not in vain—empty, or void of result and issue. You enter into the work of the Lord as the Lord Himself entered into the work given Him to do. It belongs to Him to see that your labor in His work shall not be in vain. His labor is not in vain, (1) because He has gone, in that very body, the same man precisely that He was on earth, the same man complete, to present Himself before the Father whose will He has done and whose work He has finished, saying, "Behold, I and the children whom Thou hast given Me." He asks sentence to be passed on Himself in that body, and on what He has done and suffered in that body. He asks for a judicial award. The mere bettering of His condition, as a natural consequence and gracious owning of His past and forgotten history, will not suffice. He asks for a verdict on that history, as a history not buried in oblivion's indulgent tomb, but raised for righteous judgment. (2) And then, secondly, His labor is not in vain, since not only in His risen body does He challenge judgment on Himself and His work, but with that same risen body, He takes the work up and follows it out. He carries on in heaven the work which He had on hand on earth. He resumes it that He may carry it out to its endless issues of blessedness and glory in the new heavens and the new earth, wherein dwelleth righteousness. And as the Lord's own labor in the work is thus not in vain, so yours is not in vain in Him; and that for the same twofold reason.—"Life in a Risen Saviour."

"So Teach Us to Number Our Days."—Ps. 90:12 (1062).

A young man decides on a professional career in life. Compared with its anticipated duration, his days of preparation are comparatively few. He numbers them easily enough; three years in fitting for college, four years in college, and three in the professional school. Allowing forty weeks of study to the year, on the use made of these four hundred weeks depends the good or the ill success of his whole life. The "wise" student counts carefully the weeks of each passing term, not because they are so many, but because they are so few; so almost nothing, indeed, compared with the many decades which he means to fill with useful and honorable work in the world. Gladstone is reported as having once punctuated the difference between the student who thus thoughtfully numbers his college days and one who lets them slip by carelessly unimproved, by saying, "One-third of our Oxford and Cambridge men come only because they are sent; one-third come with no other idea than that of having a good time. The other third rules England!"

If it be worth while asking, "Where and how shall I spend these few, fleeting days of my earthly life?" how vastly more to the purpose must it be to ask, "Where and how shall I spend my eternity?" It is a short problem to reduce the traditional "three-score years and ten" to the twenty-five thousand five hundred and fifty days of which they are composed. True, they do seem so definite, to be a large sum. But the point to be considered is that it is, after all, a sum—a sum-total. Each day spent takes one from the number and brings us that much nearer the end. What, then, of even the longest lived of the antediluvian patriarchs? What of Methuselah, himself? Were we, too, to be multi-centenarians, how surely would come the hour when, looking back, we would be compelled to ask, "For what is our life?" and to answer, "Verily it is but a vapor which appeareth but a little while and then vanisheth away. —Ballard.

"Seek Ye First the Kingdom of God, and His Righteousness; and All These Things Shall Be Added Unto You."—Matt. 6:33 (1063).

Get at God's purposes. Grasp His character. Accept His commandments. Come to Him and know Him. That is the purpose of life.

It is a man's work. It is worth the doing. Many men are saying today, "Give us a man's work." They find the organization of life too intricate; its details, as they present themselves, too petty. They long for what requires a larger grasp, a more heroic effort, a more prolonged and steadier purpose, than they find in the vast majority of appeals that come to them for co-operation. Here is the summons that will satisfy every need. It is, Live your life! Recognize its meaning. Understand that it is to know God; to so find Him, and believe in Him, and live for Him, that all your life shall be drawn into that purpose and controlled by it for good.

One says: "My purpose is to cultivate myself. I have a right to make the most of my talents and my opportunities." So far good. The talents and the opportunities are God's good gifts. Life as possessing them is to be lived today, for opportunities pass and talents may be lost. But is your cultivation of yourself to the end that you may know God and serve Him? Otherwise you are wrong. Your life is going astray. Another says: "My purpose is to care for my family. That is all I can do. To clothe, to house, to feed, to educate them, takes all my strength. It is my task. No other will do it." That is well. There is no better task for you. But is it that you may fit them for God; to lift them to the plane of life in which they shall know him and be fitted for His service? Are you giving them the equipment with which they shall be children of God in a larger and truer sense, if God will, then you have been yourself? Another says: "My purpose is to do good, to help men." That is well. But why are you doing it? Is your devotion to your society, or your class, or whatever may be the agency to which you are devoting yourself, for your own satisfaction or for your own glory and self-praise, or because it is yours and not another's? Is it that, or are you doing it for God to promote His kingdom and make known His love? If so, you will be humble and patient, and considerate of others, and self-sacrificing. You will find your reward and your joy in the kindness of your own heart as at the close of the day you shut yourself up alone with God to thank Him for the privilege of rendering one more day's service. Here is the real purpose of life. The man who holds and is held by it attains life; and the man who turns from it, surely he loses his life.—Stimson.

SECTION TWO.

EXTRACTS FROM
FUNERAL SERMONS AND
ADDRESSES

Contents.

SECTION TWO.

I. GENERAL REFLECTIONS ON LIFE AND DEATH.

"AS A TALE THAT IS TOLD."

REV. JAS. W. FIFIELD, D. D.

"Born of love and hope, of ecstacy and pain, of agony and fear, of tears and joy—dowered with the wealth of two united hearts—held in happy arms with lips upon life's drifted fount, blue veined and fair, where perfect peace finds perfect form—rocked by willing feet and wooed to shadowy shores of sleep by siren mother singing soft and low—looking with wonders wide and startled eyes at common things of life and day—taught by want and wish and contact with the things that touch the dimpled flesh of babes—lured by light and flame and charmed by colors wondrous robes—learning the use of feet and hands, and by love of mimicry guiled to utter speech—releasing prisoned thoughts from crabbed and curious marks on soiled and tattered leaves—puzzling the brain with crooked numbers and their changing, tangled worth—and so through years of alternating day and night, until the captive grows familiar with the chains and walls and limitations of life.

And time runs on in sun and shade, until one of all the world is wooed and won, and all the lore of love is taught and learned again.

Again a home is built with a fair chamber wherein faint dreams, like cool and shadowy vales divide the billowed hours of love. Again the miracle of birth—the pain and joy, the kiss of welcome and the cradle song, drowning the drowsy prattle of a babe.

And then the sense of obligation and of wrong—pity for those who toil and weep, tears for the imprisoned, the despised, love for the generous dead, and in the heart the rapture of a high resolve.

And then ambition, with its lust of pelf and place and power, longing to put upon its breast, distinction's worthless badge. Then keener thoughts of men and eyes that see behind the smiling mask of craft—flattered no more by the obsequious cringe of gain and greed—knowing the usefulness of hoarded gold—of honor bought from those who would charge the usury of self-respect—of power that only bends a coward's keens and forces from the lips of fear the lies of praise. Knowing at last the unstudied gesture of esteem, the reverend eyes made rich with honest thought, and holding high above all other things—high as hope's great throbbing star above the darkness of the dead—the love of wife and child and friend.

The locks of gray and growing love of other days and half remem·
bered things—the holding withered hands of those who first held his,
while over dim and loving eyes death softly presses down the lids to
rest. And so, locking in marriage-vows his children's hands and cross·
ing others on the breasts of peace with daughters' babes upon his knees,
and white hair mingling with gold, he journeys on from day to day to
the horizon where the dusk is waiting for the night—sitting by the cold
hearth of home, as the last embers change from red to gray, he falls
asleep within the arms of her he worshiped and adored, feeling upon
his pallid lips love's last and holiest kiss."

No Death.

There is no death. The great plague of many lives is unreal and has
no more substance than the banks of clouds which seem to barricade
the ongoing of the ship at sea. They hang lowering over the waters and
lift themselves far into the sky yet they are penetrateable anywhere and
the long voyage of the deep need not stop because of them. True, the
passage through the fogs is not like the journey on a sunlit sea, yet
fog is not rock and beyond their dark outline will be brightness again
and the happy coast line of home. Now death is not real. It is an
experience in the career of a life. Yet in it we do not die. It is a time
of transition. Jesus called it sleep. It has its element of mystery and
change, yet the body alone feels its power. Man's soul dies not, but
goes steadily on through this gloomy experience as it has passed through
others before. Indeed, instead of death being an hour of death it is an
hour of life. It is not evening, but morning. We begin to truly live in
the life beyond this world, in all the largeness and joys of the spirit.
At death the soul like an imprisoned dove, with the morning in its wings,
leaves its cage of flesh and enters the fuller, richer life—the life of
eternal peace and growth and joy. That is, this may be the experience.
The sting of death is not death. Its sting is sin. And sin is ever self·
limiting and self-injuring. Let the soul have its true fellowship with
God; let it be unfolding in all the gracious experiences of life; let it be
increasing into the beauty of spirit and strength of service which were
in Christ and when death comes it will be like the breaking of a new
and happy morning over a landscape and every power will be quickened
and every joy will be deepened and every moment of the deathless years
will be full of the presence and gladness of God.—Rev. Jas. W. Fifield,
D. D.

THE LIVING DEAD.
REV. MYRON W. HAYNES, D. D.

We often speak of our friends who have departed as though they
were swept out of existence. It is difficult in the hour of grief to con·
ceive that they have simply changed relations. We say of the sun at
evening, "It has gone." Gone where? It has simply faded from our
vision to shed its light on some other part of the globe. We say of the
ship that gradually sinks from sight, "It is gone." Gone where? It is

Just wending its way across pathless waters to find, ere many days, a shelter in another harbor. Our friends have gone to find rest in another harbor and to shine in another realm.

It is with something of a shudder that we stand at the grave and hear the cold thud of the dirt falling upon the casket. The earth is claiming our loved one, and the sexton stands monarch of this sepulchral realm. Yet our loved one is not being buried, and the sexton's kingship is only imaginary. He cannot bury the memory of our loved one. That may abide with us in sweet fragrance forever. He cannot bury the influence of our dear ones. Wherever our lives have been touched and our characters moulded by the one who has gone, it abides. It is a deathless influence. No one can bury it. After all what we really loved and cherished in our friends is left to us. We did not love the fleshly hand nor the face of clay. It was the indefinable something which we cannot explain, and which is really with us after all. To the purest and noblest love there is no such word as death, and to all that was best and abiding in our darling, the grave and the sexton have no claim.—Rev. Myron W. Haynes, D. D.

DEATH AS EXPRESSED IN THREE CHRISTIAN PHRASES.

REV. GEORGE WOLFE SHINN, D. D.

There are three Christian expressions which come to mind today as we meet together at this funeral service. They are descriptive of the condition of a departed Christian. They have long been used in the Christian church in speaking of those who have reached the end of their pilgrimage here. These three expressions are: "Entered into life," "Asleep in Jesus," and "Forever with the Lord."

The first of these, "Entered into Life," brings vividly before us the fact that this is not our true life, or our final life. There is something so much greater and so much more significant than the life we now live in the flesh that we can speak of entering into life when one departs hence in the Lord, in the faith of Christ. There is something beyond the present so much more important than the present that what is now is scarcely worthy to be compared with it. The present life may be thought of as the vestibule of eternity. It is the mere entrance, as the porch is to the great temple. It is like the preface to the book which is to contain many chapters. It is as the prelude to the grand composition which shall develop many a theme in wondrous harmonies. There must be the porch to the temple, but it is vastly inferior. There may be a preface to the book which shall give some idea of the writer's purpose. The prelude may contain some hints and suggestions of the grand harmonies which are to follow. But it is not the porch or the preface or the prelude which are the important features. They are insignificant in comparison with that to which they lead. And so the life that now is so vastly inferior to the life that is to be, that we may well speak of one who has gone hence in peace as having entered into life.

The second expression, "Asleep in Jesus," brings deep comfort to those who think of the condition of the departed one. He has fallen asleep. The long weary day is ended and rest comes at length. Tired with life's trials and wearied with its burdens he puts them all aside and forgets them. He is as one who sleeps—and he has gone to rest with entire confidence, for he sleeps in Jesus.

You have seen the child as the day ends falling asleep so confidently in the arms of the mother. No fear of harm. Those loving arms are open, and with a sense of perfect security the little one seeks rest there. So the Christian makes no leap in the dark, goes with no uncertain rush into the future, but calmly rests in the arms of the Lord Jesus.

But sleep implies an awakening, and as there is no slumber of the soul, we are bidden to think of the resurrection. That is the awakening for the tired, worn out body, when the Lord shall call it forth to be changed into the glory of the body of the resurrection. Blessed sleep from which none ever wakes to weep.

Then the third expression, "Forever with the Lord," indicates the conditions under which the life beyond is spent. It is life with the Lord. It is life in His nearer presence. We are, in a sense, always with the Lord. Even here in this vale of misery, but to be with Him, in this higher sense, is to know more of Him, to be more conscious of Him, to be more receptive of His presence and to become more like Him in the grace of His imparted attributes.

To be with the Lord, in a Christian sense, is to grow beneath His favor, and to take into one's self what emenates from Him, so that there is implied a steady, happy progression in the beauty and stability of a righteous character. It is growing as growth was impossible here. It is becoming what men, tried and tempted in the life that now is, could not become.

Who shall describe the graces and the gladness of the soul thus developing in the life that is forever with the Lord? What words shall indicate what the soul is to be like that takes into itself those elements of the Christ life which will authorize the statement that when He shall appear we shall be like Him? Shall be like Him! Ever growing like Him! Forever with the Lord!

And so today, as we think of the departed follower of Christ, there come to mind those three significant Christian sayings: "Entered into Life," "Asleep in Jesus," "Forever with the Lord."—Rev. George Wolfe Shinn, D. D.

"AND PHAROAH SAID UNTO JACOB, HOW OLD ART THOU?"—GEN. 47:8.

REV. PROF. GEORGE L. ROBINSON, PH. D., D. D., L. L. D.

Life is not measured by the calendar, but by experience. We may live but a few years and yet experience much. Jacob had experienced much. To Jacob life was a pilgrimage, at the end of which was Death:

for even the patriarchs who lived long and saw many years were forced to die.

I.   Life as to years of experience has two points of measurement—the cradle and the grave.   You may be twenty, thirty, forty, or fifty years from the cradle, but how many are you from the grave?   Life is a journey already begun.   The march of time resembles the onward rush of a railroad train as it leaves the Hudson of life and moves westward toward the Mississippi of death.   At one station, the train stops to take on new passengers; at another, to let some off.   Seats are vacated by one group, and filled again by others.   The process is oft-repeated, but, at last, the engine blows the whistle, the final curve is rounded and we are brought into the depot of our destination—death.   For death is the final doom of all.   There is an Arabic proverb which says, "Death is the black camel that kneels at every man's door."   Sooner or later, we, too, must die.

II.   How old art thou?   To answer this all-important question, measure life by what you have experienced of the joys of Christian service, by the faith you have in Christ, and by the hope you have of eternal life.   If your measurements are satisfactory, then all fear of death will vanish.   Wrong views of death will disappear.   There are four common attitudes of the human mind toward death.   First, there is the crouching attitude, suggesting the predominance of death.   Second, there is the attitude of flight, suggesting a hope of escape, or as Hume was wont to put it, "a leap in the dark."   A third attitude is that of conflict, intimating a prospect of vanquishing death.   Lastly, there is an attitude of reconciliation, which denies the reality of death; death being swallowed up in victory.   The last is the attitude of the Christian.   To the question, therefore, "What is life" we may answer, Life is a patient waiting; death, a falling asleep.   Life is an apprenticeship.   "Man that is born of a woman is of few days and full of trouble."   Life is a struggle; oftentimes without much light or brightness.   But Christ is in the dark room with the soul which He redeems.   Life is a vestibule: it may be narrow and lampless, but it is straight before the door.   Life is short; short at longest.

III.   But what is death?   The ancient Romans were wont to inscribe upon their costly mausoleums the Latin word abreptus, "snatched," but the Christians later wrote upon their catacombs the simple inscription dormit, "he sleeps."   Death is a falling asleep for all who have seen the risen Lord.   To such, dying is just a part of living.

Death is like a bridge, one pier of which is on the unseen shore.   Over this bridge men pass into uninvaded rest.   All is night.   But the night of death is soon passed.   It is brief; how long we do not know.   Neither know we the occupation of our loved ones between death and the resurrection.   But the period at longest is brief, and doubtless pleasant.   The dead are in Christ's keeping.

IV.   What of Eternity?   Eternity is time extended; time is "the seedplot of eternity."   Or, to change the figure: "Time writes the table of contents; eternity writes the book."   Eternity continues time.   Life there begins where it left off here.   Very little is known about heaven.   The

theme is too vast for human comprehension. There is a silent reserve
about heaven throughout Scripture. Much is left to the sanctified imagination. But we may be sure that heaven means fellowship and companionship with God and Christ, and also with friends. Heaven also
means progress and advancement—in knowledge, in wisdom, in purity
and in power. It also means service. Christ doubtless continues to
use his disciples also in heaven. He has ten thousand posts of service.
He sends our departed ones on errands of love, as ministering spirits.
Heaven also means sovereignty. To one entering His kingdom, Jesus
said, "Have thou authority over ten cities." To another, "I will make
thee ruler over many things." To his disciples, "Ye shall sit on thrones,
judging the twelve tribes of Israel." While of all the saints, he said,
"And they shall reign forever and ever."—Rev. Prof. George L. Robin-
son, Ph. D., D. D., L. L. D.

THE GRAVE AND THE GARDEN.

REV. A. B. MELDRUM, D. D.

"There was a garden, and in the garden a new sepulchre."—John
19:41.

It was part of the ambition of the old-time Jew to possess his own
grave. There was no law, as with us, that prevented him being buried
in any spot he could call his own. The thrifty Jew, therefore would
select and purchase the site that seemed to him desirable for the purpose.
Grass was sown and flowers were planted and nurtured on the thin soil.
It was regarded as a sacred place, a consecrated spot.

Jerusalem abounded in such quiet and consecrated spots. And hard
by the hill of Calvary was a garden with its sepulchre, never yet used,
hewn out of the solid limestone rock, by one, Joseph of Arimathea, a secret
disciple of Jesus.

To this new tomb in the garden not far from the cross, loving hands
bore the scarred body of the dear Lord.

One or two thoughts suggested by this text:

I. There is a grave in every garden. No garden on earth, however
fair and beautiful, but hath is sepulchre new or old. Blooming flowers
and twining ivy may hide it from other eyes, but every man who hath
come to middle life knows the corner of his life garden where, hewn
out of the rock of experience, is a tomb in which lies buried something
to which he once clung as he did to life itself. Some aspiring hope, some
scheme of daring ambition, some disappointed expectation, some well-
laid plan that went "aglee," some blighted affection, some faith slain by
doubt, some doubt slain by faith lies buried in some nook or corner of
almost every life; and ever and anon, the mind betakes itself thither in
bitterness, or in joy, in comfort or in despair, to recall the occasion which
made a break in the even tenor of life, and made it ever after, different
from what it had been before, different for better or for worse. There
are other funerals besides those which wend their way solemn and slow
through our streets to the silent city of the dead. There are other

graves besides those marked by slab or shaft in memory of those who lie beneath. There are other deaths besides those which put a term to human existence. We do not know all that happens. You may know your neighbor well, and yet in his life as in your own, there is some little space walled off, shut in, a consecrated spot in the field of his own life which you cannot explore; a garden where there is a sepulchre, in which lie the remains of that of which he thinks much, but says little.

Sometimes the wall of reserve between friends falls away, or the little gate that has "private" marked on it opens and each finds something surprising in the other. Each finds his secret matched by the secret of the other. They look into each other's faces and as they clasp hands with a tighter grip, say each to the other. "I did not know of the grave in your garden."

It would help us all to a friendlier attitude towards all men, if we only would remember that there is a grave in every garden. That grave in the garden is the great equalizer of human life. It makes all men kin. For the most part it is selfishness that lends bitterness to human sorrow. It does this by leading us to imagine that ours is the only garden in which there is a grave, that ours is the only loss, the only pain, the only defeat, that we are unlike all others in respect to the trouble that has befallen us. The cure of this selfishness is sympathy. And the spring of sympathy is the knowledge that what we bear, others are bearing, that what we have lost others have lost, that what we suffer others have suffered or are suffering, that what we have buried others have had to bury. For there is no garden that hath not its grave.

II. A garden surrounds every grave, and we should live in the garden and not in the grave.

God intends that we shall live in the open air, in the sunshine and among the trees and the flowers, not in the dark, damp atmosphere of the grave.

We should thank God for the garden that surrounds the grave, for the new flowers that bloom in the place of the old flowers that have faded, for the new hopes that have sprung up in the place of the old hopes that have vanished, for the new desires and affection and purposes which have taken the places of those which have been buried. It may not be well to forget the dead, neither is it well to forget the living. Better indeed that we should forget the dead than that we should remember them in a way that unfits us for duty to the living.

Things are never as bad as they might be. The garden helps us wonderfully to bear up even in sight of the grave. The good Lord never permits such a calamity to befall any child of His as shall forever destroy in that soul the possibility of further happiness and joy. The winter may be long and bitter, but spring cometh anon, with its singing birds and opening buds, the annual miracle of Nature's Resurrection. There may be a long winter in the soul, a winter of sorrow and loneliness, but the spring cometh again with its mild winds from the south, and its blossoms of hope and of peace, making fair and beautiful the garden which surrounds the grave.

If unbelief ever planted a flower of hope, what man ever found it? If doubt ever sowed a seed of comfort, in whose sad heart did it ever bloom? Around what grave did infidelity ever make a garden? Nay, the garden that surrounds the grave was planted by Him who came into this world with power to say, "I am the resurrection and the life, he that believeth in me shall not walk in darkness, but shall have the light of life." The Bible rings with cry, "Be of good cheer." "Let not your heart be troubled." He who calls God his father, sees some things as God sees them. To the man of faith, even the pathetic side of life, the side that is clouded, has a rich significance. He is forced to look up for help, and looking up he sees, through his streaming eyes, the garden of holy promise and hope that surrounds the grave.

III. Friends, let us try to live in the garden instead of the grave.

Yes, there are sighs and tears, but he who trusts in Christ, and strives to live the Christ-life, may even weep with hope, and his sorrow at the setting of the sun is cheered by the promise of a better morrow. There is a grave in every garden, but, blessed be the name of God, there is a garden surrounding every grave.—Rev. A. B. Meldrum, D. D.

LOVE AND DEATH.

REV. LYMAN ABBOTT, D. D.

In the famous Watts collection is a striking picture entitled "Love and Death." Death, not vindictive nor malignant, but driven forward as by the forcefulness of an irresistible fate, presses her way into the door of a humble home. Love stands before it, pushed back upon the crushed roses that clamber above the doorway, and, with upraised arm and appealing eyes, in vain endeavors to stay the calm, silent, but unappeasable and irresistible Intruder. The picture appeals to every heart that has ever known sorrow. But are we sure that it is true? Is it love that resists death? Or is it self?

Centuries ago, before Christ's words had gone out into all the world bringing life and immortality to light, and turning the piteous hope born of despair into the joyous hope born of faith, the Pagan Plutarch asked this question, and in asking answered it. "When," said he, "they mourn over those who die so untimely, do they do it upon their own account or upon that of the deceased? If upon their own, because they have lost what pleasure they thought they should have enjoyed in them, or that relief they flattered themselves they should have received from them in their old age, their self-love and personal interest prescribe the measures of their sorrow; so that upon the result they do not love the dead so much as themselves and their own interests."

Christ Himself enunciated more clearly the same truth. "If ye loved me," he said to his sorrowing friends—and in that "if" there is a tone of reproachful questioning—"if ye loved me, ye would rejoice because I said, I go unto the Father; for my Father is greater than I."

Surely, to every sorrowing mother the dying child may say this; to every husband the dying wife; to every sorrowing friend the friend who is dying. Love rejoices in death; self grieves. And whether joy or sorrow is uppermost depends on this: whether love or self is supreme in the hour of grief. Is it not so?

What is death? The separation of the soul from the body. Is that a cause for love's grieving? Is this body so excellent an aid to large and holy living that we need mourn when a loved one leaves it? Few are there whose body is free from some positive ailment and pain; fewer still who are not harassed and burdened by its infirmities; none who does not at times feel hindered by incumbrances. As the music in the soul of the organist is more than he can interpret on the keys, as the vision of the artist is more than he can embody on the canvas or in the stone, as the dream of the poet is more than the words of the poem, so the life of the spirit is more than the interpretation of that life in words or deeds. The body is a cage; the cage laments the bird, but the bird does not lament the cage. No wonder that the flesh fights hard to keep its inmate within its walls; for when the spirit is gone the body is naught. When the glory departs, the tabernacle becomes a common tent, and is straightway taken down. But to be free from the perpetual decay of the earthly tabernacle, to be released from its pains and its infirmities, to be emancipated from its clogs and its incumbrances, to have the chrysalis break and the winged soul let loose—this hour of freedom is not to be dreaded before it comes, nor mourned afterward; but to be rejoiced in. Self sits by the tenantless prison cell and mourns; but love looks up and is glad that the prisoner has escaped into the liberty of the sons of God.

Death is translation out of darkness into light! out of mystery into the clear shining of the truth. "To die—to sleep: To sleep! perchance to dream." No! no! Great poet you are wrong. Death is not sleeping; it is awaking out of sleep. Life is a sleep—a dream. "What shadows we are; what shadows we pursue!" Sometimes it is an entrancing dream of ecstatic delight, or hope more yet ecstatic. Sometimes a horrible nightmare, of bitter grief, or of fear yet bitterer. But both are shadows and both disappear: the ecstasy of pain into an ecstasy of pleasure. As in dreams so in what we call life, only the shadows do we know; the realities that cast them are always just beyond our vision. Living is dying and dying is living. For in living we are always in transition and decay; and in dying we pass from the temporal to the eternal, from the mortal to the immortal, from the seeming to the real. The plant born in the darkness struggles through the darkness toward the sunlight and the air and the sweet songs of birds and the fragrance of spring, blindly pushing its way onward and upward, not knowing what it seeks. Who will mourn when it emerges from its mystery and its darkness into the light of God? This is what we call dying; going from the darkness, the perplexity, the unsolved mystery of earth into the eternal light. To know even as we are known; to find an interpretation of all our uninterpretable longings, and in God's gift of life more than all our unutterable prayers had sought—how can love mourn that this gladness has come to the loved one?

Dying is freedom from temptation and from sin. It is escape from the double I; this I that would not and yet does, that would, yet does not. It is going from the seventh chapter of Romans into the eighth, there to abide forever. On earth our best music is dissonant, for our instrument is sadly out of tune. To die is to be set in tune of God's eternal keynote—love. It is to come into harmony with one's self, and therefore with God; it is to come into harmony with God, and therefore with one's self. What is sometimes said as descriptive of especial characters every man might well say of himself: He is his own worst enemy. Can love, pure love, unselfish love resist such emancipation when it approaches, or lament it when it has come?

Alas for him whose busy hands have harvested nothing than that which death takes away! and to whom therefore death comes as a thief in the night. But for him whose life has been one of faith and hope and love, dying is coronation. Self may weep; but love will rejoice.—Rev. Lyman Abbott, D. D.

THOUGHTS ON DEATH.

RABBI J. LEONARD LEVI, D. D.

Life is a scene of care and earth is a vale of tears. Faith in the wise counsels of God leads us to find a benevolent purpose in our cares, and His revealed will bids us to convert the valley of sorrow into a gate of hope. Most of our trials can be met in the belief that relief awaits them; but what of that great affliction that enters all homes, when the last scene of all is enacted and the angel of death bears the loved one from our side?

It is as natural to die as to be born, says the philosopher. On the day of birth man incurs a debt, of which death is the payment. The price of life is death. All that is earthly, however precious and beautiful, fades away. Youth, with its bright visions, vanishes. Health declines and strength fails. All our priceless possessions, even love and friendship, pass away, and life itself is vanquished by all-conquering death. Whether earth's journey takes us over perilous mountains and alongside yawning abysses, or through flowering meadows and by murmuring brooks, at the end all must pass through the sombre valley of the shadow of death into the silent land of the pitiless tomb. There is nothing abiding but God, nothing indestructible but the Eternal Father of Mankind, from whom we come and under the shadow of whose pinions we ultimately rest in the everlasting abode of the blessed.

It is this hope that sustains us in the dark hour of numbing grief. Man is an immortal mortal. Standing for a while on a bridge uniting the mystery of birth with the mystery of death, he finally passes into the icy arms of death, to live again in the likeness of God, though his dust-born form repose on the cold bosom of the insensate earth. Night here means light elsewhere. Sunset here means sunrise there. Darkness now means dawn hereafter. The winter of death is the precurser of the spring of unending life.

Whatever death may mean for the departed, and we believe that it means peace and rest and beatitude, it means intense grief to those who survive and live separated from their loved ones. They die, who so much long to live—the healthy and the hopeful. They die who are most needed here—the protector, the provider. They die of whom the world has so much need—the benefactor, the benignant. They die that form the charm of life—our friendships, our loves. No heat ever parched more completely, no plough ever furrowed more surely, than does death sear and leave its lines of trouble on the heart of the bereaved. The young husband or wife, conjuring up the sweet and lovely dreams of a happy future, smiling and joyous in their pure devotion, with love's halo beaming above them, and affection's tie uniting them, are suddenly parted by the grim messenger; or those who for years have been joined by bonds of tenderness, whose love has gone hand in hand with the vow made at the marriage altar, who had been all faithfulness, all devotion, all self-sacrifice, are separated by the mournful angel. Or the stricken parents clasp the cold form of their beloved child, the pride of the home, the joy of their household, who has fallen asleep in death, crying all the time, "Why, O God, hast Thou smitten us? There is no healing to us."

In the day of desolation, in the hour when around us lie the broken fragments of our hopes and joys, in the day when we speak to the unresponsive clay and weep over the motionless form, none but the abiding God can help, nothing but the hope of immortality can assuage the bitterness of our grief. And when the first intensity of pain is over and time has accustomed us to our loss, nothing will prove of greater consolation than the precious memory of the beloved, whose days were rich in blessing. The radiant picture of the sainted dead will dwell in the memory of their survivors, and though dead, they will speak; though departed, they will influence succeeding generations for God and good, for righteousness and truth.

Death has all seasons for its own. It will strike the aged oak and blast the mossy bud. With sweet lullaby it will sing to sleep the babe in its innocence; with outstretched wing it will carry away the broken form of the aged. It will bear from the valley of earth to bloom in the land of evergreens, the bride robed in her joy; it will take from the vale of tears to the gate of hope, the widow clad in mourning. It respects not the spring or the autumn, the summer or the winter of existence. Its shafts speed in the bright noonday; its arrows fly at black midnight. When suns rise and set, when oceans ebb and flow, when buds peep and fruits are mellow, death is busy. All that live must die and as the days make their unseen marks upon the dial plate of time, our turn will come.
—Rabbi J. Leonard Levi, D. D.

DEATH NO STRANGER.

REV. JAS. W. FIFIELD, D. D.

I stop to think of death as I live in all the beauty and gladness of life. About me is the music of a busy world, the singing of forms of industry and the anthem of living joy. How sad to think of death as we drink from the full cup of an overflowing life. What dark meanings it has! What unknown mysteries it contains! How it stops the music as though all the instruments were to break! Death and the sigh falls from the lips and the sorrow penetrates the heart and the sun goes down upon the scene. But let us pause and think. Can this be true? Is death a stranger to us, some enemy whom we are to lock from the palace gate? Does death come to us but once and bring only a calamity for a gift? Deeper than all this is another truth. Death is no stranger. We are continually in its presence. Death is with us like the air we breathe or as the light of mornings which cease not to come. We are always dying. In our bodies the process is working now. With every act and with each new breath we die in part. And this is that we may better live. Nature is good to us and our constant dying is so that we may be new and strong and fresh for the labors and delights of life. Why, the books of science say that in every seven years we are changed and made anew in body. As death is a physical experience we are dying all the time and die completely in every seven years. Yet we fear it not for death is the only way to life. The only difference between this continual death and death as we think of it in common speech is that one is gradual and the other is more abrupt. The process is one. Each is the making way for life. Each is in the body only. Each is as it should be in the wonderful program of nature and life.

And herein is a happy argument for immortality. If the soul has perished not in all these deaths in life we may well believe that it will not perish when the body meets its simultaneous death. When one has reached the full age of seventy the body has died ten times and yet the soul with all its powers of love and knowledge, of purpose and memory, has lived on. So will it ever live on. Man changes his coat, but lives within each garment and the body is only the garment of the soul to be put away when outworn that the eternal part may be clothed with the beautiful raiment of the spirit.—Rev. Jas. W. Fifield, D. D.

"THEN COMETH THE END."—MATT 24:14

REV. C. A. JESSUP, M. A.

A day or two ago we were watching beside a bed of pain, "waiting," so we said, "for the end." Each sign of suffering wrung our hearts; and how ready were the hands of love to supply the needed palliative to give relief to the stricken body! We watched, and waited—was it for hours, or for days, or only for minutes? We could hardly tell. In the monotony of the sickroom, time is measured by heart-throbs, not by the clock, nor even by the rising and setting sun. Then came the moment of temporary excitement, when the absent ones were hurriedly summoned, when they said "the end is near," when the struggling breath came more and more feebly, when at last the finger on the pulse detected no answering throb. Then they said, "It is over." And through our tears we answered, "Thank God, the end was peaceful."

The end! Nay, not the end. 'Twas but a turning in life's path which then was reached by the soul we love; yet round that bend in the road we may not see. But that soul still journeys on; and what seemed to us an end, seems to it (so we believe) more like a beginning. The flowers of earth bloom not beyond that turning, round which has passed our friend; but other flowers, of the spirit life, are there. The journey seems by no means ended, to those who have passed through that episode in a continuous life, to which we, in our ignorance, give the harsh name of "death." The path still stretches on before the soul which has left its bruised and stricken, perhaps its worn-out, body behind in this world—a path which it now treads earnestly, trustfully, joyfully. Another "end" is now before it, another turn in life's unbroken but ever-changing road. Toward this new end the soul turns its gaze—not without loving remembrance of those who still live in the body, not without prayers for them; but with its chiefest and its gladdest thoughts fixed on that future, when another stage of the journey will be over, another "end" reached—the end which we call "the resurrection." With the devoted sister of Bethany we say, "I know that my brother shall rise again, in the resurrection at the last day." And looking forward to that "day," we seem to see another Figure walking among the sons of men—a Figure whose presence has been felt, but not seen, before—a Figure glorious, divine, yet human. And with Him are those whom we "have loved long since, and lost awhile."

And when we question, eagerly, anxiously, "What is beyond?"—the answer comes back, "Eye hath not seen, ear hath not heard, neither hath entered into the heart of man the things which God hath prepared for them that love Him."

In these lesser endings, of certain stages in life's journey, when our loved ones or we ourselves pass the turning-point of death, let us look to that greater end, when Christ, who is our life, shall appear, and we too appear with Him in glory. Aye, let us look farther, and yet farther, even to that Great End, when our brother now departed, and we, and all that are, shall be one with God!—Rev. C. A. Jessup, M. A.

"WE KNOW NOT WHAT A DAY MAY BRING FORTH."
—REV. 27:1.

REV. ROBERT FORBES, D. D.

I. The uncertainty of life brings a moral pressure to bear upon humanity that seems to be a necessity in our present state of being. If all lives were to be extended to seventy years, the youth of twenty would probably say, I have full fifty years yet. I will not withhold my heart from any joy—time enough to think of my spiritual welfare. The busy man of forty on business bent might say, I have thirty years yet; time enough to think of religious matters, and Human Nature being as it is I fear the man of sixty might say, Have I not ten years of life yet? Time enough! Press on till wisdom is pushed out of life. God's order is better. It is ordained that smiling infancy, youthful beauty, manhood's strength and womanhood's charms as well as age and feebleness extreme, are all alike exposed to the stroke of death. One may say, If the uncertainty of life is necessary that the bad may feel the necessity of reformation, surely the good should be exempt from this uncertainty. The answer is men would then try to be good to escape the uncertainty of life and the motive being wrong the only goodness would be an impossibility. We must learn to love virtue for its own sake. Only thus can virtue be virtue.

II. Life is not a preparation for death. Life is the one great opportunity for the development of character. He is prepared for death who is prepared for life. The sacraments are not needed so much for the dying as for the living sons of men. The dying child is the one that does not need baptism. The child that is likely to live and enter the contest with the world, the flesh and the devil, is the one that needs baptism.

III. Sin and sorrow and the grave are facts, facts for the agnostic as well as for the believer. As we ponder on the facts and are bewildered in our attempt to construct a philosophy which accounts for all the racts we turn to the cross of Jesus and to the open tomb of Joseph's garden, for relief. The world admires and the church worships Him who was so tender that he took little children in His arms and blessed them, who was so sympathetic that He wept with the bereaved sisters, who was so wise that He uttered words of wisdom, such as to keep the brains of twenty centuries busy. Who was so brave and grand that He went to His cross to die without a murmur, and who was so magnanimous that He prayed for His murderers. This man died and rose again. He stood with His feet on death's cold pavement, and whispered in words tender and strong, words that have come down to us in the breezes of the centuries, "I am He that liveth and was dead and behold, I am alive for evermore." Here is the comfort, after all the earth's mourning ones.

The best manner in which we can show our respect for the dead is to take up their unfinished work and the burdens which they laid down. —Rev. Robert Forbes, D. D.

"BE YE ALSO READY."—MATT. 24:44.

LINA JEANETTE WALK.

I. It is a strange fact that we nearly all dread death. This world, transitory and unsatisfying as it is, has a wonderful influence over us. We shrink from the thought of death as though it were an enemy instead of a joyful messenger whose hand unlocks the gates of immortality. The grave is a dark, fathomless abyss to our terrified imagination, rather than the radiant vestibule of heaven through which we pass into the more luminous glories of our Father's house and the mansion prepared for us. Poor, timorous, faithless souls that we are! how groundless we shall find these fears when we come to die, if we have made preparation for death! How we shall smile at our vain alarms, when the reality has happened! When the morning cometh we shall awaken in the sunlight of God.

II. How is preparation to be made? The command given by our Saviour, "Watch," does not allude altogether, as some have understood it, to his second coming, neither was it meant to be put into practice only when the thief, or death, was expected. It was intended as a warning for all times and a continual safeguard for every-day living. Bishop Hall says, "Each day is a new life and an abridgment of the whole. I will so live as if I counted every day to be my first and my last; as if I began to live then, and should live no more afterward." His life was evidently a life of watchfulness, and therefore one of safety. Every life lived upon this principle of Christian vigilance need have no forebodings for the future. Such a life is a constant preparation for death.

Like a thief in the night the enemy of souls will seek to attack us. We must watch, therefore, that he takes us not unawares. There is no hour in our lives when we can with safety withhold our watch over self. Did we but realize this more fully there would be no spiritual languor nor slothfulness, only earnest endeavor in spiritual energy and activity. A legend is told of a man who waited at the gates of Paradise a thousand years for them to open. At the end of that time he fell asleep for a half hour. In that half hour the gates were opened and closed again, and he awoke to find himself shut out. Let us not grow weary, nor relax our efforts.—Lina Jeanette Walk.

MYSTERY.

REV. CYRUS MENDENHALL.

One need never go far to find mysteries. Our knowledge in any direction is partial; hence some things are shrouded in mystery. Many things, now pretty well understood, were entirely mysterious to the ancients.

Matters pertaining to chemistry, astronomy, the practice of medicine, and the phenomena of nature, that are now commonplace, were then magical or mysterious. The gods did everything by direct interference. Even the flight of birds, the appearance of entrails, the flash of meteors, the movement of comets, were miraculous.

While it is true we account for things in a scientific or matter-of-fact way, we have not dispelled all mystery. We cannot reduce all things to a logical sequence. The scalpel, crucible, balances, agents, and reagents, microscope and telescope, revealing so much, yet open up new marvels and spring new puzzles, so that with Carlyle, we say: "Sense knows not, faith knows not, only that it is through mystery to mystery, from God to God."

All this that is hidden inspires men to search for revelations of the mysteries, and has led to the progress and learning of today. Many hidden mysteries have been revealed, but men are so soon and so frequently balked that humility is always in order:

"A marvel seems the universe,   9
  A miracle our life and death;
A mystery which I cannot pierce,
  Around, above, beneath."

Strange things come into the most quiet and ordinary existences. At almost any step, painful or pleasurable, we may pause and ask "Why?" And can we always find an answer to the query?

We see the beginnings, and the ending is lost in the perspective. We are too near-sighted to judge. "Therefore judge nothing before the time, until the Lord come, who both will bring to light the hidden things of darkness and will make manifest the counsels of the heart."

A full solution of the problems of life, sorrow, public and private calamities, sin and its sequences, and the mystery of death, cannot be reached here. But if somewhat perplexed, we need never be in despair if we have learned through Christ to confide in a loving Father, who in the ultimate will work all things out for good.

Love is the clue to it all. And love gives us an undying inspiration to spur us on in working at the problems all around us. In our faith, our hope, our devotion, let no mystery terrify us, no marvel stand between us and the Father who, whatever else He may or may not be, is a God of love.

"O, Light Divine, we need no fuller test   7
  That all is ordered well;
We know enough to trust that all is best
  .Where love and wisdom dwell."
—Rev. Cyrus Mendenhall.

II. DEATH OF THE YOUNG.

CHRIST AND CHILDHOOD.

REV. KERR BOYCE TUPPER, D. D.

One of the most beautiful and suggestive scenes in all the earthly career of the Son of Man is that which reveals, on a certain occasion, with such delicate touches, our Lord's tender treatment of children. How picturesquely Mark—the evangelist most noted for his graphic style—presents ahe incident! "And they brought little children to Him, that He should touch them: and His disciples rebuked those that brought them. But when Jesus saw it, He was much displeased, and said unto them, Suffer the little children to come unto Me, and forbid them not: for of such is the kingdom of God. Verily I say unto you, whosoever shall not receive the kingdom of God as a little child, he shall not enter therein. And He took them up in His arms, put His hands upon them and blessed them."

Every feature of the exquisite picture attracts: the lovely flowers all about (for it is now spring-time), the charming Judean landscape, the earnest countenances of the parents, the beautiful faces of innocent childhood and the strong, manly form of the Christ, as, rebuking worthy but mistaken disciples, He takes the little ones in His arms, and speaks words of holy benediction, rich with the music of a heavenly love. Immortal picture—full of spiritual significance—which may well hang in the gallery of each of our imaginations, an inspiration and a delight!

More than simply an attractive scene, however, this Palestinian incident suggests to us some most comforting thoughts as we gather to pay a last tribute of tender affection to a little child whom God has taken to Himself in the fairer realm beyond, where every bud bursts into blossom and every blossom is filled with fruit.

I. And the first of these thoughts is this: Christ's love of childhood for childhood's sake and childhood's possibilities. When the babe Jesus opened the wondrous scenes of divinity in humanity and angels chanted their cradle-hymn over the new-born Son of Mary—then came childhood's coronation-day! As another has beautifully expressed it, "Just as the light from the child in Corregio's Holy Night illuminates all surrounding figures, so the glory of that birth sheds an unfading lustre on all the world." No wonder that our children are so tenderly loved and vigorously protected. No wonder that all over Christian lands are asylums for blind children and deaf, orphaned children and destitute. No wonder that the church, inspired by the words and deeds of its Master and Lord, regulates its worship and constructs its buildings and creates its literature largely for children. The ancient prophecy is being fulfilled, "And a little child shall lead."

To Paganism childhood has always represented only immaturity of mind and weakness of body. In other systems than that of Christianity the child is but little regarded. Writes recently a traveler in the Orient: "Two and a half years have I spent in China, but not a single monument or tomb-stone have I seen marking the grave of a child." What an astoundingly sad fact! More than a third of a million of graves are dug in China every fifty years and any token of a child's burial is an exception. Ah! the explanation is not far to seek: paganism has heard no voice from its great teachers, as Budha and Confucius, telling out the glad message, "Of such like the child is the kingdom of heaven." Take that fact and place it over against a scene like that before us this hour, or contrast it with the attitude of our Lord when, on another occasion, He declares, "Except ye become as little children ye shall not enter into the kingdom of heaven." According to this Mighty Master of the ages the child, with his simple faith and unaffected confidence and sincere love, is the most attractive type of discipleship—the child whose "angels do always behold the face of the Father in heaven."

And so it has come that to the man or woman who is a lover of the true, the beautiful and the good childhood is irresistibly attractive. "Blessed be childhood," writes, in genuine enthusiasm, the eminent mystic, Amiel, "which brings down something of heaven into the midst of our rough earthliness. These eighty thousand daily births, of which statistics tell us, represent, as it were, an effusion of innocence and freshness, struggling not only against the death of the race but against human corruption, also, and the universal gangrene of sin. All the good and wholesome feeling that is entwined with childhood and cradle is one of the secrets of the providential government of the world. Suppress this lifegiving dew, and human society would be scorched and devastated by selfish passion. Blessed be childhood: what little of paradise we see still on earth is due to its presence among us."

II. Again as Christ blest the little ones with heavenly benedictions, so should parents dedicate their children early in life to God and His holy cause. Let no parent give over the spiritual education of his child to nurse or teacher. Not enough is it that we give to those whom God has given to us, name, food, clothing, shelter, education, fortune: we owe to them, also, and above all else, sympathy, solicitude, prayer, precept, example.

III. A final thought, and one of supreme consolation: how clear, in all the scene before us in the beautiful narrative, is the implication of children's salvation in the life beyond life. Who can gaze upon the attitude and the words of Jesus here and doubt that our darlings that die in infancy go to the bosom of their Redeemer, who so loves them and so graciously embraces them in His far-reaching salvation plan? Lovely buds these children are, transplanted by death in that larger garden above, where, in pure atmosphere and with heavenly fragrance, they are to blossom through the endless cycles of a glorious eternity. Blessed, thrice blessed thought! Let it bring joy to the griefstricken spirits of all of us who have lost darling children. How many such there be!

> There is no flock, however watched and tended,
> But one dead lamb is there;
> There is no fireside, howe'er defended
> But has one vacant chair.

And when the vacancy in the home is one made by the departure of of a babe, what comfort that we can hear such words as these: "Of such is the kingdom of heaven," "Their angels do behold the face of my Father in heaven."—Rev. Kerr Boyce Tupper, D. D.

"AND HE CALLED A LITTLE CHILD UNTO HIM."—
MATT 18:2.

REV. GEO. WOLFE SHINN, D. D.

"Why did the good Lord permit it?" This question may arise in the mind of any sufferer when a great sorrow comes.

It is most likely to present itself to the parent whose child has been removed by death.

In the bewilderment occasioned by this event, and in the bitterness of grief at parting from one so tenderly loved the afflicted parent may ask: "Why could not our child have been spared to us?"

"Other children, less cared for, live and grow up—why was our child called away?"

Here are a few suggestions which may help you a little in your bewilderment and may comfort you in your grief.

Some day, through God's grace, you may be able to say, out of fullest trust and resignation: "The Lord gave and the Lord hath taken away. Blessed be the name of the Lord."

I. Your child is still living.

Your child has not been blotted out of existence. It has not ceased to live. That which died was only its body. Some day that natural body is to become a spiritual body, forever incapable of suffering and dying. In the meantime the soul of the child lives on in Paradise. The little one has simply changed its abode. It has gone to another home.

We may think of it as, in a sense, attending another school, inasmuch as it being trained and developed for higher joys and for higher service. Whenever your thoughts turn to your child do not associate it with the grave, as if that were all, for the little body you buried there was only the casket in which the soul lived for a while before God called it to Paradise.

Think of the child as living in a new home, which is a real home even though your eyes can not see it now.

2. The Child is tenderly cared for in Paradise.

You did all you could for it while it was with you here, because you loved it. It lives today surrounded by affection. Long ago when the

Lord Jesus was here on earth He called little children to Him, took them up in His arms and blessed them.

He is the same yesterday, today and forever, and He loves your child. It is safe with Him. Do not think of it as a lonely, wandering, uncared-for spirit in a dark, mysterious world, but as a happy little child in the bright Paradise of God, with pleasant companions, in the midst of brightness and joy. No day of gloom ever dawns upon it, and there is no night to bring it terror. Ah—the child is safer where it is now than if it were even in your loving arms.

"In Paradise reposing, by Life's eternal well,

The tender lambs of Jesus, in greenest pastures dwell.

The angels, once their guardians, their comrades now in grace

With them in love adoring, see God, the Father's face."

3. Your child is spared all earthly sorrow.

The child will never know trial or tribulation. It has gone out of the region where these abound. No temptation or sin will reach it. In that blessed home none ever go astray. You can always say: "Thank God my child is safe."

4. Your child sends you a message.

Not in words, but its very condition in that blessed world is a message to you. It bids you be tender and helpful to all about you who are still struggling in this earthly life.

5: Your child waits to welcome you home at last.

THE EVER OPEN ARMS OF THE LORD JESUS.
REV. GEO. WOLFE SHINN, D. D.

If we turn to the world at such a time as this for words of consolation the best the world can say to us is—"Forget your troubles. Dismiss from your minds all thought of this present affliction and absorb yourselves in something else." But we cannot forget. This sorrow is all too real, too keen, for forgetfulness. This little one brought so much gladness, awakened so many songs in these hearts—that they cannot forget. They do not want to forget. They would dwell upon the sweet memories of the past, but the very sweetness of those memories makes more vivid the affliction which has taken away the dear one. The world cannot comfort us by its opiates of forgetfulness.

We turn to the philosophy of the day. We ask of men's learning some expressions that will console us but what do we receive? They tell us of the inevitableness of death. It is an event common to all. They tell us of mighty forces working imperceptibly, of the feeble resistance we can make, and of the result that can only be postponed and not prevented. We grant it, but why did it come so soon here? Why was not this child permitted to live until the three score years and ten? Why was it not permitted to continue its blessed ministry of joy in this house?

Philosophy has no answer for such questions and philosophy gives us no comfort in such an hour of need. Where shall we turn? There is but one answer. Only in the religion of Christ shall we find the comfort we seek. Just as soon as we turn to that there looms up before us a picture of long ago. A man is surrounded by a group of other men. There came to Him parents with their children. They beg Him to bless those children. At first His friends press aside the importunate supplicants—"Trouble not the Master" they say. "Go away. Why bring your children to Him?"

But the Master Who knows all hearts is wiser and kinder than His disciples and so He says: "Suffer the little children to come unto Me." He takes them up in His arms. He blesses them. Think of that scene of long ago. Think of the little ones in His arms. Think of the gentle hand placed upon each one's head. Think of the gracious lips saying— "Bless you, little child. Your Master, your Saviour blesses you." Think of all that—and then remember that it is an object lesson for all time. Remember that there are still the same tender compassionate heart, the same powerful protecting arms, the same eternal refuge. Remember that and light begins to stream through the present dark clouds of sorrow.

The child who has gone hence has found a resting place in the arms of the Son of God. He has called the little one to Him. He has blessed it. He is blessing it. It will grow up under His benediction. It is safe. No harm can ever come to it. It is happy beneath the smile of God.

There is no need to perplex ourselves now over the mystery of death, no need to seek consolation anywhere else than in that one great truth that the child has found a place near the heart of the dear Christ.

And as in all the years to come you think of the child you can be sure that it is never out of reach of that tender watchful love. It will grow in all the beauty of likeness to Him.

By and by there will be the happy day of reunion.—Rev. Geo. Wolfe Shinn, D. D.

FUTURE LIGHT ON PRESENT LOSS.

REB. ROBERT FORBES, D. D.

Your child dies. Your heart is broken, your home is desolate, the half worn shoe, she used to wear, the toy with which she played, will awaken your slumbering sorrow again and again, when time has partially healed the wound. Be patient: He doeth all things well. If you were walking along the street holding your child by the hand, in the holy pride and unspeakable joy of motherhood, and when you reached an unpleasant or dangerous place, you took the little one in your arms and carried her over and set her safely down beyond the unpleasant or dangerous place; you have done a kindness. So it may be that the Great Father of us all, as He held your child by the hand, some place of discomfort or pain or danger or loss, and in infinite tenderness took the little one up in His loving arms and placed her safely down on the other shore.

You may some day see clearly where you are in darkness now, and in the clearer light of heaven thank Him for that act which almost excites rebellious feelings now.—Rev. Robert Forbes, D. D.

THE MAIDEN, GOD'S FLOWER.

REV. WM. RAINEY BENNETT, B. D.

It sometimes happens that the sun arises with unusual splendor. In golden armor it battles with the forces of darkness and sends them flying beyond the western hills. Each leaf hangs stuck with diamond dewdrops, each drop burning like the sun himself. Men said, this is a fair day, and hope and joy beamed from their eyes. All nature was aglow with light. The little birds caught the day spirit and sang their sweetest carols. The sky, blue and June-like, laid its warm ear close to earth to hear if it were in tune. O, what is so rare as a morn in June. But before the morning was scarce begun, a cloud arose. It came up very fast, and grew thicker and thicker. The day grew darker and darker. Not one gleam of gold could push through that stormcloud to give man one ray of hope. The day became very dark. Then came the storm—terrible, furious. It whirled through a valley of oaks, and writhed and twisted their great trunks and branches until all was waste and desolation. There was much mourning and crying in that valley of strong oaks.

Once there was a life that came in like a new born day. It brought golden light into one home, yea many homes. There was never a day in June so rare as that bright life. It gave hope and happiness to everyone. The birds sang merrier for her presence. Flowers seemed to give out their sweetest perfume for her pleasure. It was easy to be good when she was near. All was happiness, all was light.

But the storm arose suddenly. There was no warning but a heartpain, sharp as a lightning flash. Then all grew dark. Great hearts were torn and mangled. Strong men broke down and cried. It was like a battlefield of wounded, a valley of oaks after the storm. It is all lost, we say. But wait! That bright sunlit morn gave hope to a little seed. It took root and grew into a vine with luxuriant foliage and covered over ugly wounds on those strong oaks. So this morning-life has started to growing a seed of love, and it will cover over the wounded hearts with its healing leaves of memory. And, as the oak looks richer with the ivy clinging to it, so our lives will be made richer and sweeter because of the clinging love-memory of our little girl.

The wounds will not heal. The forest will never rise. The heart will always bear the scars. It will always cry. I do not tell you not to weep; let love have its way. If love says for the tears to flow, let them flow. Love knows best. Love will find a way where reason will fail. But bear just a word of reason.

Nothing can be lost. This is a law of physics. If no energy can be lost, how can love, sweetness and purity be lost? There was real worth in this young life—worth to her home, worth to the Sunday school, worth to the "Helping Hands," worth to the C. E. society, worth to the public schools; and I say it with all seriousness, worth to God. If there is anything earthly that would picture her character it is sunlight and roses. If there is anything heavenly that portrays her nature, it is love. What more does earth need? What more can heaven demand? Sunlight, roses and love—they give joy to man; they will give joy to God. Her life has been a blessing to us, though it was so very short, but

> " 'Tis better to have loved and lost,
> Than never to have loved at all."
> —Rev. Wm. Rainey Bennett, B. D.

A YOUNG GIRL'S DEATH.

HENRY WARD BEECHER.

It is a good thing to me, in looking into life, to see how that which is probably the sweetest and most intense point of human experience lies in the affections that surround childhood. There is nothing that is stirred more than the human heart—the father and mother heart—to care for the utter helplessness of childhood. There are no affections more disinterested, more helpful, more beautiful to behold, more needed by the object, and more fruitful in the outplay, than those loves which bind strength to weakness and want. Life is full of it. It is a light kindled in every house.

It is a good thing, therefore, to me, that the two or three only instances recorded of the great displeasure, of the visible and striking excitement, which Christ Jesus manifested upon earth, was in connection with little children. The thought, the feeling, was that they had been disparaged in his presence. Where they desired to come to Him, or where their parents desired to bring them to Him, and the disciples thought it was not worth while to trouble Him about little children as long as there were grown folks around about Him, and put aside the little children from His ministration—from their expression of love to Him, and their recipience of love from Him—at that point it was that His heart flamed out. He was grieved. He was offended. It was evidently one of those extraordinary displays of feeling to which at times He was subject in His earthly career.

Looking a great many times into the whole teaching of the Scriptures, I have come to feel that in the great Kingdom of God children bear a part of which we have but a very faint conception; and that their disappearance from earth, although it brings so much pain to the parental heart, is generally thought very little of in the economic world. The child is not a producer. Children are not known on the Exchange; they are not known in the market; they are not known in the ways of strife; they are not known in any way as a power or as an element of success in life. They die, and we say, "What a pity! How sad it will be for the mother! How hard it will be for the father!" and then they are as a leaf that has dropped ultimately from the stem, and wavered through the air, and rested on the ground. They were babes, they were children, and therefore they were of little account. If it had been a man, it would have been regarded differently. If it had been one who was known in human affairs, if it had been a counter of money, men would have said, "Oh, what a loss to society!" but it was only a little child.

Now, this feeling of the Saviour in regard to little children is like the feeling of the mother and father heart; but men's feeling of the unvalue of little children as measured by what they are worth to the affairs of society is akin to that of the disciples when they would hinder little children from coming to Christ; and my thought of the freshness, the unperverted, pure, royal nature that is in little children (I mean not the potential evil which is in them, but that in them which when the body drops away, discloses itself at once in the Kingdom of Heaven in beauty and in rare angelic perfection)—to my thought that element in childhood flames forth in the other world with a conspicuous and importance which we know very little of. It seems that there is a provision for it. It seems that there is a kingdom in the other life for children. It seems that there are appointed guardians for them here and that they are receiving welcome there. I take it that they as much enlarge their spheres of experience and of receptivity in going forth as little children as we do ours in going forth as adults, and that they are better off by as much as heaven in better than this world—not, however, in the vague and general sense in which we are accustomed to speak of it saying, "We have escaped temptation and sickness and various evils." That is all true; but I mean that there is a special summer in heaven, that there is a ripening spot in the other life, into which children go, where they are peculiarly blessed, and that all the touches and hints of revelation, all the glances, as it were, of Christ's eye in looking at them, and His whole mode of teaching about them, indicate that their ascent to glory is with peculiar blessings.

So I give forth my children into clouds that are both within and without rosy with light. I look upon the upgoing of the little child's spirit as perhaps the rarest and sweetest sight that the angel beholds in heaven. The entrance of these little unstained creatures into the presence of the dear Father of all—as it were, their laps from heaven, and the small segment of the circle which they describe before they light upon the boughs there—this I look upon as one of the most joyous elements of half disclosed truth.

If it be a great blessing to have our children called, received, and rendered safe, and advanced in honor, we ought not to look upon the earthware side of these phenomena—certainly not in such a way as to quite eclipse the brightness, the blessedness, the beauty and the gladness of the other and heavenly side—that of the departure of little children. For with us is the earth earthly; with us is the dishonored body, which in the battle is overthrown; and the little child, before ever it has entered the list, is outrun, as it were, and beaten. This part of it is presented to our bodily sense; but the other, that they are borne into the bosom of Christ, that they are lifted up into the eternal smile, that they are the peculiarly elect of the heavenly life, that they have come to those thrones and honors and to that blessedness which belong in heaven in a special way to little ones—this we hardly enough believe in to realize it in the time of our distress.

And yet, in a land where the monarch had it in his power to confer honor and distinction, every household would be glad to have the king send a messenger, saying, "Send thy child, thy son who is coming of age." Every household would be glad to have the queen send for a maid of honor to be in her presence. There is not a sill in the kingdom that when the messenger's feet crossed it, would not vibrate with gladness to have the royal mark of favor shown by calling to the court any child. And the house would not be empty because the child had gone forth; it would be luminous because the light of its gladness and its honor would shine back and fill the house again.

So, when our dear Lord sends to us, and is making up His heavenly company of our elect ones, when He first calls one and then another up to His presence, giving them an honor which no earthly monarch ever knew how to confer, is there no element of joy, no backward shining light, no gladness for the child, no gladness for Christ's sake, no sense of the divine goodness to us, no blessing in our loss—which is not loss? There is nothing lost. Much is changed, much is transferred, but nothing is lost; much is gained. He who plants such seed as children are, in such soil as heaven is, and under such a sun as God, is planting for a glorious harvest; and if the husbandman waits patiently from spring to autumn to see what he has planted, and what it has brought forth, how much more patiently ought we to wait to see what shall be the outcome of that which we have planted in the heavenly soil!

And so, with such thoughts as these, I do not suppose we can entirely and at once cure the sad and suffering wounds which the sudden disruption of our children from us makes; but certainly it gives to our sorrows a new direction, much healing and much comfort intermingled. Meanwhile, my dearly beloved, you are God's children, and He has not come to you in judgment; He has come to you in great mercy. The royal Hand has taken the darling, and has taken it not out of light into darkness, and not out of light into twilight, but out of small joys begun into wonderful joys; out of the humility and limitation of an earthly household into the largeness and the beauty and the fulness of the house where God is and angels are, and where sweet communion from age to age is made up of these little precious saints. The best saints, I take it, are gathered as pearls from the bottom, into the Kingdom of our God.—Henry Ward Beecher.

"FOR OF SUCH IS THE KINGDOM."—MATT. 19:14.

REV. F. T. ROUSE.

It is a time of joy when a daughter comes to the home. Not even a son can take the place of the sweet girl child that wins her way into the heart of her father and mother. I have sometimes thought that the girl wins the father most; but for father or mother it is a blessed day that brings the little girl so sweet, so dependent, so affectionate, so full of love and care.

Eleven years is long enough to bind the tendrills very tight about the heart. The various stages of early childhood have been passed through one by one. The long dresses, the short dresses, the learning to sit up, to creep, to laugh and prattle; the difficult words one by one; the learning to walk; the first toys; the inevitable doll, and dolls. The first sober thoughts—the time when the little one instead of being altogether helped, becomes a little helper; the days of those questions, and thoughts, those long, long thoughts; for a child's mind is deep like the sea. Sometimes she will come in with a question that will almost startle from its deeper meaning.

A true child's mind turns naturally to God. Prayer is as natural to a child as breathing. God is not far away to a child. The pure in heart see God, and so the pure child sees Him, better than we who have become more complex in our motives. We have much to learn from a child. Jesus took the little one as a type of what one should be who would enter the kingdom of heaven. It is the type of trustful purity and simplicity.

This is one of the lessons that childhood brings us, and if we cannot keep the child we can keep the lesson. I sometimes think that every life, however short, has had its mission. God certainly does not measure things by years. He will paint in frost beautiful pictures upon the window pain; and then the light of the sun will in a moment melt it away. And yet the picture had a purpose and fulfilled its mission. The beautiful flowers, the sweet rose bud nods its modest head kissed by the dew, and blushing at the sight of rosy dawn, then it is picked, or if it matures, its leaves fall; yet no one will say the rose has lived in vain.

This little life has not been in vain, it has been worth more than all it cost, even if we take into account this last cost of sorrow. The poet is true when he says: "It is better to have loved and lost, than never to have loved at all."—Rev. F. T. Rouse.

III. DEATH IN MATURITY AND OLD AGE.

"THE MEMORY OF THE JUST IS BLESSED."—
PROV. 10:7.

REV. S. PARKES CADMAN, D. D.

We pensively mark the lapse of time by the vanishing of faces dear and the hushing of familiar voices, but our sad abstraction is happily broken by the reflection that the day of which the prophet spoke has dawned for our fellow laborer; "that day when the Lord of Hosts shall be for a crown of glory and for a diadem of beauty unto His faithful servants."

The treasure of discipline and of love were found in the life of this honored citizen. He obtained without seeking it, an impressive weight among his fellow men because of the strength of an unusual and forcible character; a character which never coveted ease, but deliberately chose the steep and rugged path where duty led the way and useless luxuries dare not invade. The efforts thus involved were essential to the fibre of his being, and through incessant devotion to the daily round he came to his proper upward motion to the higher life where he could not be swerved from that kingly road, that "way of the just which shineth brighter and brighter unto the dawning of the day."

Unsuspected depths of hidden but sincere and steadfast love were in this man, and they mediated between the church he served and the home he cherished. In his home, that innermost circle, he loved his own well and wisely and he loved them to the end. Constant ministry shone and was reflected there in unwonted grace and thoughtful care.

If I were asked to mention the outstanding feature of his character, I should unhesitatingly reply: "It was fidelity." In things great or small, with exactitude and scrupulous honor, he kept the faith. The sense of obligation to his trusts was vital, and it helped to make him prudent in promise, but sure in performance. His profession as a Christian gentleman was not apt to dissolve into mere rhapsodies; he did not escape the present world and its burdens by postponing essential things to the eternal state beyond. He chose the better part and was "diligent in business, fervent in spirit, serving the Lord."

Conscience and intellect united in him upon one object, the truth as he understood the truth. This attribute was rooted in him, and he could not suffer it to be removed, whatever else was shaken. One does not claim that its manifestations were in a state of perfection. He would have scorned such a claim or anything approaching it. Indeed, he often did and advocated that which was opposed to his personal taste and desire, because he believed it necessary to larger interests. Such behavior had a singular power over men, whether they agreed with him or not. His valuables were not on landlocked waters, but floating on the deeps of virtue and honesty that stretch toward a just and righteous God.

Let us remember our beloved friend for what he was, but let not forget that he owed all he was to Another, to the greatest Friend there is. I know he would wish me to say little, but he certainly would wish me to say this:

> "Thou, O Christ, art all I want,
> More than all in Thee I find."

He knew and we all knew, that we cannot live a worthy life in our own strength, but we can humbly and heartily trust in our Redeemer and Lord, as he did.

The scenery of that immortal hope we can conceive of in a measure from the elements of our mortal life. Memory's peaceful retrospect is there; the satisfaction of conscience when duty has been done is there; reason delights there in its perception of the truth, and there affection feels as never before the glow of sympathy and inspiration. Combining these into one full thought glorified by the eternal presence of God and by whatever other resources the great reality beyond contains, we surrender our friend and all our loved ones to this vision of the highest which "the pure in heart" have obtained.

So let the ripe fruit fall. He goes beyond to beckon us, and with him and all who are of the assembly of the Church of the Firstborn, we may finally take our appointed place. For they are there; they who were once mourners here below and knew then as we still know that the day's burden is no dream. Now, transformed, enriched and ready for all God's perfect will, they offer their ransomed energies to a flawless and eternal service which is perfect freedom and unalloyed delight.

"Then said he, 'I am going to my Father's; and though with great difficulty I have got hither, yet now I do not repent me of all the troubles I have been at to arrive where I am. My sword I give to him that shall succeed me in my pilgrimage, and my courage and skill to him that can get it. My marks and scars I carry with me, to be a witness for me that I have fought His battles who shall now be my Redeemer.' "

"When the day that he must go hence was come, many accompanied him to the riverside, into which, as he went, he said, "Oh, Death! where is thy sting?" And as he went down deeper he said, "Oh, Grave! where is thy victory?" So he passed over, and all the trumpets sounded for him on the other side."—Rev. S. Parkes Cadman, D. D.

D. L. MOODY'S MOTHER.

(When Mrs. William R. Moody had concluded her song, "Crossing the Bar," at the funeral of Mrs. Moody, Mr. D. L. Moody rose from his place with the family, and, bearing in his hands the old family Bible and a worn book of Devotions, came forward. Standing by the body of his mother, he said:)

"It is not the custom, perhaps, for a son to take part on such an occasion. If I can control myself, I would like to say a few words. It is a great honor to be the son of such a mother. I do not know where to begin; I could not praise her enough. In the first place, my mother was a very wise woman. In one sense she was wiser than Solomon—she knew how to bring up her children. She had nine children, and they all loved their home. She won their hearts, their affections; she could do anything with them.

"Whenever I wanted real sound counsel, I used to go to my mother. I have traveled a good deal, and seen a good many mothers, but I never saw one who had such tact as she had. She so bound her children to her that it was a great calamity to have to leave home. She won her family to herself.

"And there was another thing remarkable about my mother. If she loved one child more than another no one ever found it out.

"I thought so much of my mother, I cannot say half enough. That dear face! There was no sweeter face on earth. Fifty years I have been coming back, and was always glad to get back. When I got within fifty miles of home I always grew restless, and walked up and down the car. It seemed to me as if the train would never get to Northfield. For sixty-eight years she has lived on that hill, and when I came back after dark I always looked to see the light in mother's window. When I got home last Saturday night—I was going to take the four o'clock train from New York and get here at twelve: I had some business to do; but I suppose it was the good Lord that sent me; I took the twelve o'clock train and got here at five—I went in to my mother. I was so glad I got back in time to be recognized. I said, 'Mother, do you know me?' She said, 'I guess I do!' I like that word, that Yankee word 'guess'! The children were all with her when she was taking her departure. At last I called, 'Mother, mother.' No answer. She had fallen asleep; but I shall call her again by-and-bye. Friends, it is not a time of mourning. I want you to understand we do not mourn. We are proud that we had such a mother. We have a wonderful legacy left us.

"Widow Moody's light has burned on that hill for fifty-four years to my knowledge. It has been burning there for fifty-four years in that one room. We built a room for her where she could be more comfortable, but she was not often there. There was just one room where she wanted to be. Her children were born there, her first sorrow came there, and that was where God had met her. That is the place she liked to stay, where her children liked to meet her, where she worked and toiled and wept.

"Her seven boys were like Hannibal, whose mother took him to the altar and made him swear vengeance on Rome. She took us to the altar and made us swear vengeance on whiskey, and everything that was an enemy to the human family: and we have been fighting it ever since, and will to the end of our days:

"What more can I say? You have lived with her and you know about her. I want to give you one verse, her creed. When everything went against her this was her stay—'My trust is in God.'

"I do not know—of course, we do not know—whether the departed ones are conscious of what is going on on earth. If I knew that she was, I would send her a message that we are coming on after her. She went without a pain, without a struggle, just like a person going to sleep. And now we are to lay her body away to await His coming in resurrection power. When I see her in the morning she is to have a glorious body. The body Moses had on the Mount of Transfiguration was a better body than God buried on Pisgah. When we see Elijah he will have a glorious body. That dear mother, when I see her again, is going to have a glorified body. (Looking at her face.) God bless you, mother; we love you still. Death has only increased our love. Good-bye for a little while, mother."

A GODLY MOTHER.

Another sweet and and beautiful life has gone home; but she has left us a legacy. No one can look back on her memory without feeling that there is such a life as a God-filled life. The church, home, and society loses heavily when such a life takes its flight; but there are, however, many compensations. Her many friends feel that she is the happier, and we are all made better in heart and richer in soul when we reflect on her blessed life.

No one who knew her could help but know that she had found the secret to the happy life, but not every one knows the secret. All results require a cause. Figs do not grow on thistles. There is a center—a keynote—a dominant chord in each life, whether great or small. Discover that center and all else will follow readily. Listen for that keynote and you can hear all the harmonies and discords that float around it. You can tell where that life will come out, for you have found the star that leads and the power that guides. We know the center of her life was Christ. We believe she could say with Paul, "For me to live is Christ, to die is gain." She had changed centers from self to Christ. This new centering of life's affections must come to teach person's life who lives.

Her will had become His will; her life was not only like His life, but was His life; in Him she lived and moved and had her being. Her life was hid with God. She had discovered the abundant life and made it hers every day and hour. She had made the greatest discovery of the age, yea, of all ages—life—the opulence of a God-filled life.

The best evidence of the virtue of Christianity is a Christian. When philosophy and science fail then life and love convince and convict. Let us be thankful that we can look back with a certainty on some lives redeemed and filled with love.

She had a Christian face. It was calm, strong and hopeful. In this age of doubting and disquietude, it is a boon to find a face with all the lines of care erased. A confidence in God had filled her face with a look of calm hopefulness. A pure heart and a clear conscience had given her a countenance beaming with love which looked one square in the face —ah! looked into the heart, having the effect of a loving rebuke which virtue always gives to vice.

She had a Christian language. A word has many meanings—as many as there are lips that speak it. She had that fine personality that softens words—a love that melted out all sounds harsh and cutting. Those who know say that never an unkind word fell from her lips. She had that fine Christian sense of always selecting the right word at the right time —an art almost lost to the world—an art many never learn.

She had a Christian courage. I mean by this that she had reached the state of the "affirmative intellect." It was not a factor with her what others did; she had the courage to do what she thought was right. Her conduct had gone beyond the point of being swayed by what was popular or customary. Duty was the goal, and love led the way. She had further, the culture of unselfishness which lost self in the service of others. She suffered least from her own pain and most from the sorrows of others.

She was a Christian mother. There are many mothers who are not. They care for their own as do the tigers of the jungle, and their sympathies stop with their own. Divine motherhood is as wide as the cry of human need. It mothers all children. There are some persons in whose presence we all become children. A sweet, caressing influence floats from their soul like the perfume from a rose, which seems to still us and lull us to sleep. Such was the feeling that stole over me when she was near—I was home again.

This mother had a Christian hope and fearlessness which is worth all the wealth of the world at that moment when the life forces begin to slip away like sand through the fingers. Death through her living Lord had been robbed of all its terrors. It was not a black cloud which blinded sight; she saw with the soul's eye. To her death was not a door which shut out life, but one which opened into larger life. It was a homegoing. It was a clear call; a clasping of both hands long loved and lost awhile.

She lived a beautiful life and died a beautiful death. May she have the two-fold resurrection—one into the great life beyond with her Lord and her loved ones, the other in the many lives that remain here on earth, blessed and purified by her influence.

WHAT A CHRISTIAN CARRIES INTO THE NEXT WORLD.

REV. VICTOR FRANK BROWN.

It is indeed a rare event in any city, when friends can gather as we do today at the bier of one who has lived so long a time as to have passed the four score and four-year period—and in all of whose life there has been recognized only the highest worth. Men whom the poisoned arrow of gossip has not sought at one time or another for a target, are few. But our brother, who lies before us today, lived a life that was entirely and absolutely above reproach.

In spite of the old saying, "Shrouds have no pockets," there are some things which God permits us to carry into the next world, and these things are the exact equivalents in life of the opportunities and talents that God has given us. It is true that we must all be empty-handed in the casket, and yet it is far from the truth to say that one must appear a pauper before the throne of Christ, when the "bright angel of Death" calls us to the inheritance of the blessed. Did not Jesus say: "Lay up for yourselves, treasures in heaven?"

This, our brother tried most faithfully to do, and, so far as human judgment can determine, his share of heavenly riches, is now abundant. Into the next world he carried with him.

I. A beautiful character.

II. An overflowing and happy disposition.

III. A triumphant faith in God and love for Christ and His interests among men.

IV. The ardent love of his life-long companion, and the high esteem of his friends. You all recognize our aged brother as one of your best citizens, and why? Pray, let me answer that question.

It was because he put something into life, the exact equivalent of which found expression in his sunny temper, his diligent devotion to duty, his ardent love for the church, and his high esteem for the obligations of the brotherhood of man.

And what did he put into life? What was the price he paid for these treasures which he transferred from earth to heaven? Again I want the privilege of answering. It was, first, the pure coin of faith in God.

It was, second, devotion to the church, and that for which the church stands.

The things which will enrich us in glory and which will embellish our memory after we are gone, are those which, by the Divine law of Christian growth, we have attained through great cost.

Let me urge upon you then, today this sacred lesson, learned from the beautiful life of one brother's eighty-four years sojourn on earth, more than two-thirds of which has been spent in your midst to lay up treasures in heaven, where neither moth nor rust doth corrupt and where thieves do not break through and steal.

Sometimes we all must sever the ties that bind us to this world. In that hour would you have your dying pillow soft, and your passing hour a triumphant entrance into the majestic presence of Jehovah, the King of Kings, and the Lord of Lords?

Names that live long after those who bore them are dead, are not those chiseled in marble and granite, but those which God has exalted because they have proven their right to immortality.

If in life we fail to exchange our abilities and our wealth for the coin of eternal riches, we must expect that the shroud in which we shall be laid to rest, shall contain no price with which to purchase a cherished memory among men.

This quiet and solemn hour today is most certainly a fit time for earnest thinking on the part of many who are making life an arid desert instead of transforming it into a rich and abundant garden of fruits that shall abide.—Rev. Victor Frank Brown.

IV. DEATH OF PERSONS OF PROMINENCE.

A DISTINGUISHED CITIZEN AND PHILANTROPIST.

BISHOP EDWIN H. HUGHES.

Years ago the friend who has just gone from us and myself went together to a funeral service. As we returned homeward he remarked to me: "What was said today concerning Dr. —— was all true. Nothing was overstated. I liked that feature." Then after a moment he added: "If you should speak at the services when I pass away, do not say too much. I have had my faults, and I have known them and struggled against them. I have tried through life to do my duty. Yet I fear there is not much that can be said." How much should be said now I am sure he would leave to my own sincere judgment. His underlying plea was for frankness in funeral disclosure. Therefore, I shall try to speak as if he stood here with his keen eyes fixed on my face.

No eulogy of this departed friend would be complete that did not start with the word **thoroughness**. That quality worked its way through all his life. Whatever he did was well done; that opens the secret of his career. He had small patience with any service that was scamped and slovenly. He himself obeyed, and he wanted others to obey, the Bible command: "Whatsoever thy hand findeth to do, do it with thy might."

In the more sacred associations of life this spirit of thoroughness was translated into the spirit of loyalty. Consequently he was deeply devoted in his affiliations. Toward the nation this quality flowered into a fine patriotism.

That spirit of thorough loyalty entered his domestic life. Prominent though he was, even to being the second mayor of this beautiful city, he was primarily a man of the home. He had a splendid passion of fatherhood. He would have died for his children. He bore with him a tender memory of those whom he had lost and whom, thank God, he has now found again. He simply did not know how to walk the sinuous path of the diplomatist. Like light, he always traveled in straight lines. The ends that other men gained by round-about, and perhaps righteous, methods, he sought in absolute directness. He saw things with clearness, believed in them with ardor, uttered them with fearlessness, and labored for them with intensity.

I will not be so bold as to enter into the sacred region of his husbandhood. I will only say that I had the privilege of repeated presence and prayer in his home when the companion of more than half a century of happy married life came near, so near, to the line that he has now crossed. When physicians gave up hope he never faltered; and the strong hand of his love drew his wife back to the shores of strength. His loved ones can never doubt his affection. He leaves behind the beautiful benediction of husbandhood and fatherhood.

And when his thoroughness passed out into the larger field of human endeavor, it took on the form of a vast serviceableness. Men say that he was a philanthropist; and men say well. But let us not make the mistake of thinking that he was only a financial philanthropist. It is a large temptation among the wealthy to discharge their obligation by the easy writing of a check. He accepted the doctrine of Christian stewardship; and no man that I have ever known lived it out more truly. He had the vision of the future. Once we walked together along a mountain path. A small tree had fallen across the way. I stepped over it and passed on. Speaking with no tone of rebuke in his voice and as if he were stating a common principle of his life, he said, as he removed the obstruction: "I believe it is a good plan to make it just as easy as possible for those who are to come after you." That deed was characteristic of his care over all the paths of our human life. He wanted to serve the coming people. He kept turning every day incidents into lessons of far-reaching service. In the Adirondacks we stood once beside the stump of a great pine tree. The hollowed center had given room for a slight amount of soil which had gathered either from the decay of the wood or from the bearing in of earth by the birds or the breezes. The adventurous tamarack had chosen this stump's heart as a place of growth and had pushed itself boldly up to the height of six feet. It occurred to me that in trying to grow thus upon another tree's foundation the tamarack had severely limited itself. Its tendrils soon struck the slowly decaying wood and could pierce no deeper. A wind-breath or a hand-push would dislodge the plucky sapling from its queer rooting. I remarked to Mr. Speare that the tamarack had made a mistake. He saw more deeply and said: "No! The old tree after a while will only enrich the soil for the benefit of the younger." May I not say that he has done just that! He himself lived out those fine parables of the mountains he loved. If the Saviour's word be true, that greatness has its root in service, then I affirm unwaveringly that here lies the body of a great man.

This is his past. What of his present and future? My friends, he has been a believer in Christ. Long ago he heard Him say: "In my Father's house are many mansions. I go to prepare a place for you. I will come again and receive you unto myself." The promise of the Saviour has now been fulfilled.—Bishop Edwin H. Hughes.

JOSEPH PARKER: IN MEMORIAM.

SIR W. ROBERTSON NICOLL, D. D.

I am here today in obedience to Dr. Parker's last and repeated request, and no other constraint would have induced me to speak at such a time as this. I know, however, that I speak for all, when I say that it is with songs of praise that we remember the dear father in God who has now entered the blessed and everlasting rest. We cannot but mourn that he has left us. We mourn as Christians; the whole Christian church mourns for one of the greatest preachers Christ ever called. We mourn as Free Churchmen; for we cannot but feel today how rich we have been, and how poor we are becoming. "My father, my father! the chariot of Israel, and the horsemen hereof." Only if he could speak, with what lofty and generous passion he would rebuke our misgivings, and tell us to cease from man! "Moses, my servant is dead . . . now therefore arise."

We rejoice that he has been delivered from his sufferings, that he has been unclothed from the weary weight of the body. About the middle of his illness, when he thought he might recover, he said one day, "If I were to die, I should have finished all my work, accomplished all my plans, fulfilled all my ambitions. Yes," he said meditatively, "my life is mysteriously complete. One thing only I might do: I should like to write a life of the Saviour." "Yes," I replied, "and you have known no loss of power and influence." He dwelt on this with deep gratitude, and who can wonder, for few were more alive to the comedy and tragedy of life. He had seen so many suns go down while it was yet day. He had seen the youth faint and grow weary, and the young men utterly fall. It is so rarely that we can say of a human life, "It is finished." So many toilers die on the verge, as it seems, of their achievement. They must be content to put the unfinished work and the unfulfilled hopes into God's hand again. And almost always in old age there is a period of abatement and decay. Few gifts of nature or fortune keep their brilliancy unimpaired by time. Even the gifts of grace for achievement often turn in the end into gifts for endurance. That endurance is indeed a test. Some find it hard to subside into obscurity with grace and content; some find it easy. The trial never came to our dear friend. He was at the zenith of his power and fame when he last stood in this pulpit.

"As I have grown older," he said more than once, with significant emphasis, "I have become more evangelical. I have preached Christ crucified." This was his boast—that he had been a faithful Gospel minister. Of the intellectual splendor of his preaching, of its indescribable originality, I will not try to speak. Who can analyze its magic, its wizardry, its enchantment? When we think of it, we are tempted faithlessly to say that as a preacher his like or equal will come no more. I leave that, to emphasis the burning earnestness of his evangelicalism.

He himself wrote in his latest book: "Concerning them which are asleep—that is what we want to know. We want to know all they can tell us. We are hardly content with being told, we want to see it all, and take fellowship with them that sing a new song. They will come by and by. It is all arranged. Do not suppose they are forgotten. God sends for the people just as He thinks heaven can admit them. There is no haste there, no crowding, no rushing, no clamor. Here is a man who has something to say concerning them which are asleep. He is welcome, thrice welcome. He brings us news from a far country. We have dreams and visions, and many a golden fancy, but we want to hear those who can tell us anything that can cheer our hearts. Give him time, let him take his own way in telling the tale. He will warm our hearts presently. Now, chief of the saints, mightiest of the stalwarts,

Paul, we are prepared to hear concerning them which are asleep, the old friends, the young folks, the little angels, and those who are growing old in heaven. Only there is no old age there."—Sir W. Robertson Nicoll, D. D.

ON THE DEATH OF A NOTED EDITOR.

When I learned of the departure of Mr. C——, there came quickly to mind bright characteristics which had appealed to me through twenty years of intimate friendship. And the first I name was a high and reverent thought of life. Perhaps New England shows its keen and masterful spirit in nothing more clearly than in just that. Mr. C—— came from a trained and devout New England family; among the very foremost of her thoughtful and consecrated spirits he was reared. He believed that life is a trust for a work. It would not have been like him to have said that very often, never prominently; but it was his to live it, and to show his estimate of a man's mission by the deep furrows that he cut, by some precious seed which he scattered, by the care which he gave that which he had planted, that it might find root and grow and bear fruit.

And there was wrapt up in this a remarkable thoroughness; in his early home life, all through his college life and afterwards in the editor's chair, it was his to give his best powers to that which he undertook, and to do with his might what his hands found to do. While he gathered as best he could, and as every true nature does, from the resources which our civilization has given, he put these resources into his own life; they disappeared and came back again with the stamp and finish and spirit of his own manhood, to go out and do the work of the man who gave life and utterance to them.

Another marked characteristic was a conscientious loyalty to what he believed to be right and true. This led him to seek a liberal education; this led him and strengthened him through all the years of his devotion to his college curriculum. He was not seeking honors, though he won many, and these could not but have been pleasant to him; but he was seeking that which was above honors, with which he could enrich his life and strengthen himself for bearing his part in enriching other lives.

Another characteristic was perfect sincerity. Did it ever occur to you what an expressive origin that word has? It comes from two Latin words which signify "without wax," pure honey; that is the thought that comes to me, in regard to my friend's life. Surrounded by the dissipating and clouding influences of life, I never saw, in the twenty years of our acquaintance, the least wavering from that high and pure purpose, from that manly and sincere life which characterized him from the very first. To all this sincerity and purity of purpose, bearing the mark of the noble chevalier, "without fear and without reproach," he added a courage, a persistency, hidden. but indomitable, planted in his life, and enduring even when the wasting hand of disease was laid upon him.

And then there was in it all and above it all that tender spirit of helpfulness, that grace of soul which forgets self and loses self and finds it again in the being of another. This made his home a place of joy; indeed, the very joy and spirit of his life. These friends who are here today, and many absent ones who would gladly bear their testimony, are thinking now of this ideal of a true home, where the thoughts and work of husband and wife were one because they had the same bright visions which they sought to make realities. Truly, in the thought of Longfellow, she was "sitting by the fireside of his heart feeding its flame."

The father lived until the work of a holy ambition was accomplished, until his boys had taken up the work of life as he longed to see them. But beyond his family and friends, his strong and noble thought was recognized among thinking and patriotic men, as that of a leader along the lines where humanity needs to be stirred and guided. And now to crown my humble tribute, let me give the incident which a few years ago brought to his host of friends a knowledge of the depths and tenderness of this "Great Heart." With large sympathies and masterly ability by the appeal of his pen he rescued and raised a bereaved family above want, thus commemorating by the best possible method,—but the hardest—the noble life and heroic death of a fellow-journalist. This stands, perhaps, above even his most notable achievements, as the loftiest ideal and the grandest work of his life.

The work which an editor does is not usually attached to his name; in a sense he works down out of sight, among the hidden courses; but one with such a lofty purpose, one with such a reverent spirit, cares little for the glory of a name. His glory is in seeing the triumph of that to which his life was consecrated. Could we have looked in upon his heart and have read his spirit in its highest and noblest aspirations, in its loving trust, we should have found that in all the hopes which he cherished, and in the ends which he sought, he was filled with a deep and earnest desire to meet the approval of Him "whose we are and whom we serve."

DEATH OF A PHYSICIAN.

REV. FREDERICK T. ROUSE.

When a physician lays down his work it is not like the passing of an ordinary citizen. He has held a peculiar relation to the community. He is not simply a public agent for the transaction of business. He is a public friend. He deals not with the simple external goods of men. He holds the most sacred trusts. Under his hand the strong man lies down upon the scant couch in an unconscious sleep and trusts the thread of life to his careful skill. To him the woman tells her deepest secrets and trusts implicitly to his truth and honor. He watches over our entrance and exit from the world. He is a family friend. The sick one looks impatiently for his coming, and opens the eyes with trust and hope and gratitude into his cheerful thoughtful face. His people feel that they own him; he is subject to their call by day and night. And how many

I have heard say during the last few days with that peculiar conscious-ness of this close relationship, "He was our doctor."

There seemed to come from him something more than his medi-cine; it was his personality. The patient was better before the drops were administered.

There was pathetic significance in the procession that has been com-ing to this church door during these last two days. Old and young, scantily clad and well to do, the workman and the employer, the student and the man of business. "He saved my life." "He brought my child through." "He was always willing, so gentle, so strong, so kind!"

It is no wonder that in the naming of the disciples and early Chris-tian leaders of the New Testament, while they called one the zelot, one the publican, one the son of thunder, Luke, the physician, they called "the beloved." And we realize something of the pathos, yet strength and comfort of the lonely Paul, physically weak and wrecked, when he told how all his followers save one had left him; we could guess who that one was. It was the physician, "Only Luke is with me."

How many times the pastor comes to the hush of a quiet room where perhaps an only daughter is breathing out her last with the strange sad struggle, and in the silent room with parents and family circle there is but one other, the doctor, whose very heart is bleeding because he cannot give back the precious life.

A doctor need be a good man, a true man, shall I not say a godly man, for he is often the sole counsellor to the departing spirit.

It was said in derision of the one we call the "Great Physician" that "He saved others, himself, he could not save."

Not in derision but in sad and wondering earnest we have repeated these same words during these days. While the fever has worked its dreaded way those who have been brought back to life by his skillful care would gladly have done their utmost to do for him what he had done for them, but they could not. Disease makes no discriminations and when it finds the fruitful soil and ready conditions it does its work for high and low, unskilled patient and skilful physician.

.   .   .   .

When the mysteries of life are solved; when we come to know as we are known then and then only will the sad questions that we ask today be answered. We are in the midst of mystery. This event is not the only one that is unexplained. That this life should be cut off in its prime is but a part of the unexplained workings of law of nature, of Providence. Our only way is to do our best and trust.

Our best prayer is this which I would put in your hearts and minds today:

> Lead kindly light amid the encircling gloom,
>   Lead thou me on;
> The night is dark, and I am far from home,
>   Lead thou me on;
> Keep thou my feet; I do not ask to see
>   The distant scene; one step enough for me.
>   —Rev. Frederick T. Rouse.

THE DEATH OF WENDELL PHILLIPS.

JOSEPH COOK, D. D.

Whom God crowns, let no man try to discrown. There lies dead on his shield in yonder street an unsullied soldier of unpopular reform, a spotlessly disinterested champion of the oppressed, the foremost orator of the English-speaking world in recent years, the largest and latest, let us hope not the last, of the Puritans, a servant of the Most High God, a man on the altar of whose heart the coals of fire were kindled by a breath from the Divine justice and tenderness. Wendell Phillips has gone, doubtless, to an incalculably great reward. He is with Garrison, and Sumner, and Lincoln now. He is in the company of Wilberforce and Clarkson. He has met Phocion, and Aristides, and Demosthenes, and Scipio, and the Roman Gracchi, and Howard, and John Brown, and Toussaint L'Ouverture. He is with Milton, and Cromwell, and Hampden, and Vane, and the Covenanters and Pilgrim Fathers, and the host of martyrs who, in every century, have laid down their lives that the dolorous and accursed ages might a little change their course. With the approval of this company, what cares he for our praise or blame? He cared little for it in life. Fifty years hence, history will not ask what Boston thinks of Wendell Phillips; but rather what he thought of Boston. We cannot crown him; the memory of his career crowns our civilization.

There are three periods in Mr. Phillip's life—preparation, struggle, victory. His preparation extended from his birth—or rather from some generations before it, for he inherited ancestral merit of the highest type—to the Boston mob of 1835. This period included his boyhood in the historic streets of Boston; his education in a cultured home and Boston schools and Harvard university; his study of the law, and initial, reluctant practice of it. His struggle lasted thirty years, from 1835 to 1865,—that is, from the time when he saw Mr. Garrison in danger of being murdered in your streets for anti-slavery opinions, to the day when it pleased Almighty Providence to eradicate slavery from our nation. His victory was in the last nineteen years of his life, in which he walked among us, not without occupation, indeed, but with his great purpose so thoroughly accomplished that he seemed lonely in his triumphant and peaceful days.

Is it not fair to assert that, without the forty years of this reformer's influence from the platform, our civilization might possibly have sunk so low as to make a compromise with slavery? You affirm that slavery was not abolished in his way, that he was a disunionist for years, and that, perhaps, the bitterness of his attack on human bondage precipitated the conflict between the North and the South. I maintain that slavery was abolished in Mr. Phillips' way; for after 1861 he was a defender of the Union and of all the great measures of the North in the period of the war and of reconstruction. But as to the preceding period, are you sure that, if the brilliancy of his oratory, the intensity of his moral convictions, the weight of his conscience, had not been thrown into the scale, we should have been ready when secession showed its head to crush it? Are you certain that the statesmen who were safe men would have brought us into that posture of soul in which such a degree of courage and insight became possible as to make the sacrifices of our war practicable by the will of the masses?

It is sometimes said that Wesley and Whitefield, moving up and down the Atlantic coast as shuttles, wove together the sentiments of the thirteen colonies, and made union possible by creating a national spirit. We have no national daily journals, but we have national orators, men whose words are heard from Plymouth Rock to Golden Gate; and it is on a few men who reach the whole nation that we must depend for the unification of sentiment in great crises. It is true the press echoes itself, and so fills the land, and on the highest matters is substantially a unit; but sometimes the press is not as courageous as the platform. In most great crises of unpopular reform, the platform takes the initiative. Especially in the anti-slavery contest was it notoriously true that the abolitionist platform was vastly in advance of the press and of the pulpit. It was Mr. Phillips' oratory, as I think, which imparted, more than any other weapon in the hands of one man, anti-slavery zeal to the North, and gave to the commonwealths which resisted the rebellion such moral preparation as made their victory in the Civil War possible.

Boston mobbed Wendell Phillips. Let this city now reverently, proudly, and yet penitently build his monument. Æschines said that the character of a city is determined by the character of the men it crowns. This American reformer's hands were clean from any stain of gold. He did not love place or pelf. It was to plain living and high thinking that he consecrated his life. His gains were given away in silent philanthropy. It is certain that the last person whose interest he thought of was himself. That unspeakably sacred relation of his to an invalid wife—how dare we name it in public over his open grave except as we look into the coffin through tears? More than once he said: "She was my inspiration." Was this the chief secret of his power? This man almost never unveiled to mortal gaze the holy of holies of his spirit, in which he dwelt alone with God. He said at Theodore Parker's funeral: "Mine is not Parker's faith. Mine is the old faith of New England." I heard the authoress of the "Battle Hymn of the Republic" say last night to a hushed assembly, "Wendell Phillips was orthodox of the orthodox." He would not worship with the churches of Boston; but, in the darkest days of the struggle with slavery, he and some of those who were most nearly of his own heart were accustomed to meet on the Sabbath in private homes to observe the holy service of the Lord's Supper. The faith of this servant of humanity was not a creed merely, but a life. "Blessed are the dead who die in the Lord; for they rest from their labors and their works do follow them." In this career the faith explains the works. By birth an aristocrat, by conviction a democrat, by faith a theocrat, Wendell Phillips was by Christian necessity a reformer. Let us look into our own duties through the lenses of these tears. We all are passing to the majority of souls. Lincoln, Sumner, Garrison, Emerson, Phillips, have gone,—and we are going! God grant that each of us who are alive may sell his existence as dearly as this holy soul did his¹

"Humanity sweeps onward. Where today the martyr stands,
On the morrow crouches Judas, with the silver in his hands;
Far in front the cross stands ready, and the crackling fagots burn,
While the hooting mob of yesterday in silent awe return
To gather up the scattered ashes into history's golden urn."
—Joseph Cook, D. D.

THE MIRACLE OF DIVINE LOVE.

PRESIDENT EDWARD D. EATON, D. D., LL. D.

There are some men whose lifework, as we survey it, makes the impression of solid strength and of noble serviceableness. Like the mountains which rise above the surface of the earth, they abide steadfast in their place, enriching human existence. As the mountain purifies the air and sends it cooled and renewed over the heated plains and through the streets of the city to quicken fainting humanity, so such men purify the atmosphere of daily living and animate their fellows to a more courageous struggle against evil. As the mountains are reservoirs and fountains of water and send streams leaping down their rugged slopes with a momentum that carries them far over the earth, giving fruitfulness to distant lands, and bearing afar the world's commerce, so such men are beneficent centers and sources of business activity whose influence is felt far beyond the circle of their personal acquaintance.

These men are so strong and useful that we think of them as permanent forces in the world as we know it, and almost imagine that they will remain unshaken in the midst of inevitable change. But "surely the mountain, falling, cometh to naught." The tooth of time gnaws it away, if some great convulsion does not shake it down. And the man of massive character beneficent influence yields, often suddenly, to the universal law of change and death. The place that knew him knows him no more forever.

But though such a man must fall, he does not, thank God, like the mountain, "come to naught." The strength of his personality, which is spiritual, is transferred to other spheres of service. It is our privilege to think of him as "a pillar in the Temple of our God," to be shaken nevermore. However keenly we feel the loss of his counsel and his activity here, our thought enlarges to something of the measure of his new experience, as we say with reverent joy:

"And doubtless unto thee is given
A life that bears immortal fruit,
In such great offices as suit
The full-grown energies of heaven."

After the sun has set beyond the high mountains, as shadows gather in the valleys, we look up to the summits and behold the wondrous glow which shines and burns on the far heights, departing day transfigured in glorious color. Thus when the noble life departs and we who are left behind feel thickening about us the darkness of bereavement, we may look upward and see wrought for us, in the blending of beautiful memories and ardent hopes, the miracle of divine love, the earthly life of those we have revered and cherished set in the splendor of the promise of the life immortal.—President Edward D. Eaton, D. D., LL. D.

A PROMINENT RELIGIOUS WORKER.

I should neither voice your desires, I think, friends, nor be true to my own feelings, did I not make my words at this time very largely words of personal tribute. There are times when sermons and exhortation are appropriate. But her life has already preached the sermon. And because she is silent she exhorts us with a persuasiveness that words would not strengthen. We call her dead, but she is still in very vital relations to us. And because this is so I may be allowed to speak of her, not alone as a "departed friend," in the common phrase of funeral address, I may have the privilege, I am sure, of speaking of her by the old, familiar, loved name as I try to speak of what she has been to us all.

As we think of her life we find many things that endeared her to us.

I. She was a child of the city.

II. She was a child of the church.

The church of Christ has nothing in itself of which to boast. Its power, its fruitage is of God. And yet any church may be grateful, may take heart and go forward with good courage that has been instrumental in shaping such a life as hers. Freely she received from the spiritual strength of the church, and freely she gave to it, everything that she could, for its richest upbuilding.

III. And then in charitable work outside of the church she was ready, and faithful, and increasingly useful.

IV. We find, therefore, in the outer circumstances of her life and of her death, some things that bring her near to us at this time. But there was something in her inner life that has drawn us to her far more. One thing was this: She was among us as one who ministered. Her spirit was the spirit of service.

She was not thinking of being ministered unto, but of ministering. We knew that what she was given to do would be faithfully and cheerfully done, always, and we knew that it would be done upon principle instead of impulse, also.

Her spirit was born of the Master's love for her and her love for the Master.

V. Then in these years when she has been most active among us, hers has been a growing character. It was a character sweetened and strengthened by a personal relation of loyalty and love to the Saviour Himself. It was a character that was built upon eternal foundations of truth and righteousness, and because of this it abides forever. It was a character that seemed to say, in every act, "I expect to pass this way but once, if therefore there be any kindness I can show, or any good thing I can do to my fellow human beings, let me do it now, let me not defer or neglect it, for I shall not pass this way again."

And this is our sorrow, friends, today, that she will not pass this way again. But should not joy mingle with sorrow that she has been permitted to pass this way once and to leave blessings in her pathway?

May I not bring the congratulations as well as the sympathy of this company to these brothers because their sister, like the sister of Lazarus, chose the better part of life as she passed through it,—the part that cannot be taken away from her? May I not congratulate this mother, that to her was given a daughter of whom it might be said that in home and church and society we might apply the Master's own words, "She hath done what she could." And may I not suggest this to her Sunday school class, to the Christian Endeavor society, to the church and to all who loved her and are asking "Who can take her place?" may I not say, we must take her place; not to do her work, that is done—well done—but to do our work with the willingness, the fidelity, the cheerfulness, the loyalty to principle with which she did her work; this will honor her, this will rejoice her heart more than aught else we could do, when in God's own time we shall meet with her again.

Of her life we can say in the Master's own words, "She was among us as one who served,"—"She hath done what she could." And of her death, of this sudden, unexpected and to us inexpressibly sad passing of the loved daughter and sister and church member and Christian friend, we can only say this:

"Through the deep silence of the moonless dark,
　　Leaving no footprint of the path she trod,
　　Straight as an arrow cleaving to its mark,
　　　　Her soul went home to God.

"Alas," we cry, "she never saw the morn,
　　But fell asleep outwearied with the strife."
　　Nay, rather she arose and met the Dawn
　　　　Of Everlasting Life."

DEATH OF A CONGRESSMAN.

(Eulogy Delivered by Hon. W. J. Bryan on Hon. George W. Houk of Ohio.)

Mr. Speaker, George W. Houk was my friend, and while no words of mine can add peace to his ashes or sweetness to his sleep, I beg to place on record my tribute of affection and esteem. He was one of the first members of the Fifty-second Coongress whom I met after my own election, and the acquaintance which we formed while crossing Lake Superior together in the summer of 1891 ripened into an attachment which I enjoyed during his life, and which I cherish in memory now.

He was a well-rounded man—one of the most complete men I ever knew. Some are specialists and excel in a particular line of work, or become famous because of some faculty abnormally developed. Not so with Mr. Houk. He was not a one-sided man, nor a man with but one idea or one virtue. He so blended graces and good qualities, so combined the traits and characteristics which distinguish men as to be worthy of Antony's compliment to Brutus:

> His life was gentle, and the elements
> So mixed in him, that Nature might stand up
> And say to all the world, "This was a man!"

He found his inspiration at his fireside, and approached the ideal in his domestic life. He and his faithful wife, who was both his helpmeet and companion, inhabited as tenants in common that sacred spot called home, and needed no court to define their relative rights and duties. The invisible walls which shut in that home and shut out all else had their foundations upon the earth and their battlements in the skies. No force could break them down, no poisoned arrows could cross their top, and at the gates thereof love and confidence stood ever upon guard.

In such a home the devoted parents reared a loving and dutiful family, and lived to see each son and daughter settle in life. And fortune had so smiled upon the children that the father was as far removed from anxious care concerning them as his beautiful estate, Runnymede, overlooking the Miami valley, was removed from the noise and turmoil of the busy city with whose history his achievements were entwined. He did not leave to his children that doubtful blessing, a large fortune, but he left that priceless heritage which money cannot buy—a name without a stain, a reputation without a blemish.

He was a man of surpassing geniality, and his cheerful face shed its radiance on all around him. It was my good fortune to sit by him during both terms of Congress, and I learned to look for the friendly salutation with which he greeted me every morning. He was a boon companion, and allowed no humor to escape him. He abounded in wise proverbs, in stories and in fables, and in all the affairs of life mingled with an artist's skill the lively colors with the grave. . . . .

With him citizenship was a sacred trust as well as a privilege, and in the discharge of its responsibilities he exercised the most conscientious care. He was a politician in the sense that he was a student of the science of government, and a successful legislator in that he wrought into effective law the principles in which he believed. He possessed all the characteristics of the statesman. He reasoned out each proposition that came before him with a singleness of purpose and a desire to know the right.　　.　　.　　.　　.　　.　　.　　.　　.　　.　　.

He was honest, both with himself and with others. Not only was he incorruptible so far as pecuniary influences go, but he was true to his own convictions. His fidelity to others was insured by strict adherence to the injunction—

> To thine own self be true;
> And it must follow, as the night the day
> Thou canst not then be false to any man.

He was a brave man, and dared to follow his own judgment, even
when it led him into disagreement with his party associates. His moral
courage was developed to a high degree, and he was willing to assume
responsibility for his every act, conscious of the rectitude of his purpose.
His ability was recognized by his associates in Congress, and his opinions, based upon extensive research and wide experience, illuminated
and ornamented by quotations from history, fiction and poetry, were
sought after more and more as men knew him better.

His life was one long journey upward, without a halt or backward
step. His success was not meteoric; he won his way step by step, and
pitched his tent on higher ground at the end of each day's travel. For
more than sixty-five years his home was at Dayton, Ohio. There he
attended school, taught school, read law, and practiced at the bar. There
he spent the days of his boyhood and manhood, and there, after he had
almost completed his three-score years and ten, he rests from his labors.
The sorrowing multitudes who attended his funeral testified, as no language can, to the character of the man. Their expressions of tenderness
and affection, and their gentle ministrations fitly crowned the career
which they had watched with pride and love. Truly, "The path of the
just is as the shining light, that shineth more and more unto the perfect
day."

I shall not believe that even now his light is extinguished. If the
Father deigns to touch with divine power the cold and pulseless heart of
the buried acorn, and make it to burst forth from its prison walls, will
He leave neglected in the earth the soul of man, who was made in the
image of his Creator? If He stoops to give to the rosebush, whose withered blossoms float upon the breeze, the sweet assurance of another
spring time, will He withhold the words of hope from the sons of men
when the frosts of winter come? If Matter, mute and inanimate, though
changed by the forces of Nature into a multitude of forms, can never
die, will the imperial spirit of man suffer annihilation after it has paid a
brief visit, like a royal guest, to this tenement of clay?

Rather let us believe that He who, in his apparent prodigality, wastes
not the raindrop, the blade of grass, or the evening's sighing zephyr,
but makes them all to carry out His eternal plans, has given immortality
to the mortal, and gathered to Himself the generous spirit of our friend.

Instead of mourning, let us look up and address him in the words of
the poet:

> Thy day has come, not gone;
> Thy sun has risen, not set;
> Thy life is now beyond
> The reach of death or change,
> Not ended—but begun.
> O, noble soul! O, gentle heart! Hail, and farewell.

CONGRESSIONAL EULOGIES.

BY CONGRESSMAN GRAFF, OF ILLINOIS.

I believe that after all the greatest interest in his life was the interest he took in the affairs of the community in which he lived. He moved in but one direction. He did not seek opportunity to get into the Record that he might see his name frequently appear. He made no play for public favor, he scrambled not for public notice, but moved always in the same direction, and that was in the direction of what he conceived to be his duty.

So, then, from that standpoint and analysis of his life, I say that we are justified in spending this brief hour in tribute to the memory of a man who stood as a fair type of the general level of American citizenship. He was a silent man. The silent forces of nature are the most powerful. Sound is not force. One of the greatest forces of nature is that silent one which draws the waters from the oceans, the rivers, the ponds, and the creeks of the world, and takes them to the heights from which the generous clouds distribute them to the waste places of the earth; and so this silent man could not do otherwise than by his life exert a powerful and uplifting influence for good in the community where he lived and patiently worked and died.

This man, who lived the satisfying life of content, is an example of the golden mean which is commended by Horace in the following lines:

> He that holds fast the golden mean,
> And lives contentedly between
> The little and the great,
> Feels not the wants that pinch the poor,
> Nor plagues that haunt the rich man's door,
> Embittering all his state.

> The tallest pines feel most the power
> Of wintry blasts; the loftiest tower
> Comes heaviest to the ground;
> The bolts that spare the mountain's side
> His cloud-capt eminence divide,
> And spread the ruin round.

But the pagan poet, Horace, does not fulfill my purpose of illustration or give full expression to this man's life; and his translator, the Christian poet, Cowper, carries the thought to higher heights, which the life of our colleague typified.

> And is this all? Can Reason do no more
> Than bid me shun the deep and dread the shore?
> Sweet moralist! afloat on life's rough sea,
> The Christian has an art unknown to thee;
> He holds no parley with unmanly fears;
> Where duty bids he confidently steers,
> Faces a thousand dangers at her call,
> And, trusting in his God, surmounts them all.

And, as I believe, this man, not the slave of ambition, contented in his career, fearlessly followed the commands of duty and his God.

BY CONGRESSMAN BALL, OF TEXAS.

It has been said that we are prepared for the death of the old; we can be in a measure prepared for the death of the very young, who are thereby spared the sorrows and vicissitudes of after life, but it is hard for us to reconcile ourselves to the death of those who are taken away in the flower of their usefulness. The life of such a one is sometimes pictured as a broken shaft; but, Mr. Speaker, when we have but a few years at best, and when, as individuals, we are only mere atoms in the sphere of human activity, is it for us to say when the proper time has come to die? Is it not a truth to be gleaned from all the addresses on this occasion that our brother left practically all that mortal man can hope to leave to posterity and to his family—a life well rounded in its usefulness, beautiful in its simplicity and devotion to duty; a life that has left no stain upon his memory and that is a benediction and a consolation to his friends and his family?

Death has come suddenly, but it did not meet him unprepared, for all his life had been a preparation, so living here as to deserve a higher and better life. A score of years is as nothing in the sum of eternity. The great question is, when called to die, Are you ready to meet that Creator "from out whose hand the centuries fall like grains of sand?"

Our brother was ready; as others have borne witness, he was a devoted Christian. We heard his pastor, who knew him best in life, and who can speak better than I of his Christian experience and conduct, deliver an eloquent address over the bier of our departed friend in the church of which he was an honored member in life.

BY CONGRESSMAN LLOYD, OF MISSOURI.

His chief virtue was in his moral influence and Christian manhood. His life each day was an exhibition of the truthfulness of his profession. No one doubted him. He was a forceful exemplar of right living. His words and acts brought no reflection on Christianity. Think as we may about religion, discard the Bible if it is thought best and class it with profane history, belittle the work of the church and discourage individual devotion to the tenets of Christianity, but when the coffin shall hold the body, the funeral dirge shall be sung, and mother earth receive back its own, the greatest consolation that can come to the survivors is the hope of the resurrection and eternal union of loved ones where separation never take place and tears are never known.

What a beautiful monument he has left! A structure of his own hand. The heritage of a pure and upright life. The marble shaft erected over the grave by family and friends may crumble to earth and be forgotten, but the influence of his good deeds will continue like the waves of the mighty ocean, rolling on until they break upon the farther shore. His influence will tend to strengthen and encourage long after the body has turned to dust and the marks of recognition shall be effaced.

Our friend has gone, and his untimely taking reminds me of these words:

> Death takes us unawares
> And stays our hurrying feet,
> The great design unfinished lies,
> Our lives are incomplete.

BY CONGRESSMAN GILBERT, OF KENTUCKY.

There are two consoling thoughts which are of special significance in the material universe around and about us. One is the evident fact that there is but one Architect in creation—planets, stars, and constellations have but one Builder. The other fact is that no substance can be destroyed and lost. Changes in form and combination of elements may occur, but everything is sacredly preserved. May we not, therefore, by analogy, conclude that spiritual things, which are higher than those which are material, are also preserved? I believe that nothing in the universe of God is lost. Our intellectual achievements, our mental attainments, our smiles and tears, our happiness and sorrows, our affections and hatreds are all preserved, and will be used in ascertaining our proper places when the balance sheet is made out for our starting point on the other shore. I believe that every ray of light, every emotion, and every good thing is preserved and used. In the sweet by and by we will see again the crucifixion, the landing of the Pilgrims, and whatever else has occurred in the material universe.

I believe that no flower was ever born to blush unseen, and that no flower ever wasted its sweetness upon the desert air. On the contrary, its beauty and its sweetness are preserved to ornament and perfume that house of many mansions. They are preserved along with smiles of affection and deeds of kindness which have not been seen or appreciated in this world.

BY CONGRESSMAN LAMB, OF VIRGINIA.

These occasions remind us that "it is not all of life to live, nor all of death to die."

What we call death, with all its painful apprehensions and anxious forebodings, is but a change of form and duration of existence. Religion, nature, conscience—all teach that there is a life beyond. When the frail casket that holds our better and nobler being is laid in the silent grave, the emancipated spirit will return to the Being who gave it, and we shall find homes prepared that the "eye hath not seen, nor ear heard, neither entered into the heart of man."

Though cut off in the prime of life, in the midst of an honorable and useful career, our colleague did not live in vain. His influence will survive in his country, his state, and on the pages of his country's history.

We do not agree with the couplet—

> The evil that men do lives after them;
> The good is oft interred with their bones—

But prefer to believe that the evil that men do is a signal light to warn their fellows of the breakers ahead, while the good is a friendly sign-board to point the road to higher endeavor and nobler purpose.

May these occasions, hallowed in their tendencies and time-honored as a custom, bring pure and noble thoughts to our minds as we pay tributes of respect to our departed friends. In emulating the virtues and shunning the weaknesses—if he had them—of our lamented friend, let us so live as to bring credit to ourselves and advance the interests and promote the happiness and well-being of those who have clothed us with the grave responsibilities of official position.

With tender memories of our departed colleague we pray that peace and happiness may follow those who immediately and directly bind that memory to earth.

BY HON. WILLIAM W. KITCHIN, M. C., NORTH CAROLINA.

After all, to die a Christian's death should be the great purpose of every man. Honors and riches and all else desired by mortal man shall perish away with generations and be forgotten amid the centuries, but the soul that has put its trust in the Conqueror of death, the Redeemer of the world, shall live forever. Wherever human intellect has existed there has been an earnest desire, a silent prayer, for immortality—for an eternity of existence.

The kindness and mercy of an all-wise Creator has answered that universal prayer, and so today, in accordance with the blessed doctrines of the New Testament and his faith in them, we believe that the spirit of this man is destined to eternal happiness. As we have by his death been reminded that Father Time is ever ready with his scythe to strike us down, let us take the solemn lesson ever impressed upon us and renew our devotion to the best principles of every great and worthy existence, right and justice to all and by all, strict performance of duty amid all temptations, and never-failing kindness and charity to all of God's creatures. Then may we, Mr. Speaker, when the dread summons calls us from loved ones into unknown darkness, go not alone—terrible thought, alone—but be, as we believe our friend was, accompanied by the Prince of Peace, whose mercy, love and sacrifice are sufficient for us and shall ever bless us.

BY CONGRESSMAN RANSDELL, OF LOUISIANA.

My heart bled and still bleeds for that home, but I believe the Heavenly Father, who doeth all things best, has wife and children in His keeping, and I also believe that the father and husband, though hidden to mortal eyes, still watches over his loved ones and aids them in their earthly journey.

Good-by, my friend! While here I loved thee well, and hope to meet thee some day in the valley beyond the river, where we can rest under the shade of pleasant trees and live again our happy days. Thy memory and the influence of thy pure, sweet life shall never pass from me, but I shall garner them in my holy of holies among the most precious treasures of my life.

> The monarch may forget the crown
> That on his head so late hath been;
> The bridegroom may forget the bride
> Was made his own but yester e'en;
> The mother may forget the babe
> That smiles so sweetly on her knee;
> But forget thee will I ne'er, Glencairn,
> And all that thou hast done for me.

BY CONGRESSMAN ROBINSON, OF NEBRASKA.

Mr. Speaker: So far as we have any knowledge, man is the only one of all created beings to whom is given the information that all earthly life must end in death. The experience and observation of mankind early in life impresses upon his mind the fact that death is the common lot of all the race. Through the grim gateway whose gloomy portals open upon a mystery which the yearning eyes of humanity have never penetrated or solved, all created beings which from the beginning have trod the earth in life have passed, and through that same gateway all created beings now living or hereafter to be born must surely go. This much we know to be the plan of the great Creator of the universe. The gift of earthly life brings with it the certainty of earthly death.

The promised length of days to man is three score years and ten, but certain as is death, it seems to enter but little into the plans and calculations of our life. There is within us a feeling which causes us to look with terror and aversion upon death. We shrink from contemplation of the awful mystery. So common and universal to mankind is this feeling that many join in the belief that it is part of nature's plan to guard the race in times of trial, misfortune, misery, and despair from seeking entrance through the gates of death before, in the fullness of nature's plan, they are called to go. In vain has humanity, during all the centuries, rapped at the dark and silent portals through which the countless millions have passed. The yearning desire of all mankind to know what lies beyond the tomb is only satisfied by faith as it is manifest in some of the established forms of religion upon earth.

As in the course of life youth, strength, and vigor must pass from us with the lapse of years to give way to the feebleness and helplessness of age, it would seem to be a part of nature's plan to prepare the human mind to enter into the dread "valley of the shadow of death" with resignation. But death does not always wait until the tree of life is withered, nor does it always give warning of its approach by robbing the vigorous limbs of their strength, by whitening the locks, by dimming the brightness of the eye, or causing the elastic step to become feeble and wavering. It comes at times without warning to robust youth and vigorous manhood; and so the message came to him whose untimely death we this day commemorate. When to the human eye he seemed in the full vigor of health, when, judging by his years, he was in the very prime of manhood, death placed its finger upon his heart and it was still.

BY HON. E. J. BURKETT, OF NEBRASKA.

To my mind the highest tribute that can be paid to any man is that he was loved by his fellows.

If there was one sentiment more often than all others voiced there upon the occasion of the funeral in his home city, it was the humanitarian principle and practice of our colleague. All said that he was generous even to his own detriment; that he was charitable beyond measure; that in his heart there abounded fraternity, and that he loved his fellow-men and was willing to sacrifice his personal comfort and welfare that others might be more happy. And as we stood there by his open grave, surrounded by those friends from far and near, from all walks and callings and avocations in life, the raw wind driving the sleet and snow into our very marrow, I could not help but think of that story of George Howe, in that beautiful little compilation of tales of Auld Drumtochty—Bonnie Brier Bush.

That story impresses the fact, as you remember, that to be great in death one must have merited it in life—that men are loved for what they do for others, rather than what they do for themselves. You remember George Howe sacrificed his comfort and personal tastes for poor, miserable, drunken, gutter-bedragged Andra Chaumbers. He curbed his vanity and gave others credit for his own efforts, and "made them better than himself," as one of the characters says. But in turn all loved him, and at his death they gathered together from all classes to lay him away. The rich boy from the city was there, and the fisherman's son from the seashore.

Royal blood coursed through the veins of the one, and tracing his ancestry to the "beautiful queen," he gloried in the noble pedigree. The other could see naught behind him but a stern manipulator of a fishing smack. With them, too, you remember, was poor downfallen Chaumbers. Truly it was a cosmopolitan gathering. They blended their tears and shared their sorrows—the rich and the poor, the high and the low, nobility and peasant. For each and all he had done something.

Our beloved congressman is gone. He lives now only by his example. His deeds are history. From them may we cull the good and emulate them, and thus build for ourselves lasting tablets in the memories of our fellow-men.

BY U. S. SENATOR ALLEN, OF NEBRASKA.

The dead jurist and statesman was a firm believer in the Christian religion, and he was a master of Biblical lore and Biblical history. He had an abiding faith in the immortality of the soul, and he loved to repeat the words of Longfellow:

> Life is real! life is earnest!
> And the grave is not its goal;
> Dust thou art, to dust returnest,
> Was not spoken of the soul.

Although called from time to eternity before he had lived the allotted three score and ten years, it is not within the province of his most devoted friend to say that his life work was not well finished at that time. As long as his last friend lives, the grave of this eminent citizen of my beloved state will be moistened by the tears of affection, and as often as the season returns his tomb will be bedecked with rare flowers, nature's first and most beautiful offering to spring.

Mr. President, our friend was an ambitious man withal, but his ambitions were in the right direction. He was not sordid. He was not ambitious for personal gain or personal preferment. He was ambitious that his influence might be of benefit to those around him and of benefit to the world; and he learned also this lesson from the beautiful poem of Longfellow, from which I have quoted, a few stanzas more of which he often quoted to me:

> Lives of great men all remind us
> We can make our lives sublime,
> And departing, leave behind us
> Footprints on the sands of time.

> Footprints that perhaps another,
> Sailing o'er life's solemn main,
> A forlorn and shipwrecked brother,
> Seeing, may take heart again.

> Let us, then, be up and doing,
> With a heart for any fate;
> Still achieving, still pursuing,
> Learn to labor and to wait.

Mr. President, life is but a breath; at best a span. A few days of sunshine and shadow, a few days of pleasure and pain, a few days of tears and joy and sorrow, and man lies down and fades into the future to awake on the shores of eternity.

I believe it is well with my friend, to whose memory we have dedicated the service of this hour.

BY SENATOR THURSTON, OF NEBRASKA.

Mr. President, I am not prepared to say that there is anything to regret in his early decease. His family miss him; they have suffered a great loss. His friends miss him; they have suffered a great loss. His district is deprived of his services, and the loss to the state is also great; but from the standpoint of the man I see nothing to regret in the fact that he was called, and called suddenly, in the very prime of life, in the hour of his greatest vigor and strength, to fathom the mysteries of the infinite.

Mr. President, I look upon the man who thus passes beyond the veil as a fortunate individual. I see nothing to desire in length of years— in the years that come when the strength fails, when the vigor departs, when a man becomes more or less of an onlooker by the roadside, past whom the great active procession runs and leaps. For myself, I would prefer to die as he died, before the first touch of age, before the first disappointment that must come when one realizes the failure of power— to go out at the summit and amid the successes of victorious life, to die in the harness, when all men looking on regret the loss.

So today I do not mourn for the dead. I sympathize with those whom he has left behind, but for him I do not and can not mourn. He has gone beyond, we of the Christian faith believe to a future of added usefulness, where the power and strength he has laid down here will be taken on again under better conditions, to be used in greater fields of usefulness than is possible in this temporary existence of ours.

We peer into the impenetrable shadow, but we do not see; we listen in the infinite silence and there is no sound; but the cable of human hope stretches from shore to shore. Over it we whisper our messages of love to those who have gone before, and with the ear of faith wait the answer of our prayers.

V. THE OTHER LIFE—RESURRECTION, IMMORTALITY, HEAVEN.

"IF A MAN DIE SHALL HE LIVE AGAIN?"—JOB 14:14.

REV. W. J. McLAUGHAN, D. D.

There are some questions that are prayers. Such an one is this parenthetical question of Job. There are certain places in the Alps where the Swiss peasants blow a horn to create echoes that gratify the tourist. The peasant has lived so long in the mountains that for him they have lost all their significance. As he stands there he thinks not so much of the heights of the Jungfrau or the Matterhorn, of the whiteness of their pinnacles or the grandeur of their precipices as he does of the small fee that the tourist may give him for his little performance. In other words, by living among the mountains they have become to him commonplace. He is more interested in a few cents than in all their splendor. This is all too true about our own life and many of the things that are grandest therein. The immortality of the soul is one of the greatest thoughts man knows.

We can form little conception of what it meant to the world to have no revelation of immortality, to have no conception of anything that was bright and beautiful beyond the present, to grope like blind brutes, bound in everywhere, limited by a land of shadows where all that made life worth living was lost. We need sometimes to come back to these elemental truths, these grand thoughts of the race, these mighty mountains of the human imagination that have become to us by living among them forgotten commonplaces, and realize their sublimity and their grandeur.

We find the desire for immortality everywhere. We are told that the desire being universal is no proof of immortality. There have been men and women who did not wish to be immortal; and everybody now does not wish to be immortal. The fact that there have been exceptions only proves the universality of the rule. It is by exceptions that rules are proven. Because a few people are blind that is no evidence that everybody should be blind. Because certain people cannot see a great truth, that is no evidence that everybody else ought not to be able to see it. There is more talk today perhaps than ever before about certain people not wishing to be immortal. I don't blame them. Why should they? They have lived only for themselves. They would only make immortal brutes. Why should a brute want to be immortal? While they have no wish to be immortal, I believe it is not a matter of wishing. The universality of the desire finds expression in ever form and in every land.

Let us now look at the question from another standpoint. "If a man die shall he live again?" What is the peculiar characteristic of Christ's ministry? He came to bring life and immortality to light. It was there before. All history proves that men dreamt of it; that men had an instinctive belief in it. All experience goes to show that men think of it; that life would be different without that thought, though it existed in a chaotic and indefinite shape. Jesus Christ came and He brought this thought to light in a clear, concise, complete and definite form. He did not come to answer man's desire with arguments. You cannot prove immortality any more than you can prove God. There is no system of arguments that cannot be answered that will try to prove God, and there is no system of arguments that cannot be destroyed that will try to prove immortality. Jesus Christ did not try to prove it. He made no argument on immortality. There is no argument in the Bible on either of these two unprovable questions. The Bible assumes them both. It assumes God and it assumes immortality. The Bible assumes that immortality exists irrespective of what it has got to tell; and the great reason perhaps why the Bible did not tell the old patriarchs and the Israelites more about this subject was because of the absurd descriptions of the future life that were contained in the heathen religions. All the heathen religions abounded with definite details as to what man would be like in the other world, as to what man would be doing in the other world. There is the same tendency abroad today. Jesus Christ neither argued about immortality nor went into details as to what it would be like. "In my Father's house are many mansions. If it were not so I would have told you. I go to prepare a place for you."

"If a man die shall he live again?" Yes, says Jesus. What sort of body? Jesus does not tell you. What shall he do? Jesus does not tell you. What shall he be like? Jesus does not tell you. Jesus does not tell you any of these things, but He simply says, "that where I am there ye may be also." The consciousness that God was there would have satisfied Job, would have satisfied any patriarch, for what made death so terrible to them was the breaking of the communion between God and a pious soul. The mere statement of the fact by Jesus that He would be there, would have been supreme satisfaction to Jacob or David or Isaiah, or any of the other great heroes of the olden time.

But Jesus told us more than that. He told us not only that God would be there, but He told us that love would be there in its highest and best sense. Love in God and love in one another in a way that love cannot be seen now, limited by the restrictions that are associated with the human body. Jesus tells us of these great things and enables us to build our hopes, not upon details that are trivial, that might be misrepresented and misunderstood, but upon great, broad, universal, abstract, eternal truths that cannot be questioned and cannot be denied.

"If a man die shall he live again?" All the modern movements of life go to prove the reality of immortality, go to answer this question which Job asked at a venture, which Job asked as a vague hope, and transform it into a blessed truth, a reality that cannot be denied. The evidences for this truth instead of being overturned are confirmed by all modern philosophy and science, the evidences of this truth bring home to our hearts in our hours of temptation the greatest satisfaction, and in our hours of sorrow the most sublime comfort.

There is another thought that was present to Job that is present in the world today. If God made a man for something he isn't finished when he dies. What man is? What was the use of working at a man for eighty years if that is all God can make out of him? The highest possibilities of manhood go to prove that there must be something better yet for which man is being shaped and trained.

Again, belief in justice demands immortality. The world is not just. The righteous man is punished. Was not Job being punished just then, though perfectly righteous? Yet Job did not give up his faith. This question is one of Job's efforts to pierce through the difficulty. "If God be good and if communion with God be the highest type of life, why am I left childless, why am I left helpless, why am I left poor, while on every hand there are men who deny God, and defy Him, who rejoice in their families, add to their wealth and have everything they can desire." In human hearts the desire for immortality is associated with the desire for justice. God planted in us this desire for justice. We feel that if men do wrong and seem to succeed and there be a God they ought to be punished. We know they are not punished here, and our very hearts grip on justice, and say there must be another world, there must be an immortality where these things will be equalized. Though sin carry with itself punishment it does not carry with itself an outward manifestation of punishment equivalent to the sin committed, and justice in human hearts cries out for immortality

"If a man die shall he live again?" Justice cries, he must; ideal perfection cries, he must; Jesus Christ says, he must; the Old Testament teaches that he must, and so, though there is no proof that can be syllogistically stated, no argument that is incontrovertible, all experience, all intuition, all imagination combine in answering this question of Job with an emphatic affirmative. "If a man die shall he live again?" Yes, man says from his heart of hearts; yes, humanity says in all its languages and in all its lands; yes, the Bible says in all its revelations of mystery and simplicity. God says he shall live again either with himself in glory everlasting, or where we know not, in a punishment that is in keeping with his deserving, where the injustices of earth shall be rectified, and where the sins of the world shall be punished.

THE GLORY OF THE CHRISTIAN RELIGION.

REV. WILLIAM PATTERSON, D. D.

In the Old Testament those who died in the Lord are spoken of as "gathered to their fathers," or "into the garner," as "sheaves of wheat fully ripe," with the hope of "dwelling in the house of the Lord forever."

In the New Testament death is frequently spoken of as "a sleep." By our Saviour it is referred to as going to the "house of many apartments" or "mansions," and by Paul as entering into the "house not made with hands eternal in the Heavens."

Then John draws aside the curtain and reveals the glorified to us in their new home. They are spoken of as "a great company who are innumerable," as "arrayed in white," as "joining in the song of redeeming love," as being "led by the quiet waters through the green pastures," as "free from all sorrow and rejoicing in the presence of the Lord." The place of their abode is described as containing everything that man craves for or desires, and as free from everything that man fears or dislikes. The streets are spoken of as "golden," and the gates and walls of the city as of "pearl and precious stones"—the things for which men struggle and strive on earth; and then the "night of darkness," the "sea of separation," the emblem of sorrow and unrest, the pain that racks, the sorrow that crush the heart, the tears that dim the eyes—all these things are absent from the home of those who fall asleep in Jesus.

The same Scriptures assure us that we can have a "title clear" to this home above, for while John wrote his Gospel in order that men might believe that Jesus was the Christ and have life through trusting in His name, he wrote his first epistle that the believers might know that they were redeemed and that they had "an inheritance that was sure." Paul was sure of it—so was John, and away back in the early days Job could say with confidence, "I know that my Redeemer liveth," and he had the assurance that some day he would stand in His presence.

All these Scriptures come to us for a purpose. We are warned of the brevity and of the uncertainty of life in order that "we may number our days and apply our hearts to wisdom" and do the right and serve God while while the day of opportunity lasts. We are told about the future state in order that believers may be freed from the fear of death and from the bondage that follows that fear, and in order that Christians sorrow not for their departed "as those who have no hope." These promises are intended to strengthen and encourage the Christians concerning their own future and also to comfort the hearts of the bereaved concerning their loved ones who died in the Lord.

The glory of the Christian religion is in this—that it is a religion for childhood, for manhood, for old age, for sickness, and for death—a religion for time and for eternity, for the Lord Jesus who came to save men from their sins came also to redeem their lives and to free those who through fear of death were all their lifetime subject to bondage; to plant in their hearts a hope, to be like an anchor of the soul—sure and steadfast, a hope that would purify their lives and cheer their souls in death, so that they could say as Paul did say, "for me to live is Christ and to die is gain."—Rev. William Patterson, D. D.

IS THERE ANOTHER LIFE?

REV. JOHN BALCOM SHAW, D. D.

There is no if about death. It is the great certainty of time. All men, sooner or later, without exception and without discrimination, must die. Next to the question of our origin, and ranking, perhaps, before it in practical interest, is that other momentous question of destiny: What does death mean—annihilation or promotion, the rising or the setting of the sun, the end or the beginning of life, the entrance upon an unbroken sleep or the gateway through which we pass into an endless existence? Let us attempt to frame an answer to this question.

A distinguished scholar, writing a little over a year ago in one of our leading monthlies, declared it impossible to give any definite or positive answer to the question. Man hopes to live again, and he should keep on hoping, said he, for there could be nothing more unfortunate than the shattering of this aspiration; but to justify the longing, much more to assure one's self of its fulfilment, is a logical impossibility . This, in other words, was his statement: Man is only dreaming; and whether his dreams are to come true or not, they are so delightful that it would be a pity to awake him. Let him slumber on till death either throws him into an eternal sleep or awakens him to judgment.

Is this the position we are forced to take? Are we merely surmising, dreaming, guessing, when we believe in another life? and is this the nearest we can get to the truth of things? Are there no proofs of immortality?

Three inquiries must be answered regarding the belief before it will pass muster with logic; and if these can be answered affirmatively, the belief will be found to rest upon a foundation which makes it secure and defensible, and to throw the whole burden of proof upon those who deny rather than upon those who affirm it.

1. Is it possible? is the first of these questions, and we can make short work with it. It is a fact which surely no one will deny, that the act of creation called for greater power than would the act of resuscitation. He who put life into the human body can certainly preserve it after it has left the body. What is there more mysterious than birth? If that supernatural event can take place so constantly about us as to cease to awaken wonder, though it be the most wonderful thing in human life, shall we deny the possibility of a rebirth after death, which involves not an act of creation, but merely an act of simple preservation?

A physician once told me of a unique experience of his. He was performing a simple operation that required the administration of an anaesthetic, but did not seem to him to demand the presence of a second doctor. The operation was well advanced when he discovered symptoms of collapse. He immediately examined the pulse, and found that the heart had stopped. He put his ear upon the patient's chest, and could detect no possible signs of breathing. The man to all appearances was dead; but, believing there was at least a possibility of recalling life, he instantly brought into service every known means and method of resuscitation, and after the lapse of a half hour had the immense satisfaction of seeing the patient's lips begin slightly to twitch, and the heart give evidence of the faintest flutter; an hour more, and life was fully restored. Now, if life could leave the body for a few minutes, and return, is it inconcievable that the two might be separated for centuries, and then be reunited? And if a human physician, by the use of material aids and agencies, could resuscitate life, is it difficult to believe that the Great Physician, who has all power in heaven and on earth, can bring life back into the human body at the resurrection? There can be no question, even in the minds of the most skeptical, as to the possibility of immortality.

II. But is a belief in immortality reasonable? Reason is all on its side. The nature of creation makes it reasonable. There must be—there is—a purpose in everything. What purpose would there be in man's creation, if he were made only for this brief span? The only way in which to reconcile the inequalities and injustices of human life, the reversed conditions, the abnormal relations, that now exist, is to look for another or further life, in which all this shall be readjusted or reversed. "If in this life only we have hope in Christ, we are of all men most miserable."

The nature of the soul also justifies the belief. Although the soul is now united to the body, it has a life of its own, and in an important sense is independent of it. It belongs to a wholly different sphere. Is it therefore at all unreasonable to believe that, when that part of our being which is material and belongs exclusively to this material world, dies, the other part, which we call the soul and belongs to a totally different sphere—the sphere of the unseen and immaterial—should seek its native air and still continue to exist? No more unreasonable, no less likely, than that a balloon charged with rarer air should instantly upon being released ascend to a higher altitude.

The nature of life is equally in its favor. Life is the most mysterious and subtle thing in the universe, and its escape from the body at death is quite in keeping with its character. Wherever it is found it shows a tendency to continuity, from the seed that carefully hides the life-germ away and carries it over to the succeeding season, to the traits and tendencies which heredity transmits from one generation to another. Indestructibility is no less strikingly a characteristic of life, whether seen in the successful resistance of plant life to the blight of winter or the posthumous influence that emanates from every human life and cannot be obliterated. Science tells us that while force can be diffused, it cannot be destroyed, neither is matter destructible at the hands of man; and we believe both of these statements. Does it not call for far less credulity to believe that so subtle, so mysterious, so divine a thing as life is imperishable? Surely, when all these varied considerations are taken into account, the theory of another life seems eminently reasonable.

III. Is immortality probable? That which is reasonable is always more or less probable; but add to the arguments from nature, from the character of the soul, and from the genius of life, which we have just cited to establish its reasonableness, the argument from instinct, and the probability is as strong as it could be and not become absolute certainty. Immortality is one of the two great instincts of the human heart. All men feel, in different degrees but from a universal intuition, that there is a God and that there is a hereafter. These are not the product of education or tradition, for they may be found where education and tradition have never come; but they are the innate aspiration of universal humanity.

"A solemn murmur of the soul
    Tells of the world to be,
As travelers hear the billows roll
    Before they reach the sea."

And the existence of this aspiration as fully justifies our belief in that other world as the sensations of hunger and thirst warrant a search for food and water, and make man certain that he will find them.

IV. Now, when a belief is possible, reasonable and probable, does it not come close up to the border of certainty? So reasoned Socrates and Plato; so reasoned many of the strongest minds of the race. Need there be—ought there to be—any question of certainty with us, then, when a belief so securely founded as this is found to have the unqualified sanction of Jesus Christ? When standing upon this strong foundation, we behold One next to us who saw farther into the heart of things than anyone else the world has seen; whose character is so superior to the character of other men, and whose words were so much wiser than the words of the wisest, that we must believe He came from another sphere, and upon dying went back to it again; who was pre-eminently self-poised and truthful, never having been discovered, even by His severest critics, to have once told a lie,—when we find this Divine Man standing next to us and hear Him say, with a straightforwardness and simplicity that are sublime: "In my Father's house are many mansions: if it were not so, I would have told you;" "I am the Resurrection and the Life; he that believeth in me, though he were dead, yet shall he live, and whosoever liveth and believeth in me shall never die."

How, then, should we look upon death? Not with foreboding and terror, but, if we are trusting Him who "brought life and immortality to light," with calm assurance and expectation. It shall then be a messenger of peace from the King; a chariot let down to take us to glory; a bridge thrown across the black chasm over which we shall pass in safety and triumph into the blessed life.—Rev. John Balcom Shaw, D. D.

GONE, BUT NOT FORGOTTEN.

RABBI J. LEONARD LEVY, D. D.

Thou wilt not leave my soul in the grave; neither wilt Thou suffer Thy precious one to see destruction.—Psalm 16:10.

It was customary among the ancient Romans that when one of their dear ones was dying, his relatives would gather around his bedside and carefully watch the sufferer as he breathed his last. The nearest relative would catch upon his own lips the departing breath of the dying loved one and would cry aloud the name of the departing person, repeating, each time, the word, "Vale," farewell. This word is the sol with which every human life ends. Be it pleasant or be it sad, the song of existence terminates in a minor key; its melodies conclude with a wail of lament. Over the aeolian harp of life play the winds of death and the sigh of "farewell" is the last note wrung from its trembling chords. Whether we be the most favored or forsaken, the most courageous or cowardly; whether we be lettered or ignorant, rich or poor, strong or weak, the end is the same. "Farewell" must all say to loved ones and friends, to privileges and burdens, to joys and sorrows.

Yet, is it not strange, as Alger remarks, that the terms used, in most languages, in bidding farewell, suggest not so much separation, as the implied hope of meeting again, or confidence in God's guidance and providence, or a fond and loving wish for future well-being. The Jew of old would bid farewell in a phrase which denotes "Live in peace," or "May your going out and coming in be in peace." The Greek would say, "Chairete," which signifies, "May you rejoice." The Roman said "Vale," "Mayest thou be strong." People who speak the Romance languages, Italian and French, for example, use the term, "Addio," or "Adieu," which means, "I commend you to God." The German "Lebewohl" signifies, "May you live blessedly." The English "Farewell" suggests, "May you journey pleasantly," while the word "good-bye" is a contraction of the phrase, "God be with you." But of all the expressions used when friends and loved ones part, none is stronger in its suggestion of hope and faith than the French "Au revoir," or the German, "Auf wiedersehen," (till we meet again).

The languages of mankind are, practically the pictures and emblems by means of which men make intelligible their hopes and ideals, as well as their wishes and thoughts. It is not without powerful suggestion that we fail to find in all the Old Testament literature, any term or phrase used in the sense in which we use "Good-by," in modern times. The Hebrew language seems, by this coincidence, to indicate that the sense in which we now employ the words "Farewell" or "Good-by," was unknown to our ancestors. Parting and leave-taking were associated with the blessed hope of final reunion, and if the etymology of the "parting" phrases, used by the nations, whose languages we have quoted, means anything, it suggests that the bidding of farewell has been almost everywhere intertwined with the hope of meeting again.

Wherever men take their earthly leave of dear ones, there also is found the belief that "farewell" means "Till we meet again."

The reason of man has generally refused to believe that this world is a blind alley. Mankind does not regard the grave as a cul-de-sac. It does not believe that mind and matter are the same, that body and soul are equal. All that is sweet and pure in human nature has been bound up in the hope that after life is over here, there is a higher life elsewhere and while it is possible that the general aspiration of humanity is based on a wrong interpretation of the facts of the universe, it is, nevertheless true, that the generality of mankind holds the belief dear that "God will not leave man's soul in the grave, that He will not permit His precious ones to see destruction." Dead they may be, but they live on elsewhere; gone, they may be, but they are not forgotten.

How this hope arose none can tell with certainty, but many believe that it took its origin in a mother's heart. The first human mother stricken by the affliction of death, bending low over the body of her beloved child, bathing it with her scalding tears, suffusing it with her warm kisses, found her heart growing warmer as she felt her child growing colder. And the warmth of her heart produced the hope that though her child might go, it would not be forgotten, though it might be put away upon the bosom of mother earth, from the place it held within her bosom, it could not be removed. Sleeping, she saw her child's form rise before her in the visions of the night. In her dreams, she saw her little one come back to her, and her eye met its eye with the old look of love, her lips met its lips with the former kiss of affection, her hand grasped its hand in the old, sweet way, and their interlaced bodies swayed in the passionate embrace of love. In the morning, the vision faded, but none could convince that mother that her child was gone forever beyond the power of reunion. She then dreamed a waking dream that, at some time, she would be joined with the object of her affection, when partings and farewells would be unknown, when together they would live never to be sundered.

This is generally accepted as the origin of the Immortality-hope. Today, it is regarded as one of the most reasonable of human hopes.

Over the future, near and remote, God has mercifully drawn the veil of uncertainty, and for this act of mercy, we should be eternally grateful. Were we to know what life contains for us, all action would be paralyzed. Were we to know whither the river of existence is to flow, it would be congealed at its very source. To know the future with absolute certainty would rob life of all its dramatic intensity and all its enchanting interest. All the surprises that make our existence so pleasant, all the hopes that lead us onward and upward, all the energy we exercise to reach even the noblest ends, would be blasted and killed at their very inception, if we knew what the coming days had in store for us. No enterprise would be undertaken, no new movement would be started. No man would toil and strive for the children born to him, if, beforehand, he knew the sad fate that awaited many of them. Few would care to enter upon the marriage relation if they were certain of the trials that were to fall to their lot in the future. It is well that tomorrow's events and the future's contents are hidden from our view. It is as though God had so shaped our life that today's duty should be done, honestly and confidently, leaving the working out of our destiny to the operation of God's unchanging law. It is as though God had so determined human existence that all our days on earth should be given over to the full performance of life's obligations, abiding in hope for a future beyond the grave. The immortality of the soul remains a belief, a hope and for ages to come, probably forever, it must so remain. But it is a belief supported by reason and of the highest ethical value.

Yet there are some who cannot accept this hope, simple and uplifting as it is. There are some people who cannot understand or cannot bring themselves to believe, that once dead, we can live again. Even for these people, the discovery of the "indestructibility of force" still has its powerful meaning, even though they deny that after death there is life. Every act we perform is the product of a conscious force and the consequences of the exertion of that force live on, through the influence of our character. We live through our character, through our influence, though our body dies. We live here on earth as truly as many believe we live on elsewhere. There is no termination to force and there is no end to that force in us which we call self, or character. Every act we perform goes on re-producing itself like a chain letter in which there is no break. Every deed we do goes on to all eternity working out its destiny. Every act of goodness, every seed of love we sow yields its harvest, and every act of ill, every act contrary to the moral law re-appears, sooner or later, with dire results. "The gods are just and, of our pleasant vices, make whips wherewith to scourge us." We sow wind and reap a whirlwind. The law of God, in its majesty, can never be infringed. Our deeds reproduce themselves and constitute us a source of blessing or curse to the remotest ages. In this form of immortality, we must believe. We may deny it, but God laughs at our denial and Nature mocks at us. In the continuity of God's law there is no break. Do good, and though we do not live to see it, good must come of it. Do evil and evil must be the consequence. We may doubt the immortality beyond the grave; to the immortality of human influence, none can raise a single logical objection. Sometimes as we recall the names writ large on history's pages, we think that those who failed in their day are the failures of the world. But how undeceived we are today! Nero, Alexander, Napoleon, were considered among the greatest successes of the world, in the days of their triumphs. But who, today, mentions the name of Nero without disgust? Who can regard the great military leaders in any light but that of legalized murderers? Dante was an exile, Savonarola perished at the stake in Florence, Bruno was a martyr for the cause of human reason, Lincoln was shot in the very heyday of his life. These men are deemed by many to have failed because, when the sun of happiness was still high on the horizon of their lives, it suddenly set. Yet their influence for good shall outlast the memory of such names as Nero and Napoleon, and when Alexander shall be execrated these men shall receive the grateful blessings of an uplifted humanity.

> "So live that when thy summons comes to join
> The innumerable caravan, that moves
> To that mysterious realm, where each shall take
> His chamber in the silent halls of death,
> Thou go not, like the quarry slave at night,
> Scourged to his dungeon, but, sustained and soothed
> By an unfaltering trust, approach thy grave,
> Like one who wraps the drapery of his couch
> About him, and lies down to pleasant dreams."

So live that when you are dead you shall be missed. So live that loved ones may find in you an inspiration to goodness. So live that the house of God shall be a testimony to your character. So live that religion shall find through you a witness to its great beneficence. So live that if your children do evil, they shall not be able to say: "This my father taught me; this my mother showed me." So live that you shall enjoy to its fullness the happiness of the immortality hope. So live that when gone you shall not be forgotten.

"IF A MAN DIE SHALL HE LIVE AGAIN?"—JOB 14:14.

BISHOP MATTHEW SIMPSON.

I. As to the immortality of the soul, revelation alone can give a satisfactory answer. We may reason from the mind's faculties, we may talk of its powers, and we may know the analogies that abound in nature, still the doubt comes back again—a doubt so strong that it never dispelled the fears of antiquity. Indeed, while the philosophers reasoned upon this subject, and reasoned ably, one of them, as able as any of his compeers, said that the philosophers had rather promise immortality than prove it to be true; and Julius Caesar, as many may remember, declared, in a speech delivered in the Roman Senate, that death was the end of hope, as well as the end of fear. He felt somewhat as did the Greek poet in an elegy on his friend, when he sang:

> "Alas! the tender herbs and flowery tribes,
> When crushed by Winter's unrelenting hand,
> Revive and rise when vernal showers come;
> But all the mighty, virtuous, and wise
> Bloom, fade, perish, fall; and then
> Long, dark, oblivious sleep succeeds,
> Which no propitious power dispels,
> Nor changing seasons, nor revolving years."

But how wonderful for us to turn from the mere conjectures of philosophy, from the denials of orators and poets, and the dim fancies that hang over the mind, to the clear declarations of Holy Writ! There we find that man is immortal, and that the breath which the Eternal Jehovah breathed into man shall last as long as eternity.

II. But the second question: "Shall the body be raised?" Here, too, we must appeal to the declarations of Holy Writ, for if it occur, it is beyond the power of nature, and must be by supernatural power; and hence God alone can give the answer.

Not only by explicit declaration is this doctrine taught, but it was made clear to our comprehension in the resurrection of Christ from the dead. "He died for our offences, and was raised again for our justification;" and it is said He "became the firstfruits of them that slept." The "firstfruits" was a technical expression among the Jews, very forcible to them, but not so directly forcible to us. We must place ourselves in their circumstances to appreciate its true meaning. The offering of the firstfruits was not only held by them in special reverence under the injunction of the law, but so connected itself with the harvest as to command their especial attention. A similar festival is now observed among some of our western Indian tribes, and also among other nations. The law of firstfruits was this: When the ripening grain was seen in the fields some of it was cut, and before man was allowed to eat thereof, the first ripened heads were taken up to Jerusalem and laid before the altar of God as a thank-offering, as well as a pledge of the coming harvest. Now Christ represents Himself as the firstfruits of them that slept. Here is the great human family, and God designs that a great harvest shall be gathered home.

But sometimes a difficulty occurs to us, and we ask: "Can we believe what is mysterious?" We may believe the fact, while we are not required to believe anything with regard to the manner of the production of the fact. Let us illustrate. Take the growing grass in the springtime. That the earth sends forth the grass is plain. How are the particles of earth, the sunlight, the dew, the moisture, changed into the green leaf? By what process does one blade give forth wheat and another corn? How is it that apparently the same particles are shaped into the beautiful color of the rose and the darker shade of the dahlia? The mode is mysterious, but the fact is plain. We know that the earth is covered with verdure, that the flowers bloom in the garden ,and that the trees are all beautiful with foliage; but by what process this is brought about we cannot tell. We may reason; we may proceed step by step, but the nature of the process is beyond the investigation of man. So that we believe a fact while the mode of its development is mysterious.

Look again at those Northern lights that now blush on the horizon and then ascend in variegated columns toward the zenith. Who doubts that the heavens are illumined? who doubts that he sees the phosphorescent currents flitting over the face of the sky? and yet we may ask how they are produced?

Well did Newton say, when an old man, bending under the weight of years, that he was like a little child on the ocean's beach, gathering a few pebbles from the vast heaps that lay strewn around. But we have a firm basis when we listen to the declaration of God. Still, the mind sometimes turns away and asks: "How can it be that there will be a resurrection? is it not impossible? Do not the particles of the human body enter into the composition of plants and of substances that may feed on human flesh? Can it be possible, when the body is burned, the bones ground to powder, and the ashes strewed upon the wind or sunk in the ocean's depth, that these particles will be reunited? Can they be gathered together, and shall that body in its particles coexist? I ask on what does the objection rest? If we analyze the feeling, is it not this: that God, the great Architect, cannot follow in His knowledge the particles whithersoever they go, or that He has not ability to reconstruct that frame again? I go into the shop of the silversmith and leave my watch to be repaired; the wheels are worn, the pivots no longer perform their office. If I take the watch to pieces I cannot remember the wheels well enough to replace them: he withdraws the pins, unfastens the various parts, strews them all around, lays them away, and in the laps of days or weeks takes them up, puts them piece to its piece, part to its part, and reconstitutes the framework again. And why? Because he has a knowledge of the fitness of every particle. Shall the great Architect be unable to remember the particles of our body, and watch their way wherever they may be in this wide universe? or is it in the power of man to so scatter the particles of matter that God cannot reunite them?

Again, the question whether He will, must be solved by Himself. Is it clear that He can. The silversmith knows not the particles of the watch; the shepherd knoweth not the names of his flock; the husbandman knoweth not the parts of his farm, as God knoweth and hath marked every particle of matter in this wide universe.

The Christian's faith stands on the word of God. But while we rest it there, there are analogies in nature to help our minds, and, if possible, to impress more clearly this doctrine upon us. There is the sleep of winter. The tree, which was once full of foliage, parts with its leaves at the approach of the autumnal frosts; there seems to come a death, and yet it is but partial. The tree, though bare, though covered with the ice of winter, though there is no swelling bud to be seen, yet, when the spring-time returns, the bud will enlarge, the leaves will reappear, the flowers will crown the branches, and it will bring forth fruit after its kind. Here is revivification—an awakening again. We have this same principle illustrated at night in the sleep of our body; the image of death, and the waking up to life again. Who knows but by this arrangement of nature God designs to teach us the possibility of a resurrection? These are but partial illustrations; there are others in nature. Look at the strange transformations in animal life. There is the caterpillar, an object almost of disgust, which, if noticed at all, is noticed with a feeling of aversion—watch its labors as it spins itself a web, a winding-sheet. It appears the image of death, and yet if we watch that chrysalis, by and by the ball will burst, and there will come out of it, not the caterpillar that took up its abode in the tree, that spun the thread and went to sleep, but instead of it a beautiful butterfly. If such things take place, who knows what we shall be? We may be laid in the shroud, we may be buried in the grave, we may sleep the long, long sleep—even angels may look down and see no sign of life; but the tomb shall open, the shroud shall disappear, and there shall come up from the grave, not the worm of the dust in its precise form when laid there, but a being brighter than angelic creation, and that shall dwell near to the throne of God. Here are indications even from nature to tell us there may be a resurrection. Yet these, though analogies, are not proofs; for even these creatures shall die and be no more. They are not proofs, but they are illustrations of what Almighty power can do.

But, it may be said, if these bodies shall rise, will there not be the same infirmities? I answer, the figure to which I have already alluded may teach us that there will be changes, though the same body. What these shall be I cannot tell. And yet, nature throws some light upon this point. The chemist or the mineralogist will show you that the same matter crystallizes something in different shapes, and he will explain to you what he knows of the different forms of the same substance. Let us take some varieties of it known to every one of us. Limestone and marble are essentially the same substance, yet far differently constituted. We have further illustrations of this principle. The air we breathe, the chemist tells us, is composed of oxygen and nitrogen. The school-boy knows this, taught as he is in the chemical language of the day, and yet these elements, oxygen and nitrogen, when compounded in different proportions, produce the dangerous aquafortis of our shops. There is no difference in the air which we breathe and nitric acid, except in the proportion in which those elements are mingled together. The charcoal which we trample under foot as worthless is precisely the same substance, in an impure state, as the costly diamond, both having carbon as a basis. The one is worthless, and the other brings a princely price. They are differently fashioned by Divine skill. And may not these worthless bodies of ours, that are like the dust of the earth now, when differently fashioned by Divine power, shine as diamonds in the day when God shall come to make up His jewels? Here we see the Divine power may differently fashion matter; and the apostle, in speaking of this, says: "Who shall change our vile body that it may be fashioned like unto his glorious body?"

But then, again, what says reason with regard to a resurrection from the dead? I answer, reason must say that there ought to be a resurrection of the dead. Look at the conditions of humanity. Shall I live? shall the soul be immortal? have I sinned in that frame with which the soul was united? would it not be proper that I should suffer the penalty of my sin in the same nature? Did I, because of my love for truth, allow this frame to be mangled rather than utter a falsehood? Did I suffer this tongue to be torn from my mouth; did I die as a martyr, or burn at the stake, rather than deny the Lord that bought me? How fitting that in the day of eternity I should wear a martyr's crown! that the same brow that had been pierced should be radiant with glory; that the same tongue that had been taken from my lips should be eloquent again with praise; that the same hand which was thrust into the flames rather than betray its master should receive immortal life! Is there not a beauty, a fitness, in the idea of the resurrection from the dead? There is a reasonableness, I say, in the doctrine of the resurrection of the dead, for without it Christ's triumph would be only partial, and the curse of the law would not be annulled. But when it shall be annulled, I shall rise, and then soul and body will be reunited in the New Jerusalem, with powers improved, with a nature glorified. It is then I shall enjoy the fulness of redeeming love. Even now, planting myself on the declarations of Scripture, I feel that I can put my heel on the neck of the monster, and can say: "O death! thou too shalt die; O grave! I will be thy plagues; O death! I will be thy destruction."—Bishop Matthew Simpson.

WHAT FAITH MAKES OF DEATH.

ALEXANDER MACLAREN, D. D.

"An entrance ministered abundantly. Shortly I must put off this my tabernacle. My decease."—2 Peter 1:11, 14, 15.

We are all mourners here this morning. A life of practical godliness, of bright Christian service, and, latterly, of wonderfully brave endurance, has come at last to the end to which we slowly learned to know it must come. The loving wife, who was a helper and a counsellor as well, the staunch loyal friend, the diligent worker, with her open hand, her frank cordiality, her clear insight, her resolute will, has passed from our sight, but never from our love nor our memory. The empty place in the home can only be filled by Him who has made it empty, and we all pray that He may be near. Every member of this congregation must feel that a strong stay has gone. A wider circle, for whom I may presume to speak, mourns the loss of a dear friend; a far wider one, covering the whole country, offers through my lips this morning affectionate and earnest sympathy to the stricken hearts here today.

The Bible very seldom speaks of death by its own ugly name. It rather chooses to use expressions which veil its pain and its terror; and so does common speech. But the reason in the two cases is exactly opposite. The Bible will not call death "death" because it is not a bit afraid of it; the world will not call death "death" because it is so much afraid of it.

The Christian view has robbed it of all its pain and its terror. It has limited its power to the mere outside of the man, and the conviction that death can no more touch me than a sword can hack a sunbeam, reduces it to insignificance. These thoughts are brought out in these fragmentary words which I ask you to consider now. I think you will see that they lend us some very valuable and gladdening thoughts as to the aspect in which Christian faith should regard the act of death.

I have ventured to alter their order for the sake of bringing together the two which are most closely connected.

I. I ask you, then, to look with me first, at that representation of death as putting off the tabernacle.

"Knowing that shortly I must put off this my tabernacle, even as our Lord Christ hath showed."

The expressions seem to blend the two figures, that of a tabernacle—or tent—and that of a vesture. As the Apostle Paul, in like manner, blends the same two ideas when he talks of being "clothed upon with our house which is from heaven," and unclothed from "our earthly house of this tabernacle."

To such small dimensions has Christian faith dwindled down the ugly thing, death. It has come to be nothing more than a change of vesture, a change of dwelling.

Now what lies in that metaphor? Three things that I touch upon for a moment. First of all, the rigid limitation of the region within which death has any power at all. It affects a man's vesture, his dwelling-place, something that belongs to him, something that wraps him, but nothing that is himself. This enemy may seem to come in and capture the whole fortress, but it is only the outworks that are thrown down; the citadel stands. The organ is one thing, the player on it is another; and whatever befalls that has nothing to do with what touches him. Instead of an all-mastering conqueror, then, as sense tells us that death is, and as a great deal of modern science is telling us that death is, it is only a power that touches the fringe and circumference, the wrappage and investiture of my being, and has nothing to do with that being itself. The "foolish senses" may declare that death is lord because they "see no motion in the dead." But in spite of sense and anatomist's scalpels, organization is not life. Mind and conscience, will and love, are something more than functions of the brain; and no scalpel can ever cut into self. I live, and may live—and blessed be God! I can say—shall live, apart altogether from this bodily organization.

Another thing implied in this figure, and, indeed, in all three metaphors of our text—is that life runs on unbroken and the same through and after death.

The same in direction, the same in essence, uninterrupted through the midst of the darkness, the life goes on. A man is the same whatever dress he wears. Though we know that much will be changed, and that new powers may come, and old wants and weaknesses fall away with new environment, still the essential self will be unchanged, and the life will run cn without a break, and with scarcely a deflection. There is no magic in the act of death which changes the set of a character, or the tendencies and desires of a nature. As you die so you live, and you live in your death and after your death the same man and woman that you were when the blow fell.

The last idea that is here in this first of our metaphors is that of a step in advance. "I must put off this my tabernacle." Yes! in order that instead of the nomad tent—the ragged canvas—I may put on the building, the permanent house; in order that, instead of the "vesture of decay," I may put on the fine linen, clean and white, which is the righteousness of saints, and the body which is a fit organ for the perfected spirit.

True! that does not come at once, but still the stripping off of the one is the preparation for the investiture with the other; and there is advance in the change. Death is as truly a step forward in a life's history as birth is.

II. And now we may turn to the remaining two metaphors here, which have a more close connection with each other, and yet are capable of being dealt with separately. Death is further spoken of as a departure.

This aspect of death shows it to us as seen from this side. Like the former, it minimizes its importance by making it merely a change of place—another stage in a journey.

A change of place, yes! an Exodus from bondage, as true a deliverance from captivity as that old Exodus was. Life has its chains and limitations, which are largely due to the bodily life hemming in and shackling the spirit. It is a prison house, though it be full of God's goodness. We cannot but feel that, even in health and much more in sickness, the bondage of flesh and sense, of habits rooted in the body, and of wants which it feels, weighs heavily upon us. By one swift stroke of Death's hammer the fetters are struck off. Death is a Liberator, in the profoundest sense; the Moses that leads the bondmen into a desert it may be, but to liberty and towards their own land, to their rest. It is the angel who comes in the night to God's prisoned servant, striking the fetters from his limbs, and leading him through the iron gate into the city. And so we do not need to shiver and fear for ourselves or to mourn for our dear ones, if they have passed out of the bondage of "corruption into the liberty of the glory of the children of God." Death is a departure which is an emancipation.

Again, it is a departure which is conformed to Christ's "decease," and is guided and companioned by Him.

Ah! There you touch the deepest source of all comfort and all strength.

"We can go through no darker rooms
Than He has gone before."

And the memory of His presence is comfort and light. What would it be, for instance, to a man stumbling in the polar regions, amidst eternal ice and trackless wastes, to come across the footprints of a man? What would it be if he found out that they were the footprints of his own brother? And you and I have a Brother's steps to tread in when we take that last weary journey from which flesh and sense shrink and fail.

III. The last aspect of these metaphors is that one contained in the words of our first text, "An entrance ministered abundantly." The going out is a going in; the journey has two ends, only the two ends are so very near each other that the same act is described by the two terms. Looked at from this side it is a going out; looked at from the other side it is a coming in.

So, when we see a life of which Christian faith has been the under-lying motive, and in which many graces of the Christian character have been plainly manifested, passing from amongst us, let not our love look only at the empty place on earth, but let our faith rise to the thought of the filled place in Heaven. Let us not look down to the grave, but up to the skies. Let us not dwell on the departure, but on the abundant entrance. Let us not only remember, but also hope. And as love and faith, memory and hope, follow our friend as she passes "within the veil," let us thank God that we are sure—

"She, when the bridegroom with his feastful friends
Passes to bliss, at the mid hour of night
Has gained her entrance."
—Alexander Maclaren, D. D.

THE WAY HOME.

REV. T. DE WITT TALMAGE, D. D.

"An highway shall be there."—Isa. 35:8.

Sometimes the traveler in these ancient highways would think himself perfectly secure, not knowing there was a lion by the way, bury-ing his head deep between his paws, and then, when the right moment came, under the fearful spring the man's life was gone, and there was a mauled carcass by the roadside. But, says my text, "No lion shall be there." The road spoken of is also a pleasant road. God gives a bond of indemnity against all evil to every man that treads it.

I do not care how fine a road you may put me on, I want to know where it comes out. My God declares it: "The redeemed of the Lord came to Zion." You know what Zion was. That was the King's palace. It was a mountain fastness. It was impregnable, and so heaven is the fastness of the universe. No howitzer has long enough range to shell those towers. Let all the batteries of earth and hell blaze away; they cannot break in those gates. Gibraltar was taken, Sebastopol was taken, Babylon fell; but these walls of heaven shall never surrender either to human or Satanic besiegement. The Lord God Almighty is the defense of it. Great capital of the Universe! Terminus of the King's highway!

An old Scotchman, who had been a soldier in one of the European wars, was sick and dying in one of our American hospitals. His one desire was to see Scotland and his old home, and once again walk the heather of the Highlands, and hear the bagpipes of the Scotch regiments. The night that the old Scotch soldier died, a young man, somewhat reckless, but kind-hearted, got a company of musicians to come and play under the old soldier's window, and among the instruments there was a bagpipe. The instant that the musicians began, the dying old man in delirium said: What's that, what's that? Why, it's the regiments coming home. That's the tune, yes that's the tune. Thank God, I have got home once more!" "Bonny Scotland and Bonny Doon," were the last words he uttered as he passed up to the highlands of the better country.

Hundreds and thousands are homesick for heaven: some because you have so many bereavements, some because you have so many temptations, some because you have so many ailments, homesick, very homesick, for the fatherland of heaven. At our best estate we are only pilgrims and strangers here. "Heaven is our home." Death will never knock at the door of that mansion, and in all that country there is not a single grave. How glad parents are in holiday times to gather their children home again! But I have noticed that there is almost always a son or a daughter absent—absent from home, perhaps absent from the country, perhaps absent from the world. Oh, how glad our Heavenly Father will be when He gets all His children home with Him in heaven! And how delightful it will be for brothers and sisters to meet after long separation! Once they parted at the door of the tomb; now they meet at the door of immortality. Once they saw only through a glass darkly; now it is face to face; corruption, incorruption; mortality, immortality. Where are now all their sins and sorrows and troubles? Overwhelmed in the Red Sea of Death, while they passed through dry-shod.

Gates of pearl, cap-stones of amethyst, thrones of dominion, do not stir my soul so much as the thought of home. Once there, let earthly sorrows howl like storms and roll like seas. Home! Let thrones rot and empires wither. Home! Let the world die in earthquake-struggle, and be buried amid procession of planets and dirge of spheres. Home! Let everlasting ages roll irresistible sweep. Home! No sorrow, no crying, no tears, no death. But home, sweet home; home, beautiful home, everlasting home; home with each other, home with God.

One night lying on my lounge, when very tired, my children all around me in full romp, and hilarity, and laughter—on the lounge, half awake and half asleep, I dreamed this dream: I was in a far country. It was not Persia, although more than Oriental luxuriance crowned the cities. It was not the tropics, although more than tropical fruitfulness filled the gardens. It was not Italy, although more than Italian softness filled the air. And I wandered around looking for thorns and nettles, but I found that none of them grew there, and I saw the sun rise, and I watched to see it set, but it sank not. And I saw the people in holiday attire, and I said: "When will they put off this and put on workmen's garb, and again delve in the mine or swelter at the forge?" but they never put off the holiday attire.

And I wandered in the suburbs of the city to find the place where the dead sleep, and looked all along the line of the beautiful hills, the place where the dead might most blissfully sleep, and I saw towers and castles, but not a mausoleum or a monument or a white slab could I see. I went into the chapel of the great town, and I said: "Where do the poor worship, and where are the hard benches on which they sit?" And the answer was made me, "We have no poor in this country." And then I wandered out to find the hovels of the destitute, and I found mansions of amber and ivory and gold; but not a tear could I see, not a sigh could I hear, and I was bewildered, and I sat down under the branches of a great tree, and I said, "Where am I? And whence comes all this scene?"

And then out from among the leaves, and up the flowery paths, and across the bright streams there came a beautiful group, thronging all about me, and as I saw them come I thought I knew their step, and as they shouted I thought I knew their voices; but then they were so gloriously arrayed in apparel such as I had never before witnessed that I bowed as stranger to stranger. But when again they clapped their hands and shouted "Welcome, welcome!" the mystery all vanished, and I found that time had gone and eternity had come, and we were all together again in our new home in heaven. And I looked around, and I said: "Are we all here?" and the voices of many generations responded "All here!" And while tears of gladness were raining down our cheeks, and the branches of the Lebanon cedars were clapping their hands, and the towers of the great city were chiming their welcome, we all together began to leap and shout and sing, "Home, home, home, home!"

I heard of a father and son who, among others were shipwrecked at sea. The father and the son climbed into the rigging. The father held on, but the son after a while lost his hold in the rigging and was dashed down. The father supposed he had gone hopelessly under the wave. The next day the father was brought ashore from the rigging in an exhausted state, and laid in a bed in a fisherman's hut, and after many hours had passed he came to consciousness, and saw lying beside him on the same bed his boy. Oh my friends! what a glorious thing it will be if we wake up at last to find our loved ones beside us! The one hundred and forty and four thousand, and the "great multitude that no man can number" —some of our best friends among them—we, after a while, to join the multitude! Blessed anticipation! The reunions of earth are anticipative.

We are not always going to stay here. This is not our home. O the reunion of patriarchs, and apostles, and prophets, and all our glorified kindred, and that "great multitude that no man can number!"

Does it not seem that heaven comes very near to us, as though our friends, whom we thought a great way off, are not in the distance, but close by? You have sometimes come down to a river at nightfall, and you have been surprised how easily you could hear voices across the river. You shouted over to the other side of the river, and they shouted back. It is said that when George Whitefield preached in Third Street, Philadelphia, one evening time, his voice was heard clear across to the New Jersey shore. When I was a little while chaplain in the army, 1 remember how at even-tide we could easily hear the voices of the pickets across the Potomac, just when they were using ordinary tones. And as we stand by the Jordan that divides us from our friends who are gone, it seems to me we stand on one bank and they stand on the other; and it is only a narrow stream, and our voices go and their voices come. —Rev. T. De Witt Talmage, D. D.

THE EMPTY GRAVE.
(Matt. 28:1-8.)

REV. F. W. KRUMMACHER, D. D.

Let us pass in review the different features of this highly suggestive picture. And first of all, let the mind's eye be attentively directed to the women setting out at early dawn; secondly, to the incidents which befell them at the sepulchre; thirdly, their report to the assembled disciples; as also, fourthly, the issue of their communication.

You remember that when the corpse was deposited in Elisha's tomb, it revived. In a spiritual sense, may we experience something similar! with this difference, however, that the effect wrought in us may be as much greater as the tomb we are now about to visit is greater, more sublime, and holier than was that of the prophet of Abel-Meholah.

I. Night still rested upon the holy city, and a gleam of dawn was visible in the distance, when by its aid a heart-affecting sight is presented to us in its quiet, deserted streets. It is the approach of the veiled procession. We recognize it as consisting of the female disciples of the crucified Lord. They move along with heads bowed low and eyes red with weeping. They have passed the night sleepless, or disquieted with unpleasant dreams; and now, as the Sabbath is over, they are silently moving towards the garden of Joseph, with their fine linen, their wreaths, and their spices, in order to render the last offices of love to the dear remains of their departed Friend, which had been interrupted when He was laid in the tomb.

The sorrow-stricken women move silently along. It is not until they have nearly reached the garden that a petty care unseals their lips, and we hear them say, "Who will remove the stone for us from the mouth of the sepulchre?" Thus all their wishes and desires resolved themselves into this trivial solicitude. Considering the unequivocal prophecies which they had repeatedly heard from the mouth of their Master, this seems hardly conceivable. But the fearful and bloody end of His life must have fallen like a terrific, devastating hailstorm upon the harvest-field of their hopes and recollections.

II   When these mourners reached the garden, they were still occupied with the anxious desire to know "who should remove the massive stone from the entrance to the tomb." What do they perceive there? Oh! what can it mean? Behold! the stone has already been moved aside, and the interior of the tomb lies exposed. But the spectacle plunges them in fresh perplexity. The weakness of their faith suggests that some violence had been practiced upon His dear remains. Trembling with fearful anticipation, they draw near the sepulchre! Lo! suddenly there gleams forth from it a beam of light like lightning, and by its marvellous brilliancy they discover two figures, young men clad in glittering garments, in whom they immediately recognize two beings from another world, two angels of God. Do not marvel that the resurrection should have been accompanied by such extraordinary appearances as these. Without such, as some one has truly observed, the resurrection of Christ would have been a spring without flowers, a sun without rays, a victory without a triumphal wreath. It was right that the majesty of the Almighty should be revealed in every possible way in connection with it, and holy angelic beings are truly some of the most lovely rays of His glory. Yet they were not present for the sake of pageant or parade, but, as on every other occasion, so likewise on this, for the sake of those who are heirs of salvation. They had been sent as heralds, to communicate a message. Scarcely had the women recovered from their first astonishment, when one of the angels opened his gracious lips, and speaking to the sorrowful party from within the tomb, said, "Fear not ye: for I know that ye seek Jesus, who was crucified. Why seek ye the living among the dead? He is not here. He is risen, as he said. Come, see the place where the Lord lay." There you have one of the most blessed messages ever yet heard on earth. The plain simple form in whics it presents itself to us at once stamps it with the impress of truth!

The women feel conscious of the profound significance of the angel's exclamation; but again they are so overcome by the greatness of the joyful news thus intimated, that at first they can only rejoice with trembling. They stand there dumb with wonder. But the heavenly messenger rouses them from their torpor, commanding them forthwith to go and tell the disciples of the Lord, and especially Peter, that their Master had risen, and is alive again. Truly a more glorious errand than this was never committed to any mortal! That which makes our office, the office of ambassadors for Christ, the most delightful on earth, is, that the charge committed to the minister of Christ is analogous to that given to the women. How enviable would the preacher of the gospel be, if the message which he has to declare were everywhere and at once believ ingly received!—Rev. F. W. Krummacher, D. D.

SHALL WE KNOW EACH OTHER THERE?

REV. JOHN BALCOM SHAW, D. D.

But then shall I know even as also I am known.—I. Cor. 13:12.

If we thought this was not to be the case, Heaven would lose much of its attractiveness for us. There are times in our lives, particularly after death has come into our homes and ruthlessly seized some loved one, when we almost feel that we would rather be annihilated than to live forever in a state of uncertainty as regards those to whom we have been united on earth. Better no future life, we say, than a life in which recognition is denied. It is the prospect of an unending reunion at death that has held us up through the otherwise overwhelming bereavements of life.

It gives me unspeakable comfort to believe and to say that there is no fact regarding the future life about which we can have greater confidence than concerning recognition in heaven. The idea of immortality, and the idea of recognition after death, are so closely allied, so inseparably related, as to be logically inseparable. If we are to live on in another world, our personality—that which makes us what we are, that which is our very self, and distinguishes us from others—must continue; and if our personality continues, our individuality, and therefore our identity, must abide, else that which contributes most to our essential entity, that which gives us our self-consciousness, perishes. It is a psychological truism to say that, if my ego is to exist hereafter, I shall have a self-consciousness, and if I have a self-consciousness I shall know myself from others and others from myself.

But not only are these two truths of continuity and recognition correlated, but the arguments which substantiate the one substantiate the other. It is an instinct that leads us to believe in a hereafter; equally is it an instinct which prompts our expectation of a reunion there. Go where you may, this hope, this longing, fires the human breast. Plato felt it; Virgil recorded it; the Hindu finds it in the ancient Code of Manu; the Egyptians buried their dead in the hope of it, and the Indian has ever looked forward to it as one of the assured realities of the Happy Hunting Ground. Shall such an instinct—universal, primitive, dominant— count for nothing? If it is valueless here, it is equally valueless as an argument for immortality.

Reason teaches immortality; Reason also teaches recognition. Where were the wisdom of creating these relations, enjoining and encouraging them, building the Christian Church upon them, and giving to them the sanctions of the Church, if they are simply incidental and temporary? Where were the Fatherhood of God—its reality, its sincerity—if ties so sacred and tender could be severed by death? God's relation to His Son, and the Son's relation to His Father, are constant and unfluctuating, and for that reason form an ideal and an inspiration: but of what service would they be to us, of what influence over us, if our Heavenly Father had denied the same constancy to human fatherhood? Where were the significance of the judgment, if a man loses his identity at death? We shall all stand before the throne as the same individuals that we were on earth, and receive our rewards or punishments, not as someone else or for someone else, but as and for the same persons or individuals that were on earth. Why should we keep our identity up to that point, and then, upon being directed to the right or left, suddenly lose it? Where were the imperishable law of memory, if recognition is impossible? It will be the exercise of the memory that will awaken the praises of Heaven: our delight in meeting Jesus and having communion with the Father will depend largely upon the service of the memory. An immortal soul, with no memory of the past, is a contradiction; and if we can remember one thing, why believe that we shall forget another?

Instinct and Reason, then, are both with us here, and strongly support this universal hope. There are many, however, who, after admitting and feeling the force of both arguments, are more or less influenced contrariwise by certain plausible and much emphasized objections. Three of these call for attention:

(1) That if the relationship of earth continue in Heaven, we shall cling to our loved ones with a partiality and tenacity incompatible alike with its happiness and holiness. To this I reply that such partiality God did not account an unholy or unlikely thing when He created the world, for He set the race in families, and commanded man before the fall to cleave unto his wife as unto no other; that Jesus feared no ill effects from such partiality when He selected twelve disciples, and plainly made it appear that He had three favorites among these; and what is still more significant, the blessed Trinity find nothing either inconsistent or unwholesome in entertaining a feeling for each other far closer and dearer than that held for the redeemed. What is not wrong for God or to God, surely need not be for or to us.

(2) A second objection frequently heard is, that since we shall not have corporeal senses with which or by means of which we knew each other on earth, recognition will not be possible. It is not by these alone, or even chiefly, that we know each other here, but through the inner nature, the mysterious spiritual converse and communication which one soul has with another. Even if this were not the case, every representation or suggestion which the New Testament makes of the resurrection, leads us to believe that our glorified bodies are to correspond to these which we now have. The redeemed are represented as seeing, speaking, feeling, hearing, singing; just as men and women are on earth.

(3) The strongest objection is, that we could not be happy if we missed loved ones, and knew they must be lost. Doubt and uncertainty are often worse than fact. They would certainly be so here. To know that some were saved, though others were lost, would be better than to be in doubt as to whether any were saved, as we would be if recognition were impossible. This theory, moreover, is against human and divine experience. Some of our friends are now out of the Kingdom, but it does not make us excruciatingly sad—it would be better for us if it did. God knows all, and yet He is not oppressed by it. What does not destroy our happiness now, with all the fearful consequences of sin lying just ahead of many of our kindred, and what seems never to destroy the Creator's felicity, may not be expected to counteract the joys of the

heavenly life. A sense of justice, as well as the spirit of love, will control us; and we shall be so lost in the realization of the righteousness of God—so committed to the Saviour's will, so averse to evil—that the punishment of the wicked will be accepted as a matter of fact, and approve itself to our sense of right.

The papers only the other day reported the case of a man who was drawn upon a jury that was to try his son. At first he hesitated to act, but finally yielded, and allowed the case to proceed. When the testimony had all been submitted, he retired with his fellow-jurors, and felt himself compelled in the interests of justice to vote with them for his son's conviction. This may be an unusual instance, but instances where a father's love gives place to his justice in dealing with a wayward son may be met with at every turn. Shall we have less equipoise of nature hereafter than we have here?

Our final authority is the Bible; and when the question of immortality is settled—as it must be before this second question can be approached, much less discussed—it has for us a double trustworthiness. What does the Bible say upon the subject?

It everywhere presupposes recognition after death, and in various ways:

(1) In applying names to the inhabitants of Heaven. This it does in case of the three persons of the Trinity, the angels, and many of the worthies who are represented as among the redeemed. Names are also promised to us—and a name implies individuality and identity.

(2) In revealing recognition among the members of the Trinity. If they know each other, and are known by the inhabitants of Heaven, why should not the redeemed, who are to be like them, have the same means of recognition?

(3) In recording, and thereby endorsing and justifying, the expectation of recognition. Abraham, Isaac and Jacob are all represented as desiring to be gathered to their fathers; and their burial is described as if it marked the fulfilment of that desire. David, upon the death of his cherished son, is quoted as saying: "I shall go to him, but he shall not return to me;" and the declaration is allowed to stand unchallenged.

But the Bible does more than presuppose recognition—it actually affirms it. It declares that Saul knew Samuel at a glance, when the latter came back as if to reprove him; that the three favored disciples were quick to identify Moses and Elijah—from traditional descriptions and intuition, probably; and Jesus Himself pictured Dives and Lazarus as both recognizing Abraham, and knowing each other.

And yet this is not all. The Scriptures, in the words of none other than Jesus, promise heavenly recognition. His assurance to His disciples, that He would come again, and receive them unto Himself, held out to them the prospect of renewing their relations with Him in the other life. His promise to Mary was: "Thy brother shall rise again," implying that he was to remain her kindred in the hereafter. His word to the thief, "Today shalt thou be with me in Paridise," plainly presupposed the man's ability to recognize Him there.

The Bible goes even farther than this—it illustrates or exemplifies recognition. It sets before us the person of the resurrected Christ, and bids us behold in Him the first fruits of them that sleep. He was changed after His return from the grave, but His identity was not destroyed. His name, His face, His voice, His hands, to the very wound-prints, were the same. As He arose, so we shall rise also; changed, and yet unchanged; glorified, but still recognizable; knowing even as we are known.

All this should give us perfect certitude. Nothing could be more clearly or unalterably established than our belief in future recognition. We may confidently expect to know each other there. Heaven is to be a place of reunion, and death a going home to keep it. The visions which some of our beloved have had just before leaving us, of dear ones waiting yonder to welcome them, were not hallucinations. Ere their spirits had been released, recognition was possible. A friend of mine, upon dying, called his children about him that he might bid them farewell, when, suddenly, and as if they were aware of what was transpiring on earth, the members of the family who had preceded him into the spirit land— the mother, an older son, and two daughters who had died in infancy— seemed to gather around his bed, and were as real to him as the ones who stood before him in the flesh. He knew them; they knew him. Turning from one group to the other in his conversation, and acting as a sort of medium of communication between them, he passed away, with a halo of happiness about his face, amid the salutations of the Heavenly group and the farewells of the group that still remained upon the earth. Was he dreaming? I cannot believe that he was. It was a vision as real as it was glorious. May we all have a like experience when we come to die! —Rev. John Balcom Shaw, D. D.

THE EXPERIENCES OF A REDEEMED SOUL AFTER DEATH.

REV. G. W. SHINN, D. D.

What are some of the probable experiences of a redeemed soul immediately after death?

We all recognize the fact that what is in this casket before us is only the body of our deceased friend. Something we call the soul has gone from this body. We cannot understand the connection between the soul and the body, but we have the general idea that the body is the instrument by which the soul makes itself known. The soul no longer animates this body. It has gone elsewhere. It is living elsewhere. It is not here any longer. It has gone into the spiritual realm where its activities continue under new surroundings. It has not ceased to exist, nor is it in a slumbrous condition. We are to think of it as the same soul which was once manifested through this body, but now living its life under other conditions. There must therefore have been some experiences which that soul had upon its departure hence. What are they?

I. First of all it has become convinced of the supremacy of the spiritual over the material. There is a constant struggle in the life that now is to accept spiritual verities. Material things are so insistent that they often press from us here even the thought of things spiritual. We are tempted to live as if we were only of the earth earthly. If we yield to the suggestions of some of the philosophy of the time we become materialists and know nothing of spirit and of the spiritual life. Men sometimes make their senses the only avenues of knowledge and deny whatever is not reached by their agency. If we escape the full influence of materialism we are nevertheless affected by it in some of its connections, so that it is sadly true that we must struggle hard if we would retain our belief in the spiritual life, and in the spiritual verities which are more real than things material. Now a redeemed soul that passes hence passes into the world of departed spirits, and for it there is no longer any doubt of the existence of the spiritual world. The things that were once obscure are now as plain as the day in the new light into which it has entered. But beyond this it is able to see the vastly greater importance of that which is spiritual.

II. A second experience of a redeemed soul after its entrance upon the spiritual life is, no doubt, that of realizing that its struggling with sin is over. Here the struggle was incessant. No day came without it. There was always the need of being upon the defensive. Temptations without, temptations within—this was the history of the soul here. But in that place whither it has gone there is no longer any of that which made up so large a part of its daily experience in the present life. What bliss it must be to be free from allurements to evil! What bliss to realize that there never again can be any danger of falling away from God and goodness! What bliss to know that thenceforth there shall be steady growth in righteousness without any peradventure of stumbling!

III. And this mention of growth in righteousness suggests a third part of the experiences of a redeemed soul in Paradise and that is the conviction that now it shall develop in those graces which make it unceasingly Christ like. We cannot think of a soul's remaining stationary in its attainments. There is endless progression before it. It has come into the nearer presence of vast ranges of truth. It is in condition to take into itself those elements which insure its wider and deeper development.

Boundless indeed are the resources amid which it is to live, and its receptivity is vastly increased beyond all the possibilities of the present. We are to think of it as a growing soul. Knowing more, feeling more, doing more. It will be incessantly active, because its life shall be amid surroundings free from pain and discouragement. All the conditions will invite activity and every movement must be joyous. We are to think of it as placed where the growing Christ-like shall be accelerated and where gracious results are possible which could not be realized at all here. Here there is but feeble growth. There the advance in knowledge and holiness shall be beyond our present thought.

IV. One more experience of a redeemed soul in Paradise will be that of the home feeling. The other world will not seem so strange to the soul as the present does, for it will find itself in entire sympathy with what it meets, and the blest inhabitants of that place will not be as those whom it knows not, or knows but imperfectly. The soul has gone home. It will find there a blest companionship with the good of all ages, and there cannot be the strangeness which the uncertainty, the temptations and the sorrows of the present occasion. It is here that it was a stranger. There it shall be indeed at home. The home feeling comes to it at once.

If then a soul departing hence in the Lord realizes the supremacy of the spiritual life, realizes that it has passed beyond all struggling with sin, realizes that it is to grow steadily into the likeness to Christ, and realizes that it has finally reached its true home—why should we mourn those who have died in the faith? Rather let us rejoice that they have passed out of the realm of the material, out of the power of temptation and that they have gone into the glory and the gladness of that life which knows no darkness and which is to be spent in the nearer presence of the Lord.

Note.—Some of the thoughts in this address were suggested by one of Liddon's sermons: "The First Five Minutes After Death."—Rev G. W. Shinn, D. D.

VI. CHRISTIAN COMFORT; CONFIDENCE; RESIGNATION.

GOD KNOWS—GOD PITIES.

"Like as a father pitieth his children, so the Lord pitieth them that fear him; for he knoweth our frame, he remembreth that we are dust."— Psalms 103:13, 14.

REV. I. H. WOOD.

The silver cord is loosed; the golden bowl is broken; the pitcher is broken at the fountain and the wheel at the cistern; man has gone to his long home and the mourners have gone about the streets. It is not for us to measure the length of the cord, or to tell the capacity of the bowl, or to determine the drawing power of the wheel. He who holds the water in the hollow of His hand, and metes out heaven with a span, and weighs the mountains in scales and the hills in a balance, now has the soul in His own keeping. We may not replace the pieces and say: This was the man. God alone can put the fragments together and estimate their worth.

It is not for the speaker to value this man's place in this community, or to call up memories of his career since boyhood, or to say exactly what was his strength or his weakness. Let me rather stand as one would who felt that in the casket was his own father carved in the marble of death, and it were his own mother that wept, and this was his brother and these were his own afflicted sisters, and this congregation were friends who knew and loved.

God knows our frame, He remembers our frailty, and therefore He pities us as a father his children.

I. God knows. A skillful instrument maker best knows the qualities of the product of his brain and fingers. He understands its strong points and its weak ones, for he is the creator of it all. So there is One who knows precisely where in our nature we are at fault, where the sweet, loving deeds arise, where tension is strongest, and where resistance can least be made.

He knows the body best because He fashioned it. He is fully aware of all that is involved as a result of such creation. Friends cannot appreciate us; they cannot rightly measure the good that we possess; they judge from the outward appearance; they do not see behind the result the great motive; they fail to realize that what we do is but a small proportion of what we really are. Friends may say today they regard his talents aright, but do they fathom the deeps from which the deed springs? Do they appreciate the outpush of his ambition, the splendid hopes he entertained for the future? We see the bud cut off from the plant and stop with the thought that there is only a bud. Another with better vision has already seen the beauty and the radiance of the flower that is to be. We see the bud of a life; we say that is all; but there is One above who sees the promise of fruitage, knowing what twenty or thirty years more of activity can accomplish. We see the bud; God sees the flower.

Least of all may our opponents judge us. They exaggerate defects, obscure or even forget excellencies, are prejudiced, unable to give an impartial verdict. Even a good reputation may be beaten by the scandalous flail of abuse. Nor may we know ourselves. We live for the moment; we are in a maze; we can not summon ourselves to see ourselves. We are a bundle of energies. "The soul is the enigma" to itself. What we are in the depths of our being we can not fathom. The only solution is God.

II. **God pities.** He might know us through and through. He might remember every trait and word and act, and it would be little satisfaction for us. But after His thought and remembrance He pities—as the father pities his child, only infinitely more; as the mother her infant, but with surpassingly greater tenderness. So that He invites the widow to leave her fatherless ones in His care and He will be as kind as a husband to her.

The pity of God! It shone forth in the face of His Son as He went forth on His mission. As Jesus wept at the grave of His friend, so God weeps. As when the Saviour said while they drove the iron into His quivering nerves, "Father, forgive them, for they know not what they do," so God pities His offspring even when in their blindness they oppose His will. God is affected by every tear that stains the cheek, at every moan. He aches in every heartache. He agonizes in each struggle. He loves in every noble emotion. He says, "When thou passeth through the waters, I will be with thee, and through the rivers, they shall not overflow thee." Bring your grief and your sorrow to Him, for He cares for you. Like as a father pitieth his children, so the Lord pitieth them that fear Him, for He knoweth our frame, He remembereth that we are dust.

This one died suddenly. Quick comes the call summoning the soul into the presence of the Creator. It says, "Perhaps thy turn will be the next," Are we ready? You whose hair is whitening fast, have you made wise preparation for the great change?

He would have had me say, "Forgive your enemies. Be charitable, be generous, be brotherly. Wherein I was strong and good and manly, emulate my strength. Where I was weak, be very strong. Honor God and revere His name. Turn your hope to Christ. Behold the Lamb of God."

WHO HATH ABOLISHED DEATH.—2 TIM. 1:10.

HORACE BUSHNELL, D. D.

I. How mightily is the aspect of death changed by the simple passion of our Lord! He shows us there the eternally sovereign power of goodness, and we see how weak death is, when it comes to lay its hand upon goodness. We say, speaking historically, that Christ died. And yet there seems, after all, to have been no death in the case. The terror and shrinking and grasping after life are not here. Death is only taken into the employ of goodness, and so it is made to serve where it used to reign. Captivity is taken captive by this cross. Through Christ's death upon it, He had the power of death destroyed, visibly abolished. Nor after the sight of such a transaction as the death of Christ can we look upon death as the terrible monster he was before. He is tame before love, a slave that is given to wait upon the good and open the gates of victory and life before them.

II. Again Christ, by His doctrine and by His ascension to the right hand of the Father, has opened to us another and a higher state of being, so that death is no more a realm of silence and detention, but a gate simply of transition. Death becomes twin brother of Hope, one opening to us the prospect of glory, the other opening the way. Nothing is so hopeful to the true Christian, nothing so inspiriting and animating as the scenes that are opened t ohis faith by our Saviour in the life to come. That only is true life to him, and death is but the entering into life. This life is transitional, questionable, that is life eternal. All that is gloomy, therefore, and dark and repulsive and terrible in death and the grave is overspread with light. Our faith looks above, beyond,—the evidence itself of things not seen and the substance of things hoped for.

III. Besides, it is another proof of the abolishment of death by Christ, that what remains to be called death, namely, the cessation of the body, is shown to be only the closing or completing act of redemption itself. The death we speak of is even called by an apostle the redemption of the body, that unclothing which is needful to the full clothing upon, that putting off the earthly and corrupt which is needful to the putting on of the heavenly and the incorruptible. The process of spiritual redemption could not regenerate the body. The body would still be under death because of sin, though the spirit be life because of righteousness. Therefore death shall have it, but in having it shall only become an instrument of redemption. That which sin hath marred beyond mending shall be let go and replaced, and so mortality shall be swallowed up of life—so death is gain. In this view death is even seen to be converted under the gospel and transformed into a friendly power.

IV. How different is Christianity when viewed in this light from all other known religions, how clearly eminent above them all. This is the only religion that has been able to grapple with death and bring it under mastery. Of no other can it be said that it has abolished, or even undertaken to abolish, death. If there be something of poetry in the notions of death that are offered in other religions, or something of philosophy, if they play gracefully about our imagination or offer bold conceptions to our understanding, yet they are still only fungi that grow out of the body of death, yewtrees that are rooted in men's graves. They belong to a world of death, they bring no power of life or deliverance. It may be something to a human creature with his immortal instincts to believe that he shall be a great hunter in the world of spirits, or that he shall drink wine from the skull of his enemy in the halls of Odin, or that he shall be ferried as a ghost underground across the Styx to the

Elysian Fields, paying due toll to the ghostly ferry-man; something that he shall live again on earth though it be as the soul of a beast, something to fall into Brahma and become a part of him, and be drugged with him in that delicious sleep from which he never wakes. But to be pure, a partaker of goodness and divinity even to the full, to rise out of the body as a being wholly glorious and immortal, and to have during all one's life of faith on earth a new consciousness certified of this, and to live ever in prospect of an issue so triumphant,—this is Christianity abolishing death and bringing life and immortality to light. In this eminence of Christ, in this sublime adequacy to our want, is the truly divine authorship of his gospel most signally proved.

V. Neither let us overlook the comforts given to us here in our days of mourning and the sorrow by which we are afflicted in the death of our friends. If they lived in Christ they did not die, they have only emerged into a livelier life. What we call their death is death to us but no death to them. It was only their unclothing, their entering into life, their transition to the incorruptible where God abides in complete fulness of life. And if the consciousness of God is quickened also in you, how slender a space for grief and separation is left for death to occupy. There is, to us who believe, a light that pierces the grave and opens worlds beyond. We follow our friends who die, we see them entering into life, perfect, pure, separated from pain, decreptitude and all sin's poisons. We see them emerging out of this world's wants and tears into the fulness and complete liberty of just men made perfect. They are not in the grave, they are not hid from us. They are only a day's journey ahead of us; we may see them now just passing the horizon of our day. We shall be with them tomorrow, all in life together.

The life that Christ has given us we freely yield to Him. We testify our faith in Him. We find our eternity in Him. We invite Him to reign within us by His all-renovating power, till we live in every member, We anticipate with confidence what our eyes cannot see, but what is most real to our faith, a state of purity with Him, and of youth and of glorified energy, fitly described only by the words Eternal Life.—Horace Bushnell, D. D.

NOW HE IS DEAD, WHEREFORE SHOULD I FAST? CAN I BRING HIM BACK AGAIN? I SHALL GO TO HIM; BUT HE SHALL NOT RETURN TO ME.—2 SAM. 12:23.

JOHN WESLEY.

The resolution of a wise and good man, just recovering the use of his reason and virtue, after the bitterness of soul he had tasted, from an hourly expectation of the death of a beloved son, is comprised in these few, but strong words. The reason of this strange alteration in his proceedings, as it appeared to those who were ignorant of the principles upon which he acted, he here explains, with great brevity, but in the most beautiful language, strength of thought, and energy of expression: 'Now he is dead, wherefore should I fast? Can I bring him back again? I shall go to him; but he shall not return to me.'

I. The unprofitable and bad consequences, the sinful nature, of profuse sorrowing for the dead, are easily deduced from the former part of his reflection. In the latter, we have the strongest motives to enforce our striving against it;—a remedy exactly suited to the disease;—a consideration, which, duly applied, will not fail, either to prevent this sorrow, or rescue us from this real misfortune.

Grief, in general, is the parent of so much evil, and the occasion of so little good to mankind, that it may be justly wondered how it found a place in our nature. It was, indeed, of man's own, not of God's, creation: Who may permit, but never was the author of evil The same hour gave birth to grief and sin, as the same moment will deliver us from both. For neither did exist before human nature was corrupted, nor will it continue when that is restored to its ancient perfection.

From the very nature of grief, which is an uneasiness in the mind on the apprehension of some present evil, it appears, that its arising in us, on any other occasion than that of sin, is entirely owing to our want of judgment. Are any of those accidents, in the language of men termed misfortunes, such as reproach, poverty, loss of life, or even friends, real evils? So far from it, that if we dare believe our Creator, they are often positive blessings. They all work together for our good. And our Lord accordingly commands us, even when the severest loss, that of our reputation, befals us, if it is in a good cause, as it must be our own fault if it be not, to 'rejoice, and be exceeding glad.'

II. If any species of this unprofitable passion be more particularly useless than the rest, it is that which we feel when we sorrow for the dead. We destroy the health of our body, and impair the strength of our minds, and take no price for those invaluable blessings: We give up our present, without any prospect of future advantage; without any probability of either recalling them hither or profiting them where they are. As it is an indifferent proof of our wisdom, it is still a worse of our affection for the dead. It is the property of envy, not of love, to repine at another's happiness; to weep, because all tears are wiped from their eyes. Shall it disturb us, who call ourselves his friends, that a weary wanderer has, at length, come to his wished-for home? -Nay, weep we rather for ourselves, who still want that happiness; even to whom that rest appeareth yet in prospect.

Against this fault, which is inconsistent with those virtues, and therefore tacitly forbidden in the precepts that enjoin them, St. Paul warns us in express words: 'I would not have you to be ignorant, brethren, concerning them which are asleep; that ye sorrow not, even as others who have no hope. For if we believe that Jesus died, and rose again, even so them also who sleep in Jesus will God bring with Him:—Wherefore comfort another with these words (I Thess. 4:13-18.) And these, indeed, are the only words which can give lasting comfort to a spirit, whom such an occasion hath wounded. Why should I be so unreasonable, so unkind, as to desire the return of a soul now in happiness to me;

to this habitation of sin and misery; since I know that the time will come, yea, is now at hand, when, in spite of the great gulf fixed between us, I shall take off these chains and go to him?

What he was, I am both unable to paint in suitable colors, and unwilling to attempt it. Although the chief, at least the most common argument, for those labored encomiums on the dead, which for many years have so much prevailed among us, is, that there can be no suspicion of flattery; yet we all know, that the pulpit, on those occasions, has been so frequently prostituted to those servile ends, that it is now no longer capable of serving them. Men take it for granted, that what is there said, are words of course; that the business of the speaker is to describe the beauty, not the likeness, of the picture; and so it be only well drawn, he cares not whom it resembles: In a word, that his business is to show his own wit, not the generosity of his friend, by giving him all the virtues he can think of.

At the tearing asunder of the sacred bands, well may we allow without blame, some parting pangs: but the difficulty is, to put as speedy a period to them, as reason and religion command us. What can give us sufficient ease after that rupture, which has left such an aching void in our breasts? What, indeed, but the reflection already mentioned, which can never be inculcated too often,—that we are hastening to him ourselves; that, pass but a few years, perhaps hours, which will soon be over, and not only this, but all other desires will be satisfied; when we shall exchange the gaudy shadow of pleasure we have enjoyed, for sincere, substantial, untransitory happiness?

If we are, at any time, in danger of being overcome by dwelling too long on the gloomy side of this prospect, to the giving us pain, the making us unfit for the duties and offices of life, impairing our faculties of body or mind,—which proceedings, as has been already shown, are both absurd, unprofitable, and sinful; let us immediately recur to the bright side, and reflect, with gratitude as well as humility, that our time passeth away like a shadow; and that, when we awake from this momentary dream, we shall then have a clearer view of the latter day, in which our Redeemer shall stand upon the earth: when this corruptible shall put on incorruption, and this mortal shall be clothed with immortality; and when we shall sing, with the united choirs of men and angels, "O death, where is thy sting? O grave, where is thy victory?"— —John Wesley.

"THE LORD HATH TAKEN AWAY."—JOB 1:21.

REV. JOSEPH H. CHANDLER.

We mourn today a common loss. It means much more to some of us than to others; but none here are without some sense of bereavement. The house has not simply its vacant chair at the family table; we feel the absence in every room of a dear presence. There is a place in the family circle outside the house which henceforth will be unfilled. The little children will miss those offices of love which only a mother's mother can give. Even many who are not here today, whose homes perhaps are at some distance in the surrounding country and who mingle in our society only on the streets or in places of business, when they received the tidings which brought us here were moved by the sorrow which we feel because they knew that henceforth they must miss the presence of a gracious woman going in and out among us. And yet the things which give us cause for mourning, give us reason also for gratitude. "The Lord hath taken away" and we are sorrowful; but He could not have taken had He not first given; and our loss is only great because we have been greatly blessed. The incident of death changes our future for a little time, but it does not change the past. One has been given to us, and tarried long with us, every memory of whom is a joy. While death takes from us the immediate presence of our friends and so robs us of some joy, it also gives us something which we have not had before; it sets them before us in clearer light, and because we learn to know them better it increases our occasion for gratitude that their lives have been linked with ours.

As citizens of this place we have great reason to rejoice that such a woman came here to make her home in early days. She came with rare gifts of person, mind, and heart into the wilderness. She was a brave pioneer. She never lost her high ideals. She helped to make this community what it could never have been without her. She has been an ideal inspiration to many young girls who have grown up here, and the high tone of our society is owing, more than we know, to her unconscious influence through many years.

In the church circle she has always been an example of intelligent and faithful devotion to the Kingdom of Christ. Able to appreciate the best things in architecture, music and preaching, she has never turned away from the things possible in church life in the new community. She has never held herself aloof from the humblest services or the lowest offices of ministry in the church; nor has she allowed education or wealth to separate her in sympathy and communion from any of her neighbors or fellow members in the church in different circumstances.

To those in distress she has been an intelligent friend,—never scattering alms to be seen of men, but daily doing little kindnesses for which a multitude of hearts bless her memory.

She was singular for her devotion to everything to which she once gave her heart. From the first of her making this place her home she was devoted to its interests; she was always loyal to the church of her communion; she never forgot the friends who once gained her love.

She kept daily interest not simply in those about her, but in others whose lives had touched hers in past years. The friends who came here in early days were friends always; the former pastors of the church gone were not forgotten. Her friendships were such as to outlast death's partings. She had a love which many waters could not quench. It was stronger than death. Can we believe that a heart that has loved so steadfastly is left desolate on the other shore? Some of her friends have gone before and what brings for a time sadness here must bring joy yonder.

We cannot stop the heartache nor dry the tears that come unbidden today. But even before the pain of separation is softened by the healing touch of time, we may help ourselves to patience if not to gladness by remembering how much we have been blessed in these years in which she has been with us. And let me add this word, let not our gratitude be hindered by vain repining because death came when it did. The Lord gave graciously, and in love and wisdom He has brought the end of one stage of life, and the beginning of another. Let us not be too much disturbed by death for what is it but a second birth?—Rev. Joseph H. Chandler.

CHRISTIANITY A RELIGION OF COMFORT.

PRESIDENT SAMUEL PLANTZ, D. D.

"Let not your hearts be troubled."—John 14:1.

Life is by no means all sunshine, and often is cloud and thunderstorm. Optimism is only a half truth. In spite of us we cannot always walk on the sunny side of the street. The ills of life are as real as its joys. Sorrow is as sure a factor in experience as peace. Homer complained that of all that lives and moves, nothing on earth is sadder than man. This may be an exaggeration, but it suggests a truth. Our existence is full of contradictions, and sorrow and death lurk along our track. The longest life, as far as this world is concerned, is brief. In the Hohenzollern museum at Berlin the cradle in which Frederick the Great was rocked, stands by the side of the chair in which he died. There is no city that has so many inhabitants as the city of graves. In the Berlin picture gallery is a great painting entitled, "Der Zug des Todes." It represents a long procession passing over the hills, the end of which is lost in the distance. In that procession we see little children with locks of golden hair shining in the sun; young girls just blooming into womanhood; the bride with her wedding veil; the business man in the full strength of mature years; the mother with her babe on her breast; the aged with wrinkled face and tottering on their staffs, and the apparently healthy and strong, and the sallow cheeked victims of disease; all are there, members of that endless procession, marching over the hills of time; and at its head, leading the line, is the skeleton form of Death, who rings his bell as he passes along. On the side of the road there are aged and decrepid ones imploring to be taken, but they are left; and there are the young and strong, shrinking back and asking to be left and they taken. "Pause and remember thy days, for they are numbered."

We are in a world where the lights go out; where friends and loved ones are constantly being called to swell Death's great procession: and where we too in a few days or months or years must surrender to God the life which He has given.

I. In a world of such transient experiences, in surroundings where grief and sorrow and pain and death ever enter, what can be said, what consolation can be given to keep the rainbow still in the sky, and drive away the dark visage of despair? Can philosophy comfort us? The ancient Stoics said yes, and a modern French philosopher has put forth the doctrine that by a correct philosophy one can conquer all the woes and ills of life. But experience shows that this is a very weak crutch to lean upon and that it gives way when trials and sorrows really come. Dr. Johnson in his Rasselas represents this, when he tells us of the young man who went to hear a philosopher speak and became infatuated with his doctrines. He taught him how he might subdue his passions and rise above all difficulties and trials. The youth thought he had found a true light shining in darkness. However the next day he went to hear his teacher discourse, but was not admitted; later when he was ushered into the philosopher's presence he found him wringing his hands and wailing in deepest distress. "Why this grief," asked Rasselas. "Oh," said the teacher, "my only daughter, the light of my home and the comfort of my old age is dead!" But certainly," said Rasselas, "the philosophy which you eloquently descanted on yesterday, comforts you now?" "Oh, no," cried the philosopher, "what can philosophy say to me now, except to show me that my condition is inevitable and incurable?" Rasselas went to Imlac and told him what he had heard and he replied: "They preach like angels, but they live like men."

But how is it with the world's religions other than our own? Have not they a balm for sorrow; cannot they give comfort and peace in the midst of the world's sufferings, afflictions and ills? The greatest of these religions is Buddhism. Its founder, "The Light of Asia," so called, spent his life pondering this problem of the world's ill and built up his system to solve it. It was the sorrows of life which drove him from home into the forest, and it was this problem to which he thought he saw the answer when under the sacred tree, he felt the struggle was over and the realm had come. And what was his solution   We can find it in one of the stories told of the great teacher which stated that one day there came to him a woman, wailing and weeping, as she bore her dead child in her arms. She asked for help, for words of comfort. The Buddha told her to wipe her tears, and go to some home and get him a handful of mustard seed, and he would raise the child to life; but she must get the mustard seed from a home in which no sorrow, no trouble, no affliction had ever come. The woman left in gladness, and sought for the mustard seed. She found plenty of it, but found no home into which some affliction had not entered; and, at last, weary and in despair, she came back to the Buddha, already guessing his meaning, when he said to her: "My sister, endure! You have now seen that what has come to you is only the common experience of man." This is the wisest word the religions of the world can speak; endure put your strength against the inevitable facts of existence, callous your soul by resolution against life's ills.

II. In the Christian religion, however, there is a different solution to the problem of evil. Christ came to a burdened race that he might give it light and cheer. He healed broken hearts and set at liberty them that were bound. He put silver and golden linings in the dark clouds. He made a rainbow of hope and promise shine brightly in the sky. He taught the true meaning of suffering and of death. Those who have fully believed in Him, have, in all ages, found comfort and strength in the darkest hours of human experience, when the smart has been keenest and the burden heaviest to bear. They may have wept, but beneath the external manifestation of sorrow, there has been confidence and abiding peace.

1. This comes first from the character of the God which Christianity teaches. It does not put behind human life a blind fate which holds us to its Ixion wheel. It does not give us a God lost in Nature, a great All of existence, without mind to know or heart to feel. It does not give us gods many, some of whom perhaps, when we are in need are in sleep or off on a journey. But it gives us a God immanent in the world, whose essential nature is love and who conducts his government in righteousness and truth. This God knows us all by name, he leads his flock like a shepherd, takes the lambs in his arms and folds them to his bosom. His name is Jehovah, the fellowship-God, who tabernacles with men, and whose ear is ever open to our cry.

> "O, wondrous story of deathless love!
> Each child is dear to that heart above;
> He fights for me when I cannot fight;
> He comforts me in the gloom of night.
> He lifts the burden, for He is strong;
> He stills the sigh and awakens the song.
> The sorrows that bowed us down, he bears,
> And loves and pardons, because he cares."

With such a God, one who loves us and means us good, one who has in His hands the rule of the world, we can be reconciled to the apparent contradiction of things, the pains and sorrows and heartaches that come to us, and say, "All things work together for good," although we see and understand it not.

2. But again, with our confidence in God's wisdom and love, there goes the inner strengthening of His grace. Christianity is an inner, not an outer, life, one which is righteousness, peace and joy in the Holy Ghost, not prosperity, friends, pleasures. We can lose the latter and yet be confident and strong. Often there is a storm, without the wind rages, the thunder speaks, the lightning flashes in the sky, but within the home there is laughter, happiness and good will. So in the realm of man's outer life there may be disappointment, sorrow, affliction, and yet we may have such a grasp of faith, such inner strengthening, such a consciousness of the presence of God's grace, that we can say, "Thy will be done," and see light and peace in the darkness of our day. Indeed, it is promised that as our day is, so shall our strength be, and that though the waters come up against us they shall not overflow us, and though we pass through the fire we shall not be burned. Did not Stephen's face shine and did he not see the heavens open when the stones were pelting his body? Did not Paul sing in the inner prison when his back was lacerated by the scourge and his feet were made fast in the stocks? Did not the martyrs sing at the stake? And have not thousands and thou-

sands of Christians in all ages dried their tears as there has come to them the sweet consciousness that round about them were the everlasting arms?

3. But besides what I have mentioned the Christian doctrine of immortality is a source of great comfort and consolation. We know that when our friends pass from us it is not like the emptying of a bottle in the sea. It is not like blowing out a candle. It is not like tearing up the flower by the roots. Death is only an illusion. God is not the annihilator, but the Creator. The soul lives and lives forever. Christ, the conqueror, carries the keys of death and the grave in his girdle. "We shall not sleep, but we shall be changed." If the house of our own earthly tabernacle be dissolved we have a building of God, a house not made with hands, eternal in the heavens. Moses and Elias appeared and communed with Christ upon the mount. Lazar s came forth from the tomb. The son of the widow of Nain rose from the bier. Jesus said, "Let not your hearts be troubled. Ye believe in me. In My Father's house are many mansions. If it were not so I would have told you. I go to prepare a place for you, and if I go a I will come again and receive you unto myself." Here is comfort for sorrow which no pagan religion nor human philosophy can give. In the light of it humanity has dried its tears. It has strengthened souls in the dying hour. A number of years ago, a sister-in-law of the writer, just maturing into womanhood, was stricken with disease. Her father, Dr. T. A. Goodwin, in his "Mode of Man's Immortality," has thus described the parting scene: "Calmly and patiently through months of intense suffering, she approached the final hour with many expressions of trust in God, which would have done honor to a war-worn veteran. The last day finally came after a night of indescribable pain: cold limbs, a failing pulse and difficult breathing all indicated the closing scene. Addressing her mother she said: 'You will not have to watch with me tonight, for this poor suffering body will be at rest, but I shall be with the Saviour.'' Shortly afterward, having taken an affectionate farewell of the family, she reached out her hand, cold in death, as if to embrace someone unseen by the rest. With a smile of recognition she began to call by name departed members of the family, and others of her acquaintance who had died, adding after some minutes such greetings: 'Here we are an unbroken family in heaven, washed in the blood of the Lamb. Washed, washed, washed!' and in a few moments she was in the spirit world. Certainly "these Christians die well," and they do so because they see before them a city that needs no light of the sun, for God is the light of it, and where all tears shall be wiped from their eyes. The hope of immortality is a comfort to those who are passing over, and it is comfort to those who remain, for they feel that in a brighter world, on some glad day, the broken ties will be reunited, and partings will no longer need to be said. The religion of Jesus is a religion for the dark day as well as the light. It gives us hope and strength and comfort as we make our way through this veil of tears.
—President Samuel Plantz, D. D.

"SO HE GIVETH HIS BELOVED SLEEP."—PSALM 127:2.

ROBERT STUART McARTHUR, D. D.

These words are beautiful as a strain of music from a celestial choir. The language softens and sweetens death where it is introduced on the sacred page. Sleep is the twin-brother of death. The great dramatist says, "After life's fitful fever he sleeps well." This language applies with absolute literality to the death of every true believer. Even the old heathen poets saw some likeness between death and sleep; but they described sleep as iron, as brazen, and not as coming in softness, gentleness and blissfulness as it is described in the New Testament. Homer said of one of his heroes:

> "He slept an iron sleep,
> Slain fighting for his country."

This is a very different sleep from that described by the Apostle Paul, and in the familiar hymn, "Asleep in Jesus." Sleep implies an awakening. Thus, the term sleep suggests the doctrine of the resurrection. The atheists who at the time of the French Revolution put on their tombs the words "Death is an eternal sleep," were guilty of a gross rhetorical blunder, not to speak of their sin against truth and God. Their language was self-contradictory. They utterly stultified themselves as logicians. They were mere sciologists and not true scientists. If death be sleep, then death is not eternal. If death be sleep, then death is temporal. Then the night will end and the morning will come. Then the graves of our beloved dead will one day be empty, as was Joseph's tomb from which our divine Lord rose in glorious triumph on the first blessed Easter morning.

How divine is the blessing, when the awful monster Death, is transformed into the sweet messenger, Sleep! Then life is robbed of its gloom, and the grave becomes simply the dressing chamber in which we lay aside the garments of earth and put on the robes of heaven. Truthful as beautiful, and finally illustrative of the transformed meaning of death, are the soulful words of Elizabeth Barrett Browning:

> "Of all the thoughts of God that are
> Borne inward unto souls afar,
>   Along the Psalmist's music deep,
> Now tell me if that any is,
> For gift or grace surpassing this—
>   He giveth His beloved sleep?"

Comforting are these words of the poet and the psalmist when spoken in the rooms of our sick, and gloriously inspiring are they when uttered over the graves of our dead. With these words in our thought, we can, with the apostle Paul, triumphantly ask, "O death, where is thy sting?"

We cannot too strongly emphasize the idea that the sleep of death is God's personal gift. He gently closes the eye-lids; he graciously loosens the silver cord; He lovingly takes down the earthly house of this tabernacle. "Like as a father pitieth his children, so the Lord pitieth them that fear him." Here the fatherly side of God's nature is gloriously displayed, but God is mother as well as father to those who trust Him. We have, therefore, in Isaiah 66:13, in the words, "As one whom his mother comforteth, so will I comfort you," the picture of God as a mother bending over the cradle of a tired child, and soothing the little one to peaceful rest. The sleep of death occupies God's thought, both as to the time and the manner of its coming. We read that, "Precious in the sight of the Lord is the death of his saints." Death never comes as an accident; there are no accidents in God's providence. No saint of God dies too soon; no saint of God lives too long. To God's view there are no broken shafts in God's acre. If we could see as God sees, we would do exactly as God does. Let us trust Him where we cannot trace Him. If we cannot now say, "Thy will be done," let us patiently wait until our lips will joyously utter those words. The assurance that sleep is God's personal gift, takes much of the pain away from disease and takes all the dishonor away from death. God personally bestows the gift of sleep, the sleep of death, upon his beloved. God, with his own hand, rocks the cradle and puts His beloved to sleep.

Then let us who are believers not fear the approach of death. Dry your tears, ye that mourn. Your departed are not dead, but sleep. A hand, gentler than that of wife or mother, is closing their eyes. A voice, sweeter than that of angels, whispers, "So, He giveth his beloved sleep." And, above all these voices is that of our divine Lord and Savior Himself, saying, "I go that I may awake them out of sleep." The morning dawns; the cloudless day has come. All God's beloved shall awake out of sleep; shall awake in His likeness; shall see Him face to face and shall be with Him in His own immediate presence. This is bliss unspeakable; this will be reunion inseparable; this will be glory indescribable. This is life without sleep and day without night. This is heaven.—Rev. Robert Stuart McArthur, D. D.

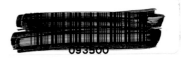